KU-186-620

SIX CENTURIES

OF

WORK AND WAGES

The History of English Labour

BY

JAMES E. THOROLD ROGERS, M.P.

London

SWAN SONNENSCHEIN AND CO., Lim.

25 HIGH STREET, BLOOMSBURY

1909

G 2768 15/- 4.66

FIRST EDITION, *February*, 1884; SECOND, *December,* 1885; THIRD, *November*, 1889; FOURTH, *August,* 1894; FIFTH, *January*, 1901; SIXTH, *December*, 1901; SEVENTH, *May*, 1903; EIGHTH, *March*, 1906; NINTH, *March*, 1908; TENTH, *July*, 1909.

PREFACE.

SINCE I published, nearly eighteen years ago, the first two volumes of my history of agriculture and prices, I have been frequently urged to extract and exhibit those parts of my researches which illustrate the history of labour and wages. To have done this to any purpose, it was necessary that I should have in my possession such a continuous record of wages actually earned as would enable me to traverse the whole of the six centuries which intervene between the time at which the first information begins and that at which our present experience concludes. I have already published the facts which bear on more than half the whole period, *i.e.*, for 324 years, and I have collected evidence, as yet unpublished, for 120 years more, *i.e.*, for the 444 years which begin with the forty-third year of Henry III., 1258-9, and conclude with the first of Anne, 1702-3. Sufficient information for the residue has been supplied from the writings of Arthur Young and Sir Frederic Eden in the eighteenth century, and from numerous writers in the nineteenth, the principal authority in the latter period being Porter.

It would have been of little value to have collected evidence as to the wages of labour unless I had also been in possession of adequate information as to general prices from which to estimate precisely what was the purchasing power of wages. Now I have published the prices of food from 1259 to 1582, and from 1582 a record of wheat and malt prices has been registered every six months at four important centres, Oxford, Cambridge, Windsor, and Winchester, under the statute 18 Eliz. cap. 6. Besides, for the purposes of my inquiry, I am sufficiently provided with the evidence of such other prices as enables me to translate money wages actually paid into the necessaries of life. I cannot, indeed, in the later period exhibit the position of the labourer with the same exactness which is in my power for the period during which I have compiled and published the evidence of wages which were actually paid, and provisions which were actually purchased or sold. In the period which intervenes between the first record of wages and the death of Henry VIII. (1547), during which the condition of the labourer was progressively good for more than a century and a half, and stationary at the highest level for nearly the whole of Henry's reign, more than thirty-seven years in duration, it is possible to follow the course of wages as exactly as that of any other article which is bought or sold, and to represent them by their power over all kinds of commodities. After this date, when they declined greatly in value, and the degradation of labour, owing to causes which I hope to make clear, began, I possess nearly the same continuous and minute knowledge for more than a century and a half, some being published, some being in notes. But except for about fifty years in the earlier part of the eighteenth century, the wages of labour have been a bare subsistence, constantly supplemented by the poor rate, till, in modern times, a considerable amelioration in the condition of some kinds of labour, owing, I believe, to a peculiar cause, has been effected. I have attempted to point out what that cause has been, and to suggest that it should be extended and encouraged.

It may perhaps be objected, that though I have dealt with a subject which is entirely new, I have appended no notes and have given no authorities for my facts. But for half the period

I could have made no reference except to my own publications, and for another century and more I can refer only to my unpublished notes, and the tabular statements which I have drawn up from them. The difficulty is an exceptional one, for no one has entered on this field of research but myself, or has even, to the best of my knowledge, attempted to make use of what I have published for purposes like those which are before me in compiling the present volume. I could, if it were needed, however, give ample verification for all that I have alleged, not, indeed, from the original sources, for those are contained in muniment rooms, in the Record Office, and in public libraries, but from my own transcripts and averages. For the later period, the authorities, as I have said, are chiefly Young, Eden, and Porter.

Again it may be objected, that I reiterate particulars in dealing with the topic before me. But in the reconstruction of the social state of England six centuries ago, and in the narrative of its history or development, it is frequently the case, especially when there is seen to be no marked change in the process under which men lived and worked, except in so far as the interests of the class about which I am writing are raised or depressed, that one has to piece out the picture which one attempts to draw from details which may need to be restated in the narrative, but were characteristic of an earlier as well as of a later epoch. Thus there is little change in the economy of rural life, as far as the labourer is concerned, from the days of the third Henry till the days of the eighth, and illustrations of the labourer's condition may be safely taken from any part of the period.

The plan which I put before myself was to devote the first chapters of the book to a sketch of early English society up to and during the latter half of the thirteenth century. In handling this part of my subject, I had to deal with the pursuits of the Englishman at this time, and especially with that which was the business of the vast majority of our people, agriculture ; land in England, as one can gather by a wide induction from the facts contained in existing records, having been divided in nearly equal moieties between manorial lords and tenants at fixed rents and with permanent holdings. Having dealt with the pursuits of this vast majority, it remained that I should say a little about life in towns and the processes by which trade was carried on. This is followed by an account of the several classes who made up mediæval society, all these subjects being handled in the first six chapters.

The remainder of the work deals particularly with the history of labour and wages, though I have felt myself constrained to touch on the general history of agriculture, and to dwell on some few particulars in the political history of the country, in connection with the main topic of my inquiry. But I have designedly abstained from entering on the new system of taxation which, beginning with Cecil's book of rates and continuing through the excise and customs system of the Protectorate, the Restoration, and the Revolution, at last imposed nearly all the burden of taxation on those whose resources were crippled, and whose freedom was taken away by a variety of enactments imposed in the interests of a narrow but powerful class.

I have attempted to show that the pauperism and the degradation of the English labourer were the result of a series of Acts of Parliament and acts of government, which were designed or adopted with the express purpose of compelling the labourer to work at the lowest rates of wages possible, and which succeeded at last in effecting that purpose. These Acts have become historical, and except in so far as they are responsible for the existence of much that is difficult and regrettable in the condition of the working classes now, they have no existence at the present time. We have long since ceased to regulate wages by Acts of Parliament and the ordinances reform, and even by enriching them through the machinery of the reform, I venture on predicting that some of those who have raised the question will regret that they were rash enough to have stirred in the matter.

Fortunately for all, the leaders of English labour have sought to better the condition of their followers by processes which the most rigid of economists cannot condemn. I have taken occasion to point out what, in my opinion, is the economical significance of a trade union or labour partnership. That this principle may be extended so as to embrace all labour, should, I am convinced, be the wish of every one who desires to save his country from the spread of doctrines which are as pernicious to the true interests of labour as they are destructive of all progress, and ultimately of all hope. Nothing would be more fatal than the despair which might succeed in reconstructing society from its foundations.

Since this book has been written,—since, indeed, the foregoing part of the preface has been written—I have had the advantage of seeing the very able and intelligent essay of Mr. Giffen, the President of the Statistical Society, on the progress of the working classes during the last half-century —*i.e.*, from 1833, speaking generally, to 1883. A great deal of what Mr. Giffen has collected by way of material for his conclusions is of very unequal value. Many of his inferences are perhaps too hopeful, many of his economical principles are of very doubtful cogency, and I have, indeed, read nothing lately the result ... to debate

hat

the old school and the judges had revived them in the very worst form and with the most malignant pedantry. I need only refer to the conviction of the six Dorsetshire labourers in July 1834, their transportation for a perfectly innocent act, their pardon, and the concealment of the pardon from them, in consideration, I presume, of the vested interest to which the Sydney Government had sold them at a pound a head. It is, I think, to be regretted that Mr. Giffen did not describe, as he certainly could have done, what was the condition of wages in relation to profits fifty years ago. I hope that I have sufficiently stated it; I am certain that I have done so with much restraint and moderation in the following pages. That wages have risen I thankfully admit. Water rises in an artesian well. But the physicist who explains the rise has to take account of the pressure which previously kept the water below its just level. In the case of labour, the economist should have announced and deplored it.

It is noteworthy, too, that the kinds of labour for which Mr. Giffen has adduced evidence have all been aided and protected by trade unions. I refer to those which are tabulated in page 5 of his address. The inference from those paid for seamen is more doubtful; for the comparison is between wages paid in sailing and in steam vessels, two callings which are only nominally one. Most doubtful is the estimate of Sir James Caird as to the wages of agricultural labourers. Here we do not know whether the 60 per cent. means the rate of wages or the cost of labour. We do not know, as w
real w
the

farm labourers. There must have been some meaning in the plea, or it would hardly have been put forward. I speak of responsible writers ; no reasonable person notices anonymous critics, least of all those who take the wages of a publisher's review.

The question, in fact, of the present position of labour cannot be discussed in a short essay. But no comment, however slight or superficial, will be other than misleading which does not give an estimate of the English labourer's condition fifty years ago, when it dwells on the progress which he has made since that period. What the state of this country would have been, if he had not made progress, is pretty certain ; and I am afraid that we shall not entirely escape the speculative evils on which most far-sighted people are now dwelling, if he is not made to realise that other and considerable reforms are forthcoming in the near future.

In the interval, despite the interest which is felt in speculative novelties and startling theories of reconstruction, the English workman, in his best and most thoughtful forms, is more intent on seeking out and adapting the process by which the interests of employer and employed should be harmonized than in striving after an entirely new departure. The Continental socialist has hitherto owned that England is a barren field, which bears none of his fruit, and seems unable even to make the seed which he sows germinate. This indifference to theory is not due to selfishness or to the deadening effects of competition, for it is the essential characteristic of the trade unionist that he sacrifices himself to the good of the voluntary corporation with which he has associated himself, to an extent which foreigners do not understand or imitate. According to those who are entitled to speak with authority on the subject, the English unionist readily subscribes for the purpose of his organization fully two-and-a-half per cent. of his income, and sometimes more. The Continental artizan, it would seem, can with difficulty be persuaded to contribute a sixth of the sum. I do not, therefore, infer, with my friend M. Laveleye, that the English workman is yielding to Continental ideas, for I find that the essence of all foreign schemes, as portrayed in M. Laveleye's excellent work, "Le Socialisme," is the sacrifice of others, while the English workman essays to achieve the solution of his problems by the preliminary sacrifice of himself; partially, imperfectly, and unequally, I grant, but still consistently and on principle. Above all, he does not invoke the aid of the State.

For my part, I believe that as the English people has taught other nations the machinery of parliament and representative government, has slowly, after many struggles, and after having been long made the experiment of insincere factions, won, or is winning, the admission of all who deserve it to the constitution, and has constantly falsified those sinister predictions about a hungry and angry democracy which have been the stock-in-trade of reactionaries, so it is likely hereafter to solve the far more important question as to the true harmony between the rights of property and the rights of labour. We have been confidently warned that the power of the people will be the spoliation of the rich. Nothing of the kind has happened as yet; nothing of the kind has been threatened; nothing of the kind has been hinted at. The democracy of the towns have formulated no claim, instructed no representative in this direction. They wish to distribute property, but by the honest operation of an equitable purchase. They wish to better the wages of the workman, but by the equally equitable interpretation of the market, of the goods which they produce, and the price which the consumer is prepared to give for them. They are singularly, generously oblivious of past ill-usage, and seem to have no animosity against the classes and the institutions to which their fathers owed the miseries deliberately inflicted on their lot. They contrast favourably with many of their critics, who do not disguise their desire for reaction. But the best hope of the future lies in the existence of a temper among the people, which is equally removed from the temptation to revenge and is contemptuous of the sophistries which a narrow self-interest is ventilating.

I am well aware that these views will seem paradoxical. But in political matters it has been long since proved that aristocratical government is a failure and its prolongation a mischief and a menace. It forms wrong judgments, and when it is right by accident in its ends, it adopts wrong means, or inverts the order in which its grudging and tardy reforms should be effected. Nor has the franchise of a more extended and real kind than that which existed from the Restoration to the first Reform Bill done much better. This country owes much to the Parliaments which sat between 1832 and 1868. But they would have done far better had the franchise been that of 1867. They will do better still when the peasant is allowed to express his judgment on the policy of Government.

But the value of popular opinion on the policy of Parliament and the administration is as nothing to the usefulness of combined action on the part of labour with regard to social questions. "The crowd," says Aristotle, the wisest interpreter of ancient political forces under the clearest circumstances in which they have ever been estimated, "makes better general judgments than any individual whatsoever. It is in the main incorruptible. Like a large sheet of water, the multitude is less liable to sinister influences than the few, for when the individual is influenced by passion or any similar impulse, his judgment must be distorted, while it is hard for all collectively to be led by passion or to err."

The difficulty is not to get wise action, but to get any

action at all. The mass of persons in England take a languid interest in political action, and a capricious line on social questions. They have had reason to believe that politics are the mere game of two hereditary and privileged parties, in which it signifies little which gets a temporary ascendency. They are convinced of the hollowness of political cries, and are under the impression that the public service is a phrase by which politicians mean private advantage. Since 1867, they have made few demands on Parliament, apparently because they have seen that Parliament is more busy in arbitrating between rival interests of a special character than in considering the general good. They may do more in the future. They may, like Jonathan in the day of battle, taste the wild honey in the wood and find their eyes enlightened. But I for one do not fear that, like the rest of the people, they will fly upon the spoil.

JAMES E. THOROLD ROGERS.

House of Commons.

CONTENTS.

CHAPTER I.

CHAPTER I.

INTRODUCTION.

Archives of English History—Number and Copiousness of—Domesday, and the Blank which follows it—Commencement of Economical Archives—Degradation of the Anglo-Saxon Nobility—The English the Allies of the King—He is the largest Landowner—The Ministers of the Sovereign, Churchmen—The King's Principal Revenues—The Exchequer, a Source of Power and Object of Attack —The Method of the Exchequer Audit copied in private Accounts—These Accounts Evidence of Title, and therefore preserved—Henry the Second's Position and Abilities—Effects of Becket's Murder—The Liability to Military Service at the bidding of the Crown—The Origin and Effects of Escuage—The English Army, its Character and Traditions—Open to Villeins, though the Militia was not—The Story of Sale in 1381—The Contrast of England with other Nations in Western Europe—The Treatment of the English King by his Subjects—The Commutation of Military Service for Money .imitated in Domestic Matters between Lord and Serf—Matthew Paris—His Value as an Interpreter of Public Opinion and Social life—The Beginnings of Hostility to the Roman Court—Henry III.—His Character, and that of his Reign.

THE archives of English history are more copious and more continuous than those of any other people. The record of public events begins with the Teutonic invasion of the fifth century, and is prolonged, with scarcely a break, down to our own times. There are periods in which the information is scanty. The events of the reign of Edward IV. have not been preserved in such abundance as those of Edward I. We know more about the life and times of Archbishop Becket than we do about the life and times of Archbishop Morton. But we are rarely left without contemporary annalists, and those authoritative materials by which the historian can give continuity and vivacity to his narrative. As the political history of England can be written from its beginnings, so can the history of its laws, which are founded on the customs of the Teutonic races. Again, the constitutional history of our people has been traced back to customs which long precede

2

the Conquest. Its financial history is contained in a series of documents engrossed annually from the days of the first Plantagenet to those of the fifth monarch of the House of Hanover, which exist in unbroken continuity in the great collection of national archives. No other country possesses such a wealth of public records. But those, for the last three centuries at least, are supplemented by still more abundant materials in private collections, the quantity and value of which are not yet estimated, though research into them has frequently thrown a new light on public events, or suggested a new theory of public policy, or modified the traditional judgments which have been promulgated about public men.

The economical history of England is illustrated with singular clearness towards the end of the eleventh century, by that great survey of the whole kingdom, with the exception of the four northern counties and part of Lancashire, which is known as Domesday Book. This unique and invaluable record, which has never yet been adequately analysed, is a register of landowners and tenants, describes the changes which had been effected by the Conquest, and exhibits the economical condition of the English under the government of William. But the social history of England is almost a blank for nearly two centuries afterwards, except for the little which may be gathered from the chroniclers. The new light which is thrown on the economic and social condition of the country at the time when continuous archives inform us of the facts, reveals a very different state of things from that which is exhibited in Domesday.

The information from which the economical history of England and the facts of its material progress can be derived, becomes plentiful, and remains continuously numerous from about the last ten or twelve years of the reign of Henry III. Before this time there is not, I believe, a farm account or manor roll in existence. Suddenly these documents, from which this aspect of English history can be constructed, are found abundantly. It is noteworthy that changes of practice in the conduct of business occur almost simultaneously all over the country. Even changes of handwriting are discovered at widely different places, but with singular uniformity of time. An expert in the common hand of the English scribe will tell the date of a document within a few years, whether its origin be Lancashire, Kent, Warwickshire, Norfolk, or Northumberland. It is plain that the intercourse of Englishmen in the so-called middle ages must have been frequent and familiar, even if there were not abundant evidence to show how general was the habit of travel with certain classes of the community. But such an intercourse is the principal factor of what is called public opinion, that sentiment which has been so difficult to interpret, still more to anticipate, in the political action of this country, but which has, at various epochs of English history, startled sovereigns and governments by the suddenness of its action and the intensity of its purpose.

The Norman Conquest appears to have almost completely supplanted the aristocracy of the Anglo-Saxon race, and to have put the adventurers who accompanied William into the place of those nobles who had ruled the peasantry. It seems that the lower classes were no better off, and no worse off, after the Conquest than they had been before it. The thane had his villeins and slaves; and there is no reason to believe that the Norman baron was a worse master than the Saxon thane whom he superseded. William changed the local administrators in Church and State; and he had to deal with those whom he had dispossessed. The disinherited had their partisans; and naturally there was partisan warfare wherever it was likely to be successful,—in the morasses of Ely and the fells of the Northern borders. The outlaws of the Conquest, when resistance became hopeless, assassinated the intrusive Norman; and William imposed a serious liability on the district in which the outrage was committed. By a series of accidents, the collective importance of which cannot, in the interests of administrative government, be over-estimated, any murder, the doer of which was not taken red hand, became an affair of the King's court; for the hundred was liable to a penalty of from £36 to £44 in case the culprit were not found out and surrendered.

With few exceptions, the Anglo-Saxon lords were de-graded, and assumed a lower social position, or were wholly dispossessed, and sought their fortunes in other countries. But the higher social element of the residual English was still strong enough to be useful to the sovereign in an emergency, and the lower retained and clung to their local institutions. It was therefore easy for the king to appeal to his English subjects, and to use their services against rebellious barons and their retainers and, if he were strong enough, to secure them, after he won his victory, against notable outrages. He soon saw that it was wise to keep entire a force which might be employed against the dangers which his own aristocracy might cause him. Experience confirmed his anticipation. The second and third Norman kings found their most useful allies in their English subjects; and the *savants* of the Norman and Plantagenet sovereigns soon began to protect the tenants of the Norman lords, by the machinery of the law courts, against the arbitrary authority of their superiors.

The English king was the largest landowner in the kingdom, and he stood to his tenants in the same position that any great landowner did to his. But great as his estate was in comparison with that of others, it was scanty in amount compared with that of his great lords, if they acted in concert, and it was liable to demands to which they were not exposed. The king had to undertake the expenses of administration, of justice, and of police, except in so far as the machinery of local self-government relieved him from such duties. Besides, in order to keep up his own influence, he had to conciliate his advocates, his officials, and his partisans with gifts. In other words, he had to construct, maintain, and occasionally to revive a royal party. Such a policy required mature vigour and incessant care. The Crown was enfeebled and the country im-poverished and irritated whenever these conditions were not observed. It cannot be by accident that social discontent and disorder always followed on the reign of a sovereign who succeeded to the throne in his minority. The government of the country was put to its severest strain in the reigns of Henry III., Richard II., Henry VI., and Edward VI. The certainty that the same result would ensue in the contingency of Edward V. reigning under tutelage, is the sole apology for Richard the Third's usurpation. It is probable that the danger of a child-king was present to the minds of those who brought about the Revolution of 1688 ; and that the position which English statesmen for four centuries have successfully insisted on, that the office of regent is in the gift of Parliament, and can be exercised only under such conditions as Parliament may impose, has been constantly affirmed.

The king was led, for many reasons, to employ such persons as could be rewarded for their services from the revenues of the Church. At the Conquest, the dignitaries of the old monarchy were constrained to retire, but the patrimony of the Church was not diminished. Its bishoprics, deaneries, canonries, and benefices were frequently the reward of secular service on the Crown's behalf. When the Papacy arrived at despotism over Christendom, as absolute, as far reaching, and as aggressive as that of the old Roman Empire, through agencies which it believed to be moral, but later criticism has declared to have been superstitious, and a short experience proved to have speedily become dishonest, it saw with unerring instinct that the bestowal of benefices for political services was the principal obstacle which must be removed before these aims could be achieved. When it found that it could not succeed in the war against investitures, it most adroitly and with far greater success insisted on the right of provision, that is, of nominating to ecclesiastical offices in expectancy, or of taking advantage of technical flaws in an election, the legal right to which was in certain hands, in order to establish its own nominee. Sometimes the king was disappointed, sometimes the pope. Henry II. thought that he had secured a courtier prelate in Becket, and owed all the misfortunes of his reign to the miscalculation which he made in his man. Innocent III. imagined that he secured a papal prelate in Langton, and found that his hold over England was irrecoverably loosened by the man of his choice.

Beyond the profits which he derived from his private estate, the king was in receipt of certain dues from his subjects. He was the heir of all escheats—that is, of all estates in which there was a failure of legal heirs, and of all forfeitures—that is, of all estates, the owners of which had committed such crimes as involved the destruction of rights in property. The former, in an age of violence and risk, were probably more frequent than the latter, though for feiture was by no means uncommon, unless the partisans of a rebellion were too numerous and too united to be disinherited. But whether the estate was escheated or forfeited, the grants of the former possessor were respected, and the king succeeded to those rights only which the misfortune or the misconduct of the owner could extinguish.

The king had also the right of claiming fixed and casual dues from those of his inferiors who stood in certain relations to him. The tendency in the mind of his subjects was to make all dues, with some exceptions, fixed, to estimate them once for all in an unchangeable quantity of money, to resent or resist all attempts to collect more than was due, and to exercise a discretion as to the frequency of collection. In the first Great Charter, that of John, the assent of the kingdom is to be required for all extraordinary grants; and though this condition was omitted in some subsequent editions of the Charter, it was never forgotten, was suspended for special reasons, and was ultimately acknowledged to be a fundamental right of the subject.

The king had trivial dues on exports and imports, called customs. It is obvious that, in the first place, the trade of the time was too small to make such sources of revenue lucrative, and that in the next, there neither did nor could exist any adequate police for the collection of other than small dues at the principal ports. In all likelihood the imports and exports at the numberless smaller ports were necessarily neglected.

He derived, however, and in consideration of very solid advantages secured to the subject, a considerable income from fees of court for conveyances. From very early times, the conveyances of estates by what were called fines, were registered and carefully recorded in the archives of the Court.

The convenience of an indefeasible title was obvious, the guarantee of the register was complete, and there was no part, perhaps, of the business of the great office of the Exchequer, in which the whole revenue of the sovereign was collected and audited, which excited so little dissatisfaction as that by which the estates of the great landowners were conveyed and assured.

But the Exchequer was felt to be armed against every one, to be constantly watching for the rights of the Crown, and to be actively vigorous in the vindication of these rights. The Crown and its officers knew that it was dangerous to rouse discontent by any general usurpation, and that it could only attempt oppression where oppression roused no sympathy for its victim. The Crown could alternately caress and fleece the Jew; but the Jew was held to be the private enemy of all debtors. It could assail successfully those whom the nobles hated, or the people distrusted and disliked. It was often incapable of defending its own instruments or favourites, but this was when it transgressed prudence in administration and excited general dislike. Individuals were wronged and outraged, and public opinion was not arrayed against the ill-doer. But it was a very different thing if the Crown attempted to oppress the whole people, to levy contributions at its own discretion, or to increase the amount of that which had been conceded. The Exchequer was the principal instrument of government, the real centre of the administration, which was always striving to increase its business and the king's revenue. Against this ever present and ever prying institution, baron and franklin, esquire and yeoman, were united. When a revolution occurred, sometimes when a revolution was avoided, the principal objects of popular indignation were the ministers of the revenue.

The great audit of the king's revenue was imitated in the account taken of the receipts and outgoings of a manor. These were made up annually, and always in the same form. The scribe who wrote out the annual roll examined the rough notes and tallies of the bailiff, and reduced the particulars to an exact profit and loss account; and on the back of the roll entered all the stock, live and dead, on the estate, giving an account of the whole. In the same way a register was kept of the manor services and dues. The names of the tenants, the extent of their holding, the amount and value of their services, were all entered. The receipts of the lord from the police of the manor, the fines paid for offences, for assaults, for trade frauds, were all duly recorded, just as in the great roll of the Exchequer the multifarious sources of royal revenue were all duly entered, and on audit, credited to the officer whose duty it was to collect them. This system came suddenly into use all over England a few years before Henry the Third's death.

Only a few thousands of these documents survive. They had, it would appear, only an ephemeral interest. The account of one year had no importance, it would seem, to the owner of the estate, except in so far as the undischarged liabilities of the bailiff or other agent whom he employed are noted. But the universal practice of drawing up an annual account of receipts and disbursements, of assets and liabilities, of stock-taking, besides the engrossing of the manor-roll, and in the case of large properties or large establishments, other exact accounts of household expenditure, must have involved a large amount of clerical work at certain times of the year. The scribe must have been nearly as universal a person as the smith, and the number of persons who were competent to draw up a balance-sheet of numerous particulars must have been very large. There is a general impression that few persons in the later middle ages knew how to read and write. But the prodigious amount of documents penned yearly, and penned precisely, and at nearly the same time of the year, just before Michaelmas, proves that education must have been far more widely diffused than is commonly imagined. It is probable that the bailiff was not uneducated either. I have occasionally found the accounts of this personage, accounts which the scribe examined, verified and copied fairly out. It is remarkable, too, that, with hardly an exception, the accounts are written in Latin. The Latin is, of course, barbarous, full of English words with Latin terminations; but it is always grammatical. I cannot believe that the language into which his annual balance-sheet was rendered was an unknown tongue to the bailiff, or that he would have been content to allow his liabilities to be expressed in a form which he could not understand. But I must return to this topic hereafter.

These documents, I do not doubt, were preserved because they formed evidence of title. The courts of law had laid down the rule, that no title could be shaken by adverse evidence of an earlier date than 1189. But evidence would be admitted subsequent to that date; and therefore any proof of continuous possession was valuable. At the beginning of the present century, one of the Oxford colleges attempted to establish an ancient right to tithe in an Essex parish, and supported their claim by presenting in court a number of their most ancient rolls of receipt and expenditure. It was customary, too, for a purchaser to receive from a vendor all the evidence of which the latter might be possessed. Thus the founder of an Oxford college bought an estate from an Oxfordshire family at the latter end of the fourteenth century, and received with it a number of accounts which go back to the latter part of the thirteenth. Another founder, nearly a century later, succeeded in procuring the suppression of a wealthy priory in Hampshire, the character of which was not very good, and carried to the record room of his college a number of accounts of this religious house, which run back for a long period before the suppression. The great abbey of Sion contained a number of documents which illustrate the domestic history of many among these alien priories, with the estates of which this fifteenth century religious house was endowed.

It is well known that the construction of the Exchequer was the work of Henry II., and that he was assisted in the elaboration of its machinery by the unwearied services of certain ecclesiastics who were devoted to the Crown and the interests of the Crown. The most eminent of these persons were of one family, which had long held bishoprics as the reward of their fidelity to their employer and his policy.

Henry had every opportunity for the work which he set before himself. The country was exhausted by a war of succession, which had degenerated into mere brigandage. Englishman and Norman were equally anxious to secure quiet and good government, to live under the same laws, and to aid in maintaining the king's peace. The miserable experience of anarchy and disorder had united the two nations against common foes. England is almost the only European country in which the nobles, the gentry, the yeomen, and the burghers have for ages made common cause against public dangers, whether the danger was a foreign enemy introduced into the kingdom by a tyrannical ruler, as was the case under John, or a reckless waste of the resources of government, as was the case in the reigns of Henry III. and Henry VI., or the peril of unworthy favourites, whom the experience of the country detected in the times of Edward II. and Richard II., or the development of an arbitrary system of government such as that which made opposition to the king irresistible in 1641 and 1688. In those emergencies the whole body of the English people were of one mind, as they have been in the defence of governments which were not indeed perfect, but interpreted the true interests of the country.

Henry II. was a man whose political instincts were far in advance of his age, and he owed his troubles to the fact that he yielded to them and strove to do what was premature. He came to the conclusion that he was strong enough to do battle with the Church in the interests of good government. That he nominated Becket to the see of Canterbury under the conviction that he had a thorough-going partisan of the royal power and policy in him is plain. That the hesitation of Becket in taking the office was understood by Henry to be mere prudery is equally manifest. That Henry's suspicions were aroused when Becket instantly divested himself of his secular offices, and determined to give himself up wholly to his ecclesiastical duties, was the natural result of the disappointment which he felt at the error which he committed and of the foresight with which he anticipated trouble to come,

He might have temporized with the new archbishop, and have employed him in the correction of those ecclesiastical abuses which he saw were scandalous and increasing, as his great-grandfather employed Lanfranc, under the cloak that by so doing the archbishop could strengthen the Church. He might have delayed his action till he had assured himself of success in the project which he had set his heart on. He was fully assured, as the event proved, that all the other bishops would support him, and he concluded that Becket would not stand away from his brethren. As it is well known, Becket at first subscribed to the Constitutions of Clarendon, a summary of customs which would have anticipated the changes brought about by Henry VIII. nearly four centuries afterwards, repented of his compliance, sought the pope's pardon, and irretrievably quarrelled with the king. Henry might have thought that the pope, who had quarrelled with the Emperor Frederic, and was denounced by an anti-pope, would not support Becket; and many persons must have thought with him, at times even Becket himself. But the pope strove to effect a reconciliation, and did effect it. The issue of Becket's restoration was the murder of the prelate.

I do not doubt that Henry's horror and alarm at Becket's death was genuine. He must have foreseen that the whole of his projected reforms in the Church, and his cherished hope that he would make the clergy obedient to the law, were indefinitely postponed. He had not only miscalculated the forces to which he was opposed, but he had given them, by his indiscreet language, and through the agency of Becket's murderers, who thought they were doing his bidding, an almost irresistible power against him. Henceforth the only means by which the Crown could succeed in checking the power of the ecclesiastical party, was by rousing its interests in national purposes against those of the Roman Court; and it generally did this unwillingly. Sometimes the higher clergy take part with the people against the misgovernment of the king, as Langton did against John, and many of the prelates did against his son. Sometimes the bishops are incensed against the Papal court, by reason of its exactions and the scandals which its favourites caused. Sometimes the monks are the objects of hostility, for their privileges and immunities were derived from the action of the Roman court, and were a perpetual grievance to the bishops and the secular clergy. At last Edward I. seized the opportunity, when both regular and secular clergy were unpopular, and were indiscreet enough to shelter themselves under the mandate of Boniface and his bull forbidding payments of taxes by the clergy, to frighten them so thoroughly that henceforth, with rare exceptions, the authorities of the Church became as docile to the Crown as they had been refractory in earlier days.

By his marriage with Eleanor of Guienne, Henry had acquired nearly the whole sea-board of France from the mouth of the Seine to Bayonne, and claimed rights of inheritance over the greater part of the Mediterranean sea-board. He inherited Normandy, which had a sort of suzerainty over Brittany, from his mother, and the territories which lay between Normandy and Guienne, and formed, as was found in the fifteenth century, a necessary connection between the two great duchies, from his father. Guienne came to him with his wife, who had also claims on Toulouse. He prepared to vindicate these claims in 1159, and took his chancellor Becket, now his dearest friend and soon to be his principal foe, with him on the expedition. He laid siege to the town, but soon abandoned the attempt, through good feeling towards the French king, who held the duchy by a claim inferior, as some jurists asserted, to those of Henry's wife. It is said that he thought it unwise to attack the French king, his feudal superior in respect of his foreign possessions, on territory which he was holding by a disputed title indeed, but by one of considerable duration. But the attempt led to results which no one could have anticipated at the time.

The universal rule under which military tenants held their possessions from the Crown was that they should give their personal attendance on the king during his wars, for a given time, exclusive of that required for going to and returning from the seat of war. When the English baronage marched to the Scotch or Welsh frontier, the charges of the journey were comparatively slight, and were endurable. The peculiar character, too, of the double tenure in England and Normandy which the comrades of the Conqueror and their descendants possessed, made the transit from one country to another natural and easy, though in course of time it plainly became the custom for the English and French possessions of the family to be divided between descendants of the same degree, so that one should hold the former, another the latter. But the obligation imposed upon an English baron to travel on his own charges from Yorkshire or Cheshire to Toulouse might well seem intolerable. It was, and it remained to a very late period, a popular impression that the foreign possessions of the Crown were an advantage to the English people, that their revenues lightened the charge of government and increased the estate of the Crown, and more reasonably, that the intercourse between the producers and traders of England and the transmarine possessions of the king was of signal importance to the former. This was especially the case with Guienne, as I shall show hereafter. But the burden of defending those distant territories, cast on the English tenants in chief, was a great, an unfair, an intolerable load. A commutation of this payment in kind for a payment in money, which should be a fair and equal assessment, would be an advantage to all parties. It would relieve the baronage from a most unequal incident, it would give the king a manageable revenue.

Becket is understood to have been the agent in negotiating this commutation, which is known under the name of scutage or escuage. The bargain was effected, as usual, on a fixed and uniform rate, and the tenants of the Crown were made familiar with taxes levied in lieu of personal services, and at a fixed rate. In course of time the scutage is dropped, and a subsidy based on a valuation, made in the time of Edward I., and revised in that of Edward III., was substituted for it. But the fact remained,—a money contribution in lieu of personal service. The contribution again was extracted from those who were alone liable to it,—the immediate tenants of the Crown, *i.e.*, to all persons, whether holding of the

Crown or not, whether military tenants or socagers, from persons who held by a rent, and from those who held by a base tenure, as is proved by the taxing rolls or assessments of Edward I.

The funds derived from this money commutation enabled the English monarch to maintain a military force of picked and trained volunteers, whose efficiency contrasted strongly with that of the continental or ordinary feudal levies. I do not assert that at the commencement of the system such a military force was developed and maintained, but it certainly was in course of time. Nor does it appear that Henry II. used to the full the new instrument which was put into his hands. As is known, he regulated the militia of freeholders ; and probably found in the wars which he undertook, most of which were for the defence of his continental dominions, that the ordinary feudal force was sufficient for his purpose. Richard was hardly at all in England. But John appears to have exacted the scutage from his English tenants constantly. He had a plea in the loss of Normandy and in the peril to which his mother's duchy was exposed. He employed the funds which he extorted in maintaining an army of mercenaries on the English soil, which he had collected for foreign service, and on the plea of foreign service had used for the oppression of his English subjects.

That at some time or other the English prelates, baronage, and commonalty would make common cause against the Crown, and assert that they must be consulted before the king was competent to levy the military tax was to be expected. This was done in 1216, and the principle of popular assent to all extraordinary taxes was affirmed in the Great Charter, was confirmed subsequently, and was never lost sight of. The right of the subject to examine into and interpret the needs of the Crown, to give or refuse subsidies, was the origin, and remained the essence of Parliamentary government. Several times, during the reign of Henry III., and before Parliamentary institutions had been formed and developed, the great council summoned by Henry debated the king's necessities and gave or refused to give assistance to the

Exchequer. To have acknowledged that the king was the sole judge of the extent to which his necessities should be relieved, would have been to surrender the fortunes of the whole of England to his discretion. To have merely received the king's message, and to have directed a scutage or a subsidy in accordance with the royal wish, would have been only the same result disguised. Debate involved the inherent right of refusal, and Matthew Paris shows that the refusal was not infrequent. It is known that the improvidence of the king, the difficulties in which the Exchequer was placed by his action, and the fact that the country was compromised, formed the apology for the association at the head of which were Simon de Montfort and Clare, and for the Barons' War. The king could not be trusted; and an attempt, temporarily futile, was made to exact guarantees from him. It is a mistake to imagine that the relations of the king and his people remained the same after the victory of Lewes and the defeat of Evesham. If Henry was anxious to grasp all that he had before these events, he found that others, especially his son, knew better, and saw that there must be a new departure. The commutation of personal service for money was the germ of the Parliamentary system, of the power of the Commons over the public purse and of the appropriation of supply. It took centuries to develop these results, but they were in the beginnings of Parliament as surely as the forest oak is in the seedling.

The army formed out of these parliamentary grants was developed during the "hundred years' war" with France. Its efficiency was remarkable. It constantly broke in pieces armies infinitely more numerous than itself, if it were only properly trained, disciplined, and handled. It was always, or nearly always, victorious in the field, though it was too small to permanently occupy the country which it conquered. But from the Battle of Crecy to the Treaty of Picquigny, an English army was the terror of continental militias. From the defeat of Charles the Bold to the battle of Marignano, the Swiss were the most renowned and formidable soldiers in Europe. From the decline of the Swiss power till the latter end of the sixteenth century, the Spanish foot-soldier took the first place in the military force of Europe. Cromwell's New Model was founded on the same principle as that which had, nearly three centuries before, been adopted by Edward III.; as was also the British army of the Revolution and the war of the Spanish Succession, as was that which Wellington formed and commanded.

None but freeholders could serve in the militia, as constructed by the Assize of Northampton. But servile birth was no obstacle to enlistment in the king's own army, and we get, incidentally, evidence of the fact. When in 1381, the uprising of the serfs took place, and the siege of Norwich was undertaken by Littlestreet, Sir Robert Sale was captain-general of the city. The insurgents tried to induce him to desert and become their leader. He had been born of villein descent, had enlisted in the king's army, had served in France, had been knighted, and raised to high military command. The rebels argued that as he was no gentleman born, but, like themselves, the son of a villein, he should and ought to lead them. They proposed, as a reward for his compliance, to put a quarter of England under his obedience, for it was Tyler's plan to govern England in the king's name, by military officers set over various districts of the country. Sale refused to comply, and remained faithful to the king's service. Perhaps the reasoning employed by the insurgents was not the most prudent and convincing that might have been suggested. He defended himself as long as he could, till, notwithstanding his gigantic strength, he was overpowered by numbers. But the story shows that a serf could rise to knighthood during the wars of Edward, at a time when it was difficult indeed to overcome obstacles of birth, and knighthood appeared to be peculiarly the privilege of the well born. The royal army, like the Church, effaced distinctions of birth, in the case of those who entered its ranks. A Sale could become a general, just as a century or more before a Grostête could become a bishop. Hence while in France and Germany the distinction between the noble and the peasant or burgher was intensified as time went on, in England the nobility was constantly recruited from the lower orders through the army, and in course of time through trade. I do not recall any instance in which the collateral relatives of Churchmen were ennobled by the wealth of prelates or other opulent ecclesiastics, but it is clear that the brothers of Chichele, perhaps the kinsmen of Wykeham, were enriched by the fortunes of their clerical relatives, though both these personages devoted a large part of their wealth to the foundation of colleges in Oxford and elsewhere.

We may therefore trace the germ of great political and social results in the commutation for personal service on the foreign possessions of the English kings,—possessions, it will be remembered, which to a greater or less extent were united to the English Crown, for nearly four centuries, *i.e.*, from the Conquest in 1066 to the final expulsion of the English from France in 1453. The commutation led directly to the formation of parliamentary institutions, which bargained for the development of public liberties and private rights by grants in aid of the Crown. It created an army which from time to time has had no parallel in efficiency. It broke down the distinction of race and birth, and ultimately made the tenure of the peasant more desirable than that of the knight and noble ; so that in the end the higher qualities of land were transformed into the semblance of the lower. It united all parties, the nobles fitfully and last of all, against the extravagant pretensions of the prerogative, so that England at a very early period was the theatre of very singular political events. A change of dynasty owing to the decadence of a reigning house and the rise of a powerful subject was effected thrice in French history. The balance of power in the German Empire was so nicely dubious in German history, that at one time the interposition of the pope was able to ruin an imperial family ; and at another time the ambition of the German princes led to the complete degradation of the imperial authority, during the period which intervenes between the fall of the House of Suabia and the rise of the House of Austria. But in England the whole people has deposed the reigning monarch six times, selecting in five of these cases some other member of the same family to fill the room of the dethroned king. On two occasions, earlier than any of these instances, it strove to dethrone the king. The first attempt would probably have been successful had not the king died in the midst of the crisis; for John appears to have been reduced to almost the lowest extremity at the time of his opportune death. In the other case there was a counter revolution, effected, as is manifest, by the singular tact and ability of the heir to the throne; for Edward I. was as vigorous and far-sighted a ruler as his father, Henry III., was irresolute and imprudent. Now it does not seem that this unity of purpose, frequently recurring in English history, so puzzling to foreigners that they called the English "the disloyal nation," could have been developed except there had not only been a community of interest, but familiarity with the agency by which discontent could be effectively expressed. In the course of this inquiry we shall find some instances of a similar intensity of opinion influencing the action of large masses of the common people.

The commutation of precarious service for fixed money payments became the rule. The charters of self-government accorded to the towns were always accompanied by an obligation on the part of the town to pay the fee farm rent of the municipality to the sovereign; and these annual payments, fixed in amount, were in early times an important part of the king's income. Nor could the lords of the serfs avoid following the example. It may be the case that Madox is right in his interpretation of those entries in John's pipe-rolls, which seem to indicate the actual sale of serfs and their families. I am disposed to interpret these entries as implying that the services of these persons were sold, or the customary payments made by them in lieu of service were farmed out—a practice which prevailed long after the period to which Madox refers. But in the many thousands of bailiffs' and manor rolls which I have read, I have never met with a single instance of the sale of a serf. Nor have I discovered any labour-rent for which an equivalent money-payment could not be substituted. That the base tenure of these serfs, villeins, and ultimately tenants by copy or custom, involved certain very disadvantageous contingencies and some very humiliating liabilities is certain, and I shall have hereafter to comment on them. Most of these nearly cease at or about the middle of the fifteenth century, for reasons which I hope I can explain hereafter. It was by these contingencies and liabilities that the tenure of the copyholder differed at a very early period from that of the socager, who paid a fixed money, or fee-farm rent, for his holding, who had fixity of tenure, but who was liable to distraint or even eviction on the non-payment of his permanent annual charges as late as the sixteenth century.

Any one who reads the work of the ablest and most instructive of our chroniclers, Matthew Paris, will find how marked a change has come over English life between the accession of John and the rise of the opposition to the government of Henry III. During John's reign, there was but little organization against the arbitrary action of the Crown, and every class in England was in turn the victim of its rapacity. John defied the pope, but was brought on his knees only because his people were deserting him. When he made England a fief of the Roman see, he imagined for a time that he could hold his people in complete subjection by the assistance of the pontiff; but the whole nation rose against him, extorted the liberties of the Great Charter, and, with Langton at their head, defied both pope and king. But John, thanks to the mercenaries whom he levied and paid was able to resist them, till they invited Louis of France to wrest the crown from the unworthy king. It seems that the action of the pope in John's reign, and in that of his son, in interfering on the side of the king with the universal demands of the people, is the beginning of that deep-seated hostility to the Roman court which is so marked in the best and most zealous Churchmen during the thirteenth, fourteenth, and fifteenth centuries. But it is also clear that John was far more autocratic than any of the sovereigns who followed him, and that the confederates of Runnymede did much more than extort a charter, for they organized a permanent opposition to the government.

Langton and Pembroke contrived to free England from Louis and from John's mercenaries. The policy of these great men was followed by the Justiciary, Hubert de Burgh, and the king's peace was generally maintained. Fortunately for England, the death of Philip Augustus was soon followed by that of his son, Louis VIII., and the accession of a child, Louis IX., the management of whose minority occupied all the anxieties of the queen-regent. There was, on the whole, peace between England and France, and, on the whole, peace between England and Scotland. During this reign, prosperity was general. The grant of a fifteenth was conceded, under the express condition that the charter of the forests should be granted in return,—a precedent for similar bargains, not always completed, and for constant wrangling, when the king made his poverty the plea for demands on his subjects.

It is possible that during the minority of Henry III. the estate of the Crown was lessened. Henry was always in pecuniary difficulties. His debts grew, payments to his household were in arrears ; and on one occasion we are told of the brigandage which disgraced Hampshire, the head-quarters of which were at Alton, that not a few of the culprits were Henry's own servants, driven to these acts in consequence of the non-payment of their wages. The king gave away largely, not to say lavishly, to his favourites, especially to his half-brothers and to his wife's relations. He was fond of splendid entertainments, and indulged in a passion for building. He engaged recklessly in undertakings which were certain to be costly, and unlikely to be successful. The English were not only perpetually importuned for money, but were pillaged by the papal emissaries, and fleeced by intrusive nominees of the pope. The court of Rome had prohibited, under the plea that the transaction was almost certain to be simoniacal, the nomination of prelates by the prince, only to appropriate the collation of these benefices on behalf of his own creatures, and the king was passive or consenting. The plainest language is employed by Matthew Paris to describe and denounce the king's administration, who is openly rebuked for his wilful and wanton extravagance by his nobles and clergy, Matthew himself having constantly told the king his mind about Henry's conduct.

Though generally good-natured and easy-tempered, Henry was liable to violent fits of passion. He was served faithfully by Hubert de Burgh, but turned upon him at last savagely, stripped him of his property, threatened his life, compelled him to take sanctuary, and dragged him from his refuge. In the end, however, he was reconciled to his minister, and restored him to his property. He furthered the marriage of his sister Eleanor with Simon de Montfort, employed Simon in several important offices, but at last quarrelled with both, assailed his sister in the coarsest language, drove her and her husband from court, and, after a time, made up the quarrel. Never was man more capricious and uncertain, more violent and more placable. He was easy, but perfidious. The morality of the Roman court assumed to free sovereigns from the obligations of an oath; and Henry constantly availed himself of the opportunities to which his own interests prompted him, and papal dispensations made obvious and easy. He tried to manage all the affairs of his kingdom, and so directed all the unpopularity of his administration against himself, till at last every one, even his brother, whom he had so enriched that he was credited with being the wealthiest noble in Europe, took part at first with the malcontents against him.

It is, I believe, a rule that dissatisfaction with a government, and a determination to reform the conduct of affairs, are ordinarily shown when a community is generally prosperous, and that those uprisings which are the outbreak of despair, lack that organization which attains the end which it purposes. From the scanty notes which contemporary writers make of the seasons, it appears that the middle of Henry's reign was a period of plenty, owing to propitious seasons. In the later years of his activity Matthew Paris generally gives some account of the weather and crops of each year. In four of these years—1244, 1245, 1247, and 1248—this author informs us that the harvest was exceedingly abundant, the price of wheat falling to two shillings a quarter.

CHAPTER II.

RURAL ENGLAND—SOCIAL LIFE.

The Contrast between Town and Country Life early Established—Some English Towns maintained themselves and their Institutions during the Teutonic Conquest—Ranks in the English Manor—The Tenants at Cuxham, their Rents and Services, with the Money Equivalents of such Rent—The Bailiff and Serf—Ibstone Tenants, and their Services—These Services finally commuted for Money—The Money Payments carefully Exacted—The Disabilities of the Serf—Bye Industries in the Villages—Cultivation of Land Universal among all Classes—The Bailiff's Annual Roll—Leases occasionally granted for Terms—Social and Political Effects of this Practice of great Lords cultivating their own Property—The Agriculture of the small Tenants identical with that of larger Holdings—The "Rent" of the Thirteenth Century—Wheat the Principal Product of English Agriculture, and the Principal Food of the People—Facts and Reasons for this Opinion—The Lord of the Manor—The Rector of the Parish, his Revenues—The Miller—The Free and Serf Tenants—The Parish Church—The Houses of the Yeomen and the Cottagers—The Social Opportunities of the Peasantry—Their Power of Organization—Past and Present.

IT is necessary, in order to arrive at a fairly accurate conception of the economical condition and the social life of our forefathers in the thirteenth century, to attempt the description of rural and of town life up to this century. The country parish had constantly remained, with some modifications, the Teutonic settlement of the sixth century. The town, however, had acquired municipal rights, and the management, under certain conditions, of its own affairs, and was striving to attain that comparative independence and freedom from external authority which the municipalities of Roman origin had, it seems, continuously enjoyed or exercised. It is impossible to doubt that English merchants and travellers journeying to Flanders, to the towns of southern France and of Italy, or those of Rhenish Germany, should have noted what they saw in those foreign regions, and have striven to develop the institutions which had given freedom and opulence to those cities. It is likely, too, that some of the English towns, which had a distinct history during the Roman occupation, and contrived to maintain their existence continuously during the days of the Saxon conquest and the Saxon monarchies, also retained during this obscure period some of those institutions which the system of imperial Rome had long made universal. London and York, Lincoln and Winchester, Exeter and Bath, have been inhabited cities from the days of Suetonius and Agricola. They remained, as the great military roads of the Roman occupation remained, in existence, if not in their ancient efficiency and form.

The English village, or manor, as the earliest court rolls inform us, contained several orders of social life. At the head of the settlement was the lord, to whom belonged the manor house, the demesne, which was a several estate, enclosed and occupied exclusively by him, and such rights over the inhabitants or tenants of the manor as ancient compact or more ancient custom secured to him. Sometimes these tenants held military fees, and were bound to such obligations as tenancy in knight service defined. Thus the Warden and Scholars of Merton College, in Oxford, at the close of the thirteenth century, were lords of Cuxham manor, in Oxfordshire, and its demesne, with divers rents and services. The two principal tenants, Quartermain and Pageham, each hold the fourth part of a military fee within the limits of the manor. If a scutage is imposed, they have each to pay 10*s*., *i.e.*, the fourth part of the assessment on an entire fee. They made suit in the court. If their heirs are under age, the college has the guardianship of those heirs; if they have a female heir, the same persons have the right of disposing of her in marriage. The Prior of Holy Trinity, of Wallingford, holds a messuage, a mill, and six acres of land in free alms, *i.e.*, under no other obligation or liability than the offering of prayers on behalf of the donor. A free tenant has a messuage, with three and three quarter acres, the portion of his wife. The rent of this is 3*s*. a year. He has another messuage with nine acres, for which he pays annually

a pound of pepper, the cost of which at the time was about
1*s.* or 1*s.* 6*d.* The rector of the parish church has part of a
furrow—*i.e.*, one of the divisions by which the common arable
field is parcelled out. For this he pays 2*d.* a year. Another
tenant holds a cottage in the demesne under the obligation of
keeping two lamps lighted in the church. Another person is
tenant at will of the parish mill, at 40*s.* a year. The rest of the
tenants are serfs (*nativi*), or cottagers (*coterelli*)—thirteen of
the former, and eight of the latter. Five of these tenants
appear to be widows, and the whole manor, omitting the two
tenants of military fees, appears to have contained twenty-
four households.

Each of the serfs has a messuage and half a virgate of
land at least, *i.e.*, certainly not less than twelve acres of
arable. His rent is almost entirely corn and labour, though
he makes two money payments,—a halfpenny on Nov. 12th,
and a penny whenever he brews. He is to pay a quarter of
seed-wheat at Michaelmas, a peck of wheat, four bushels of
oats, and three hens on Nov. 12th; and at Christmas a cock
and two hens, and two pennyworth of bread. He is to
plough, sow, and till half an acre of his lord's land, and give
his services, as he is bidden by the bailiff, except on Sundays
and feast days. He is to reap three days with one man at
his own charges in harvest time. He is not to marry son or
daughter, to sell ox, calf, horse, or colt, to cut down oak
or ash, without the lord's consent. If one estimates these
services and payments in money of the time, they amount
to near 9*s.*, of which 3*s.* at least must be set down for the
house and curtilage about it. The labour rent for the land is
therefore about sixpence an acre in money value. The soil
at Cuxham is very good wheat land, a loam lying at the base
of the Chiltern Hills, and yielding in good harvests what was
at that time a very full return, viz., thirteen bushels of wheat
to the acre, twenty of barley, sixteen of oats, and fourteen of
peas. This production is far in excess of other land, the
exact produce of which has come under my observation, and
will be commented on.

Some of these tenants hold, besides their virgate, some other plots of land. For these allotments they have to make hay for one day, with a comrade, and receive a halfpenny; to mow with a comrade for three days in harvest time, but at their own charges, and three other days, receiving at the latter the lord's food. The nature of these labour payments and allowances being calculated, is about 2*s*. 4*d*.; and the plot was therefore almost certainly between four and five acres in extent.

The actual rent paid in this indirect way is the ordinary amount paid for fairly good arable land. After their harvest work they are to have together sixpennyworth of beer, and each a loaf of bread. The amount of the bread given to all is to be the produce of three bushels of wheat. Every evening, after the hours are over, each of the reapers is entitled to carry off as large a sheaf of corn as he can lift on his sickle.

The cottagers pay from 2*s*. to 1*s*. 2*d*. a year for their tenements, and have to give a day or two to haymaking, receiving a halfpenny for the service. They are also bound to harvest work for from one to four days, during which they are fed at the lord's table. During the rest of the year they are free labourers, earning wages on the lord's demesne, tending cattle, sheep, or pigs on the common of the manor or in the woods, and engaged in the various crafts which were customary in the village, or might be required by the more opulent employers. The village probably contained from sixty to seventy inhabitants. The parish of Cuxham is small, containing only 487 acres at the present time. But it is noteworthy that the tenants in knight service hold their tenements in Chalgrove; and it will be seen that in the thirteenth century the arable and common land in the neighbourhood contained a far larger area than the modern dimensions of the parish would imply.

The average amount cultivated by the college, who are the lords of the carucates in the manor, is, during four years for which accounts have been exactly preserved, 181½ acres. No doubt fully one-third of the arable land in these two carucates was in fallow, which brings the total to about 242 acres the land held by the serfs amounts to about 170 acres ; and the other tenements probably absorbed 30 acres more, so that from 440 to 450 acres of the present area were, in the thirteenth century, under tillage or permanent occupation. But it is perfectly clear that there must have been originally a far larger amount of common land for pasture than is implied in the residue of the present area.

For at least three generations one of the serfs of the manor was the bailiff of the college, cultivated its estate, exacted its rents and services from the other tenants, and supplied accurate accounts at the annual audit of receipts and disbursements. The office was transmitted from father to son, and many transactions of moment were entrusted to this serf-bailiff. But at last he and all his perished in the plague of 1348-9, for the name disappears from the college records, and the college inherits the chattels of the family.

The manor of Ibstone, which is partly in Oxfordshire, partly in Bucks, was also one of the estates of Merton College. Here also the college had two carucates, which were let to farm during part of the period for which information has been supplied for the Cuxham estate. They were let, indeed, for nearly forty years. At the latter part of the thirteenth century, the college cultivated its own property by a bailiff. The modern area of the parish is 1121 acres. The freehold tenants are twenty in number, the serfs four, the cottagers four.

One of these freeholders holds a virgate by charter, and pays a penny yearly at Christmas. His liabilities are—to ride with his lord when there is war between England and Wales,—the conditions of tenure were evidently old, for Wales was thoroughly subdued in 1298, the date of the rental,—to be armed with iron helmet, breastplate, and lance, and to remain with his lord, at his own charges, for forty days. If his services are required for a longer period, he is to remain with his lord at the lord's expense. He is also to do suit in the lord's court. Besides, he holds a croft, for which he pays 8*d.* yearly. A second has two half-virgates. He pays 5*s.* 6*d.* yearly, and three capons. For the first of these half-virgates, he is to find at his own cost a reaper for three days in harvest time, is to carry his lord's corn in harvest for a day and a half, receiving as pay a sheaf of corn, and to annually carry a load to Henley-on-Thames. For the second half-virgate he is to pay 5s. a year. Another tenant is under the same liabilities for a similar extent of land, but he also pays a fee of 20s. for getting possession. Some of the parcels of land are at higher, some at lower rates, and from his name one of the tenants appears to be by origin at least a resident in Oxford. A few hold for a term of life.

The serfs (*nativi*) all hold half a virgate of land, for which they have to pay the following, in money or labour : 4½d. each quarter, 4½d. on Nov. 12th, and 1s. on Christmas-eve, a hen at Christmas, ten eggs at Easter, and a goose on August 1st. During one week in harvest the tenant (in this case a woman) is to find two reapers on Monday and Friday, and on Tuesday, Wednesday, and Thursday to cut half an acre of corn daily, unless any day be a feast-day. On another week she is to find two reapers on Monday, and one on Friday. She is, at the lord's discretion, to find two men during harvest, who are to be boarded by the lord. Every fourth week, between September 29th and August 1st, save Saturdays and feast-days, she is to work with one other person. She is to take part in washing and shearing the lord's sheep. She is to plough six measures of land, every fourth Sunday, if notice be given on the Saturday, and during the same period to plough and hoe half an acre of land sown in winter, half an acre of Lent land, and half an acre for fallow. The other three tenants have exactly similar duties, so that it would seem that the labour rents of the four serfs provided the farm labour of eight persons from Michaelmas to August 1st, and four weeks' harvest work, abundant time being given to the tenants for getting in their own produce. The tenancy is more onerous than that at Cuxham, but the rents paid for the supplementary crofts and acres is low.

The four cottagers got their homes and curtilages at very low rents. But they have to reap for three days in harvest time, sometimes for one day in each of four weeks, receiving a sheaf of corn every day for their labour. Two of them have to help in washing and shearing the sheep, and to carry five hurdles when the fold is pitched in a fresh spot.

I have given these rents, in money, in produce, and in labour, partly because they exhibit the social economy of the time, and show how the services, which in the early part of the next century were entirely commuted for money payments, were imposed on freeholders and serfs respectively ; partly to point out that, onerous as these labour-rents occasionally were, they indicate a real bargain between lord and serf, and, by implication, point to an arrangement which is very far removed from that ideal state of villeinage which is described in our law books, and has been incautiously accepted by those who have written on the social state of England. According to these authorities, the serf had no rights of property or person against his lord. But as long as these dues were satisfied, it is plain the tenant was secure from dispossession. Within a little more than half a century of the period of which I am writing, when these labour-rents had been universally commuted for money payments, the same tenants are described as copyholders or customary tenants.

Mr. Hallam, the most shrewd and judicious of writers on early English history, is misled by the emphasis with which lawyers in the middle ages comment on the dependent condition of the serfs, and therefore conceived that they owed their emancipation from thraldom, and all negation of rights and property as regards their lords, to the good-natured contempt with which a noble would look upon the miserable savings of his serf, and his unwillingness to appropriate so poor a spoil. No opinion can be more mistaken. The noble and the lord of a manor gathered, through their bailiffs, stewards, and collectors of rent, every farthing and half-farthing which was due to them. When the custom of cultivation by the lord was abandoned, and land was let for terms of years, or upon a yearly tenancy, the collection of these ancient and minute rents became the principal business of the landlord's agent. Occasionally they were farmed out for a lump sum to any cultivator who hired the lord's demesne. They were, no doubt, frequently bought up by the copyholders. The last trace of them disappears in the reign of Elizabeth, though fee farm rents, which have very likely taken the place, in copyholds of inheritance, of these ancient liabilities, remain to our own day.

The serf was disabled from migrating to any other habitation than the manor of his settlement. He could not bear arms in the militia. He could not enter into religior or become a secular priest, without the license of his lord, though it is very unlikely, if he furtively professed himself that the Church would, at least in the thirteenth century, suffer him to be seized and handed back to his lord. The prohibition of the villein's ordination is one of the Constitutions of Clarendon, and the enactment points to a systematic evasion of villeinage in the middle of the twelfth century.

If the serf obtained leave of his lord to live away from the manor, he paid a small annual tax, called capitagium or chivage. These items of income are long recognised and entered among the bailiff's liabilities. They may have constantly hindered the absent serf from obtaining the privileges of burghers in the towns. But in course of time the chivage was capitalised and bought up. Sometimes the tax is, contemptuously perhaps, called culage, for this expression is not solely applied to women.

The serf was, as I have said, disabled from marrying his daughter without license and fine. Very numerous instances are found of these kinds of payment, under the name of mercheta, in the earlier times. Similarly fines are paid for marrying a daughter outside the manor, for marrying a nief, *i.e.* a female serf, who was possessed of property, and by men of another manor for marrying a female serf from her lord's manor. I have found traces of this custom, though they become very infrequent, far on into the fifteenth century. Sometimes the serf purchases his chivage and his license to marry at the same time, and is thereafter quit of all obligations.

The serf's son was unable to get instruction and enter orders, regular or secular, without his lord's consent. Entries of fines paid for going to the schools and entering the Church are exceedingly common in the manor rolls of the thirteenth and fourteenth centuries, though they become increasingly rare and finally disappear in the fifteenth. These payments, degrading as they may seem, are indirect proof, occurring early, that the chattels of a serf were safe, at an early date, from arbitrary forfeiture to the lord. In 1394, at a village in Hunts, a serf had committed homicide and abjured the realm. His chattels, forfeited to his lord, the Abbot of Ramsey, are valued at £5 0s. 8d. We may be sure that he had carried away with him as much of his movables as he could. The sum, supposed to be recoverable, represents fairly enough the stock of a small farmer, the actual value of his holding, after his dues were deducted, not being more than a third or fourth of this sum.

A thirteenth century village then contained some sixty to eighty inhabitants, most of whom were constantly engaged in husbandry, all, indeed, for certain periods of the year. There were few handicraftsmen, for probably common carpenter's work was undertaken by ordinary farm hands, as we know it was by the small farmers four or five centuries later than the thirteenth. The most important artificer, indeed, was the smith; but it is plain from the records which have been preserved, that the smith's work, even on the demesne estate, was not sufficient to maintain a smith in any manor, and that the same person served the needs of three or four. When the bailiff of one of these Oxfordshire parishes makes a large purchase of millstones in London, and brings them by water to Henley, he hires the smith at this town to complete the necessary work on his purchase, before he carries them by road from Henley to their destination at Cuxham and Oxford.

It is only by casual notices that we learn anything about the existence of other industries besides agriculture in the rural districts. But it may be taken for granted that weaving was a bye product in nearly all villages, and the tanning or tawing of leather in most. Coarse linen and woollen clothing were doubtlessly manufactured in the cottages of the peasantry, for we occasionally find that flax or hemp was purchased in a raw state, and given in the villages to be woven, the former much more rarely than the latter. The fact that woollen cloth is so rarely found in the charges of agriculture, especially at a time when payments in kind are so general, except when the purchase is made for a great noble or a wealthy corporation, suggests that homespun fabrics were generally available. The same inference is implied in the sale of locks and refuse wool in the neighbourhood of the farm. But it is also contained in the fact, though the evidence is of a later date, that many small and obscure villages in the south of England had flourishing manufactures of textile fabrics, at a period long preceding the migration of part of the Norfolk industries to the west of England, from whence, in comparatively recent times, they have travelled to the north. Even in Norfolk, which was their special home in the thirteenth century, they were carried on in villages where agriculture must have been a principal employment. The yeoman and the labourer undoubtedly fashioned for themselves in winter time, as we learn from the earliest works on husbandry, most of the tools which were needed for their calling,—all, in short, which were not made of iron or steel, or shod with iron.

The first information which we get as to the occupations of the people in rural districts discloses to us the fact that almost every one not only possessed land, but that he cultivated it. The king was not only the largest landowner in the realm, but the most extensive agriculturist, the wealthiest owner of live and dead stock. The estates of such magnates as the Earls of Norfolk and Gloucester were nearly all cultivated by their lords; and I owe to the accident of the surrender of Bigod's lands at the beginning of the fourteenth century, and to the escheat of other and similar estates, and to the preservation of some few fragments of what must have been at one time exceedingly abundant in the public archives, that I have been able to discover so much of the economical condition of mediæval England. On nearly every manor there was a bailiff, who cultivated the soil for his lord, made purchases of necessary stock and materials, hired labour, sold produce, and submitted his account in an exact and elaborate balance sheet yearly. The form which this account takes is uniform, whatever part of the country it comes from. No manuscripts of the middle ages are commoner, and frequently none are better preserved than the handy books of those legal and commercial forms which were adopted universally. Among copies of the statutes and forms of writs and covenants, one generally finds the form in which the annual balance sheet of the lord's profit and loss and capital account is to be rendered by the bailiff.

The name of the estate is engrossed on the head of the roll of parchment, front and back. Then follows the name of the bailiff, provost, seneschal, or receiver of rents, as the case may be, with the date, generally the regnal year of the king, though in the case of some monastic houses the date of the abbot's or abbess's election is substituted for the regnal year, or taken with it. Generally the date is from Michaelmas to Michaelmas, rarely a little later, more frequently a little earlier. I will illustrate the facts by the Cuxham bailiff's roll of 1316-17. The first entry is the arrears with which the bailiff is debited. Then follow the rents of assize, that is, the fixed payments of the tenants. At Cuxham, these amounted to 38s. 10¾d. In the rental they amount to 38s., with a variable tax on domestic brewing. Then follows the rent of the two mills, one for grinding corn, the other a fulling mill, a proof, by the way, of the prevalence of these domestic industries to which I have referred. Next follow the corn sales, the sales of stock, the exits of the manor, *i.e.*, commutations for labour rents, sales of farm produce, except those of the dairy, which follow under the next heading, and sales of wool. Then come manorial fines on entry, heriots, the pleas of court, and sundries. This completes the schedule of receipts.

Next come the expenses. The first item is always the bad debts of the estate and the charges payable to others. Then the charge of the ploughs, the carts, small purchases, charges of the dairy, and purchases of corn and stock. Next we have the cost of the buildings. Then comes the bill for wages, for threshing and winnowing, hoeing and mowing, harvest work, servants' yearly wages, and extraordinary expenses. The last item is foreign charges, *i.e.*, items which cannot be reduced to any of the foregoing heads. The whole is reckoned up. Then the bailiff notes the sums which he has paid to his employers, and what he has paid on their account. Among these items, but under a separate head, are occasionally tallies for wheat taken by the king's purveyor. This concludes the entries on the face of the roll.

The back of the roll contains an exact account of all the stock and produce of the farm, of all that was on it at the conclusion of the last audit, of all that has been produced in the current year, of all that has been disposed of by sale or otherwise, and of all that remains as a liability against the bailiff. Besides sales, there is the seed corn, that used for domestic consumption, and that in payments to farm servants. The tailings of the wheat—it is a year of famine—are mixed, in the proportion of two to one, with coarse barley and pea meal. The same exact account of the sale or consumption of every peck of any other kind of grain is rendered. Then follows an account of the live stock on the estate—horses, cattle, sheep, pigs, and poultry; the produce of cheese, of woolfels, and wool. Each of the several particulars is balanced after the statement, for the account is more minute and exact than any modern account. Printed in full, it requires twelve pages of closely ranged type in a full-sized octavo page.

The figures are all Roman. I have found Arabic numerals as early as the middle of the thirteenth century; but their use in accounts is not familiar before the latter part of Elizabeth's reign. This is a curious but not an isolated illustration of the conservative habits of the age in all matters of business. One would have thought that the obvious convenience of a decimal system in calculation would have commended the practice in accounts which are so minute and elaborate as those which I have described, especially as this practice of account keeping and stock taking was so general. The account is drawn up by a "clerk," who is paid a moderate fee for his trouble. The demand for the services of such scribes must have been considerable between the latter end of July and the beginning of November. Frequently similar or analogous accounts were rendered at other times of the year, as, for instance, on the vacancy of the bailiff's office before the time of the annual audit came round, or for general stock taking over the whole estate of a noble or a monastery or a college. The bailiff's audit was only one of the numerous schedules of receipt and expenditure which were constantly being compiled. There could have been no lack of scribes during this period, and no cessation of employment. The art of account keeping and engrossing must have been very generally known considering the demand which must have been made on the scribes' labours, and instruction must have been far more readily accessible than modern writers are apt to imagine.

Though the custom of landholders cultivating their own estates was general, it was not invariable. The corporate owners of a small estate would probably not be opulent enough to incur the charges and the risks of an agricultural occupancy, and probably let their lands, as a rule, to tenants. But even the more opulent corporations created leases on some of their estates. Thus the fellows of Merton College let their Ibstone estate for thirty-five years, and their Gamlingay estate for fourteen years from the year 1300. They let their Basingstoke estate for twenty-one years from 1310, and their Wolford estate before that date. The property which they possessed in Northumberland and Durham was let as early as 1280, and they never cultivated their estates in Leicestershire. But in all but the last, they let land and stock, alive and dead, together, stipulating that at the termination of the lease all their chattels should be replaced in good and sound condition, or that a fixed price should be paid for all that was deficient or deteriorated. This land and stock lease is so significant in the history of English agriculture that I shall have to comment on it at greater length hereafter.

Several very significant consequences followed from this all but universal practice on the part of landowners of cultivating their own estates with their own capital and at their own risk.

1. The practice made every one anxious to keep the peace and to put down marauders. Every owner of property was

interested in an efficient police. There was plenty of crime and violence in the middle ages, not a little brigandage from time to time, for highway robberies and the organization of gangs of plunderers were not unknown. But it is remarkable how very seldom one reads in these farm accounts (and I have read very many thousands) of agrarian robberies. Even in years of great dearth, such as the terrible time 1315-1321, when there was a veritable famine in England, and many perished from want, we read indeed of alarm that the dire pressure might induce thefts of live stock, but there have been no instances in my reading of that period, the evidence being plentiful, that agrarian robberies were actually committed. There is a well-known complaint of the younger Despenser about the outrages and losses which he suffered at the hands of marauders; but it will be remembered that Despenser was looked upon by a very powerful faction as a public enemy, whom it was lawful, and even meritorious, to harry. Long after the distress to which I have referred ceased, there remained a feeling of respect, even in the most disturbed times, for agricultural property. We read of no complaints of plundering during the war of succession, except when Margaret of Anjou's northern army, in the beginning of the year 1461, did not refrain from pillage; an act of folly as well as of violence, for it raised Edward IV. to the throne. The fact is further illustrated by the special characteristic of English agriculture,—the extensive maintenance of sheep. I know no reason why France, the Low Countries, and the Valley of the Rhine should not have bred sheep as successfully as the English farmer did from the middle of the thirteenth century, except in the fact that a sheep is a very defenceless animal, and needs for his continued existence that he should live without the risks of violence. It seems to me that the comparative success of English agriculture in early times is due to the general conviction that every person was interested in preserving agricultural property from theft or violence.

2. The custom which prevailed materially modified the effects of primogeniture. It is easy to explain the origin and motive of the English law of succession to real estate, though

it is not so easy to follow its growth. But during the period
in which landowners cultivated their own estates, a great part
of the harshness and mischief of the custom was obviated.
On ordinary arable land in the thirteenth century, stock was
three times the value of the land, when adequate stock and
farm implements were kept upon the land. Water or warped
meadow was always very valuable. But ordinary arable
land, yielding, when let to farm, rarely more than 6d. an
acre rent, was worth, to buy or sell, little more than from
6s. to 8s. an acre; while the stock on the land, live and
dead, the cost of labour, and the amount of capital held in
suspense, was from 18s. to 20s. an acre. Now, the younger
children shared with their elder brother in the personal
estate of their ancestor, unless, indeed, they were deprived
of it by an ancestor's will. Hence the phenomenon of an
opulent younger son is seen commonly enough during the
time that the ancient custom lasted; while the appearance
of the impecunious younger son, who is to be provided for
by war, or the Church, or the public treasury, is synchronous
with the abandonment of the ancient practice.

3. The system under which owners of land were generally
capitalist cultivators must have regularly and materially
assisted the distribution of land. It is true that in the time
of which I am writing the ownership of real estate—often,
I admit, under onerous conditions—was all but universal.
A landless man was an outlaw, a stranger; one registered in
no manor, a thief. There were owners of real estate whose
possessions were limited to a cottage and curtilage about it,
a cow's grass on the common, or at least grass for geese and
fowls, since, as I have already shown, cottagers had to pay
poultry rents, just as villeins at half a virgate did. But I
am thinking of something more—of the necessity under
which the eldest son was put of making such terms with his
brothers, perhaps his sisters, as would enable them to exchange
portions of the stock which came to them by inheritance or
by will for the land which came to the eldest son by
inheritance, and could not come to him or his brothers by
will. I make no doubt that it was the custom to arrive at

these arrangements by subinfeudation—*i.e.*, by the elder brother granting the younger, lands to be held of the elder as superior lord; and that when it was thought to be public policy to put an end to subinfeudation by the statute known as *quia emptores*, it was necessary to give the owner of land full powers of alienation, in order to make it possible that these bargains should be negotiated and completed. For we do not hear of the poverty of younger sons till a far later period ; and we hear of it most of all after the risks of the civil wars during the last half of the fifteenth century encouraged the extension of entails from the small and few holders of such estates to the great nobles, and further suggested the additional security of what was called a use —*i.e.*, the introduction of a trustee whose estate might endure for others, and thus the penalties of forfeiture might be avoided.

4. As the tradition of a time in which the great noble was the capitalist cultivator of land survived after the practice ceased, as is proved by the care shown for the farmer's interest, even during the heats of civil discord and actual war, so it early suggested legislative aid to the agricultural interest. The attempt so frequently made, so long unsuccessful, and so successful finally, when a combination of circumstances made it possible to make labour abundant and cheap for the farmers, was not, for a century and a half, an effort made to keep up rents in the interests of the landowners, for these were virtually stationary long after landlord agriculture had entirely ceased, but was an attempt to give the farmer a chance, and probably to increase the area of arable land by enclosures, the object of all writers on agriculture during the seventeenth century. Nor do I believe that the purpose of the landowner during the early part of the eighteenth, in the bounties and corn laws, which were enacted and extended, was his own direct advantage, except in so far as he got the lion's share in the enclosure, but was the encouragement of arable farming. Any student of Adam Smith will find that his fear that free trade doctrines could not and would not be accepted, in spite of their justice and wisdom, was not

derived from the attitude of the landowners, but from that of the manufacturing, and still more from that of the mercantile classes. In fact, it was only after the great rise in rents, consequent on the continental war, that the landowner became passionately protectionist.

5. The custom of capitalist cultivation by the landowner led again to that peculiarity in the relations of landlord and tenant which has been called the English system. Under this, the landowner was expected to do all repairs, to effect all permanent improvements, other than those which were conceived to be in the course of good husbandry, and, in the earlier days of the landlord and tenant system, to insure his tenant against extraordinary losses of stock, especially sheep. The relations of landlord and tenant began, as I shall show, at the beginning of the sixteenth century, to be unsatisfactory, particularly in the fact that good husbandry, which seems an obvious duty of the tenant, was discouraged by raising rent on the sitting tenant, to use a modern phrase, in proportion to the excellence of his husbandry, the eagerness with which he adopted improvements in the process of his art, and the difficulty he had of extricating his capital from his holding on its determination. But the principle that the landowner should do repairs, and contribute all permanent additions to fixed capital in land, has been for ages the practice, and was in early times a far wider practice than it has been for the last century. Without such a custom it would have been impossible to have maintained the English land system. Agriculture would have hopelessly stagnated, and there would have been either discontent as fierce as that in Ireland, and as violent, or the farmers would have entered into some combination which would have had the effect of establishing either a customary rent by the submission of the landowner, or one fixed by a general understanding among occupiers, and determined in the same way that trades unions fix wages and capitalists in certain industries fix prices. Combination may neutralize competition in the rent of land as effectually as it does in railway rates and in divers trades.

The lord did no repairs to the holdings of his freehold tenants or to those of his serfs. The annual accounts of bailiffs are silent about such repairs, though the rents due from cottages are duly entered along with other rents of assize. It would even seem that the rent of cottages was a payment made to the lord for permission to erect and maintain a hovel. But the amount of the rent was unalterable, and thus was an equivalent of the concession. But the fact that such tenants on fixed rents were liable to repairs on their holding—they were generally allowed to obtain the raw material from forest or close or common—was a reason why tenants-at-will or on short leases, or even on long leases, should look to the landlord for all repairs. In town houses these repairs were constantly very costly, and made the difference between gross and net rent very large indeed. On farms they would not be so considerable; but the repairs on the lands occupied by precarious tenants are found, as time passes on, and rackrenting, or its nearest equivalent, became general, to be a very serious item in the rent collector's schedule of expenses. And when we add to this the insurance of stock, which must have been a grave outlook in years when sheep-rot was general, as, for instance, in 1448, the cost to the landowner of recouping his tenant for these losses to his stock, when the loss exceeded a certain amount, might have reduced the gross rent of land to almost as great an extent as the charge for repairs lowered the actual rent received for house property in towns.

We have, as may be expected, no account of the produce obtained from the holdings of these small freeholders and serfs. But there is no reason to doubt that it was identical in character with that produced, manipulated, and sold by the lord's bailiff. The peasant's homestead, barns, and byres were the microcosm of the greater estate, and were probably quite as productive and even better cultivated. In my native village in Hampshire there was in my youth no tenant-farmer at all, though one sale of an outlying farm to a non-resident landlord was effected just before I came to the university. The holdings of these yeomen varied, the land being generally light, from forty to eight hundred acres. But the parish contained fully twice as many homesteads as there were several estates, all with yards and barns about them, though the farmhouses had been cut up into tenements for agricultural labourers. The process of accumulation by owning occupiers had been going on for seventy or eighty years, as I learnt from the talk of old people in the village, and it is certain that if one could have gone back to the earlier rentals —the copyhold of the manor, then only a small part of the parish, was held under somewhat onerous conditions—we should have found that there were far more yeoman land-holders than in the period within living memory, that there were sixty original proprietors, while in the time I speak of there was evidence of no more than thirty. In this village the system of cultivation carried on by the smaller proprietors was exactly identical with that which was practised by the larger, and the system under which labour, supplementary to that of the yeoman, was hired. Generally speaking, too, there was the same simplicity of life, unchanged, I believe, except in a few particulars, from that which was general in a far earlier age. Nor were these yeomen unprosperous when they were active, temperate, and thrifty. The greatest peril they ran was in purchasing land with their savings, mortgaging it to obtain possession, and, up to this having committed no serious error, cultivating the land with insufficient capital. I have known several yeomen, who, having fallen into this mistake, have lived a life of extreme labour and thrift, and, having enlarged their estate, were poorer at their death than they were when they began their career. And in this day I believe that agricultural distress is, and has been for some years past, due to the double cause of enlarged domestic expenditure and insufficient capital for the extent of land occupied.

In the thirteenth century there was no rent paid, in the ordinary economical sense of the word. There was no com-petition for holdings in that state of society in which the great landowner cultivated his property with his own capital, and the smaller tenants had a genuine fixity of tenure under traditional, customary, and certain payments. There were occasions, it is true, in which from an early period land were let to farm. But these tenancies, to which allusion has been made above, were land and stock leases, on really beneficial terms to the tenant; for the estimated value of the stock, or its compensation, in case the tenant failed to restore it at the termination of his lease, was from thirty to forty per cent. below the market value, unless, as is highly improbable, the stock on such land was far inferior in quality to that for which market prices are recorded. Besides, such leases were for the convenience of the landowner or from his necessity, and consequently would be negotiated on terms which were as low as, or probably lower than, customary holdings at a fixed rent. This at least is the inference which I gather from the rate at which stock and land are let together when the custom becomes general. The only apparent illustration of the existence of competitive rents is the fine which is occasionally paid for admission to the property of an outgoing tenant. Instances of the payment of such a fine are rare. It is sometimes called a fine, occasionally gersinna, or gersuma. In all cases, however, it appears to be a payment made either for entering on the estate of an ancestor, and therefore is indirect evidence that the tenancy even of a serf was of a beneficial kind, or for acquiring the exhausted or abandoned tenancy of some other occupier in the manor. But a competition which is practically limited to the tenants of the same manor could hardly be called a competition at all. These fines correspond in amount generally to the two years' value of the tenancy, which ultimately became the maximum fine on succession or alienation in manors. As I deal farther with the subject of genuine farmers' rents, I shall be able to point out when competitive rents arose, and with what consequence to the tenant and to English agriculture.

In point of fact, the rent of the tenant in the time immediately before me may have been, and probably was, in its origin, as the Dialogue on the Exchequer (i. 10) states, a license to live on and cultivate the soil, always, indeed, less than a competitive rent, and perhaps, in its beginning, a precarious tenure. But in course of time the tenancy became permanent, the rent remaining fixed. It was as full, indeed, as could be obtained, for I find that when land is let on lease for short periods, or for life, the rent is no higher than that paid by freeholders and copyholders, but it is not as much as could be paid, seeing that the tenants were constantly able to add to their tenancies, and were frequently called upon for extraordinary payments, which could not have been yielded from a genuine rack rent. And it is a proof of Adam Smith's sagacity, that without the materials before him from which the facts could be demonstrated, he saw that rent was originally a tax, and that a long interval must have occurred before farmers' rents became real and oppressive.

I have commented above on the rents paid by the Cuxham and Ibstone tenants at the latter part of the thirteenth century. I could illustrate the topic further by quotations from rentals of a later date, and in other parts of England, from tenancies far larger in extent than those which I have dealt with, and from holdings in which serf-labour is regularly commuted for money payments. In some cases the labour rents have entirely disappeared and fee farm rents have taken their place at a very early date. This is especially the case in the north of England. But in all, or nearly all, a small amount being deducted for house and curtilage, the maximum rent paid is 6*d.* an acre. On one estate in Durham seven tenants hold over two oxgangs, each equal to a carucate, or hide, and containing at least 120 acres, four a single oxgang, and one holding thirty-three acres, a toft, and a cottage. Here there are coterells with cottages, and pieces of land ranging from nine acres to two. These instances could be multiplied indefinitely, and prove how general was the distribution of land, and how the tenant of the small estates was husbandman as well as possibly labourer, if not in his own person in that of his sons and daughters. Indeed, it is frequently found that the principal servants on a farm, the bailiff, the shepherd, and the carter, were tenants of the manor, and held land and stock, having dealings on their own account with the lord, derived but apart from their relations to him as his farm hands. Their occupation and their industry were identical in kind, but differed only in extent from those of the lord himself.

There is a general impression that the Englishman in the days of the Plantagenets lived on the coarser and inferior kinds of grain. That most of the best wheat went to market, supplied the towns, and was even exported to foreign countries, is probable, or even certain, especially during the fifteenth century. But over the greater part of England, over all, indeed, which has come under my inquiry, even as far north as the county of Durham, the staple produce of agriculture, and by implication the staple food of the people, was wheat, though oats are also consumed as the food of man in those northern regions. From the earliest times wheat has been the principal grain on which the English have lived. No better proof of this can be given than an account of the acreage devoted to the different kinds of grain on various estates. It will be plain that the crop with the widest area was the staple produce, and had the widest market. Now the proof of this is forthcoming, for by an accident the account of the acreage, the seed sown, and the produce obtained for four years during the first half of the fourteenth century, on eleven estates belonging to one corporation, have been preserved. I say by accident, for the record had nothing but a temporary interest, and is probably one surviving from a long series of similar documents which have perished.

1. During the four years 1333-1336, Merton College, Oxford, was cultivating with its own capital eleven of its own estates. Three of them are in Surrey, one in Kent, two in Cambridgeshire, one in Bucks, one in Warwickshire, two in Oxfordshire, and one in Hants. In the first of these years 1,206 acres were under cultivation for grain; in the second, 1,315½ acres; in the third, 1,457 acres; and in the last 1,440¼ acres. But in the first year 527 acres are sown with wheat; in the second, 460; in the third, 560½; and in the fourth, 510¼; so that the acreage of wheat is nearly 44 per cent. in the first year, nearly 35 in the second, about 39 per cent. in the third, and nearly 35½ per cent. in the fourth.

The next most considerable crop is that of oats, the acreage of which is 333, 330, 299½, and 335¼ for the four several years. Oats are very slightly the food of man in southern and central England. They are chiefly used for horses.

The two kinds of barley, ordinary barley with two rows of grain, and the coarse kind of four rows, called bigg or bere in modern husbandry, but anciently known most frequently under the name of drage, a term now entirely obsolete, occupy 263 acres in the first year, 310 in the second, 396½ in the third, 352½ in the fourth. Of these the former was used for beer almost exclusively, the latter for beer occasionally, but most commonly for feeding pigs and poultry. It entirely disappears from cultivation at about the middle of the fifteenth century.

Rye is more scantily cultivated than any of the cereals. In the first and second years, 52½ acres are sown with it; in the third, 50; in the fourth, 72. The only places where it forms a considerable crop are at Gamlingay in Cambridgeshire, and in the immediate neighbourhood of Oxford. It is occasionally mixed with wheat for the manufacture of bread. But it almost disappears as a grain crop in southern and central England at or about the middle of the fifteenth century. Sometimes, under the name of mixtil, wheat and rye are sown together. During the four years under examination, 7½ acres are sown in the first, 19 in the second, 14½ in the third, and 13¾ in the fourth.

The three kinds of leguminous plants cultivated at this time, beans, peas, and vetches, occupy in the area of cultivation for the four years, 113, 144, 136¼, and 156½ acres respectively. Among these is a small amount of white peas on one estate, three acres in one year and five in another. These are used for human food. Beans and vetches are horse food ; grey peas are generally given to pigs. It will, I think, be clear from this analysis of farm produce that the production of wheat for human food, and barley for malting purposes, was the principal and most important part of arable cultivation. There are, however, certain other facts, which prove the same position, that the Englishman of the middle ages subsisted on wheaten bread and barley beer.

2. The monastic chroniclers constantly give, though one

must set little store by their figures, amounts of prices in years of special plenty or exceptional dearth. I have already adverted to a nearly continuous account of the harvests in England, noted by Matthew Paris, during the last fifteen years of this author's literary labours. In every case, the only grain on which the writer thinks proper to comment is wheat. What is true of Paris is true of other authors, of the notes made by farmers and corporations. Corn with them is wheat, and they note the dearness or cheapness of this exclusively, as the main or the principal agricultural interest.

3. In the research which I have made into agricultural values, the amount of information obtained as to wheat prices, whether one takes the record of production and sale on cultivated land, or that of consumption by corporations and individuals, the number of the entries of wheat and malt grains far transcends that of any other information, though the quantities and prices of other kinds of grain are sufficient, as is proved by the maintenance of the ratio of value between them, for the purposes of inference. I have collected, between 1259 and 1583, in my published volumes, 13,313 prices of wheat, 5,172 prices of barley, 4,344 prices of malt, and 6,494 prices of oats. The prices of wheat recorded in these volumes are more than double those of any other kind of grain.

4. At an early period, so early that the statute is reputed to be the oldest after the Great Charter, if, indeed, it be not earlier still, for no date is assigned to the enactment, the assize of bread was made an English law, and every locality had a police for making it effective. But the assize takes no account of any but wheaten bread, and when it is extended to malt, contemplates only that manufactured from barley. I cannot but think in the provident care which the legislature took at so early an epoch of the interests of the consumers,— a care which it has not wholly abandoned in our own day, —attention would have been given to rye, or oaten, or barley bread, if these had been in early times the food of the people.

5. With the same purpose the legislature prohibited the exportation of corn when the price of the quarter exceeded a certain amount. Thus in the year 1438-9, the petitions in

Parliament request that permission should be granted to facilitate the inland distribution of wheat and malt by water carriage, the year being one of severe dearth. The petition was refused on the ground that advantage would be taken of the concession to export English produce to foreign countries where the dearth was as severe as it was in England. But as before, the restraint is only on wheat, barley, and malt, the latter being generally sold at nearly the same price as the former, since the manufactured article fills more space than the natural grain.

6. The extreme rarity of famine in England. I have no doubt that there were local scarcities, possibly local famines, though, as I shall show hereafter, the means of communication between the producer and the market were good, and the cost of carriage, as might be expected in a country of numerous small proprietors, was very low. But I know of only one distinct period of famine in the whole economical history of England, in so far as contemporaneous and statistical evidence demonstrates the facts. This is the seven years 1315-21, especially in the first two and the last. Then famine prevailed, the people perished for lack of food, and the most conclusive proof of famine is afforded, for wages obtained a real and a permanent rise, owing to a scarcity of hands, prolonged for a considerable time, and thereupon effecting a lasting increase of wages; for temporary dearth rather depresses wages. It needs a considerable reduction in the number of those who seek employment to bring about a real increase of wages, and this state o things must last till the increased rate becomes familiar or customary.

Now it is a fundamental principle in the theory of population and wages, that the former does not increase beyond what is the customary food of the people, and that the latter do not fall below the amount necessary for the labourer and his family to subsist on, during the less advantageous part of the labour year. Hence a high standard of subsistence is a more important factor in the theory of population, than any of those checks which Malthus has enumerated. The economist who treats of the social state of any country should note in the

very first instance what is the customary food of the people.
Famine is, or has been, periodical in Ireland and India, for the
mass of the people in those countries feed on an agricultural
produce which is the cheapest of any, and is most affected by
contingencies of climate or weather. Scarcity has occurred
from time to time in England, frequently in the fourteenth
century; in only one year of the fifteenth, at least in any
marked degree; seriously in the middle of the sixteenth and
seventeenth centuries, being aggravated in the former of these
epochs by the scandalous state of the currency; in the latter
part of the sixteenth and eighteenth centuries; and during the
first fifteen years of the present, when, perhaps, the dearth more
nearly approached famine than at any period since the great
famine which is referred to above, the only example in the
statistical history of England.

I have dwelt in detail on these facts, and have given this
evidence of the condition of the English peasantry, in order
that I may, if possible, once for all show how untenable the
opinion is which doubts that, as far as the mere means of life
were concerned, the Englishman of the middle ages lived in
ordinary times in coarse plenty. I shall, in a subsequent part
of this work, treat of his wages and their power of purchase,
and of the profits which were obtained from agriculture. I do
not indeed myself doubt that the comforts of all but the most
destitute dwellers in cities have been increased by the growth
of society and the diffusion of knowledge, that the continuity
of comfort is more secure, and that the workman has shared in
the advantages of economical progress. But the landowner,
the capitalist, and the trader have done infinitely better than
he has, and for a longer period. I am convinced that at no
period of English history for which authentic records exist,
was the condition of manual labour worse than it was in the
forty years from 1782 to 1821, the period in which manufacturers and merchants accumulated fortune rapidly, and in
which the rent of agricultural land was doubled.

Even though the lord did not reside within his manor, the
principal house in the village belonged to him, and was
inhabited by his bailiff. Here the court baron and court leet

were held, the former of freeholders, and concerned with civil proceedings, the latter of all tenants, free and serf, whose principal business it was to be a jury for the trial or acquittal of offenders. Such manor houses are still to be found, the building of which goes back nearly to the thirteenth century. Many have been expanded into larger homes, or been partly razed for the building of country houses, or have been turned into farm houses. In my native place the latter result has occurred; but the antiquary can discover in the walls of the yeoman's homestead unmistakable relics of thirteenth or fourteenth century work, when the house was the residence of the lord of a single manor. This manor house was generally near the church. Sometimes the church and churchyard were within the private grounds of the lord. His ancestors had probably built the church, and he was the patron of the advowson, as well as the principal parishioner. If he was the lord of other manors, he paid periodical visits to his manor house, at least to take the audit of his bailiff, perhaps for a temporary residence there.

The next most important personage in the parish was the rector. We will suppose that some neighbouring monastery has not been able to secure the impropriation of the benefice, and to serve the parish with the offices of some starved vicar or ordained monk. This rector has generally a fair share of glebe land, as well as tithes and dues. As the owner of the glebe, he is, like the rest of the inhabitants, an agriculturist; as the tithe owner, he keeps his eye on the yeoman's corn strips or closes, on his lambing fold, his shearing stead, and his poultry yard. As the receiver of dues for ecclesiastical offices, he exacts his fee, graduated according to the means of his parishioner, on churchings, weddings, and burials, claims his Easter dues from every home, and his price for obits and masses. For one of the most singular features in the particulars of mediæval estates is the permanent charges which are imposed on the tenant. We have seen what was the character of those which were exacted in the interest of the lord. Very likely the lord's estate, beyond what was due to the Crown, was charged with some payment to a monastery

some exhibition to a college, some annual pension for a
chantry, as well as with dower to a widow, and portions, to
be realized from the sale of stock, or by a rent charge, for
brothers and sisters.

We learn from information given us at a later period than
that on which I am immediately commenting, that some of
these rectors had large incomes from the benefices. Gascoigne, writing in the fifteenth century, tells of some which
were worth £100 a year, and the Rolls of Parliament contemplate others at £200. These must have been parishes in
which the glebe and the dues were very large, for the tithe of
no ordinary parish could have nearly reached this sum. Such
benefices were eagerly coveted by the monks, and were
frequently, as we are told, impropriated, that is, the larger
revenues from tithe of corn and wool were secured to the
monastery, while the vicar was left with the smaller tithes and
the fees. Sometimes, if the monastery were near, even the fees
were absorbed. Thus the monks of Bicester acquired the
rectory of the town, and all its ecclesiastical revenues. The
record of their gains from this source has been preserved for
two years of the fourteenth century. The fee for churchings
varies from 1s. 10d. to 1s. 0½d. ; for weddings, from 5s. 3d.
to 2s.; for burials, from 9s. 3d. to ¾d. The fellows of Oriel
College, Oxford, obtained the principal church of St. Mary in
High Street, and derived no small part of their corporate
income from religious offices, and from trafficking in wax
tapers, which they manufactured and sold to devotees. It is
no wonder that the king, knowing how large were the profits
of the parochial clergy and the monasteries, insisted on liberal
contributions from them towards public necessities, and that
the clergy should have striven to obtain the powerful aid of
the pope, in order to escape from these exactions.

The most important lay tenant of the manor was the
miller. Every parish had its watermill,—sometimes more
than one, if there were a stream to turn the wheel,—or a
windmill, if there were no running water. The mill was the
lord's franchise, and the use of the manor mill was an obligation on the tenants. The lord, therefore, repaired the mill,

5

the wheels, or the sails, and found—often a most costly purchase—the mill-stones. Sometimes the homage at the court baron supervises the contract with the local carpenter for the labour needed in constructing the mill wheel; sometimes the jury of the court leet presents the miller for using a false measure and for taking excessive toll. The miller figures in the legends and ballads of the time as the opulent villager, who is keen after his gains, and not over honest in the collection of them.

The residue of the tenants generally inhabited the principal street or road of the village, near the stream, if one ran through the settlement. There were to be sure isolated farmhouses, and these probably in early times; but, as a rule, I believe the building of these distant homesteads followed on the enclosures, and was not usual as long as the system of open arable fields remained. The houses of the cottagers were also generally in the principal street; but some, even at an early date, were in remote parts of the manor.

The parish church, even in the most thoroughly rural districts, was far larger than the needs of the population would seem to require. It is certain that villages with less than fifty or a hundred inhabitants possessed edifices which would hold a congregation of five or even ten times that number. But it will be remembered that the church was the common hall, perhaps even the common market-place, of the parish. The parish vestry is said to be the most ancient of our social institutions, and a vestry of the whole inhabitants could be summoned at the discretion of the rector. Here, too, mysteries are performed, processions marshalled, and perhaps even secular plays exhibited. When the Host and portable altar were removed, the church could be employed for all uses. Sometimes it was employed as a storehouse for grain and wool, a small fee being paid to the parson for this convenience. The tower, especially in the more exposed districts near the sea, was a place of refuge, the castle of the inhabitants. As late as the time of the Parliamentary wars, the royalists of a Hampshire town garrisoned the parish church, and stood a siege and cannonade in it.

The houses of these villagers were mean and dirty. Brick-making was a lost art, stone was found only in a few places, and, though cheap enough, was certainly not generally employed, even where it was plentiful and within reach. The better class of yeomen had timber houses—housebote was a customary right of the tenants—built on a frame, the spaces being either lathed and plastered within and without, or filled with clay kneaded up with chopped straw. The floor was the bare earth, though it was sometimes pitched with split flints. The sleeping apartments under the thatched roof were reached by a ladder or rude staircase. A few chests were ranged round the walls, the bacon-rack was fastened to the timbers overhead, and the walls of the homestead were garnished with agricultural implements. The wood fire was on a hob of clay. Chimneys were unknown, except in castles and manor houses, and the smoke escaped through the door or whatever other aperture it could reach. Artificial light was too costly for common use, for the hard fats were four times as dear as the meat of animals, and a pound of candles could only have been procured at nearly the price of a day's work.

The floor of the homestead was filthy enough, but the surroundings were filthier still. Close by the door stood the mixen, a collection of every abomination,—streams from which, in rainy weather, fertilized the lower meadows, generally the lord's several pasture, and polluted the stream. Two centuries and a half after the time of which I am writing, the earliest English writer on husbandry comments on the waste, the unwholesomeness, and the agricultural value of these dunghills.

The house of the peasant cottager was ruder still. Most of them were probably built of posts wattled and plastered with clay or mud, with an upper storey of poles, reached by a ladder. In the taxing rolls of Edward I., preserved numerously in the Record Office, the household furniture of such cottages is inventoried, and valued at a very few shillings. It consists of a few articles of furniture, generally of home manufacture, some coarse bedding, and a few domestic implements, mostly earthenware. The most valuable articles in use were copper or brass pots, and a few common iron utensils, all metals being exceedingly dear; and iron, relatively speaking, being the dearest of all.

Rude, however, and coarse as village life was, it must not be imagined that it was without its hopes and aspirations. The serf could arrange with his lord to remove to a neighbouring town, and there prosecute his fortunes, perhaps emancipate himself. The king, when war arose, would look out the likeliest and most adventurous of the youth of all ranks, and employ them in his army with good pay, and prospects of plunder and ransom. The parish priest would encourage some bright and quick child to devote himself to the schools, to the university, to the service of the Church in the monastery, or in parochial offices. Many a peasant had heard doubtless of the learned Grostête, the son of a serf, the most distinguished scholar of thirteenth century Oxford, of the Oxford which existed long before a college was founded, —the friend of the reforming friars, the enemy of the Roman court, the advocate of England for the English; and was eager, out of his scanty means, to buy the license, that his son might go to the schools and take orders. Perhaps with these openings for himself and his kind, the yoke of dependency did not press very heavily on him. But the lord must beware of breaking the customary bargain between himself and his serf. He once attempted to do so, and a sudden and unexpected revolution shook England to its centre, and, though organized by serfs, was a memorable and perpetual warning.

I am far from forgetting that in many material points the man in our day, who lives by manual labour, is better off than his ancestor of the thirteenth century, just as he is better off than his ancestor of the eighteenth. One of the earliest objects to which wealth has given encouragement is the science of health. I do not know that they who welcomed this great change in the conditions of human life thought or cared that it should be extended beyond their own interests. To judge from the indifference with which the housing of the poor in cities is recognised and permitted, I should conclude that the desire for health is not beneficent, even when reflection points out that for one's own sake it is better to be one's brother's keeper. I am aware also that all classes, though at a period long after that of which I am now speaking, shared the benefits of those great improvements in agriculture, under which fresh food is supplied all the year round ; and that many forms of inveterate disease, which once afflicted humanity, have been banished, and life has been rendered easier and longer. The means of life were as plentiful, considering the population, in the thirteenth century, as they were in the eighteenth, the continuity of labour was secured, and the prospects of those who lived by manual toil as good. The age had its drawbacks, as every age has, but it had its advantages; and I hope to be able to show that the peasant of the thirteenth century, though he did not possess, and therefore did not desire, much that his descendant had in the eighteenth, had some solid elements of present advantage and not a few hopes of future advancement.

CHAPTER III.

RURAL ENGLAND—AGRICULTURE.

THERE is a single essay on English agriculture which was written before the middle of the thirteenth century. This essay is by Walter de Henley. The earliest copy of this work is contained in a lawyer's handy book, written at the conclusion of the thirteenth century; though a few additions have been made to the volume up to the latter part of Edward II.'s reign by a later scribe, as the book contains the Statute of York. The work is in Norman French; and the copy which I have used is considerably later than the author's own age. There is a story that it was translated into Latin by the great Bishop Grostête; and a Latin version of the work is also found. "La Dite de Hosbanderye" was a handy book of agriculture; and, as is probable, was frequently copied in one or the other language. It was not superseded till the sixteenth century, when the English work of Fitzherbert makes its appearance.

The date of Walter de Henley's work cannot be exactly
ascertained. It contains a careful description of the diseases
to which sheep are liable, but it makes no mention of "scab."
Now we know that this disease did not make its appearance
till about the beginning of the last quarter of the thirteenth
century. Again, the treatise contains on the last three leaves
a remarkable list of certain English towns and other localities,
each of which is designated by some characteristic; and a
schedule of the English bishoprics, with the various counties
of which they are composed. From internal evidence, the
list of towns appears to have been compiled shortly after the
year 1249. The schedule of the bishoprics appears to refer
to even an earlier date, as the counties of Northumberland,
Cumberland, and Westmoreland are grouped under the
common name Northumbria. I shall have occasion to revert
to this list of towns in a later chapter, and shall treat of Walter
de Henley's account of English husbandry as I have occasion
to refer to what was the actual practice of the agriculturist.

As I stated in the preceding chapter, wheat was cultivated
on every estate, a larger breadth being sown than there was
even on those which cultivated rye. The following is the
acreage of all the land under tillage in the eleven estates
referred to before. At Maldon the average under cultivation
for the four years is 268½ acres; at Leatherhead, 148¾ acres;
at Farley, 182 acres; at Elham, which was chiefly a horse
breeding estate, 15¼ acres; at Cambridge, 86½ acres; at
Gamlingay, 153¼ acres; at Cheddington, 123 acres; at Wolford, 72¾ acres; at Cuxham, 181¾ acres; at Holywell, Oxford,
118½ acres; and at Basingstoke, 100¼ acres. The average
amount of arable land in cultivation on the whole eleven
estates for the four years is therefore 1,448½ acres. The same
inventories give us an account of the live stock on the estates.
Horses are found everywhere. But there are others called
stotts, a word used at Maldon and Cambridge only, and
affers, a word used on all the estates except Elham. Both
probably mean the breeds of coarse large ponies, which are
occasionally found in country places at present. The average
on all the estates is thirty horses, eight stotts, and thirty-eight

affers. These animals are kept principally for draught, but were probably employed for ploughing also. The average number of oxen and cows kept on ten of the estates is 215, Elham possessing none. No sheep are kept at Elham, Holywell, and Cambridge. But on the other eight estates an average of 1,133 sheep and lambs are kept in stock, the largest number being wethers. They are known as ewes, muttons, hoggs, rams, and lambs. About 9 rams are kept to 287 ewes. An average of twenty-one calves is given in the audit. There are on an average 159 pigs, and 137 store pigs. There are in the same way 246 geese, 146 capons, 281 fowls, and 103 ducks.

The stock does not, it is clear, represent the maximum of the year, but the amount on all the farms at the date of the audit. The list, therefore, does not account for the sales nor for the purchases. But the enumeration is not only suggestive of the amount of stock on a series of estates, but it shows how general stock keeping was, how necessary it was to have other resources for maintaining such a stock beyond common pasture or the balks in the open fields, and that there must be implied in the amount of arable land occupied by the tenant a considerable further area of several pasture. These were the crofts and closes, which are generally added to the virgate or half virgate of the freeholder or serf.

Taken at the average values of the four years, the live stock on the farms, as accounted for by the several bailiffs, is of the money value of £291 19s. 1½d. But the same record informs us that the average floating balance left in the several bailiffs' hands was £115 12s. 8½d.—a sum in live stock and working expenses of £407 10s. 10d. The dead stock and seed amount to at least £200, and the rental of the land alone to £75 more. The capital invested in the farm buildings mills, and similar property cannot be less than £800 more, so that a capital sum, in fixed and floating form, of more than £1,482 was required in order to take in hand and manage properly the amount of 1,448 acres of land in cultivation on an average of years. Now, in the period before me, arable land was not worth more than fourteen years' purchase,—*i.e.*, land yielding 6*d.* an acre rent was worth about 7*s.* an acre,—and, as the foregoing calculation points out, the stock, capital, and buildings on an arable farm were three times the value of the land when taken apart from their necessary conditions. Even if we omit the buildings and rent, the necessary floating capital is considerably in excess of the value of the land, and the position which I laid down before is worked out, that the system of landlord cultivation, with its vast amount of floating capital, divisible in equal parts among the representatives of a common ancestor, and open to distribution by will, must have considerably modified the effects of the custom of primogeniture.

Speaking generally, the arable lands of a manor were divided pretty equally between the lord and the tenants of the manor. There were, however, certain advantages possessed by the lord, some of them of very solid significance indeed, some vexatious and injurious to the tenants rather than profitable to him.

1. Whenever there existed natural meadow, regularly warped or watered by streams, it was, as a rule, the property of the lord, and held by him in severalty. In the entire absence of all artificial grasses and winter roots, this kind of land bore a very high rent. About Oxford it is constantly let at 7*s.*, 8*s.*, or 9*s.* an acre; aftermath, or rowens, called *rewannum* in its Latinised form, being let at 2*s.* 6*d.* Now, taken generally, the value of grain has risen about twelve times in nominal value since the period before me, and such water meadow as let at the high rates referred to five or six centuries ago has risen to from about £4 4*s.* to £5 10*s.* an acre— *i.e.*, in about the same proportion, while ordinary arable land has risen from fifty to sixty times. For the same reason— viz., the singular importance of water or natural meadows— sales of hay are very rarely found in the bailiff's account, though they are occasionally seen in the account of consumption by nobles and great corporations. In later times, when nearly all the information procurable as to prices is from the records of consumption, entries of the price of hay are common enough

2. The tenants of the manor had a right generally to the use of wood from the lord's timber for the repair or enlargement of their homesteads, for their agricultural implements, and, to a limited extent, for their fires.   On the other hand, as we have seen, they are prohibited from cutting oak or ash, even on their own holdings, without the lord's consent. Now it was generally the case that the manor contained, especially on its boundaries, a considerable and extensive belt of wood.   For example, the northern slopes of the South Downs were generally covered with beech woods, and the higher grounds on the north were similarly over-grown with coppice, oak, and ash.   The sales of fuel from this wood were a very considerable source of income to their owners.   After the great rise in prices occurred, during the latter half of the sixteenth century, though rents remained provokingly stationary, the profits of coppices and forests were a welcome advantage to landowners, who often found in the rise on the price of their woods that there was some compensation for the stagnation of agricultural rents.   Besides, they got payments for the grass in the spring, and the pannage of pigs in the autumn.   One can quite understand, then, how indignant the nobles in the seventeenth century were, when the examination and claim of the Crown's forestal rights so seriously lessened the estates of some among the nobility, and greatly curtailed a lucrative source of income.   Of course, much wood and forest was held by private owners and in severalty.

3. Generally the use of the common pasture was without stint—*i.e.*, any tenant could put as many beasts as he liked on it.   It is a common subject of complaint that the lord, being possessed of several meadows, saved his pasture for hay or summer feed, and cropped the land bare by the multitude of cattle and sheep which he put on the common pasture.   Such a common without stint exists still near Oxford, in the large space known as Port Meadow—a piece of ground which belonged to the inhabitants of Oxford as long ago as Domesday, the sole use of which was subsequently usurped by the citizens, who, indeed, after the city got its

charter, were the principal, or at least the permanent, residents in the borough.

4. Generally, also, the lord had or claimed the right of erecting a dovecot or pigeon-house on his demesne. Prodigious numbers of these birds were kept, and though they doubtlessly plundered the lord's fields, they must have been a greater nuisance to the tenants. Even if there were no evidence of the number accounted for in the bailiff's roll as sold or sent to the lord, the price, about a farthing each, would show how common they were. There was hardly a manor without its dovecot. The right to keep a pigeon-house was confined to lords of manors, who could punish in their own courts any one who imitated their practice. When, as was sometimes the case, the same parish contained two or more manors, the loss and inconvenience must have been great to the other tenants' crops. In the year 1332, the bailiff of one estate accounts for the sale of nearly 700 pigeons.

An estate under the plough was divided into three parts, and the ploughing of each part had its own name. Ordinary ploughing was undertaken in the autumn, and was called hyvernagium; the second plough-time was in April, and was called warectatio; the third was at midsummer, and was called rebinatio. The la t should be undertaken when the ground is dusty. The fu ws should be a foot apart, and the plough should go two dig.. deep, no more. Now in order to traverse this space of an acre, there will be thirty-three journeys made. Walter de Henley advises thirty-six. It will be found that the whole space traversed in order to plough two acres will be nine miles—he says six leagues ; and he says that it would be a poor stott or ox which could not do an acre in a day. He concludes, therefore, that a carucate of land, *i.e.*, the amount which a team of horses or oxen could plough, is from a hundred and sixty to a hundred and eighty acres in the year, taking forty-four weeks in the year, and omitting eight for marketing and other hindrances. By this he means, not that a team is engaged in ploughing all the year round, but that if it were so engaged, it would cover the space of an acre a day. But he is willing to allow three and

a half roods for the first, and one acre for the second ploughing.

Land should be ploughed three times, unless it be such a
soil or such parts of the soil as will bear a crop every year.
After sowing, the young plants should be hoed, and drawn
out of the furrows to the ridge.   Always get seed from some
other estate.   If you doubt my advice, try half your land with
foreign seed, half with that of your own growth, and you will
see the wisdom of my counsel.   Plough with two oxen and
two horses together.   You will do better than with horse
ploughing alone, unless the ground is very stony, when oxen
find it difficult to get a grip at the ground with their hoofs.
During the time of ploughing, whatever be its kind, the farm
bailiff, or head reaper, or head man, should be constantly about
the plough, to see that the serf do his work well ; see at the
end of the day's work what they have done, and that they
keep up to the amount every day afterwards, unless they are
able to account for a deficiency by some hindrance.   Servants
and customary tenants shirk their work, and you must be on
your guard against their rogueries.   Besides, the head reaper
must look after them daily, and the bailiff see to them all
that they do their work well, for if they do not they should
be chidden and punished.

The ox was considered a far cheaper and, on the whole,
more effective animal for the plough and for other kinds of
farm work than the horse, though it is true that ploughing by
horses is speedier.   The cost of a horse between Oct. 18th
and May 3rd, the period during which they cannot graze, was
reckoned as nearly four times that of the ox.   Besides, when
an ox grows old, he may be fattened for the table, and his
hide will fetch a good price, whereas there is no such economy
possible in a horse, whose flesh is useless and hide of little
value.   Oxen were shod, though the shoe is far cheaper than
that of the horse.

The agriculturist of the thirteenth century was quite alive
to the importance of stock keeping.   When you can do so,
says my author, stock your land to the full extent which it
will bear, for you may be certain that if your land be wel

stocked, if your stock be well kept and properly handled, your land will give you a threefold return ; by which I presume is meant over arable farming only. I shall be able hereafter, by an examination of the balance-sheet of farms, to show what was the rate of profit obtained.

The cost of arable farming in the thirteenth century, when the crop is wheat, is thus reckoned :— The land is ploughed thrice at the cost of 6*d.* an acre ; hoeing costs 1*d.* an acre ; two bushels of seed at Michaelmas, 1*s.* ; a second hoeing, ½*d.* an acre; reaping, 5*d.* an acre; carriage, 1*d.* an acre. The straw or forage will pay for the threshing. In this account of the cost, taken from Walter de Henley, no estimate is made of rent ; but my author infers that at 4*s.* a quarter, unless more than six bushels are reaped, there will be a loss on the operation of 1½*d.*

The hoeing of land was generally undertaken by women. There was full opportunity for this employment till the middle of the fourteenth century, after which the outdoor employment of women almost disappears for a long time. In harvest time, women worked at piece work, as the men did, and generally at the same rates. I refer to these facts at the present time only to illustrate the course of husbandry, not to anticipate what I have to say on the wages of labour and the general condition of those who lived by hired labour, at least in the main.

I have already referred to the amount of stock kept on 1,448 acres under the plough, and bearing crops. It is now desirable to deal with the several kinds of animals kept on land.

Oxen and Cows.—The ox was kept for plough and draught, a few were kept for fatting, but I conclude that the amount of stock regularly fatted for the table was a very small percentage of the whole. They would be consumed only by wealthy nobles and wealthy corporations, and, as a matter of fact, fresh beef was put on table only for a few months in the year. Much was killed and salted in November, but this beef was of grass-fed cattle. The ox, quit of skin, head, and offal, did not weigh on an average more than 400 pounds, and was worth about 11s. to sell. The hide of an ox was worth at least 2s., and the head and offal amply paid the services of the butcher. The meat was therefore worth about a farthing a pound. It was lean, for the hard fats were worth four times the price of meat; and tough, for it was neither young nor stall fed. Whatever stock the agriculturist could not keep during the winter or dispose of to opulent consumers in town and country, was killed, and put into the powdering tub at Martinmas.

There was no attempt to improve breeds of cattle. The proof is the low price of bulls. A collateral proof is the low price of cows. The ox was valued for his work and for his flesh. The maintenance of the bull was a necessity, and the use of the cow was for the dairy. At the same time I do not assert that there were not different breeds, but I am sure that the difference was in the size, not in the quality of the animals, and that there was no distinction made in the character of the breeds. In point of fact, the scarcity of winter food and its poor nutritive powers, the absence of all winter roots, even carrots and parsnips, and the change from the scanty pasture of the summer to the straw-yard in the winter, must have brought about that all breeds were on the same level in point of size and quality, unless they were the few animals kept for the consumption of wealthy persons.

Sheep.—The mainstay of English agriculture was the sheep, at once for the profit which its wool supplied, and for the value of its droppings to the fields. It is well known that England had virtually the monopoly of the wool trade from the earliest records till at least the middle of the seventeenth century. The unrestrained export of wool, by which I do not mean the taxation of the export, but the permission to export under a heavy customs duty, more than once determined the policy of the Low Countries, and was the subject of numberless diplomatic arrangements. If supplied freely and plentifully, the Flemish burghers throve accordingly; if it were curtailed or prohibited, discontent was sure to arise in those manufacturing towns of the middle ages. The burgher life of Ghent, Bruges, Malines, a thousand towns, depended on this important raw staple. It is almost the only article, as far as I have been able to discover, on which an export duty could be put, the whole of which was paid by the foreign consumer. Financiers have always desired to find some product possessed of those qualities which will, without harm to the domestic producer, render it possible for the foreign consumer to inevitably pay a tax levied on the material. The conditions are four :—It must be a necessity ; there must be no substitute for it ; there must be no other source of supply ; and there can be little or no economy practised in the use of it. Such an article in the middle ages was English wool. It was a necessary material for clothing, and no other material could be used in its stead. It was produced, efficiently at least, in no other European country, for the Spanish wool, scanty in quantity, was so weak a fibre that it could not be woven without an admixture of the English material, and the Saxony supply was not yet developed. And although it is possible that the dearness of woollen garments may have led to some economies in their use, these could not have been considerable. Hence the Government was able to constantly impose, in times of emergency, a cent. per cent. *ad valorem* duty on the export of average wool, such, for instance, as the produce of Lincoln-shire, Gloucester, and ordinary Hereford. The foreign wars of the Edwards and the Henrys were carried on mainly by the proceeds of wool taxes, and the enormous revenues which from the thirteenth to the fifteenth centuries were exacted from England by the Papal Court and the Italian ecclesiastics who were quartered on English benefices, were transmitted in the shape of wool by the Lombard exchangers to Flanders, and thence by a cross exchange to Italy.

There were a great number of breeds of sheep, and it is evident that pains were taken to improve the breed. This is proved by the high price of rams, whom our forefathers called hurtards (the butters) ; very often much more being paid for rams than for the best wethers. There is other testimony to the fact in a remarkable petition presented to Parliament in 1454. The Commons present a schedule of forty-four qualities of English wool, designated by the locality of their origin, the money value of which ranges from £13 the sack of 364 lbs. for wool grown near Leominster, the highest, to that of £2 10s. the sack for wool grown in Sussex, the lowest. And the prayer of the petition is that no quality should be exported, except at the prices in the schedule, under a penalty of £40 the sack. The petition was rejected. Now in the fifteenth century it was a very common expedient for Parliament to impose an export duty of 100s. the sack on wool, without distinction of quality. But it was not found to be so easy to put export duties on the last of hides, another important English export. To have imposed too high a duty on hides would have driven the trade to other countries. I have no doubt that these forty-four kinds were so many brands, as we should say, of English wool, which were fully recognised in the Flemish market, and I am the more convinced of this because the names of some of the qualities are taken from very narrow districts.

The wool was coarse and full of hairs. I say this because I have seen cloth manufactured from fourteenth century wool, in which the quality of the raw material is very discernible, though from the use made of it the cloth was almost certainly the best procurable. The fleece, too, was light, an average from many entries which I have made giving 1 lb. 7¾ oz. to the fleece. But the unimproved sheep of the eighteenth century gave nearly 5 lbs. to the fleece. Hence the animal must have been small, and I think I may certainly say that a wether in good condition weighed a good deal less than forty pounds

The sheep master was liable to heavy losses on his stock. I mentioned above that an average of 1,133 sheep of all kinds was kept on eight of the sheep-breeding estates. In one year the losses were 308 ; in another, 242 ; in a third, 300 ; in a fourth,—a more fortunate year,—34. But the average is 221, or close upon 20 per cent. of the stock. No doubt there were considerable losses in lambing time, but the rot made the most serious ravages. Our forefathers, who comprehended all cattle diseases under the generic name of murrain, were well aware of the risks they ran from rot, and give the symptoms with the precision of a modern farmer. "There are," says Walter de Henley, "several means by which shepherds profess to discover the existence of rot:—(1) They look at the veins under the eyelids; if they are red, the sheep is sound; if white, unsound. (2) They pull at the wool on the ribs; if it holds firmly to the skin, the sign is good; if it tears off easily, it is bad. (3) If the skin reddens on rubbing, the sheep is sound; if it keeps pale, the animal is rotten. (4) If in November the hoar-frost in the morning is found to cling to the wool, it is a good sign; but if it be melted, it is a sign that the animal is suffering from an unnatural heat, and that it is probably unsound." Experienced farmers have told me that it is not easy to better the exactness of these symptoms. The farmer of the earliest period had a vague idea that the presence of a small white snail on the grass was dangerous, and the most modern experiments have proved that a water snail is the carrier of the fluke. Our forefathers advised that sheep should be kept under cover from November to April and should not be allowed to go on the ground between mid-August and November, till the sun had well purified the ground. They were fed under cover on coarse hay, wheat and oat straw, or, failing these, on pea or vetch haulm.

The most valuable product of the sheep, his fleece,—and the fleece is often worth half the value of the animal when shorn, —was liable from the latter part of the thirteenth century to a new disease, the scab. We can almost define the year— 1280—in which this disease first appeared, by the simultaneous record of the medicines employed for its cure. At first the agriculturist tried sulphate of iron, verdigris, mercurial ointments, and occasionally arsenical washes. Soon, however, the use of these articles was abandoned for that of tar, which begins to be imported for this purpose in the southern and eastern counties at the end of the thirteenth century, after which it was used as a specific for all skin diseases in sheep, "The shepherd," says a writer of the early sixteenth century 'should never be without his tar-box."

The hardships of the winter must have generally baffled the efforts of the husbandman to improve his breeds of sheep.

It appears that the goodness of wool in England is not so much a matter of breed as of soil, and I am told that the localities which supplied the best English produce in the fifteenth century and in the centuries before that period are characterized by analogous excellence in the nineteenth. The sheep were washed ; the wool appears to have been sorted or picked, for "locks" and "refuse" are always at a much lower price than the rest of the fleece. Black wool, used for russet and dyed cloth, bore as high a price as white wool, and lambs' wool is generally a great deal cheaper than that of the sheep.

Sheep were occasionally hired to lie on the ground. This must evidently have been done in enclosures. A hundred and fifty sheep were folded on an acre at from 1s. 4d. to 2s. the acre, or two hundred sheep were kept on a field at 8d. a week, for eight weeks. It would seem, then, that such a flock was kept on land from three to eight weeks, in order to fertilise it, the owner, of course, feeding them.

Swine.—It is to be expected that swine were, for general use and consumption, the most important object of all English agriculture in the thirteenth century, and for many a century afterwards. The pig is a saveall, a universal consumer, and as universal a producer. It was kept by the peasantry throughout the whole parish ; the sow, during farrowing time, in the sty, the only period, except during that in which the animal was fatted, when it was of any immediate cost to the owner. The object of the agriculturist was to have his herd in such a position as that there should be three farrowing times in the year ; and we are expressly informed that care was taken in the selection of breeds.

The pigs were the scavengers of the mediæval village. In the autumn they were turned into the cornfields after the crop was carried, and into the woods to gather mast and acorns. The ringing of pigs, in order to prevent their uprooting the ground, was known, though not perhaps universally practised. The whole of the parish stock was put under the charge of a single swineherd, who, receiving a payment from the owner of every pig under his charge, had a smaller wage from the lord of the manor, to whom he was also a servant. It is said that the pannage of pigs, *i.e.,* the practice of feeding hogs on mast and acorns in the woods, was not a matter of original right, but had to be granted by deed. But the concession was very general, and the payment was ordinarily fixed at a penny or halfpenny for each head of swine. Pigs are often said to be leprous; but most of the diseases to which they are liable are classed under measles, properly entozoa. Three centuries after the time on which I am commenting, the pious and patriotic Tusser recommends that when the disease is very prevalent, the animals should be slain, salted, packed, and the pork sold to the Flemings.

The fatted boar was a lordly dish, and though often the principal item in the Christmas feast, was even served up at Midsummer. Large quantities of barley, bere, beans, and peas were consumed in order to bring these animals into condition. But ordinarily the pig in the sty was put into saleable form at the cost of from two to four bushels of grain. The boar sometimes consumed ten times the larger amount before he was ready for the feast. Store pigs, when ordinary food was scarce, were fed largely on brewer's grains, which were purchased at a few pence the quarter. But as every peasant was frequently brewing ale,—it will be remembered that the drink was not hopped, and was therefore of rapid consumption,—such food was generally forthcoming Some idea can be formed of the condition of the ordinary pig from the fact that the lard of thirty-five of these animals was a little over five pounds a piece. The meat was, as now, salted as pork or smoke-dried as bacon. Wild boars are occasionally mentioned; and it may be added that salted or smoked pork was slightly higher in price than other kinds of meat, certainly than other kinds of salted meat. There can be no doubt that, in the thirteenth century, every peasant had his pig in the sty.

Poultry.—It is even more certain that he had his fowl in the pot. Poultry keeping was universal, and poultry and egg rents were the very commonest form of rendering dues. Fowls are found everywhere, the cocks rather cheaper than hens, and pullets cheapest of all. Geese and ducks were also well-nigh universal, the former called green when they were stubble fed, but often put into coops and fattened on oats. Capons, which are exceedingly common, are about double the price of ordinary poultry, being always fattened in coops. That they were found everywhere is shown by the fact that " capon's grease" is constantly used for cart wheels and sheep dressing. In modern times, one might as reasonably prescribe hare's fat as so costly a lubricant. Swans and peacocks were occasionally kept by the wealthy, and were sold at high prices.

It may not be amiss to refer here to the singularly high price of rabbits. I am convinced that they had lately been introduced to the country; that they were found in very few localities, and were often procured from a considerable distance. In the last half of the thirteenth century a rabbit was often sold at one-third the price of a wether. At the end of the fourteenth, they were as dear as geese, were purchased at a spot which was more than sixty miles from the place for which they were procured, and were carried at considerable cost. The rabbit warren is known to Fleta, but it is not mentioned in Domesday. It may be added that the bailiff, who is ready to explain any extraordinary cost or failure, has never, in the thousands of accounts which I have investigated, set down losses to the ravages of ground game. I may add, too, that, save in years of exceptional dearth, he rarely speaks of losses of poultry by theft, though he has to account for all deficiencies in stock,—a pretty clear proof that his neighbours, even the poorest, had similar property of their own, and were therefore interested in a police over property, or were removed from the temptation to pilfer.

Such was the live stock of the mediæval farmer, whether he were landlord or peasant. I have taken for granted that the husbandry of the peasant was like that of the lord, and that the servants of the manor house, save that they were more secure in the income which they received in wages and allowances, lived with and in the same manner as their fellow villagers. Except that the thirteenth century villager was greatly better off, there was little change induced on the rustic's condition in many parts of England from the middle of the thirteenth to the beginning of the nineteenth century. Sixty years ago there was many a village, in the south of England at least, which was out of the way of the great high roads, in which few of the yeomen knew how to read and write, and scarcely one of the labourers. For five centuries and a half, for fifteen or sixteen generations, there was no appreciable alteration in the condition of these people. The discipline of the manor court had passed over to the justice's room, and perhaps was more severe after the custom, that no one could be prosecuted as an offender except at the action of his peers, was exchanged for the information of the master, the game-keeper, or the constable. The village weaver made homespun cloth from the hempen or woollen yarns a century ago as he did six centuries ago. The year witnessed the same unvaried round of occupation that it was when the third Henry was king. Only there was a change in the land of the parish, now generally enclosed. The ancient rights of the villagers were extinguished as these several properties were created. But in many parishes the loss of communal privileges had long been forgotten. In one place, the enclosure might have dated back to the age of the last Plantagenet; in another, to that of the Tudors. If the commons had endured beyond these several spoliations, or some residue of them had been left, they were gradually absorbed by those numerous Acts of Parliament which, beginning with the age of Anne, were the principal private bill legislation of the eighteenth century. Now and then the peasantry had risen in insurrection against those who invaded their ancient privileges. There had been the uprisings of Tyler, of Cade, of Kett. But since the days of the clubmen, the dwellers in rural England have been apathetic.

Changes of dynasty, civil wars, changes in religion, had occurred without making a break, or leaving a memory in the routine of rural existence. The church of the mediæval village became the church of the Reformed Establishment. The parish priest of the old faith was succeeded, though with a greatly shorn income, by the rector of Cranmer's and Cromwell's, of Parker's and Grindal's, models. Sometimes, perhaps, in the days after the Reformation a more than ordinarily opulent ecclesiastic, having no family ties, would train up some clever rustic child, teach him, and help him on to the university. But, as a rule, since that event, there was no educated person in the parish beyond the parson, and he had the anxieties of a narrow fortune and a numerous family. The villagers frequented the same ale-house as that at which their forefathers had caroused for generations, held the parish feast on the same day—generally the name-day of the church, or of that on which the parish guild was founded—as that which had been set apart when the old church was a new one, or the guild was started in the days of the third Henry, or in those of his great-grandson, or during the prosperous epoch of the fifteenth century; and, except for slow, trivial, and insensible changes, everything was continued as it was when the beginnings of that constitution were effected, outside which the mass of Englishmen remained, or from which they had, in the fifteenth century, been excluded. There is, I believe, no part of the Western world in which so little change was induced on the fortunes, on the life, and on the habits of the people, as there has been in rural England from the peaceful reign of Henry III. to the earlier years of George III.

I stated above that one of the estates from which I have taken my facts as to the husbandry and live stock was employed for the breeding of horses. In one year of the fourteenth century, the bailiff of this estate buys twelve horses for 157*s.* 9*d.*, and sells them for 180*s.* 8*d.*, besides getting rid of eighteen of his own rearing. These were cart or ordinary saddle horses. The war charger was a much more expensive affair, and frequently cost more than a dozen others.

Dead Stock and Tools.—The estate of Holywell, Oxford, the whole of which, with the exception of some twelve acres, possessed by a monastery, and a few tenements inhabited by cottagers, was the property of one owner, lay outside the north wall of the city. It had been possessed by its owner in severalty, and had been enclosed in the middle of the thirteenth century, and was about two-thirds arable and one-third pasture, the latter being regularly warped by the Cherwell. The pasture, as I have stated above, was very valuable and the land, lying near a great city, fortress, royal palace, and university, was as well placed as land in the middle ages could be. Oxford was a favourite residence of the first Angevin king. Two of his sons were born there, and the palace occupied a considerable space in another district to the north of the city, from which point, indeed, the place was alone assailable. But a legend had grown into shape, that a residence in Oxford was dangerous to the English king, and the palace was almost deserted in the thirteenth century.

The arable land under cultivation in Holywell was, on an average, nearly 120 acres. It was divided into at least twelve corn fields, six of which were called furlongs. The principal articles employed on the farm are :—Four iron-bound carts, and four cart frames, with four sets of rope harness ; four forks for lifting trusses, and one long one for the rick ; three ploughs, six iron dung-forks, three hoes, a reaphook and a scythe, two mattocks, two wheelbarrows, a seed cod, two axes, a saw, two winnowing fans, three pairs of leg chains, divers measures and kitchen utensils, three milk buckets, a butter churn, three cheese vats with cheese cloths, and a variety of other articles. Of these the most costly were the carts. Speaking generally, the dead stock on the farm must have been worth in money of the time at least £25. The inventory was made up on the occasion of the appointment of a new bailiff, and is an exhaustive account. But it was the practice to enumerate the principal articles on the farm in the annual roll.

The most formidable item of expenditure in the supply of necessary dead stock was the annual cost of iron. Relatively speaking, iron was considerably dearer than lead, and frequently nearly as costly as copper, tin, and brass. It was generally bought, whether it were of English or of foreign origin, in bars of about four pounds in weight. This was ordinarily purchased at one of the great fairs, and carefully preserved by the bailiff, being served out for the local smith to fashion into what was needed, and the weight being debited to him on each occasion. Sometimes, but rarely, it is bought in mass. Steel, which was employed to tip the cutting edges of iron tools, was four times as dear as iron. Over and over again, the bailiff seems to apologize for the large consumption of iron in his ordinary operations, by the dryness of the seasons, and the consequent wear of the material. The high cost of iron explains the fact that cart-wheels were frequently unprotected, being made from the section of a full-sized tree. Again I must repeat that harrowing with a frame set with stout iron pins was unknown or unpractised. Nearly three centuries after the time on which I am writing, when the practice was generally known and adopted, the principal writer on English husbandry states that the agriculturist cannot afford iron-toothed harrows in stony ground, and recommends the use of strong oaken pegs in their place. The share, too, must have been a very slight affair,—I judge by its price,—little more, indeed, than an iron point to a wooden frame, the frame being protected by clouts or plates of iron nailed to it. The principal source of foreign iron was Spain, the produce of which was about one-third dearer than that of home manufacture. What is called Osemond iron is as dear as steel, and appears to be identical with it. The cost of working iron or steel into the requisite implements was about as much as that of the raw material. The shoes with which horses and oxen were shod were exceedingly light.

The arable land of the manor was generally communal, *i.e.*, each of the tenants possessed a certain number of furrows in a common field, the several divisions being separated by balks of unploughed ground, on which the grass was suffered to grow. The system, which was all but universal in the thirteenth century, has survived in certain districts up to living memory, though generally it gave way to enclosures, effected at a more or less remote period. The system has been traced back to remote antiquity. The ownership of these several strips was limited to certain months of the year, generally from Lady Day to Michaelmas, and for the remaining six months the land was common pasture. The communal cultivation had its advantages for the poorer tenants, since the area of their pasture was increased. But at the latter end of the seventeenth century it was denounced as a wasteful and barbarous system, and wholly unsuited to any improved system of agriculture.

In Fitzherbert's treatise on surveying, a work of the early part of the sixteenth century, a description is given of these communal districts. The work, though two centuries and a half later than the period on which I am speaking, deals with a system which is of immemorial antiquity, and was probably entirely unchanged from what had prevailed in the earlier epoch. There is, he says, a field, which he calls Dale Furlong, in which the several inhabitants have "lands." In this field the parson has two strips, the lord three, a tenant one, another two, a third one, the lord four, the prior two, the parson one, a fourth tenant two, a fifth one, a sixth one, a seventh two, the prior three, the lord two and one headland, the parson having the other. The rest of the fields, of which he gives four names, are similarly divided.

He then treats of a long meadow containing 122 acres, which is similarly staked and bounded. This appears to be devoted to hay, and the several tenants mow and stack their portions. In this typical manor there are also closes of various dimensions. Every husbandman, in addition to his share in the communal field, has six of these closes,—three for corn, and the others for pasture and hay. The rental of the communal land is sixpence an acre, of the enclosed eight-pence, the difference in the value being derived from its being possible to let oxen lie on it. This rent illustrates what I have said above as to the average rental of arable land. It is unchanged from the thirteenth to the sixteenth century.

Besides his several closes, and his use after harvest of the communal fields, the husbandman had access to three kinds of common of pasture :—(1) In many places, where closes and pastures exist in severalty, there is often a common close, taken in out of the common or fields by tenants of the same place—and I conclude by the action of the homage—for oxen, kine, or other cattle, in which close every man is stinted from the lord downwards. (2) The plain champaign country, where the cattle go daily before the herdsman, this lying near the common fields. Here again each person who has the right of use should be stinted; and a suggestion is made that the principle of the stint should be determined by the extent of the tenant's holding. (3) The lord's outwoods, moors, and heaths, which have never been under the plough. Here the lord should not be stinted, for the soil is his; but his tenants should be, for they have no certain parcel of this district annexed to their holdings, but only bit of mouth with their cattle. The stint of cattle, we are told, is necessary, in order to prevent the rich man from buying sheep and cattle in the beginning of summer, getting them into condition, and selling them, all the while sparing his own pasture, and so defrauding the poor man. As an equitable adjustment of the stint, it is proposed that the tenant's right should be proportioned to the amount of cattle which he can maintain in the winter from the amount of hay and straw housed during the season from his several holding. These passages make it clear that the interest of the mediæval tenant was by no means limited to the acreage with which he is credited in the manor survey; and that, under proper regulations, his common of pasture was necessary and valuable.

The division of communal fields into lands, or regular plots of equal length and breadth, as far at least as the unit is concerned, of which the several owners had multiples, necessitated, after the practice of tenant farming became general, an accurate survey and terrier of the different interests in the field. As long as cultivation was carried on by the owner, whether lord or tenant, identification was easy, and boundary disputes rare. But when the occupier ceased to be the owner, a great deal of care and frequent visits were necessary to prevent fraud or encroachment. The owner of one strip in freehold might be the tenant on a short term of years on another strip, and would be strongly tempted to edge on his landlord's property. This is curiously illustrated by some of the bad debts which landowners made in later times. They had defaulting tenants, whose property was insufficient to meet the debts which they had incurred. But the remedy of distress, the common law process, by which the lord could recover his rent, appears to have been available only on the land from which the rent issued; and if by any means the boundaries of it were lost or obscured, the landowner might be unable to recover, because he could not find the precise spot from which his rent issued. Now it was a common practice in later times to let different strips for various terms; and thus the tenant, not taking his holding in the aggregate, but piecemeal, could with difficulty be dispossessed. It also became difficult to discover, unless the area of the several strips was accurately registered, to find out what plot was liable for overdue rent. I have constantly found, in the accounts presented by rent collectors, that arrears extending over a long period of years, especially in the fifteenth century, are described as not recovered because the collector cannot identify the land from which the rent issues. It was, I believe, to meet such contingencies as these that the old remedy of distress was supplemented by the action for covenant and the action for debt; and thus that the rights of the landowner have been made a far more secure debt than they were under the ancient system.

The system of communal tenure, it must be admitted, was hostile to permanent or even transient improvement, because it left the personal advantage of outlay on such land insecure. The argument may be pressed with great force in favour of the tenant under the modern system; and it is certain, as we shall see hereafter, that as soon as ever it was possible to apply new methods of cultivation, and to enhance by such methods the natural capacity of the soil, the complaint arose that the landlord entered on the benefit of the tenant's improvements, deprived him of them by the exaltation of rent, and therefore discouraged agriculture. This complaint, which begins in the sixteenth century, is exceedingly common in the seventeenth, when English agriculture was making rapid progress.

Still, improvements were made in the thirteenth century. These consist of ditching, draining, and ridging wet land, of marling and claying stiff or poor soils.

Ditching was generally contracted for by the pole, and, to judge from the price, a pole of ditching was about a day's work. I should gather, however, that this is not the cost of the first construction, but of subsequent cleansing. Draining was practised on wet lands by digging a trench and laying angular stones in the cavity, or, in some cases, by setting an arch of stone through the length of the trench, provision being made for an exit into the ditch, or even by laying hollowed alder stems in the trench. Ridging was practised on wet arable land or meadows, and sometimes the ridge is raised to a considerable elevation. This is the most indestructible of agricultural improvements ; and districts may be found where, time out of mind after arable cultivation has ceased on the land, the artificial ridge of the ancient field is as marked as ever.

Much more important, however, is the marling and claying of light and poor lands. If in marls the proportion of calcareous matter is large, it is said to be a good dressing for clay soils; if the amount of clay is large, it is good for light, sandy soil. It was extensively adopted at Maldon, in Surrey, one of the eleven estates on which I have so frequently commented ; the operation extending over thirty-seven years, and nearly 143 acres having been gradually treated in this manner. Maldon is in the sandy district of Surrey.

It was a costly operation. It appears that about one hundred loads were spread to the acre, and that the cost—I am speaking of Maldon only—was from 3*s.* to 3*s.* 6*d.* an acre, that is, nearly half the value of the fee simple of ordinary arable land. Sometimes it cost more to the acre, the charge rising in the case of one estate to 7*s.* an acre, and in another to nearly 8*s.* The effect in altering the texture and increasing the fertility of the soil was supposed to be very great, and the value of marl pits was generally recognised. There is no reason to doubt that the freehold and copyhold tenants, whose rents and services were fixed, followed the example of the lord in improving their property, especially as the cost of carriage, owing to the fact that so many beasts of burden, relatively speaking, were kept, was exceedingly light.

Writing two centuries and a half afterwards, Fitzherbert tells us that the most useful process for mending ground is marling, and that generally, when such a material exists within convenient reach, marl pits have long been opened. Latterly, he adds, the practice of marling has become uncommon. Two causes are assigned for this change of agricultural custom. One is "that tenants"—he is speaking now of tenants at will, or on short lease—"be so doubtful of their landlords, that if they should marl and make their holdings much better, they fear lest they should be put out, or make a great fine, or else pay more rent. And if a lord do so, meseemeth he is unreasonable, seeing that it is done all at the cost of the tenant, and not at his. The second cause is that men be disposed to idleness, and will not labour, as they have done in times past; but it meseemeth a freeholder should not be of that condition, for he is in a security, for his chief lord cannot put him out doing his duty. And he knoweth well that he shall take the whole profit while he liveth, and his heirs after him ; a courage to improve his own, the which is as good as he had purchased as much as the improvement cometh to. And one man thus doing would give other men the courage and a good example to follow the same. Marl mends all manner of ground, but it is costly." He goes on to say that in Cheshire and Lancashire the process of marling has doubled the value of the land.

While marling was the expedient, according to the quality of the article, for sandy land and some kinds of clay, lime was employed for the destruction of moss and some kinds of insects, and for altering the texture of heavy clays. Lime was manufactured, the owner supplying kilns, fuel, and raw material, at about $1\frac{1}{2}d.$ the quarter, or at about $2d.$ the day, when the service is not paid by the piece, and the operation was carried on at bye times of the year. I find no record of the amount needed for the acre; it probably varied, and was frequently employed as a dressing. Our forefathers seem to have sometimes committed the error of mixing it with stable dung, and thereby of liberating the ammonia in their manures. The sort of liming of course varies with the proximity of the estate to chalkpits or limestone.

The Dairy.—Cheese and butter were abundant and cheap. The proof is that, except kitchen stuff, butter is the cheapest of the fats. Both appear to be produced on every farm. But information in detail, such as the statistician would require, is defective. Cheese is generally sold by tale, not by weight. It is made up into three shapes, great, middle, and small, and the weight of the aggregate is rarely found. So, again, butter is frequently sold in pats. Again, it was a common practice to let out the cows, the owner supplying food, at 5s. to 6s. 8d. a year, and the ewes at about 1s., to the dairyman, who had the calves, often repurchased by the bailiff, as part of his bargain. The dairyman, or deye, engaged to restore the animal in sound condition at the end of the year. Here it is worth noting that such a bargain implied not only a power of contracting on the part of persons whom the law books describe as having no rights of their own against the lord and his agent, but the possession of a considerable amount of private resources on the part of the contractor, who is generally a farm servant. The custom, in short, is proof that the condition and means of persons who entered into hired service on annual wages and allowances with the lord's bailiff, were far better than anything of which our modern experience informs us as to the condition of farm labourers in our time, or, indeed, within recorded memory. Butter was worth about three farthings, cheese about a half-penny the pound. It appears that butter was occasionally melted, as it is sold frequently by the gallon. This may be accounted for by the high price of salt.

The manufacture of cheese generally commenced at Christmas, and was continued to Michaelmas. Within these nine months, two cows should produce, in fair pasture, a wey (224 lb.) of cheese, and about 19 gallons of butter. It seems, then, that cheese was made of skimmed milk, or, at least, that a portion of the butter was abstracted from it. If the pasture is light, as in woods, meadows after mowing, or in stubble, three cows were required for the same produce. Now, says Walter de Henley, if a cow produces, as it may, 3½d. worth of cheese and 1d. worth of butter weekly, its gross annual return, deducting the cost of keep, will be 9s. a year, and, therefore, it is strongly advisable that cows should be kept. Ten ewes were considered to be equal in productiveness to one cow. Goats, for obvious reasons, were rarely kept. In the open country they would have been entirely unmanageable.

Rennet was employed (generally the produce of the farm, but occasionally purchased) for manufacturing cheese. The curd was put into a vat and pressed through cloths. The charge for vats and cheese-cloths is found on every farm. The cheese thus manufactured seems to have been sold at once, if possible, in the nearest town, and the sale was continued through the whole season. It appears that the produce of certain dairies was stamped, not probably as evidence of quality, but of ownership. It was the practice, as I have said, to make cheeses into three shapes. These seem to have been, to infer from the prices, six, four, and two pounds respectively. In a later period we find very different qualities of cheese, the practice being to make them into larger shapes. The best cheese at this time came from the eastern counties; the cheapest from the southern.

Butter is generally sold by the gallon. Of course this may have been salted and pressed into earthenware pans or small barrels, which were very cheap,—the art of the cooper, like his name, being universal,—or, as I have suggested, it may have been melted. Its use for purposes which could hardly bear salt argues that the melting of butter was not unknown. At any rate it was abundant.

Salt.—In connection with these articles of agricultural produce, salt should be referred to. It was a matter of necessity to an extent which we cannot conceive, and the acquisition of a good quality of the article was as important as its cheapness and plenty. For five or six months in the year, our ancestors, at least the majority of the people, lived on salted provisions. The wealthy had game, fish from their stores, and even fresh meat from their farms, though the latter in varying quantity; for it was plainly a piece of extravagance to habitually consume fresh meat in the winter. But the mass of the people had to live on salted meat, or to go without meat at all. The pig was doubtless the principal food; but salted beef, and even mutton and poultry, were common articles of diet. The usages of the Church prescribed that just before the coming of spring all should live on salted fish, and, as a consequence, there was a great and most important trade in salted sea-fish, the earliest maritime adventure being directed towards the discovery of new and more abundant fishing-grounds. Now, in the absence of all winter roots and herbs, beyond a few onions, a diet on salted provisions, extended over so long a period, would be sure to engender disease, even though the salt were of the best quality; and as a matter of fact, scurvy and leprosy, the invariable results of an unwholesome diet, were endemic, the latter malignant and infectious, in mediæval England. The virulence of these diseases, due, in the first instance, to unwholesome food, was aggravated by the inconceivably filthy habits of the people.

The salt, however, with which the provisions were seasoned made matters even worse. It was entirely produced by solar evaporation in the southern counties, in so far as it was an English product. That the Romans made use of the brine springs of Worcestershire and Cheshire I can well believe ; that the English did not, before the beginning of the eighteenth century, I am quite certain ; for the best authorities at the time, those on the spot, declare they did not. English salt, therefore, was full of impurities. It contained, or was likely to contain, all those salts which the skill of the modern chemist easily separates from the staple product. It contained sand and dirt besides. " White " salt was very properly a good deal dearer than grey or black salt ; salt that was used for the dairy than that which was supplied to the servants. Great or bay salt was the dearest of all English products.

The acquisition of salt, therefore, from such foreign regions as could supply a purer article, was a great consideration. Such a supply could come from the south-west coast of France. As long as Guienne was parcel of the English Crown, and trade was regular between the district and England, salt and wine were the principal exports to this country. In 1450, Guienne, after being annexed to the

English Crown, though with some interruptions, for three centuries, was lost. The French king, knowing how important the export of salt and wine was to England, ventured on imposing an export duty on these commodities. The Gascons rebelled in 1452; and were supported by the English Parliament and the force under Talbot for very good reasons. Talbot and his son were slain at Chatillon in 1453, and Guienne was irretrievably lost. Thenceforward the English kings strove to negotiate commercial treaties in which the free exportation of the salt of Guienne was stipulated for.

I have said that English salt was always produced by solar heat. The proof of this fact is to be found in the exaltation of the price when the summer was wet. The price of salt is even a better index of the rainfall during harvest time than the price of wheat; for the latter might recover, even when August rains were heavy, since it was cut high up on the stalk; but the lost heat was never regained. The stocks were generally, it would seem, larger; and the exaltation of price is always, or nearly always, seen in the year following on the agricultural scarcity. In what was a matter of necessity, this was to be expected.

My reader will be now able to construct for himself the picture of an English village in the thirteenth century : of its timber or stone manor house,—brick-making, we must remember, was a lost art, and was not revived till the middle of the fifteenth century,—of the rough buildings in which the peasant owners lived, and the still ruder huts of the peasant labourers. From childhood to old age, all labour. There is no change in their career, their industry, their experience, from generation to generation. Sometimes, indeed, an enterprising or favoured village youth quits his rustic home, and, successful in war or the Church,—a Sale or a Wykeham or a Fox,—is knighted or raised to episcopal dignity and such wealth as to enable him to say, as Fox is said to have predicted, that the whole village would not serve for his kitchen. But though a few persons became opulent in the middle ages,—exceedingly opulent by way of contrast with their countrymen,—the mass of men in the rural districts were

7

removed equally from excessive poverty and from the prospect
of much wealth. They could and did make their savings add
strip to strip, accumulate the wages of the harvest, and—
there being little to tempt them to expenditure—constantly
invest their earnings in plots of land.

Doubtlessly the court days, when all were summoned on
pain of fine for non-appearance at the manor hall, to serve
on the homage or court leet as the case might be, were
occasional breaks in their monotonous lives. There they presented scolds for wrangling; there the miller who took
advantage of his monopoly was indicted and punished; the
widow was allotted her charge on the land; the baker or
brewer, who had broken the assize or outraged the discipline
of the manor, was fined; ambitious fathers bargained for permission to send their sons to school; and mothers got leave
to marry their daughters. The labourer who is defrauded of
his wages is permitted to distrain on his employer's goods and
even household chattels; and poachers are mulcted for their
offences. Sometimes the whole parish strives to emancipate
itself from the obligation of grinding its corn at the lord's
mill, and is amerced for so heinous a breach of manor law.
The common carrier is summoned for failing to deliver goods
trusted to him, and is constrained to make compensation
A woman is fined for harbouring a stranger in her house.
A son comes into court, and, on succeeding to his father's
tenement, not only fines in a mark for quiet entry, but
acknowledges that he is bound to pay an annuity to his
mother for her whole life—of a quarter of wheat, another of
barley, another of peas, and forty pence; proffering, as
sureties for the due performance of his obligation, two other
residents. The parish priest is generally the peacemaker.
These courts are held about three times a year, and seem
always to have had a day's business to do.

At harvest time, again, there is a glimpse of the outer world.
The lord of the manor comes to take audit of his bailiff's
doings through the past year, and perhaps to reside temporarily in the manor house. The parson hires labour, super-
intends the reaping of his own lands, and collects the tithe of

the produce into the huge barns which stand by his manse on the close of his glebe. The busy Benedictine from some convent is there, to watch over the harvest of his portion and to look covetously on the rector's lands and tithes, with a view, if possible, of getting the impropriation of the benefice out of the hands of the secular, and into the grasp of the regular, clergy. Sometimes the parish is visited by the begging friars, the revivalists of the thirteenth century, now in the height of their reputation for piety and self-abnegation, and therefore encouraged to contrast their labours with the lives of luxurious monks and worldly clergymen. When the harvest is over there are processions to the village cross, hard by the church, with thanksgivings for past benefits, and with litanies deprecatory of real or impending calamities.

Grave offences against life and property are exceedingly rare, else the penalties inflicted for these would have been recorded in that exact and faithful transcript of the year's accounts, the bailiff's roll. But it is quite likely that though the little community was generally at peace within its own borders, and property was so generally distributed that none was imperilled, it heard with indifference that strangers were robbed on the high roads, and was even pleased that the foreigner was not allowed to have his way in England. An incident in Matthew Paris is so characteristic that I am induced to quote it at length, the more so because it is strange that so curious a narrative is omitted from the current histories of England. The scene is Winchester and Alton in Hampshire, two places which are equidistant from what is probably the scene of the transactions in question. The date is 1249.

The king, who had taken the whole conduct of affairs into his own hands, and had neither Justiciary, Chancellor, nor Treasurer under him, was residing in Winchester during Lent, when two merchants of Brabant complained to him that they had been robbed of two hundred marks in money by certain highwaymen, whom they thought they could identify. The culprits were arrested, and being put to the test of compurgation, were set free by the oaths of their own neighbours. The whole county was an accomplice in the robbery, and was agreed to convict no one; so that the efforts of the judge to detect the scandal were fruitless. The despoiled merchants pressed the king, assuring him that the Duke of Brabant would certainly grant reprisals against English merchants in Flanders, and thus amicable relations, then of great importance, between England and the Low Countries would be seriously interrupted, or at least imperilled.

So the king summoned the bailiffs and freemen of the county of Southampton to him. Looking angrily at them he said, "What is this that I hear of you ? The cry of those who are robbed reaches me, and I must needs come down. There is no county or district in the whole of England so scandalous or so stained with crimes as yours. Even when I am here, in this city, its suburbs or its neighbourhood, robberies and murders are committed. Even this is not enough. My own wine in my own casks is stolen by grinning and drunken thieves. I am ashamed and disgusted at the abominations of this city and its neighbourhood. I was born in this city, and yet have never been so dishonoured in any place as here. It is probable, credible, nay, all but certain, that you are confederates and accomplices with these criminals. But I will deal with you. Shut the gates, and let none go forth ! "

After certain expostulations from the bishop, who was present and excommunicated the offenders, a jury of twelve was appointed out of Winchester and Hampshire men. They were kept under strict custody, and held long debate. Summoned at last, they could make no mention of the thieves. The king was exceedingly enraged, for he knew they were well acquainted with the facts. So he cried out, "Seize these cunning traitors, and put them heavily ironed into the lowest prison. They are concealing what they ought to tell. Then choose another jury of twelve from the same district, who will be willing to tell the truth." After a long and secret colloquy, these came forward, and disclosed the crimes and offences of many persons from Alton and the bishop's liberty of Tanton. The result was that many persons of substance, numerous bailiffs and servants of the king, and some even of the king's household, were convicted and hanged. Among these thieves was one William Pope, whose house, when searched, was found to have no less than fifteen tuns of wine in it. More than sixty were executed for their offences. Such brigands must have lurked in the numerous forests which covered much ground in the south-west, centre, and north-east of Hampshire. The villages, however, would have cared little for the calamities of a Flemish merchant or a papal collector. The story, moreover, illustrates the state of society and the process by which justice was done through the agency of a jury of witnesses and compurgators.

The winter and the summer were in violent contrast. The former was dark and cheerless, for the cost of artificial light was disproportionately high—a time in which the peasant lived perforce on unsavoury and unwholesome food. Such clothing, too, as could be obtained was inadequate to repel the cold. Hence the chroniclers comment on severe winters as the most serious calamity of the year. But, on the other hand, the freshness and glory of spring was heightened by the rudeness of the season which it followed. The earliest English poetry is that of the spring-time and its surroundings.

It is probable that the summer of the thirteenth century and for some generations later, was better than that of modern experience. Wheat was grown much farther north than it was in the eighteenth century. Vineyards are found in Norfolk, and wine, manufactured from English grapes, is sold at a price not much less than that given for ordinary Bordeaux. There are traditions of similar plantations over many of the southern counties. In the fifteenth century, wine was made in Devonshire, and in the sixteenth, after the dissolution of the monasteries, a vineyard of five acres is scheduled as part of the possessions of Barking nunnery. In the thirteenth, as in the nineteenth century, the danger of English agriculture was in unseasonable wet in summer. A wet harvest is the cause of every famine and dearth in the agricultural history of England.

CHAPTER IV.

TOWN LIFE.

Many Roman Colonies survived the Saxon Conquest—Many grew up round Monasteries, some Ports—Southampton in the Twelfth Century—Charters granted to the Towns—List of English Towns in the Thirteenth Century, with the Characteristics of each. The Guilds—were possessed of a Monopoly—adopted and Enforced Apprenticeship; supplied a Military System to the Towns, and in London gave great Political Influence; were Benefit Societies; had to be cautious how they admitted Serfs—London, a perpetual Market—Attachment of Londoners to the City—Trade in London Illustrated by a par.icular Purchase—Political Activity in England—Relative Opulence of London in 1341, 1453, 1503, as compared with other Towns—Population of the Principal Towns in 1377—Difficulties in the Estimate of Population—The Population of England and Wales, and the Principle on which it has been Estimated—Population and Occupations at Colchester in 1301—The whole Population engaged in the Harvest—The Commerce of the Towns.

DURING the slow progress of the Teutonic invasion and occupation, many a Roman colony perished. The sites of some are now entirely lost, and some have been recently, as Uriconium, Silchester, and the like, discovered. Roman England was dotted over with villas, the foundations of which are now and then exposed in places which have long since been abandoned to tillage. Saxon England was not a settlement of towns, but of villages and communal customs. Even most of the bishoprics were settled in places which never could have been considerable. The seat of the bishop whose jurisdiction extended from the Humber to the Thames was an Oxfordshire village, which grew round an ancient monastery, founded within the walls of a Roman town. The Bishop of the West had his see at the hamlet of Crediton, that of the Central and East at Elmham. A few were from the first placed in the ancient colonies of Roman England, as at London, Winchester, York, and Worcester.

Even if the names did not prove the fact, some of the cities of Roman Britain clearly survived the ruin of the second conquest, and must have had a continuous existence. The sites of London, of York, of Lincoln, Winchester, Exeter, Chester, Gloucester, and several others could never have been abandoned. In the fragments of history which throw a little light on the annals of the petty Saxon kingdoms, there are a few hints of the independent existence of London, and of a corporate vitality there. This was to be expected. Unless the town offered an obstinate resistance, the invaders might well be content to spare those places which they had no mind to occupy. It is true that the desolation of Roman Britain was more thorough than that of Roman Gaul ; but it is more than probable that the towns which the Saxon tolerated he found useful afterwards ; that the Saxon king discovered in these towns some means for strengthening his authority, and that Edward the Elder was not the first king who made the successful merchant "who had passed thrice over the sea by his own means" thegn worthy. From various notices in the Codex Diplomaticus, London appears to have been included in the kingdom of Mercia. Nor can it be doubted that when the intercourse between the England of this and even a remoter age and France began, men learned about the Roman municipalities which survived. These became the patterns of the chartered towns which were so numerously enfranchised in the early Plantagenet period.

Many of the English towns grew up round monasteries The piety of the converted Saxons led them to spend lavishly in the foundation of these institutions, and the principal part of the documents which have been preserved from a period antecedent to the Conquest refer to these early monasteries. Thus the town of Oxford grew up under the shadow of the great monasteries of St. Frideswide and Osney. Such was the origin of Abingdon, of Reading, of St. Albans, of Coventry, of Durham. Some, when trade was developed or restored, owed their existence to the convenience of the site for com-

merce. Such must have been the origin of Southampton,
which migrated from the Roman Clausentum to the eastern
side of the Itchen ; of Bristol, and of Norwich. Some were the
havens of fishermen, as Yarmouth, Grimsby, and Scarborough.
In the beginning of Richard the First's reign, Southampton must
have been a thriving town, for the possessions of God's House,
a charity for decayed merchants, founded in 1189, were exceedingly extensive. The hospital holds houses, shops, and
lands in the parishes of Holy Cross, St. John, St. Michael, St.
Lawrence, All Saints, St. Mary's, and in the district outside
the Bars. In point of fact, Southampton was the chief port
of southern England, with which the principal part of the
French trade was carried on, especially that in wines. It did
not recover for many generations the ruin which fell on it when
the French landed and burnt it on October 6th, 1338. The
names in the Southampton rental of the twelfth century
imply a considerable population of foreigners, especially of
Flemings ; and it appears from documents that there was a
constant immigration from North-west Germany into the
Eastern Counties.

The towns which depended on the Crown were liable to
certain annual payments, which were collected by the sheriff.
In the twelfth and thirteenth centuries, the custom began of
entrusting the town with the collection of its fee farm payments, and of confirming and enlarging the jurisdiction which
the authorities of the town had over their own burghers.
These were granted very extensively by Richard I. and John,
and generally contain exemptions from harassing and vexatious charges, the right of self-government, of the election of
their own officers, and the power of forming guilds and
enacting bye-laws for their government. The municipal
privileges of London are even recognised in a charter of
William the Conqueror. Most of the charters are confirmations of privileges which were alleged to have existed from
ancient times. The permanent and fixed sources of income
which the Crown enjoyed from these chartered towns were
occasionally charged with payments to other permanent
institutions. One of the principal sources of income pos-

sessed by the King's Hall of Cambridge, the predecessor of Trinity College, was a portion of the fee farm rent of the town of Scarborough.

In a lawyer's handy-book of the thirteenth century, the compilation of which was clearly made at or about 1250, and which contains the earliest copy which I have found of Walter de Henley's work on husbandry, though, as the corrections show, it is a copy of a still earlier original, is a list of English towns and similar places, each with some marked characteristic annexed to it. Thus we have the Baronage of London, a phrase which seems to point to that period in the earlier recorded history of the great city when the artizans and traders were struggling against the dominant influence of the local nobles, and the Fitzosberts were seeking to give method to their discontent and their efforts. The relics of Westminster, the pardons of St. Paul's, the approach to Thorney, perhaps the enclosure of the old Palace of Westminster, if not the isle of Ely Abbey, and the prostitutes of Charing, designate the characteristics of localities near London. With the exception of Berwick, York, and Chester, no place north of the Humber is named.

Oxford is renowned for its schools, Cambridge for its eels—a proof that the list was compiled before the latter University was recognized. Manufactures of cloth are noted :—Scarlet at Lincoln (Nichol); blanket at Bligh ; burnet at Beverley ; russet at Colchester (eight weavers are enumerated at this town in the rolls of Parliament under the year 1301); produce of linen fabrics at Shaftesbury, Lewes, and Aylesham ; of cord at Warwick and Bridport, the latter being also quoted for its hempen fabrics ; of fine bread at Wycombe, Hungerford, and St. Albans ; of knives at Maxstead ; of needles at Wilton ; of razors at Leicester. Banbury is distinguished for its drink, Hitchin for its mead, and Ely for its ale. Gloucester is the mart for iron, Bristol for leather, Coventry for soap, Doncaster for horse girths, Chester and Shrewsbury for skins and furs, Corfe for marble, Cornwall for tin. Grimsby is famous for cod, Rye for whiting, Yarmouth for herrings, Berwick for salmon, Ripon is a horse market, as it was in the sixteenth century, and gloves are bought at Haverhill, while oxen are sold at Nottingham, and, unless I am mistaken, saddlery at Northampton.

Southampton is famed for its navy, Norwich for its harbour, Stamford and Dunstable for inns. Some towns are indicated by uncomplimentary characteristics—as the robbers of Alton, in allusion, doubtless, to the story of brigandage in that neighbourhood recounted in the last chapter—butchers at Winchester, and villeins at Tamworth. The plains of Salisbury, the hot springs at Bath, the cloister at Lichfield, the marvel of Stonehenge, the passage of Chelmsford, the ferry of Tilbury, the warren of Walton, the prairie of Waltham, the mills of Dunwich, the forest of Sherwood, the chase of Englewood, the forest of Windsor, the manor of Woodstock, the castle of Dover, and the marsh of Ramsey, are natural or artificial objects which made the localities famous. The courage of the Cinque Ports probably refers to the battle with Eustace the Monk in 1217, when these ports bore the brunt of the struggle, and made the cause of Louis of France hopeless.

The inhabitants of these towns were merchants and artizans. London was, no doubt, from the earliest times wholly unlike any other English town, as well for its magnitude, its opulence, as for its singular political importance, for its military defences, and for the energy with which it strove to free itself from the overpowering influence of the magnates within its walls. But the essence of the mediæval town was the formation of the guilds of merchants and craftsmen; and if the town was large enough, of craftsmen who represented each and every calling which was carried on in the locality. There was every motive for the creation of these guilds, for the establishment of rules for their private governance, for jealous supervision over those who had the privileges of these corporate bodies, and for care lest an unauthorized person should intrude on what was a valued right, which might be and was watched with suspicion and alarm by other forces in the state.

1. Within the limits of the corporation, the guild had the monopoly of manufacture or trade. Such a privilege was

entirely in accordance with the fundamental characteristic
of these societies which constituted the parish or manor of
rural England. There were no strangers in the manor. It
was an offence, punishable with fine, to harbour one. If a
tenement changed hands, it was generally to some other
villager. For generations it was no easy matter to import a
stranger; and when competitive rents began, this virtual
exclusion of strangers checked for a long time the development of such rents. In the same way, and from the same
ancient feeling, centuries after the period on which I am
writing, the first law of parochial settlement, under which
the peasant labourer was formally declared to be *adscriptus
glebæ*, or a serf without land, who might be debarred from
seeking employment in any other place than that of his birth
or settlement, and dragged back to his native field of labour,
did not seem unnatural or unjust. It was not, therefore,
remarkable that, apart from the obvious but secondary motive
of self-interest, the guild should number its members on the
lines of a register in the decenna, or tithing, and should put
effectual hindrances on the introduction of strangers. Membership in a guild was a birthright, an inheritance.

2. But it was also a great advantage. The members of the
guild had paid good money for their privileges in their
collective capacity. They had, as individuals, contributed to
the common stock, not, perhaps, always in fair proportion.
for the contribution in all likelihood, as in modern times,
pressed hardly on the poorer among the fraternity; but the
privilege was all the more valuable because it had been gained
by solid sacrifices. They alone who were of the fraternity
had the right to manufacture and sell within the precinct.
They took care that this right should not become obsolete.
They insisted, as one of the hindrances to the too free
distribution of the privilege, that new-comers should undergo
a long period of servitude or apprenticeship. This custom, or
innovation, which was rightly interpreted by Adam Smith,
required that a considerable time should elapse before the
workman or trader should be able to set up for himself, his
services during the time of his apprenticeship being the

property of his master. The object of the rule was to restrain competition, and the restraint was further enforced by limiting the number of apprentices which the master could take. The rules of trade were copied by the Inns of Court and the Universities, who enacted that no one should be free to practise in a court or to lecture in the University till seven years had elapsed from his entrance to the initial privileges of the order. In some corporations it was prescribed by byelaws, which had the effect of public laws, that the apprentice should work for a period after his probation had elapsed as a journeyman to his employer. He was a freeman to the guild, but not in the trade. Hence the celebrated statute of 5 Elizabeth was merely declaratory of custom, was in reality only a re-enactment of 7 Hen. IV., with the fact that the machinery for enforcing the law was applied.

3. The organization of the guilds bestowed that military system on the London artizans, and similarly on the guilds of other trading towns, which the circumstances of the time seemed to demand. The London apprentices and train bands were a force, not indeed considerable enough to withstand the charge of regular soldiers, as was proved at the battle of Lewes, but as good as the militia, and for purposes of defence entirely adequate on ordinary occasions. The wealth of London was great, and naturally provoked the angry comment of Henry III., when, in 1248, his "parliament" of nobles having refused to assist him in one of his recurrent straits of poverty, and his foreign possessions being wasted, he sold his plate and jewels for what they would fetch, and found they were bought in London: "I know that if the treasure of Imperial Rome was to be sold, that London would take and buy it all. These London clowns, who call themselves barons, are rich to loathing. The city is an inexhaustible well." And so he bethought himself of spoiling the citizens, and the citizens to arm the companies, till at last they ranged themselves on De Montfort's side in the civil war, as they had nearly fifty years before taken part with Langton and the barons in the exaction of the Great Charter.

During the many political dissensions of the middle ages

the side which London took was always in the end, and
generally at an early period, victorious. To pass over the
uprisings in the reigns of John and Henry, they joined in
deposing Edward II. and Richard II. They put away the
House of Lancaster in 1461. When the rapacity of his
courtiers and the poverty of his exchequer led the guardians
of Edward VI. to despoil the guilds in the country towns, they
were prudent enough to spare the possessions of the London
guilds, which still exist, though with very different objects
from those for which they were first incorporated. The
indignation of the robbed and ruined traders overset the
calculations of Northumberland, extinguished the project of
setting Jane Grey on the throne, though she had a parliamentary title, and affirmed the right of Mary Tudor. The
adherence of London to the cause of Parliament during the
long struggle which began with the book of rates, and was
concluded by the battle of Naseby, made the issue of the
conflict manifest to all foresighted persons. And lastly, when
Charles was bent on despotism, and discovered the best means
by which to attain his ends, at least for a time, he employed
legal chicanery to rob the citizens of their liberties, which he
never could have destroyed by violence. The situation of
the city was doubtlessly very strong. It was protected on
the north by extensive marshes, on the south by the river
and a lofty bank, on the west by other fortifications and the
Fleet stream. But the strength of mediæval London lay in
the sturdy determination and military spirit of its citizens.
For centuries it held the balance of power in England.

4. The guilds were the benefit societies in the middle ages.
It does not follow that they were under a legal obligation
to relieve their destitute members, as they are in those modern
cities of Europe in which the guild system has continued to
our own day, as at Munich. But it was a common practice
for the wealthier members of a guild to give or devise sums
of money to the guild, the proceeds of which were lent without interest to struggling members of the fraternity, adequate
pledges or securities being exacted from the borrowers. Such
gifts were frequently made to the University of Oxford in its

earlier days, the trustees being the University officials, and the money being deposited in chests or hutches in the University church, where also the pledges were left. The college in Oxford which is now reputed the earliest, though its incorporation was much later than that of Merton College, began with the proceeds of such a hutch, limited to a certain number of beneficiaries. These gifts are common in London and other cities, both to guilds and parishes, and constitute a large part of their estates, purchases of real estate being made with the benefactions which belong to the companies and the parishes, often from nameless donors. Still more frequently the members of guilds devised lands, tenements, and moneys, the proceeds of which were to be charged first with the cost of religious offices for the repose of the dead, the residue being devoted to the common purposes of the guild. Sometimes the benefactor founded an almshouse for destitute or decayed members of the guild, their widows and orphans. Such almshouses, though unconnected with guilds, were founded near Canterbury by Lanfranc and Anselm in the reigns of the Conqueror and Rufus ; by Henry de Blois, near Winchester, in the reign of Stephen ; and by Stephen's wife, Matilda, in London. The condition that prayers should be said for the deceased was the plea on which those guild lands were confiscated in 1547, though the court did not dissolve the London companies, and the colleges in Oxford and Cambridge were allowed to retain their chantries discharged of the trust. Besides these funds, there were fines on admission, payments for membership, and penalties for breaches of the corporation bye-laws. The accumulation must have been considerable at an early date, for in the fourteenth century two Cambridge guilds contributed from their funds to found a new college in the University. The origin of the trading companies, their revenues and their statutes, are almost exactly like those of academical colleges.

5. The guilds had to be careful in the bestowal of their privileges. Residence for a year and a day in a corporate town precluded a lord from regaining his serf ; and we have seen that the lords, by exacting an annual fine on absentees

of base origin, were not remiss in claiming their rights. It might have been dangerous for the guilds to openly defy the feudal lords by making their fraternities an asylum for runaway serfs. We may conclude that not only selfish motives, but those of reasonable prudence would have made them cautious in welcoming strangers. Still they would not put up with an invasion of any right which was or seemed to them clear in the case of any enrolled member of their order. In 1381, Sir Simon Burley gave no slight stimulus to Tyler's insurrection by imprisoning a Gravesend burgess on a plea of villeinage. It is not easy to see indeed how the suit against a runaway villein could be prosecuted, except he had taken refuge in a town.

6. London was a perpetual market. If goods were sold in open market, it is an ancient custom that the owner of stolen property has no remedy against an innocent purchaser. Hence it was throughout the year what the great fairs were at stated intervals. The market for heavy goods, especially of foreign origin, was below the city walls on the river wharves. Within the city walls were great open spaces, now built over, no doubt because the tolls of these markets were the property of the city, of individuals, or of companies ; spaces like those which are still to be seen in Nottingham and Norwich, the last of which cities in the thirteenth century was only second to London, though at a great interval behind it. London, in fact, was a perpetual fair, the localities of whose trades are still discernible in the Cornhill, the Cheapside, the Poultry, the Leadenhall, or designated in literature, as Bucklersbury and Smithfield are.

7. Macaulay, in a well-known passage, has dwelt upon the intensity of feeling with which a Londoner looked upon his city and its privileges at the conclusion of the seventeenth century. The feeling must have been keener in the thirteenth and fourteenth, when it did not contain a population of over 40,000 persons, even before fire and plague had desolated it. The streets were narrow, and the upper stories, projecting from the timber frames, nearly touched each other. But in the rear of the houses were trim gardens, in which the citizen

sat in the summer evenings. I have often noticed the charges
to which corporations are put in repairing the fences and
walls in the gardens of their London tenements. These
gardens are now occupied by courts and lofty buildings, the
value of which is estimated by the square foot, the rental of
one such court being in nominal amount equal to the whole
fee farm rent which London, in the middle ages, paid her
Plantagenet kings. But London in these times was a *rus in
urbe,* as nearly all the walled towns in England were, the
inhabitants of which were densely enough packed in the
buildings which they occupied, but had open spaces in
abundance within the walls, and in the ward without, the
western outskirt of the city. The attachment which the
merchant princes of the seventeenth century felt for London
was a feeble sentiment beside that which the " barons " of the
thirteenth entertained towards their home and their stronghold. There was little opportunity for handsome houses, or
for costly furniture, such as might be seen in the Italian cities,
perhaps in Flanders and the free towns of the Rhine; the
tale of domestic goods is scanty and mean, but the burghers
accumulated wealth, which they liked to expend, as the piety
of the age dictated, in handsome churches, in splendid presents
to the shrines of saints, and in the pomp of religious worship.
Fitzstephen, a century before the time of which I write, is
eloquent about the opulence of London, and how it constantly
recovered after the disastrous fires with which it was frequently
visited. The churchyard of the great cathedral might be in
ordinary times the burial-ground of the whole city, as its vast
aisles and nave were for the chief citizens, the ecclesiastics on
its establishment, and some of the nobles ; but there were
numberless city churches and monasteries where space was
ample for all the burials of the inhabitants.

There is an entry in one of the accounts of Cuxham which,
with very little effort of the imagination, may give one a picture
of those daily mercantile transactions of magnitude which
were carried on in London. In the summer of 1331, the lords of
Cuxham and Holywell determined to make an extensive purchase of the best millstones procurable for the purpose of sup-

plying their mills at the village and at Oxford. These stones were formed probably from the chert which is found in the neighbourhood of Paris, or were perhaps quarried at Andernach on the Rhine, the two localities from which, it appears, the best foreign millstones were procured, and still are. At daybreak, therefore, the bailiff, who, like his father, was a serf of the manor, started on the road to London, some forty-five miles distant, over the Chiltern Hills, through Wycombe and Uxbridge to London, along one of the most beautiful highways in England. He arrives in London, with servants and horses, and takes up his lodging at one of the numerous inns in the city or in Southwark, and, according to the fashion of the time, goes out to purchase provisions for man and horse, for the inn did not necessarily provide travellers with more than lodging and sleeping accommodation. Early next day he sets about the business on which he had come, inspects the warehouses on the wharf below the southern wall of the city, and finds the five stones which will suit his own and the Oxford mill. Having chosen them, he adjourns with the merchant to some tavern near, in which to discuss the terms of his bargain. The chaffering was doubtlessly long and anxious. In so large an affair it was worth while to stint neither time nor money, and the bailiff debates the price over the exceptional and extensive order of five gallons of Bordeaux wine. The business, too, is worth the merchant's while, for the order is also a considerable affair to him, since it is plain that the bailiff wants the best articles in the warehouse. At last the bargain is struck, the price first asked abated, the luck penny—"God's silver"—is delivered. There are witnesses to the transaction, and the bailiff delivers his acknowledgment of debt. Next morning the bailiff returns to his farm and his duties, and communicates the terms of his purchase to his lords and employers. Shortly afterwards he makes a second journey to London, to pay for his mill-stones,—the five cost £15 16s. 8d.,—and to make a bargain for their carriage by water. Two days are spent in London on this business, and more potations, now cheaper, as he is dealing with sailors and wharfingers, are found necessary. At

last they are set on board, a considerable sum being paid for
shipping them.   Dues are claimed for wharfage and murage,
tolls for maintaining the bank and the city wall, and the bailiff
rides back to his home on the fourth morning of the second
visit.   The vessel with its freight passes up the river, through
the swans and salmon fisheries and the forest of Windsor, as
it is emphatically called, which was still a mere hunting seat,
though soon to be crowned with the palace which the young
king erected on Wykeham's designs.   At Maidenhead the
boat pays a second murage, perhaps because the jurisdiction
of the city over the Thames extended as far as this.   Then it
passed along the horseshoe of the Thames till the boat rested
at Henley, beyond which it is probable that the navigation of
the river did not extend, at least in summer.   Here the stones
are bored for the use of the mills, and two are carried in hired
carts to Cuxham.   The Oxford servants looked after what
was needed for their wants.

On his road to and from London, Oldman, the bailiff, passed
Tyburn brook, which had been employed a century before to
supply water for the growing necessities of London, a supply
which sufficed till more than a century after the journey which
I have described, when springs at Paddington were added,
now, I believe, collected in the Serpentine.   A few months
before, Mortimer had been hanged at Tyburn, the place
which was for many a century to be notorious in the annals
of metropolitan crime.   The downfall of the foolish, disreputable Edward had not been followed by the reforms which the
nation expected, the dignity of the English Crown demanded,
and the interests of the English exchequer required.   Mortimer had been the queen's paramour, and had made peace
with the Scots, even selling the young king's sister to the
son of the detested Bruce.   He had suffered the claims of the
English monarch to be neglected in France.   But this was
over, since Mortimer's righteous execution.

It cannot, I think, be doubted, as we shall see when we come
to deal with subsequent events, that political questions were
discussed among the peasantry with great freedom and
keenness.   The mass of men had that interest in public affairs

which is bred by the possession of property and by the habits of self-government in the manor courts. In the days of Henry III., the Parliament was, as far as the record informs us, of prelates and nobles only, and it was to them that Henry appealed on the frequent occasions of his importunate mendicancy for aid. That the charge of this taxation, when a grant was made, was paid from the moneys of the nobles alone cannot be believed, unless, indeed, it were a scutage. But, at any rate, the commons are summoned in 1259, not only to assent to certain proceedings, but to undertake responsibilities; and when the full Parliamentary system is adopted in Edward's reign, we find that direct taxation of all householders is forthwith introduced. And as the possession of property and the habit of self-government predispose to political debate, so the incidence of direct taxation stimulates it, and I make no doubt that the domestic and foreign policy of the English sovereign, involving as it did a sensible contribution from the peasants' hoard, in order that his crops, his stock, and his household goods should be ransomed, was discussed with eagerness, and opinion, sometimes adverse, sometimes dangerous, was formed, which burst out occasionally with unexpected violence.

In 1341, the first year in which I have been able to find any trustworthy evidence on which to infer as to the comparative opulence of the English counties and principal towns, the city of London, exclusive of the county of Middlesex, was rated at less than one fourth of the whole county of Norfolk, inclusive of Norwich, which was probably, for its size, the second city in the kingdom in point of wealth, and about as much as the counties of Berks, Cambridge, Devon, or Northampton. The assessment is more than ten times that of the "city of the county of York," about seven-and-a-half times that of Newcastle-on-Tyne, and about eight times that of Bristol, these being the only municipalities which are severally assessed, and each being thus assessed for special reasons, for in each of them a considerable district in the neighbourhood was included in the city liberties, or put under the direction of the local authorities. The assessment of the county of Norfolk is far in excess, estimated ratably by the acreage, of that of any other county; the next to it, though at a considerable distance, being Oxfordshire and Middlesex, exclusive of London. The cause is the inclusion of the opulent city of Norwich within the assessment.

In 1453, another assessment of an equally unsuspicious character exists. In this, the next city to London is York; the rate of London being about seven-and-a-half times more than that of York. London is about nine-and-a-half times as opulent as Norwich, the second city; twelve times more wealthy than Bristol, the third; fifteen times more than Coventry, the fourth; twenty-one-and-a-half times more than Newcastle; nearly twenty-three times more than Kingston-on-Hull; twenty-four-and-a-half times more than Lincoln; nearly twenty-eight times more than Southampton; and thirty-eight times more opulent than Nottingham, the lowest on the list. Some of these facts are to be accounted for, notably York and Coventry, by political and temporary causes. York was one of the headquarters of the Yorkist faction; and Coventry, the special stronghold of the Lancastrians, had been latterly enriched and extended by Margaret.

Fifty years later another and a similarly unsuspicious assessment can be found. In this seventeen cities and towns are separately valued. On this occasion, Bristol, which had been greatly enriched by the trade with Ireland and the North Sea, was the second city in the kingdom. London is assessed at only three-and-three-quarter times over Bristol; but there had been a great conflagration in London in the same year. Next comes York, with nearly one-fourth the amount. London is about five-and-a-half times richer than Lincoln. The next is Gloucester, with less than a sixth of the London quota. But London is seven-and-a-half times richer than Norwich, the manufacturers of which were now migrating southwards and westwards. Shrewsbury has nearly the same assessment as Norwich. The assessment of Oxford is a little more than a ninth that of London. That of Salisbury and Coventry about a ninth; of Hull less than a tenth; of Canterbury a little more than a tenth; of South-

ampton a little more than a twelfth; of Nottingham about
a seventeenth; of Worcester and Southwark about a thirty-
fourth; and of Bath, the lowest, about a forty-seventh that of
London.

In 1377, the Parliament granted the king a poll-tax of
fourpence a head on all lay persons over fourteen years of
age, none but known beggars being exempted. Beneficed
clergymen paid a shilling; and other ecclesiastics, except
mendicant friars, paid fourpence. The number who paid the
tax in each of the principal towns is preserved. If the
number of those under sixteen is taken as one-third of the
population, the estimate made a century ago, and one-third
is therefore added to the amount, the population of London
was 35,000; and next to it York, with near 11,000. Bristol
had about 9,500, Coventry a little over 7,000, Norwich near
6,000, Lincoln about 5,000. No other English town had over
5,000 inhabitants.

In this record, the counties of Bedford, Surrey, Dorset,
Middlesex, exclusive of London, Westmoreland, Rutland,
Cornwall, Berkshire, Herts, Hunts, Bucks, and Lancashire,
do not appear to have contained any town which was thought
worthy of particular enumeration. It is to be expected that
the relative opulence of London was greater per head of
population than that of any other city, and the facts of the
poll-tax square with such an estimate. The same rule will
apply to towns like Norwich, which were conspicuous for
their manufactures, and others, like Bristol, which had already
become eminent for their commerce.

There is no topic in political arithmetic on which persons
who are inexperienced in the art of interpreting figures are
more likely to be deceived than they are in the population
of any given country, or any given city, when a direct
enumeration of the inhabitants is not at hand. Guesses have
been made as to the populousness of English towns, and
indeed of England itself, during the middle ages, which would
be ludicrous, if they were not misleading and mischievous,
because they suggest economical results which a more minute
inquiry into the facts of the case will show to be impossible.

Now to estimate the real progress which this country has made, it is expedient that we should attempt to arrive at precise information as to what was the product of English agriculture; for we may be pretty sure that no importation of food worth speaking of was regularly made into England till very recent times; that what was produced in the country was the measure of its possible population; and that if an estimate is formed from vague surmises and still vaguer numbers, the inferences which are based on such estimates are sure to be delusive.

The estimate given above, which adds one-third to the number of persons liable to the tax in consideration of those who were under fourteen years of age, and raised to sixteen years in order to cover the probability that in the collection of the tax there were many evasions, may be taken exception to as too low an estimate of the untaxed population.   It is true, that at present the number of persons under fifteen years of age, as compared with all above that age, is as nearly as possible in the proportion of 9 to 11, instead of 6·33 to 13·66.   But it must be remembered that in the middle ages the risks of life from disease were far greater than they are at present, that medical skill was almost non-existent; that the conditions of life were eminently unwholesome; that the diet of the people, during fully one-half of the year, though abundant, was insalubrious; and that when human life is shortened by unfavourable circumstances, the mortality is far greater in the young than it is in those who, having escaped the perils of childhood, are, so to speak, selected and hardened.   Besides, there was a large part of the population which was, by ecclesiastical rule, obliged to celibacy and chastity; and however much we may give ear to the gossip about monks and nuns, and the secret marriages or open concubinage of the secular clergy, public opinion and discipline must have exercised a very considerable check on the contribution of the clergy to the population of the middle ages.   I am therefore disposed to conclude that the calculation made by Mr. Topham, in the seventh volume of the *Archæologia*, from whom I have borrowed the facts and the estimate of the English towns in the fourteenth century, is as correct as can well be imagined, and that it would not be probable if any other basis of addition than that of one-third were made in determining the population of the towns.

When I published my first two volumes of the history of agriculture and prices, I was led to investigate the grounds on which estimates were made of the population of England in the thirteenth and fourteenth centuries, and to give the grounds on which I arrived at my own. My reasoning was nearly as follows :—" There were generally as many people existing in this country as there have been, on an average, quarters of wheat to feed them with. The evidence supplied from the produce of arable land of average quantity gives about a quarter an acre. At present it is about from three to four quarters an acre ; and this food is supplemented by other products which were unknown in the thirteenth century or for many centuries afterwards." I concluded, that setting the amount of land which has been devoted to towns, roads, and pleasure-grounds, in modern times, against that which was not broken up or cultivated six centuries ago, the possible wheat-growing land of the thirteenth century was about three million acres, and that from this must be deducted—though I admit that by far the greatest breadth sown was wheat— about a sixth of the average wheat-land—much more of which could be given under modern rotation to other crops—which would lie in fallow. I therefore concluded that about two-and-a-half millions of population was the maximum that could be reckoned with any probability for England, and that it was possibly even less. The view which I took was challenged with some acerbity, chiefly on the strength of certain numerical accounts given at the time or soon afterwards as to the loss of life in the great plague of the fourteenth century. After a brief controversy, I dropped the subject, for I know no time which is lost more thoroughly than that devoted to arguing on matters of fact with a disputant who has no facts, but only very strong convictions.

I had a singular confirmation of my inferences on the

subject in the actual enumeration of certain Kentish hundreds, nine in number, the facts of which I discovered in the Record Office. The document is undated, but is clearly of the time of Henry VIII., among the state papers of whose reign it was found. The hundreds are on the south-east side of Kent, and the enumeration, besides the population, contains an account, taken after the middle of the agricultural year, *i.e.*, about the beginning of April, of the stock of corn in the various hundreds. It may be observed here that there is no rye grown, the principal crops being wheat, barley, and oats. Kent at this time was one of the most thriving and populous parts of England, and these hundreds are in the richest agricultural district of the county. They contained no large town at that time, and contain none now. They are fair specimens of what was the wealthiest part of agricultural England in the later middle ages. Now the population of these hundreds in the first half of the sixteenth century (14,813) is almost exactly one-sixth of that at which it stood in 1861 (88,080). It will be seen that the population almost precisely corresponds to that which I stated, from an estimate of the rate of production, was the maximum population of England, and that this population was almost stationary for three centuries and a half. There is further evidence that the rate of production had not increased, and that, in fact, no improvement whatever had been made in the art of agriculture.

These inferences are signally confirmed by the estimate which is made from the record of the poll tax in 1377. The forty-two towns, with the addition of one-third to the actual numbers paying the tax, contained a population of 168,720 persons. The rest of the population is 1,207,722, together making 1,376,442. Durham and Chester are reckoned at 51,083, a very large, perhaps excessive estimate, Wales with Monmouth, at 131,040. The two Counties Palatine were separately assessed, and the return is not included, and Wales with Monmouth is not assessed at all. This gives a total of 1,558,565. By adding a third for the children, and making a very liberal allowance for ecclesiastics and mendicants, no less than 162,153, Mr. Topham concludes that the whole population of England and Wales, in the last year of Edward the Third's reign, was two and a half millions. I cannot but think that three calculations, two of them being from matters of fact, could not be so exactly similar in their results and be merely fortuitous coincidences.

The distribution of occupations in a town of some magnitude, Colchester, estimated in 1377 to contain a population of 4,432, as it had a taxable number of 2,955, and is reckoned a tenth in the list, is curiously illustrated by the rolls of Parliament of the years 1296 and 1305. The first is, I imagine imperfect, only 251 persons being specified in it, while 391 are found in the second. If we take five persons to a family, and consider the last enumeration to be exhaustive, there must have been about 2,000 persons residing in Colchester and its vills in 1301, and the population must have doubled within three-quarters of a century. It is very possible that certain of the eastern towns made considerable progress, as during Edward's wars an active agricultural trade, and no little purely commercial intercourse, took place between the eastern counties on the one hand, and the Hanse and Flemish towns on the other.

In the second list, there are 229 persons, whose calling is not specially designated. Besides these, there are twelve clergymen, ten persons of considerable substance, sixteen shoemakers, thirteen tanners, ten smiths, eight weavers, eight butchers, seven bakers, six fullers, six girdlers, five mariners, four millers, four tailors, three dyers, three fishermen, three carpenters, and three spicers or grocers. The following trades are also enumerated :—cooper, white leather seller, potter, parchment maker, furrier, cook, tiler, bowyer, barber, mustarder, woolcomber, lorimer, wood-turner, linen draper, wheelwright, glover, fuel dealer, old clothes dealer, sea-coal dealer, glazier, brewer, ironmonger, and vintner. Two of the girdlers were also mercers, and one sold verdigris and quicksilver (for shoe dressing). It will be noticed that the number of tanners is large, as also of shoemakers. The fact points to a local manufacture and handicraft. Essex contained a large amount of forest, and especially oak forest, and the town was therefore well placed for a leather industry.

The activity of the townsfolk was not confined to their special craft or trade. In harvest time they poured out of the towns into the country. When the king dismisses his parliament in the middle ages, he sends the nobles to their sports, the commons to their harvest, and makes no distinction in his directions between knights of the shire and burgesses. So, we are told, the long vacation in the courts and the universities was extended from July to October, in order that such persons as followed the pursuits of law and letters might have ample leisure for the all-important work of the harvest. It is true that the aggregate of the town population was not of much account in the mass of the rural folk, and for the purposes of the harvest. But beyond doubt the land in the immediate neighbourhood of towns was better dressed and more heavily manured than that at a distance from any considerable centre of population, and the spare hands from the town were welcome to the larger proprietors.

The chief port of England was London, as it was the centre, and, in a great degree, the controller of the government. It would seem, however, from the accounts which have been preserved as to the accommodation which the ports were able to supply to the Government on emergencies, that London did not possess the greatest number of vessels. In the enumeration of the contingents which each English port provided in 1346 towards the siege of Calais, the largest contribution to the south fleet was Fowey, with forty-seven vessels, each manned with a little over sixteen men; and Yarmouth for the north, with forty-three ships, each with more than twenty-five men on an average. London sends twenty-five vessels, each with twenty-six men.

The principal English ports, some few on the east coast, with Bristol on the west excepted, are in the south, for the southern contingent is more than double that of the northern, the former being the district south of the Thames and Severn. The principal southern ports are Dartmouth, Plymouth, Bristol, Sandwich, Winchelsea, Southampton

Weymouth, Looe, Shoreham, Dover, and Margate. Those
of the north are Newcastle, Boston, Hull, Lynn, and Har-
wich, in addition to those in each district which have been
referred to above as supplying the largest number of vessels.
The total number of sailors in the employment of private
individuals is 13,732, or at least that number with the ships
(700) were impressed, together with the vessels in which they
were employed and rated. Most of the southern ports were
engaged in the French and Flemish trade. They may have
ventured to the coast of Spain, though as late as the middle
of the sixteenth century it does not appear that the English
mercantile mariner passed the straits of Gibraltar. It was,
however, especially with the coasting trade that the English
mariners were concerned ; and if we may trust the calumnies
of their French enemies, they did not scruple to maintain
their supremacy in the narrow seas by acts of piracy, and by
a total abstention from the duty of checking Mohammedan
corsairs, who had, even in early times, gained a detested
notoriety. It is said that towards the close of the fourteenth
century a Genoese merchant offered the government of
Richard II., that if he were allowed to store his property in
the castle at Southampton he could make it the principal port
of the Oriental produce which the Genoese used to despatch to
the Flemish, Norman, and Breton marts, and that the London
merchants put an end to the plan by murdering the projector. The story may be, probably is, merely monkish
gossip, but it shows what were reputed to be the capacities
of Southampton, and the convenience which belonged to its
port.

Bristol was the principal port for Ireland and the western
fisheries, especially for the salmon of the Severn, then and
for a long time after the source of the best of this fish. We
learn also that it was a great mart for hides, derived probably
from Wales and Ireland. But the number and importance
of these southern ports must be explained by the favourable
position in which they stood for the trade with France and
eastern Europe, and by the fact that, owing to the lightness
of their draught, the small craft which swarmed upon the

coast found abundant shelter in the numerous creeks and rivers of southern England.

Still, the northern, and especially the eastern, marine of England had a considerable mercantile trade for the time. Newcastle from early times was the centre of the coasting supply of coal. The central coal-fields of England, except those in the valley of the Trent, were unknown. But early in the thirteenth century, sea-coal, probably as ballast, was carried as far south and west as Southampton. The vessels in which they were conveyed were under forty tons burden, and the trade, on which a ratable toll was paid to the king, became so general and so important in the fifteenth century that frauds were practised on the revenue by returning the tonnage at less than its actual amount.

Many of the eastern ports, from Hull to Colchester, were connected with the Flemish, Norwegian, and Baltic trade. Lynn, as the list of towns quoted above informs us, was a considerable resort for merchants, especially during the time of Stourbridge fair. Norwich is designated for its haven, and barley and malt were largely exported from it. So was also wool, notably from Hull. The small craft ran across the German Ocean during the fine weather of the summer months, and traded extensively with the Continent.

But the most important industry of the eastern ports was the fishing trade. Yarmouth was, as now, the chief centre of the herring fishery; Grimsby of cod, such at least as was caught in the neighbourhood ; and Berwick of salmon. The greatest enterprize was, however, shown by Scarborough. This little town coasted along Scotland to Aberdeen, from which they brought fish, the name of which, Haberdens, implies the origin of the take, though it has long been a puzzle. They went on to the Orkney and Shetland Islands, and even to Iceland, where they gained great store. At last, in the fifteenth century, the Bristol fisherman, fired by trade emulation, and now acquainted with the mariner's compass, reached the same goal through the stormy Hebrides, and competed successfully with their eastern rivals.

English towns were generally commanded by castles. The

most important of these were in the king's hands, and were garrisoned by his captains and troops. Such were the castles, for example, of Oxford, Wallingford, and Windsor, which commanded the most important points in the Thames valley. Of these the two first were supposed to have the highest strategic value. It is noteworthy, that when the articles of impeachment were drawn up against Suffolk in 1450, the fact that, while he held Wallingford castle nominally for the king, he had garrisoned and victualled it really for himself, was emphatically insisted on as proof of his treasonable intentions and designs against the reigning family. But these castles, though frequently held by nobles as part of their private estate, were in reality licensed by the king; and it appears that, when the authority of the administration was unimpaired, it was held that the power which gave license to fortify a dwelling-house was competent to rescind the permission.

I do not find, in searching through the records of mediæval business, that complaint is made of rapine or wrong-doing, either by the king's deputies or by the nobles who had those fortified habitations. The castle does not appear to have often been, even after the use of gunpowder became familiar, furnished with artillery, though it was and remained in the immediate possession of the Crown. The establishment of a private fort would, I conceive, be looked on with the gravest suspicion, and be conceived to be evidence of sinister designs. It is remarkable, too, after the general demolition of castles on the accession of Henry II., that mediæval warfare in England was rarely characterized by sieges, though in the war between king and parliament the fortified house, doubtlessly under royal license or command, is constantly assailed, defended, and captured, or successfully held. These castles were useful in maintaining the peace, as quarters for such soldiers as the king habitually kept under arms, and as residences for the sovereign and his court. Thus, on the Scotch and Welsh borders, they were important instruments for checking marauders; and, as is well known, the line of fortified castles from Flint to Carnarvon was part of the machinery by which Edward held the Principality in a firm grasp. But it does not appear that the castle was conceived to be a means for controlling the king's subjects.

The towns themselves were walled, and the castle was almost always outside the circle of the city wall and moat, though connected with it by an outwork. It was the duty, too, of the citizens or townsfolk to keep their own walls in repair. The king could also make a requisition, it appears, on the vicinage of his castles, or on the inferior tenants, for money or labour towards the repair of such castles, when they were conceived to be part of the public defences. Sometimes charters were given, expressly relieving the tenants from this liability. But the fortifications of the town were in the hands of the burghers, and we may be sure that the Crown would encourage them in forming, as far as they could, an equipoise to a powerful or turbulent noble. I am persuaded, that had the possession of these fortified places been abused, the dismantling of them, which became the necessary policy of the Parliamentary army, would have been anticipated centuries before.

Though the king was entitled to demand the assistance of his subjects, or at least of his tenants, towards the repair of his castles, I do not find that the demand is made, or the expense of satisfying it recorded. There is, however, a good deal of evidence still existing, through the thirteenth, fourteenth, and fifteenth centuries, of the charges to which the king's personal revenue was put in maintaining these public defences. It is probable that not a few towns in England rose under the walls, and on account of the protection of the castle.

Many English towns, long since decayed, owed their origin to the development of some local industry. It is well known that many settlements, which afterwards grew into towns, were gifted subsequently with parliamentary representation, though not with municipal institutions, in consequence of a special manufacture carried on in them. Such were several of the Sussex towns, where, as late as the reign of Anne, iron of high quality was manufactured. So, again, not a few of the western towns became the seats of the cloth manufacture, though it has become extinct in them now.

On the other hand, the most populous and busy districts of our day were the fens and moors, scantily peopled by a rude race. Lancashire was one of the poorest English counties, as was also the West Riding of York. As late as the end of the seventeenth century, these two counties were nearly at the bottom of the list in opulence. Population was scanty in them, and wages low. The Mersey was still a silent estuary; the Irwell a mountain stream. There were forges and cutlery works in Hallamshire, and Bradford was a cloth mart in early times. But the greater part of the district, now so densely inhabited, which lies within the circuit of twenty miles from Leeds, was occupied by wild animals and lawless men, the latter hardly kept in order by swift justice. The maiden of Halifax is the type of a jurisdiction which had long been obsolete in the more settled parts of England.

CHAPTER V,

THE DISTRIBUTION OF WEALTH AND TRADE,

Source of the "Distribution" of Wealth—Comparative Wealth of English Counties
—Norfolk and Oxfordshire the most Opulent—Poverty of the North and
West—Present Condition of Agricultural Counties—Markets—English Roads
in the Thirteenth Century—Carriage of Goods—The Common Carrier—The
Scattered Character of Estates—English Inns—The Control of Markets—The
Assize of Weights—The Assize of Bread—The Regulation of Labour Prices
—Usury Laws, their Origin—Bankruptcy—Forestalling and Regrating—The
Absence of Middle Men—Low Cost of Building—Bargains Universal—Fairs
and their Origin—The Discipline of Fairs—Their Object and Place in the
Middle Ages—Their Usefulness even to Recent Times—Stourbridge Fair—
Its Magnitude and Importance—Routes by which Foreign Produce reached
Europe—The Hanse Towns—The Spice Trade with India—Routes in the
Thirteenth Century—The Discoveries of the Cape Passage and the New
World—The Conquest of Egypt in the Sixteenth Century.

ECONOMISTS understand by the distribution of wealth
that share which each of the factors in production is
able to secure for himself out of the gross total of objects
possessing value in exchange. I purpose to postpone this
interesting subject to later chapters, as I have discussed the
distribution of social privileges, in so far as it was relative to
the occupancy of land, in an earlier chapter, and in the present
to deal with the comparative opulence of different districts in
England, with the locality of other than agricultural industry,
with the relations of England to domestic and foreign trade,
with the fair at home and the centres of commerce abroad,
and with the machinery by which Eastern produce was carried
to England and acquired by the consumer.

I have already adverted to the relative position in which
the principal cities and towns of England stood at different
times in the various documents which supply us with evidence

on the subject. This comparison is instructive, because it indicates at once the amount of the population which could be spared, in the thirteenth and succeeding centuries, from the primary aim of all human industry,—the acquisition of food, and suggests, by a contrast between population and taxation, what were the opportunities of accumulation which particular towns possessed. In the fourteenth century, the urban stood to the rural population in the proportion of 1 to 12.34; and many of the towns enumerated are mere villages according to present ideas.

The comparative wealth of the different English counties is to be learnt from such assessments of taxation as have been referred to in the previous chapter. The boundaries of the counties have not been materially changed for centuries. There was no motive to alter these boundaries ; indeed, there was every motive to keep them strictly, for the administration of the district, and its liabilities to taxation, of whatever kind it were, would have been rendered uncertain had not the boundaries been defined. It is true that some counties, particularly northern Norfolk, eastern Kent, and the coast of Sussex, have lost by denudation, or perhaps by gradual subsidence. But it is not likely that this incident has materially altered them, and perhaps the loss has been compensated by accretion. I have therefore, in estimating the relative opulence of the several counties, taken the existing acreage, and have calculated a past burden, and the past means of bearing it on the present area.

Including London, Middlesex is, of course, the most opulent of the English counties, though, even if London is excluded from it, the wealth of Middlesex is considerable. It would naturally, as being in proximity to the principal market of England, from which it could get its wants supplied at the cheapest rates, and in which it could sell its produce at the best price, possess advantages from which remoter districts would be excluded. Nor does it follow that because a comparative decline in the relative opulence of London and Middlesex seems to take place, that the city and the home county had become poorer. If a fixed sum is to be raised by

9

way of taxation, a town or district may seem worse off, when in reality its contingent is lessened by other towns and districts being better off. In the earliest valuation for taxation which I have been able to obtain and analyse, the opulence of Middlesex, without London, was equal to that of the second county. In later assessments it falls, under the same circumstances, to the eighth or tenth place.

In the earliest assessment, Norfolk, excluding Middlesex with London, was the most opulent county in England. The explanation of the fact is that, in the thirteenth and the first half of the fourteenth centuries, it was for the time densely peopled, being the principal seat of the woollen manufacture, a considerable place for linen manufacture, and in close relations with the Low Countries. It grew large quantities of barley, which was exported, either raw or malted, to Flanders. The cloth manufacture was carried on in many villages and small towns ; the linen was principally woven at Aylsham. Even when the woollen manufacture spread to the west and north, Norfolk was still largely employed in this industry, and though it declined relatively, and, indeed, absolutely, after the second half of the fourteenth century, it remained till the sixteenth the second county for opulence in England. It is noteworthy that it was the head-quarters of Lollardy in the century preceding the Reformation, and the most deeply imbued with the tenets of the Gospellers at and after the Reformation. The victims of those new opinions seem to have been more numerous in Norfolk than in the whole of the rest of England during the persecutions of the fifteenth and sixteenth centuries.

My reader may be perhaps surprised to hear that, in the earliest assessment, Oxfordshire was only a little behind Norfolk, and soon surpassed it, though it does not appear to have had any local manufactures, and must have owed its wealth entirely to its agriculture. But an inspection of the county will explain the fact. It had only one or two inconsiderable forests, one not very extensive fen, and very little waste land. The county is generally flat, and watered by two important rivers and their affluents. The amount of natural pasture in this county is probably larger than in any other. The soil, except in the south-east, is exceptionally fertile, and adapted to heavy crops of wheat and beans. The character of the county, even in remote times, is indicated by the extreme paucity of roads. When land was of little value, even though the district was near the metropolis, as in Surrey, roads are very abundant, the gravel or stone lying near the surface, and a track being made without offence or hindrance. The next counties are Bedfordshire, Rutlandshire, and Berkshire. In early times, Kent takes a higher place than it does later on. The soil of the first of these counties is not unlike that of Oxfordshire, though there is more chalk and gravel in Berks. Hunts, Cambridgeshire, Wilts, Northants, Lincolnshire, and Gloucestershire form the next group. Then come Herts, Suffolk, Somerset, Warwickshire, Leicestershire, and Bucks; Somerset, if we include Bristol, and the East Riding of Yorkshire, if York be included in it. A fifth division contains Dorset, Notts, and Hampshire. A sixth includes Surrey, Sussex, and Essex, to which may be added Worcester. The ratable value of the remaining counties and divisions of counties rapidly declines. The least unprosperous of them are Hereford, Stafford, Shropshire, Derby, Devon, and Cornwall, but the opulence of the best off of these is not much more, acre for acre, than a fourth of the Oxfordshire rating, and of the poorest, little more than a sixth. The North and West Ridings of Yorkshire and Westmoreland come next. Far behind these come Lancashire, Northumberland, and Cumberland, though in the earliest assessment Northumberland stood thirty-first in the assessment, while, later on, it is uniformly thirty-eight. At the same time Lancashire is the poorest English county. But in the assessments of 1375, 1453, and 1503, Cumberland is at the bottom. Cheshire and Durham were never valued, being taxed by a different machinery, and being unrepresented in Parliament. The extreme south-west, the northern counties, and the Welsh marches, were the poorest districts of mediæval England, while the east and those which lie within the Thames valley system were the most wealthy. Wilts, Northants, Gloucester, and Lincolnshire owe their position to other causes. The first two in all the assessments are nearly stationary. The last two occupy a much higher position in the sixteenth than they do in the fourteenth century.

The comparative poverty of the northern counties and the Welsh marches is, I make no doubt, to be ascribed to the unsettled condition of a district which was engaged in a constant struggle against the incursion of plunderers over the border. The princes of Wales had been extirpated, and the Principality could put no force in the field which could cope with an English army. But the spirit of independence was not dead, and the Welsh were troublesome neighbours. The prolonged revolt of Owen Glendower in the fifteenth century was, no doubt, preceded by frequent incursions of the Welshmen from the hills. And on the Scotch border there was incessant warfare, hardly lessened by the engagements which the Scottish kings made on behalf of their subjects.

If we take the twenty English counties which are principally engaged with agriculture at the present time, we shall find, excluding Westmoreland, the poorest ; Cornwall, the assessment of which is double that of Westmoreland, Cumberland, and Dorset, that there is no material difference in the ratable value of the property, ranging as it does between £1 15s. an acre, the valuation of Wilts and Rutland, and £2 8s., the valuation of Herts, which, by the way, is not unaffected by proximity to London. After Hertfordshire, the next highest is Cambridge, at £2 7s.; Berks, at £2 5s. 6d.; and Oxford, at £2 4s. The progress of agriculture has done much towards eliminating such hindrances to the adequate cultivation of the soil as were present to the imperfect husbandry of a bygone age, and of rendering agriculture possible where pasture seemed to be often the only use which could be made of land. A range, however, of only 13s. an acre, to be accounted for in part by other than purely agricultural operations, indicates the direction which agricultural improvement has taken. Nor do I see any reason to doubt that, according to their lights, our ancestors, six centuries ago, did not willingly neglect to cultivate that which their experience showed to be likely to return a fair compensation for their labour.

The cultivation of England in the middle ages demanded the establishment of markets at which the villager could purchase what he needed for his calling, obtain the few necessaries which his domestic industry could not supply, and sell his own produce. In order that he might do all this the more conveniently, it was necessary that he should be able to find sufficiently serviceable roads.

It is a general impression, gathered, I suspect, from the scandalous condition of the English highways at about the middle of the eighteenth century, just before the General Turnpike Act (1773) was passed, that at an earlier age the means of communication between places was difficult at all times of the year, and all but impossible at certain periods. This opinion, I am persuaded, is a mistake. The proof that communications were good in the time of which I am writing is partly to be explained by the rapidity with which journeys were effected, partly by evidence as to the cost of carrying goods over known or ascertainable distances.

Many of the English roads were a survival of the Roman empire, in which the construction of highways was a military and political necessity. Great lines of road traversed Roman Britain from its principal colonies, London and York, to the other settlements. Roman villas are constantly discovered in secluded spots, but near those great roads, which ran in rigid lines. Now we are told that, among other ancient obligations, the maintenance of existing roads was one of the earliest and most lasting. They were from remote times under the authority and protection of the king,—were his highways. As new towns sprung up, like Oxford, Coventry, Reading, Abingdon, under the shadow of great monasteries, though probably the last two were always Saxon villages, roads were constructed from such towns to the main or ancient roads. Generally, however, the houses of the villages were grouped on either side of the old road, where such a road was in existence, or on the new road, when it was necessary to connect the settlement with the old system of communication. The roads of England are roughly exhibited in a fourteenth century map still preserved in the Bodleian

Library, and are identical with many of the highways which we know familiarly. In time these highways fell out of repair, and were put, as I have said, in the last century under the Turn-pike Acts, when they were repaired. But comparatively little of the mileage of English roads is modern. What has been constructed has generally been some shorter and easier routes, for in the days of the stage coaches it was highly expedient to equalise the stages.

I set no particular store by the evidence which may be found in plenty as to the rapidity with which journeys on horseback were effected during summer. The head of an Oxford or Cambridge College was able to travel to London in a single day in summer, and would take two days in winter. The journey from Oxford to Newcastle-on-Tyne, near which one of these colleges had two valuable estates, occupied six days, one other being a day of rest, five being occupied in reaching Thirsk. In the thirteenth century, the Earl of Gloucester takes three days in journeying from London to Leicester, and three from Melton Mowbray to London, fifteen days from Lincoln to Carnarvon, and seven from Shrewsbury to the Isle of Axholm. And to extend this record, the traveller bound to the court of Avignon in the winter, started on Monday, Jan. 23rd, and reached Dover by Satur-day, got to Paris on the following Saturday, and to Avignon by the end of a fortnight. The return journey occupied eighteen days from Avignon to Calais, and a week more from Calais to Oxford. In the journey of the Earl of Gloucester there were no doubt some wheeled carriages in attendance.

The cost of carrying heavy goods by land is about a penny per ton per mile, whenever the journey backwards and forwards could be accomplished within a single day. If the carrier were employed over night, of course the charge was somewhat greater, as the traveller had to be lodged, though this was always at a cheap rate, for, as I have already stated, he purchased or carried with him his own provisions. The lowness of the charge, which continued till the great rise in prices in the sixteenth century, is, I have no doubt, to be ccounted for by the fact that the freeholders and tenants in villages were numerous; that horse and cart, or oxen and cart, were part of the equipment of any holding beyond mere cottage farming, and that, therefore, plenty of the service was readily available. Even after the great rise in prices, land and water carriage, especially the former, were disproportionately cheap. We find this fact in the carriage of stone, bricks, and other building materials, in that of wood and charcoal and analogous kinds of fuel, and in the low price which is constantly paid for the conveyance of farm produce to market.

The ultimate test is the rate paid for carriage by the common carrier. Here, however, it should be remembered that the carrier was by common law a bailee of the goods, and liable to the consignor for their safe delivery. Hence his charges involved a variable sum for insurance. When he conveys money his rate is high, as it also is, though in a less degree, when he conveys, as he sometimes does, personal baggage. Now an excellent test of the cost of carriage over known distances is the charge for conveying wine, for the distance is considerable at any inland town, and the carrier may, in some cases must, have passed several days and nights on the road. The article is bulky, packed with labour and difficulty, and is peculiarly liable to being pilfered. I find that it was conveyed in winter time at about $3\frac{1}{2}$d. per ton per mile for the double journey; and I think that no article could be found of more difficult and laborious conveyance than a tun of wine (252 gallons) in bulk during winter, over the ancient road from Southampton to Oxford, with the loading from the wharf, and unloading at the place of destination.

The very existence of a class of common carriers, who got their living by conveying the most valuable kinds of goods, and by regularly traversing the country from Southampton and Winchester to Oxford, from the midland counties to Stourbridge fair, near Cambridge, and even from Oxford to Newcastle-on-Tyne, is proof, not only that there was a demand for the carrier, but that the means of communication were fairly good, and the principal roads, even in winter time, were kept in decent repair. Nor were the motives for such a practice, the adequate maintenance of highways, wanting. Estates even of wealthy noblemen were rarely in a ring fence, but were greatly scattered. Persons living at a considerable distance had often for that time important interests in the matter of rent charges on the estates of others, rent charges frequently paid in kind. This was especially the case with the monasteries. A religious house was in the first place endowed with an estate immediately adjacent to the site on which the conventual buildings were erected. In course of time, piety or fear endowed the monastery with scattered and outlying portions of an estate, a few strips in this communal field, a close and house in that parish, a mill and curtilage in another. As time went on, it became a custom to enrich monastic and collegiate foundations, and lastly, academic colleges, with the great tithes of valuable livings, for the impropriation of which the consent of king, bishop, and pope was necessary, or at least so convenient that prudent persons would not neglect the precaution. In Fitzherbert's time, just before the dissolution of the monasteries, the Benedictine was everywhere looking after his rents, his produce, and his tithes, and the Cistercian after the woolpacks of the conventual sheep farms. The earliest foundation of Balliol College, in Oxford, was from the great tithes of a Yorkshire benefice. The fellows of Merton College took long journeys to Avignon and Northumberland in order to procure the appropriation of the great tithes in a large parish on the Scotch border. And if we add to these the annual circuits of the authorities, three a year, one of which, that in autumn, was carried out in great detail, we can understand, in an age when cultivation by owners was universal, and the collection of dues, rents, and produce a matter of great interest, how important it was to have adequate and regular means of communication.

In the more sparsely peopled and outlying districts it is probable that accommodation was afforded on long journeys by the monasteries, though I am sure that people, mistaking, as they constantly do, concurrent facts for causes, exaggerated the use of these conveniences after or at the Reformation, and ascribed to the Dissolution that rapid interruption of

accommodation and the means of transit from place to place
which certainly ensued on that event. But England from the
very earliest times was a country full of inns. In the year
1332, the Warden of Merton, Robert Trenge, and two of the
fellows, make a journey to Northumberland, for the purpose
of inducing the bishop to acquiesce in the impropriation of a
benefice to which the papal consent had been given the year
before. They leave Oxford on Monday, Jan. 5th, and are
absent for ten weeks, till March 16th. During the greater
part of this time—indeed, the whole of the time, except
when they are resident on their own manor—they stay for
the night at inns, where they pay a small sum for lodging,
and buy provisions, beer, wine, fuel, light, for their own wants,
with corn and hay for their horses. They feast the bishop's
commissioner for a week, and the parishioners for a Sunday ;
and though the most costly articles of the feast are procured
at Newcastle-on-Tyne, and even the better beer, the wine
appears to have been purchased on the spot. I know no
trade, indeed, which has clung longer to special localities
than that of the innkeeper. Not a few of the Oxford inns can
be traced back for centuries. The constant tradition was
that an ancient inn frequented by Shakspeare stood in one
street, from which it was removed only a few years ago to
make room for the newer buildings of a neighbouring inn.
Another, opposite St. Mary Magdalene Church, which I have
been able to trace to the fifteenth century under the same
sign, was removed only twenty years ago. One great Oxford
inn, near the Four Ways, was in existence as the principal
hostel for five centuries, under the name of the Fleur-de-
Lys, and the names of many others bear evidence of a
remote antiquity. Indeed, the signs of inns are constant
proof of the period in collateral history when the site was
dedicated to a hostel. The Tumble Down Dick and the
Royal Oak are specimens of the manner in which partisans,
contemptuous or loyal, ridiculed Richard Cromwell and
welcomed back the Stuarts, as the Boulogne Gate and the
Boulogne Mouth refer to the expedition of Henry in 1544,
the Blue Boar to the short-lived reign of Richard III. The

sign was not, indeed, confined to the inn. It was the advertisement to all shops ; not, I believe, for the reason which has been absurdly guessed, that the arts of reading and writing were comparatively unknown, but because the eye could be caught and informed as to the kind of goods which were to be found in the low dark shop. There is certainly no country where elementary teaching is more general than in the eastern cities of the American Union, there is none in which the goods in shop or store are more openly displayed, and there is certainly none in which the use of signs designed to attract the eye is more general.

The establishment and control of the town market was the most universal and the most valued of municipal privileges. The market in London was perpetual, and the market spaces were the property of the Corporation. In Norwich, which was said to have received its first charter from Stephen in 1147, there were many markets in the square where the Guildhall is built, and, indeed, elsewhere, the tolls of which were regularly collected under separate schedules, and formed part of the corporate income of the city. The same was the case in Oxford, where there was a conflict of jurisdiction between the University and the city, which ultimately ended in a compromise, under which the discipline of the provision market was conferred on academical officials, and the tolls were divided between the two corporations. The two days of the Oxford market, Wednesday and Saturday, can be traced back to the thirteenth century.

The control of the market was undertaken for a treble purpose,—to prevent frauds, to regulate the cost of manufacturing products, and to ensure what was believed to be a natural price. The assize of weights and measures, that of bread and beer, and the enactments directed against forestalling and regrating, are examples of the mode in which our forefathers exercised the police of the market. The first, which has, without objection, remained to our own day, is a statute so early that its date is lost. The repression of false weights and measures was part of the police of every manor, village, or town. The ale-seller and miller, the two perma-

nent traders or craftsmen of the village, were constantly
under the control of the court leet, and were frequently
presented for frauds. An attempt was made to guarantee
the quality of the drink served, as well as to regulate its just
quantity, by giving authority to two officers of the manor,
called ale-tasters, to certify to the character of the ale which
was to be sold. Their function was to prevent adulteration.
So there was a corporation in Norwich whose business it was
to see that woollen goods were up to quality, measure, and
weight, and to amerce offenders. It was generally part of the
business of a London company, in consideration of the privileges bestowed on it, to see that the public was not defrauded
by dishonest craftsmen and traders. A survival or two of
this universal duty is to be found in the Hall marking of the
Goldsmiths' Company, and the control which the Fishmongers
are supposed to exercise over the supplies of Billingsgate.

We leave manufacturers to charge what they please for the
process of transforming raw material into consumable articles,
with the conviction that competition will be a greater check
to excessive rates than market regulations could be. But in
the middle ages such a notion would have been repudiated,
and justly so. Even now it is doubtful whether competition
is of universal efficacy, and whether it is not more correct to
say that where combination is possible, competition is inoperative. Hence we subject some callings to regulated
prices, and it may be doubted whether the progress of opinion
will not hereafter enlarge the area of regulated prices. Still
the inclination of people is as yet to let prices find their level
by competition in every case where distinct proof is not
given that such a concession would be unsafe or unfair. In
the middle ages, to regulate prices was thought to be the only
safe course whenever what was sold was a necessary of life,
or a necessary agent in industry. Hence our forefathers fixed
the prices of provisions, and tried to fix the price of labour
and money.

We have seen that the early history of municipal institutions was identified and associated with the principles of
self-government and a regulated monopoly. The munici-

pality was permitted to frame bye-laws for its own conduct, such bye-laws to be not adverse to the general well-being, and the guilds were similarly allowed to limit, on definite and well understood conditions, entrance into and a share in the business which was to be done. A mediæval guild, in short, was not unlike the regulated company of the seventeenth century, into which admission was allowed on the payment of a fine, and the individual so admitted was left to carry on his calling as his means, his abilities, and his reputation gave him opportunities. Where that which he produced and sold was a matter of optional use, the custom of the middle ages gave him the discretion of bargaining and exacting such a price as the needs of the purchaser might fix, though it is probable that the guild would look suspiciously on under-selling, as it did on buying over the heads of other members. But no police of the middle ages would allow a producer of the necessaries of life to fix his charges by the needs of the individual, or, in economical language, to allow supplies to be absolutely interpreted by demand. The law did not fix the price of the raw material, wheat or barley. It allowed this to be determined by scarcity or plenty; interpreted, not by the individual's needs, but by the range of the whole market. But it fixed the value of the labour which must be expended on wheat and barley in order to make them into bread and ale. Not to do this would have been to the mind of the thirteenth century, and for many a century afterwards, to surrender the price of food to a combination of bakers and brewers, or to allow a rapacious dealer to starve the public. It was thought that whenever the value, or part of the value, of a necessary commodity was wholly deter-minable by human agencies, it was possible to appraise these agencies, and that it was just and necessary to do so. That we have tacitly relinquished the practice of our forefathers is, I repeat, the result of the experience that competition is sufficient for the protection of the consumer. But I am disposed to believe that, if a contrary experience were to become sensible, we should discredit our present practice, and revive, it may be, the past, at least in some directions.

The history of usury laws is curiously illustrative of the manner in which society interprets contracts. I think I am right in saying that, without exception, in the infancy of social organization, contracts, even involving the severest consequences, were enforced with rigour. The Athenian and Roman law of debt, and the stringency with which principal and interest were exacted by the law, are well known. It is said that much of the slavery which prevailed in early English history was the punishment for unfulfilled contracts, the compensation for debts that could not be paid. The earliest mercantile law of England permitted the borrower to pledge his land, and to render his person liable for unpaid debts. It was felt, I do not assert that it was said, that when men discovered that trade and commerce made credit a necessity, stringent penalties were necessary in order to educate people into the habit of not making default in contracts. The acknowledgment that a debt is a binding obligation, and the cultivation of commercial integrity, are, I believe, two of the most difficult and important lessons which civilized society teaches, and are far more difficult to learn than the control of passion and deference to custom. In course of time it is found that the rigid interpretation of contracts for loans of money may lead to outrageous oppression, to the slavery of many defaulters, and to grave social perils. We know that in Athens and Rome the inconvenience led from discontent to revolution, and that usury laws were enacted. Now it is easy to say and prove that, in a later stage of society, usury pretends to assist the debtor, and in reality makes the loan more onerous, because it compels the lender to exact a further price for his risk, or to compensate him for breaking the law. Our forefathers saw that there were some loans to which, from their point of view, the usury laws should not apply; for loans on bottomry were always exempt from these enactments, and the equity of redemption was always implied in mortgages.

No doubt the remedy is to be found in the equitable nterpretation of contracts. It is one thing to forbid a contract, except under certain conditions, another to see whether the situation under which one of the parties to a contract has made it, has not been abused by the other party. The English law relieves the borrower on the expectancy of the reversion to a settled estate against usurious bargains; and it might very possibly extend its power of interpreting contracts equitably to other bargains. The legislature has recently decided to interpret contracts for the use of agricultural land on equitable principles, partly on the plea of the public food, partly on the ground that the occupier is in a position of disadvantage, and therefore is disabled from making a perfect contract. But the principal difficulty in the equitable interpretation of contracts is to find a competent arbitrator. The Irish landlords accuse the Land Commissioners, under the Act of 1881, of scandalous favouritism towards the tenants; and the advocates of the Irish tenants accuse the same persons of scandalous favouritism towards the landlords. Arbitrators on disputed questions are pretty certain to be criticised adversely by those whose interests are contrariant. It may be the case that the usury of the Jewish, or Greek, or Armenian money lenders in Eastern Europe, in Egypt, in India, in countries where the law gives unlimited protection to lenders, is producing discontent and violence, or is threatening social revolution. But if the persons could be found who could adjudicate between borrowers and lenders on equitable grounds, it might be expedient to make use of such agencies, even at the risk of being charged with the virtual revival of the usury laws.

In this country we have, though in a clumsy and indirect way, and of late years to the serious injury of commercial morality, given effect to what is a usury law, or perhaps an equitable interpretation of contracts, by our bankruptcy system. A law of bankruptcy, even in the more stringent form in which it has latterly been re-enacted, differs economically from a usury law, in the fact that the latter extinguishes a portion of the interest, the former a portion of the principal. Every person who buys on credit gives a price for the credit, whether he borrows money or goods, and it makes no difference to the economical position of credit as a factor in trade, and to the rate at which credit is accorded, if the law intervenes to cut off a portion of the creditor's interest, or to call upon him to give his debtor a quittance on the payment of part of his principal. The evils which Bentham alleged to be the consequent of the usury laws are equally consequent on the bankruptcy law, which relieves a debtor of his liabilities. It is true that usury laws may put a heavier burden on perfectly solvent borrowers than they would have to bear in the absence of such laws ; but the burden is exceptional and temporary, and does not differ from an exalted price due to temporary scarcity or exceptional demand ; but a bankruptcy law must require, however severely it is administered, that all losses in trade must be paid either in the enhanced profits of dealers or in enhanced prices to consumers, the latter being in effect the same process as the former. But this is what the opponents of the usury laws have always alleged to be the inevitable effects of such legislation.

Our forefathers in their market regulations were always anxious to ensure what I may call natural cheapness. They did not, as I have said, except in some commodities,—money, labour, and certain labour processes,—attempt to fix the price of articles the plenty or scarcity of which depended on the abundance or the dearth of the seasons, for the assize of bread and ale contemplated the extremes of either cheapness or dearness. But they strove to prevent the artificial enhancement of price. Hence the offences of forestalling, that is, the purchase of corn on the road to the market, and of regrating, *i.e.,* the resale of corn in the same market at an increased price. The first offence was probably a double one ; it lessened the dues of the market, as well as seeming to curtail supply. The second was thought to be an offence against the consumer. The criticism of these obsolete statutes and, as they have been called, imaginary offences is well known. To forbid traffic in articles of prime necessity is to encourage waste when plenty prevails, to induce famine when dearth is near. The corn dealer equalizes supply, and if by withholding his corn from market he makes it dearer, he also makes it cheaper than it would be by bringing it out when it otherwise would be scarce. Now this is certainly true. But though our forefathers doubtlessly erred in making these practices an offence, they did not compel sales, and I find that producers were very acute during the middle ages, and for the matter of that, buyers, too, in doling out their supplies to the market, or in making purchases, according to their interpretation of the amount in hand or available for sale. The most critical sales of the year are those effected in early summer, when the amount of the last year's produce was known pretty correctly, and the prospects of the ensuing harvest could be fairly guessed.

The Englishman of the middle ages disliked intermediaries in trade, and strove to dispense with them as far as possible. He did his best to buy all his goods at first hand. He had his stock of iron for tools, and doled it out for fashioning to the local smith. He bought his stock of tar for sheep dressing in bulk. If he wished to have some article of luxury, as a silver cup, he purchased the metal, and paid the craftsman for his labour, weighing what he gave out and got back, as the merchant in Shakspeare's comedy is invited to do. A great corporation or a wealthy noble purchased their cloth and linen in large quantities, and hired tailor and seamstress to shape and sew them. If an opulent person resolved on building castle or church or convent, he rented a quarry for stone, and hired labourers and carts by the day to dig and carry it ; he burnt lime with his own wood and in his own kiln, paying for the services of the lime-burners. He had trees cut down in his own forest or park, and shaped them by the hands he hired himself. He hired sawyers to prepare planks for floors, bought cranes to lift the materials and raw iron for the bars and frames of the windows. He got, in short, all the materials together, and frequently supplied the plans of the building and superintended the work of his labourers himself. As a consequence, the cost of building was inconceivably low — so low that, though wages and materials were at full relative prices, the ultimate cost of the building is far less than could be expected from any ordinary multiple which could be supplied with fair accuracy for the materials and labour. I have constantly inspected the accounts of buildings, in which a multiple of twelve would give good modern prices for materials and labour; while one of thirty or forty would do no more than meet the cost in our present experience of the completed structure. It is the fashion with economists to speak of the functions of middlemen with admiration or complacency, as cheapening agents. I can only say that in many building operations, if I am to judge from mediæval prices, they have trebled the natural cost of the object produced, and, as far as I can see, with only one advantage, rapidity of construction—a result often more than compensated by scamped work, bad masonry, and other shameful frauds. The whole cost of building the bell tower at Merton College, Oxford, in the two years— May 1448 to May 1450—was under £142; this including the cost of three cranes, amounting to £6 6s. I do not believe that at present it could be built for less than £5,000, perhaps for not less than £6,000, though at a multiple of twelve the masons employed would have had 40s. a week for ten months of the year, and 34s. for December and January; the carpenters 24s. I shall comment on this hereafter.

The essence of mediæval trade was the bargain. It was no doubt as long and as anxiously discussed as it now is in an eastern town. The importance of it, when hands were struck on it, was indicated by the gift of the luck penny—God's silver, as it was called—the earnest or pledge of the contract. The custom survives, or did survive till recently, in the acceptance of the king's shilling by recruits. There might be witnesses to the transaction, and there was frequently a memorandum of the purchase exchanged by indenture between the parties when the business done was of importance. Such acknowledgments of purchase are sometimes discovered tacked on to annual rolls, and thus preserved from the destruction which would be the lot of mere temporary engagements.

As important, however, as markets in the economy of mediæval society were fairs. It is not easy to understand their origin. They were often held on land which lay outside the mark or manor or parish, as was the great fair on the north hundred of the city of Oxford,—the barbican of its mediæval fortification, the only point at which the fortress was assailable by the acts of mediæval warfare. Hence in the middle ages the custody of the north hundred was entrusted to some trusted subject. It was on the side of the north hundred that Cromwell attempted his siege of Oxford after it had been the king's head-quarters. Sometimes they were part of the franchise of a great monastery. As late as Hearne's time, there was a fortnight's fair in Oxford called St. Frideswide's Fair, at which I find that, in the sixteenth century, the sale of books was carried on. Occasionally there were fairs for special objects, as at Leeds for cloth, at Weyhill for cheese. It is difficult for us, in the very general decline of these institutions, to understand how important they were in the middle ages. As I have said, London was a perpetual market, and yet there were fairs within the precinct of the city.

The franchise of a fair was one of great significance to the possessor thereof. It was always supposed to have originated with a grant from the Crown, or to be of prescriptive antiquity, and, consequently, to imply such a grant. If it were obvious or convenient to do so, the fair was associated with some church or religious house, and was opened at some convenient time at or after the day of dedication. Hence they were sometimes held in churchyards, till the practice was forbidden by a statute of Edward I.

A universal incident to a fair was what was called the court of pie-powder. The wayfarer, with " dusty foot," coming to the fair, and bargaining, might dispute with the vendor of goods, and words might go on to blows. There were consequently always judges, or at least a judge, to arbitrate on bargains, to keep the peace and to punish offenders. Of course it was an obligation on the authorities that just weights and measures should be used. There was a summary jurisdiction on ill-doers, perhaps the highest ; for it is reasonable to conclude that a right, constantly conferred on lords of manors, to punish offenders, should be appurtenant to these great gatherings. The receipt of toll for what was sold—no toll could be taken on what was not sold, and the payment of toll therefore rested with the buyer—was the profit of the franchise. But if the owner of the franchise attempted foolishly to take excessive toll, he was liable to action, even though he was destroying his own profits.

The object of the fair was twofold. It was to supply a market in which goods, which could not be found in the ordinary town market, would be procurable, and in which there would be a wider market for ordinary goods. The trader did not exist in the villages. In most villages he hardly existed at the beginning of the present century. In my native village the first shop was opened, for general trade, about sixty years ago, as I have heard, and, for many a year afterwards, the wants of the villagers were supplied by pack-men and pedlars, or, in the case of the more opulent, by carts which came periodically from the nearest towns for orders. In the thirteenth century, all but the largest towns were less than modern villages. In 1377, the taxable population of Oxford was a little under 2,500 persons. It was probably not much more populous at the beginning of the fifteenth century. In 1411, Beaufort, Wykeham's successor, paid a sudden visit to New College, the foundation of Wykeham, and the college was called upon to entertain its visitor and lord, who was the king's brother and the Bishop of Winchester, and a possible benefactor, for the Oxford college always was on the look-out for him. Now pepper was an ingredient in every feast, and the college was out of the spice. The fellows had to buy half a pound of the Oxford grocer, and they paid a price for it which is entirely without parallel. Except in London, it was not possible to get foreign produce, other than wine, at a reasonable rate, and the purchaser of such produce obtained it more cheaply at the great fairs than he did in London itself.

Again, there were products sold in most towns which could be purchased in the greatest variety and at the lowest rates at the great fairs. The landowner gained the best market for his wool at the mart to which traders thronged from all parts of the world. But he had to lay in his own stock, either by exchange for his produce or with his own money. For forty days he lived on fish; here he could buy herrings and salt fish at the lowest prices. He needed to put up his own winter store in the powdering tub, and he purchased salt at half the rate which the country dealer demanded, and of much better quality. He wanted sheep medicines, verdigris and copperas, or, best of all, tar, and he could buy it by the barrel at half the retail price. Cloth and leather, linen and fur, kitchen vessels of iron or brass,—I am writing of what I find was actually bought,—could be obtained here at reasonable or natural prices. Nothing was too cumbrous or too costly for a mediæval fair, for if the dealer did not find customers here, he could find them nowhere else. It was frequented by noble and serf, by churchman and soldier, by merchant or trader, and peasant, by monk and craftsman. And it was at these gatherings, a veritable parliament of the people, that discontent ripened into action; that doings in church and state were discussed; that Straw and Ball laid their plans, and the Lollards whispered their doubts. Only the king was exempt from toll, and it was said that his tenants in ancient demesne shared the privilege. But that the court of pie-powder, or the lord of the franchise, showed much consideration to these favoured tenants may well be doubted.

I am drawing no imaginative picture. Sixty years ago, a visit to an autumn fair, for the sake of laying in winter supplies, was part of the ordinary life of a small country gentleman or a wealthy yeoman. Here he got bales of West of England cloth for his household, hides and uppers for shoes and boots, cheese in districts where dairy farming was not practised, and a host of conveniences and rare luxuries. Some of Wedgwood's finest pottery was regularly sold over southern England at village fairs; and in the old days of differential and sumptuary duties, upright and pious men, who would have defrauded no man consciously, thought it no harm if, in the inner recess of the booth, they bargained for a keg of French brandy, or a case of Hollands, or a roll of ribbon, or a yard of lace. So a century and a half before, or over two centuries, books, which would have hardly found a sale by any modern means, were circulated, even when they were unlicensed. In a curious day-book of an Oxford book-seller of the sixteenth century, preserved in Corpus College library, the pious dealer notes his sale of books at St. Frides-wide's and St. Giles' fairs, and I have constantly met with entries in the annual account of receipt and expenditure of books purchased for college libraries at these universal and important marts. I cannot, indeed, conceive how the writings of such an author as Prynne could have been disposed of except at the places which were at once so open and so secret, where every one was welcome, and those who were unwelcome could, with common prudence, so easily escape detection. For in a fair, where all were strangers, no one was a stranger.

None of the English fairs were so important as the great and famous fair of Stourbridge, whose reputation was ex-tended over all Europe, probably in places where no European had been seen, for we are told that not only was it a mart for European goods, but for Eastern produce—for everything which could be bought at the time.

Stourbridge fair was held in a field near the monastery of Barnwell, about a mile from Cambridge, and for the profit of the corporation of that town. Its origin is unknown, the stories as to the cause of its first establishment being obviously idle. The situation of the fair was excellent. It was within easy distance of the two busy mediæval ports of Lynn and Blakeney, and was accessible by the river from the sea. Lynn, in the list of towns which I have referred to as drawn up in the middle of the thirteenth century, was the "town of merchants," and there was great activity at it. The fair was commenced and concluded with peculiar solemnity.

It was proclaimed on the 4th of September, for, in old times, the proclamation of a fair was an essential condition of the franchise. It was opened on the eighth, and the business was continued for three weeks. The field in which it was held was what is called Lammas, *i.e.*, was open and common ground during part of the year. The temporary wooden buildings erected for the purposes of the fair were commenced by custom on St. Bartholomew's Day (Aug. 24th), and the builders of these houses were allowed to destroy corn grown on the spot with impunity if it were not cleared before that day. On the other hand, the owner of the field was empowered to destroy the booths on Michaelmas day, if they were not cleared before that time. The space allotted to the fair, about half a square mile, was divided into streets, which were named, sometimes by nations, and in each of these streets some special trade was carried on, the principal being foreign spices and fruits, ironmongery, fish, metal goods, cloth, wool, leather, and, latterly, books. But every conceivable commodity was brought hither for sale, for I have found records of every article in use at the time as purchased at Stourbridge fair. On Sept. 25th, late in the period allotted to the fair, the chief business was the purchase and sale of horses.

Purchasers frequented Stourbridge fair even from the vicinity of London, as, for example, from the religious house of Sion. The Oxford colleges bought here their stock of winter herrings and Lent fish, as well as their spices. Here they laid in salt and tar, olive oil, wax, and frankincense. As the time for closing the fair drew on, strings of waggons laden with goods were despatched to all parts of England, and the carriers bargained for the rates at which they conveyed the goods to their destination. Had I made a collection of the articles which are noted in mediæval accounts, and even later, as purchased at Stourbridge, the list would have included nearly all kinds of such goods as were purchased out of the village. It was as famous in its day as Novgorod, or Leipsic. There were few households which were possessed of any wealth which did not send a purchaser or give a commission for Stourbridge fair.

The Lombard exchanger was present to assist in the sale of goods, and to facilitate commercial transactions, for at the close of the thirteenth century the Jew was expelled from England, and lingered in such places only as could, from their great privileges, give him a secure asylum. It is stated that a Jewish colony in Oxford remained under the protection of the great University. The Venetian and Genoese merchants brought with them precious store of Eastern produce, silks and velvets, stores of delicate glass and jewellery, cotton and alum. The Flemish manufacturers from Bruges and Liège, from Ghent and Mechlin, brought their linens and lawns, their diapers and holland. The Spaniard supplied iron and the best kinds of the wine which the country grew, while the commoner and cheaper growths of Guienne were abundant; and even those of Greece and Crete were found. There were currants, raisins, and almonds from the Levant, and occasionally cocoa-nuts, whose shells were fashioned into cups, and adorned with gold or silver. The Norwegian brought tar and pitch, the Hanse towns furs and amber, copper, and the choicest iron, bow-staves for the English archers, flax and thread, fustian, buckram and canvas, and the finest kinds of ornamental timber. These towns were the channel by which the precious stones of the East, set unpolished in mitre and coronet, on rings and jewelled gloves, came to the West through the markets of Russia. And these were probably the means by which the porcelain of the farthest and earliest East, the fragments of which are occasionally found in the most unlikely places, were exposed for sale in these booths. To assist in this great and varied activity, the eastern harbours were full of foreign vessels, while eastern England grew rich by the traffic. Can we doubt the interest with which franklin and bailiff, cellarer and bursar, priest and knight, frequenting this scene of unusual bustle, talked of the wonderful world before them, and discussed the geography and politics of the known world?

To this great fair came the huge wool-packs, which then formed the wealth of rural England, and were the envy of surrounding nations, on which monarchs did not disdain to trade and jest. Hither came the produce of the Cornish tin mines, stamped with the sign of the rich earl who had just bought the German empire, though his purchase was only a barren title. Here was lead from the mines of Derbyshire, and iron from the Sussex forges. Here also bargains were made for the barley of the eastern counties, to be transported, if the price fell low enough, and therefore the law, provident for plenty among the people, permitted the export to the Flemish breweries, which more than two centuries later taught Englishmen to flavour and preserve their ale with hops.

In order to regulate the currency, to prevent the loss of specie, always an object of concern to the statesman of the middle ages, and with more reason, in order to exclude spurious or defaced coin, the officers of the king's exchange examined into the mercantile transactions of the foreign traders, and the servants of the king's exchequer collected their dues on exported products, the wool and the hides on which the foreign manufacturer depended. To supply a ready remedy against fraud and violence, against disputes on contracts and breaches of bargains, the mayor sat at his court "of the dusty feet." All classes were busy; the nobles securing what their wealth could give them in articles of luxury, their velvet robes, their costly furs, their armour from Milan, their war-horses from Spain. I have found that even the purchase of high-priced rams, doubtlessly to improve the breed of sheep and the quality of wool, was negotiated at this fair. And on holidays and Sundays some one of the numerous clergy in the diocese of Ely,—for there were more in this than in any other diocese,—or one of the monks from the neighbouring priory, said mass in the ancient chapel which still stands near the spot, the most notable relic of the greatness of this fair, now long departed and forgotten. In a less degree there were many other such gatherings in England, and Walter de Henley may have reasonably assigned eight weeks in the year as required by the farmer who frequents fairs and markets.

Ten or twelve generations ago these fairs were a necessity, three or four a great convenience, with which the country could ill dispense. At present the importance which they once possessed has passed away, and their significance is forgotten. There is no part of English social life which has been so totally altered by improved means of communication as trade, especially trade in the country. Two generations ago pedlars carried tea about in packs on their shoulders. At the present time a country grocer can one evening bid his agent by letter free a chest of tea from bond, and the next day he can have it in stock. Goods can be carried at one-tenth the cost, time, and risk, from the centres of trade to distant villages. Migratory trade has, therefore, become superfluous and obsolete, and the great marts of the Plantagenets, of the Tudors, of the Stuarts, and of the early reigns of the later family, have degenerated into scenes of coarse amusement, and after having been granted and protected as the highest and most necessary franchises, have been tolerated for the sake of their traditions, and are now being generally suppressed as nuisances.

It remains that I should describe, as far as the existing information enables me to do so, what were the routes by which foreign, and especially Eastern, produce was introduced into this country. I need not dwell here on the coasting trade between the English ports and the Continent, from Bristol on the west, from the long coast line commencing with Fowey and ending with Dover on the south, and from the eastern ports along the coast of Kent as far north as Hull, where there were innumerable ports, some silted up and forgotten, some perhaps buried in the German Ocean. It is probable that few English vessels ventured far from Bayonne in the thirteenth century, though after the conquest of Spain at the latter end of the fifteenth, they seem to have traded as far as "the crane of Seville." I am at present concerned with the trade of the Hanse towns, and that of the routes to India.

Towards the latter end of the thirteenth century the Hanse towns appear to have been recognised by the English sovereigns; to have been established in the neighbourhood of the Tower under the name of the Alderman and Merchants of the Steelyard; and to have maintained their position, though with some reverses, till their institution was suppressed, and their representatives expelled from the kingdom by Elizabeth at the conclusion of her reign. They were an association of free towns carrying on trade, with a staple at Bergen and a treasury at Wisby, who were united for purposes of mutual protection. They appear to have been at the height of their influence in the early part of the fifteenth century, just at the time that the Teutonic knights were extending their rule over Lithuania and Old Prussia by sheer violence and outrage. They were leagued together against these and other lawless chiefs of Eastern Europe, as the League of the Rhine was against the robber barons of the great German waterway. Their trade was in the produce of Scandinavia, of the Baltic, and of Muscovy; one of the confederation from early times till the middle of the sixteenth century being the ancient republic of Novgorod. That they were of great importance in English trade is proved by the protection accorded to them by the Court, despite the jealousy and the remonstrances of those London merchants who were not in this privileged class. They seem to have had settlements not only in London, but at Boston and Lynn. The chief cities of the four divisions into which the various Hanse towns were ranged were Lübeck, Cologne, Brunswick, and Dantzic, and the principal factories were Novgorod, London, Bruges, and Bergen. The opulence of Hanseatic prosperity is well seen in the numerous and costly churches of the town of Lübeck. This association of trading cities is a notable phenomenon in the age of feudalism and chivalry; and it is to be regretted that its history has not been better told than in the works of Mallet, Schözer, and Lappenberg.

More immediately significant, however, is the trade with the East by caravan routes and a sea passage. It is difficult for us to imagine the eagerness with which our forefathers, as far as they could afford the luxury, sought after the spices of the East. But the appetite was natural enough. Their diet was coarse; and, owing to the absence of winter food for cattle, unwholesome. They seem to have had few native condiments. It is certain that they were excessively fond of spices, and used them, when they could be procured, in all their dishes, as the cookery books of the Plantagenets testify. Spiced wine, called Hippocras, was a present to princes; and a seat near the spice box was a greater privilege than one above the salt.

The Crusades and the decline of the Eastern Empire, the latter due more than to anything else to the scandalous capture of Constantinople by the Latins, stimulated the fanaticism of the tribes which inhabited Central Asia, and soon made that caravan trade which was common and easy enough in the twelfth century all but impossible in the thirteenth. The numerous channels of trade were dried up, especially over land, and but three routes remained. In two of these, goods from India, *i.e.*, from the western coasts, were conveyed by water to Bagdad. Thence they were carried by the Tigris till a point could be reached in the river which was nearest to Seleucia and Antioch. This was in the early period the chief and most convenient course of trade. But it had been rendered dangerous, and finally blocked, by the ferocious and fanatical tribes of Mesopotamia.

The second route was from the same point to the highlands of Asia Minor and Armenia to Trebizond. This course of trade must have passed over the same, or nearly the same, ground which Xenophon travelled with his famous ten thousand. This, the most difficult and precarious route, was not so dangerously blocked as that to the Orontes and the Mediterranean. It was the opinion of Sanuto, to whom we are indebted for the narrative of the facts, that by energetic action these two ancient and convenient lines of traffic could be restored, reopened, and sufficiently guarded, if Europe in general, and the pope in particular (he is writing to one of the Avignon Popes, John XXI.) were united and public spirited. It is needless to say that the hope was disappointed.

The third route was that from Western India to Aden, thence across the desert by a nine days' journey to Chus on the Nile, from thence by a fifteen days' river transit to Babylon, *i.e.* Cairo, and thence by a canal, two hundred miles long, to Alexandria. From Aden this route went through the Sultan of Egypt's dominions; and we are informed that a toll of thirty-three per cent. was levied on all the goods which went this way. Hence the writer concludes, although the cost of package and land carriage across the old routes were large, the tolls, if the caravan transit could be restored, were small. The spices, too, which passed through Egypt were damaged and adulterated; so that articles of the greatest value—cloves, nutmegs, and mace—went by the land road, notwithstanding the perils of the way; while pepper, ginger, frankincense, and canella, go through Egypt. The trade, too, is not one-sided. Egypt depends greatly on Europe for many products, and entirely for iron, timber, and pitch. Sanuto concludes, therefore, that by the equipment of a competent fleet, the Sultan of Egypt might be compelled to respect the feeling of Europe, and even be starved into submission.

The greater part of this Eastern trade, whether it passed into the Black Sea or the Mediterranean, by Antioch or by Alexandria, fell into the hands of the Italian cities, especially Genoa and Venice. Thence it was conveyed to western Europe, along the Upper Danube and its tributaries, and down the Rhine. The stream of commerce was slender enough, but it enriched the free cities on the banks—Ratisbon, Nüremberg, Coblentz, Mayence, and Cologne. The opulence and power of the burghers raised the cupidity and envy, and after a time secured the association, of the nobles in the neighbourhood. As the wealth of the West was poured into the lap of the Court of Rome, so the treasures of the East were distributed by the cities which lay on the road. I conclude that, heavy as the tolls were which the Sultan extorted, he must have known that the trade was too advantageous to be destroyed without a permanent loss, and too reciprocal to be sacrificed without serious danger. And so the trade went on, and in some directions flourished. For example, the manufacture of cane sugar, a very costly article, and at first confined to Sicily, was set up in Alexandria, and within a hundred years, *i.e.*, between the beginning and end of the fifteenth century, the later price sank to less than one-eighth of the rate at which it stood at the earlier date.

Still the conquest of Constantinople, the progress of the Turkish arms, and the total desolation and block of Central Asia, made the trade centres of Western Europe uneasy. The march of the Turks seemed to the fifteenth century like that of a devouring pestilence, or of the sword of God. The battle of Belgrade was a great deliverance, but only for a time. At any rate, it was of supreme importance to get to the rear of these warlike savages, and so reach India. Hence the efforts of Henry of Portugal, a grandson of our John of Gaunt, to discover a sea passage round Africa, in the first half of the fifteenth century; the voyages of Vasco di Gama, of Columbus, and of Cabot in the second half. As is well known, the discovery of the Cape Passage and of the New World were almost simultaneous.

The discovery was not too soon. Between 1512 and 1520, Selim I., the most active and ferocious of the Turkish sultans, conquered Mesopotamia, got possession of the holy places of Arabia, and annexed Egypt to his empire. The last ancient route to the East was blocked, and though the region of spices had been opened by Portuguese enterprise to the Western world for some years, the voyage was long, dangerous, and uncertain. The price of Eastern produce rose rapidly to famine rates. The trade with the East was successively appropriated by Portugal, Spain, Holland, England; and in our own day, under better conditions, the old road of the Pharaohs and Ptolemies has been reopened, and the border of Egypt has become the water-way of India.

Before this epoch could be dreamed of, the commercial ruin of Italy set in, and with it the decline of those great cities which had been the carriers and distributors of Eastern produce. The wealth of the burghers and the resources of princes dwindled, though it is likely that few saw the causes of the decline, or could trace them to their proper origin. As the nobles grew poorer—for the trade was starved before it was annihilated—they began to oppress the peasants, and the Boors' war broke out. The discontent of town and country alike had no little influence on the temper which gave Luther a hearing and the theses of Wittenberg an ominous significance. The decline of trade, the pressure of poverty, the discontent engendered by distress, the angry inquiry into the causes of these unexplained calamities, the reference of these distresses to papal extortion and extravagance, and the outburst of a passionate longing for reform in the Church, are not remotely connected with the battles which Selim won at Cairo and the Pyramids, and with the break which those victories made in the commerce of the East. Then the inquiry into the causes of commercial and social decay became wider, and the discontent with authority more marked. The Western world revolted. Germany, a century after Luther's age, lay wasted and bleeding at the feet of the Austrian emperor. France was torn by wars of religion, and finally succumbed to a central despotism, while England began anew that struggle for constitutional liberty which has now, we trust, been founded securely, and to be wisely progressing, though two centuries elapsed before the mass of the people were emancipated from injurious laws,—a people which is not yet re-admitted to the constitution.

CHAPTER VI.

SOCIETY—WAGES—PROFITS.

The Labour of an Agriculturist always leaves a Margin for others—The Nobles and the Clergy—Number of the Clergy—The Incidence of Tithe in the Middle Ages, and its Proportion to Agricultural Profits and Rent—The Position of the Clergy—The Use of the learned Monk and Chronicler—Education was probably Diffused—Proofs thereof—Education of Girls in Nunneries—Oxford, its Reputation—Number of Students there—Merton's Foundations—The Fortunes of Oxford—Wages of Labour—Of Farm Hinds—Payments for Threshing—Wages high in the Eastern Counties and London—Wages in the Irish Pale—The general Distribution of Land, and its Effect on Wages—Comparison of wages in the Thirteenth and Eighteenth Centuries—The Profits of small Proprietors Estimated, and their Expenditure—Artizans few, and all Work on Raw Materials hired by Employers—Working Days in the Year—Money Wages of Artizans—Farm and Domestic Servants—Wages of Clerks and Scribes.

IT is certain that the agriculturist must earn more than is necessary for his own support before any other person can contrive to exist. It was with some reason, therefore, that the economists and Adam Smith put him in the first rank of productive labourers. However scanty may be his share in the distribution of wealth, except he abide in the ship, none can be safe. It is true that in the rudest agricultural, and even in the rudest pastoral age, the labour of the individual always produces more than is requisite for himself and his family. He can therefore be made to maintain others on his labour. Some of these consumers will benefit him, by increasing his comforts, by allowing him to devote his undivided attention to his own industry or calling, and by furnishing him with economies in the conduct of his business. Some will quarter themselves as of right or by force on his labours and their produce, and will colour their usurpation by alleging that he owes them allegiance or duty. These claims are always most insolent and incessant when society is barbarous. As it becomes civilized, people reiterate, with apparent reason, that only the criminal and the utterly destitute are burdens on society, and that they who provide the pageantry, or are recognised as the ornaments of civil life, represent the highest utilities. It is to be hoped that labour and poverty are satisfied with this assurance, and are convinced that these pretensions are founded on a solid basis of facts. It will be found in the course of English social history that the assurance has been occasionally disputed, and the pretensions severely criticised. It is possible that the temper which disputes or criticises may occur in force hereafter, when it is not anticipated or expected.

The nobles and the clergy were the two powers in the middle ages which enforced the subjection or affirmed the duty of those who lived by labour. As both orders were engaged in industry of the same kind as that of the mass of the people, as landowner, priest, and monk were all employed on husbandry, and were all adding to the sum of visible wealth, there was a harmony of purpose and interest which made Grostête and De Montfort, the barons of London and the franklins of Kent, the monks of St. Benedict and the parson of Dale, the lord of the manor and the serf under him, all toiling and spinning, impatient critics of a foolish king, who would have no responsible councillors; and of foreign favourites, who drew income out of that to which they contributed nothing,—the Mansels, the De Valences, the herd of the Savoyards and the Poictevins. In two or three generations afterwards there begins the struggle between labour and ease, between obligations and privileges,—a struggle which commenced five centuries ago under Tyler and Ball, and has continued under various leaders and various phases into this our present unsatisfied condition.

The clergy of the thirteenth century were very numerous. There were certainly as many as in the fourteenth, when the poll-tax, which excludes the most popular and growing class of the regular clergy, the begging friars, makes them 29,161.

or about one in fifty-two of the population, male and female, which was above fourteen years of age. It is probable, indeed, that the numbers of the clergy, secular and regular, had been greatly reduced in the third quarter of the fourteenth century by the great plague and the drain which Edward's wars laid on the population.

It will be obvious that the more costly the process of agriculture, the more ungrateful the soil, and the more scanty the produce, the more onerous is the impost of a tithe of the produce, even though it may seem to supply but a small income to the recipient. The average tithe of the produce in corn and wool on the eleven estates of Merton College in the year 1333, as taken from the return of produce in that year, rendered by the bailiffs on all the farms which are cultivated by the college, and estimated at the current prices of the year, is about £4. But not more than half of the titheable area was ordinarily in the hands of the lord. The income of the parson was therefore, on an average of corn and wool, and, on this produce only, at least £8. To this must be added a further £4 at least, for the tithe on stock, and, finally, the dues, ordinary or extraordinary, payable to the rector. Now I find that, taking one estate with the others and setting the profit of bailiff cultivation, inclusive of the rents and dues paid by the tenants, at 20 per cent. on the capital (and there is good reason for believing that such a rate was realised on the average), the receipts of each estate were, on an average, £36 a year, while I have calculated the average receipts of the parson at about £15. The parson therefore received from each estate under cultivation rather more than two-fifths of the income of the lord; this income, it should be remembered, being in part derived from the agricultural operations of others, and often supplemented by the profits of glebe lands. In towns, benefices are of far greater value. Gascoigne speaks from his own knowledge of rectors who had £100 a year of annual income.

My readers may now see why the pope and the king claimed a heavier percentage tax on the clergy than they did on the laity. Unlike the rest of the community, they subsisted on the produce of other men's labour. They often held, as I have said, glebes in addition to their tithes. These, with their personal goods, appear to have been taxed at the same rate as lay tenements and chattels, as were also lands held by spiritual persons in mortmain, and by the consent of the Crown since the 20th year of Edward I. (1292).

The estates of the monasteries are said over and over again to have comprised a third of the knight's fees in England. Most of these religious houses were founded before the close of the thirteenth century, many of them in the early ages of the Saxon polity. Only a few were founded in later times. Besides these monastic estates, the bishops and the chapters held large possessions. They added to them, especially in the fifteenth century, by procuring, through the action of the Roman court and with the connivance of the Crown, the great tithes of valuable livings, while they left a pittance to the vicar, or served the church by one of their own monks or chaplains, in which case they appropriated the fees which the piety of the age conferred on the clergy, or usage secured to their order. Hence the king, who had enacted over and over again, in the interests of the Crown, and, indeed, of the public at large, that the clergy should be debarred from adding to the real estate which they already possessed, claimed on various occasions large contributions from the religious orders and the secular clergy, and once in the thirteenth century put a novel but very effective kind of pressure on them, by withdrawing from them the protection of the king's peace, and subjecting them to a virtual outlawry.

Large as the proportion of the clergy is to the rest of the community, and it is stated that the numbers given are not exhaustive, it must be remembered that the clergy, in the widest sense of the term, contained nearly the whole of what we should call the professional classes. The architects, the physicians, the lawyers, the scribes, the teachers of the middle ages, were almost always clergymen, and when employed in these callings, were rewarded for their services with benefices. We know but few of the men who designed the great cathedrals, churches, and castles of the middle ages,—those buildings which are the wonder of our age for their vastness, their exquisite proportions, and their equally exquisite detail. But when we do know, as it were by accident, who the builder was, he is almost always a clergyman. It seems as though skill in architecture, and intimate acquaintance with all which was necessary, not only for the design of the structure, but for good workmanship and endurance, were so common an accomplishment, that no one was at the pains to proclaim his own reputation or to record the reputation of another. It is known that we owe the designs of Rochester Castle and the Tower to one ecclesiastic. It is recorded that William of Wykeham was Edward the Third's architect at Windsor, as well as his own at Winchester and Oxford, and of various handsome churches which were built during his long episcopate. It is probable that Wayneflete designed the beautiful buildings at Magdalen College; and it is alleged that Wolsey, in his youth, planned the matchless tower, which has charmed every spectator for nearly four centuries. But no one knows who designed and carried out a thousand of those poems in stone which were the glory of the middle ages, and have been made the subjects of servile and stupid imitation in our own.

The monks were the men of letters in the middle ages, the historians, the jurists, the philosophers, the physicians, the students of nature. It is owing to their labours that we know anything of our annals, of the events by which the political history of England is interpreted. They were often frivolous, frequently credulous, but they collected the facts to the best of their ability. It is true that the material which they put into shape is far less in quantity than those voluminous archives are which are preserved in our national collection. But these, though of great collateral value, would have but little constructive importance in the absence of the chronicles which the monks compiled. This is abundantly illustrated by the history of the fifteenth century and part of the sixteenth. The archives of this time are exceedingly copious. Public documents are numerous, the rolls of Parliament are full and precise, the record of legal proceedings is very large, and there is no lack of private memoranda.

But the chronicler has disappeared, to the regret of the few authors of the time. Gascoigne, the Oxford Chancellor, is constantly indignant at the fact that the literary monk is nowhere found, that the *scriptorium* of the abbey is deserted, and chronicles are no longer compiled. He suggests the sternest measures, fine and even confiscation, for such a neglect of duty. But owing to the absence of such chronicles, the history of England from the middle of Henry the Sixth's reign to the beginning of Henry the Eighth's, between sixty and seventy years, is as dark a period as any in our annals. We depend, to a great extent, for our own history on the works of foreign authors.

In our sense of the word, these chronicles were not published. They were copied over and over in the same monastery; they were frequently inspected by monks of other houses or other orders; but they do not appear to have been accessible to a public, if any, which could read them. Hence the authors of these books are exceedingly plain spoken. Matthew Paris writes of Henry III., with whom he seems to have had more than a personal acquaintance, with a candid severity which was certainly never designed for the royal eye. But they do not, like some memoirs, appear to have been composed with a view of postponing that information to posterity which might be given when the writer was out of the reach of all who might resent his calumnies, or when a cynical avowal of licentiousness and malignity could be safely made. That the reflections of the monk took a colour from his surroundings was natural; that the indignant critic of the Roman court should have been equally angry with Grostête for striving to make the monks amenable to discipline was an intelligible inconsistency; but on the whole, when his abilities were equal to the task, the literary monk addressed himself to his labours fearlessly and honestly.

The monasteries do not appear to have become scandalous in the thirteenth century, as they were in the latter part of the fourteenth and the whole of the fifteenth. But they lacked zeal. Wealth had made them negligent, if not corrupt. Without becoming absolutely unpopular, they had ceased to be an ideal of religious life, and piety no longer expended itself in founding establishments for the older orders. But for a time, especially in the thirteenth century, two new orders, those of Francis and Dominic, were popular, energetic, and influential, and had a great reputation for saintliness. One of the old military orders was, on the other hand, about to fall, and give the first precedent for the dissolution of a religious society, and the confiscation of its possessions.

It is a common opinion, but, I believe, a common error, that education, in the sense of reading and writing, was hardly ever acquired out of the ranks of the clergy. I cannot account for the universal practice of keeping elaborate and exact accounts if the bailiffs were wholly illiterate. I decline to believe that an official in an estate could carry in his head or verify by tallies the exceedingly numerous details which he must have supplied in order to get his assets and liabilities balanced at the end of the year to a farthing. I have seen from time to time, but rarely, a rough set of entries, evidently scrawled by a very different person from the neat and accomplished scribe who finally indites the roll. Again, we are told that schools were universal. I have alluded to them in London. I am convinced that they were attached to every monastery, and that the extraordinary number of foundation schools established just after the Reformation of 1547 was not a new zeal for a new learning, but the fresh and very inadequate supply of that which had been so suddenly and disastrously extinguished.

The bills presented by artizans and mechanics in the early period of this inquiry would not be worth keeping. But for several years during the fifteenth century, New College, in Oxford, preserved by some accident, filed and rolled up in a scrap of parchment, the tradesmen's bills which were presented and paid before the audit. They are rudely written, and are evidently the composition of persons who were not adept penmen; but they are evidence that artizans in the fifteenth century knew how to write out an account.

During the course of the same century I find it was the practice of country gentlefolks to send their daughters for education to the nunneries, and to pay a certain sum for their board. A number of such persons are enumerated as living *en pension* at the small nunnery of Swyn in Yorkshire. Only one roll of expenditure for this religious house survives in the Record Office, but it is quite sufficient to prove and illustrate the custom. The eagerness, too, with which the Lollards treasured, copied, and disseminated the Bible and the controversial works of their sect, is proof that reading and writing were not strange accomplishments among the Norwich weavers, who were the head-quarters of the Lollard movement, and offered an asylum to the proscribed and hunted teachers of the sect. The Lollards' Pit, on the other side of the Cathedral Close at Norwich, had probably as many victims as Smithfield, though the chronicle of their sufferings has not been written. It is probable, too, that Latin, such as it was, was not unfamiliar to all. The bailiff's accounts are invariably written in it. That the monks and academics should universally employ Latin was intelligible enough; but it is surely unreasonable to conclude that bailiff and lord, master and servant, should have agreed to record transactions of vital importance and minute detail in a tongue which neither of them understood, or either was ignorant of. The likelihood that Latin was generally understood is further enforced by the frequency of political songs in Latin or in a maccaroni of Latin and English. Nor were these bailiffs men in any superior position. The bailiffs of Cuxham, father and son, from the days when Merton College became possessed of the estate to the time when the whole family perished in the plague and their chattels became the property of the lords of the manor, were serfs, and so described. Inventories of chattels also designate books frequently, though they are generally of small value in the estimate.

In the middle of the thirteenth century, Oxford, which had been in existence for at least a hundred years, was at the height of its reputation as a university. "The schools"—by which title the University was generally known—were situated on part of what is now Bodley's Library, the ground floor of which when built was devoted to the same uses as the older structure was. Oxford appears to have attracted students from all parts of the world. The reputation of Grostête, the famous bishop of Lincoln, whom succeeding ages reverenced as the greatest of English saints, though uncanonized, was reflected on the University in which he lived and taught for the greater part of his life. This was during the first half of the thirteenth century. The situation was admirable. The town is placed on a slight eminence above the river, which embraces nearly three sides of it. It is naturally protected. It possessed one or two ancient and opulent monasteries, founded in Anglo-Saxon times, and others of more recent date. On the north of the town was the royal palace of the Plantagenets, where two kings of England, Richard and John, were born. Near it was the park and manor of Woodstock. The circuit of the walls was densely packed with houses, in which students lodged, the dedication of buildings to their use greatly enhancing the value of the tenements in which they dwelt.

In the fifteenth century, Gascoigne tells us that he inspected the records of his predecessors, Chancellors of Oxford, and found that before the Great Plague, the University had thirty thousand students within its liberties. I confess that, with every respect for this pious and estimable person, the number seems to me absolutely incredible,—to be, in short, ten times more than the possible truth. That the majority of the clergy studied here is almost certain. That a large proportion of the monks were here also as students during their novitiate is proved, for large establishments, sometimes collective, as Gloucester Hall, sometimes single, as Durham College, were entirely devoted to the reception of monks. That students came from all parts of Europe is clear. It is far from unlikely that many a poor foreigner, after studying in Oxford, as Alexander V. did, returned to his country and reached the papal chair.

In the latter part of the thirteenth century, an ecclesiastic, who had long been engaged in secular business, and when advanced in life was made bishop of the small see of

Rochester, being possessed of considerable private means. and being high in favour with the king, his brother, and his sons, and even with the barons of the popular party, determined to found a house of students. At first he placed it in a Surrey village, but soon removed it to Oxford. He gave it very considerable possessions, estates indeed numerous and valuable enough for an abbey, these being partly his patrimony, partly purchases, partly donations from the king, the King of the Romans, and the younger brother of Edward I. He founded it for a warden and as many fellows as the revenues could maintain, provided for religious offices in or near the building, and prescribed that the fellows should for ever maintain a school in which his kinsfolk and others should be taught. He put certain geographical limits to the area from which his fellows should be eligible, but no other conditions. Only they should be at once excluded from the benefits of his foundation if they became monks. They were not bound to become secular clergy, or to betake themselves to any particular calling, but to be students and men of business. To use a modern phrase, the liberality of the views entertained by Merton is amazing in a thirteenth century ecclesiastic.

This foundation became the type of the Oxford colleges. It was speedily imitated at Cambridge, the earliest house of that university having statutes copied almost literally from those of the first among the Oxford colleges. For a long time, however, these institutions were almost unimportant members of the academical system into which they were planted. As Grostête attracted students from all parts of the world in the thirteenth century, so did Wiklif in the fourteenth. In the fifteenth, Oxford began to decay. At the beginning of the sixteenth it seemed likely, under the influence of Erasmus and the Humanists, to revive. But the Reformation came, and it was almost ruined, and far more seriously compromised than Cambridge was. In the seventeenth it fell under the baneful influence of Laud. In the eighteenth it sunk to its lowest degradation. It has been successively the prey of Jacobites, obscurantists, and adventurers from the beginning of those evil days. There never has been an English institution which has been at times so noble and at times so ignoble, in which partizanship has been so contemptible and public opinion so dead.

During the epoch of its occasional reputation, the University of Oxford must have powerfully leavened English life. It is remarkable that it has developed every great religious movement in English history. The teaching of its students was carried to Bohemia in the fourteenth century, and to the Mississippi in the eighteenth. Chaucer has sketched its clerks in their student days ; Gascoigne in the decline of letters. During the short-lived ascendency of the Commonwealth, it founded what became the Royal Society. It has never been entirely without witnesses. In the eighteenth century it had great astronomers. In the nineteenth it had a great scholar. But though these men had a vast reputation outside it, they never leavened the inert mass within it. It has constantly stoned its prophets, but has never even built their sepulchres, and hardly knows their names.

The leisure classes in England in the thirteenth century were therefore a few nobles, a few opulent ecclesiastics, and a large number of clergy and scholars. The supplementary industries were those of the traders and artizans in the towns, and a very few, and those very scattered, smiths and carpenters in the villages. Even these persons, in rural districts at least, united the functions of the husbandman or labourer to that of the craft which they practised. There were, indeed, very few of the population which were wholly dissociated from agriculture. The fellows of a college, the monks in the monastery, all took their part at times in supervising at least the work of the fields. And though agriculture was unprogressive, the husbandman was diligent. His wants were few, and most of them were satisfied on the spot, and it was quite possible, by thrift and painstaking, not only to satisfy the claims of his lord and the charges of the tax collectors, but to make a store, with which to gratify his paternal ambition or to enlarge his holding.

Agricultural labourers were rarely paid by the day, but

generally by piecework. The bailiff hired hands by the year, but these were constantly paid in allowances of grain and a small sum of money. Where one does find day work paid for, it is at about the rate of 2*d.* a day for men, 1*d.* for women, ½*d.* for boys. Now it must be remembered that a penny contained at that time three times as much silver as a penny now would contain, if a pound of silver were coined into 720 pieces, instead of being, as it would be now, if silver pence were minted, cut into 792 pieces. I need not trouble my reader here with the difference between the Tower pound and the Troy pound, beyond saying that the former stood to the latter in the proportion of 15 to 16. The rarity of payment by the day is indirect evidence that the great majority of the labourers were occupied on their own holdings during a considerable part of the year. Omitting exceptional rates paid for piecework, the wages of an agricultural labourer would be at a rate of £2 11*s.* 8*d.* a year, or taking, besides Sundays, twenty days for church holidays, £2 10*s.* In harvest and hay-making time, which may have well lasted five weeks, his wages would be doubled, and this would raise them to £2 15*s.* His wife was paid for harvest piecework as well as he was, and could earn another five shillings, raising his amount to £3. If he had two children fit for employment, at their rates they might raise the total earnings of the family to £3 15*s.* or £4.

When the hinds were hired by the year, they received a quarter of corn, at say 4*s.* every eight weeks, and 6*s.* money wages, *i.e.*, about the value of 32*s.* a year. They were always, however, boarded in harvest time and at periods of exceptional employment. This board, as I find from other sources, was reputed to cost from 1¼*d.* to 1½*d.* a day, and if we take six weeks as the time thus employed, the real wages which they received would be in the aggregate about 35*s.* 8*d.* a year. Such hinds were undoubtedly single men. Occasionally the labourer serves more masters than one, and his allowances and money are therefore reduced. Thus the swineherd is the servant of the whole village; the deye, or dairy servant, of more than one or two; the shepherd frequently of two persons. During the

harvest quarter the money wages are always three times the
amount of what is paid in the other quarters. This rule is of
course adopted in order to prevent the hind from deserting
his employment during the most profitable time of the
labourer's year, and is indirect evidence of the voluntariness
of the engagement. Had the labour of the resident serf been
entirely at his lord's discretion, such a distribution of money
wages would have been a superfluous precaution.

The wages of agricultural labour were higher in the Eastern
counties and the neighbourhood of London than in the rest
of England. So copious has been the information which I
have collected as to the price of agricultural labour and
produce in England at the close of the thirteenth and through
the greater part of the fourteenth century, that I have found
it in my power to construct a table of the prices of one kind
of labour from five districts of England,—east, west, south,
midland, and north. The labour which I took as an illustration was that of threshing a quarter of the three kinds of corn—
wheat, barley, and oats—in the several districts. The rate of
payment is, speaking generally, that of 3, 2, and 1. No better
illustration of labour by the piece could be conceived. The
process was in universal demand, and was not, as far as I
have seen, provided by customary labour. It is that kind of
labour which is, relatively speaking, the cheapest, for it can
be carried on at all times of the year under cover, in good and
bad weather, and at the discretion of the employer and
labourer. It was comparatively easy work, for our forefathers
cut their corn high on the stalk, leaving the straw for a second
reaping or mowing at their convenience or discretion, or even
for ploughing in. All corn was, as a rule, reaped, little or none
was mown; and as the reaper took only such a length of straw
to his sickle as would be sufficient to bind by, it is clear that
it was easily spread and threshed. The labour of threshing
the three principal kinds of corn-growing grasses differs with
the difficulty of separating the seed from the husk, and the
graduated rate of payment expresses the difficulty with exactness. It is 3*d.* for wheat, 2*d.* for barley, 1*d.* for oats. Winnowing was performed by the women, at about a farthing the

quarter, the fan being provided by the employer, as, indeed, most tools and implements are.

The higher rates paid in the eastern counties are to be explained by the competition of manufacturing labour, just in the same way as now the wages paid to agricultural labourers in the manufacturing districts of England are far in excess of those customary in purely rural parts, and would, if they were familiar to the farmers of the south, become another of those foolish and futile cries by which English agriculturists habitually deafen and blind themselves to those facts which have to be comprehended before the agricultural problems of our own time can be solved. It does not, however, appear that the price of agricultural products is higher in the east than it was elsewhere. On the contrary, Norfolk prices are generally low, especially for its staple product, barley. Again, London wages are high, for prices are high in or about London, and it is reasonable to conclude that the strongest and the most skilful labour gravitated towards the metropolis, or was to be regularly found there. I may add here that the Anglicised part of Ireland, in which Roger Bigod had several estates, and in which there were thriving manufactures, paid as high wages as England did. The glimpse which the preservation of the bailiff's accounts from Bigod's Irish estates gives us as to the position of the English pale in Ireland during the last few years of the thirteenth century is instructive, and, I believe, unique. These estates were in the counties of Wexford, Carlow, and Kildare. Now in Arthur Young's time (Southern Tour, p. 81) threshing near Braintree was paid at the rate of 2s. a quarter for wheat, and 1s. for barley and oats. If we take the multiple of twelve as a fair and, on the whole, exact representative of the rise in the price of provisions and the other necessaries of life between the years 1260 and 1760, the labourer in the time of Henry III. was paid better than he was in the first year of George III. I reckoned, when estimating the position of the mediæval labourer by the side of his descendants in the eighteenth century, that the former received for the labour of threshing rather more than one-eighteenth of the wheat he threshed, rather more than a twenty-second part of barley, and rather less than a fourteenth part of oats, taking the rate of wages and the price of grain as the factors in the calculation. In the eighteenth century, the peasant got one twenty-fourth part of wheat and barley, and a one-and-twentieth part of the oats he threshed.

I have little doubt that the comparative price of labour at these remote periods, separated by five centuries, and the relatively advantageous position which the peasant occupied at this period, are to be ascribed to the general distribution of land. When persons are engaged in a calling which regularly demands a particular kind of labour for its conduct, and an external demand as regularly arises for the same kind of labour, the tendency of the market for labour is to rise, *i.e.*, the labourer is able to require and obtain more than he would if he had no identical calling of his own to follow. It has been noticed that in a country of small agricultural proprietors hired labour is always absolutely or relatively dear, and that contracts with labourers for harvest or other work were always to the advantage of the labourer. But if the labour given by the small proprietors is a bye occupation, *i.e.*, it is followed when the requirements of the labourer's ordinary calling are satisfied, the remuneration is low. Hence Adam Smith (Book I., Chap. x.) declines to admit such kinds of labour into his estimate of the causes which determine the rate of wages. Agricultural labour, hired by employers, would be dear ; home industries, such as spinning and weaving and similar employments, would be carried on for a small or an inappreciable remuneration.

The facts to which I have referred will be further illustrated by an examination into the prices paid for such kinds of labour as that for which there was or might be a comparatively urgent demand. The persons who first fixed labour rents were shrewd enough to see that it was most important for them to tie their tenants to the obligations of ploughing, hoeing, mowing, and reaping, because three at least of these operations had to be undertaken at what might be a critical time for the agriculturist, and certainly would be in districts where there were numerous peasant holders. Now it is clear that this customary labour, judiciously exacted, would tend to depress the price at which it would be hired in the open market. For the lord and his bailiff had only to bargain for such services as were over and above what would be afforded by the regular hinds on the farm and the customary labour of the tenants. The latter they could exact, the former they secured by larger money allowances, by giving board in addition to payments in corn and money, and by a few luxuries in harvest time. They knew, to be sure, that the enforced labour was not of a satisfactory kind, hence they were always ready to commute it for a reasonable money payment, with consequences which we shall see hereafter.

In the thirteenth century, wheat was reaped at a fraction over 5*d.* an acre, barley at 5½*d.*, oats and rye at 4½*d.* Beans, peas, and vetches at 5*d.*, or a fraction less. Hay was mown at 5*d.* an acre. The discrepancy between the price at which rye and oats, on the one hand, and wheat and barley on the other, were reaped, is to be accounted for by the fact that the rye crop, always a small and unimportant one, comes to maturity earlier than any other kind of grain, and therefore at a time when there is a less energetic demand for hands, while oats can lie out with less injury than any other kind of grain during wet. Barley, too, was a heavier crop than wheat.

In Arthur Young's time, to revert to a comparison made above, the average price, compiled from very numerous entries made in his various tours, paid for the service of reaping wheat was 5*s.* 6*d.* an acre, *i.e.*, a little over twelve times what was paid five centuries before; but so little over that the rate may be considered, in view of the multiple employed before, as inappreciable. Estimated in the price of wheat, the reaper of the thirteenth century received about one-twelfth of a quarter for his labour. During the period of Young's tours, which were made during the remarkable abundance which characterized the first three-quarters of the eighteenth century, the receipts of the reaper of wheat were about one-ninth of a quarter. But in the eighteenth century, all other kinds of corn were mown, the labourer receiving, on an average, 1*s.* 2*d.* an acre for corn and hay; while the

thirteenth-century peasant received, again taking twelve as
the multiplier, over 5s. an acre for his labour. Now the
average price of the other kinds of grain, which were paid at
the higher rate, is 3s. 6d. a quarter, and for this part of his
work the labourer received in value about the eighth of a
quarter, or a bushel of grain for the labour of reaping a
quarter of the produce. This cost of labour corresponds with
that given in Walter de Henley's estimate, who sets the
whole cost of cultivating an acre of corn at 3s. 1½d. an acre,
and reckons the reaping at 5d., the carrying at 1d. But
taking the average price of barley, oats, and beans in Arthur
Young's time, we shall find that the labourer earned, on an
average, not more than the nineteenth of a quarter for the
labour of mowing them. It is clear, moreover, that the
average crop of the eighteenth century was more than
double that of the thirteenth, as may be readily discovered
from a very hasty examination of what I have shown in my
history of agriculture and prices on the one hand, and the
facts of English husbandry which Arthur Young has so
copiously collected on the other.

It remains that I should attempt to point out what were
the profits of such a small proprietor as is described on the
Cuxham and Ibstone manors, as having a holding, for which
he pays a quit-rent, or a quit-rent and service, at about 6d. an
acre; his holding being about twenty acres of arable land.
If he carried on his cultivation in the same way and to the
same advantage, one thing being put against the other, as the
lord did on the land which he held in his own hands and
cultivated by his bailiff with the assistance of hired labourers,
though we might expect with reason that his small husbandry
would be more profitable, he should expect to obtain, by a
capital of about £15, about £3 10s. profit, out of which he
would have to pay 10s. for rent and dues. In addition to
his land, and contributing to the profit which he earned,
would be his pasture rights in common, field, waste, and wood.
These would be after the rate obtained by the lord, though he
might have to pay a few pence for the pannage of his hogs.
If, in addition to the labour which he gives to his own little

homestead, he, his wife, and his boys take their share in harvest work and winter threshing, in hoeing, and similar avocations, he would find, as the evidence of numberless records testify, no difficulty in bringing his aggregate earnings up to £4 annually, or even more; for I have shown above that this sum was not unattainable by the free labourer who had only a cottage and curtilage, but got regular farm work at day wages. I am content, however, to take the less sum.

The distribution of his income would be as follows :— Taking the average price of wheat, and assuming that four quarters a year were sufficient for the support of the farmer and his family, the first and heaviest charge on his resources will be £1 3*s*. 6*d*. for bread. I have taken the price of the best wheat which comes to market, and has been screened from the lighter produce. Let us suppose that he uses the inferior produce for home consumption, and, with a very liberal margin, the difference between the price of the best and of inferior corn, fully 25 per cent., will be amply sufficient to reimburse the miller for his labour and his toll. Two quarters of second quality malt may be allowed for the home manufacture of beer. This allowance, nearly a bushel of malt every three weeks among the members of a small family, though liberal, is not excessive, for it gives about four gallons of tolerably sound ale weekly to the whole number. The cost of malt will be 7*s*. 7*d*. Now if we allow 800 lbs. of meat at the rate of ¼*d*. per lb., its ordinary price in the thirteenth century, as we may find from the weight and prices of oxen and sheep, a further sum will be expended on beef, mutton, and bacon of 16*s*. 8*d*. This puts the cost of maintenance on a somewhat liberal scale of £2 7*s*. 9*d*. a year. The residue of his charges would be for clothing. But much of this was homespun russet cloth, and hempen or linen shirting; a pair of rude boots, worth about 2*s*., and of leather gaskins, which do not cost more than 1*s*. 6*d*., being all that was necessary for him to purchase, though substitutes of home manufacture would doubtlessly be found even for these. But if we take the whole of his purchases together, they will not amount to more than 12*s*. 3*d*., the sum needed to raise his expenditure to £3. He might, therefore, be supplied abundantly from the produce of his farm, debiting himself with the cost of his own produce, and laying aside 20s. a year, with which hereafter, as opportunity might arise, he might increase his holding, portion his daughters, provide for his widowed mother, or put forward his son in the Church, or any similarly advantageous calling.

Such may be fairly taken to represent the receipts and expenditure of these small landowners, who were, as I have frequently stated, so numerous in the thirteenth century. I have taken the schedule of profit and loss which a lord's accounts supply as the basis on which to estimate a tenant's income and outgoings, and I have gathered my inferences from years of undoubted prosperity, though not of exceedingly low prices. I have taken the expenditure not from the prices of a few years or of one or two years, but from the general average of the thirteenth and fourteenth centuries, and so have allowed for a considerable margin. Again, I have included only the simplest necessaries in the family expenditure. Even after I have reckoned £3 as farming profit, there is certain to have been some produce of cheese, milk, and butter, which was consumed by the family, besides poultry and eggs, which would hardly have been reckoned cost or loss by the small proprietor. And lastly, in order to avoid the suspicion of exaggeration, I have taken the quantity of earnings from a period preceding the great change in the circumstances of the labourer and yeoman, to which I shall presently allude, though I have gathered the estimate of his expenditure from a period which includes the rise in prices consequent on that change. That a working farmer with his wife and children could find opportunity for more labour than that required to cultivate twenty acres of arable land, I have taken for granted. In Arthur Young's time, when agriculture was far more developed and land was much more highly cultivated than was thought possible, or, indeed, expedient, in a previous age, twenty acres per head of labour is reckoned the standard of excellent management. It is clear, too, that there was a periodical demand for labour, since the Statute of Labourers, passed in the middle of the fourteenth century, though it strove to prevent peasants from migrating from one parish to the other in search of higher wages, made an exception in favour of those who temporarily travelled from the north to the south in quest of harvest work. The statute, though enacted in favour and with a view to control the prices of labour, is evidence of a custom with which agriculturists had been long familiar.

I am sensible that these arithmetical calculations, which I have indeed reduced to the narrowest limits consistent with accuracy, will, after all, be deterrent to the general reader, if any such care to examine what I have written, and will be distasteful even to the student of economical history. But I have no choice in presenting them. Had the views which I have proved elsewhere, which are the result of long and careful calculations, gathered from very numerous and unquestionable facts, been already incorporated into the history of the English race, in place of those absurd fables and careless guesses which have hitherto been taken as the history of the English people,—if there had been any inclination to search into the life and doings of the great mass of our forefathers, instead of skimming the froth of foreign policy, of wars, of royal marriages and successions, and the personal character of the puppets who have strutted on the stage of public life, I might have dispensed with this marshalling of facts and figures. But even in English political history, writers have only attempted to deal with the antiquities of forms, and not with the realities which lie beneath these forms ; much less have they attempted to revive, as Hallam wished, though he thought the wish hopeless, the life of a single village in mediæval England. To do this, even when the materials are discovered, is impossible without facts and figures, and the student of what is the genuine life of our forefathers, and withal the conditions under which modern society has been instructed and developed, may well comfort himself with the conviction, which will be overwhelmingly demonstrated as he labours honestly and fairly on his materials, that the man who first formulated the statement that "nothing is more false than facts, except figures," uttered a shallow epigram. The falsehood is in the incompetent use of them.

The number of artizans in mediæval England must have been very small. In my early researches, I was under the impression that the smith was in every village, the carpenter in most. But I seldom find these personages enumerated in the rent-rolls of the manors, and I am persuaded that their trade would have been designated had they been generally present. Nearly every village had its miller, but he was a privileged person, sturdy in defence of rights, for which he paid the lord handsomely, and reputed to be not over honest in his calling. The miller, if the village stream was a scanty one, had always a standing quarrel with the owners of the upper water meadows, whom he accused of keeping back his supplies, and against whose interests, in the dry season, he was charged with furtively raising his weir. But the smith and the carpenter served, I suspect, several villages together, as the country doctor does now.

In almost all cases the artizan supplied labour only, and not materials. Even where costly and elaborate iron work is designed and constructed, the smith receives the iron from his employer, fashions it from designs supplied to him, or perhaps devised by himself, accounts for the residue of the raw material, and receives his pay for the work. His stock-in-trade was his forge and bellows, his hammers, anvils, and pincers. That he wrought up scrap-iron is certain, for one product of his craft is always bought in a manufactured state, lath-nails, and frequently other kinds of nails. So the carpenter and wheelwright fashion the manor timber, the mason uses the stone and lime which his employer has bought; and lead in pigs, with solder for joints, is served out in bulk or mass, is rolled, or cast and smelted by the plumber. Even the glazier receives the purchases of his employer, and fits them into casement or frame. As might be expected, the Eastern counties and London are the earliest localities in which the capitalist artizan who deals in finished goods is to be found, and his transactions are generally with opulent individuals or with wealthy corporations. The capitalist employer, the first middle man, is entirely unknown till the seventeenth century, and the capitalist purchaser of raw materials, the later middle man, is later still in the economy of society.

Hence the wages of the artizan are generally reckoned by the day, more rarely by the piece, though where piecework can be conveniently given, it is found. Thus the pair of sawyers are constantly paid by the day, but nearly as often by the hundred of boards sawn, this quantity being about the amount an average pair of sawyers could turn out in a day's work. In the thirteenth century we find traces of a different quality in carpenter's labour, the best being paid at 3½*d.* a day, the ordinary at 3*d.* Artizans' wages are from 25 to 60 per cent. higher in London, where they reach 4*d.* and 5*d.* A pair of sawyers will get 7*d.* a day together, or from 7*d.* to 8*d.* the hundred. Where labour is of special quality, or impressed, the rate rises in the country to 4*d.* or even 5*d.* The master mason or master carpenter received slightly higher wages, and sometimes in addition to his weekly earnings a yearly fee. At the building of Newgate Gaol in 1281, one set of carpenters receives 5½*d.*, another 5*d.*, a third 4*d.* ; the sawyers have 9½*d.* the pair, and the masons 5*d.* a day each.

From 312 to 252 or 235 days are reckoned in the mason's year. That of the carpenter, who is independent of the weather, and can work under cover continuously, is as long as the first of these quantities. The winter's wages are about 25 per cent. less than those of the other seasons ; but the winter seems to have been limited to the months of December and January. This fact, which I have frequently noticed, is proof that the hours of labour were not long. They seem to have been not more than eight hours a day, and at a later period in the economical history of labour the eight hours' day seems to be indicated by the fact that extra hours are paid at such a rate as corresponds to the ordinary pay per hour for eight hours, being a little in excess. Hence the artizan, if he were minded to do so, would have time during summer for some agricultural employment. It would seem that this occupation of spare time was not unusual, for I have found employers of artizans occasionally purchasing agricultural produce from the mason and carpenter, or from their wives. Extra hours are often paid for when the work is pressing and time was an object. On the other hand, employers reckoned halves of days, and when the artizan was in regular employment carefully noted and deducted his absences. These facts are more noticeable when the workmen are employed by the king, who generally pays a higher wage for his men than his subjects do, and if he impressed them at a distance for his service, paid an allowance for their journey to and from their homes.

The mediæval labourer took very few holidays. There is a general impression that, previous to the Reformation, much of the labourer's time was wasted in the compulsory idleness of religious festivals. How far this is true in foreign countries, I do not know, but it is certainly not true of mediæval England. An employment for 312 days leaves only one holiday besides the Sundays. Walter de Henley reckons the working days of the year as 308, which gives only five holidays. In all the continuous accounts which I have seen of labour payments for work extending over a long period, the workmen, with the exception of one set, cease from working on Sundays. The exception is the building accounts of Henry VIII. Here the clerk of the works draws out the list of all persons in the king's employ, and presumes that they will work six days in the week only, and cease from labour on Sundays and certain holidays. But the hurry in which the king was, put such pressure on the men, that they not only worked extra hours, but many of them by night, and constantly on Sundays and holidays. I cannot but think that if there was conceived to be anything very unusual or highly improper in this, the king would not have allowed such work, especially as the practice begins, as far as the accounts give me information, after Henry's quarrel with the Pope, and during the time when his conscience constrained him to compensate for his schism by the severity of his orthodoxy. But work on holidays was paid at rather higher rates than that done on ordinary days. It is singular that in these

account books, four of the principal artizans sign every page,
as though they were a check on the clerk of works.

It is not always easy to determine whether the artizan was
boarded as well as paid. At times he is certainly not. At
times it is stated that he is boarded, and the cost of his board,
generally about half his ordinary wages, is noted. But very
often, especially when the job for which he is engaged is a
short one, the work of a day or two, and he is employed by a
corporation where an abundant table is kept, and the servants
have their separate meal, the labourer appears to get his meal
also. In the fifteenth century, the abbot of St. Edmund's-
Bury engages an architect for certain new work. He and
his servant are to be boarded, lodged, and each to have a
livery by the year, and £10 for the two. The architect's
board is to be that of a gentleman, his servant's to be that
of a yeoman, *i.e.*, the architect is to sit at the table where the
gentlemen-in-waiting of this opulent abbot were fed, and the
man is also to be provided at the upper servants' table. He
and his man were to be fined at a fixed rate if they were
absent more than two days in each quarter of the year. But
in every case workmen had an allowance of beer and bread,
which went by the name of Nonschenes, a word which, I presume, is the origin of our modern luncheon.

An artizan, therefore, if he worked for 300 days in the
year, was able to earn from £3 15s. to £4 7s. 6d., according
to the reputation which he possessed as a workman, or even,
in exceptional cases, as much as £5. In London, his pay
might be as much as £6 5s. to £6 17s. 6d. a year. It may,
however, be doubted whether artizans could safely count on
such continuous employment. In such a case there was the
recourse to agricultural operations, in which we may be certain
that almost every adult was experienced and competent.

The ordinary hired servants on a farm for a year were, besides the bailiff, three ploughmen, three drivers, a carter, a reaper,
a swineherd, a shepherd, a cowherd or dairywoman, and a cook.
This was the establishment on a farm of two carucates, *i.e.*, of
about 240 acres. In places where horses were bred, there
were grooms, or breakers, and stable men, one of whom acts

as marshal or farrier to the stud. The domestic servants of a private house or college were few, beyond the ordinary officials,—butler, porter, steward or manciple, cook, and sewer, with their under servants. If the college had a garden they had servants there, and if the house kept horses, grooms. But attendance at table seems to have been performed by poorer students or servitors, perhaps even waiting in chambers and cleaning them. A large society keeps rarely more than one laundress, and, if we may judge by her usual rate of remuneration, the labours of her calling were not incessant or onerous.

As compared with ordinary servants in husbandry, the domestics in a large house or an opulent corporation were well paid. They were boarded, lodged, provided with a livery annually, the quality and quantity of the cloth being inferior to that served out to the other inhabitants of the house or corporation, and received wages in money, ranging from 40s. a year, the highest generally paid, to 13s. 4d., the lowest. Such servants frequently saved money, and obtained a start for their children. It has constantly been my chance to see the names of college servants, which appear in the next generation as traders in the university, and, later on, as the founders of county families.

On the other hand the wages of clerks and scribes were very low. The scribe who writes out the long account of the Cuxham bailiff, a document which fills thirteen closely printed octavo pages, and balances all the items, gets only two shillings for his trouble, though a further present of a similar sum is given him by favour. A clerk of works is not so well paid as an artizan. The labour of copying and illuminating is very poorly remunerated. The three chaplains whom Henry III. maintained at his hunting lodge of Woodstock get only 50s. a year each; while an advocate, retained to defend a will, is remunerated by 6s. 8d., and the fees to attorneys were very small. I have found one fee paid for conducting a case, which is also 6s. 8d.

My reader therefore, if he has the patience to pursue this dull account, will see that the life of our ancestors, though laborious, was not without its hopes. All the necessaries of life in ordinary years, when there was no dearth, were abundant and cheap, and even in dear years, the margin of wages, or profits, over the bare wants of life was considerable enough to fill up the void, even though the labourer had to subsist for a time on some cheaper food than wheaten bread. Meat was plentiful; poultry found everywhere; eggs cheapest of all. The poorest and meanest man had no absolute and insurmountable impediment put on his career, if he would seize his opportunity and make use of it.

I am well aware that in many particulars he was far behind his descendants in the conveniences and comforts of life. His diet, as I have allowed, was coarse, though plentiful, and during great part of the year was unwholesome. It took three centuries before the Dutch, who were for a long time the centre of economical civilization, were able to discover and adopt those succulent and wholesome roots which have given health to man by banishing the loathsome diseases of the middle ages, and have rendered it possible to improve the breeds of cattle. I am well aware that such medical skill is now at the service of the poorest as princes and prelates desired, but were entirely without, in the middle ages. I am quite familiar, as we all are, with the victories which human ingenuity has acquired over nature, and how man's skill has forced into his service the most common and the most unlikely agencies. I know that four grains of wheat and barley, or any other grain, are produced by modern tillage where one was with difficulty raised before; that the ox has been selected, bred, and fed from 400 lbs. or less to 1,200 or more; that sheep which once yielded a pound of wool precariously now produce seven or nine pounds; that the powerful cart-horse has taken the place of the wretched and stunted pony of the old English breed, and that all other animals which are destined to the service of man have been selected, till there seems nothing to desire in their shape, size, and utility. I see in all directions that human toil has been supplemented, and sometimes superseded, by mechanical agencies, which genius has invented and patience has elaborated. I know that many of our fellow countrymen have exchanged squalid habitations and uncleanly

practices for houses built by the newest lights of sanitary science, and for fastidious cleanliness. I am alive to the fact that what were once the luxuries of the very few have often become the habitual comforts of the many, and that enterprize has scoured the earth in order to make these and newer luxuries abundant and cheap. I know that owing to the spread of knowledge, the adaptation of industry, the energy of invention, and the extension of trade, the population of England and Wales is tenfold what it was six centuries ago; that trim gardens, magnificent mansions, noble parks, rows of handsome houses, vast and splendid cities, occupy sites which were covered by squalid hovels or frequented by wild boars, curlews, and bitterns, or were marshy fens and wild moors. I can see, without being reminded, that the most lofty and subtle pleasures, those of literature, are now common and profuse, and that the world of civilization is so strong that there seems no possible danger of its becoming destroyed by a new incursion of barbarians, not even of those barbarians whom it creates. The inhabitants of this country, at least those whom the historian and the politician think worth instructing and consulting, enjoy the refined pleasure of criticising, and, as many of them believe, conducting in no small degree the affairs of their own country, and even of other peoples, and have got far away from the time when the Englishman believed it his interest to support his sovereign's dream of foreign conquest, because in this way, as he fondly fancied, he could lighten his own burdens at home. I do not need to be told that the wealth of London is such, that a single block of buildings pays a higher rent to its fortunate owner than was derived from the whole customs of the port in the days of the Plantagenets and Tudors; that in a few hours a loan could be raised in London sufficient to equip and provision an army more numerous than all the men-at-arms were in mediæval Europe, and this probably without deranging the course of trade or materially interfering with the functions of credit. And I suspect that when we are invited to consider all these things and more of the same nature, as the prodigious strength of modern governments, the bound-

less resources of modern societies, the enormous accumulations of inherited opulence, the priceless collections of art and letters, the ceaseless activity of enterprise, and the ever increasing discoveries of science, it is fancied that a complete answer is given to those who entertain misgivings, because they believe that there is a reverse to the picture, another side to the shield, which those triumphant eulogies on modern progress would have us conceal or forget. But I am convinced that modern civilization will be judged, not by what it has done, but by what it has left undone; not by what it has remedied, but by what it has failed to heal, or at least to have relieved; not by its successes, but by its shortcomings. It may be that the progress of some has been more than counterbalanced by the distresses and sorrows of many, that the opulence and strength of modern times mocks the poverty and misery which are bound up with and surround them, and that there is an uneasy and increasing consciousness that the other side hates and threatens.

It may be well the case, and there is every reason to fear it is the case, that there is collected a population in our great towns which equals in amount the whole of those who lived in England and Wales six centuries ago; but whose condition is more destitute, whose homes are more squalid, whose means are more uncertain, whose prospects are more hopeless than those of the poorest serfs of the middle ages and the meanest drudges of the mediæval cities. The arm of the law is strong enough to keep them under, and society has no reason to fear their despair; but I refuse to accept the superficial answer, that a man is an admirer of the good old times because he insists that the vaunts of civilization should be examined along with, and not apart from, its failures. It is not possible to give the solution of one problem, the growth of opulence, and to refuse all attention to the other problem, the growth of penury.

I do not assert that my researches into the economical history of England will throw a clear light on these complex and contradictory phenomena; but I am convinced that till we learn how it was that this society has grown and been

collected, and how wealth has been distributed between labourer, capitalist employer, and those who enter on the rest of the inheritance which labour has earned, we shall only be dealing with the most superficial elements and the least important problems of social life; we shall be offered remedies which are more dangerous than the disease; we shall be invited to adopt, as a complete solution of a profound difficulty, that which would make the confusion more inextricable, and the prospect of unravelling it more hopelessly remote. if we accepted it without reserve, examination, or anxiety.

CHAPTER VII.

THE KING AND HIS EXTRAORDINARY REVENUES.

Death of Henry—Legislation of Edward—The Statute of Entails and of Free Sale—Mortmain—The Creation of the House of Commons—The Conquest of Wales and Scotland—Edward's Struggle with the Church—Edward II. : his Political Errors—The Murder of Stapledon—The Claim of Edward III. to the French Throne—The Acquisition of Calais, of Boulogne, and Dunkirk —The English Troops—The Distress of the French Peasant—The French Nobility—The English Peasant—The Cost of the Hundred Years' War— Richard's Reign—The Finance of the War with France—Fifteenths and Tenths—The Wool Tax, the Aid, the Tax on the Parishes—The Poll Tax —The Incidence and Percentage of Fourteenth Century Taxation—Taxes for the King, for the Pope—The Wages of Proctors and Members—Taxation necessarily direct—Attempts to escape Taxation.

THE last years of Henry III. were passed in profound quiet. The rebellious barons were pardoned, the administration was improved, and the king made peace with all. So safe seemed the State, that the king's eldest son and successor, the warlike and politic Edward, had left England on the last crusade, and did not return to his country and kingdom till nearly two years after his father's death.

The reign of Edward is well known as an epoch in land legislation. It also saw the commencement of regular parliaments, to which the prelates and lords, the knights of the shire, the citizens and burgesses of the cities and towns, and the barons of the Cinque Ports were summoned. The king conquered and garrisoned Wales, almost conquered and garrisoned Scotland. He published, with or without the authority of his parliaments, a variety of statutes, many of which affect the law of England to this day. He banished

the Jews from England. He quarrelled with the clergy, and treated them in so peremptory a fashion that he broke their spirit. He confirmed the charters of his predecessors, and surrendered the right of tallaging his proper subjects at his will.

The land legislation of Edward, under which entails were permitted, and subinfeudation was forbidden, is well known. The former law is memorable from the importance which the practice of entail assumed in later times ; the latter, because it made a sale of lands common, and extinguished the creation of manors. I am persuaded that in early times, and for many years after Edward's legislation, entails were few, unimportant, and small, and that the condition which the statute declared to be for ever binding, and not obsolete when it was satisfied, was intended to secure the status of a new body of small military tenants, almost always of the male sex, who would be perpetually dependent on their lord, called the donor of their estate, and whose interests would revert to the lords when male heirs failed the object of the gift. It is, I think, impossible that I should have never found instances in rentals of such tenancies in tail, if, as is assumed, these were freely and largely created. We are told, indeed, that during the great war of succession, as soon as the combatants discovered that defeat might involve forfeiture, it became the practice to entail the great estates, and as tenancies in tail were protected from forfeiture as well as incapable of alienation, that the entail became a precaution. If this be the fact, the protection was not enduring, for Margaret began the system of parliamentary attainder,—a precedent which was followed by sovereign after sovereign, till by an enactment of Henry VIII. the forfeiture of entails followed on a judicial conviction of treason.

The plea for the statute under which subinfeudation was put an end to, and manors could no longer be created, was the loss of dues to the lord, owing to the multiplicity of interests carved out of the estate which was subject to such dues. It is said to have been passed at the instance of the nobles. It provided that the purchaser of an estate, to whose action it gives full freedom, should hold of the same person as that from whom the vendor held his estate, and that no more mesne or middle lords should be created. That it immediately served the interests of the nobles is probable, and this, indeed, is the avowed motive of the enactment; but it seems to me still more markedly, though more remotely, to have served the interest of the Crown, since escheats would finally come to the Crown, and anything which limited the number of subordinate interests in the same estate must have aided in securing the rights of the only person who was ultimate heir of every subject. But I think it cannot be doubted that by stereotyping the existing manors and their tenancies, it gave an additional security to the lowest class of tenants, those in villeinage, whose status would now be defined and even published, or at least be open to inspection. We are told, and I can well believe it, that the lawyers favoured the legal irremovability of the serfs, and materially assisted them in becoming what they were styled, a generation or two later, tenants by copy, or by custom of the manor. But though this famous statute stopped subinfeudation, the old practice was virtually revived in the practice which rapidly grew of charging estates with grants, annuities, rent-charges, and analogous burdens, so that in many cases the nominal receipts of the owner were largely diminished by the liabilities which he had created, or inherited, or had to accept when he purchased. Thus, to quote an example, when Wykeham was founding his colleges at Oxford and Winchester, he purchased an estate in Oxfordshire from the family of Lisle. As usual, the old bailiffs' rolls, some of them going back to the commencement of the first Edward's reign, were handed over at the time of purchase, and are preserved, with those which were drawn up after the property came into the possession of New College. One of the Lisles had charged this estate with the payment of five quarters of wheat on November 1st to the monks of Bicester; and the liability is continued to the purchaser, for the fellows of New College purchase and pay the monastery this quantity of wheat for more than a century, when they finally commute it for a money payment. But it seems manifest that if the present possessor of an estate were able to charge it with all manner of dues and payments, he was doing that which this famous statute was seeking to prevent, and was creating interests out of a property which were dependent on himself, his heirs and successors.

More effectual than either of these statutes, and, as it appears, more necessary, was the statute directed against gifts in mortmain. Grants to religious houses were made void by the Great Charter, the plea, as before, being the loss of dues and services. But the Act of Edward inflicted a penalty on such transactions by introducing the interest of the Crown as a reversioner on such grants, when the giver or his heirs were indisposed to claim them, or the intermediate lord was negligent in setting up his right. But the devices by which the monastic orders strove to evade the Statutes of Mortmain, and the sleights by which they sought to cover their acquisitions, are well known to students of English law. As time went on, they contrived to get possession of charges, annuities, rents, and finally impropriations, where they were often out of the reach of any statutes.

As Edward has been called the English Justinian, so he is credited with being the author of the English House of Commons. The precedent had been set him by De Montfort, who seems to have wished to make the counties and towns, as well as his party among the nobles, accomplices in his designs. But I cannot imagine that Edward intended or foresaw that his Commons would take part in legislative action, then or thereafter. It is plain that the grants made to Henry were conceded by the nobles and prelates. It is certain that the taxes paid to Edward were contributed from valuations of all persons, their household goods, chattels, and corn in stock, serf as well as free, for the taxing rolls of Edward I. almost amount to a census of the families. It would appear, then, that the knights and burgesses were summoned to grant and distribute the tax, perhaps even to assess it. That they would inevitably, in time, criticize the occasion on which the tax was granted, that they would consider themselves entitled to withhold or refuse it, or burden it with conditions, any

statesman of the age might anticipate.   But Edward, though
he is constantly asking for taxes, constantly gets what he
wants.   There are several occasions on which Edward disregarded differences of tenure, and therefore of liability, and
strove to bring all his subjects under the same liabilities.   The
right of the Commons to a place in Parliament, under the
condition that enactments were not valid except with the
consent of the Commons, was affirmed for the first time at
York in 1322, when Edward's son was striving to restore the
Despensers, who had been banished by the Peers the year
before.

The principality of Wales had long acknowledged the
feudal superiority of the English Crown ; the kingdom of
Scotland had done so periodically.   Thus the suzerainty of
England was admitted in the reign of Henry II., remitted in
that of Richard.   But I presume that Edward's claim, fruitful
of so many miseries to both kingdoms, though it undoubtedly
had a great influence in moulding the national character of
the Scotch, was derived from the reputed claims of those
early English princes of whom the Norman conquerors
affected to be the rightful successors.   It is probably for
some reason of this kind that Edward is sometimes called
Edward IV., and his son Edward V.   The Lowland Scotch
were more strongly Teutonic in their origin than the English
themselves.   Perhaps there is no English king who has been
more variously depicted by his foes and by his subjects than
Edward.   With the one he is the greatest of the Plantagenets;
with the other he is an implacable and ruthless tyrant, who
trampled on the most sacred rights of nations and the most
undoubted title of his pupil, his subject, and his rebel, for
Robert Bruce was a Norman noble, who had been educated
and promoted by Edward, who had solemnly pledged his
allegiance to him, who was seduced by the prospect of a
crown, and murdered one nearer in blood than himself to that
crown, in order that he might, it appears, remove a rival
out of the way.

The administrative and military abilities of Edward were
plainly of a very high order.   He was reputed to be studiously

true to his word, to have been conspicuous in his own age for his integrity and good faith, and to have exacted similar fidelity from all who were under obligations to him. Hence his confirmation of the charters, and his pledges to levy taxes only with his subjects' consent, were concessions from which he did not mean to swerve, but to honourably keep. His reign is therefore an epoch in English history on which constitutional antiquaries love to dwell, and in which politicians of later ages have thought they could detect the development of English institutions.

The most successful part of Edward's administration was his short and decisive struggle with the Church. The time was favourable to him, for Boniface, whose pretensions were as exalted as those of any among his predecessors at the beginning of the century, had contrived to quarrel with Philip IV. of France ; and France has always been the most inconvenient foe which the Papacy has ever wrestled with. Deceived by the belief that Boniface could shelter them from Edward's authority, the English prelates seem to have determined to defy the king, perhaps to have obtained the very bull which forbade their obedience to his demands. The king put them out of his peace, that is, refused them the protection of the law, and excluded the bishops from Parliament. In the end they submitted, and granted the king his demands. But it is remarkable that this is the last occasion on which the clergy, as an order, resisted the authority of the Crown. In some particulars the occasion was favourable to them, for the quarrel with the bishops and clergy was simultaneous with the famous altercation of Edward with the two earls. But there appears to have been no party in the country which was willing to side with the Church, and it is only a pious belief that they had a notable part in the solemn confirmation of the charters.

The great reputation of Edward I. was followed by the scandals which marked the career of his foolish and disreputable son. Edward of Carnarvon was a person of considerable accomplishments, of graceful manners, and of genial temper. But from the first he roused to fury a party among his

13

nobles by his unseemly attachment to scandalous favourites. The gossip of the time affirmed that he was not the true son of the Hammer of the Scots, but that the real royal infant had been mutilated in his cradle by some animal, hog or dog, and that the nurse, fearing the king's displeasure at her carelessness, had substituted her own son. In just the same way, when his great-grandson, Richard II., became unpopular, a story was current that he was not the son of the Black Prince, but a supposititious or even adulterine child. Edward's reign was marked by unheard-of calamities. England suffered a famine to which there has not been before or since a parallel. To the disgust of the English people, his army was hopelessly defeated at Bannockburn, and all hope of recovering Scotland was lost. But, worst of all, the king was incurably attached to utterly hateful persons. Gaveston had been banished by the old king, and was instantly restored when death had removed the obstacle to Edward's affection for his favourite. He is again banished, and again restored; again driven into exile, again recalled, and finally murdered by the discontented lords. Edward vowed vengeance on his cousin, the ringleader of the party, and found the opportunity of satisfying his revenge nine years afterwards.

In the later years of the king's reign, the Despensers were the king's favourites, especially the younger. They excited the same animosity which had been roused by Gaveston, were banished, restored, and finally fell with their master. In the first attack on the Despensers, they were charged with usurping royal power. I find, in many accounts of the time, that they exercised the privilege of purveyance, *i.e.*, the compulsory purchase of agricultural products and merchants' goods, at fixed rates, paying for them by orders on the Exchequer; and the accounts frequently mention that bribes were given them in order to escape their exactions. Purveyance was an ancient right of the Crown, but I do not find that it was generally abused. It was occasionally inconvenient for the bailiff or farmer to have his stock entirely cleared out, even when full market prices were given for what was taken, but the bailiff rarely, if ever, notes that his master's goods were seized by the royal officers without payment, or for nominal sums. After the accession of the Stuarts, purveyance became a real grievance, for the Crown declared the contingent of live stock or provisions which a county should supply, fixed the price, often at one-third of the real value, and then called on the county to provide for the demand.

Edward was deposed on Jan. 7th, 1327, by the Lords and Commons in Parliament, after articles had been exhibited against him. Commissioners were sent from Westminster to Kenilworth, where he was, to inform him that his subjects had renounced their allegiance to him, and were no longer bound by their oaths. An oath of adherence to Isabella's quarrel was exacted from the nobles in Guildhall. Edward resigned, and his son was proclaimed. The Despensers, the king's favourites, were executed; the chancellor, Baldock, who had fled with the king, was thrown into prison; and Stapledon, Bishop of Exeter and Lord High Treasurer, was murdered by the London mob. This kind of violence shows that the people were irritated by fiscal oppression, for the public anger is directed against the officials of the Exchequer. The murder of Stapledon is a strong indication of the change which had come over the mind of Englishmen. It was an act of sacrilege, from which, a generation or two before, every one would have recoiled with horror. At the beginning of the next century, an archbishop was executed after judicial process; and fifty years after Scrope's death, two English bishops attached to the Court were murdered by infuriated mobs. In Edward's reign, too, the order of the Knights Templars was dissolved; and though these military ecclesiastics did not, in England, suffer the atrocious punishments which were inflicted on them in France, their possessions were confiscated, and a precedent given for dealing with the property of religious organizations.

The principal events of Edward the Third's reign are contained in his claim to the throne of France, and the great war of the French Succession, which continued, with interruptions of truce, from the Battle of Sluys to that of Chatillon. There were persons who believed, even in France, that

Edward's title was valid. Stated briefly, it was that he was the nearest male heir of Charles IV. Some historians, in commenting on the nature of Edward's claim, observe that Charles of Navarre was nearer in blood to the last king of the older stock; but this personage was not in existence when Edward's claim, whatever it was worth, accrued. The effect of this claim was a war which lasted, with intervals, for more than a hundred years, during which, at one time, the great province of Aquitaine, less, indeed, than the ancient dominions of Henry of Anjou, was annexed to the English crown by the Treaty of Bretigni; at another time, the succession in France was altered and transferred to Henry VI.

The English people were under the impression that the possession or acquisition of considerable transmarine dominions by the English king would lessen the burdens which the exigencies of the king's exchequer called upon them to bear. The more reasonable advocates of foreign empire pointed to the benefits which would accrue to trade by the possession of a country, the supplies of whose produce was a matter of high necessity to England, and whose people might be purchasers of English produce. In any case, it was of great military importance that the country should have for itself some means of entry into France. Thus Calais was conceived to be of the greatest value to England. It was garrisoned with extraordinary care. The charge of maintaining it was a heavy burden on the English exchequer. It was made the principal mart for English produce, or, in the phraseology of the time, the staple was fixed there. The custody of Calais was the highest office of trust which the king could confer on any subject. The acquisition of Boulogne by Henry VIII., in the latter part of his reign, was also conceived to be of supreme military significance. The loss of Calais was a sign, though not the cause, of the decline of English influence on the Continent. When Elizabeth succeeded, she affected to be anxious for its recovery. But this wise queen knew that the recovery of it would be a most serious burden on her finances, and that political strength does not always consist in the possession of strong places. When, during the splendid career of Cromwell, Dunkirk was captured from the Spanish Netherlands, no part of the Protector's career, not even the capture of the Plate fleet, excited so much enthusiasm as the acquisition of this town on the French border. When, after the Restoration, Charles prudently, but meanly, sold it, at Clarendon's instigation, as was believed, to the King of France, the English public was excited to extreme wrath at the event, nicknamed Clarendon's new mansion Dunkirk House, pretended to believe that it was built out of the bribes given for the surrender of the town, and drove the owner into exile.

The wars of Edward took place at a time in which the spirit of ancient feudalism was breaking down, and a military system was supplanting it. Edward had taken advantage of the latter before France had rid itself of the former. Hence his armies, composed of selected men, taken from every class of the community where likely recruits could be found, were picked, drilled, and kept under discipline. Though they were numerically always inferior, the chivalry of France was scattered in confusion before them. They were taken to Spain, and the Spanish militia was easily routed at Navaretto. For generations they were the best troops in Europe. Sometimes a captain of the companies, when employment at the seat of war was scanty and pay was not to be had, migrated to Italy or Germany. Thus Sir John Hawkwood, one of Edward's captains, served the republic of Florence. These companies were the scourge of France, pillaging friend or foe indifferently. The French peasantry rose in insurrection against them, committed horrible atrocities on the chivalry which had oppressed them, and made havoc where they could. The combatants suspended their hostilities, made common cause against the peasants, and drove them back into even more abject misery.

The oppression of the French roturier dates from the evil days of the first war of the French Succession. The miseries of the Thirty Year's War in Germany were not, I believe, more terrible than the calamitous times of Philip of Valois, John, and Charles V. While the English yeoman was growing in

opulence and spirit, and even the English serf was attaining
a legal tenancy, the French peasant was becoming more and
more degraded, more hopelessly ground down between the
two great millstones of the king and the aristocracy. In
France, from the days of Philip Augustus to those of
Louis XIV., the struggle was always between king and
nobles, for the French king never had the wit to make the
people his friends. At one time the great feudatories, Normandy, Toulouse, and Guienne, were striving after independence, and seeking to limit the kings of the House of Capet
to the city and outskirts of Paris, as generations before
the kings of the House of Charles the Great were confined
to Laon and its suburbs. At another, a party of nobles is
willing, for its own ends, to give the crown to a foreigner.
The most sagacious act of Edward was to accept Aquitaine,
which he could manage, in lieu of the throne of France, where,
even if he had exterminated every pretender of the House of
Valois, he would have had an incessant struggle with the
turbulent chivalry of the kingdom. A generation or two
later, and the crown of France is the prize which the Bur-
gundians and Armagnacs were ready to offer to the claimant
which would give them the best price for the splendid bauble,
while either would make the acquisition intolerable to the
king of their choice. The King of England, sometime King
of France, is expelled, and the faction fight revives, under the
grotesque name of the War of the Public Good, the most impudent fiction which a party has ever assumed. In the next
century the conspiracy of the nobles against the sovereign is
that of the Huguenots and the faction of the House of Guise.
The genius and contempt of Henry curbs the factions for a time,
and the traditions of his policy are inherited, though with far
inferior sagacity, by Richelieu, who succeeded in discovering
a *modus vivendi* with the Huguenots, while he strengthened
the central authority. He and his wretched, selfish, callous
master, Louis XIII., whose brother was even baser than he
was, pass away, and again the ever-present conspiracy breaks
out in the war of the Fronde. That the French have endured
a monarch or a despot is intelligible, for he has been the

symbol of order and government. But I can well understand that a Frenchman who had the most superficial knowledge of his own country's history, or had even experienced a traditional instinct, should have loathed his aristocrats, and should have rent them, even when, as in 1789, they postured on behalf of the people's rights.

I know nothing in history which is sadder than the story of the French peasant. The picture which Michelet gives of him in his better days implies and contains the accumulated tragedy of generations. From century to century the gulf between him and the privileged classes grew deeper and deeper. He bore all the burdens of government, taxes in money, taxes in produce, taxes in blood, and was treated, as time went on, with increasing brutality and contempt. The France of the writer of memoirs and novels is the country of fine ladies and gentlemen, in which the mass of Frenchmen counts for absolutely nothing, except to be robbed and cudgelled. When the economists urged a reform in the laws which regulated husbandry and its products, they had nothing to say about the rights of the roturier, but dwelt on the supreme utility of his industry. But in England the case was very different. The yeoman and the noble were on the same level as regards the law and the Crown. The former was constantly being levelled up to the latter, till at last the incidents of the farmer's tenancy being found to be more convenient and less onerous than those of the military occupant, the estate of the noble and the knight was levelled down to that of the yeoman and the peasant. The picture which Fortescue in the fifteenth century gives of the English franklins and freeholders, and the contrast which he draws between their condition and the beggarly poverty of the French husbandman, where the civil law is supreme, and the kingdom is not "political," as he calls a constitutional monarchy,—borrowing the term from the politics of Aristotle, —but one which is absolute in theory and arbitrary in practice, shows that even at this time the difference between the husbandmen of the two nations was striking and appreciated.

The war of the French Succession inflicted excessive misery

on France and permanent degradation on her peasantry. But it also did England the mischief of creating that most dangerous of all classes,—the professional soldier. This inconvenience is not so manifest in the fourteenth as it was in the fifteenth century, when the hired partizans of the two factions literally destroyed each other, and England for a century became a despotism under parliamentary forms.

The constant want of money for his foreign campaigns made Edward more than ever dependent on his Parliaments. In course of time the chambers are separated, and sit apart. In course of time the function of granting taxes is left to the Commons, for as the king sat with his lords, the debate as to the king's necessities was best carried on in a chamber from which he was absent, and from which, as far as possible, the ministers of the Crown were excluded. At last the king himself consults his Commons on questions of public policy. Thus, in 1366, he put the question to them, what course of action they should recommend, in case the pope put his threat into execution of citing the king to Avignon, to make answer for default in the non-payment of the tribute granted by John for the realm of England and the lordship of Ireland ; and in 1369, the Parliament is asked whether, in their opinion, the King of England should resume the title of King of France, *i.e.*, engage afresh in war at their expense. At the conclusion of the king's reign they revive or invent the process of Parliamentary impeachment, or, at least, energetic criticism in Parliament on the conduct of the king's ministers. The declining years of Edward were clouded by military reverses and domestic troubles. His eldest son, who had declared himself on the side of the popular discontents, predeceased him, leaving an heir only ten years old. His third son, John of Gaunt, the titular King of Castile, through whom the claims of Philip of Spain to the English throne were derived, was credited with ambitious aims, and with having proposed that the issue of females should be declared to be out of the royal succession.

The old king was succeeded by a child. The natural guardian of the realm during the king's minority was John of Gaunt. But the custody of the king's person and the administration of affairs appears to have been left in the hands of his mother. The war in France languished ; there were quarrels, becoming more and more bitter, among the members of the royal house ; and the Duke of Gloucester took the position of a regular opposition to the king, which the Earl of Lancaster had taken in opposition to the king's great-grandfather. Already the precedent of that reign was talked about. As early as 1386, Richard was threatened with a sentence of deposition. In the same year the Commons proceed to the impeachment of an unpopular minister. In the next, the king's attempt to obtain a legal decision in favour of his prerogative, and the premature disclosure of his design led to the uprising of the lords appellants. But the combination of the nobles was soon broken up, and Richard regained his authority. For some years he remained on terms of apparent amity with his former enemies, but nourished his animosity towards them with that patient dissimulation which is the only sign of persistent vigour in a man whose character is otherwise weak and uncertain. At last he found himself able to strike. Gloucester was arrested and murdered at Calais ; Arundel was executed after trial ; and the Archbishop of Canterbury was banished. Soon after this followed the banishment of Norfolk and Bolingbroke, the unlucky expedition to Ireland, the death of John of Gaunt, whose possessions the king unwisely and illegally confiscated, the return of Bolingbroke, the general uprising of the nation against Richard and his government, and the king's formal deposition.

The political troubles of Richard's reign were, I am convinced, greatly inflamed by the number of military adventurers whom the cessation of the French war had brought back to England. In the early years of Richard, we read that formidable bands of brigands had established themselves in various parts of England, especially in Lancashire and Cheshire, which were under a special jurisdiction, and that they committed incredible atrocities. The Commons explain the great insurrection of 1381, to which I shall hereafter refer in detail, to the existence of these lawless bands, and to the impunity with which they committed their crimes. But they also complain of the grievance of purveyance, and the discontent which it caused among the peasantry. It is highly probable that during the non-age of the king, the principal servants of the Crown may have abused their power, and that the king's half-brothers, the Holands, may have committed the offences of which the Despensers were guilty. But I see also in these banditti, as well as in the rapidity with which the discontented nobles could collect an army, that there must have been a large body of persons in the country who had followed the profession of arms, who were ready to be enlisted by any one who could offer them pay, and quite prepared for acts of violence. Still we do not hear that the peasantry was plundered.

The long war with France, though from many notices in the rolls of Parliament it seems to have been certainly popular, was attended with great expense. The principal source from which supplies were derived was an assessment on the personal estate of every householder. When such a tax was granted in Parliament, assessors were appointed to value property and collect the proceeds. It is possible that the duty of this assessment and collection was originally imposed on the representatives who assented to the tax. If so, the practice was found inconvenient, for in the parliament of 1352, a grant by the Commons is made on the condition that no knight, citizen, or burgess of parliament should be a collector of the aid so granted. This limitation is frequently repeated on subsequent occasions.

Parliaments were held constantly during Edward the Third's reign for financial and legislative purposes. Even in the early part of it, a promise was made that Parliament should sit every year once, and even oftener, if necessary. From the time, too, in which Edward began to prosecute his claims, first in Scotland and next in France, he was constantly appealing to his subjects for assistance,—the counties, the towns, and the clergy. The general rule was that a fifteenth should be levied on the counties, a tenth on the cities and the boroughs and the clergy. These fifteenths and tenths were granted at least eleven times during the reign, as well as seven other contributions designated as grants, or subsidies, or aids.

In 1339 and 1340, when the war was beginning, very great efforts were made. In the first year a tithe was given to the king of corn, fleeces, and lambs; and in the second, the grant of a ninth of each of these agricultural products was conceded for two years. On both occasions the "bondmen" of the lords were exempted from the charge. The inhabitants of towns were to pay an equivalent.

But the most novel and important financial expedients are those adopted in 1341, in addition to the tithe named above, in 1371 and in 1377. Each of these requires a short comment.

In the first of these years, the king having warned his parliament and the clergy three years before that he was about to enter on a most serious and costly war, besides the large grants in produce, which were of course redeemed at market rates, the Commons offer an aid of 30,000 sacks of wool, under certain conditions. In order to assist the king's credit, they pledge themselves in any case to guarantee 2,500 sacks, which they make a free gift to him. It is clear, then, that in the case of a grant like this, perhaps in the case of any grant, the king anticipated the revenue which he should receive by borrowing money on the security of future income. We know that he did this to a great extent, that two Florentine houses made considerable advances to him, and that they suffered great losses when, subsequently, he was unable to meet his engagements. There was, however, no grant which was of greater value for the purpose of negotiating commercial bills than wool, for it was always saleable, especially in Flanders, where the king at this time had amicable relations with the popular leaders.

It might be supposed that the grant of so large an amount of the staple produce of England at such a crisis, to be disposed of by a sudden sale, in case the payment were made in kind or redeemed at market rates, in the event of the obligation being met in such a manner, as it was from those who were not sheep-masters, would have materially reduced the market value of the article. But no such result ensues ; wool had indeed been cheap for some years past, about 25 per cent. below what had been the average for half a century ; but immediately on the settlement of this financial operation, the price rose to nearly the old average, and remained comparatively high. The fact is, the monopoly of this produce was so absolute, and the necessity of procuring it was so urgent, that even so large a quantity as 30,000 sacks, which I conclude to have been nearly a tenth of the annual produce of the kingdom, though made the basis probably of a single or, at any rate, a concerted commercial transaction, was put on the market, or at least was known to be forthcoming, without the price of the article being adversely affected. As I have stated, the price immediately rose.

The average price of wool during the nine years 1349-47 was 3*s.* 6½*d.* the stone of fourteen pounds ; while the average prices for the seventy years 1261-1330 was 4*s.* 8½*d.* Hence the sack of wool was worth at the time of the grant about 92*s.* This closely corresponds to the average of the values given to the different kinds of wool by Parliament in 1452, when the Commons petitioned that wool of the qualities named and priced in the schedule should not be exported at less than the price quoted, under a penalty of £40 the sack. In the year 1452, I find that the average value of wool was 3*s.* 4*d.* the stone, according to such sales as I have found, or 86*s.* 8*d.* the sack. The average of the Parliamentary schedule is 90*s.* 3*d.*

The Commons, or some commissioners appointed for the purpose, scheduled the several counties and four towns, London, Bristol, Newcastle, and York, omitting, as usual, Durham and Chester, the two counties palatine, which were not represented in Parliament, but were undoubtedly assessed and taxed by the proper authorities. The assessment is exceedingly minute, descending to quarters of pounds, and is undoubtedly, according to the lights of the time, an exact and equitable distribution of an exceptional tax proportionately to the reputed wealth of the several counties. I have

already commented by anticipation on this and similar assessments, when I was treating of the comparative opulence or
poverty of the several English counties in the fourteenth
century. For this purpose any value might have been assigned to the sack of wool, and I accordingly took 80s. as the
market value of the unit, since it formed a convenient multiple, and, according to the practice constantly adopted by
statisticians, I added a unit to the gross sum when the fraction
was over half, and omitted all notice of it when it was less.

The quantity of wool assessed over the thirty-seven counties
and four towns is a good deal less than the grant. It amounts
to 20,376 sacks, and, at 80s. the sack, it is valued at £81,504.
It is quite possible that the king accepted a less amount than
the Commons offered in their burst of enthusiasm after the
great naval victory of Sluys, as more than a century later
Henry VI., or his advisers, accepted a less grant than his
Commons were willing to give him after the revolt of Guienne.
But it will be seen that, taking the actual price of wool at the
time, the grant amounted in money value to £138,000, an
enormous sum, and far in excess of any similar grant, for the
subsidy of a fifteenth and tenth on the property of laymen
amounted to about £38,176; and this, as the war went on,
was conceived a reasonable annual contribution to its
expenses.

It does not follow that the tax was paid in kind. In the
case of the towns it is improbable that it should have been;
and as the grant of the tax is unaccompanied by an equivalent
contribution from the districts where, as Parliament says on
other occasions, corn and sheep are not found, the payment
in kind could have been no possible convenience to the king,
and would have been a very great inconvenience to the
burgesses. In accordance with such an hypothesis I find
that the fellows of Merton College paid on their Cambridge
and Chesterton property certain sums in two instalments—on
the former of 40s., on the latter of 5s.—as their contribution to
the great wool tax of 1340-1. It is plain that these were not
only money payments, but assessments in money.

In 1346, the king claimed the aid which was payable out of

every knight's fee on the occasion of his eldest son being made a knight. He demanded 40s.; but the Commons answered that by the Statute of Westminster the first, this aid had been fixed at 20s. Such a sum was, I find, actually paid from two of the Merton College estates on this ground. But at another of these estates the quarter of a knight's fee pays 10s. It is noteworthy that an aid for knighting the king's eldest son was not paid again by the military tenants of the Crown till 1503, when Henry VII. demanded it on behalf of Arthur, who had actually died three years before. If, as was stated commonly,—for instance, in Wynkyn de Worde's "Chronicle of England," printed in 1489,—the knights' fees in England were 75,000, of which the "men of religion" had 27,015, the receipts from this aid were a very notable sum. But numbers are habitually exaggerated in these estimates. The next tax on which I shall comment is a well-known instance of the untrustworthiness of early statistical calculations.

In 1371, the Commons give the king a round sum of £50,000 in an assessment of an average of 22s. 3d. on each parish in England. This estimated the number of English parishes at nearly 44,950. But it was speedily found that the number of parishes had been absurdly miscalculated, and they at once amended their grant by assessing the parishes at an average of 106s., which gives about 9,434 as the real number. This is probably accurate. I find several entries of taxes to a large amount paid during this year; but as the clergy gave an equal sum of £50,000 from their revenues, and two, at least, of the payments are from impropriate tithe, and a third maybe, the amount is from too uncertain a source to be suggestive. The payment from a fourth is undoubtedly from a lay holding, and is twenty-five per cent. above the amount ordinarily paid on account of a subsidy.

The third of these financial expedients is the poll-tax of 1377. It was 4d. on all persons of both sexes over fourteen years of age, mere mendicants excepted; a shilling on all beneficed clergy; and 4d. on all non-beneficed clergy. I have already referred to this tax, as it gives information about the amount of the population in England, and supplies other valuable statistics for the fourteenth century. The tax, if we can rely on the numbers, must have brought in a little less than £24,000; but its unfairness could hardly fail of being irritating. Even when the poll-tax was graduated in the next reign, it became the immediate, though not the real, cause of Tyler's insurrection. Probably, however, the Commons were at their wits' end for expedients, and a tax which was suggested by the charge for enrolling names on the manor record, and which treated the whole of the king's subjects as the members of a vast manor, appeared obvious and natural. The threefold payment made by the beneficed clergy accords with the view which, as we have seen, generally prevailed, that the proportion contributed by them ought to be larger than that of the laity.

It may be convenient at this point to say a little about the incidence of taxation, and the proportion which it bore to income. I have never, as my reader will anticipate, found an unbroken series of accounts from any manor or parish. There are gaps in them all, even though care was originally taken for their preservation. The wonder is rather that so many have survived in muniment rooms, when all interest in their existence had passed away, and they were often thrown in heaps on damp stone or tiled floors. Thus for the fifty years of Edward the Third's reign, of the annual rolls of one estate, constantly cultivated by its owners, up to the last year of Edward's reign, twenty-nine alone survive; and in nineteen of these years, the estate pays a fifteenth to the king, in one the tax twice over, the impost of two years having been probably collected in one. It is probable also that in not a few cases the lord paid the tax to the collector at his own audit when he was in receipt of money.

On one particular estate, the farming profits of which I have exactly estimated, and which amount to about £30 a year, the amount of a fifteenth imposed by Parliament is, on an average of three years, about 30s., or five per cent.; and this I should conclude was the ordinary incidence of a fourteenth century subsidy. The wool tax, however, if it had been paid in full and assessed proportionately, would have been between three

and four times the amount of the ordinary subsidy, or about
18 per cent. of the annual profits of the estate. And this I
find is nearly verified by the amount of taxation paid on other
properties. A fifteenth on an estate at Cambridge is 10s. ; the
wool tax, as I stated above, is 40s.

The rolls of Parliament, from which we derive all our
knowledge of public business from the thirteenth to the beginning of the sixteenth century, are far from perfect. Many
of the records have been lost. When the journals of the two
Houses began with the reign of Henry VIII., that of the
Lords, though the early years exist, has large gaps in its continuity, while that of the Commons is lost for Henry's reign, the
record commencing with the reign of Edward VI. In consequence, my accounts, though I did not record the payment of
taxes on any but the Merton College properties and one or
two besides, give me many more taxes than the rolls of Parliament grant to the king. There are only eight out of the fifty
years of Edward's reign in which one or the other of these
estates is not represented as paying the king a tenth or fifteenth
as a tax or a subsidy. The estate at Leatherhead, which pays
nineteen taxes in the twenty-nine years for which its accounts
are preserved, had about 160 acres under the plough, earned
about the same profit, some £30 a year, from its agricultural
operations, and pays about five per cent. on its profits when it
contributes to a subsidy. After the Great Plague, its payments
drop to half their original amount. The same shrinkage of
taxable property is observed in other estates, and it is therefore possible that the amount of a subsidy in the later years of
Edward is considerably less than the amount which was
collected before that great social convulsion occurred. At
any rate, if the wool tax of 1340-1 represented a charge of
18 per cent. on the annual profits of labour and capital, the
net income of the English people at the time was probably
about £766,600 a year, or a little over 6s. a head, to be saved
by labour, or appropriated by the non-producing classes.

The taxes paid to the king were by no means the whole
of the charges which were imposed upon the fourteenth
century Englishman. The pope and his minions, the car-

dinals, the archbishop, the bishop, and the archdeacon levy their charges, generally in the form of a percentage on receipts. The amount varies considerably. It is sometimes as much as two-and-a-half per cent. on the taxpayer's income, in this case the recipient of an ecclesiastical revenue, sometimes at no more than a halfpenny in the mark. The payments to the pope are most noticeable during the weak reign of Edward II., who, we are informed, paid John's tribute regularly. Thus on one estate in Cambridgeshire a payment is made to the pope in 1314 for six years, *i.e.*, for the whole period during which Edward had been reigning. These taxes to foreign ecclesiastics became rarer during Edward the Third's reign, but do not disappear. I find them up to the close of his reign.

Sometimes the estate pays a regular tax, quite distinct from those which are levied by authority of Parliament. Thus one pays a fixed sum under the head of foreign service, another a tax called the king's gabelle. In each case the amount is precisely, or almost precisely, the half of the ordinary fifteenth. I find no record in the rolls of Parliament of a tax of the twentieth sack of wool given in 1347, amounting to nearly three times the ordinary fifteenth, and paid in several places. So sometimes a locality is charged with the maintenance of soldiers, to repel an invasion or raid of the Scotch; or a levy is made upon inland counties for the "ward of the sea," the precedent for Noy's ship money. Similar to these are a contribution made by a Cambridgeshire parish for the burial of the dead in Scotland in 1321, the year in which Edward made his second foolish expedition into that kingdom. But these charges are exceptional and rare.

When the Parliament became a regular institution, and the Convocations of the two provinces were summoned and duly warned of the obligation that they must meet, to discuss the king's necessities and supply the requisite means for the defence of the kingdom and the maintenance of the king's estate and rights, the parties represented were bound to pay wages to the knights, citizens, and burgesses who appeared for the laity, and the proctors who appeared for the Convocation

14

of the clergy. The prelates were in both assemblies, in a double capacity and under a double duty, as lords of parliament and peers. They held by barony, and were liable to the ordinary obligations of the Crown's vassals. As the recipients of incomes derived from estates in free alms or other benefices, they were of the clergy, and made their grants for such estates in Convocation. It seems that for this reason a distinction is constantly drawn between two kinds of clerical estates, or rather estates held by clergymen. Some of these are said to be amortized at or after a given date; some to have been in the hands of these dignitaries from time immemorial. It was an object with the ecclesiastics to escape what might be, perhaps was, a double risk. The Abbot of Osney, in Oxford, and the Abbot of Thorney, in Cambridgeshire, constantly claim to be relieved of attendance at secular assemblies. They sometimes succeed in proving a license of exemption; but it is clear that there is an adviser of the Crown, who counsels the permanent officials that this is a disputable shift, and that the abbots must come to parliament, all objections notwithstanding. In point of fact, absence from parliament is a sign of disaffection among the lay lords and of evasion among the spiritual peers; and just as absentees were treated with considerable severity if they were nobles, and with very significant threats, even of confiscation, if they were ecclesiastical dignitaries, so it is clear that the Government was clearly alive to the wisdom of compelling an appearance and submission to the general rule.

The payment made to the proctor in Convocation is generally a rate. The ordinary amount is a halfpenny per mark of income; and probably if these payments, in which a sum is given, could be referred to known quantities, it would be found that the basis of the payment was always a fixed amount. In the case of lay representation, the amount could not be anticipated in this way.

The Member of Parliament had daily wages; the knights or county members receiving more—the amount is not invariable—than the burgesses. When the Parliament was prorogued or dismissed (it is premature to use the word dissolved), the writs for payment were made out, and the time during which the House sat was exactly calculated. Now it is plain that the charge put by representation on a small town was a far more onerous burden on the inhabitants than that imposed on a county. Hence the burgesses were frequently dismissed, in the early days of Parliament, long before the knights were, though we may, I think, conclude that the former would be held to their attendance if duties common to town and county were before parliament. To many of the towns representation was a formidable burden, was most unwillingly borne, and was gladly evaded. Even in the counties there was a struggle, which lasted for a century, and which the Crown always refused to decide at the instance of the Commons, under which the old tenants of the Crown, those in ancient demesne, were relieved from contribution to the wages of the knights of the shire, though these tenants had long been taxed by the same Act and on the same principle as other people had. But with the towns the cost was always grudged. Even in the opulent city of Norwich the expense was serious. The cost of representation is a considerable item in the municipal accounts.

If I am correct in my conclusion that the direct taxation of the fourteenth century, though frequent, and during the war almost annual in its imposition, was not more than five per cent. on the net profits of agriculture, and probably less on manufactures and trade, one cannot but be struck at the discontent and impatience with which the appeals to Parliament are received. The Commons plead that they are impoverished and wasted by incessant subsidies; that the country cannot bear the charges which the Government seeks to impose on it; and that the patience of the people is taxed beyond endurance. Part of these complaints are, no doubt, the real expression of those who found they had but a very narrow margin of receipts over expenditure, and felt the urgency of any drain. But most of this dissatisfaction is due to the form which taxation took—the ransom, namely, of one's chattels from an inquisitive and rapacious inquiry. Our forefathers, too, were under the impression that, except on rare occasions, when it was certainly the duty of the subject to aid his king, the king could live, and ought to live, on his hereditary revenue, ample if properly husbanded, and constantly receiving accretions from well-known and obvious sources. The prince, they argued, has a vast estate. If he is so weak and lavish that his wealth, which he possesses in order that his subjects may not be harassed by exactions, is wasted on favourites, it is intolerable that his people should be the victims of his or their waste. His household should be ordained, his expenditure controlled, his grants resumed, his favourites banished. So before the deposition of Edward and Richard, attempts were made to reduce the royal expenditure by an interference in the king's private affairs and by the sumptuary regulations of his palace. Above all things, the Englishman of the middle ages disliked any indefinite risk in his liabilities. Hence in Edward's time the amount which was to be paid in a subsidy was finally fixed, and grants were made on condition that there should be no alteration whatever in the assessment. The grant once conceded, the locality distributed the charge over those who were liable to it. This ancient and continuous precedent was followed in the last of these grants, the land-tax of the Revolution, which has remained on the assessment of 1692.

It is always difficult to raise a revenue from direct taxation in a country where industry is mainly agricultural. The financier of the middle ages had no other resource, besides land and goods, on which to lay his charges. Even if the scanty consumption of foreign articles could have borne any check beyond the trifling import duties which were imposed on it, the charge of collecting the customs would have exhausted, perhaps have exceeded, the receipts. Besides, the customs duties were virtually an octroi on the larger towns. The south and east of England are full of creeks into which the light vessels of the time could easily run and discharge a cargo without risk of detection. After the Union of England and Scotland was effected, it was necessary to put the northern kingdom under the English revenue laws, for otherwise Scotland would have a free port for smugglers. But for nearly a century the receipts of the Scotch custom houses, according to Macpherson, were quite insufficient to satisfy the charges incurred in collecting the duties on imports. It is probable that with a view to the king's revenue, particular towns were designated as staple ports for various products, and the sale of such products to the foreign exporter was forbidden in any other locality. In the fourteenth century the English financier had not yet learned how important and elastic a source of revenue was the export duty on wool.

Constant attempts were made to obtain a release from the payment of direct taxation by petition to the Crown. In the year 1347, the warden and fellows of Merton College, Oxford, prayed the king that their land should be relieved from all tallages, fifteenths, and prises, and every other charge beyond the tithes of their churches, and that they might hold all their possessions in free alms. On this the king, by his son Lionel, the Warden of England, directs that an inquisition should be held by the escheator of the county of Oxford, and a return made of all the lands and tenements which they possess in the county, a similar inquiry being directed, no doubt, to the proper official in other counties where they held possessions. The inquiry was also to include information as to the injury which the king or others would receive if the prayer of the petitioners were granted. There is indirect evidence that the inquiry was duly held, and direct proof that the application was unsuccessful, for the College after this time pays these taxes to the Crown on its Oxford property from which it prayed to be relieved.

Later on it became a common custom to insert exemptions in Parliamentary grants. Thus the Colleges of Eton and Winchester and the Universities of Oxford and Cambridge are frequently, and at last regularly, excused from taxation. The same favour is shown to certain towns whose, revenues had diminished, or which had otherwise become impoverished.

In some cases payments of money are made to the assessors

which are obviously bribes to secure a favourable valuation. The knowledge that this risk was always run, perhaps an occasional detection of the culprits, would have materially aided the demand that the assessment of the fifteenth should be a fixed and invariable quantity, and should be distributed, though not collected, by those who made the grant and earned the wages of a public service.

CHAPTER VIII.

THF FAMINE AND THE PLAGUE.

THE average price of a quarter of wheat for the 280 years, 1261-1540, is 5s. 11¼d. During this long period there were years of exceptional plenty and of exceptional scarcity, the range being from 2s. 10½d., the average of the year 1287, the lowest, and 16s. in 1316, the highest recorded. The latter year is, however, one of famine. In 1315, the average was about 1s. 2d. lower. In 1438, the price was 14s. 7½d. In 1527, it is nearly 13s. On two other occasions it nearly reaches 12s. On four occasions it is a little over 10s. Four shillings, according to Walter de Henley, was a price below remuneration, unless the crop was more than six bushels to the acre. In ordinary years, the price varies between 4s. 6d. and 6s. 6d. There are, of course, prices paid which are greatly above the highest average, and others which are a great deal below the lowest. The highest price which I have found during the whole period is a sale on May 30th, 1316, at Leatherhead, where two quarters are sold at 26s. 8d. If there be any scarcity, the market is always at its highest in May, because the stock of the past harvest is falling low, and the prospects of the next are uncertain. In this case, the harvest of 1315 was found after Christmas to have been exceedingly deficient. That of 1316 was as bad, so low that the scarcity was hardly lightened during any part of the period between harvest and harvest. The highest quotation of wheat in modern English history was in March 1801, when it was returned at 156s. 2d. This, however, is not much more than double the customary price of the time. In the two years 1315-16, the average was nearly three times, and on the occasion quoted above, five times, the ordinary price.

I do not think, however, that the climate of England from the forty-fifth year of Henry III. to the thirty-first of Henry VIII., 280 years in all, could be treated as extraordinarily capricious or treacherous, since in only ten of the years did the price of wheat nearly reach or exceed double the average, the two greatest scarcities of 1316 and 1438 being separated by an interval of 122 years, and the third, that of 1527, occurring after an interval of eighty-nine years. It may be stated, too, that when the harvest is bad, it is always worst on a belt which lies between the Thames and the Wash, and includes the Midland and Eastern Counties. Hence the whole of the country is seldom similarly affected, South Wales and the southern promontory of Cornwall and Devon being generally more favoured when bad harvests afflict the Midland and Eastern Counties. This is even seen at the commencement of the great famine of 1315-16, for during the first year, the Welsh and extreme West were not so seriously injured. In the second year, the ruin is universal. As may be expected, corn is generally cheapest in the early winter, dearest in the early summer, even when the price is at an average, unless the previous year has been one of comparative scarcity, when the purchase of seed always affects the average. If the prospects of the coming year are of abundance, the rise in May and June is very slight, and hardly appreciable. There is, I think, reason to conclude, on looking at the course of the wheat markets, that information as to the aggregate crop was very widely diffused, and that corn was sent to very considerable distances for sale. There were horses and carts in plenty, the rate of carriage was low, and the bailiff could easily reach a market where there was a demand. Beyond question, the surplus produce of country places was taken to the nearest towns, and sometimes to those which were at a distance.

The cause of bad harvests is always excessive rain. In the years 1315-16, we are told that the wet was incessant, and much of the corn never ripened. Contemporary writers tell us that the poorer classes were constrained to live on unwholesome or disgusting food, and that numbers of them perished from famine. An attempt was made to procure corn from the Continent, and ordinances were published fixing maximum prices—of course without avail, and prohibiting the consumption of beer, as was done in 1800 with the distilleries. To add to the distress, a pestilential murrain broke out among the cattle, and the bailiffs' rolls bear testimony to the universality of the disease, and the magnitude of the losses. It is said by chroniclers, that in the universal scarcity, numbers of servants and domestics were discharged; that, made desperate, these people became banditti; and that the country folk were constrained to associate themselves in arms, in order to check the depredations of those starving outlaws.

That the famines of this unfortunate period led to a considerable loss of life is proved by the unquestionable rise in the rate of agricultural wages after their occurrence. This is visible in the payments made for threshing corn, and still more markedly in those for reaping, where the rise is fully a penny an acre, the exaltation in the rates for oats and rye, previously the lowest paid, being the most considerable. The same rise is seen in payments for mowing, for thatching, and for women's labour. Now it is generally the case that, unless the labourer is paid at a rate which leaves him no margin over his necessary subsistence, an increase in the price of his food is not followed by an increase in the rate of wages, this result being arrived at only when there is a scarcity of hands. We shall see, when we come to deal with the wages of the sixteenth century, how slight was the rise in their amount compared with that of other values. Now the exigencies of the weather put certain opportunities within the reach of the labourers which, as their numbers had now become scantier, they could easily use. The immediate rise in the wages of labour after the famine of Edward the Second's reign is as much as from 23 to 30 per cent., and a considerable amount of this becomes a permanent charge on the costs of agriculture. That part which is permanent amounts to 20 per cent. on an average.

The habit of cutting corn high up on the straw, and therefore of avoiding weeds, must have materially shortened the drying process, and subsequently that of threshing out the grain. Hence I conclude, if the corn only ripened, the mere presence of rain was not so injurious as it came to be, when, at a later period, the corn was cut low with the weeds. That this change took place is proved by the statement of Fitzherbert, who advises that corn used for home consumption should not be screened too carefully, as the seeds of many weeds in corn supply a notable quantity of meal which might well be saved for flour. In Arthur Young's times, it is again clear that wheat was cut high on the stalk.

During the reign of Edward II., the practice became increasingly general to accept money compensations in lieu of labour rents, and by the end of the first quarter of the century the rule had become almost universal. It was to the interest of both parties that these commutations should be effected. It was a vexation to the tenant that he should be called away from the work of his own holding to do the lord's labour. It is plain, from Walter de Henley's statement, quoted above, that the bailiff had no little trouble in getting the due quota of work from the tenant, some three roods of first ploughing a day, or an acre of second stirring. Hence, if the lord could get a fair money compensation for the labour, he could spare the cost of the bailiff's supervision over unwilling labourers. And as money was more useful than the work he got, as well as perhaps more profitable in the end, he would be induced to make liberal terms with his tenants in villeinage, even if he were not morally constrained to take the alternative in money, which was prescribed as an alternative in case the labourer, for any cause, made default in the field. At the same time he could, unless he made a special bargain, save the allowances which he made of bread and beer, and the license of every day taking as large a sheaf as the serf could lift on his sickle from the corn crops. These commutations would be entered on the manor rental, and would tend to assimilate the tenure of the serf, now increasingly called a tenant by copy or custom, with that of the freeholder who sat at a fee farm rent, besides familiarising all parties with the redemption of those contingencies which affected the status of a serf. Ultimately the money payments would be deemed to be fixed and determinate liabilities, the satisfaction of which was a discharge of all the old labour rents, and the proffer of which was a tender which the steward was bound to accept. I do not mean to say that the change was invariable, for there is evidence that the monasteries clung to the old system longer than lay lords did, and it is alleged that, while the regular clergy urged on these lords the expediency and humanity of enfranchising their serfs, they failed to practise in their own persons the moderation which they commended to their patrons and their penitents.

The period which intervened between the last of three bad harvests and the great event to which I shall next advert was one of exceptional prosperity. The harvests were generally abundant, the wages of labour had been permanently improved, and all kinds of produce were cheap. The early days of the great war did not impair the general well-being of the English people. The supremacy of England on the sea was assured, and the famous battle of Crecy was fought, less considerable in its immediate consequences than in the exalted reputation which it conferred on English arms. But this country, and all Europe with it, was on the verge of a great calamity, the most extensive in its immediate incidence, and the most significant in its ultimate effects, of all events which have happened in the history of this country, and, indeed, of all Europe.

The Black Death is alleged to have had its origin in the

centre of China, in or about the year 1333, and is reported
to have been accompanied by various phenomena in the earth
and atmosphere of a very novel and destructive character,
such, indeed, as were noticed as long ago as in the plagues
of Athens and the simultaneous visitations at Rome, or the
mortality which prevailed in northern Europe near three
centuries before our era, and at the terrible pestilence which
visited the known world in the age of Justinian. So in later
times the cholera and the influenza were traced to particular
spots in India or China, which had been desolated by earth-
quakes, as Justinian's plague was said to have had its origin
at Pelusium. Nearly every infectious or contagious disease
which has desolated mankind appears to have had its origin
in the farthest East, and to have travelled along thence to
Europe, though the yellow fever is said to be a product of
the West. It is alleged, that before it reached the West, the
Black Death exhausted itself in the place of its origin. Like
most other plagues, it was infinitely more destructive at the
commencement of its career than after it had endured for
a time. This is not to be accounted for by the fact that the
weakest members of the community naturally succumbed the
first, for we are told that it killed the strong, and that, just
as with the Asiatic cholera, when it is most virulent, many
of those attacked perished speedily, and before the disease
had developed its most characteristic symptoms. It appears,
indeed, and the impression is confirmed by scientific research,
that when some new infection or contagion is developed, the
whole population is specially liable to the assaults of the
disease, and that sometimes it may totally perish, as in all
likelihood the ancient occupants of the ruined cities in Central
America have disappeared without leaving any sign, other
than their stupendous buildings, of their existence. So also
diseases familiar to us in England, and now become mild, are
specially deadly to those races into which they have been
for the first time introduced. In course of time, either the
original virus of the disease is weakened, or those who are
most susceptible of it are removed by death, or remedial
measures are discovered which check or extinguish it. For

more than three centuries the plague wasted England, though at no time, it seems, so seriously as at its first and last visitations.

The Black Death, as our forefathers called it, from the dark purple blotches which appeared on the skin, when the blood and tissues had become wholly disorganized through the virulence of the disorder, still lingers in the East, under the name of the Levant, or Oriental, plague. Even now we are occasionally informed of some outbreak in an Eastern plague spot, where the hateful Turk has reduced every one to squalid poverty and misery, and whence Europe is again threatened. But the progress of sanitary science has probably put an end to the worst ravages of a disease which was so terrible more than five centuries ago. In England it does not seem to have been assisted by any prevalent distress among the people, as the Athenian plague was by overcrowding, as that of Cadiz was in 1800, or as the last visitation of small-pox was by the miseries of the Franco-German war. The period just before the plague was one of prosperity and abundance; and though our forefathers were immeasurably unclean in their habits and surroundings, and remained unclean for centuries afterwards, the best conditions of life do not appear to have given an immunity from the plague. Among the victims of the first year were one of Edward's daughters and three Archbishops of Canterbury. So the narrative given us by Boccacio proves that all classes were equally affected, for the ladies and gentlemen who retire in the Decameron to tell each other stories in a country house on the road to Fiesole had all of them lost relations by the plague. The Black Death visited Christ Church, Canterbury, very lightly, for a century before the prior had laid on pure water from the hills to the monastery.

The Black Death first attacked Europe in Cyprus at about the end of the year 1347, and was accompanied by great convulsions of the earth, and by atmospheric disturbances. Many persons who were seized with the disorder died instantly. The plague seemed not only to the frightened imagination of the people, but even to the more sober observation of such men of science as lived at the time, to be moving forward with slow progress from the desolated East, under the form of a dark and fœtid mist, which settled on the garden of the Lord, and left it a howling wilderness.   On January 25th, 1348, an earthquake had laid waste great part of the peninsulas of Italy and Greece.   Meanwhile the mischief was steadily progressing along the basin of the Mediterranean, for the caravan traffic was carrying it everywhere, as the pilgrimages to and from Mecca disseminate disease in the homes and cities of returning devotees.   The Black Death appeared at Avignon in January 1348, was in Florence by the middle of April, and had thoroughly penetrated France and Germany by August.   It entered Poland in 1349, reached Sweden in the winter of the same year, and Norway, by infection from England, at about the same time.   It spread even to Iceland and Greenland,—the former, a well-wooded country and fairly flourishing colony of Norse origin; the latter a region with which communications had been kept up for centuries.   We are told that, among the physical changes which ensued from the Black Death, or preceded and aided it, vast icebergs were formed on the eastern side of Iceland and on the whole coast of Greenland, and effectually cut off all communication between the Old World and those parts of the New which heretofore had been familiarly visited.   In 1351 it reached Russia, after having inflicted its first severities on the rest of Europe, and having taken the circuit of the Mediterranean.   It is probable that the caravan trade through Russia had been at this time suspended, and that the natural spread of the disease had been checked by the barrier of the Caucasus.

On the 1st of August, 1348, the disease made its appearance in the seaport towns of Dorsetshire, and travelled slowly westwards and northwards, through Devon and Somerset, to Bristol.   In order to arrest the progress of the mortality, the authorities of Gloucestershire prohibited all intercourse with the citizens of Bristol.   It was in vain; the plague spread to Oxford, where it was terribly destructive, and travelling slowly in the same measured way, reached London by the

1st of November.　It appeared in Norwich on the 1st of January, and thence spread northwards.　Later in the year 1349, the Scotch made one of their customary raids into England, and, as they ravaged the north, invented an oath, "By the foul death of the English."　On their retreat they were attacked by the pestilence in the forest of Selkirk, and the northern part of the island suffered as seriously as the more populous south.

The mortality was no doubt enormous and appalling.　It is probable that one-third of the population perished.　To be sure, panic always exaggerates numbers.　One chronicler says that nine out of ten died.　Similar amplifications, which have been heedlessly accepted by writers who are inexperienced in possibilities, are found in all the chroniclers. We are told that sixty thousand persons perished in Norwich between January and July, 1349.　Norwich was probably the second city in the kingdom at the time, and Norfolk was certainly the richest county; but the number is twice as much as the population of both city and county at the time. Joshua Barnes, the author of a diffuse life of Edward III., pretends to give exact information as to the persons who died in the principal English cities.　His numbers are undoubtedly untrustworthy.　The nearest estimate to likelihood which I have seen is that of Knighton.　He was a canon of Leicester, and lived a short time after the events.　He tells us that the deaths in the three parishes of Leicester town were 1480. Even this number I believe to be exaggerated, for there is reason to conclude that at this time the population of Leicester was under 3,500.

Every town had its plague-pit.　That of London was a spot afterwards occupied by the Charterhouse, and purchased for the purpose of sepulture by Sir Walter Manny, one of Edward's captains.　Some years ago, being at Cambridge while the foundations of the new Divinity School were being laid, I saw that the ground was full of skeletons, thrown in without any attempt at order, and I divined that this must have been a Cambridge plague-pit. I have no doubt that the principal place of burial for the

Oxford victims was at some part of New College garden, for when Wykeham bought the site, it appears to have been one which had been previously populous, but was deserted some thirty years before during the plague, and apparently made a burial-ground by the survivors of the calamity. Hecker estimates the loss of population in Europe at twenty-five millions, a moderate and probable calculation.

No doubt the ravages of the pestilence were more general among the poorer classes. But, as I have already stated, the more opulent were not unaffected by it. The disease made havoc among the secular and regular clergy, and we are told that a notable decline of learning and morals was thenceforward observed among the clergy, many persons of mean acquirements and low character stepping into the vacant benefices. Even now the cloister of Westminster Abbey is said to contain a monument in the great flat stone, which we are told was laid over the remains of the many monks who perished in the great death. The novelist Boccacio dwells on the effect which the mortality caused in the character of the survivors, and how panic or despair made men callous, reckless, superstitious, heartless, cruel, and licentious ; and Sismondi, in his great history of the French people, and of the Italian Republics, has collected contemporaneous evidence to the same effect.

The Black Death formed an epoch, and, for many years afterwards, facts were computed according to their nearness from the great pestilence. A century after the event, Gascoigne makes it the era of the new departure in Oxford, after which learning, morality, and the adequate discharge of duties began to wane ; the universities were, relatively speaking, deserted, and the whole spirit of society was changed. It is said by Sir Harris Nicolas that of the three years, 1349, 1361, and 1369, in which note was made of the extraordinary virulence of a disease now become sporadic, the first pestilence was said to have lasted four months; the second through the winter, for eight months and nineteen days ; the third for nearly three months. These dates of duration, given centuries after the event, cannot be accepted as authentic, but they are indirect testimony of the singular impression which the ca amity left on the mind of England. I have been struck with the fact, from more trustworthy sources, when I have noted certain entries made in the records of several Hertfordshire manors, where the plague appears to have been specially deadly. In these manors it was the practice for thirty years to head the schedule of expenditure with an enumeration of the lives which were lost and the tenancies which were vacated after the great death of 1348. Nor have I any doubt, if some antiquary were to have the patience to peruse and tabulate the taxing rolls of Edward I., and compare the names of residents in the several manors with the entries of tax-paying inhabitants resident in the same manors after the great plague, he would find that thousands of names perish from the manor registers, as that of the Oldmans did from Cuxham. It may be noted that the foundation of colleges in Oxford, which was rapidly proceeding before this stupendous event, ceased for many years, when it was taken up with renewed vigour.

At first, as is constantly the case in times of panic, there was a suspicion that the disease was the work of human agencies. As usual, the Jews were credited with having contrived the calamity. They were charged with poisoning the wells, and throughout France, Switzerland, and Germany, thousands of these unhappy people were destroyed on evidence derived from confessions obtained under torture, or even from the fact of their religion and origin. They were protected as far as possible by the Emperor, Charles IV., whose own influence in Germany was very circumscribed. They escaped persecution, too, in the dominions of Albrecht of Austria. It is said that the large Jewish population of Poland is due to the fact that Casimir the Great was induced, by the entreaties of Esther, a favourite Jewish mistress, to give them harbour and shelter in his kingdom. The story is curiously corroborated by the respect which is still paid by the Podolian Jews at the present time to the memory of this second Esther, who, being taken into the harem of another king, also alien to the race of Israel, remembered her kindred in the day of their trouble, and to the generosity of the Polish

15

monarch who yielded to her wish. It ought to be added that
Clement VI. forbad the persecution of the Jews at Avignon,
where the pope was still residing. The English people was
saved from being tempted to the crime of murdering the
Jews, because the king's grandfather had expelled the whole
race from England. And yet, in this our own day, one sometimes wonders whether we have really escaped from the contingency, even in countries calling themselves civilised, of
witnessing again the bigotry, the malignity, the spirit of hatred
which accepts impossible lies, for which there was the excuse
of ignorance in the middle ages, but not the shadow of an
excuse now.

We learn from contemporary accounts, and here we can
trust them, that a rapid growth of population followed on the
destruction of the Black Death. It is said that after this
event, double and triple births were frequent; that marriages
were singularly fertile; and that, in a short time, the void
made by the pestilence was no longer visible. The repressive
check of a high standard of living was removed by the ease
with which the survivors could obtain that standard, and
accumulate from a considerable margin beyond it. The
physiologists of the time, however, averred that the human
race suffered a permanent diminution in the number of teeth,
which had been always possessed by those who were born
before the visitation of the Black Death. I make no doubt
that the population speedily righted itself, as it has done on
many other occasions when a sudden or abnormal destruction of human life has occurred in a people and the people has
a recuperative power. That they had this power is proved by
the events which followed.

I stated above that probably a third of the population
perished. Froissart made the same estimate a generation
later, when fear had ceased to disturb the judgment; and,
as I have said, it is described as having been peculiarly deadly
to persons in the vigour of life. It is certain that the immediate consequence of the plague was a dearth of labour, an
excessive enhancement of wages, and a serious difficulty in
collecting the harvests of those landowners who depended on

a supply of hired labour for the purpose of getting in their crops. We are told that these crops were often suffered to rot in the fields for want of hands; that cattle and sheep roamed at large over the country for lack of herdsmen; that land went out of cultivation; and that the grandees were utterly impoverished. I have referred already to the collateral evidence of an extraordinary falling off in the assessments under customary taxes. Many of the lords excused their tenants' rents lest they should quit their holdings from a want of labour and the increasing and excessive cost of materials; the omission of rent sometimes extending to a half, sometimes for a term of years, as the landowner could arrange with the tenant. So, says Knighton, "they who had let lands on labour-rents to tenants, such rents as are customary in villeinage, were compelled to relieve and remit such labour, and either to utterly excuse them or to rehabilitate their tenants on easier terms and less payments, lest the loss and ruin should become irreparable and the land lie utterly uncultivated." It appears, therefore, that in the panic, the confusion, and the loss which ensued on the Great Plague, that process which, as I said before, was going on already, the commutation of labour-rents for money payments, was precipitated; that the lords readily gave in to compositions; and that even less than had hitherto been demanded in exchange for the service was arranged for the future. The plague, in short, had almost emancipated the surviving serfs.

I shall point out below what were the actual effects of this great and sudden scarcity of labour. At present I merely continue the narrative. Parliament was broken up when the plague was raging. The king, however, issued a proclamation, which he addressed to William, the primate, and circulated among the sheriffs of the different counties, in which he directed all officials that no higher than customary wages should be paid, under the penalties of amercement. The king's mandate, however, was universally disobeyed, for the farmers were compelled to leave their crops ungathered, or to comply with the demands of the labourers. When the king found that his proclamation was unavailing, he laid, we are told, heavy penalties on abbots, priors, barons, crown tenants, and those who held land under mesne lords, if they paid more than customary rates. But the labourers remained masters of the situation. Many were said to have been thrown into prison for disobedience ; many, to avoid punishment or restraint, fled into forests, where they were occasionally captured. The captives were fined, and obliged to disavow under oath that they would take higher than customary wages for the future. But the expedients were vain, labour remained scarce, and wages, according to all previous experience, excessive.

As soon as Parliament could meet, the proclamation was reduced to the form of a statute, which remained, with the proclamation, a law, till both were formally repealed by 5 Elizabeth, Cap. 4. The statute contained eight clauses :— (1) No person under sixty years of age, whether serf or free, shall decline to undertake farm labour at the wages which had been customary in the king's twentieth year (1347), except they lived by merchandize, were regularly engaged in some mechanical craft, were possessed of private means, or were occupiers of land. The lord was to have the first claim to the labour of his serfs, and those who declined to work for him or for others are to be sent to the common gaol. (2) Imprisonment is decreed against all persons who may quit service before the time which is fixed in their agreements. (3) No other than the old wages are to be given, and the remedy against those who seek to get more is to be sought in the lord's court. (4) Lords of manors paying more than the customary amount are to be liable to treble damages. (5) Artificers are to be liable to the same conditions, the artificers enumerated being saddlers, tanners, farriers, shoemakers, tailors, smiths, carpenters, masons, tilers, pargetters, carters, and others. (6) Food must be sold at reasonable prices. (7) Alms are strictly forbidden to able-bodied labourers. (8) Any excess of wages taken or paid can be seized for the king's use towards the payment of a fifteenth and tenth lately granted. The statute provides for the difference between summer and winter wages, and guards against the emigration of the town population to country places in summer. In answer to com-

plaints from the employers of labour, the Statute of Labourers
is constantly re-enacted, with accumulated penalties and
precautions,—penalties sometimes laid on the labourer only,
sometimes on the employer, sometimes on both. An attempt,
which was, I believe, premature, was made to enforce apprenticeship in handicrafts at the beginning of the fifteenth
century, with the view of making the agricultural labourers
an ever-increasing residuum, and thereby securing cheap
labour for the tenant and the lord.

The Statute of Labourers may have induced some slight
effect on the wages of farm labourers. The peasantry were
under the eye of the lord's steward or bailiff, and might have
been denounced and punished if they claimed more than the
law allowed them. But they had great power of combination,—
a power which they used, perhaps, in a manner which made it
very difficult to enforce the statute, for the enforcement of it
is given to the manor court, where the goodwill of the tenants
was essential to harmonious action between lord and tenants.
This combination the statute called the " malice of servants in
husbandry." But there was the pretence of submission to the
statute in the bailiffs' rolls, which might have been taken in
evidence. After the Black Death, payments are frequently
entered in these rolls, at a particular rate, and this a very
exalted one. These payments are drawn through with a pen,
and a less sum substituted. Thus, in 1349, on one estate, the
bailiff enters 5*d.* as the price at which wheat was threshed.
A line is drawn through the figure and 3*d.* substituted. In
the next year, wheat, rye, peas, and vetches are threshed at 6*d.*,
barley at 3*d.*, oats at 2*d.* But a pen is drawn through these
rates, and 2½*d.*, 1½*d.* and 1*d.* are substituted. In the same
year, barley is reaped at 1*s.* 2*d.* at first, but the sum is altered
to 1*s.* Very many of these instances could be quoted. Occasionally, but rarely, the hirer of labour makes similar changes
in artizans' labour, as though to show obedience to the
statute.

I cannot help thinking that these transparent erasures are
simulated, and that they point to evasions of the statute.
The labourer, if he did not receive his full money wages, was

compensated in some covert way to the full extent of the previous entry, and by some means which would not come under the penalties of the law, and the process by which these penalties might be enforced. There might be larger allowances at harvest time, a more liberal concession of common rights, or, as I have often seen, a license given to a shepherd to turn his own sheep into the lord's pasture, or some analogous equivalent to a necessary, but, under the statute, an illegal money payment. Even though we take the substituted entries, we shall find that a great rise in the wages of labour was effected. We know that this rise was in direct contravention of the law,—a law created in the interest of those who employed labour, and, therefore, who wished to have it cheap, and who might be within the risk of the penalties imposed on employers for violating that law which they had probably been instrumental in enacting, but were compelled to incur. Besides, the wages of many kinds of labourers whose callings were enumerated in the statute were not affected by the law at all. These men took their full increase. It was no marvel that Parliament constantly complained that the Statute of Labourers was not kept. The marvel is that they did not see that it could not possibly be kept. But the straits in which the capitalist landowner found himself were sufficiently serious for any one; and the landowner might be pardoned for believing, that if he could fix, as he thought he could, the price of provisions and materials, he could also fix the price of labour. He clung to this delusion for centuries, and at one time he seemed to have achieved what he desired. But he paid for his remedy in a far more ruinous way than that of giving what would have been in the end cheaper labour than he actually procured.

I mentioned in a previous chapter that the rate of profit derived from agricultural operations, after all charges had been deducted and an average allowance had been made for rent, when the occupier was also lord, was about 20 per cent. on the capital invested, about 2 per cent. being represented by the rents of assize and manorial receipts. This estimate has been taken from an actual balance-sheet, in a year of average, or rather more than average, fertility, but when the price of stock was, on the other hand, rather high, and so returned more than the ordinary profit to the farmer. Still, it will be remembered that the superintendence by the bailiff was a heavy charge on the owner's profits, or, at least, was a charge from which the small proprietor was free. It will be obvious that, with such a rate of profit before them, land-owners, who possessed by inheritance a large amount of live and dead stock, would naturally cultivate their land them-selves. There was, indeed, no way in which they could use their property to equal advantage.

In the year which I have taken, 1332-3, the outlay, though in some particulars large, is, on the whole, very much an average. The charges which come under the head of neces-sary expenses are rather high, but the bad debts are very low, and the cost of labour is so small as to suggest that some part of the regular cost of farm labour must have been omitted or put under another head. In another year we shall find a large cost incurred for fittings to the mill; in a second, a serious loss in customary or ordinary rents; in a third, a heavy loss of stock, and the consequent necessity of large purchases. An enormous quantity of cider was this year produced from the orchard, and, therefore, the spring must have been mild and the summer genial. On the whole I cannot but think that the year was in no way excep-tional, and that the rate of profit on agricultural operations was neither unduly exalted nor unduly depressed.

Now if we take the balance-sheet of the same estate in the year 1350-1, we shall see the full effects of the loss of life and the scarcity of hands which ensued from the plague. The whole family of the bailiff, as I have more than once said, had perished. The rents of assize have sunk to one-third their former amount. The fulling mill is abandoned; there is no tenant for it. No one will give more than 22s. for the corn-mill—the previous rent having been 50s. ; and next year there is no tenant to be found at all. The exits of the manor are a little more than a fourth of the sum previously received, and the profit of the court is not a tenth. The harvest had been poor, for notwithstanding the loss of population, the price of wheat was 50 per cent. above the average, and the crop was small, the sales being less than two-thirds of the earlier year. The profits of the dairy are about three-fifths of those in 1332, and about half the amount of stock is sold. On the other hand, the expenses are very heavy. The outlay is cut down ; but little is spent on repairs, nothing but what is absolutely necessary in order that farm operations should be carried on is bought. Labour in harvest time and in the manor house costs three times what it did in 1332. There is a great increase in the cost of all services, and of such articles as depend mainly on labour for their manufactured value.

The expenses exceeded the receipts. The new bailiff, however, possesses a quantity of wool, the accumulations of two years. He had no doubt kept it in hand in the hopes of more remunerative prices. He had good reason for this caution, for wool had been sold at little more than three-fifths the money value which it realised in 1332. Then there were some of the chattels of the deceased bailiff and his family, which could hardly be reckoned among the profits of the farm, but an accidental escheat. Without them the profit for the year is only 4 per cent., with them it is 5½. In all these calculations I have taken corn and stock at their average prices for the year, when the actual value of any item is not given, as is of course the case with anything except what is actually bought and sold. In the next year the owners of the estate did not lose heart, they sowed a larger breadth of corn than usual, and strove to carry on their operations, only to meet with a second failure. Four years later, in 1354, there were lower prices and greater plenty. But the old rates of profit on such farming operations as had been carried on by the capitalist landowner had entirely passed away, never to be recovered, at least to their full amount. Sooner or later, labour must be hired at the old prices, or a new system must be adopted.

Although I am by no means convinced that the erased figures were not paid to the labourer, and that the substituted amounts were, I have always assumed that the after-thought was the real payment. Even under these circumstances the rise in agricultural labour was enormous; and if, as we are told, the young and healthy were the principal victims of the disease, the quality of the labour must have been considerably deteriorated.

In the autumn of the year 1349, the fullest effect is induced on the price of agricultural labour, in the Eastern, Midland, and Southern Counties. The cost of threshing wheat is nearly doubled in the first division, that of barley and oats considerably more than doubled. In the Midland and Southern Counties the rise is even greater for wheat and barley, but oats, in the south, are still threshed at the old rates. The price in the west is raised, but in a far less degree, and, indeed, it appears that Western England did not suffer so much from the disease and the consequent paucity of hands as the greater part of the rest of the country did. But the prices of this year are panic rates. Even if the Statute of Labourers had not been passed, a fall would have ensued, though the price of labour, proclamations and statutes notwithstanding, did not ever fall to its old rates.

If we take the whole period from 1350 to 1400, when the prices paid for labour had been steadied by custom, and examine the divisions of England which it will be convenient to take, we shall find that the final rise in the prices of threshing, taking the three principal kinds of grain together, is 60 per cent. in the Eastern Counties, 73 in the Midland, 48 in the Southern, 37 in the Western, and 59 in the Northern. The most notable rise is that in the payment for threshing oats. But the prices paid for this service had been very low, and, as may be expected, the dearth of hands told far more on low-priced labour than it did on high-priced. This is strikingly illustrated in the price of women's labour. Before the plague, women were employed in field work, as in reaping straw after the corn was cut, in hoeing, in planting beans, in washing sheep, and sometimes in serving the thatcher and tiler. Generally they are paid at the rate of a penny a day, but sometimes less. After the plague, women's labour is rarely recorded, but they are seldom paid less than twopence, sometimes as much as threepence, a day. The same facts are observed in boys' labour, which becomes much dearer.

The rise in the wages of harvest work is equally suggestive. Naturally the increase should be less as the rate in the old time was higher. But against this is to be set the opportunity which the labourer had of pressing his claim in a time of urgency. In the first place, the rate is equalised, or nearly so. Before this event, the highest price was paid for barley, the lowest for rye and oats. Now the same, or nearly the same, rate is secured for all. The price, too, is constantly rising. The old average was about $5\frac{1}{2}d$. an acre. It rises at once to $7d$. and $7\frac{1}{2}d$., and soon is much more, so that it is evident that the Statute of Labourers was from the first entirely inoperative as regards harvest work. For the ten years 1371-80, it is more than double what it was before the plague. We shall see hereafter how serious were the consequences which ensued from this progressive exaltation in the price of harvest labour. About 1770, as Young tells us in his "Eastern Tour," vol. iii., the rate for reaping wheat, the only corn reaped, was $5s$. an acre; for mowing other corn, $1s$. In the decade I am referring to it is $10d$. all round, though nearly every kind of grain was below the average price. With corn of all kinds at an average of $3s$. $8\frac{1}{2}d$., and reaping at $10d$. the acre, the peasant in Young's time got a little more than one-tenth of the price of a quarter of wheat for his labour, and the fourteenth century peasant about two-ninths of the value of the whole produce.

The general rise of harvest work, however, if we omit the exceptional period 1371-90, is $59\frac{1}{2}$ per cent., the reaping of the acre of wheat and barley rising by 51, bigg by 44, rye by 47, beans, peas, and vetches by 59, and oats by 69, per cent. But after the plague, the cultivation of bigg and rye becomes increasingly rare. Had this not occurred, I am convinced that the invariable rule in prices, whether of labour or food ; that in a general rise of anything in demand, what was paid for or purchased at the lowest rate previously gets the largest increase subsequently, would have been again exhibited. The rise effected in the labour of mowing grass is not so considerable. But it is found to be 34 per cent. above the old rates. I should not expect that so notable an increase would be effected in the rate at which grass was mowed by the acre, as in ordinary harvest work. The mower is hired at a time when—I am speaking of the fourteenth century, when early summer ploughing for root-crops was unknown—agricultural labour is least in demand, and, therefore, better bargains could be made for it. But at the same time, if we refer to the parallel already cited, the prices paid for labour in the middle of the third quarter of the eighteenth century, the facts when compared are very striking. The rate paid for mowing grass, on the authority of this writer, Arthur Young, was a maximum of 2s. 6d. an acre, but was ordinarily 2s. At the latter rate the labourer received no more than the equivalent of a twenty-fourth part of a quarter of wheat; at the former rate it was about a nineteenth; whereas before the plague the rate was about a thirteenth of the quarter; and in the latter part, *i.e.*, after the plague, it rose to one-tenth. I have already observed that in the eighteenth century the price paid for mowing an acre of corn is far less than that given for mowing an acre of grass.

The price paid for the thatcher's labour is equally suggestive. He was practically a farm-servant, employed to keep buildings in repair, when the thatch was worn out or imperfect, as occasion required, but constantly to cover stacks after harvest, and hayricks before harvest. His labour attains a slight and permanent rise after the great famines of 1315-21, but a far greater rise afterwards. He is always accompanied by a help or *homo*. This assistant is ordinarily a woman, and the wages are frequently paid conjointly, though sometimes separately. This is explained by the fact that the help was very often the thatcher's wife or daughter, or perhaps young son. When the wages are paid separately before the plague, the rate is about a penny a day : afterwards it rises to $2\frac{1}{2}d$., or by an increase of 125 per cent.

Now we might expect that a thatcher's employment was influenced generally by the two causes which affected or moderated labour prices. His services were occasionally needed when the roofing of houses and barns was to be done, and if his wages were over high, this demand might be economized. But no such economy was possible in the roofing of ricks and haystacks. Hence we should expect that the rise in his wages would not equal that of other kinds of farm labour. It is actually 48 per cent. But if we take the payments made to himself and his help together, the proportion is sure to be enhanced by the extraordinary increase made for the helper's services. It is found to amount to 79 per cent. Even this is less than the amount paid for the two services taken separately. I conclude, that if the help was, as I have said, his wife, daughter, or young son, a slightly lower rate of remuneration would be agreed on than that demanded or paid when the bailiff or employer was hiring two persons whose bargains with him were independent.

It is necessary to follow out the facts in the wages of artizans. These are chiefly the carpenter, the mason, the tiler, the tiler and help, the slater, the slater and help, and the sawyer, either by the day and the couple, or by the hundred feet of plank; this latter, the only kind of piece work which can be conveniently handled, being taken as almost identical with the day's work of a pair of sawyers. The others are paid by the day.

There are two kinds of carpenters regularly employed. The one is engaged on ordinary farm work, and was in frequent requisition. The other was employed for the more difficult business of house building, and the more delicate business of joinery, for which there was plenty of occupation in the domestic buildings of the more opulent classes. The best paid carpenter gets about 25 per cent. above the average paid to common carpenters, though, in taking a general average, I have thought it fair to include the former's wages with those of all others, as he may have been engaged at lower rates, or even the same rate if he were a good workman, on commoner kinds of employment. Here the same facts appear. He gets a slight permanent rise after the great famines, and a large one after the great plague. The common carpenter's wages experience an enhancement

of 48 per cent., and, exactly in accordance with the rule laid
down as the regulator of prices, the highest kind of carpenter's work gets a rise of only 42 per cent. Masons, however,
are more fortunate. The rise in their wages is 60 per cent.
It is very probable that the combination which these
artizans were able to effect, the regulations by which they
might govern their trade, and the manner in which they
were certainly associated together under the title of free
masons (as is proved by the fact that these combinations
were made felony by 3 Hen. VI., cap. 1), would have enabled
them to take full advantage of the situation. The tilers'
wages rose only 34 per cent. But the joint wages of the
tiler and help rose 90 per cent. The evidence of the slaters'
wages is less clear. The calling was confined to some of the
Midland Counties, where fissile oolite had long been used for
roofing, and, as we have seen, the general rise in the rate of
wages was very great. It would seem that the increase is 60
per cent. in this kind of labour. The rise in the wages of
the pair of sawyers is 70 per cent., and that of sawing by
the hundred feet is nearly the same amount.

The rise in agricultural labour is, all kinds of men's work
being taken together, about 50 per cent ; and of women's
work, fully 100 per cent. When taken together, the rise in
the wages of artizans' labour is almost exactly the same as
that effected in the case of the husbandmen. The result is
marked, universal, permanent, and conclusive, even if we had
not on record the complaints of the landowners in Parliament that the Statute of Labourers was entirely inoperative.

The peculiarity of the situation is that, while every kind of
agricultural produce experiences no rise, everything to which
labour adds its principal value is exalted proportionately.
Thus the price of wool, though temporarily depressed, re-
covers, though only to its old rate. There is no appreciable
alteration in the market value of cheese, butter, and eggs, in
the price of the different kinds of fat and candles. The price
of wax and cider remain the same; and so does that of firewood, except during the very height of the plague. But
there is a rise of 50 per cent. in the price of charcoal.

The price of salt is nearly doubled, that of lime and iron more than doubled. The price of laths rises 60 per cent., of tiles 75. Crests, *i.e.*, ridge tiles, are three times as dear as they were before the plague ; and the different kinds of nails, such as were fashioned by the town smith, and sold by retail to his customers, are proportionately enhanced. Quite as great is the exaltation in the price of millstones, articles which the lord was constrained to buy if he were to get the profits of his most lucrative franchise, the manor mill. The price of hurdles, which are generally purchased, is exactly doubled ; of horse-shoes more than doubled, as are also horse-shoe nails and plough gear. The share and the shoe are almost doubled. The iron clouts, by which the frame and axles of a cart are strengthened, are nearly trebled in cost ; and the nails by which they were fastened rose as other nails did. Plain wheels—that is, wheels formed from the trunk of a tree, with holes bored through them for the axles to run on—are more than doubled in price. Wheelwrights' wheels are nearly trebled ; and the iron framework of a pair of cart-wheels, one of the most costly parts of agricultural furniture, rose by 130 per cent. There was scarce an article needed for agricultural operations, the cost of which was not doubled instantly after the calamity occurred, and which did not remain at these exalted and ruinous rates. Even the coarse canvas, which was employed for fans, mill-sails, and sacks, was nearly doubled in price. The hair-cloth used for drying malt was more than doubled, as was linen for shirts and sheets, and that which was used for table, with most of which probably, if not with all of which, the peasant dispensed. The least rise was effected in woollen cloth, one of the indirect illustrations of the fact that the domestic manufacture of woollen goods was a very general, and also what is called a bye industry. Lead, again, a metal used very frequently and generally in the middle ages, was more than doubled in price. Tin, pewter, or solder articles, substantially the same, rose 50 per cent. ; while little increase occurred in the price of brass and copper vessels. They were probably economized, and, lasting a long time, few purchases were made of them.

I have stated before that in the face of these serious changes in the value of these articles, on the regular and cheap supply of which the success of capitalist agriculture in the fourteenth century so largely depended, there was no corresponding rise in the price of provisions. The different kinds of grain are not appreciably dearer, beyond what is occasionally due to the unfavourable character of the seasons. Oxen and cows are a little dearer, but in no such degree as to suggest that there was any rise of general prices to account for the change. The price of horses is absolutely stationary. There is no change in the price of sheep or in that of pigs. Poultry, too, is similarly unchanged in money value. The loss of the agriculturist was confined to the cost of labour and the products of labour, and the only thing which could have been sacrificed was rent, or rather, under the circumstances which prevailed at the time, the profits of capitalist husbandry. The fact that these profits had to bear the first shock of the crisis, and therefore that a little time intervened in which the landowner could look round him, and probably take some new departure, and so keep his fixed rents, probably saved English society from a severer shock than it would have otherwise experienced. No doubt, as we indeed have seen, these fixed rents were at first reduced and generally imperilled. In many cases, where the landowner had leased his land, and had abandoned cultivation on his own account, he was constrained to remit a portion, or even, as Knighton says, to effect a new and permanent composition with his old tenants ; for just as rent, when agriculture improves and a country progresses, is a constantly increasing quantity, so when a serious reverse takes place, when labour is dearer and deteriorates, or capital is lost or scanty, or agricultural profits are otherwise depressed, it is natural, nay, inevitable, that rent should have its reverses, and decline in value and quantity, even for a time to a vanishing point. We shall see hereafter how the English landowners of the fourteenth and fifteenth centuries applied themselves, when they found that parliamentary regulations were futile and misleading, to the solution of the great problem which lay before them.

One article of food rose greatly in price, was, in fact, doubled in amount. This was fish, especially herrings, an article which derives all its value from human labour, the raw material, so to speak, being free to all. The consumption of herrings was all but universal, even in the inland counties of England, large numbers of them being salted and smoked, r pickled without being smoked, and called in the former case red, in the latter white, herring. It would seem that the barrel or cade of smoked herring was marketed earlier than the barrel of white herring; for the former is found in the purchases long before the latter. But in the thirteenth and fourteenth centuries the art of the fish-curer had not reached that amount of skill and variety which was common in the fifteenth, and we know from various sources that much capital and enterprise were devoted to deep-sea fishing in many of the eastern ports and at Bristol during the reigns of the House of Lancaster.

All at once, then, and as by a stroke, the labourer, both peasant and artizan, became the master of the situation in England. The change was as universal as it was sudden. The lord found on all sides a stationary or retrograde market for every kind of produce, in which he dealt as a seller, and a rapidly advancing market for everything he needed as a buyer. Even if he should succeed, after making desperate efforts, in recovering labour at the old prices; if the old but deep-seated delusion that law can regulate prices should turn out in the end to be possible as regards the wages of farm hands; should the police of the manor be only armed with sufficient power for the purpose, he was still confronted with the difficulty that everything he wished to buy, beyond the labour employed on his own fields, had risen by 50 or 100 or even 200 per cent. Even on his estate nearly one-half of the charges of cultivation set down to the credit side of the bailiff's account are derived from outlay, over the amount of which no proclamation, statute, or ordinance could have had any influence whatever, and the exaltation of price on these items alone would reduce his profits to a minimum. If the value of his own produce had risen to an equivalent, the void would be filled, but no Act of Parliament could be devised by which the producer should be able to compel the consumer to pay 50 or 100 or 200 per cent. more for bread and beer, beef and mutton, pork and poultry. Besides, he was not the only dealer. A number of industrious and prosperous tenants were settled round his manor house, who tilled their own lands, from which they could not be evicted; on the profits and improvements of which he could not, as long as they paid their dues, lay his clutches, and it was certain that if he strove to force an enhanced price for what his bailiff had to sell, they would undersell him. They were protected against him, as he was against the king, by custom,—a custom which he dared not break if he could, and could not if he dared. No position could be more unsatisfactory. If he left matters as they were, ruin to all appearance was imminent. If he strove to remedy the mischief by violent or unusual means, the danger was serious. We shall see, by-and-by, that he tried the remedy of force, and signally failed.

The peasant farmer shared the new charges which were put on his calling, but not in the same degree. The costs of the harvest to the lord amounted to £3 13s. 9d. before the plague, they are swollen to £12 19s. 10d. in the year following it. From this charge the surviving peasant farmer was free. He found his own labour on his own holding, and hired none. Besides, he could, after his work was over, hire himself and his children out at the enhanced rates; or, if he had thriven and saved, he could double his own holding, and that on easy terms, for the lord was seeking tenants, not tenants seeking lords. Perhaps the household of the miller was desolate and without inhabitants, and he was one of those who offered less than half the old rent for it; or, maybe, he aspired to the bailiff's vacant place, for the lord was not going to desert his old calling without an effort. Only he could now save his wife and daughter from field labour, and set them to spinning and weaving for the household; perhaps do better at that than they did at the drudgery of the field. The tools had become dear, the sickle and scythe were doubled in price, and the shares and plough-shoes were going the same way.

16

But he would patch up his stock of husbandry tools in the winter, and rub along for a time with the old, as his lord did.

The free labourer, and for the matter of that, the serf, was, in his way, still better off. Everything he needed was as cheap as ever, and his labour was daily rising in value. He had bargained for his labour rent, and was free to seek his market. If the bailiff would give him his price, well; if not, there were plenty of hands wanted in the next village, or a short distance off. If an attempt was made to restrain him, the Chiltern Hills and the woods were near, and he could soon get into another county. There was no fear in these times that the lord could spare to follow him, or that they who wanted his service would freely give him up. He had slaved and laboured at the farm, and now his chance was come, and he intended to use it. So the peasant farmer and the labourer were to try conclusions with the landlord. We shall see how the struggle was fought out. The machinery which the former used had been long in preparation, though no one guessed its efficiency.

CHAPTER IX.

DISCONTENT—COMBINATION—INSURRECTION.

Growing Discontent with the Papal Court—Sections of the English Church—The Party of the Fourteenth Century—The Secession to Avignon—Attitude of England to the Pope in the French War—The Mission of Wiklif—His Residence in Oxford, and Safety in the University—The Poor Priests, and Wiklif's Theory of their Office—The Relative Condition of Landowners, Peasant Proprietors, and Labourers—The Course of Events after the First Statute of Labourers—Counter Organization of the Labourers—The Need of Agents—The Attitude of the Lords—The Teaching of the Poor Priests—The Outbreak—The Trivial Causes of it—The First Movement in Kent—Events in London—The Conference at Mile End and in Smithfield—The Insurrection Collapses—The Outbreak at Norwich—The Energy of the Bishop—The Serfs of St. Albans—The Prosecution and Punishment of the Leaders—The discovery of the Organization—Proceedings in Parliament—The Attitude of the Government—The Mayor of Cambridge and the University—Resistance to Reform—Arguments against and for it—The Demands of the Serfs Conceded—The Persecution of the Lollards—Causes of the Success of Religious Movements—Discontent, the Outbreak of Prosperous Times—The Continuity of the Lollard Movement in the Fifteenth Century—Its Influence at the Reformation.

FOR many years the English people had been getting discontented with the Papal Court. In the days of Becket, this court, though it had to take account with an antipope, was too strong even for so vigorous a monarch as Henry II., because the people still bowed to the authority and believed in the sanctity of the Holy See. At the beginning of the thirteenth century it was even more powerful than in the days of Hildebrand; and the influence it possessed was laboriously exercised by the active genius of Innocent III. His successor, Honorius III., was able to use the machinery which Innocent had devised. But soon afterwards the inherent vices of the Papal Court weakened the pope's influence ; and, except in purely spiritual matters, on which as yet no general interest was felt, all hostility to which was perhaps exterminated for a time, the influence of the papacy was rapidly declining. The excommunications and interdicts, at which a generation or two before the boldest trembled, had become far less terrible. When the pope could excommunicate Grostête for maintaining the discipline of the Church against a scandalous act of nepotism, and Grostête could afford to disregard the censures of the pontiff as long as he knew he was in the right, to denounce the unrighteous and greedy harpies of the pope's court, and, while still professing veneration for the spiritual functions of the father of Christendom, to repudiate his authority in secular affairs, a great change had come over men's minds. The position of a ruler who shares his authority, or divides his responsibility with his ministers or his court, is safer than that of one who controls everything himself. But the ruler who delegates his authority, soon ceases to be infallible and autocratic. The same nation, which in the twelfth century would have sided with the pope in the quarrel about clerical privilege against the second Henry, would have agreed in the thirteenth to a Statute of Provisors if the third Henry had been energetic enough, or perhaps independent enough, to take action in this direction.

Towards the latter end of the thirteenth century, the English clergy, with the connivance or at the instigation of the pope, refused to make a grant to Edward I., tried conclusions with him, and were signally worsted. Thenceforward they take care not to provoke the king, and the papal party in England ceases to be a dangerous power to the State. The English Church had indeed always three sections within it :—One, which busied itself with affairs of state, and supplied from time to time some very able and energetic politicians, was, to anticipate a word from later ecclesiastical history, profoundly Erastian, and exceedingly secular in its sympathies. Examples of this party were the clerical officials of the Exchequer. At the time of Becket's elevation they were all of this mind it seems, for they were willing to accept the Constitutions of Clarendon, which they must have been aware were not only distasteful to the pope, but were a naked submission of the English Church to the royal authority.   Such persons were always found in the English Church, and as long as it remains an establishment, always will be found.   Such men were Roger of Salisbury in the twelfth, and Wolsey in the sixteenth century.   The second party in the English Church is essentially Anglican. It stands aloof equally from secular subservience and from foreign complications.   This element, again, has always been present.   Langton and Grostête are among its earliest types. Gardiner and Bonner represented it at the Reformation. Laud revived it in the seventeenth century; and Atterbury was a type of it in the eighteenth, till he became the dupe or the tempter of Harley and St. John.   It has been revived in our own day, and is vigorous and pretentious. The third is that which sincerely allied itself with Rome, and saw in submission to the papacy the unity of Christendom. In the thirteenth century this was an active and not a very creditable party.   In the fourteenth, and on to the Reformation, it consisted mainly of the monks, especially of those orders on whom the pope had conferred great immunities.

In the fourteenth century there sprung up a fourth party in the Church, which was at first favoured, then silenced, and finally persecuted by the other three.   Disagreeing in other particulars, the Official, the Anglican, and the Papal clergy were ultimately agreed in striving to suppress the Lollards. The annals of these obscure but enthusiastic sectaries have never been written; perhaps the materials for the history could not be collected.   But there is enough known to show that they were numerous and formidable; that they were credited with political and social aims which were highly distasteful, and perhaps dangerous to existing authorities and powerful interests; and that the tenets of the sect were widely disseminated, enthusiastically adopted, and doggedly retained.   As might be expected, they had the greatest hold in the towns, and especially in the manufacturing districts. That the persecution directed against them constrained them to make their tenets and their rites a secret is highly probable ; but it would be a very incorrect estimate of human nature to imagine that the hierarchy succeeded in extirpating that which they hated so heartily. The hatred felt by the clergy to the Lollards was naturally heightened by their own enforced submission to the Crown.

Early in the fourteenth century the popes migrated from Rome to Avignon. The city of Rome had not escaped the infection of that passionate desire for liberty which animated Italy in the fourteenth century, which made it the scene of so much intellectual activity, of such furious feuds, and ultimately of so degraded a servitude. Rome was no pleasant place for a pontiff to live in, and Boniface VIII. had troubles enough. His next successor but one migrated to Avignon; and for more than seventy years the pontiffs lived in a town in the south of France, were all Frenchmen, and were thoroughly devoted to, or dependents on, the French king. Still, so great was the force of habit, that the rest of the European states acquiesced in the attitude taken by their spiritual head, who was fortunately, except for a short time, not troubled with an antipope. I cannot but think that the indifference shown at this voluntary residence in Avignon is a symptom of the decline of the papal authority. At the beginning of the fifteenth century it had become a pious opinion with most good and devout men, that a general council was superior in articles of faith and Church government to the pope himself,—an opinion which would have been strangely unnatural a century before. The pope had been a reformer, he then became a despot, and he was rapidly sinking into being a huckster of spiritual wares.

The long course of the French war, and its alternate successes and reverses, during which it was alleged that the Avignon pope was on the side of the English enemy, prepared the minds of the English people for a revolt against the papal authority, and especially against the encroachments of the Roman see and court. The pope most inopportunely claimed the arrears of the tribute promised by John, and its punctual payment for the future ; and the king, shrewdly appealing to his parliament, enlisted public opinion against the claim. Great discontent was felt at the practice long adopted by the pope of nominating his creatures to benefices, and even to sees, before they were vacant; or, as it was technically called, making such dignities the subject of provision. This practice had always been unpopular, and the opportunity for putting an end to it seemed to have come. Hence, in 1350, a statute was passed, prohibiting the practice, and enacting fine and ransom, with imprisonment, on those who procured such letters from the pope. But it was one thing to pass a statute curtailing the pope's power, another to secure obedience to it; and the Statute of Provisors was very indifferently kept. In point of fact, the elections to bishoprics and deaneries was theoretically, and by the Great Charter, in the hands of close corporations. But the king was always anxious to nominate to them, and frequently did not scruple to invoke the aid of the very power against which he had procured the enactment of the law. At last, in July 1374, Edward sent a kind of legation, of seven persons in all, to Bruges, with a view towards effecting a settlement of the question with the pope. These persons succeeded in obtaining an authoritative document from the Roman see, in which the practice was surrendered, and a compromise was effected. But it was by no means a final act. Martin V. threatened to put England under an interdict, near sixty years afterwards, in case this obnoxious Statute of Provisors was not repealed, and it was supposed that but for his opportune death he would have put his threat into execution. One of the commissioners was the celebrated Wiklif.

This personage has had a more extensive influence in England and Europe generally than any other English ecclesiastic before or since. He was born in or about the year 1324, at a small village in Yorkshire, from which his name was derived. It is said that his kinsfolk resided in the manor house till the seventeenth century, and that they remained strict papists after the Reformation. He went to study at Oxford, where is not known. But he was a fellow of

Merton College in 1357, and master of Balliol in 1361.   After several preferments, during the tenure of which he generally resided at the University of Oxford, he was appointed to the benefice of Lutterworth, whither he ultimately retired.   Here he died on Dec. 31st, 1384.   He received this living from the king, as a reward for his services on the embassy to Bruges. Wiklif is well known as a theologian, who evidently aspired to the influence in Oxford which Grostête had wielded a century before.   In this capacity he had a vast following, and was the author of Lollardy, the repudiator of the pope's authority, the translator of the Bible, and the precursor of the Reformation.   Crowds came to hear him from all parts of the world.   Among them were many Bohemians, who, carrying his books and tenets back to their native country, and being proscribed with their leaders and teachers at the Council of Constance, provoked the war of the Hussites, as their descendants did the terrible strife of the Thirty Years' War two centuries later.   But I am not concerned with Wiklif's religious opinions, except in so far as they are necessarily connected with his social and political theories.

The first objects of Wiklif's attack were the monks and the friars.   The older orders had long become wealthy, worldly, luxurious, and, it was whispered, profligate.   They were generally exempt from the authority of the bishop, and their independence was not favourable to their reputation. In order to purify the Church and counteract the vices of these older orders, Francis and Dominic, a century and a half before, had founded their famous fraternities of begging and preaching friars.   These men were prohibited from acquiring any permanent property.   Even the houses in which they lived were held in trust for them, and so popular were they in the early days of their career, that the town corporations eagerly became their trustees. They tended the sick, especially those who were affected with loathsome diseases, such as leprosy, which was then very common. As they could acquire no gain, they became the unsuspected confessors of the wealthy.   They were exceedingly popular, especially the Dominicans, as preachers, and their homely, earnest discourses were much sought after. Still, a century and a half of popularity had corrupted the friars and had diminished their reputation. Upon these monks and friars, and upon the secular clergy, whose lives and conduct the mission of the friars was supposed to rebuke, came the frightful calamity of the plague, with all the moral evil which such a social convulsion was sure to produce. Benefices were vacated and ignorant men were thrust into them, cloisters were emptied, and new monks, wholly unworthy of their calling, were professed. It seemed as though Satan were let loose, as the Apocalypse had predicted.

The University in which Wiklif resided was assured of its independence by the bulls of popes and the charters of kings. No bishop or archbishop, said the Chancellor of Oxford in Wiklif's time, has any authority over the University in matters of belief. It was, therefore, if a man could get an audience, a place where speculative novelties were tolerated. The fashion of the University, in which the graduates disputed against each other on all topics, aided in developing an inquiring, perhaps a sceptical habit of mind. So far was it from being an ecclesiastical foundation, that it was for a long time the only safe refuge for heterodox opinion. Now Wiklif's teaching was national. He despised the pope, and denounced the usurpations of the Roman Court. He argued that all ecclesiastics should be subject to the civil power. He made no distinction, says Melancthon, between the gospel and the state. He told the king, in a time of financial difficulty, when counselled as to the transmission of English money to the papal coffers, that the prohibition of such an operation was not only justifiable, but a public duty. He denounced the friars as the emissaries of the pope. He advocated the heavy taxation, perhaps the confiscation of the monasteries. He probably suggested the fable which he makes a lord tell in the Parliament of 1371, to the effect that a featherless owl came to an assembly of birds, and begged a feather from each bird present. In compassion they give him a plumage, when he suddenly turns into a hawk and begins to harry them. So they demanded their feathers back again, and reduced him to the bare and beggarly condition in which he was when he first came as a mendicant. "This," said the lord, "is the history of the monks' wealth; and, if we are wise, we shall make them bare again." He probably urged that ecclesiastics should be excluded from secular offices, and formulated the petition to that effect which was presented to the king. As time went on, Wiklif, protected by John of Gaunt and his party, and by many noblemen who relished the courage and plainness with which he attacked the over-grown wealth of the clergy, uttered louder and bolder denunciations of the moral and political evils which, in his opinion, the papacy necessarily induced. As is well known, he was persecuted for these opinions, and practically silenced.

He had, however, before this occurred, taken a step, the effects of which neither he nor his contemporaries foresaw. In order to counteract the influence of the begging friars, who were as devoted to the pope as the Jesuits were after-wards, he established an order of persons whom he called poor priests, whom he had clothed in russet, that is, in cloth made of undyed black wool, and sent about barefoot to preach, and rouse men to good works. These men were to be entrusted at their discretion with the function of address-ing the people, were responsible to no authority, and were provided with no credentials beyond their own zeal and convictions. It does not seem that they were to make any place their special residence, nor were they to report them-selves to any person, nor to have any restraint put on their utterances. The pope, Wiklif held, had no more spiritual authority than any other ordained minister. The monks had no more intrinsic holiness by virtue of their profession than a wall has solidity because it has been whitewashed. No man should be imprisoned or hindered for conscience' sake. A wealthy Church is sure to be corrupt. Dominion is founded in grace, by which the reformer intended that allegiance to authority is due only when it is guaranteed by deserts and that authority is founded on merit. It is easy to see how passionate, earnest, and sympathetic men could gain influence by these teachings, and how terribly they might abuse their influence. Wiklif had created an order of ecclesiastics on whom he had imposed no discipline; and these men speedily emancipated themselves from all control. Their violence of language, their contempt of authority, their advocacy of equality, in its coarsest and homeliest form, soon distinguished them, and disgusted those who had at first favoured the movement. Occasionally their vehemence exhausted itself. Some of the most violent of Wiklif's poor priests ultimately deserted the cause they had taken up, conformed to the existing order of things anew, rose to high rank in the Church, and persecuted that which they had aforetime preached.

My readers will remember that the crisis of the Black Death left the great landowners in very evil case, with rents and profits reduced, the latter almost to a nullity. The small proprietors had to bear some part of these exalted prices; but these were more than compensated by the advantages immediate and prospective of their position. But the labourers gained all which the landowners lost, and could extort what terms they liked from the necessities of their employers. This attitude was met by the Statute of Labourers, and the attempt to restrain wages to the rates which prevailed in 1347. The attempt failed. Year after year, almost century after century, the Parliament complained that the Statute of Labourers was not kept, re-enacted it, strove to make it effective, were baffled, adopted new and harsher expedients, and were disappointed. They tried to keep up the old system of capitalist cultivation, but gradually dropped it. Some, as the college from which I have derived so much information, let out all their lands to lease within ten years of the great plague. Some, more conservative, more hopeful, or more successful, continued the system a little way into the fifteenth century. Some of the landlords, especially those who lived near hill pastures, took extensively to sheep farming. A few, especially the monasteries, kept home farms in cultivation, mainly for the convenience which it was to them in order to supply their houses with certain kinds of produce. But sooner or later, in the great majority of cases very soon, the old system was abandoned in despair, and the land was leased in a peculiar fashion, to which I shall refer hereafter, to tenants for terms of years.

Still, ineffectual as the enactments were, they were intended to be effectual, and were certain to be irritating. The peasants met the law by combinations. They organized themselves, subscribed, as we are expressly told, considerable sums of money for the defence and protection of the serfs, perhaps for the payment of fines. In plain modern English, the serfs entered into what are now called trades unions, and supported each other in resistance to the law and in demands for higher wages. This is especially noticeable among the peasantry, the upland folk, as they were called, to distinguish them from artizans and townspeople generally. These facts are proved by the averages of agricultural wages. At first it is only occasionally that the price of their services is excessively high in comparison with what had been customary. When such demands are effectual, they are so chiefly on harvest labour, when, naturally, the greatest pressure could be employed and felt. At last, twenty years after the first incidence of the plague, the combination appears to have been completely successful, and the price of harvest labour is more than double what it was before the plague, all kinds of reaping being paid for at the same excessive rate. This lasts without a break, except in one year, till the time of Tyler's insurrection, after which, though the price is still high, it is less than it was. The wages of other labour were steady at the enhanced rate which was obtained at and after the year 1350.

Now a combination such as that which is described by contemporary writers, and which the chroniclers certainly could not have invented, must have needed agents who were competent to organize, who could be trusted, and who could keep the particulars of their organization secret, if they could not the fact. But the peasants could not have done this among themselves. Any conference which they might have held would have been detected, suspected, and punished. The essence of mediæval society was that, in every manor, everyone knew everything about his neighbour. The lords,

armed with the force of law, would never have suffered a
conspiracy against the interests of property to have been
hatched at their doors. They would have brought their
retainers, or some of the discharged soldiers, down on these
wretched, isolated helots, and have slain them without
mercy, if they had found that they were collecting money,
making deposits of arms, and conspiring against the state.
In their opinion, the revolt of the serfs, even the bare suspicion of a revolt, would have justified a massacre; and if
we had no other evidence, we might be quite certain that
the peasants would do all they could to avert suspicion from
themselves.

When I first began to examine the social condition of
England, as it is described by those who wrote at the time,
and, afterwards, when I corrected the narrative by the unerring evidence of those statistical facts which bear on the
circumstances of the case, the meaning of which was a secret
to those who recorded them, I stated, though I had no doubts
myself, what I thought was the course of events and the
causes of what ultimately happened, as an hypothesis. Larger
investigations, and, I may add, the general agreement of all
who have studied the subject with me, convince me that the
lords attempted, in despair of getting back to the old wages
by law, to reverse the customary commutations of money for
labour by force. Let me state, or re-state, the case. The
lord had agreed to take, when labour, especially harvest
labour, was plentiful and cheap, small sums of money in
lieu of labour. Such labour was sure to be half-hearted, and
had to be habitually watched by the bailiff or overlooker, in
order that the serfs might not shirk their work. Besides,
there were a number of ways in which a sullen or discontented
serf might disappoint his employer or avenge himself. Money
in hand would be better than unwilling labour, and so the
commutation took place on very favourable terms to the serf,
even when compared with the old labour prices. Now,
however, it was urged, these people are demanding for the
work which they were bound to do, and their lord's good
nature has remitted, for an insignificant consideration, three

times the amount of the commutation. It is very possible also that perfidious lawyers, bailiffs, and agents pointed out to the impoverished and angry lords that, after all, in law and in past times these serfs had no rights at all; that they possessed what they had by the good-natured easiness of their superiors; and that their black ingratitude should be punished by resuming those lands and that liberty which had been so grossly abused. At any rate, they argued, we may well imagine, as follows: " The experiment is worth trying. The landed interest is perishing, and with it the ancient nobility, the chivalry, the gentry of the kingdom, its culture, its honour, its institutions, all that makes its character, enterprize, and prestige, and this by the malice and malignity of a mob of clowns, whose fancied rights we have, of all people, no reason to respect." Guided by these counsels, or of their own motion, they certainly strove to reverse the bargain which they had made with their serfs, and had engrossed on their manor rolls, determining to reduce them to villeinage again, or, at least, to exact the old labour rents.

They could not have anticipated, when they came to this determination and began to put it cautiously into execution, how the poor priests, who alone could traverse the country by right and without suspicion, would advise their followers. They could not have seen that these were precisely the persons who would organize resistance among the serfs, could win and keep their confidence, and could be trusted with their subscriptions, their plans, and their communications. Wiklif's poor priests had honeycombed the minds of the upland folk with what may be called religious socialism. By Wiklif's labours, the Bible men had been introduced to the new world of the Old Testament, to the history of the human race, to the primeval garden and the young world, where the first parents of all mankind lived by simple toil, and were the ancestors of the proud noble and knight, as well as of the down-trodden serf and despised burgher. They read of the brave times when there was no king in Israel, when every man did that which was right in his own eyes, and sat under his own vine and his own fig-tree, none daring to make him afraid. They read how God, through His prophet, had warned Israel of the evils which would come to them when a king should rule over them, and how speedily this was verified in the conduct of the young Rehoboam, with his depraved and foolish counsellors, of how woe had been predicted to the people over whom a child should rule. The God of Israel had bade His people be husbandmen, and not mounted knights and men-at-arms. But, most of all, the preacher would dwell on his own prototype, on the man of God, the wise prophet who denounced kings and princes and high-priests, and, by God's commission, made them like a potter's vessel in the day of His wrath, or on those bold judges, who were zealous even to slaying. For with this book, so old, yet so new, the peasant preacher—we are told that many learnt to read when they were old that they might tell the Bible story—could stir up the souls of these clowns with the true narrative of another people, and would be sure that his way to their hearts and their confidence would be, as it always has been with the leaders of a religious revival, by entirely sympathising with their wrongs, their sufferings, and their hopes. And when they told them that the lords had determined to drag them back to their old serfdom, the preacher could discourse to them of the natural equality of man, of the fact that all, kings, lords, and priests, live by the fruits of the earth and the labour of the husbandman, and that it would be better for them to die with arms in their hands than to be thrust back, without an effort on their part, into the shameful slavery from which they had been delivered. And as their eyes kindled, and they grasped their staves, he could tell them to keep their ears open for the news of their deliverance, that on the password being given, they were at once to hie to the appointed place, where a great work could be done for God's people by His appointed servant. Sometimes the preacher was denounced, detected, and imprisoned, for Ball, one of the most active and outspoken of these poor priests, had been put into Maidstone gaol in consequence of his violent harangues.

This was the way in which the communications were kept

up, and the organization made ready to be called into activity at a moment's notice. The secret was well kept. The storm, which no politician of the time anticipated, burst on June 10th, 1381. The uprising of the upland folk was simultaneous. It extended from the coast of Kent to Scarborough, all through the Eastern towns. Norwich, the richest English town of the fourteenth century after London, full of thriving artizans, who were the disciples of the poor priests, as the county was subsequently their hiding-place, fully shared in the insurrection, for the rioters took Norwich and stormed the castle. On the west it extended from Hampshire to Lancashire. The story of the insurrection is told by all the chroniclers. They connect the outbreak, it is true, with a trivial incident,—the outrage on Tyler's daughter and the Roman vengeance which he took on the ill-doer. Others ascribe the discontent to the poll-tax. It is true that the first was very unfair, being an equal contribution from all persons except beggars and mendicant friars, a triple tax being demanded from beneficed clergymen. This tax, however, though exacted at the time when combinations were general, seems to have caused no open expression of feeling. The second tax was graduated, was levied on the king's uncles as well as on the peasantry, for the dukes of royal blood and the archbishops were rated at five hundred and twenty times the tax of the labourer. The tax, too, was not imposed on married women. The third poll-tax, synchronous with Tyler's insurrection, was not so fair, for the maximum payment was sixty groats, the minimum, one. The limit of age in the first poll-tax was fourteen, in the second sixteen, in the third fifteen years of age.

The cause was far more deep-seated than a personal grievance and a personal outrage, as we might conclude from the evident concert with which the uprising was carried out. The true cause was the incidents of villeinage, and the dissatisfaction felt at revived oppression. It is noteworthy that Kent takes the lead in the movement. But there were no serfs in Kent. To have been born in that county, and to prove one's birth there, was a bar to the proceedings by which a lord claimed the recovery of his serf. In the many accounts which I have read from the county of Kent, there is no trace of the serf-tenure or of the serf. The foremost place, then, which the men of Kent took, must be assigned to their sympathy with popular movements. It was traditional in the county. Kent was the headquarters of Cade's revolt in 1450, and took action in almost all considerable events up to the days of the Commonwealth. Under Tyler the commons of Kent liberated Ball from Maidstone gaol, and a burgess of Gravesend, who had been imprisoned by Sir Simon Burley on a plea of villeinage. They marched to London, occupied Blackheath and Southwark, and constrained Sir John Manly to communicate their demands to the king. Then they crossed the bridge and entered London, a thing which would have been impossible, unless divided counsels had distracted the city. There they burned John of Gaunt's new palace and sacked the hospital of St. John. Their animosity was specially directed against the Flemings, whom they dragged from the churches. In all likelihood this was the work of their associates in the city, with whom the Flemish merchants were always unpopular. These events took place on the 11th, 12th, and 13th of June. On the last of these days, Thursday, the insurgents encamped in London, probably in the open space near St. Paul's, or in Smithfield.

The city took counsel on Thursday evening. It is said that the mayor and some of the aldermen were anxious to attack the rebels by night, but that they were dissuaded by the Earl of Salisbury, who was, by the way, a partizan of Wiklif and the reforming party, on the ground that if the attack was repulsed everything would be lost. Three of the aldermen and certain of the council are said to have been friendly to the movement. During this night of terror, the young king, his mother, his two half-brothers, some of the nobles, and Simon Sudbury, Archbishop of Canterbury and Chancellor, were lodged in the Tower, with only a slender garrison. On Friday morning the insurgents presented themselves at the Tower, and informed the king, who was not yet fifteen years old, that unless he granted them a conference

17

they would attack the Tower, capture it, and slay all that were in it. To satisfy them, the king left the Tower with his two brothers, and appointed the place of conference at Mile End. He sent his two brothers out of the way, for the Earl of Kent and Sir John Holand had already become notorious for their misdeeds. He had no sooner left the Tower than the rebels burst in, seized the Archbishop and certain others, and forthwith put them to death. In the sudden capture of the Tower, we must, I think, see that Tyler's insurrection was aided by old soldiers of the French wars ; and in the murder of the archbishop, as in that of Stapledon fifty-four years before, the hatred entertained towards the officers of the Exchequer.

The king, it is said, with courage beyond his years, gave audience to the rioters at Mile End, and demanded what they wanted. They answered, "We will that you make us free for ever, ourselves, our heirs, and our lands, and that we be called no more bond, or so reputed." The king immediately assented. He bade them return to their homes, leaving two or three from each village, who should receive and carry back the charters. Many of the insurgents, misled it would seem by so prompt a compliance, obeyed, and quitted the city, and the king assigned one of his banners to each of the counties which had furnished complainants. It is more probable that Tyler was quite willing to reduce his forces into manageable dimensions, for we are told that thirty thousand men, a number far in excess of the adult male population of the city at the time, remained under arms. The king, in all appearance anxious to fulfil his pledge, set thirty clerks to work in writing out and sealing the patents of manumission. One of these, dated June 15th, is preserved in Walsingham, being that addressed to the authorities of Hertfordshire. It frees all the king's subjects in the county of bondage, and makes them quit, *i.e.*, free of any charge accruing from the past, pardons them all offences committed, and assures them of the king's peace. Hertfordshire was the county in which Walsingham's abbey, St. Albans, was situate. In these matters the king was probably advised by the Earl of Salisbury. At the same time Richard had in his company a youth of exactly his own age, his own cousin, who was hereafter to depose him, and be the indirect instrument of his murder—Henry Bolingbroke, Earl of Derby.

On Saturday morning Tyler occupied Smithfield in force. The king was attempting to escape from London, though one can hardly see whither he would have fled, as the whole country was insurgent. He found the peasants under arms, halted at St. Bartholomew's Abbey, and prepared to parley with them. As he came near, Tyler bade his men fall back, and advanced to confer with the king. Then Tyler was slain by Walworth, the mayor, who seems to have gathered a number of partizans together, and perhaps to have made them simulate sympathy with the rebels and mingle with them. The king appeased the enraged crowd by riding up to them at the peril of his life, declaring himself their monarch and their friend. He checked Walworth and Knolles, who wished to attack them. He is said to have ordered the banners and charters of manumission to be given up, and to have destroyed whatever were surrendered; but this part of the narrative we must assuredly disbelieve. The army of the rebels returned to London, satisfied with his assurance, and soon after, for here the details of the story fail us, seems to have dispersed. But though Richard spoke them fair, he assured his counsellors, with a dissimulation which could hardly be credited in so young a person, that he would take full vengeance on them hereafter. But the longing for revenge, dissimulated by a show of patient acquiescence and even friendship, was the one steady feature in Richard's character. He returned to the Tower, and when his mother congratulated him on his safety in the evening, he told her that he had well-nigh lost and actually gained his crown on that memorable morning Before the evening he issued a proclamation, commanding the departure of all the country folk from London. We are told that the order was obeyed.

The insurrection broke out in Norwich on June 13th, under the command or guidance of Littlestreet. The captain-general of the city, Sir Robert Sale, had been born a serf,

but had risen to knighthood and an office of great trust.
The insurgents invited him to join them, and offered to
put a third of England under his obedience if he would consent. He refused, and fell overpowered by numbers. But
they did not long retain possession of their advantages. The
cathedral close and buildings at Norwich are a fortress by
themselves, isolated from the rest of the city. The young
and warlike Henry Spenser, one of the aristocratic prelates
who were beginning to occupy the highest offices in the
Church, collected an army of his retainers and others, attacked
the entrenchments of the rebels by surprise, forced them, and
routed the enemy. He slew many of them with his own
hand, and ordered to instant execution all those who escaped
the carnage and were taken prisoners. Among these was
Littlestreet. A short time afterwards Spenser led an army
into the Low Countries, where he was not so successful as he
was in dealing with the Norfolk peasants.

If the chronicles compiled in the writing rooms of the
several abbeys had all been preserved or continued (for only
a portion of these annals has come down to us), we should
have learned how universal the panic was, and how frequent
were complaints like that which comes to us from St. Albans.
The serfs who held of the monastery surrounded the abbey,
and claimed an audience of the abbot. They averred that
a charter had been granted long since in their favour, in
which their liberties had been secured, but that this had been
secreted by the monks, and they demanded that it should
be surrendered to them. The abbot made promises in
abundance, and ordered the seal to be affixed to the document required. But when the seal was pressed on the wax,
we are told that it could not be pulled away from the
impression, and the monks thereupon inferred that the
patron saint of the abbey, the proto-martyr of the British
Church in Roman days, was unfavourable to the demand
for the emancipation of the serfs. One would like to know
the serfs' account of the transaction.

The peasants' war was over in a week, if we are to trust
the account given of the events. And now the authorities

began to discover the process by which the insurrection was fomented, organized, and developed. A letter of an enigmatical but sufficiently intelligible kind addressed by one Schep, formerly a priest of York, but latterly of Colchester, to the confederates was discovered and has been preserved. It speaks of John Nameless, and John the Miller, and John Carter, Piers Plowman, and John Trueman, bids them beware of guile in borough, and to stand together in God's name. Piers Plowman is to do his work, and chastise Hob the robber. The confederates are assured that the king's son in heaven shall pay for all, and the circular ends with a few lines of doggerel. Richard did not long delay his vengeance. A commission was sent into the disturbed districts, and the movers of sedition were claimed from the chief persons in the towns and villages. The culprits were hanged, some say gibbeted in chains. It is stated that fifteen hundred suffered death in the various counties. Ball was taken to prison at Coventry, condemned by Tressilian, and executed. Seven years after Tressilian was himself hanged at the instance of the Duke of Gloucester, as was also Sir Simon Burley, who had given occasion to the Kentish and Essex insurgents by imprisoning the Gravesend burgess. The rolls of Parliament give a list of the several leaders in the insurrection with a view to their being indicted. These are probably persons who had not been captured in the assize of the judges. Seventeen are set down to Norfolk, twenty (four of whom are beneficed clergymen) to Suffolk, four to Cambridge, eleven to Essex, four to Herts, twenty-three to Middlesex, one hundred and fifty one to London, eight to Winchester, twenty to Kent, eight to Sussex, eleven to Somerset, and eight to Canterbury. Most of the London leaders are craftsmen and artizans. But I conceive that the harshness with which the rioters were treated by the law did not break the spirit of the people, or make them tamely submissive to authority, as it has not at other times. The bloody assizes of Jefferies were of no little assistance to the march of William of Orange, while he was in the West of England.

Tyler according to the judgment of his enemies (the unsuccessful leaders of insurrections have no friends), was a man of ready abilities and sound sense. He seems to have kept those who were under him in good order and discipline. He had probably seen military service, and kept a guard of picked followers about him, whom he was unwise enough to leave in the rear when he advanced to the parley in Smithfield. It is said, on the confession of some among his companions, that he intended to secure the King's person, to overset the system of feudal dependence, and to establish in its room a government of county districts, over each of which was to be put a person of like principles with himself. The monasteries would provide ample funds for these major-generals of the fourteenth century. It is curious that the scheme was that adopted in the seventeenth century by Cromwell, and shows at least that the purposes of the leaders in this insurrection were far more extensive than the remedy of mere personal wrongs, and that they contemplated even more than the extinction of services in villeinage,—a scheme, namely, for the reconstruction of English society. I admit that the confessions of criminals are always suspicious, but there is just the probability in this confession that the plan is one of singular political foresight, and could never have been invented by a foolish monk.

The Essex serfs sent certain delegates to the king, praying that the charters of manumission should be confirmed. We are told that he answered the petitioners savagely, in language which was suggested by the reply of the rash Rehoboam. The story is exceedingly improbable. It is not likely that, when the embers of insurrection were still smouldering, he would have told the serfs that he " would so order with them and their descendants that the generations to come should curse the memory of those who had provoked the insurrection." Besides, it is clear that the best of his counsellors would have gladly seen the charters confirmed by Parliament, as is proved by the authentic record of proceedings contained in the Rolls. He had, perhaps, revoked the charters of manumission. They were not legal and could not be binding. It was and is a plain maxim of law, that no grant or remission on the part of the king could be allowed to injure another. The king could remit a forfeiture, the benefit of which would accrue to the Exchequer, but not an escheat, the benefit of which might accrue to a lord. He could pardon a murderer convicted in his court by a jury summoned to try an offender against the Crown ; he could not pardon a criminal, even one who had been pardoned after a first conviction, who was convicted on an appeal of blood at the instance of the nearest relative of the deceased. The charters could not be considered valid. Seventy years afterwards, when Cade's insurrection occurred, and the artifice of a promise of pardon was employed to disperse the insurgents, we are informed by Gascoigne, no mean judge of contemporary events, that Cade hesitated to take the proffered pledge on the ground that it needed the confirmation of Parliament.

Parliament met on Sept. 16th, and the situation was immediately put before it. The Treasurer, Sir Hugh Segrave, informs the Commons that "the king had been forced to grant the insurgents letters patent under the Great Seal, enfranchising to a considerable extent those who were only bond servants and villeins of the realm, for which the king, knowing it to be against law, directs them to seek remedy and provide for the confirmation or revocation thereof. If they desire to enfranchise and manumit their villeins by common consent, he will assent to it." The answer given unanimously is, "That all grants of liberties and manumission to the said villeins and bond tenants, obtained by force, are in disherison of them, the Lords and Commons, and to the destruction of the realm, and therefore null and void ;" and they add, that "this consent they would never give to save themselves from perishing all together in one day."

Language such as the above, employed by the king or his councillors; suggestions so generous as those proposed to the Commons by the Crown, and, I may add, so much in accordance with the policy of the Government afterwards, are inconsistent with the threats and reproaches which Walsingham puts in the mouth of Richard a few weeks

before. We know that the policy of the Government was by
no means unfriendly to the emancipation of the serfs, that
every construction which lawyers could put upon usage or
statute was favourable to their freedom, and that in after
years the king put his veto on those petitions of the Commons by which he is entreated to impose social disabilities
on the condition of villeinage. Thus in 1391, ten years after
the insurrection, the king declines to accede to the request
that the sons of serfs should not be allowed to frequent the
universities, or to listen to the complaint that "they fly to
cities and boroughs and are there harboured, and that the
lord, on attempting to recover his serf, is hindered by the
people." The Commons suggest in their prayer that the lord
should be allowed the remedy of allowing the serf to be
seized without regard to the franchise of the place in which
he has taken refuge.

In singular contrast to this outbreak, and yet to some
extent in harmony with its temper, is an account of an
outrage committed by the Mayor of Cambridge, one Lystere,
and four of the bailiffs of the same town, on April 30th, 1381,
some six weeks before Tyler's outbreak. These officials of
the city were dissatisfied with the charters granted to the
University. So they set on the University authorities, compelled them to deliver up all charters conferring franchises
and privileges on the students, which they burnt on the spot,
and further constrained them to execute a formal renunciation of all their rights by an instrument under their common
seal. The citizens for this outrage were fined 101 marks.
The act was certainly not so alarming as the insurrection of
the peasants, and did not portend such serious consequences;
and the penalty was, perhaps, even for a town of nearly three
thousand inhabitants at this time, light; but it shows that
passionate demonstrations against privileges or usurpations
were not confined to the lower orders, but were encouraged
even among the burgesses of an east county town. Cambridge was probably at this time, like its neighbour counties,
strongly leavened with those doctrines of equality which the
poor priests had been preaching.

The peasants were dispersed and defeated ; their leaders were tried, sentenced, and hanged ; but the solid fruits of victory rested with the insurgents of June 1381. It may have been the case that the discontent was too widespread. The peril had been so great, and the success of the insurrection was so near, that wise men saw it was better to silently grant that which they stoutly refused in Parliament to concede. It has always been so, and, until social man has solved every problem, an impossible Utopia, it always will be the case that wise men counsel concession when the less far-sighted clamour for resistance. The history of the English Parliament is full of examples, instructive in the highest degree, of the fact. There have been constantly persons who affirm that the grant of the commonest justice will bring about "that they all will perish in one day," as the Commons of 1381 predicted, when the English landowners were in the most grievous strait that has ever occurred in their history. It is true that in the great majority of cases, and till comparatively recent times, the efforts of those who have led the way in reform have been directed towards the maintenance of those public liberties from which, in the nature of things, the wealthy and well-to-do reap more benefit than the poor and the anxious. This is not, indeed, to be regretted, for till liberty and equal law are granted to all, the amendment of the poor man's lot is indefinitely postponed, though, when that earliest justice is done, the righting of other wrongs may be remote, but is within the ken of the true statesman. When wreck was made of Parliamentary institutions in the great war of the English Succession, and a despotism, not, indeed, absolute, but therefore more dangerous, was induced over every part of an Englishman's life, except his memory, it took two centuries and a half before even the shadow of the fifteenth-century Parliament was restored. Since that time, we of this generation and our fathers have been striving for fifty years to secure some of those acts of justice and wisdom which are essential to the well-being, the progress, the moral health of our countrymen. If any one were to collect the predictions which have been uttered as to the certain ruin of our institutions and our fortunes should this or that be conceded; if one were to narrate the intrigues, to expose the falsehoods, to unravel the diplomacy, to reveal the hypocrisy, to excuse the timidity of those who have resisted wholesome change, we should be telling the history of the English Parliament for the last fifty years. Liberty and property, the two conditions of social order, have been invoked as names, by those who know nothing of any liberty but their own privilege to do wrong, and no property but that which custom has allowed them to appropriate and fence.

It would not be difficult for one to exhibit in modern argument the defence of serfage and the attack on the institution, for the slight echoes which have come to us from the strife of tongues in 1381 are no way different, except in the faintness of the sound, from those which are ringing loudly in our memories five centuries later. The advocates of the old order would allege, that "on the foundations of submission had grown up marvellously noble institutions, a beautified land, full of handsome churches, served by a devout and faithful priesthood, whose labours were supplemented by the prayers of holy and religious monks, within whose cloisters the young of all classes are taught and promoted, and the annals of the kingdom are faithfully transcribed. The country is embellished with noble castles, not now an offence, but a protection; and every parish has its manor-house, in which justice is done, agriculture is fostered, and the ancient institutions of England are maintained. The owners of these possessions feed the hungry, give employment to the needy, a career to the active and bold. When the heir of the ancestral house comes of age, the country side is feasted, and the salt is put below the tenants of the lordship and the manors. It may be the case that, in some degree, we live by the earnings of our tenants, but we have made the name of England terrible in Palestine and Egypt, in Sicily and Spain, and have overthrown the proudest chivalry of Europe. Is it nothing that the English king has been offered the imperial crown, and that we hold the balance of power in Europe; that the king's eldest uncle is the rightful king of Spain, as our king is the rightful heir of France, in the just recovery of which he will imitate the deeds of his glorious father and grandfather ? Take from us, who have been the pioneers of England's greatness, the means by which we can maintain the traditions of the race, and England will be the last of nations, as she has been the first. If we do not hold our grip upon what we possess, and regain what we should possess, our supremacy is gone, our place in the councils of Europe will be forgotten, and trade will desert the flag to which we fail to rally. Besides, it is the lot of the poor to labour, and their duty to be patient."

On the other hand, it might be alleged that "contracts must not be one-sided, but equitable ; that they should be, in the interests of all, faithfully kept by both parties ; that the peasant, who has improved his holding at his own cost, cannot safely, without wrecking the real fortunes of the people, be discouraged from that toil which, one way or other, continues and adds to the wealth of the nation ; that discontent, fostered by unjust dealing, is more dangerous than any foreign foe ; and that in no case should the misfortunes of one class be made a pretext for wronging all others. All have suffered, they might continue, from a grievous visitation. There is no home in England which does not mourn its losses. Is it wrong that the survivors should make the best of their condition ; or, at least, is it not reasonable that they should enjoy the fruits of those agreements which you have voluntarily, and in what appeared to be your interests, extended ? The effects of the calamity will pass away, and you will find that your difficulties will be also transient. Besides, you have another remedy. Your ancestors founded those lordships which opulent abbots possess. Valuable as their prayers may be, it was never intended that those prayers should be endowed so richly as to reduce the kingdom to penury. These holy men have a third of the land of England in fee. They were far holier when they were poorer. English honour and English power could be supported abroad by a portion of their superfluities, and, if the worst comes, knights and nobles enough could be maintained on the lands of the monks. The poor priests went too far, but they have been chastised   Those who took up arms have been dispersed. But you will never break the spirit of an Englishman, and it is far better to drop that which you cannot justly claim and you could not safely exact." I can imagine a Salisbury of the Montacute race arguing in this fashion, if not publicly, yet earnestly in private or in the lobbies; and I can easily conceive an unanimous vote against that which, a short time afterwards, would be churlishly granted, or more wisely conceded in silence. For in those times *le Roy s'avisera* meant the opposition of the Government.

That the claims of the serfs were conceded, or, if you please, the claims of the landlords were dropped, is absolutely certain. The Parliament cried " No surrender ! " in September, and began to surrender immediately. " Snap resolutions " were no doubt made ten years or less afterwards, but the Government evaded them, and declined to give effect to the petition, as they called it in those days, convinced that matters would turn out better than malcontents and reactionaries imagined. The custom of commuting the old labour rents for money payments became universal; the serfs became copy-holders, and the insurrection of Tyler, once a terrible memory, became in the later annals the mere outbreak of a mob, which had been stirred to indignation by a brutal tax-gatherer, or an insurrection of frantic communism, or, as one of our later philosophers has described it, " The outcome of an age in which social inequality was over keenly felt." The wiser contemporaries of the movement agreed to abandon its provocations, and consign it to oblivion or misconception.

But the Court and the Government could not forgive the Lollards. They drove them from Oxford, and threatened to extinguish the University itself, unless they were suppressed. In appearance Oxford submitted. It displaced the Lollard chancellor, and elected one of Wiklif's colleagues at Bruges. The preachers were silenced, which means that they were rendered cautious. Many went across the sea, and spread the new Gospel of the Bible-men to the furthest confines of the Christian world. Some recanted, and became bishops, cardinals, and persecutors. But many remained. You cannot meet, said one of the monkish historians, five people talking together, but three of them are Lollards. The Archbishop of Canterbury, who was noble, orthodox, and treasonable, said that there were wild vines in the University, and therefore little grapes; that tares are constantly sown among the pure wheat, and that the whole University is leavened with heresy. Nor do I doubt that when Henry IV. came to the throne, he still remembered the scene in Smithfield, and putting cause and effect together, though he had no ill-will to the country-folk, to whom he conceded the largest franchise, a franchise not yet restored, that he had little love to the Lollard priests, and readily put the duty on the sheriffs in boroughs and mayors in towns of burning such heretics as the clergy had handed over to the secular arm.

Two inferences beyond these which fall within the domain of ordinary politics can be gathered from the causes which preceded the outbreak of 1381, and from the consequences which ensued after the storm was over. One of them has often been noticed, the other I think rarely, if ever.

1. The success of a religious movement has generally, if not invariably, been associated with a movement for improving the moral and secular advantage of those whom it seeks to benefit. In this permanent condition lies the difference between a superstition and a religion, between the slavery and the freedom of dogmas. The teachings of Buddha and Zoroaster, of Christianity and of Islam, are based on the principles of freedom, of the giving liberty to the captives, of the opening of the prison to them that have been bound. They invariably contain the doctrine of the equality of man, if not before the secular ruler, at least in the sight of God, and for the saving of men's souls, and have as regularly been a reaction or protest against tenets which are intended to serve limited interests. It is possible to carry out what you may call a reformation, an entire and wholesale purification or abscission of dogmas, but if in the end it is felt or seen that the process is merely intended to serve the functions of government, or to bolster up an existing order, or to control personal but devout freedom, it never commands sympathy

and never has a lasting influence. It has over and over again been the fate of national churches, created in what seemed to be the interests of order, to fade gradually out of all living reality, and to become extinct forms. The institution may be useful, it may be respectable, it may from time to time become the rallying ground of vehement party spirit, but it never becomes the inner life of its disciple, the object of his existence. This is curiously illustrated in the history of Scotch Presbyterianism, for certain reasons the most national of religions, and its numerous sects.

Now Lollardy in the fourteenth and fifteenth centuries was a religion which associated itself directly with the moral and material interests of its disciples. It was probably sour and opinionative. It certainly made no scruple in scoffing at and insulting the State creed, and in the few records we have of the doings of these poor and obscure sectaries, the fact is noted. "All the Lollards," says one chronicler, "hated images ; they even called the image of our Lady at Lincoln, the witch of Lincoln." One of the poor priests is said to have lighted the fire at the lepers' chapel at Leicester with an image of St. Catherine. A number of these Lollards cut down the crucifix in the parish of Westcheam, tied it to the tails of horses, and threw it into a sewer at Kingston-on-Thames. Very likely persecution bred hatred and outrage. But these sectaries inculcated those virtues of social life which among active men give a solid earnest of religious hope. The Lollard would sacrifice his worldly possessions, even his life, to his creed; but while he was allowed or permitted to cherish his creed, or his creed escaped detection, he did not disdain the assistance which his religion gave him towards prosperity in his calling. Hence they were thought to be disaffected men, who wanted an opportunity, but had no excuse for wishing it.

2. Such political movements as are organized and developed with any hope of effecting their object ultimately and permanently are always the outcome of times in which prosperity, or at least relative comfort, is general. The forces of society always make easy work of the outbreak

which despair sometimes instigates. The Jacquerie in France, the Peasants' War in Germany, were desperate efforts, ferocious reprisals, but futile struggles. The years which preceded the Peasants' War in England were times of high wages and low prices. The means of life were abundant, the earnings of the labourer exceptionally great. The teachings of the poor priests were addressed to men whose prospects were far higher than those of their fathers, whose opportunities were greater and more immediate than those of their remote descendants. What is the use of preaching social equality to the indigent and miserable? How can men combine and organize when their one thought is for their daily bread, and that is only secure for the day? The message of Wiklif's priests would have seemed a mockery to the destitute. How can the starving contend for their rights? The overmastering sense of a struggle for bare life leaves no room for any other thought. I am persuaded that the most remarkable religious movement of which we have accurate and continuous information, that of Wesley, with its unlimited sympathy and easily attainable optimism, would have fallen on deaf ears in other times than those of the extraordinary plenty which marked the first half of the eighteenth century, and agriculture became a favourite calling. But this plenty was as nothing to the golden times of the fifteenth, when the earth brought forth by handsful, and the yeomanry were planted in England.

Once in the history of England only, once, perhaps, only in the history of the world, peasants and artizans attempted to effect a revolution by force. They nearly succeeded; at least they became, for a short time, the masters of the situation. That they would have held the advantages they gained at Mile End, had they provided against the tragedy of Smithfield, is improbable. But they caused such terror by what they actually did, that they gained all that they claimed, and that speedily. The English labourer, for a century or more, became virtually free and constantly prosperous. The machinery with which they began their efforts still existed

I have no doubt that the services which the poor priests, Bible-men, and Lollard preachers had done in and after the great crisis of 1381, is the explanation, in some degree at least, of the passionate persistence with which Lollard tenets were secretly cherished during the whole of the fifteenth century. It was due to the fact that the upland folk and the village artizans favoured, protected, and concealed an organization which was reputed to be hostile to the rights of property, that the influential laity at the beginning of this century made no serious demur to the unconstitutional statute under which convicted heretics were, after trial in the spiritual courts, handed over for execution to the secular authorities, who were compelled to carry out the decrees of the bishops and their deputies. That this statute would have been rescinded if it had not been conceived supremely useful is, I am convinced, certain, if one takes account of what the temper of the English laity was at the time. But the working classes identified the Lollard teachers with their emancipation in the past and their progress in the present. It is known, obscure as the annals of fifteenth-century Lollardy are, that one of the most audacious of these preachers laboured long in his calling, and so constantly eluded his persecutors that he seemed to bear a charmed life. William White, who had for years preached in Norfolk, disguised and hidden by the weavers, was at last captured in 1427, and burnt at Norwich. He left successors to his teaching, who were as much trouble, more than a century later, to Somerset and Cranmer as he and his had been to Bedford and Chicheley. But what was a disservice and a danger to property, was a service and a security to labour. The villagers and craftsmen whispered the names of those men with respect and affection whom the landowners and the clergy had proscribed. They hid them in the day of peril, though their means of concealment must have been imperfect, just as they secreted those fragments of the Bible and their comments on its teaching which seemed to them to be the irreversible charter of their liberties and of their hopes.

They who have discussed the history of religious movements in England have discovered in the vigorous courage of those who began and continued the Puritan movement in England, immediately after the Reformation, and especially that early off-shoot from it, the Independent or Congregational organization, nothing but the influence of Genevan experiences in the exiles of the Marian persecution. To my mind, and in the light of what I have read, this explanation is quite insufficient, though I can readily allow it a proper force. Geneva would have produced little fruit in the minds of the better off peasantry and the artizans unless it had found the soil already prepared by the teaching of Lollardy. Wiklif is infinitely more the father of English Protestantism than Cromwell and Cranmer, Parker and Grindal were. There is a saying that Cambridge bred the founders of the English Reformation, and Oxford burnt them. There is a grain of truth in the statement. The English Reformation took root in the minds of the people in the Eastern Counties not because State Anglicanism was developed in the younger University, but because for nearly a couple of centuries the poor priests of Wiklif's school had pursued their obscure but effectual labours in the east of England, and had familiarized the minds of men with an organization which was first bitterly hostile to Rome, and afterwards as irreconcilable with Canterbury

CHAPTER X.

THE LANDLORD'S REMEDIES.

THE old system of cultivation by the capitalist landlord
was hopelessly doomed. Wages were rising, profits and
prices were falling. During the twenty years between 1371
and 1390 the labourer was engaged in stereotyping his new
rate of remuneration, and during the best part of a generation
had accustomed himself to a scale of living and saving, which
was far in excess of previous experience. During the last
twenty years of the fourteenth century, the price of corn was
greatly below the average, though it must be allowed that,
when compared with the twenty years to which reference has
so often been made, labour was a little cheaper. The fact is,
a new class of farmers had become, or was fast becoming, the
employers of labour,—those who were occupiers on a lease, and
such persons were capable of striking a harder bargain in the
open market than the old capitalist landowner was. The rate
of wages is always lower when the principal employers are

small tenant farmers, if the number of labourers seeking for work and wages is considerable enough to compete against each other for employment. An Irish labourer gets very poor wages from an Irish farmer, an American farm hand gets good wages from an American occupier. But the reason is that the labourers are many in the former case, the employment scanty, and the bargain hard. In the latter the field labourers are comparatively few, and, in consequence, the labourer is often better off than the small farmer. In fourteenth and fifteenth-century England, the labourer was not indeed poorly paid ; far from it, but had it been possible for the old system to have continued, he would have been better off than he was under that which succeeded to the old.

The price of live stock was stationary. There is hardly a sensible difference between the old rates at which farm stock is sold, and those at which it changes hands during the last twenty years of the fourteenth century. On the whole, the rate rather declines than rises ; for we must remember that as landlord farming passes away, the record becomes one of consumable rather than of store stock, which it largely was at first, because the evidence of market values is chiefly that supplied by purchasers. The price of wool is still that of production, and is slightly lower. Dairy products are a little cheaper. The other articles which were essential to the conduct of husbandry are even dearer ; such, for instance, a iron. Fifty years had elapsed since the Great Plague, and the habitually adverse balance on the producer's side of the account, and there was no prospect that the conditions would be altered. The same facts apply to agricultural implements, to the various materials used for building, and, in short, to all articles which, being produced by labour and sold to the best purchaser, could command the market price without restraint.

I am quite aware that the weight of the silver penny was reduced by about ten per cent., *i.e.*, from $22\frac{1}{2}$ grains to 20 grains during the century. But it is also clear that if the lessening of the weight in the coin effected, as it would seem natural that it should, a rise in prices, it ought to have had the effect all round. But we find that the price of food is lessened ; while in the price of labour, and all articles whose value is related to labour only, by which I mean in which there was no element of rent or profit against which the tendency to rise would operate, there is a rise which is wholly disproportionate to, and in excess of, the lessening of the silver unit. Whatever effect, then, the action of the mint might have had, or however much the concurrent circulation of gold, either of foreign origin or of English mintage, should have had an effect on the price of silver, it is plain that it did not produce the result of heightening prices all round. The ingenious explanation, then, of Adam Smith, that silver was gradually becoming scarcer,—a conclusion he arrived at by noticing, in the very scanty evidence which was supplied him, a constantly decreasing price of food, and the principal necessaries of private life—is untenable, as Smith would himself have declared had information as to the wages of labour during this period been in his possession.

The English government was keenly alive to the risk which it imagined that it ran from the depletion of the precious metals. In the interpretation of the painful problem before them, though the English landowners set sufficient importance on the factor which was represented by the enhanced rate of wages, they are willing enough to believe that the scarcity of silver increased the mischief. Long before the trouble came, however, the king established, in 1335, the office of the King's Exchanger, appointing William de la Pole, a Hull and London merchant, to the office, with the duty of superintending the import and export of the precious metals at the various staples. In the same reign, but shortly afterwards, the offence of coining and clipping was made high treason, and I cannot believe that Parliament, which was keenly awake to grievances, would have quietly acquiesced in the reduction of the penny by ten per cent. if the value of the piece had been, as we conclude it would have been, sensibly diminished, or the older and heavier coins had disappeared, as they should have done, and it appears did not.

It would be a long and tedious business to state the arguments which have persuaded me that from the earliest times till after the issue of base money under Henry VIII., payments in England were not made by tale but by weight, and that consequently it was of no great importance that the size of the piece should be uniform or continuous. I do not affirm that my reasons are entirely conclusive, for they lack the proof of direct evidence, but the circumstances are so probable, and the facts are so inexplicable on any other interpretation, that I feel myself compelled to conclude in the manner which I have indicated. I cannot conceive that for the temporary advantage which the fraud of reducing the weight would have given, the Crown would have committed the extraordinary folly of reducing the whole of its revenue which was derived from fixed sources, and represented by fixed payments for ever, or that the most patient and the most supine body of landowners, and such the nobles, knights, and gentry of the fourteenth and fifteenth centuries were certainly not, would have acquiesced in the permanent and irreversible reduction of all their dues and rents.

For many years before the Great Plague, landowners had been occasionally in the habit of letting land on lease. If the estate were too distant for convenient access, it was found advisable to adopt this expedient. Thus Merton College possessed estates in the counties of Durham and Northumberland, the latter having been a gift to the founder of the college by Edmond of Lancaster. At first the college cultivated these estates with its own capital and under the supervision of its own bailiffs, as Lancaster had done before them. But the place was very distant, and could not be brought under that constant supervision of the owner which the bailiff system required. Again, the estate was near the border, and constantly liable to be overrun. Fraudulent bailiffs were not unknown, and it would have been easy to magnify or even invent a loss. Hence the college determined, at a very early date, to lease these lands. Sometimes, again, the owner succeeded to, or purchased, an estate in which the lease of the whole manor, under the ordinary process of granting perpetual tenancies at fixed rents, had been already effected—a system in which the commutation of labour for money was a necessity, since the labour rent could have been turned to no account if the lord had no land in his own hands. Sometimes the owner, for reasons of his own, which it is now impossible to discover, granted a lease of lands which, under ordinary circumstances, he had cultivated himself, to some tenant for a varying term of years, and when the term was over, resumed the property, and resumed the old system of bailiff cultivation with the landlord's capital. I have already illustrated this practice. It takes place in property near as well as remote, and was probably due either to the fact that the landlord had advantageous offers, or it was difficult to find a sufficiently trustworthy bailiff, or because the land-owner was suffering from some temporary straitening of his circumstances, and was glad to avoid a large immediate outlay and unproductive arrears, for the arrears which were necessarily in the hands of the bailiff were often very con-siderable. Occasionally these leases were long, thirty years or more. Sometimes they were short, for five or seven. Sometimes the lord would let the arable land and retain the pasture, especially if he kept stock, and determined on a sheep, cattle, or horse-breeding farm ; for it is clear that the supervision of a stock farm would need beyond what was sunk in the stock, a less working capital, and should represent fewer arrears.

The abandonment of landlord cultivation takes place at various times after the plague. This is partly due to the conservative feeling of certain proprietors, who struggled against the change, hoping things would mend, or that they should get cheaper labour, or that they might find Acts of Parliament and royal ordinances efficacious. Sometimes it would seem that in cases where the landowners—in this case a corporation of an ecclesiastical or quasi-ecclesiastical kind —were possessed of tithes as well as land, or land held with tithe as part of the ecclesiastical endowment, they kept the system up because it was difficult to separate the tithe and the lay estate, or because they found it all but impossible to find a lessee. In the end they generally granted a lease of the tithes to their vicar, and as generally, also, on very advantageous terms,—so advantageous occasionally as in some degree to make the impropriation little more than a moderate rent charge. But everything goes at last, and the tenant farmer takes the place of the landlord. The last *bonâ fide* cultivation of the old kind that I have seen is in 1433-4; and here I suspect that the amount of land held by the lord had been considerably cut down before the residue was leased. Sometimes it is true that the corporation retained home farms in its hands. Battle and Sion Abbeys do so up to the beginning of the sixteenth century.

When, during the prevalence of the old system, a landlord occasionally let his lands to farm, he invariably let his stock, live and dead, with them. The stock—never quite as copious as during the landlord's occupation, and, to judge from the valuation assigned to it, never of so high a quality—was carefully recorded on the lease which the tenant and landlord executed, and as regularly entered on the back of the tenant's roll of account, for such tenants rendered audit annually, just as the old bailiffs did, and had to exhibit their stock to the collector or steward. It is probable that at the creation of one of these stock and land leases the landowner disposed of the household effects and the best of the herd and flock, leaving only such a quantity as the tenant would take, or would find necessary in order to supplement the deficiency of his own capital. The landlord generally leases along with the live and dead stock a certain amount of seed corn, occasionally corn for wages and food. All this the tenant covenants to restore at the conclusion of his time in good condition, reasonable depreciation excepted, at a fixed price for every quarter of corn, head of cattle, sheep, and poultry, with the assessed value of the dead stock left on the farm. As I have said, the valuation is generally low.

Now in the old times, the stock and land lease, as it had its occasional utility to the landlord and its necessity to the tenant, was also an inevitable arrangement for the landlord. Such a lease was essentially a temporary bargain. The landlord always might, and generally did, contemplate the resumption of his estate and its renewed cultivation under the old capitalist landlord system. To have got entirely rid of his stock would have made it difficult for him to resume his old relations. He might have wished, when he called in his arrears, and either exacted his debts or wrote them off as irrecoverable, to put himself in funds by the sale of his best or superfluous stock. But he would not entirely abandon the means of renewing, perhaps under more favourable conditions, the advantageous and profitable system which was so general.

There was, indeed, one kind of stock leasing which was of immemorial antiquity,—that of letting cows to dairy farmers. It was exceedingly common in the middle ages,—so common that it was the rule on many estates ; and thus the records of dairy produce are frequently absent from such estates as kept considerable herds of cattle. It endured longer than any custom which was handed down from the middle ages, for it is constantly referred to by Arthur Young, not only as a practice but as an index of profit on good pastures. In the older agriculture, the lessee of the cows, sometimes of the oxen, is the deye, *i.e.*, the dairyman or maid, and the fact bears testimony to the growth of property among those who had belonged to the servile classes.

The new stock and land lease was generally for a short period, from seven to ten years. The advantage of this was obvious, not that the lord was likely to get better terms, but that he had better security for the due return of his stock at the end of the period. The lord always covenants to keep the buildings in repair, for in this the lessee on a term differed from the tenant on a fee farm rent ; but he also stipulated to insure the tenant against the losses by murrain in his sheep, the word used generically for all diseases which are fatal to animals. On the other hand, the tenant took the risks of scab, which the farriery of the time conceived to be curable by proper precautions and remedies. The risk was not trivial, though it imposed a minimum loss on the tenant. The maximum which the tenant had to bear appears to have been ten per cent. of the stock ; and the landlord frequently had to compensate him to the extent of twenty per cent. more. Besides this the landlord was expected to assist the tenant, either when the price of corn was very low, or when the farmer had suffered serious losses in his own harvest or in the quality of his crops. In short, the landlord learnt early that he had to submit to part of those casualties which the tenant affirmed that he had endured, for under a stock and land lease the amount of goods on which the landlord could distrain was necessarily limited to the tenant's crops and property.

Adam Smith (Book III. chap. ii.) saw that such a form of tenure as that which I have described must have existed in England at some period between that in which the small tenancies in villeinage existed, and the holdings of tenant farmers cultivating land with stock of their own commenced. He compares it to the metayer tenancy, which in his time prevailed, and for a much longer time, which probably prevails now in Southern France and Northern Italy. It differs from *métairie* in the fact (1) that it was essentially a temporary expedient, (2) that the rent was open to periodical adjustment, *i.e.*, was not a fixed quantity, and (3) that the stock was valued to the tenant, and had to be restored by him on the determination of the lease. A metayer tenancy is a virtual partnership between landowner and tenant, by which, in consideration of certain advances of stock made and renewed, the landowner receives a certain share of the produce, whatever the amount may be. In the land and stock lease, the tenant, subject to the regular insurance and the occasional help alluded to above, took his chance of the seasons and the markets, and made what he could by his land. We are told by Adam Smith that even in his time such farmers existed in Scotland, under the name of steel bow tenants. They had a much shorter existence in England, for they had passed away so completely, and had become so much a matter of distant tradition, that the law-writers of modern times who commented on them entirely misunderstood their meaning.

The stock and land lease was a necessity to both landlord and tenant, but it was an advantage to both. It enabled the latter to increase his holding, his margin of profit, his savings, and to become either a tenant with his own capital, or the purchaser of freehold or copyhold estate for himself. It is plain that the former must have been the result of the system, or the capitalist tenant would never have been developed. It is equally clear that the latter was no infrequent consequence, or we should not see how very large the number of the freeholders was in the fifteenth, sixteenth, and seventeenth centuries. An occupying freeholder of eighty acres with rights of common was, if we may conclude from the rent rolls and manor records, in the fourteenth century and earlier, a comparatively rare personage ; in the fifteenth he becomes numerous enough to form the basis of a new political system, and in the seventeenth he gives that system solidity and strength. That this tenant made the best bargain he possibly could with the landlord we may be quite sure ; that he was not slow to take advantage of the landlord's necessities, to get stock at the lowest possible rate, and to exaggerate his losses in fold and market, we may be also quite certain ; but it is even more certain that he was thriving, and that the business of the agriculturist was eminently profitable in the fifteenth century. In about seventy years, with rare exceptions, land which is hitherto let on the stock and land system is turned into the holding of an ordinary capitalist tenant farmer. It was naturally kept up longest where the landlords were the easiest, and it is noted that the practice continued with some of the monastic lands to the time of the Reformation, as we find from the sales of monastic chattels, the accounts of which are preserved in the Record Office. These show by the prices at which the stock is sold that they were either forced sales, or that great allowances were made to the tenants in purchasing them.

We are fortunately able to determine what the profit of a stock and land lease was to the landowner. I have printed in my third volume of the " History of Agriculture and Prices" (pages 705-8), the stock on a farm let on a land and stock lease at Alton Barnes, in Wilts, in the year 1455, and at a rental of £14.

The farm contains the manor and domain lands, except

meadows and pasture at the manor. It is said, at the end of the account, to amount to 108 acres of the second ploughing, of which 44 have been composted by sheep. The tenant has, however, been for some time in possession of the tenancy. The stock is corn, live stock and dead stock, most of the live stock and some of the dead being valued. The corn will be taken at market prices near the locality, where it is very cheap, and the few other articles which are not valued will be estimated. It is to be observed that the quantity of corn left on the estate is far in excess of any requirements of seed, and is to be interpreted as a stock for the exigencies of the year, from Michaelmas to Michaelmas, just as under the old bailiff farming a considerable amount of corn and stock is treated as working capital independently of the arrears. The collector of rents has arrears in his hand, the particulars of which are not given. The amount, however, proves that the collector had succeeded some one who is very remiss. The arrears amount to £13 11s. 2d. The rents of assize are £5 10s. 8d. The farmer's rent is £14, and the collector's total liabilities are £32 1s. 10d. He is allowed for void and excused holdings 19s. 11d.; and in external expenses, including his own fee of 5s. 6d., 7s. 8d. The warden's visit to the manor involves a cost of 4s. 4½d. He pays £25 6s. 10d. in two sums to his employers. The college allows the farmer £2 4s. 5½d. off his arrears, on the ground that his farm for previous years has yielded unsatisfactory crops. He pays £20 rent and arrears in part, a further allowance of £2 being made for this year, and acknowledges a liability of £1 18s. 7d.

Now the corn which the tenant takes over is worth, at the nearest place in Wilts, £11 8s. 6½d.; the live stock, five horses, eleven oxen, a bull, three cows, two heifers, and two yearlings, are valued at £13 2s. 4d.; the sheep, 571 (it is specially a sheep farm, with extensive hill pastures, long since enclosed), at £39 9s. 6d.; the rest of the live stock at 15s. 4d.; and the whole live stock is, therefore, valued at £64 15s. 4½d. The dead stock, which partly is priced, is put at £3 15s. 2d. There are, however, a large number of other articles which the tenant takes over under the same conditions, and the whole amounts to £68 10s. 6½d. To this must be added the purchase value of the land, which at 6d. an acre rent and twenty years' purchase, the ordinary payment for unstocked land, and the purchase value of land at or about the time that the lease was delivered, brings the capital value of the holding, land, and stock, up to £122 10s. 6½d. Here I must also add the unvalued dead stock. Besides ordinary farm implements, ploughs, rakes, prongs, hoes, a sickle, a scythe, wood-hooks, and similar articles, it comprises a brass cover and basin, a brass four-gallon pot, a spit weighing 20 lb., and 20 lb. of raw iron for repairing the ploughs. We shall deal fairly with the sum total if we raise it to £125, by including the value of these articles.

I have taken the prices nearest the estate. They are very low this year. Wheat is only 4s., barley 2s. 4d., pulse 2s., and oats 1s. 8d. a quarter. I think it would be reasonable, in estimating what was in the mind of the owner when he made his bargain with his tenant (especially as he allows him a considerable sum in consequence of unremunerative prices), to take better prices. The average of the decade in the midst of which this year stands would raise the corn prices £5 higher, and the tenant would thus be paying a little under eleven per cent. of its capital value for a land and stock farm in the middle of the fifteenth century. It is true that the landowner is still under a risk. By the terms of his agreement, the tenant is to restore every article enumerated in his holding in good condition,—the corn in the quantities specified, the live stock similarly,—the landlord having the right to claim their pecuniary valuation at his discretion. In theory the owner's property is therefore indestructible. But the following clause is inserted in the document after the enumeration and assessment of the sheep :—" And be it known that if the wethers (284) die of common murrain in a year to the number of 28 or less, the ewes (160) to the number of 16 or less, the hoggs (120) to the number of 12 or less, the farmer shall bear the loss himself. But whatever die in excess of these numbers, the landlord shall bear the loss of them." The landlord, therefore, guarantees his tenant in all loss of sheep over ten per cent. This was no slight contingency. Three years before the landlord paid on 46, seven years before on 116, eight years before on 63. These charges would reduce the rent payable materially.

In the year 1530, the same person, one John Benger, is at once farmer and rent collector, as Richard Benger, his father, had been in 1484. The land and stock lease is still in operation, for his arrears are limited to the stock, and his indebtedness at the end of the year is also said to be the stock. His rent is now £15 10s. and a quarter of oats. But his tenancy now includes the meadow, pasture, and close of the manor house, which appear to have been excluded in the lease of 1455. The rents of assize are 5s. 4d. less than they were 75 years previously, but just the same as they were 46 years before. Considering that the tenant has now a fair quantity of meadow land, we may conclude that there is no appreciable rise in the rental of this farm for three-quarters of a century. The clause of insurance is not inserted in the subsequent accounts, but neither are the particulars of the stock. They had undoubtedly been continued on this hypothetical basis of indestructibility with the condition previously stated during this very lengthened period.

So prolonged a land and stock lease is, however, very exceptional, at least in such accounts as I have seen, and these amount to many thousands. In the great majority of cases the land is ultimately let for short terms. Thus, in an estate belonging to the same proprietors with that which I have described above, and in Oxfordshire, the three manors contained within the parish, or within the range of the collector's labours, are severally let, one for a term of ten years, the other two for a year certain only. In the last two cases the farmer takes the rents of the other tenants, *i.e.*, stipulates as part of the tenure which he has to guarantee to the landlord his rents of assize for the term. The lessee of the third manor lands does not undertake the collection of the rent. They pay £8 13s. 4d., £12., and £16 respectively. It is impossible to separate the particulars of these holdings, for the dimensions of farms since the days of enclosures no way

correspond with their ancient limits.   They have been quoted
partly to show that leases on terms and for a year certain
were familiar, and also for another cause.

The rent could not be levied, or in case of default, the
tenant could not be distrained, unless the precise ground
from which the rent or service issued was known and defined.
This perpetually reappears, for instance, in the Oxfordshire
account before me.   " There is a deficiency of 28s. 2d. in the
rents of divers customary tenants, because one does not know
from what lands and tenements to levy them."   " Seven
capons should come from tenants there, and one does not
know whence to collect them."   " There is a particular field
called ' Matchyngbernys,' but the rent is not forthcoming,
amounting to £1 6s. 8d., because we do not know what land
to distrain on."   But the list of arrears is far more formidable.
" There is a sum of £56 13s. 4d., an arrear of 95 years, and
we do not know what to distrain on."   Collectors make
default, nine of them successively in the collective amount
of £86 9s. 10d.   Two of the farmers make default, or are
in arrears, to a sum which is over £50, while the whole
value of this very considerable estate appears to amount to
£102 4s. 6d.

I have referred to these particulars, tedious and technical
though they may seem to be, because they illustrate the
difficulties in which the landlord was put.   If he had a tenant
farmer on a stock and land lease, he was perpetually called
on to put his hand in his pocket, for repairs, for trade losses,
and for what were called in these days, as well as in ours, times
of agricultural distress, " *debilitas annorum.*"   If, on the other
hand, he leased his land without stock, he had to be exceedingly careful with his terriers and his rentals, in order to
secure his remedy of distress, and he ran the risk after all
of dishonest agents and defaulting tenants.   That circulation
of capital which involves competition for occupancies was
certainly in its infancy, if, indeed, it were known at all.   Except
as a purchaser, and then he would prefer his place of birth,
the occupying farmer was very unlikely to go far in order to
find a holding, and by parity of reasoning, when he did apply

for a holding in his native place, he was very unlikely to find a competitor from a distance. Even in London, offers of rent over another person's head were exceedingly distasteful. The annals of the Grocers' Company in the fifteenth century contain the record of fines of £10 each inflicted on two free-men of the Company for having offered a higher rent than a sitting tenant, and so having rented his house over him.

The exceedingly scattered character of the several lands in the common fields of manors must have been a serious incon-venience to the non-resident landowner, who had to employ, in addition to his own labour of supervision, the charge and risk of a collector of rents. When the old system prevailed, the bailiff was not only a trusted servant in constant commu-nication with his employers, but was conversant with every furrow which belonged to the domain, and constantly on the alert for his master's interests. But when the direct interest, and hitherto uninterrupted relations of the landowner with his estate, had come to a sudden end, especially with the memories of the past in their minds, and with the constant irritation of the Statute of Labourers, the small farmers, who were mere peasants, must have sympathised with everything which would weaken the hold of the landlord over property; and the landlord, as we shall see, was very keenly alive to any chance which the tenant gave him of increasing the rent of the occupier, and appropriating the benefits of his skill or industry.

During the fifteenth century, however, and notwithstanding the difficulties and losses of the landowner, the value of land rose rapidly. In the fourteenth century it was constantly obtained for ten years' purchase, the amount of land in the market being probably so abundant, and the competition for its purchase so slight, that it easily changed hands at such a rate. There was also no purchasing as yet on the part of the small proprietors, and it is always the case, that when land is made accessible to small buyers, the price rises rapidly, whereas if a country is one of large holders only, and hin-drances in the way of the acquisition of land prevent small purchasers from buying or even discourage them, a panic in the land market leads to a most disastrous depreciation. At the present time, if one may anticipate or deal with such a subject, while, under certain agricultural difficulties, the market price of land in England has fallen by thirty per cent. at least below what it was a dozen years ago, and in the opinion of some, a further fall is imminent, a late return from France shows that in almost every part of that country the price of land is still notably rising, though the agricultural calamities which have affected England affect France, besides what has been superadded in the disastrous diseases which have visited the vine, and in a less degree the silkworm. In England the opportunity and inclination for purchasing are seriously cramped by the absurd system of English conveyances and the preposterous charges which are imposed by the legal profession on the purchase and sale of land.

Land was valued at twenty years' purchase in the middle of the fifteenth century. In 1469 a valuation was made of Lord Cromwell's property. His lands were estimated at a capital value of £41,940 9s. 0½d., that is, he was considered to have a rental of £2,097 a year. In his lifetime he had made gifts to Tattenhall College, in money, of over £15,000; in land and goods of more than £7,500; and in jewels of £3,000; so that he had inherited and collected an estate of £67,440. Cromwell was Lord High Treasurer in 1433, and was subsequently an ardent Yorkist. The same rate of purchase is indicated by the amount of money which divers benefactors gave to certain of the Oxford colleges with a view of settling a fixed stipend on the object of their benefaction, the investment being generally directed to be made in land.

The passion for acquiring land, and the habit of constantly purchasing it in parcels, led, during the fifteenth century, to the purchase of copyholds by persons of good means and position. Such a practice must have considerably raised copyholds in social value. No doubt they purchased or extinguished the baser parts of the tenure, perhaps repudiated them, and were powerful enough to do so with impunity. I do not doubt that the transaction under which the dues of the Abbess of Sion, in the manor of Cheltenham, were reduced from £10 to ten marks (£6 13s. 4d.) by the arbitration of Sir Ralph Cotiller and others—an award which I discovered in the Record Office—was only a type of many such. Here Sir Ralph Cotiller, who, with others, undertakes the duty, appears to me to have the interest of a tenant in the manor. The award takes place at Cheltenham, in the presence of no less than twelve "esquires and many others." It is difficult to explain such a gathering for such an object, unless there had been interests influencing the assembly which are not stated on the record. But whatever may have been the motive, the change from the position of persons holding by a base tenure in 1381 must have been immeasurably different from what it was in 1452, when in the latter year the tenants were able, not only to force the Abbess of Sion into a renunciation of a third of her dues, but to enlist so powerful a body as the Prior of Deerhurst, Sir Ralph Cotiller, and others, to assist at and enforce the reduction of these liabilities.

It must not be imagined that the landowners and capitalists of the fifteenth century were indifferent to gain, and solely concerned with military operations. One of the most renowned captains of Henry's wars, Sir John Fastolfe, after having amassed a very considerable fortune in the wars and having settled in Norfolk, engaged very actively in the business of a corn dealer with the Low Countries. Many of his papers after his death came into the hands of Waynflete, the founder of Magdalene College, Oxford, and a *protégé* of Henry VI. He was appointed by this king his first master at Eton College, and, on Beaufort's death, to the bishopric of Winchester. He appears to have been Fastolfe's executor, and to have succeeded in diverting a portion of the funds, which the deceased captain intended for a very different foundation, to the opulent college in Oxford which he was endowing. From these papers, still preserved in the archives of the college, we find that Fastolfe sent large consignments of malt from Norfolk to Flanders, with which country it is probable that such transactions were habitually carried on. The price of barley and malt was exceedingly low in the Eastern Counties during the greater part of the fifteenth century; and as the law permitted its exportation when the price was below a certain amount, the trade was constantly brisk. The malt appears to have generally been shipped from the port of Norwich. In return, the Flemings taught the Eastern Counties the use of hops, which appear to have been employed in that region for flavouring beer nearly half a century before they became known to the rest of England. It is highly probable that the practice, of which the accidental preservation of Fastolfe's accounts informed me, was very general, and that not a little, we may hope, of Cromwell's fortune was procured from this innocent source.

The passion for acquiring land was further stimulated by the success with which trade was carried on in the fifteenth century, certainly for that early part of it which preceded the loss of the French and Gascon seaboard. I shall take occasion hereafter to point out what the nature of that trade was, how it was extended, and how the Cannyngs and the Chicheles were the prosperous successors of the Poles, the Walworths, and the Whittingtons. But the principal evidence of the opulence of England in the fifteenth century is to be found in its splendid churches and handsome residences. The castle gives way in the greater part of the country to the embattled house, built when the owner was wealthy and luxurious, if he could afford it, of the new and costly material, brick. And such brick it was. After four centuries it is as good and sharp as when it was first turned out of the kilns. Arches were turned in it, which might, for their flatness and the strength of their crowns, well excite the envy of the modern builder, or rather of the modern householder. The vast and solid churches, too, with their lofty towers, are a special result of the wealth and taste of the fifteenth century, more costly, more business-like, but far less full of that poetry in stone which marks the exquisite structures of the earlier generations. These places, like York Cathedral, were long in building, for the great minster was being slowly raised through the greater part of the fifteenth century, and, if all told is true, this noble church was paid for by expedients which were so scandalous that they gave no slight motive to the Reformation. But there is no building of this age which is marked by the beauties and the luxury of the time so fully as the gift of the pious Cannyngs, the church of St. Mary's, Redcliffe. Successful trade was no doubt a great source of English wealth in the time before me, but it was by no means the only source. The architectural antiquary can illustrate the fact more fully than I can pretend to do, or, for the matter of that, the professional architect.

It is more important for me to consider the consequences which ensued from the extinction of the capitalist landlord, and the decline of stock and land letting in England. They are so significant and become so permanent that they form an epoch in the social and economical condition of the country.

In the first place, they materially altered and ultimately destroyed those qualifications in the crude law of primogeniture which had for a long time modified its stringency. Whether it were by ordinance or custom, matters not; whether it arose at the epoch of the Conquest, or during that obscure period when the Norman and Saxon customs were being amalgamated in order to give effect to an aristocratical system, is not probably discoverable; but it is certain that the rule of giving the whole fee to the eldest son was early established, not only in the military tenures, but in that which we are advised the Norman settler would have disdained,—the estate of the free socager. The Kentish landowner kept his custom of equal division among all heirs of the same degree. There were manors where the serf was allowed to partition his holding, and some in which the parody of primogeniture, the succession of the youngest, under the name of borough English, was allowed, not without coarse guesses at the origin of the practice, to prevail, or was, maybe, constrained, in order that the lord might have the longest possible succession in the labour of his serf. But, with these exceptions, the whole land was under the custom of primogeniture. I have stated above that this custom was virtually modified under the system of capitalist cultivation by landlords. As long as the stock and land lease existed, it was in a less degree alleviated. But as soon as ever the farmer's tenancy came into existence, and the farmer's capital superseded the earlier systems, the custom of primogeniture became absolute and dominant.

We know now, from the records of religious and secular corporations, that the stock and land lease was not infrequent with such proprietors. We know that even the old system of capitalist cultivation survived among some corporate land-owners. But the majority of corporate estates, and almost all private estates, were, after a varying period, which averages some sixty or seventy years, according to the date at which the custom began, let to ordinary tenant farmers on short leases, who cultivated the land with their own capital, because they had succeeded in saving so much from the profits of a business, in which three times the value of the land was needed as capital in the older days, when land was cheap, and one-and-a-half times at least in later times was needed, as to either purchase their holdings out and out, of course with the old rents, or to cultivate a lease with their own property. My reader may perhaps think that this is an extravagant interpretation of the facts; but he will remember, if he has followed what I have pointed out pretty often, that there was little difference between a terminable and a perpetual lease, as far as the charge on the lessee was concerned, and that the real difference, discovered later on, when the money value of a fee farm rent was seen to be fixed, and that of a renewable lease was seen to be elastic, lay in the precarious nature of the latter. In point of fact, the way in which, on a demise, the lord could raise the letting value of his estate to a temporary tenant, was by mulcting him of a part of the average profits of agriculture, under the threat of eviction. When a considerable number of the tenants were freeholders at a full fee farm rent, by which I mean a rent not at all below what the tenant on a lease would pay, no grievance would arise in the mind of the lessee on a term; but when the landlord succeeded in exacting, under threat of eviction, an increased rent, that result ensued which Fitz-hubert deprecates and Latimer denounces,—the raising of the rent on the tenant, so that he dared not improve, and perhaps could hardly live.

It is not surprising that the landowner strove to screw his tenants. It is certain that during the fifteenth century the landowner was unable to screw them directly, and that the rack rent is a product of the early part of the sixteenth century. There is good reason to believe that the manorial lords enclosed largely where they could, and so curtailed the common pasture. This was the natural process by which a sheep farm was constructed, and sheep farms were common in the fifteenth century. But the lord had also to provide for his own. Any person who cares to study the *Fasti Anglicani,* by which the editors of that laborious publication mean the succession of the English bishops and deans, will see how the younger son after the Great Plague was quartered on the English Church. Even in the fourteenth century we find the names of Arundel, Courtney, Grandison, Nevil, Percy, Spenser, Stratford, Wentworth. They were more numerous in the fifteenth.

The great resource of the younger son, without land or means, and therefore sure to be quartered on the English people, was the army. The great war with France was maintained in the interest of the younger son. When the war was over he was to be a hanger on at the elder brother's house, or at the Court. For generations he was a mischievous, and sometimes a hateful adventurer. But as long as the stock and land lease lasted, he had his prospects in the division of the family estate. When it was no longer his share, he became a soldier of fortune. No one, I think, can doubt this, when he compares the aristocratic feuds of the reign of Richard II. with those of Henry VI. They were as bitter in the former reign as in the latter. I find it difficult to discover any more savage family vendetta than that between the house of Lancaster and the house of Norfolk after 1397. It endured for nearly a century, and was suspected; and, suspicion always awakening vengeance, punished for nearly a century more. It is true that the rivals in the fourteenth and fifteenth centuries abstained from harrying the peasant. But it is quite certain that they fought the battle out among themselves till both were nearly exhausted, and that Richard was only able to levy a poor following when he met the latest adventurer at Bosworth.

The perils of the war of succession, or, as I should prefer to name it, the war of the nobles, who had not the hypocrisy to call it, as the French at the same epoch did, the war of the public good, led to the general use of entails and the adoption of the civil law expedient of trusts. The mischief of the former, as far as the political result went, was obviated by parliamentary attainder; that of the latter, under the name of uses, was more immediately unmanageable and more permanently disastrous. I am disposed to believe that parliamentary attainder was much more a threat than a reality, more a proclamation that loss would ensue if partizanship in arms were persisted in, than a real risk to combatants. On any other hypothesis I cannot understand how it was that on petition, at least in the reign of Edward IV., a parliamentary attainder was always remitted by the king. We are told that Edward was suspicious and vindictive. And much might have made him so. He had to deal with a bitter faction, once dominant, and only lately repressed or proscribed. He had to count with the creatures of his own folly, a new nobility and political nepotism. He subdued the defection of those to whom he owed much, and who thought he owed them much more—the most dangerous enemies with whom any man has to deal, and with whom a ruler can hardly make any terms. He lived in an age when the revenge of injuries had risen to the dignity of a moral virtue, to be corrected only with the pretence of forgiveness and the exaction of the fullest usury for the delay. He had to deal with the hardest struggle of all, the treachery of his own brother, the only person whom he could not forgive. But he forgave every one else, excused their hostility, remitted their forfeitures. But he was expensive and poor. His grandson remitted nothing which came within the reach of his clutches.

But the use, or the trust, as it was subsequently called,

was a different matter. It was the origin of the true law of entail, under which the possession of land may be a danger, and is the means of fraud. It perpetuated the poverty of the younger son and the system of quartering him on the public purse. It was the origin of the principle of vested interests, perhaps the most anti-social and danger-ous doctrine which has pretended to justify the robbery of all labour, and will justify the antagonism of all labour to privilege. The development of the younger son as a social pauper and a social leech, is at the bottom of most of the financial extravagances and all the financial meanness of the English administrations to our own day. It is difficult to be thrifty in the public expenditure where one should be, and impossible to be generous where one ought to be. It is true that the most glaring scandals of the old system have been put out of sight, but not a few of the indirect incon-veniences remain, and among them especially the retention of sham offices in the public service.

In the fifteenth century these law-made paupers appear to have been quartered on the royal revenues, especially on the hereditary estate of the Crown. In a later age they were put on such fixed sources of revenue as were considered to be permanent, such as the post-office or the civil list. Hence the constant outcry in the fifteenth century, when the poverty of the Crown rendered an appeal to Parliament almost annual, or at least as frequent as the meeting of Parliament, that grants should be resumed. The prayer is often answered affirmatively, but the exceptions are so numerous that the remedy is one of little efficacy. My readers will be familiar with the history of the struggle between Parliament and William III., when that king, with very pardonable feelings, wished to reward and enrich the Dutch gentlemen who had followed and served him.

The leases which were granted to tenants were, as I have said, generally short,—from six to ten years. This rule was, I conceive, not adopted in the hope that rents might be raised at the termination of the period, since the rent for the mere use of land was singularly invariable from the earliest times till close upon the end of the sixteenth century, but in order to secure the constant verification of the property from which the rent issued. It is a curious fact, too, that these tenancies were generally made up of a number of plots, the terms for which ran out at different periods. Thus a farmer might have five or six separate holdings from the same landlord, the demise of which might, and constantly did, run over the whole period for which he held his longest lease. His tenure would cease, say, in one plot, in two years from a given date; in another, the remainder would be three years; in another, four; in another, five, and so on, so that his leases were constantly falling in and being renewed or transferred to another tenant. It seems probable that such a system arose by the fact that the small tenants extended their holdings as opportunities offered, taking a strip here, a land there, a close in another place, a meadow in a fourth place, at different dates. The custom, much more frequent in ordinary estates than it was in those of corporations, must have indirectly given the tenant a hold on his tenancy which he would not have had if the whole estate were entered on at once, and all the parcels of the occupancy were for the same term. I do not imagine that, provided his rent was paid, the tenant was often disturbed, as it was not till the sixteenth century that attempts at rack-renting began.

Grants of freehold estate for life are by no means uncommon in the earliest times. But these tenancies I generally find were additions made to the holding of some existing freeholder in fee of inheritance, in consideration of some service rendered, or in satisfaction of some debt, or for any other private reason of the lord's own. Thus, at Ibstone, in 1298, one of the free tenants, who holds a half-virgate by deed, under conditions of certain payments in money, kind, and labour, holds also a couple of crofts containing another half-virgate for the term of his life, at a rent, but without service. But it is unlikely that life estates were, in early times, or for a long time subsequently, common. An instance apparently to the contrary occurs to me in a tenure of the fifteenth century. In 1441, John Franke, Master of the Rolls, devised

£1,000 to his executors in order to purchase lands for the benefit of Oriel College. The college acquired, with commendable self-denial, the reversionary interest in a Berkshire estate, then held for life by John Norris and his wife Alice, and were a good deal disappointed at the prolonged period during which the widow's life was protracted. It is, however, quite possible that these persons, being childless, had themselves purchased the freehold as an annuity, as the best means for investing their funds, or savings, since the college purchased their interest from the reversioners.

It is said that the monastic houses, foreseeing the dissolution which threatened them, and for which there were very ominous precedents during the fifteenth century in the confiscation of the alien priories, and the not infrequent suppression of individual religious houses on the plea of misconduct, began to grant long leases of forty years or more. It is, I believe, well ascertained that, at the general dissolution, such leases were found to have been very frequent, and that in consequence the spoil in land was far less in actual value than had been anticipated, though the chattels of the religious houses must have been relatively of enormous value. This is confirmed by the fact that very shortly after the dissolution Henry was in as great pecuniary difficulties as ever, an incredible result had he not only acquired the chattels, much of which probably went to pay his debts, but the lands, which are over and over again said to have been one-third of the whole area of the kingdom. The reversionary interest in these lands was very large, but even this appears to have been soon lost or alienated from the Crown.

The practice of the religious corporations was followed by the secular clergy and the colleges, who adopted the system of granting long leases of lands, renewable at fixed periods on the payment of a fine. Originally these fines were very small, probably only a handsel, or earnest money, or a complimentary present to the principal authorities of the corporation. The fine for entrance was familiar enough in the case of copyholders or tenants in villeinage, and instances could be multiplied of such payments by such tenants on the entry or succession to customary estates. But they are not entered on the earlier college accounts, either because they were trivial and treated as the perquisites of the officials, or because they were not paid at all. The earliest price for entry by a personage who must have entered on one of these leases is a payment of £50 made by the Earl of Derby to King's College for the *introit* into Prescot in the year 1533-4.

There was, however, one considerable source of income besides sheep farming, to which allusion has been made already. I refer to the profits obtained from the sale of firewood and timber. The more opulent and better-built houses had long possessed chimneys, and with the use of the new material, brick, these conveniences became general and even necessary; the purchases of bricks in places where the article was not, as in the Eastern Counties, largely manufactured, being generally described as for fireplaces. I find andirons in the Eastern part of England early in the beginning of the fifteenth century. In these fireplaces wood, called generally tall-wood, was burnt, as also what was called logs and great wood, the trimmings of timber. Faggots, reed, sedge, and turf were burnt in open grates, but most commonly were employed, it seems, for heating ovens.

The most important kind of fuel, however, was charcoal. The trade of the charcoal-burner was very ancient and very common, considerable districts where wood was abundant being occupied by colliers, and the price of the article rapidly rising. The most common way for warming the large halls of mansions and colleges was by a charcoal-burner set in the middle of the hall and filled with glowing embers, the fumes of the burning mass escaping through a lantern in the roof. These vast charcoal grates have been continued within modern memory in some of the Cambridge colleges, and must have been exceedingly common at an earlier period. I have constantly found, in examining the accounts of colleges in Oxford and Cambridge, that the amount received from the woods of these corporations rapidly became equal to and gradually exceeded the rent derivable from the lands let to farm or lease, till at last the profits on their woods became the most important source of income.

One other expedient was adopted, peculiar, as far as I have been able to discover, to the Eastern Counties, where rents were as stationary and inelastic as elsewhere. This was to stipulate that, in place of money, the tenant should pay a certain amount of wheat, barley, or malt, and a number of sheep at fixed rates. Thus a corporation would require twenty quarters of wheat and an equal amount of barley to be supplied to them at 5s. and 4s. a quarter, when the market value of these commodities would be three times as great. So they would demand the delivery of fifty sheep at 1s. 6d. or 2s. each, as the case may be, when the market prices show a similar rise in the true price of mutton. This practice begins very early, and even before the rise of prices, which I shall comment on hereafter. It seems to me to be an attempt to get in an indirect way that increase of rent which the landowner evidently thought he ought to obtain, but which he was hopeless of obtaining in money. At last, as far as Oxford and Cambridge and the two great schools of Winchester and Eton were concerned, the practice was enforced by law, under the celebrated statute of 1576. This statute is supposed to have been due to the prescience of Burleigh, but the principle had been adopted many years before in that part of England with which Burleigh in his earlier days was familiar, and in which the spoils of the Cecils had been accumulated. That it had not been adopted in other parts of England was not, I conclude, from want of will, but from want of opportunity, or from the jealously conservative attitude of the tenant farmers.

CHAPTER XI.

THE DEVELOPMENT OF TAXATION.

The Particular Scope of Economical History—The Revolutions of 1399 and 1668 Compared—The Parliaments of Henry IV.—The Career and Character of Henry V.—The Taxes of the Time—The Character of Henry VI.—The Wealth of the Aristocracy and the Poverty of the King—The Speaker's Function—Income Taxes—The Allowance for Impoverished Towns—The Speakership of Tresham—The Unpopularity of the Bishops—Cade's Rebellion —The Imprisonment and Death of Henry—Tresham's Finance—Thorpe's Budget—Edward IV. and his Revenue—Benevolences—Henry VII. ; his Income Tax—The Aid of 1503—The Expedients of Henry—The Treaty of Commerce—The Succession of Henry VIII.—His Extravagance—The Dissolution of the Monasteries—The Acquisitions soon squandered—The Debasement of the Currency.

IN dealing with the history of agriculture and wages, I am not immediately concerned with those topics on which historians ordinarily dilate. The struggles of bygone diplomacy, the claims of extinct dynasties, the exploits of historical heroes, the rivalries of buried factions, the ambitions of mythical statesmanship, the plans of obsolete policy, the enmities and friendships, the intrigues, the victories, the defeats of kings, generals, and ministers, are nearly all out of that which I propose to myself. They are properly recorded and dwelt on by historians. It may be that not a single force in politics is wasted, as we are told none are in nature, and that if we could trace the effect of those political occurrences, which are not wholly superficial, we should be able to follow them into the life of our own age. It is sometimes, indeed, the fortune of the historian to detect some such results, and to trace them back to their veritable causes,—as, for example, the development of the Burgundian duchy of the fifteenth century, and its influence on the politics of Western Europe even up to recent times. But the narrative of the historian rarely aids the science of politics, and only occasionally the philosophy of society.

But the knowledge of what a nation's industry and economy have been, the discovery of the processes by which the facts and purposes of the past have been developed into the habits, the traditions, the pursuits, and the energies of the present, is the true history of the race. Unfortunately, no age, except by accident, takes cognizance designedly of contemporaneous practice, and the economical historian has to piece his particulars together, when he can obtain them, with the same care which the naturalist adopts (though, unfortunately, he cannot do it with the same conviction) who builds up a skeleton and an organism from a few fragments of bone. Here, however, all facts have their place and relevancy ; for it is more certain that the existing generation of Englishmen have received their habits, their practices, and their public character from a series of continuous and abiding influences, than it even is that they have inherited capacities and tendencies from the generations of whom they are the descendants. It is, however, necessary that I should give a sketch of the leading political events of the age which I am treating, partly because the action of governments always has its influence on the economical condition of the nation, however much the genius of a people can modify the effect induced by the administration of its public affairs, and partly because the financial expedients of government illustrate the social condition of the people. The fifteenth century, moreover, has a peculiar interest to English students. In it the most important constitutional principles were affirmed and the most important parliamentary precedents established, so that the patriots of the first Stuart kings could claim that they were restoring the fabric of a bygone age when they were resisting the forces of despotism and the conspiracies of the Court and the Church.

The Revolution of 1399 bears a strong resemblance to that of 1688—the difference of time and manners considered. In both cases, a sovereign, who a little while before appeared to have a secure throne, was suddenly deposed from his dignity and found to be entirely friendless.   In both cases a powerful faction of nobles and churchmen prepared the revolution, and for a time the whole country acquiesced in it.   In both it was found necessary, if the change were to be made, to supersede an infant heir of higher claim than the sovereign who was actually accepted.   In both cases, the reaction commenced immediately after the throne appeared to be settled. In both cases, the new king had to reckon with a discontented faction of nobles and churchmen.   In both cases, the worst enemy of the new monarch was a man whom he had loaded with benefits but could not satisfy, who had aided the revolution by his dissimulation and strove to reverse it by his perfidy; for Northumberland was as false and as treacherous as Marlborough, and though Henry was constrained to keep peace abroad in order to maintain himself at home, and William's life was, except for a short period, engaged in an incessant struggle with the French king, yet each reign was followed by a succession of splendid victories, which in the end were barren.   And, to make the parallel complete even in particulars, the first Parliament of Henry was summoned under circumstances not unlike those of the Convention Parliament under William.

Whether it was that the Commons of the fifteenth century thought that the Parliament which changed the succession and put Henry on the throne was entitled to be consulted in the conduct of all affairs and to be strengthened in its privileges, or the peculiar character of the times aided their pretensions, it is certain that at no time before, and, for many generations, at no time subsequently, did the Parliament obtain so large a place in the government.   They claim to have a conference with a Committee of the Lords; they go some distance in taking cognizance of their own returns; they insist on privilege of Parliament; they claim the right of sending for and amending the Lords' Bills; they provide that due notice shall be given of elections; they extend the county franchise to suitors in the county court and all others, which seems to bestow a universal suffrage in the counties; they attempt to exercise an absolute control over the administration and the estates of the Crown, and appear to have secured to themselves the right of originating grants. If, as was stated at the time, the execution of Scrope was followed immediately by Henry's sickening with leprosy, we may conclude, perhaps, that the public opinion of the age considered that Henry's treatment of his cousin, which was said to have been signally perfidious, was visited by the displeasure of Providence. It is not unlikely, too, that Henry had found it necessary to bribe his partizans in the revolution with lavish grants from the Crown estates, as he was constantly appealing to his subjects for money, and they for their part ordered a resumption of his grants, and prohibited in the future that any person should receive part of the ancient inheritance of the Crown without the consent of Parliament. And yet the king had added to the ordinary estate of the Crown the extensive possessions of the duchy of Lancaster, which remained a separate domain till it was united to the Crown by Edward IV., though it was kept, as it is to this day, under an independent administration.

But whether the unpopularity of Henry was due to the defects of his title, to the perjuries by which he had won his crown, and to the harshness of the means which he employed to make his position secure, or to the compliances and concessions which he made in order to disarm opposition, or to the blight and disease which came upon his life, and cut him off at an early age—he was a little over forty-seven years old at his death—everything was forgotten in the splendid career of his son. Henry of Monmouth was twelve years old at the time of Richard's deposition, and only sixteen when he fought with Percy at Shrewsbury. If the stories of his youthful dissipations are not pure inventions, they are probably heightened by contrast with the stern morality of his riper years, and were perhaps invented by the Lollards, whom he felt himself constrained to persecute. No English monarch was ever more popular than Henry. He had to meet a conspiracy at the beginning of his reign, but it was put down with little difficulty. He had previously escaped from a conspiracy of some desperate and fanatical Lollards, whom persecution had driven to fury, and whose rank in society shows how the teachings of the Wiklifite party had permeated the most unlikely persons.

Henry united those qualities which the English have always admired but have rarely witnessed even in their best kings. He was strictly orthodox and severely just, tenacious of his right, and loyal to his word.   He was a model of private virtue, of knightly courage, of military skill, who conquered fortune rather than was favoured by her.   He seems to have entered on the French war not merely to recover what was lost by the violated peace of Bretigni, perhaps to revive and enforce his claim of descent, but more to correct the frightful scandals of the French Court and society.   He announces his purposes and his motives in language like that of some Puritan commander in the early days of the Parliamentary War, as though he had been sent by God to chastise the guilty.   His army, well schooled, drilled, and invincible, was kept under rigid discipline, and, as far as the king could make it, was as pious as Cromwell's Ironsides, as confident as they were in the genius of its general, as staunch in the hour of battle, and as severe in that of victory.   Nor was Henry simply influenced by the lust of conquest.   He was beyond measure anxious to heal the scandals which troubled the Church and the schism which distracted it.   He did all in his power to hasten the assemblage of the Council of Constance, and to constrain all heretics and schismatics, from the Pope to the Hussites, to obey the will of Christendom in that assembly of kings and prelates and doctors of law.   He could not suffer the Lollards, whose tenets he believed to be subversive of society as well as dishonouring to God.   But he condescended to argue with these sectaries, and to show them, as he thought, the more excellent way, lamenting that their obstinacy left him no alternative to the punishment which the law inflicted on them.

The demands of the first two Henries of the House of Lancaster were met by grants of fifteenths and tenths, by taxes on wool and hides, differential duties being levied on these materials when exported by aliens, and by increased *ad valorem* duties on exports and imports. These fifteenths and tenths were granted nearly every year. During the first twelve years of the century, the price of wool is exceedingly high, and though after this the value falls slightly, it keeps high for the first thirty years. It is plain, therefore, that the export duty did not lower the price of the article or materially check its use, and that, therefore, it was practically paid by the foreign consumer. If, as I stated above, a fifteenth and tenth amount to 5 per cent. on lay incomes, and something less than 10 per cent. on clerical incomes, the direct taxation of the war amounted to nearly 10 per cent. on the laity, and nearly double that on the clergy. But no discontent is expressed at these burdens as long as the war was successful or not unprosperous. The total revenue derived from the customs and the wool tax appears to have been a little over £40,000, of which £30,000 was derived from wool.

The French War lasted with hardly a truce from Aug. 11th, 1415, when Henry sailed from Southampton, till July 17th, 1453, when Talbot and his son fell before Chatillon. The charges of the war did not exhaust the wealth of England, for one sees in a thousand ways how great was the opulence and abundance of the country, if one gathered it only from the style of living and in the expenditure of great corporations before and after the change which took place in the sixteenth century. But it demoralised an influential section of the English people, and it filled the country, after the struggle with France was over, with military adventurers, who were eager to enter into the service of those nobles who, now divided by rancorous feuds, some of them continued from the days of the Lords Appellants, were ready for civil war, with or without a genuine pretext.

As long as the alliance with Burgundy lasted and the Duke of Bedford lived, the war in France seemed likely to be successful, or at least to be open to a settlement on terms favourable to the English claims. But the English were expelled from Paris in April 1436, the year after Bedford died. The utmost that they could expect was to retain Normandy and Guienne, the connecting links of which were Anjou and Maine. The successors of Bedford were Suffolk, Somerset, and York.

While the war in France was being carried on, the principal figure in English society was a prince whom every one revered, no one consulted, and every one, who could do so, pillaged. Born on December 6th, 1421, he was less than nine months old at his father's death, and he had been brought up by the old Earl of Warwick, who had scourged all his spirit out in his youth. In business, especially the business of the kingdom, Henry was always a child. He seems to have taken no part in it, but always to have remained indifferent and passive in the hands of those who administered his affairs, whether it were Beaufort or Gloucester, Suffolk or Somerset or York. To the English he was a saint, perhaps almost the only saint of the fifteenth century. He was not a monk, for the monk of this age had become a gross and greedy voluptuary, whom every one wished to get rid of, though no one saw how to do without him decently. Henry was no ascetic, nor did he pretend to disclaim natural affections. He was loving to his mother, he was generous to his half-brothers, whose education and advancement he took care of; he was warm-hearted to all his kinsfolk; he conferred great benefits on the man who was afterwards his rival; he heaped honours on the Neviles, who owed everything to his family; on the Mowbrays, who were his hereditary foes; on the Beauforts, the Percies, and the Poles, who were his parasites and who ruined him. He was gentle and affectionate to the furious woman whom he married, who, like one of those mysterious persons in ancient tragedies, was the evil genius of his house, the reputed murderess of his last surviving uncle, and who made it at last impossible that he should reign, since, under his name, she was bent on destroying all those whom she hated. The king's delight seems to have been in reconciling foes, in hearing mass (his courtiers would allow him to hear no sermons which they had not previously perused and approved), in watching the boys for whom he had provided at Eton, in giving them kindly and affectionate advice, and in surprising those whom he met and with whom he conversed by his exceeding simplicity and unworldliness. Before he was twelve years old, the estate of the Crown had been nearly squandered, and the king was hopelessly impoverished. The annual regular expenditure had become more than five times the hereditary income of the king, and nearly four years of this expenditure were in arrear.

Henry was the most unlucky of English monarchs. After such a minority, no abilities could have saved him, and he had none. He inherited a war in which he took no share, except as part of a pageant. The lord of two kingdoms, he had no authority in either. The war which made others rich made him a pauper. Fastolfe and Cromwell gathered gigantic fortunes from the spoils of office, from the spoils of war, and from lucrative trade. The opulence of the great houses of the Neviles, with their fortunate marriages, their numerous titles, their vast estates; of the Beauforts, the Holands, the Poles, and the rest, was prodigious. The riches of the great English houses were amazing even to men like De Commines, who had been familiar with the opulence of the House of Burgundy and the wealth of the great Flemish burghers. When acts of resumption were passed, we can see in the exceptions the noble mob who were squabbling over the plunder of the Crown, and were soon to fly at each others' throats like wild beasts.

A curse seemed to hang over the House of Lancaster. When, in 1406, the Parliament settled the crown on the king's sons successively, it might have seemed that there was every prospect of numerous issue to the House of John of Gaunt. Four sons (the daughters are passed over in the Act), the Prince, Clarence, Bedford, and Gloucester would hardly be childless. But the eldest had died leaving one child; the next was slain in battle; and the other two, both married twice, had died without issue, the youngest not without suspicion of foul play. The king was married in 1445, when he was in his twenty-fourth year. But there was no child of the marriage for more than eight years, and it seemed likely that the family would become extinct. From certain statements in the rolls of Parliament it seems as though the succession in 1450 was supposed to be in the Beauforts. It is probable, however, that others looked to the Duke of York. The animosity which existed between the House of York and that of Somerset was certainly first developed during the time in which Henry was childless, and the title of the presumptive heir to the crown was necessarily discussed. But it is noteworthy that during the whole of Gascoigne's life, though he was plainly unfriendly to the administration, and had little respect for the person of his king, this writer does not give a hint of the superior claims of the House of York, nor, indeed, of any claim other than that of the king in possession. Now Gascoigne died on March 12th, 1458, and was writing certainly up to within three months of his death.

In the early days of parliamentary history, the Speaker was, to use a modern phrase, the Chancellor of the Exchequer. He framed budgets and announced grants, and, it may be noted that up to the date of the Union, the Speaker of the Irish Commons always held this office. That he took counsel with the House of Commons is undoubted, but the initiative in taxation having been now tacitly resigned to the Commons, since it would have been inconvenient, if not indecent, to discuss the question in the Lords, and before the king, the Speaker announced his plans for the consideration of his fellows. That they were in the main his own is, I think, clear from the various expedients which different Speakers adopted. On Dec. 23rd, 1435, John Bowes, Member for Notts, and Speaker, gave, among several other grants, the first income tax that I have read of to the service of the Crown. It is graduated, and in three schedules. The minimum taxable income derived from manors, lands, tenements, rents, annuities, and offices, and all other temporal possessions of freehold, is £5 a year. On this income and others up to £100 a year, the tax is to be 6*d.* in the pound. Between £100 a year and £400, the tax is to be 8*d.* in the pound. On incomes above £400 a year, 2*s.* in the pound. It is noteworthy that this income tax, like the others of the fifteenth century, satisfies the conditions of Adam Smith's "First Law of Taxation," that it claims from those who pay it a sum proportionate to what they are enjoying under the protection of the State; a graduated income tax levied on permanent revenue being the only tax which exactly squares with Smith's rule. It may be observed that Pitt's first income tax was graduated, though the maximum stopped at a very low amount.

It is possible that a laborious search in the pipe rolls would give the amount collected under this tax, and nothing would be more instructive than a tabulated account of the persons who came under the three schedules, and the amounts paid in the several counties. We may, however, I think, conclude that a considerable number of persons must have been ranged under each of the schedules in order to have given the financial expedient any significance or value, and that this applies even to incomes over £400 a year, since, large as the residual tax is, we must conclude that Bowes intended to raise a revenue by it. Again, it seems plain that the tax was intended to catch the grantees of the Crown, such as those who are mentioned in Cromwell's schedule of the king's liabilities as quartered on the revenue. It should be added that ecclesiastics, though they were allowed to tax themselves on their ancient possessions, were made liable to the income tax on all lands which they had acquired by license of mortmain from the Crown since 20 Edward I. (1292). But I have no doubt that this income tax supplied a notable revenue. The wealth of the country had grown rapidly during the fifteenth century already, to grow more rapidly as the century progressed. Any one who reads, as I have read by hundreds, the daily bills of fare of not very wealthy monasteries and colleges, can understand how sumptuously people fared in this singularly prosperous age, when Jeshurun waxed fat and kicked.

Tenths and fifteenths were always the favourite property tax. But in 1433, a curious custom begins of deducting a sum (£4,000) from the amount given, and, as I have often said, fixed, for the purpose of enabling the commissioners to relieve any particular town, or even village, from its contribution.   In the great majority of cases the commissioners are plainly left to their own discretion, though they were no doubt aided by the representations of the members from the less opulent districts, who very likely gave the commissioners of the Exchequer some trouble, and were probably sent to the authorities to scramble and lobby for these remissions.   But there are always some places named whose claims for exemption must have been examined and allowed in Parliament. Thus in the first year Lincoln and Great Yarmouth were so designated.   In 1435, Andover and Lincoln are named ; in 1437, Lincoln, Elm, Wisbeach, and two villages in Cambridgeshire with it, Andover and Alresford ; in 1442, Lincoln, Cheltenham at half it assessment, Alresford, Scarborough and Headington (near Oxford) ; while Great Yarmouth is to pay a quarter of its ordinary liabilities.   These arrangements in Parliament imply not only that the House of Commons was dealing with the details of finance, but that there was a considerable amount of intelligence and method in the way in which the House manipulated public business, and in the general pressure, was ready to allow for exceptional emergency.   In the same way we can trace not obscurely the practice of appropriating supply.   In 1445, the exemption rises from £4,000 to £6,000.   The king was married in this year, and it seems that for a time loyalty was predominant.   In 1446, Gloucester died, as was supposed murdered by Margaret's order, at Bury.   Between this year and 1450, nearly all the possessions of the English in France were wrested from them.   The Norman towns capitulated, and Guienne was overrun.   The conquests of Henry V. were lost by the treason or incompetence of those who succeeded to the inheritance of the great victor and his brother. The nation was thoroughly angry with the administration, with the Court, and with the commanders in France.   Parliament met six days after the capitulation of Rouen, on Nov. 6th, 1449, determined to take vengeance on those who had brought English affairs to so shameful a pass.   They did not, however, as they did later on, fall into the trap of factious opposition. They elected, for the fourth time, William Tresham as Speaker. This man, as we can see for a few months through the mists of that time, when the passions were being roused and the feuds engendered which were to be extinguished only after thirty years of bloodshed, was one of the ablest statesmen of the fifteenth century. He was a member of the king's household, and his family remained zealous Lancastrians. It is clear that his re-appointment to the high office which he had so often held before was a proof that Parliament was not yet hostile to the House of Lancaster, and that it was thought possible that remedies could be found for the alarming state of public affairs. Somerset was in France, York in Ireland.

The Parliament of 1449 is singularly like that of 1640 in its temper and policy. In both Parliaments the country had been stirred to its very centre, and an extraordinary number of new men, instructed to find a full and complete remedy for the mismanagement of public affairs, was sent to Westminster. In both, for a time at least, the Commons were practically unanimous. In both the House insisted on the redress of grievances before the grant of supply. From Nov. 6th to Dec. 17th, the Commons debated public affairs. In both an attempt was made by the Court to force on those topics only, which the administration put before them. In both the king's ministers and the bishops were the objects of absolute detestation. In both the Court was surprised and staggered by the unanimity with which the Commons insisted on their own course, and by the complete accord between the two Houses. In both the Commons resolved to destroy a powerful minister, whom they considered responsible for all the disorders that had happened, and to establish a precedent of Parliamentary impeachment which should be a warning to all bad ministers in future. The difference between the results of these two great Parliaments is in the subsequent course of events. Just before the Parliament met after the Christmas recess, one of the King's ministers, the Bishop of Chichester, was seized at Portsmouth, put to a kind of trial, and executed by the populace. Suffolk was impeached, imprisoned, released, banished, intercepted, and slain after the pretence of a trial. The king's counsellors were trying to browbeat the Parliament, while the Parliament was resolved on reforming the royal household and the administration. While this was going on at Leicester, where Parliament was sitting, a sudden insurrection, which has been strangely misrepresented by historians, broke out under Cade. The bishops fled from London, one into his own diocese, where he was murdered. The battles of Sevenoaks and London Bridge were fought, and Cade entered London. Here Fiennes and his son-in-law were put to death. But the insurgents dispersed, as Tyler's did, and Cade was slain. In the autumn the great Speaker was murdered as he was on his way to a conference with the Duke of York, and the civil war virtually began. There is no doubt that Tresham was assassinated at the instance of that faction which is particularly identified with Margaret, that of the Percies, Beauforts, and Cliffords,—a faction, namely, within the wider Lancastrian party. I do not dwell on this most interesting and significant part of English history, that in which the effects follow clearly and closely on the causes, because the strife of the civil war is essentially of Margaret and York and the partizans of both, and the struggle does not appear to have in the least degree affected the ordinary life of England.

Had the errors of the administration been in any way chargeable to Henry, his throne would have certainly passed away in the autumn of 1450. Personally the king was entirely blameless. No one thought of setting any of the mischief down to him. When partizanship became furious, vindictive, implacable, he was no partizan, but was trying in his poor, gentle way to reconcile enemies. The king's blamelessness touched all strangely. The Houses would not depose him, even after the Coventry Parliament had made parties irreconcilable. He owed his deposition at last to the mad fury of his wife. And I make no doubt that he was used well during the nine years of his residence in the Tower. While he lived, every one reverenced the saintly and patient son of the great Henry. Nor do I believe that he was done to death after Tewkesbury. The story of his assassination in the Tower is, I am persuaded, a Tudor calumny; I prefer to conclude that nature, which had hid his misfortunes from him more than once in his life by a lethargy which seemed almost like death, at last released him in the same merciful fashion from the recurrent sorrows of his life. It is not surprising that the heir of his house should have encouraged the belief that the saint was not only a confessor, but a martyr.

Tresham, who had previously conducted, though a member of the king's household, the prosecution of Suffolk, as he was bound to do in duty to the house whose servant and spokesman he was, revived the income tax for which Bowes had given a precedent fifteen years before. But he takes a much lower taxable unit, though, as before, he makes three schedules. Freehold estates in lands, tenements, rents, services, annuities, offices, fees, pensions, or temporal commodities are declared liable. In this income tax also persons having an income for term of life, or, in an annuity not issuing from a certain place, all persons having occupation in ancient demesne (previously exempt from taxes) or elsewhere, and all having estates by copy of court roll or custom of the manor, are chargeable. The first schedule is from twenty shillings to twenty pounds annual income. This pays two-and-a-half per cent. The next is between £20 and £200 annual revenue, which is to pay five per cent. The third is on incomes of £200 per year and upwards, which are to pay ten per cent. on all income over £200. The guardians of tenants in ward are to pay. Every person having an office, wages, fee or fees, or term of years is to come under the schedules, but the first is to begin at forty shillings a year. Four paid commissioners are to receive the tax, but no Member of Parliament is to be a commissioner. The Lords agreed to this searching and remarkable Property Tax, declaring it reasonable. They seem to have had fairer views about taxation in the fifteenth than they have in the nineteenth century. The next Parliament, which had for its Speaker a partizan of Cade, was far more hostile to the Court than its predecessor was. It continued the income tax, but heightened the minimum, beginning with forty shillings revenue from freehold and copyhold lands instead of twenty, and £3 a year from offices instead of £2. No such tax is granted again till the accession of the Tudor dynasty.

In 1452, the revolt of the Gascons occurred, the nomination of Shrewsbury to the lieutenancy of Guienne, and the hope that Aquitaine would be recovered. The hope was short-lived, the disappointment at its failure great, and the reaction thorough. But in the interval all was loyalty, enthusiasm, and confidence. Thorpe was appointed Speaker. This man was a zealous Lancastrian, and in the retinue of Somerset. A tenth and fifteenth were granted ; export and import duties, some of them raised, are given for the king's life. The taxes on the export of wool and hides are increased, to a greater extent, as events proved, than they would bear, a license duty is put on aliens, and a charge of 13,000 archers for six months (the Commons offered 20,000) is put virtually on the towns and counties. They supplemented these grants by that of a half-fifteenth and a half-tenth. The last grant was on July 2nd, 1453. On July 17th occurred the battle of Chatillon, the deaths of Talbot and his son, and the total wreck of the campaign. The entire amount of the grants must have exceeded £130,000. Had the king accepted the whole force which the Commons gave him, it would have exceeded £160,000, the largest sum ever offered by the Commons in one year during the middle ages.

On the re-assembling of Parliament, Thorpe, the Speaker, was in prison, along with Walter Raleigh, knight of Devonshire. The history of this transaction is entirely misconceived. Thorpe had been convicted in his own court of a trespass, accompanied by a breach of the peace,—offences for which there never was privilege of Parliament. The king was insane, no doubt through the disasters which had occurred during the summer. Tiptoft, afterwards a zealous and ferocious Yorkist, was made the king's lieutenant; but two days afterwards the Duke of York superseded him. It is probable that there was a palace revolution, which

Margaret and her party could not resist. Her son had been born in the previous October, during the king's insanity. The story of Henry's dementia is told minutely in the rolls of Parliament. The Battle of the Kites and the Crows commences with the affair of St. Albans, May 22nd, 1455, and Parliament becomes the toy of faction.

I have referred to the financial expedients of the great war with France at some length. They indicate, first, that finance was attempted on system and on principles. It is true that the fiscal system of the time was mainly direct, no other being, I conceive, possible under the circumstances. But it is clear also that the Commons did their best, while they called on all to contribute, to make those pay who could best afford it, by imposing a graduated income-tax on the property of the wealthier classes, and this when there is no reason to doubt that the knights of the shire at least belonged to this class themselves. I do not pretend to admire the virtue or the honour of public men in the fifteenth century, though it is clear to me that the laity were infinitely better than the clergy; but the English gentry, who put these heavy burdens on themselves at a crisis of the nation's affairs, will contrast very favourably with their descendants, who, when Pitt proposed to tax real estate with legacy duty at the same rate as personalty, compelled him to withdraw that part of his budget, while they cheerfully taxed the small savings of industry, under the threat of turning him out of office,—a threat to which he ignobly yielded. Again, when he ventured to adopt in a slight degree the principle of a graduated income tax, they compelled him also to relinquish that, though the suffering and sacrifice in England were far greater in the beginning of the nineteenth than they were in the middle of the fifteenth century, and the danger to the country was incomparably more threatening. The great war with France in the days of our fathers and grandfathers was fought with the blood and sweat of the industrial classes, while the profits and the vaunts went to the propertied and capitalist few. And, again, the enormous amount, relatively speaking, of taxation which the English Parliament gladly offered when it seemed that it might be spent worthily, is a proof of how singularly prosperous England was during the fifteenth century. It was, indeed, said that the taxes on wool were too heavy, and depressed the price. They were speedily reduced to a more moderate amount.

Edward IV. asked his people for very few taxes, if we can rely on the rolls of Parliament. There are only four grants of fifteenths and tenths. In view of the expedition which was concluded by the Peace of Pecquigni, Edward obtained the grant of the 13,000 archers which was promised nineteen years before. I entirely discredit the stories told of this king's tyranny and suspiciousness. All the evidence of his reign is against the charge. He never refuses a petition for pardon; while the errors and misfortunes of his reign, and the calamities which came upon his house, appear to have resulted from the neglect of the commonest precautions and an overmastering confidence in his own genius and good fortune. He lived with most treacherous men in a most treacherous age, when political perfidy was being gradually developed into a science by such masters in the craft as Louis of France and the Italian princes, while he had to be on his guard against enemies in his own household, as well as against the rancorous relics of the Lancastrian party, when the bishops were more sordid, time-serving, and false than at any period in the history of Churchmen. In the midst of this quicksand of politics he was gay, dissipated, negligent, and supine. It would seem that Edward was unwilling to risk his popularity with his subjects by asking for parliamentary grants.

He is credited with having devised the famous benevolences. These were gifts or loans from wealthy citizens and others, pressed for with importunity and exacted with disguised force. Such gifts had constantly been made to kings in earlier times, but Edward is reported to have systematised the custom. The appeal to these wealthy persons may have been disagreeable, but it is very likely that the gift or loan carried with it countervailing advantages of a solid kind, analogous to those patents of monopolies which were so freely granted a century and more afterwards. Nor do I set much store by the statute of Richard III., in which these benevolences are declared illegal, or on the language which, according to the rolls of Parliament, was employed to Richard by those who urged him to usurp the crown. The terms of this address are general, and need not apply to benevolences at all, but to be a mere criticism of the last reign and its administration; and we should remember that Richard's partizans were chiefly in the city of London, where, if the benevolence were compensated by a monopoly, the mass of traders would resent the favour; and if it were not, but were a merely disguised tax on the rich, the wealthier citizens would be dissatisfied under the exaction. This seems to be the more reasonable because the practice of exacting these gifts or loans was resumed by Henry VII. on the plea that a usurper's statutes had no authority, though it is quite certain that Henry had every motive to conciliate his subjects, and, after all, passed a very uneasy and anxious reign.

In the early part of Henry Tudor's reign, considerable demands are made on the people through Parliament. Among these is the equipment and pay for 10,000 archers for twelve months, the cost of which is estimated at £100,000. This sum it is proposed to raise by an income tax of £75,000 on the estates of commoners, the remaining £25,000 being derived from a property tax on all chattels over ten marks of a very small amount. The income tax was supposed to be ten per cent. But the particulars are not given, and we do not know whether, like the taxes of Henry VI., it was graduated. The collection of the tax was resented, and its produce was said to have been disappointing. If the estimate made was a correct one, the taxable income of the Commons was £750,000 a year. In 1503, three years after his son Arthur's death, Henry bethought him of the aid due on making his eldest son a knight, and marrying Margaret to the King of the Scots. There had been no opportunity for making this claim for a century and a half. The last aid of this character was granted to Edward III. for the knightage of the Black Prince, and subsequent kings could not claim it, as their sons were either knighted before the succession, as was the case in Henry the Fourth's reign, or their children were below age, as was the case with Henry V. and Henry VI., Edward IV., and Richard III. Henry estimated the aid at £40,000. As, however, the full exaction of the tax would press heavily on the poor, he declares himself willing to remit £10,000, and be content with £30,000. The tax is to be paid by all who had over twenty shillings a year in "free charter lands," or above twenty-six shillings and eightpence in lands "held by will," which is afterwards explained to mean copyholds. Cattle used for the plough, stock, and implements of husbandry are exempt, but farm produce, corn harvested and stock-in-trade, are declared ratable. Nothing shows more clearly how entirely obsolete the aid had become than Henry's claim to include copyholds, goods, and stock-in-trade in the ratable elements of an aid, which was originally leviable from lands in knight service only. A very large number of commissioners, whose names are given, are appointed to assess and collect the aid, who are paid two per cent. on the whole amount. It is illustrative of Henry's character that, in distributing the assessment, he took care that it should realise a little more than £1,000, after all costs are deducted, over the estimated total. The claim is demanded in the Parliament of 1504, when Dudley, the father of Northumberland and the grandfather of Leicester, was Speaker. It was very likely suggested by this instrument of Henry's exactions.

Henry called but few Parliaments and asked for few grants. But he was penurious and avaricious, greedy and mean. He practised severe economy in his household,—I have studied his accounts,—and he involved his people in no foreign wars of importance. His reign, as far as the materials of ordinary history go, is sordid and uneventful. But his people prospered. Food is plentiful and cheap. In the last year of his reign, wheat falls to a price which had not been known for 222 years, when two years of similar plenty prevailed. Nor do I imagine that Henry was unpopular with the mass of his subjects, although it was still possible, since the ferment of the great war of succession had not entirely ceased, for adventurers and pretenders to disturb his quiet. But with the noble and wealthy he was odious. He seems to have been the first English king who improved his revenue by expedients which would have been discreditable to a low sharper or a pettifogging attorney. He began the practice of setting his agents to ferret out any claim which the Crown could make and a subservient judge would affirm. The Stuart kings improved on the meanness and knavery of Henry's expedients, and they added this much, that by beginning the practice of making their judges' patents depend on the royal pleasure, they made their lawyers the cringing, rapacious, and unprincipled crew, who dishonoured the sixteenth and seventeenth centuries, with very rare exceptions, and could not, as a profession, be made tolerably honest, except by giving them well paid freeholds in their offices. The judges of the Plantagenet kings used their office for the best ends,—the maintenance of civil rights and the extension of liberty. Those of the Tudors and Stuarts, under the teaching of the crafty adventurer who won at Bosworth, were the persistent and malignant enemies of all right and all liberty. No profession has had meaner representatives than Empson and Dudley, Cowell and Noy. The English bench sank to the lowest depths of turpitude, by the continuous selection of the basest, till it produced Williams and Jeffries.

The mean projects of Henry, his meaner expedients, and utterly mean agencies were relieved by one act of consummate but accidental statesmanship. He was troubled by adventurers, whom Edward's sister, the Dowager Duchess of Burgundy, widow of Charles the Bold, harboured and helped. It is impossible to prove that Warbeck was an impostor. It is quite certain than Simnel was, and that if the former was the Duke of York, Mary of Burgundy had done one genuine nephew irretrievable injury by countenancing another person, who was assuredly not her nephew. Now Henry believed, and he lived and died in the belief, that private interest was the one thing to which people are faithful.

The commercial relations of England and Flanders had been intimate since the days of Arteveldt and Edward III., and were interrupted only to the injury of both, and by the ambition or passions of princes. It would be well, he argued, if these interests were enlisted for the safety of princes. Hence the king concluded that he could protect his government and dynasty—for Henry was an affectionate father—by associating with his own ends the material advantage of Englishman and Fleming.

The great Intercourse (I suppose this is Bacon's own name for the treaty of commerce with Flanders executed in 1496) is sensible and practical, and some of its provisions have been acknowledged as part of that comity of civilized peoples which is called international law in very modern times only. The particulars are to be found in all works which deal with the true history of human civilization, and are, therefore, seldom studied. But the effects of this treaty were marked. It led, despite some modifications which Henry made in this treaty in 1506, to a continuance of friendly relations between England and the Low Countries for more than a century, and predisposed England, though in a halting and imperfect, perhaps a higgling fashion, to aid in the heroic struggle for independence which those Lowlanders fought for and part of them won,—a struggle as noble, as difficult, as important as that of Greece against Persia, and infinitely more prolonged and fertile. It would have been greatly to the reputation of England if, returning good for good, she had not taken for her policy the one most foolish act of Selden's great career, the paradoxes of the *mare clausum*, and had not been led into the one most unpardonable crime of Cromwell's Government, one which was, it seems, against that great man's judgment, the war with the Dutch. Selden's folly led to the martyrdom of Barneveldt, the crowning wickedness of the House of Orange, and Cromwell's blunder to the trickeries of Charles and his crew of profligate sharpers, and to the murder of the De Witts. If Dutchmen in our day had a spark of their forefathers' merits, they would see their ghosts in the Binnenhof, and atone for their ancestors' evil doings by setting up the statues of their prophets. But waning nations have nothing but the sepulchres of their great men.

Henry Tudor died, and his son came after him. Never was a contrast more violent than that between father and son. The one was penurious as no other English king had been, the other was extravagant to such a degree that he succeeded in ruining the unfortunate people over whom he reigned. The foreign policy of the father was cautious, prudent, and, on the whole, successful, that of the son was reckless, blundering, and disastrous. Henry VIII. succeeded to a position of great strength. He held the balance of power in Western Europe. At the conclusion of his reign, England was of no more account in the political system of the time than Portugal or Naples. Sovereign and people were alike impoverished. The wastefulness of Henry was incredible. The establishments of each of his infant daughters were more costly than the whole annual expenses of his thrifty father. He had fifty palaces, whims of the hour, in which profusion was constantly going on. He was incessantly building, altering, pulling down, by day and night, on Sundays and festivals, from year to year. As Wolsey said of him, " Rather than miss any part of his will, he will endanger one half of his kingdom." By the conclusion of his reign he had endangered the whole of it.

The earliest taxes of Henry, besides the customary fifteenths and tenths, are poll and property taxes. The former ranges from ten marks, payable by dukes, to a shilling, which is to be contributed by all. The latter is an equal or nearly equal percentage on income. The maximum is £800 and over, the minimum, 40s.; but labourers, whose annual earnings are from 40s. to 20s., are to pay 6d.; those less, 4d. No one is to be exempt, except married women and beggars. The assessment was estimated to yield £160,000, but it only reached £50,000; and Parliament granted 2½ per cent. on all income and wages above 20s. a year, and on all personalty over 40s. But this tax did not even yield so much as the previous income tax, either because Parliament miscalculated the resources of the kingdom, or because it was found impossible to extort the money. In 1523, a property tax of 5 per cent.

21

on the rent of all lands held by natives, and a double rate in the case of aliens, was imposed for two years; but if the income was less than £20 a year the tax is to be 2½ per cent. In the third year, 1525, the tax of 5 per cent. is levied on those incomes only which are over £50 a year. It was in the Parliament which granted these last taxes that the well-known scene occurred between Wolsey and More the Speaker.

I am persuaded that the ever-increasing necessities of Henry and his vast expenditure would have led to the suppression of the monasteries, or the confiscation of their wealth, even if the king had not quarrelled with the Pope. The religious orders had, one and all, long been discredited with the people. The abbeys and convents were, with few and well-known exceptions, dens of gluttony and vice. Nearly a century before their suppression, Gascoigne gives them the worst of characters for profuse and luxurious living, and tells tales of worse practices or theories. If only a portion of what was told of them by the visitors is true, they were stained with the vilest debauchery. Besides, they had been pointed out as the natural prey of the Government, both in and out of Parliament, by nobles and knights as well as by Lollards and Bible-men. The pious and devout Henry V. confiscated all the alien priories on the plea that they succoured his enemies, and, in 1524, Wolsey obtained permission of pope and king to suppress more than forty monasteries and nunneries, chiefly Augustinian and Benedictine, in order to found his colleges at Oxford and Ipswich. Henry affected to be scrupulous at the time, but eleven years afterwards he took the spoil of all religious houses whose income was under £200 a year. Four years later, the larger houses were dissolved and confiscated. Six years after this, and an Act was passed by which all colleges, free chapels, chantries, hospitals, fraternities, brotherhoods, guilds, and endowments for stipendiary priests were vested with their lands in the Crown. The execution of this Act was, however, delayed till the reign of his son.

The annual value of the monastic lands was estimated at over £160,000. This is certainly not an exaggeration, if, as is so frequently alleged, these institutions held a third of the land in the kingdom, and that not the least fertile portion. But it may be the net value, after the charges on the property, created by Henry himself; for he gave handsome pensions to the dispossessed abbots, officials, and monks, if they surrendered peaceably; and after the beneficial leases, which the corporations were said to have extensively granted in view of the coming storm, are deducted or allowed for. The king intended to have created a number of new bishoprics and a variety of educational institutions, perhaps some public charities. But his necessities, probably the situation in which he found himself placed, and the need to have associates in the plunder, perhaps his debts, made him stay his hand and abate his purpose. He founded a new nobility on the ruins of the mediæval Church, the descendants of whom are among the most ancient of our peers. But the mass of movable property which these religious houses possessed, the accumulations of ages, was immense. The shrine of Becket must have resembled the treasury of Delphi when Herodotus saw it, or before the Phocians plundered it. But all the spoil was rapidly wasted. Whatever wealth came into Henry's hands soon disappeared, as the treasure did which Bunyan saw poured into the lap of Passion, and change to rags. The wonder is what became of it. In three or four years it was nearly all gone, and Henry was forced to seek fresh plunder by even baser means.

The dissolution of the monasteries must have been, even from the fact of so vast an amount of property being suddenly transferred from one set of owners to a new and needy aristocracy, the cause of much disturbance in the economical condition of England. I have stated above that the custom of land and stock leasing remained with the corporations, especially the religious houses, much later than it did with the ordinary lay proprietors, for the reason that it was the most advantageous mode in which the landowner could get profit from his property. As the corporation was not mortal, the personal estate continued with the successors of each generation of monks; while, in the case of lay owners, such personalty would always be divided, and was probably devised, after the death of the proprietor. Now though the alienees or allottees of the monastic estate got the lands, they certainly did not get the chattels; for the register of such properties as they had possessed, other than their plate and jewels, which soon disappeared, still exists, and is a long inventory of the Crown's property in the early days of Edward VI. It is almost certain that the Crown respected the stock and land leases which the monks had granted, and dealt with the chattels on the land only as the leases expired. The only wonder is, that when the heirs of the founders were still in existence, the dissolved abbeys did not revert to them, but were at once vested in the Crown. It may be that these heirs, when they were found, were compensated, and that only a few of them had survived from the slaughter of the war of succession. In the fifteenth century, Gascoigne suggests that if the monasteries continue their lazy and gluttonous course, the heirs of the founders, who are their natural visitors, should coerce and, if need be, dispossess them, as if this were a power which such persons legally retained. But it is certain that the aristocracy of Henry's day was far too much broken and cowed to make head against the imperious, suspicious, and unforgiving king. He had used the terrible power of parliamentary attainder which Margaret, in an evil hour for the English nobles, invented, and employed a docile majority in the Lords, now to execute a Surrey or a Buckingham, and at another time to delight the old nobility with the slaughter of the upstart Essex.

Four years after the dissolution of the larger monasteries, Henry, who seems to have prudently dreaded the discontent of a Parliament which might well suppose that his new acquisitions ought to have been sufficient for his wants, and would therefore hesitate before they made him grants, hit on a new expedient for supplying his necessities. He began to debase the currency, the gravest crime which a king or ruler can commit against his subjects, the mischief and misery of which is rapid and sure. But the consequences of this act, which was more deep and lasting than any event in English economical history, except perhaps the Great Plague of 1348-9, and the details of the transaction itself, must be reserved for separate treatment in a subsequent chapter. Henry's offence was hidden from his subjects, for the evil was exaggerated as well as detected in his son's days. He was popular,—wasteful people generally are,—and he was the instrument of a reform which was greatly desired by the best men of his own day, was a source of wealth to those who shared in the plunder, and a great opportunity for political intrigue. Besides, the course of events connected the ecclesiastical policy of Henry, halting and contradictory as it was, with the cause of the Reformation, and gave him credit for what he never designed nor anticipated.

It is said that Henry spent part of his spoils in fortifications on the south coast of England and in building a navy. It may be so, and with the results of such expenditure, Pitt and Palmerston built fortifications which have become nuisances. What Henry's fortifications were was shown in his elder daughter's reign. I have read an account—it was among the waste papers of Henry's reign—of one of his big ships. It was built on as costly a scale as his palaces were, and was not seaworthy. The fight with the Armada was won by other structures than he made, and by other men than he degraded.

CHAPTER XII.

LABOUR AND WAGES.

The Fifteenth Century the best Time for the Labourer—The Working Hours of the Day, and Yearly Wages—The Labourers' Board—Spread of Piecework —The Wages of the Agricultural Labourer—The Impressment of Labourers, and Journey Allowances—Prices of Food do not increase, while Labourers' Wages are increasing—The Great Plague—The Civil War—The Effect of the latter on Husbandry and Wages imperceptible, and the People indifferent— The Lollards probably friendly to the House of York—The Sweating Sickness—The Capitalist Artizan in the Fifteenth Century—The Decay of Towns —The Increase of Sheep Feeding in the Sixteenth Century—The Debasement of the Currency—Its Effect on Wages—The Confiscation of the Guild Lands—The Origin and Uses of their Property—The Guilds like the Oxford Colleges—Induced Weakness of the English Labourer—No Rise in Rents, and the Reason—The Statute of Apprenticeship—The Result of these Changes, Pauperism—The Cost of maintaining Labour illustrated—Elizabeth's Expedient of making the Coin only Two-thirds its nominal Value.

I HAVE stated more than once that the fifteenth century and the first quarter of the sixteenth were the golden age of the English labourer, if we are to interpret the wages which he earned by the cost of the necessaries of life. At no time were wages, relatively speaking, so high, and at no time was food so cheap. Attempts were constantly made to reduce these wages by Act of Parliament, the legislature frequently insisting that the Statute of Labourers should be kept. But these efforts were futile; the rate keeps steadily high, and finally becomes customary, and was recognised by Parliament. It is possible, that as the distribution of land became more general, and the tenancy of land for terms of years became habitual, the phenomenon which has often been noticed as characteristic of peasant proprietorship, a high rate of wages paid to the free labourer, may have been exhibited in the period on which I am commenting.

The wages of the artizan during the period to which I refer were generally, and through the year, about 6*d.* a day. Those of the agricultural labourer were about 4*d.* I am referring to ordinary artizans and ordinary labourers. Persons who plied a craft in which greater skill was needed, perhaps one which was rarely procurable except from a distance, received more Thus, the carpenter, taken generally, gets a little under—it is a very small fraction—6*d.* He was constantly employed in agricultural operations and for domestic business. But the plumber, who might not be so regularly employed or was hired from a distance, gets 6½*d.* on an average. The mason, whose labour was likely to be suspended during winter time or in very bad weather, gets the full average. The joiner, who is employed in finer carpentry, is better paid than the average carpenter. It should be noted, too, that as the century goes on, the wages of labour tend decidedly upwards. Nor is there any material difference, with one notable exception, in the payments made for labour all over England. It is equally well paid throughout the whole country. The exception is London, where the wages were from twenty-five to thirty per cent. over the rates paid in other places. This increase may be due either to the cause that the guilds made labour in London comparatively scarce, or to the greater cost of living in London, for general prices are, as a rule, higher in or near the metropolis ; or to the fact that the best crafts-men sought London as a place of employment, and were better paid, because worth more than elsewhere.

There is no reason to think that these labourers were paid well because their employment was precarious. Men got just as good wages in the fifteenth century, whether they were employed for a day or a year. Nor, as I have already observed, were the hours long. It is plain that the day was one of eight hours. Nor was the period of winter wages, when the pay was lessened, considerable, for the short-pay season is, when such a period is specified, only the months of December and January. Sometimes the labourer is paid for every day in the year, though it is certain that he did not work on Sundays and the principal holidays. Thus, at

Windsor, in 1408, four carpenters got 6*d.* a day, and six got
5*d.*, for 365 days in the year, *i.e.*, the former receive £9 2*s.* 6*d.*
for their year's wages, the latter £7 12*s.* 1*d.*, the rate per day
and the amount for the year being specified in each case.
These men were no doubt in the service of the king, and the
king, as I shall show presently, was a very good paymaster;
but he is not the only person who hires labour on these
liberal terms. At York cathedral, six masons got £8 8*s.* a
year each; six others, £7 16*s.*; six more, £6 3*s.*; and one
carpenter gets £7 5*s.* 4*d.* This is in 1415, when the prices
of labour had not risen to their full amount.

Very often the labourer is fed. In this case, the cost of
maintenance is put down at from 6*d.* to 8*d.* a week. Sometimes the labourer is paid as though he were fed, and a
further allowance for his board is given him, this probably
being paid to some person who has contracted to feed him at
a rate. Sometimes the food is given in, and the labourer's
wages are paid at the full average. This is especially the
case when the workman is hired by opulent corporations and
on their premises. There was always a servants' table in these
establishments, and the workman is bidden to it without
stint or grudging. I find, for example, at some of the Oxford
colleges that ordinary rates are paid, and the workman is fed
into the bargain. Food was so abundant and cheap that it
was no great matter to throw it in with wages.

Piece work becomes more common in artizans' labour. In
the earlier time, for instance, the pair of sawyers were generally paid by the day, occasionally by the hundred feet, *i.e.*,
the long hundred of 120, the pair evidently being understood
to be competent to get through such a quantity in a day. In
the earlier time the piece price is a little less than the day
price. In the fifteenth century it is a little more. This is
evidence of an upward tendency. When the reaction, on
which I shall hereafter comment, begins, the former state of
things is reversed in an exaggerated form, piece work falling
below the remuneration of day work. So laying tiles and
slates by the thousand, splitting laths by the hundred, walling
by the yard, casting and rolling lead by the hundred-weight,

making plate by the ounce, and doing ceiling work by the yard, are found, and are generally well paid.

The agricultural labourer gets about 4*d.* a day for his work; but in harvest time 6*d.* The practice of paying this person by the day instead of by the piece becomes commoner than it was. But piece payments are progressively higher than they were in the dearest period of the fourteenth century. The man (*homo*) who is employed as a help to the thatcher or tiler, and often to the mason, later on to the bricklayer, is paid at the rate of agricultural labourers in ordinary times, or a little less. This help was sometimes a woman, as was generally the case in the earlier period; and thus it is seen that women's work, when of what we may call an unskilled kind, was equally well paid with that of men. Piece work in the harvest field was paid at even higher rates than during the famous years of the fourteenth century, in which the labourer's combinations were so effectual and so alarming to employers. The full price of a labourer's board was a shilling a week, often considerably less; his wages were twice or three times the cost of his maintenance under contract. In 1467, two girls are hired to work, and are paid twopence a day. They are also boarded, and this is put at twopence a day more. In the same year, at Selborne Priory, in Hampshire, the board of men is put at 2*d.*, of women at 1½*d.*

The king, who pressed labour at his pleasure, and from all parts of England, for he sends for workmen from distances of 150 miles, paid his agent in the business handsomely. This official sometimes also got a handsel for not taking workmen who were employed by private individuals and on works where despatch and convenience were important. But he cannot succeed in misusing the king's press, as Falstaff does, for he is paid by results, and would no doubt run considerable risks if he sent inefficient workmen. The men are also well paid. They are frequently boarded on contract, and we shall see presently how important is the information which these contracts give. They were also paid a *viaticum* on coming to and going from their work, at so much per mile of distance.

One reads, too, of free-masons who get a slightly higher pay than ordinary craftsmen do; of principal masons, who receive an annual fee, besides their daily wages; and of master masons, like that one at York in 1423, who was paid £10 a year.

From 1260 to 1400 inclusive, the price of wheat is 5s. 10¾d. a quarter. From 1401 to 1540 inclusive, it is 5s. 11¾d., and this slight increase of a penny a quarter is due to the dearer years of the period, 1521-1540. Had it not been for the rise induced on the general average, the price would have been 5s. 8¾d., or 3d. a quarter less. But, including these dearer years in the average, every kind of grain, except wheat and peas, is cheaper in the fifteenth and part of the sixteenth centuries than it was in the thirteenth and fourteenth. Now, notwithstanding the extraordinary cheapness of provisions (a fact to which public men turned their attention in the sixteenth century, by comparing the prices of the past with current experiences), there is no evidence that the wages of labour were depressed, or that the payment for service was the least affected by the low price of food. I do not, indeed, imagine that the economist who duly corrects his inferences from a wide range of facts, would be under the impression that such a result would necessarily ensue, or, indeed, unless there were other causes at work, conclude that the tendency of population would be to grow up to the limits of subsistence, as it grew for special causes in the seventeenth and eighteenth centuries. We shall see in the course of this inquiry that an excess of population is quite compatible with no increase in numbers, and that the misery of the working classes can be frequently ascribed to other causes besides their own improvidence and recklessness.

There occurred during this long period from the accession of Henry IV. to the dissolution of the great monasteries a number of social facts to which one should refer. And, in the first place, to the waste of human life by pestilence and other causes.

The Great Plague was said to have visited England twice in the fourteenth century after its first appearance, in 1361 and in 1369   But there is no information of a contemporary

kind as to its ravages on these subsequent occasions, and
though it is exceedingly likely that the disease remained
endemic, it does not appear to have recurred with alarming
severity.   The farm accounts of the time make reference abundantly to the losses of 1348, but none speak of the return of the
disease at the later dates, though we are told that the summer
of 1361-2 was exceedingly hot and dry, and we know that
though the price of wheat was low, that of other kinds of
grain was abnormally high.   But in 1369-70, all kinds of
grain were very dear,—dearer than at any time since the
great famine of 1315 and 1316, a convincing proof that the
summer and autumn were cold and wet, and that, therefore,
the temperature was unfavourable to the spread of contagion;
and I therefore set little store by the computation given by
Sir Harris Nicolas, on the authority of a King-at-arms in the
reign of Charles I., as to the duration, and even as to the
occurrence, of these visitations.   The notes I find of plagues
in the fifteenth century are in 1477, 1478, and 1479, when
unusual mortality seems to have prevailed in the Eastern
Counties ; and during the sixteenth, in 1521, in 1538, in 1545
and 1546, when it was at Cambridge and Oxford; in 1555 and
1556, in 1570 and in 1579.   All these are re-appearances of
the Levant plague ; for another disease, which occurred for
the first time in the fifteenth century, will be treated separately.   In some of these cases, the note is of precautions
taken against a possible visitation ; but in 1579, the Norwich
register expressly states that 4,918 people died, a loss of life
which must have been as serious as that in the first attack.
But I cannot discover that the wages of labour were affected
by any of these occurrences of the fifteenth century, nor in
those of the sixteenth, until the general change in money
values puts it out of one's power to infer anything from
such events.   I conclude, therefore, that the steadiness
with which high relative wages were secured was in no
sense due to the losses which labour suffered from pestilence.
The existence of this formidable disease may have checked
the growth of population ; but if abundant evidence as to
the rate of wages and silence as to the loss of life are to go

for anything, it did not create a sensible void in the number of labourers.

From 1455 to 1485, the country suffered from civil war. I doubt the statements made in chronicles as to the number of combatants engaged in the struggle. In the first battle of St. Albans we have been told that five thousand persons were slain. It is almost certain that not much more than half that number were in action. It was an accidental skirmish, provoked, as is alleged by contemporary writers and even eye-witnesses, by the king's party. Henry had liberated Somerset from the Tower, and York felt, or professed to feel, that his life was in danger. Nor do I doubt that, if we could arrive at the actual facts of the case, the combatants in the other battles were far fewer than the narrative affirms.

There was abundance of wealth in England possessed by the partizans, especially by the Duke of York's party, which was strong in London and the Eastern Counties. In the first period of the war, indeed till after the battle of Wakefield and the second fight at St. Albans, the sole purpose of the Yorkist party seems to have been the reform of abuses in the administration. It is true that the unfortunate murder of Tresham, and the development of violent partizan feeling in the Commons, made men, I conclude, despair of constitutional remedies against misgovernment. Matters were further complicated by the fact that, after Parliament had appointed York Protector, and had continued his office till he should be discharged of it by Parliament, Margaret contrived to create such a diversion in favour of the royal party that York surrendered his authority little more than two months after he had it granted him, and the queen went off with her husband and son into the county of Chester,—by which I believe is meant the city of Coventry,—the stronghold of the Lancastrian party, and there undertook the management of affairs. I make no doubt that during this period the Yorkist faction settled their differences and consolidated their plans.

The soldiers of fortune, who had long been familiar with partizan warfare in France and had now returned to England, were numerous enough for the armies of the rivals. In this the Yorkist party had an advantage, for Warwick was in command of the fleet and was governor of Calais—offices which he would certainly not have retained if the king's party had at all suspected the direction to which affairs were tending. When they were discovered, Margaret took the decisive step of summoning the Coventry Parliament, which was said to have been packed, and in which Tresham's son was Speaker, and of passing a sweeping bill of attainder by which York and all his partizans were proscribed.

We are told that house was divided against house, that families were rent by factions, and that partizanship invaded even monasteries and colleges. Our great dramatist, as is well known, has illustrated the passions of the day with tragic incidents in his plays of Henry VI. But in this I suspect there is the special pleading of the Tudor writers, who wished to represent in the strongest way how great were the blessings which came in with the accession of the family under which they lived, and how healing had been the pacific policy of the first Tudor prince. I can only say, that though I have read hundreds of private documents compiled for private inspection only during the whole of this period, I have never met with any significant allusion to the troubles which were impending or the scenes which were enacted. It is true that, in the summer of 1460, between June 26th and July 8th, just before the battle of Northampton, where Grey de Ruthin, the murderer of Tresham, deserted to the Yorkist party, and so ensured the defeat of the king's troops, the provost and fellows of King's College, Cambridge, who had despatched two of their number to Coventry the year before, and had induced the University of Cambridge to celebrate the obsequies of the king's warrior father, were exceedingly anxious for news, and sent no less than eight times in the twelve days to obtain information as to the king's affairs and his doings. It was natural enough; the college was Henry's favourite foundation, which a year before had received its last statutes from the king, in which all disciples of the heretics Wiklif and Pecok were proscribed. Besides, the chapel was unfinished, and the king was making an annual grant for its completion.

During the struggle between the rival houses, it seems to me that the people were absolutely indifferent. It was not a war of sieges but of battles, in which the combatants appear to have sought out some secluded spot, and to have fought out the combat. I have never seen or read of any injury done to neutrals, except the outrages of Margaret's northern army in the beginning of 1461,—deeds which led to the instant deposition of Henry and the coronation of Edward. The war, as I believe, was as distant from the great mass of English people, and was as little injurious in its immediate effects, as summer lightning is. If it was followed by the destruction of human life, the loss did not fall on the working men of England, but on the nobles and professional *condottieri*. It had no bearing on work and wages. At the same time it is not wonderful if the partizans on either side believed that the rest of the country took sides in their struggles. One of the commonest and most persistent delusions into which parties fall is that of imagining that the rest of the world has as keen an interest in their affairs as they have themselves. A strong upheaval of national feeling is a rare event. Its continuity beyond the occasion of its first activity is rarer still. The farmer and workman, during the last half of the fifteenth century, must have had only a transient and languid interest in the faction fight which was going on around them.

It is exceedingly likely that the Lollards were active enemies of the House of Lancaster when the issue was fairly before them. John of Gaunt had been the friend and the patron of Wiklif; and the reforming party, who finally overthrew the Government and put an end to the reign of Richard II., was identified with those who had been willing to strip the Church of its overgrown wealth. But Henry Bolingbroke had made his peace with the persecutors, and compelled, in deference to them, the civil authorities to execute the sentences of ecclesiastical tribunals. The Lollards' pit at Norwich always had its stake and faggots ready, and we may be pretty sure that the Norwich weavers had no love for their persecutors, whom they identified with Henry and his bishops. So I can quite understand that the authorities of the city were doing no unpopular act when they clothed and paid forty hired soldiers to join the king at Tewkesbury fight, and aid in the final discomfiture of the House of Lancaster and its chiefs, as they had sheltered the queen and her daughter a short time before the king's triumphant return. So the same citizens the year following gave a handsome present to the Duke of Gloucester in a gilded purse, fed his actors, and put in prison those who spoke evil of the duke and the king.

After the battle of Bosworth, a new and fatal disease occurred in England. It is remarkable that for a long period it was confined to this country, or to Englishmen, though at last it broke out in Germany and the Low Countries. Its appearance was at special and well-defined periods, its duration being on each occasion brief. While it lasted, it was specially destructive, especially in the towns. So local was it that it did not reach Scotland or Ireland. The Sweating Sickness broke out in Henry's army during its march to London. It appears to have had its origin, according to the chroniclers of the time, in the Welsh mountains, and to have been primarily due to the privations which Henry's army underwent before he reached his foe and gained the timely treason of the Stanleys. The disease was a violent inflammatory fever, accompanied by great prostration, general disorder of the viscera, great oppression of the brain, a lethargic sleep, and a profuse fetid perspiration, which flowed from the patient in streams. "So deadly was it," says Holinshed, copying the exaggerated language of the older annalists, "that not one in a hundred recovered." The course of the disease was very brief, the crisis being always over in a day and a night. Men who had been quite well at evening were often dead in the morning. It attacked robust and vigorous people more frequently than the weak, and went from east to west through the kingdom. Two lord mayors and six aldermen were victims to the disease in a week.

It visited the country again in 1506, though on this occasion the malady was not so severe. As before, its ravages were confined to England. In 1517, it appeared for a third time, when it was as destructive as it had been thirty years before, and was particularly deadly in the Universities. It also attacked Calais, but it was noticed that it affected only the English inhabitants of the town. The fourth visitation was in 1528 and 1529. It was so destructive that the time was known afterwards as the Great Mortality. The period was one of scarcity, almost of famine, and it was noticed that the "smut" first appeared in wheat in this year. On this occasion it attacked Northern Germany, beginning at Hamburg, where it is said that 1,100 persons died in twenty-two days. Thence it spread to Dantzic, Cologne, and the Low Countries, and afterwards to Amsterdam, Copenhagen, and Stockholm. The last visitation of the disease was in 1551, when it was described by Dr. Keyes, or Caius, the founder of a well-known and distinguished Cambridge college. Since that time it has not re-appeared in England, though epidemics closely resembling the described symptoms of the sweating sickness have occurred in modern times, especially in Northern Germany and North-eastern France.

The sweating sickness, though alarming for its virulence and the rapidity of its course, was not so destructive of human life as the plague had been and still was. Still it is desirable to give a brief account of it, because not only are the effects of pestilence marked on the social condition and moral character of nations, but the many economical consequences of plagues are more lasting and more significant than those of famines. Famine, indeed, has rarely occurred in England, for a reason which I have frequently given. But the habits of the people were favourable to pestilence. Every writer during the fifteenth and sixteenth centuries who makes his comments on the customs and practices of English life, adverts to the profuseness of their diet and the extraordinary uncleanliness of their habits and their persons. The floor of an ordinary Englishman's house, as Erasmus describes it, was inconceivably filthy, in London filthier than elsewhere, for centuries after these events. The streets and open ditches of the towns were polluted and noisome beyond measure. The Englishman disdained all the conditions of health, and in the large towns the deaths, to judge from the returns up to the eighteenth century, greatly exceeded the births. When pestilence was abroad, the town folk, not always welcome visitors, hurried into the country; the students of colleges sought their country seats, generally provided by the foundation against those occasional risks of town life, and there perhaps encountered nothing much more serious than a dunghill heaped with all sorts of festering offal at their doors. But the residence was only temporary, the townsman and the student had no love for country life, and when the danger was over, the shop-keeper and artizan returned to their guild houses, the student and the monk to common hall and refectory.

I cannot, therefore, conclude that either the civil disturbances of the fifteenth century or the visitation of disease, sporadic from the re-appearance of the old pestilence, or endemic at times from the occurrence of the new, materially affected the population of England during the period before me. It must not be imagined that the outbreak of a new disease such as the sweating sickness is evidence by itself of a low vitality among the people. We are expressly told that the victims of this disease were constantly the strong and healthy, not the weakly, the infirm, or the young. The disease, it is supposed, sprung from the privations to which Henry Tudor's army were exposed. But it is constantly the case that an epidemic which has its origin in the privations of one set of people, or even in a foreign nation, may seriously affect those who have not been brought under the conditions to which the first outbreak of the disorder is due. It is, I think, admitted that the severe and destructive outbreak of small-pox which passed through many parts of Europe, and our own country in particular, some ten years ago, was directly traceable to the sufferings which the French and German armies underwent in the war of 1870, just as it is probable that the ravages of the same disease at the conclusion of the seventeenth century were not obscurely connected with the wars of Louis XIV.

One notable fact in the economy of the fifteenth century is the development of the capitalist artizan. At a previous period of social history in England, this personage has scarcely an existence. The farmer, landowner, or noble, the monastery, or lay corporation, when it wants products on which the craftsman's labour is required, buys the material in a raw state, and hires the smith or other artizan to fashion it. Thus iron and steel, lead and copper, or brass, stone, and lime are either purchased raw and in bulk, or, as in the case of the latter articles named, are manufactured from chalk or limestone, or quarried by the person who requires to use them. There are always, indeed, some articles which the purchaser buys ready made. Such, for instance, are lath nails, and, in certain parts of England, particularly the Eastern Counties, other nails, these being, I am convinced, manufactured by the local smith, when he is not being engaged in regular employment by others. But other iron articles were, at the commencement of the century, regularly manufactured from the employer's material. In course of time finished articles were more and more purchased from what is evidently the stock of the craftsman. Take, for instance, a farmer's waggon. In early times, every part of this is constantly fashioned on the spot as I have described. In course of time, the farmer buys the cart frame from one person, the wheels from another, and the iron-work, the most costly part of the whole, from a third. Later on he purchases the whole article complete from the wheelwright. The same is the case with ordinary ironwork. First he hires the smith to fashion it from his stock; then he buys the article from the smith by weight; then he bargains for the article he needs at a price, without reference to weight. The special department in which the custom of buying materials lasts the longest is in building. In the Midland Counties the purchase of bricks and tiles, stone and lime, is continued, though often with special con-tracts for particular work, in which the items are not given, till the epoch of the Parliamentary wars. In the Eastern

Counties, the old system lasted longer. But in the middle of the fifteenth century, small repairs were often done by craftsmen, who send in their charges with a bill of particulars. Now the growth of this system proves that the artizan was beginning to accumulate such capital as would enable him to wait for and deal with customers, and therefore is indirect evidence that wealth was growing.

I have referred before to the fact, that in the first half of the fifteenth century, grants of fifteenths and tenths were made with a fixed deduction from the total, afterwards increased, for the relief of towns which were decayed or temporarily impoverished, and that generally certain towns were named. It is highly probable that some of this decay is due to the spread of woollen and linen manufactories into country places, where the charges of the town dues and the restrictions of the guilds did not apply. But in the year 1515 (by 6 Henry VIII., cap. vi.), complaint is made of the decay of towns and the growth of pastures. The Act states that, in "places where there used to be two hundred persons, men, women, and children, who used to be occupied and also lived by the growing of corn and other grain, and the herding of cattle, and the increase of man's sustenance, the number is lessened, and that husbandry, which is the greatest commodity of the realm for the sustenance of man, is greatly decayed, that churches are destroyed, divine offices neglected or suspended, and that public health and safety are endangered, by various causes," pointing to urban depopulation. The owners of these houses are bidden to rebuild them under pain of forfeiture to the king or the lord, and the pasture lands are to be restored to tillage. The statute is re-enacted in the following year.

Acts of Parliament in the sixteenth century complain that enclosures of arable and common fields are made for the purposes of laying them down in pasture, and that there is a serious increase in sheep breeding, accompanied by a great enhancement in the price of sheep and wool. The complaint about enclosures is as old as the fifteenth century, when the land hunger of the age led to encroachment on common pastures, and the forcible extinction of rights over common land. I do not, indeed, find that the price of sheep has risen generally as high as the Act of 1533 asserts it to have been, but wool was undoubtedly dear, being in some places nearly 8s. the tod,—a price, however, which was frequently reached as early as the beginning of the fifteenth century. The preamble to the Act states that some persons keep as many as 24,000 sheep, and some from 20,000 to 5,000, and the statute enacts that hereafter no one shall keep more than 2,000, and in order to avoid the ambiguity in the number implied by a hundred, which sometimes means the long hundred of six-score, the sum shall be five-score only, and any breach of the Act shall be followed by a penalty of 3s. 4d. on every head above the legal number, to be recovered by any informer, who shall receive half the penalty, the other moiety going to the king. The adoption of sheep farming in lieu of ordinary tillage was due to the greater profit gained by sheep raising, especially as the importation of wheat and rye from the Baltic had already attracted the notice of the legislature.

Twenty years afterwards, in 1536, in order to prevent the decay of agriculture, a new statute orders that the owners of land taken by tenants to farm shall provide proper farm buildings for every holding from fifty to thirty acres which were so let. The Act is made to apply principally to the Midland Counties, twelve of which are specified, to Lincolnshire, and to the Isle of Wight. These counties had been, in the assessments made at different times, among the most prosperous in the country. In the same year, and in divers Acts of Parliament between this year and 1545, lists of towns are given which are said to be greatly decayed. There is scarcely a town in England which is not in a declining condition, if we can rely on the statements contained in these Acts. Complaints are made that the decay of some of these towns is due to the fact that the country people have set up the business for themselves which had hitherto been the staple of the town, and the practice is forbidden. Thus the town of Bridport is protected in rope making, and the towns of

Worcestershire in cloth weaving. But I do not discover that the rate of wages falls, though the price of wheat keeps continually, though slightly, rising. Complaint is made by the city of London that foreign manufactures are injuriously imported, and that English agricultural produce is extensively exported, and that remedy should be supplied.

It would have been well for the English labourer and artizan if no worse fortune had been before them than was apprehended in these several Acts of Parliament, and provided for, on paper at least, by these regulations. Henry had spent his own substance and that of his people. The treasures of the religious houses had been squandered in an incredibly short time, hurled away in the wanton waste of his boundless extravagance. In the short remainder of his life he inflicted two wrongs on his people, the mischief of which was incalculable, the effects of which lasted for centuries. They were the debasement of the currency and the confiscation of the guild revenues. It is possible that the king did not understand the mischief which he was doing, for his apologist certainly does not.

It has been stated before that at various periods of English history the English sovereigns lessened the weight of the unit, the silver penny, till, in the year 1464, the penny of Edward IV. was almost exactly half the weight of the penny of Edward I. It is remarkable, that notwithstanding these successive diminutions, no effect is traceable in the price of commodities, and no discontent is expressed at the action of the Crown. If anything, after the last change, commodities became cheaper, and yet all those persons who were receiving fee farm or fixed rents, the amount of which had not varied from the thirteenth century, were receiving contentedly, and without the consciousness of change, about half the money in the fifteenth which their ancestor received in the thirteenth century. The king, too, whose fifteenths and tenths, whose dues and aids had long been a fixed sum, had deliberately, and for the sake of a temporary gain, from time to time deprived himself of half his income. Now Adam Smith, imperfect as his materials were for the interpretation of prices, saw that when the weight of the coin was diminished no appreciable rise of prices ensued, and he came to the conclusion that silver, measured in commodities, was becoming increasingly dearer in the fifteenth and earlier part of the sixteenth century. But it is difficult to understand why it was that the increase of value and immobility of prices corresponded with chronological precision to the several changes which were made by the indentures of the mint, and how the issue of new light money was not followed by the immediate disappearance of all the old heavy money. And if it be alleged that the force of Government is constantly able, provided the country is not affected by the foreign exchanges, to give a nominal value to a legal currency, it may be answered that the commercial transactions of England in the fifteenth century were considerable, especially with Antwerp, at that time the principal centre of trade, and that every effort was made by Government to regulate the exchanges, as was supposed, in the English interest.

I cannot explain the facts given above, except on the hypothesis already stated, that payments were ordinarily made by weight. This appears to be confirmed by the price paid for silver plate. In the very year in which the penny is reduced to one-half the amount it stood at in the thirteenth century, plate is bought at 3*s*. and 2*s*. 11*d*. the ounce. In 1493, an Oxford college purchases a quantity of new plate, some of it gilt (and mediæval gilding was very substantial), at 2*s*. 9½*d*. the ounce. But it is difficult to understand how raw silver could be purchased at anything li these prices, and the cost of manufacturing plate, when the goldsmith was on the premises and had his commons, was not less than 8*d*. an ounce, and gilding assuredly doubled the cost of workmanship at least, and, on many occasions, more than trebled it. Such low prices are inconsistent with a payment by tale, but are perfectly intelligible if they are estimates by weight.

In 1543, Henry put out his first debased money. Hitherto the coin had contained eighteen pennyweights of alloy in the twelve ounces of metal, and the pound was coined into forty-five shillings. In the issue of 1543, the debasement was two ounces in twelve in 1545, it was six ounces in twelve; in

1546, it was eight ounces in twelve. This vile mixture was coined into forty-eight pieces. The process was continued by the guardians of Edward VI. In 1549, the alloy was six ounces, and in 1551 nine ounces, the pieces now being seventy-two in the pound, and the nominal shilling possessing less than $5\frac{1}{2}d$. worth of silver in the one, and less than $2\frac{3}{4}d$. worth in the other. In the last year of Edward's reign, 1552, an issue was put out of nearly the standard fineness, and nearly the weight of the later currency. But there is no doubt that this coinage was made in order to enable Edward to negotiate for the payment of his debts at Antwerp, through the agency of Gresham, who was his factor there.

When Elizabeth reformed the currency in 1560, restoring the old standard, and coining the pound Troy into sixty shillings, the amount of base money by weight received at the Mint was nearly 632,000 lbs. Its nominal value is said to have been a little more than £638,000, which gives an additional illustration to my theory that payments were made by weight and not by tale. The actual amount of sterling silver contained in the mixture was 244,416 lbs., and the average debasement was therefore 60 per cent., or a little more than seven ounces in twelve. Elizabeth coined £733,248 in the new coinage out of the silver she refined. She was supposed to have made a profit on the transaction. I shall show hereafter that the difference between the actual and the reputed value of the old base currency was almost exactly the ratio between the price of provisions and the general necessaries of life, before the debasement occurred, and after it had taken full effect.

Now it is clear that prices were rising, though slowly and moderately, during the first forty years of the sixteenth century. In the first decade the money value of the principal necessaries of life, corn and wheat, were at the rates, speaking generally, at which they had stood for two centuries. In the last decade they had risen by twenty to forty per cent.; and the rise was recognised and wondered at, being set down to the changes which had been made, as I have already stated, in agriculture. But the knowledge of the fact should have

stayed Henry's hand, when he contemplated the great fraud
which he practised on his people.   Silver, probably owing
to the conquest of Mexico, was getting progressively cheaper ;
and had Henry not taken the step he did in 1543, the rise in
prices, inevitable after the discovery of the New World, would
nave been as slow and regular as it was during the period to
which I have referred, as foreign trade gradually distributed
the fruits of the Spanish conquests over Europe.

It is not possible, I believe, to determine the precise extent
to which a government may exact a seigniorage on a metallic
currency, or issue an inconvertible paper, which it professes
that it will afterwards redeem, without seriously disturbing
internal prices.   It may easily render its paper valueless, as
the French did with their assignats and mandats at the time
of the Revolution.   It may lower the actual value of its
metallic currency while it gives it a nominal value, till it
stimulates private coining, either at home or abroad.   In the
interval, however, it may give an appearance of prosperity to
a country where such a policy is adopted, for the price of
exports may be raised, while the money value of products in
the home market may remain unaltered.   It is very likely
that the operation of Henry's issues was disguised for a time
at home, and it is remarkable that corn was very cheap in
1547, and not dear, as matters now ruled, in 1546 and 1548,
perhaps owing to very plentiful harvests.   The monetary
history of all countries is full of instances which illustrate the
rapidity with which people fall into the delusion that high
prices, due to over issues of paper, the coinage of an over-
valued metal, or to excessive speculation, are evidence of
prosperity.   Our English Parliament in the present century
endorsed the follies of Vansittart and repudiated the truths
which were announced by the Bullion Committee and Lord
King.   But the issue of base money is rapidly and irreme-
diably mischievous.   It affects all, except those who are
quick at measuring the exact extent of the fraud, and, by
turning the base coin into an article of traffic, can trade on
the knowledge and skill which they possess.   To the poor,
and, indeed, to all who live by wages and fixed salaries, it is

speedily ruinous. The effect of Henry's and Edward's base money, though it lasted only sixteen years, was potent enough to dominate in the history of labour and wages from the sixteenth century to the present time, so enduring are the causes which influence the economical history of a nation. Whether payments were made by weight or not before the debasement, they were certainly made by tale speedily afterwards, and when Elizabeth reformed the currency, the new system, to her evident disappointment, was permanently adopted.

The proportionate money value of meat is nearly three times the old rates, that of corn nearly two and a half times, that of dairy produce, two and a half times. But the rise in wages is a little more than one and a half times. In other words, if a labourer's wages rose from 6d. a day to 9d., he had to pay 3s. for meat, 2s. 5d. for bread, and 2s. 6d. for butter or cheese, where he paid 1s. before. And the same facts are visible in those products whose value depends almost entirely on the labour which renders them fit for the market. The price of fish, of prepared fuel, of building materials, rises but a little above the rate at which labour rises. The producer of animal food, grain, and other agricultural necessaries commanded a better market than the dealer in any other article of value did, while labour, and those products the value of which is principally derived from the outlay of labour, partook in the least degree in the rise of prices. Henry and his son had at last, though unwittingly given effect to the Statute of Labourers.

Had the offence of issuing base money not been committed, and had prices risen through the distribution of the precious metals over the civilized world, the condition of the labourer would have still been impaired, for when prices are raised without there being any increased demand for labour, wages very slowly follow the rise. The general inflation of prices which I have pointed out as taking place in the forty years which followed Henry's base money have their particular explanation. But between the middle of Elizabeth's reign and the breaking out of the Parliamentary War, a period of sixty years, general prices were more than doubled, while a very miserable percentage of increase is effected in the wages of labour, certainly not more than twenty per cent. Wages are raised first by an increased demand for labour; secondly, by a limitation of those who compete for employment, and, thirdly, by the regulative action of labour partnerships, or trade unions as they are commonly called. Wages may rise when profits are stagnant or even declining.

The second injury which Henry put on his people was the destruction of the guilds and the confiscation of their property. The sums he had received from the monasteries, and the profits which he made by debasing the currency, were still insufficient for his wants, and he resolved on confiscating the rest of the corporate revenues which still survived. In the last year but one of his reign a Bill was actually passed by both Houses for the dissolution of all colleges, chantries, hospitals, free chapels, etc. ; and it is probable that the universities, the colleges, and the public schools would have been swept away into the all-devouring exchequer, had not Henry died before the Act was carried out.

The corporate existence of the town long preceded that of the guild. It is possible that associations of traders, voluntarily united or recognised by some external authority, were active from very remote times, from the merely gregarious instinct of human beings. They are traced to a period before the Conquest. It is probable, for instance, that the guild of goldsmiths in London was an association at a date earlier than the earliest extant charter of the city, just as it is probable that in the town of Oxford associations of students preceded the foundation of the University. But the chartered town or city was antecedent to the chartered guild. In course of time the associations of traders obtained charters, but were obscure and feeble societies, though rallying places for the burghers against the urban aristocracy. In time they united in a guild-hall; in time they constrained all the inhabitants of the city to enter in one or the other of the companies, and ultimately obtained the exclusive franchise. But the relics of an older constituency remained in the residential electorate of the wards. In just the same way the Oxford and Cambridge colleges, which were in the first instance tolerated excrescences on the academical system, became finally the monopolists of education and academical authority.

The guilds gradually acquired property, sometimes entirely for their own ends, more generally as interested in the remainder of a trust. A brother of the craft would give house and lands to better the annual feast, which the craft always held ; or he might found a school, an hospital, or an almshouse, and after defining the amount of his benefaction, would leave the surplus, if any, to the discretion of the guild. Or he would make the guild the trustees of the fund from which the mass priest should receive his stipend for spiritual offices, the residue being left to the guild as remuneration for management. Occasionally the corporation bargained for the amount of the spiritual service, and refused to agree to a proposal which might be too costly for the fund to bear. They exacted fees for apprenticeship, for taking up freedom by inheritance or servitude, and more lately for admission into the guild by purchase. Like prudent men, who might be liable to occasional charges, they saved and invested these funds, as also gifts for lending without usury to poorer citizens, for apprenticing poor boys or girls, or for marriage portions, or for widows' pensions, or for the relief of the destitute members of the craft, the first and the most enduring duty of the guild. The guild estates, the chest of the company, its revenues and rents, were, like the endowments of an academical college, at once the support of the fraternity and the means by which the discipline of the order or craft was maintained. The analogy between the guild and the college was close, and perhaps this was fully understood. Two guilds in the town of Cambridge founded out of their resources one of the older colleges in that University. Sometimes the permanent revenues of the guild or college were scraped together from the savings of the fees which bygone generations of applicants had paid, and the college or guild had hoarded.

Somerset, Edward the Sixth's uncle, procured the Act by which these guild lands were confiscated, on the plea of the " superstitious use " with which they were generally associated. He did not, indeed, venture on appropriating the estates of the London guilds, for London had it in its power to make revolutions, and they were spared, after ransom paid, under the plea that the guild did service to trade. Similarly the chantries annexed to the Oxford and Cambridge colleges were not reft from these institutions, but allowed, discharged of the duty. I conceive that most of the outlying bits of land in the urban boundaries of Oxford and Cambridge which were possessed by the pre-Reformation colleges are mainly chantry lands. These guild lands were in the aggregate considerable, and the confiscation made Somerset and the Reformation unpopular. After Somerset's execution, the rapacity of Northumberland made the Reformation still more odious; and when this schemer attempted to set Jane Grey on the throne, the most Protestant district of England rose against the new order of things, protected Mary, who trusted herself to them, and made her queen, to be repaid by fire and faggot. For anything which Northumberland, the son of Henry the Seventh's hateful instrument, the father of Elizabeth's worthless favourite, had touched, was tainted. He had secured, in the last year of Edward's reign, the surrender of the see of Durham, with the regalian rights of the County Palatine. He intended to appropriate this to himself, and to dismember northern England by making an independent principality, which should include the Northern Counties, and probably York, to ally with the Scots, and to procure the hand of Mary Stuart for his son Robert. In this case he would be able to defy all attempts to dispossess him. But Edward's death disconcerted his plans, and the hatred of all parties cowed him.

The issue of the base money was recognised to be the cause of dearth in the realm. Latimer preached before the king and lamented that the silver had become dross. All the good money disappeared, of course, and the king's credit with it. Pauperism began to show itself, and the people were exhorted to charity and almsgiving by proclamations which issued from a gang of coiners and smashers. In Mary's days the rich who declined to give were to be denounced to the ordinary as heretics. It may be doubted whether, even if she had reformed the currency in her reign, the old prices would have been restored. Elizabeth effected the reformation, but the facts were too strong for her, the wages of labour possessed less and less purchasing power, and pauperism increased. The great queen's government strove to stay it by insisting on the creation of peasant holdings, or by supplementing wages with land allotments of four acres to each cottage. But the evil was too far gone for the remedies of legislation, and a poor law, under which the relief of destitution was guaranteed, was the only expedient before her government when it was left face to face with the irremediable poverty of labour.

The English labourer, then, in the sixteenth century was almost simultaneously assailed on two sides. The money which he received for his wages was debased, and the assistance which his benefit society gave him in times of difficulty, which allowed him loans without interest, apprenticed his son, or pensioned his widow, was confiscated. All the necessaries of life, as I have already stated, rose in value in the proportion generally of 1 to $2\frac{1}{2}$, while the wages of labour rose to little more than from 1 to $1\frac{1}{2}$. His ordinary means of life were curtailed. The considerable advantage which the London labourer and artizan had over his country fellow in the calling disappeared, and the wages of country and London hands were nearly equalised. This was indeed to be expected, for in the virtual decline of wages, the advantage of the better paid or selected hands would certainly be lost. But the deterioration of his condition was not confined to the loss of money wages. He lost his insurance also, the fund destined to support him and his during the period of youth and age, when work is not open to the imperfect powers of youth, and has become impossible to the enfeebled powers of age. Nor is the extent of the loss which the working classes suffered by the confiscation of the guild lands to be estimated by the value which was set upon the capital fund, as we may see from the enormous amount to which those funds have increased in London, where they were spared, for it is admitted that most of the guild or corporate estates of the city companies are of pre-Reformation origin. The estates of the guilds in country towns might not have nearly reached the value of the London property belonging to the companies, but they would hardly have been so entirely perverted from their original objects as they have been in the city, and would have remained, in some degree at least, to fulfil the original purposes of the donors. The country guilds, though not formally suppressed after being plundered, were practically superseded by the corporate action of the burgesses, who appropriated such income as was left, from fees and fines, to the common purse of the freemen.

The purpose which the legislature had before it for two centuries had now become possible. The Statute of Labourers had been passed, re-enacted, invoked, and put into execution in vain. There is hardly a trace in the history of English labour and wages that the passionate desire of the employers of labour that workmen should be constrained to accept reasonable wages had been satisfied. The rise in wages, and what was even more significant, of articles the price of which no law could pretend to control, had changed the form of English husbandry from capitalist cultivation on a large scale to the stock and land lease, and thence to tenancies of the ordinary farm kind on short lease, or to tenancies at will. But though there was a formidable increase in prices after the full effect of the debased currency was reached, there was no rise in rents. The landowner was paying nearly three times as much in the first years of Elizabeth's reign as he paid in the first years of her father's reign, and receiving no more rent in the later than he did in the earlier period. This is proved by the evidence given of corporate income at the two periods when the income is the source of the corporation's existence. For a long time the revenues of King's College, Cambridge, and New College, All Souls, or Merton, Oxford, show no increase in amount. The Cambridge College, it is true, tries to remedy the loss by demanding its rents in kind, but the Oxford societies either did not attempt the expedient or found that their tenants could resist it. The bishoprics were opulent before the Reformation, but poor after it, not so much because they had generally been shorn of their possessions by the greedy courtiers of the later Tudor princes, though this took place, as because rents had remained stationary while prices had been rising. Nor is the cause far to seek. Rents do not rise because prices rise, for the power of the tenant to pay an enhanced rent which the rise in the price of farm produce will give him may be entirely neutralized by the rise in the price of that which he must purchase in order to carry on his industry. This is made clear at the present (1883) time. The high price of meat and dairy products is more than a compensation for the low price of corn, if one is to interpret the power of a tenant to pay rent by the price of agricultural produce. But all farmers will tell us that, owing to the great price of lean stock, no profit, or little profit beyond manure, attends stock keeping. Nor would the difference between high and low wages materially diminish or increase the power of paying rent, apart from other causes. Wages may be high, and profits may remain high, because demand is great and supply indefinite. This is the common case when there is great activity in manufactures, and it arises from the fact that business has become more brisk, that the industry is for the time capable of indefinite extension, or that a great and notable economy has been induced on the process of production. Wages may be high and profits low, not because, as some economists have absurdly argued, wages trench on profits, but because an increasing number of persons compete for an inelastic or stationary amount of business, and therefore at once overbuy each other in the wages market and undersell each other in the produce market.

In mediæval agriculture the greatest outlay, as I have frequently said, was on stock, live and dead. It is not easy, in the old system of capitalist farming, to precisely figure the wages of labour, because the tenants of the manor frequently paid the rents for their small holdings in labour, and an estimate of this would have to be given in any interpretation

of the cost of labour in the earlier husbandry. But in the
small tenancies which followed, this kind of labour is extinguished, and it is not easy, in the absence of direct
evidence, to determine what additional cost the tenant would
be at. Still the farmer gave, as in older times, his own
labour and that of his household to his holding, and would
not be as likely to employ independent labour as the capitalist farmer was, except in harvest time and under urgency.
And it will be clear, that unless hired labour formed a
considerable item in the costs of the tenant farmer, a fall in
wages would not of itself render him, under such altered
circumstances, able and willing to pay an enhanced rent.
There is only one cause for a rise in rent, and this cause has
manifested itself at well-defined periods in the history of
English agricultural industry.

This is an economy in the process of production due to
improvements in the process of agriculture. From the days
of Henry III. to those of James I., no such economy or
improvement occurred. It is probable that some processes
by which land was tilled were neglected or forgotten. It
is not unlikely that the care which had been taken to improve
breeds of sheep had been remitted. Only one new kind of
agricultural industry had been introduced,—the cultivation
of the hop; and this was suspected and even denounced.
But from the time of James I., especially after the middle
of his reign, large and important improvements are made
in agriculture, great economies discovered, and a rapid rise
in rent ensues. These will be subsequently commented on.
It is to be regretted, though it is not to be wondered at,
that these improvements and economies had no beneficial
effect on the wages of labour.

The government of Elizabeth was, however, convinced that
the legal restraint of wages was a necessity or a benefit, or
both. Hence the Statute 5 Eliz., cap. 4 (which enacts that
no person shall, under a penalty of forty shillings a month,
use or occupy any art, mystery, or manual occupation
without a previous seven years' apprenticeship), seems to
favour traders and artizans at the expense of labourers in

husbandry, by limiting the number of the former and making the latter the residuum of all non-apprenticed labour. But the favour is more apparent than real in the case of the artizan ; for what the statute gives with one hand it takes away with another. The justices in Quarter Sessions are empowered to fix the rate of wages in husbandry and in handicrafts, and they do not let their powers lie idle. The great collection of Elizabeth's proclamations now in the Bodleian Library, a volume which probably once belonged to Cecil, gives two of these exhaustive assessments,—one for the county of Rutland, which seems to have been published as a type for the southern counties, and one for that of Lancashire, which is probably a guide for the northern counties. There are others in existence.

This expedient was at last successful, and was the third in the set of causes from which pauperism was the inevitable effect. The two former, the base money and the confis-cation of the benefit societies' funds, are economical, and can be so interpreted. The third is capable of historical proof. The wages of labour do conform, notwithstanding the con-tinual increase in the price of the necessaries of life, to the assessments of the Quarter Sessions, and the system is continued under legal sanction till 1812, and by a sufficient understanding for long after that date. It seems that as long as the practice remained, under which the wages of the peasant were eked out by land allowances and commonable rights, he continued to subsist, though but poorly, under the system ; but that when the enclosures of the eighteenth century began, and the full influence of the corn laws was felt, during the fourth quarter of that century and the first quarter of the nineteenth, it became necessary to supplement his wages by an allowance from the parish fund, and thus to indirectly qualify the assessment which the magistrates had established.

Had, however, the first two acts to which I have so often referred not been committed, the third would have, I am per-suaded, been nugatory. It was nothing more than had been enacted in the reign of Henry IV., and had been wholly

23

inoperative, at any rate in the direction which it was intended
to take—the reduction of agricultural wages; for these, as
we have seen, improve after the enactment. But it was a
very different thing when the workman had been weakened,
and he had been constrained for half a generation to submit
to a base currency and to undergo other losses.

The altered condition of the labourers is further illustrated
by the rise in the price of their maintenance. In the early part
of the fifteenth century the average cost of a labourer's board
is 9*d*. a week. In the famine year of the fifteenth century,
1348-9, it rose to an average of 1*s*. 6*d*., a proof that the rates
which I have given were contract prices. Nor is there much
variation in the rate till after the issue of the base money. In
1542, board and lodging are put at 1*s*. a week; but in ten years
from this time it rises to an average of 3*s*. a week. In 1562,
1563, and 1570, Elizabeth makes quarterly contracts for
victualling her workmen in her dockyards at Deptford and
Portsmouth. In the first year the contract is at an average
of 4*s*. 0½*d*.; in the second, at 4*s*. 6*d*.; in the third, at 3*s*. 11*d*.;
the first and third being a cheap, the second a dear year. The
Queen also rents lodgings at 2*d*. a week, the contract being
that the men should have feather beds, that two should lie in
a bed, and that the Queen should find sheets and pay for
washing them at 1*d*. the pair. Similar contracts are made at
4*s*. in 1573; at 4*s*. 8½*d*. in 1577; at 4*s*. 3*d*. in 1578. These
prices represent the highest increases of any, for I find that
in 1562 the average price of labour was 4*s*. 9½*d*. the week; in
1563, 4*s*. 0½*d*.; in 1570, 4*s*. 7*d*.; in 1573, 4*s*. 11½*d*.; in 1577
4*s*. 10¾*d*.; and in 1578, 4*s*. 8*d*.; these average rates of
wages, taken from eight different kinds of labour, five
artizans and three ordinary or unskilled, being only a very little
in excess of the amounts for which Elizabeth contracted in
the same years to board her artizans at the docks.

Elizabeth soon discovered that one of the causes which was
impoverishing her people was making her also poor. The rents
and dues of the Crown, the subsidies, tenths and fifteenths,
all the revenues of the Crown, except, perhaps, customs, were
fixed in amount. The purchasing power of the revenue had

fallen to about one-third of its ancient capacity, and the Queen strove to meet the difficulty by declaring that the new currency should run at only two-thirds its nominal value— *i.e.*, that the shilling should be current at 8*d.*, and so on. But the proclamation, though drafted, was not issued, probably because the Queen's advisers feared that the step would be unpopular, and would suggest that the Crown was trying arbitrarily to enhance its rights against its debtors.

The enactment and development of the English poor law, unique among legislative enactments, must be treated in a separate chapter. But I must remind my reader that it by no means follows that population had increased because there was a virtual decline in wages. Low wages may be the con-comitant of a scanty population, high wages of an abundant one. Nay, unhappily, society may make notable progress in wealth, and wages may remain low, misery may be general, and discontent may be imminent. The mass of English workmen are far better off now than they were two generations ago, though population has greatly increased. But relatively speaking, the working man of to-day is not so well off as he was in the fifteenth century, when the population was not one-tenth of what it is now.

CHAPTER XIII.

THE CLERGY TILL THE REFORMATION.

The Merits and Action of the Mediæval Church—Reformers, their Zeal and
Ferocity—The Seats of Resistance to the Church—The Treatment of Ec-
clesiastical History by Ecclesiastics—The State of England in the Monastic
Age—The Affair of ·1297—The Meeting at Canterbury—The Policy of the
Pope—The Residence at Avignon—The Schism—The Prosperity of the
People, and the Mismanagement of Government—The Bishops of the
Fifteenth Century—Arundel, Chichele, Stafford, Kemp, Bourchier, Scrope,
Booth, Wykeham, Beaufort, Waynflete, De Molyns, Ayscough, Pecok—The
Position of the Latter, His Books, His Trial and Condemnation—The Clergy
and the Monks—The Progress of Church Reform from the Days of the
Oxford Reformers to the Settlement of Elizabeth—The Ordinary History
of the Fifteenth Century, as that of the latter part of the Seventeenth,
Superficial.

NO inquiry into the economical history of England would
be complete which did not give some account of the
clergy. During a long time they were the most powerful
factors in the progress of civilization, were the principal
instruments by which the very memory of ancient literature
was preserved, and some of its relics treasured; were the only
historians of the age, the only educators of the people, the
only refuge from tyranny and violence, the asylum of the
past, the hope of the future. At one time the national
and secular clergy performed, to the best of their power, these
high functions; at another time, the protection of society
becomes the business of monasteries, though often uncon-
sciously; at another, the papacy is the ark of refuge; at
another, the hierarchy of different European states was compelled to save the corporate Church from the ambition, the
vices, the incapacity of its chief; at another, the authors of
schisms within the order were the agents in working out the

higher destinies of mankind. As they preserved the relics of culture, of order, of law, of obedience to a common purpose ; as they maintained a bold front against the degrading and debasing selfishness of a turbulent aristocracy, the common foe of the administration, of trade, of religion, of morality, of every national and every private interest, so they were the principal cause why England became thoroughly settled and occupied, that agriculture was safely and, for the times, successfully carried on, and that the husbandman was not utterly trodden down and impoverished. No body of persons has played a more important part in the history of English progress than the English clergy have, especially when they were at once Englishmen, and yet had higher and more far-reaching aims than the mere political interests of the day or the mere ends of their order. The visitor to the cathedral church of Canterbury will see that the grave of the greatest English prelate, Stephen Langton, lies partly within and partly without the church. Perhaps it is an accident that, an addition having been made to the fabric after Langton was laid in the grave, the architect of the Warriors' Chapel would not disturb the remains of the great statesman and bishop who saved England from John in the first instance, and from Innocent and Honorius in the second, but arched the grave over with the wall which he was constructing. But the place of Langton's grave is an apt symbol of what the work of the best churchmen was. It is at once of and in the Church, and of and in the world ; in the Church of the past, and in the world of the past, but in what was Church and world together, the ancestor of that of which our present England is the descendant. A century after Langton's time, and the Church has become the handmaid of the regal authority, without spirit and without a policy, and the forces were slowly gathering which weakened its influence, overset its power, confiscated its revenues, and claimed to inherit its ancient rights over all men, for the policy of the Puritan in the middle of the seventeenth century had been the policy of the Lollard in the latter part of the fourteenth—an attempt to supersede one ecclesiastical dynasty by another.

The Church of the middle ages conferred inestimable
benefits on mankind, and especially on England, from the
days of Lanfranc to those of Grostête; but it inflicted enormous mischief in other ways.   It was in the last degree
intolerant to all who would not agree with its tenets and
its policy.   As it became more zealous it became more implacable.   It educated the human mind, but only on its own
lines, and, though it allowed it growth, it stunted and distorted
it.   It had no patience with those who challenged its authority
and the means by which it thought fit to maintain its authority.
It put out the most shameless fictions in order to vindicate
its claims.   It forged a whole body of law that it might
maintain, first, the appellate, and, next, the original jurisdiction of the papal court.   It forged charters innumerable,
in order to give the pretence of independence for its action
and status.   It forged miracles by thousands, in order that
it might at once enslave the people and fill its coffers.
Mr. Hallam has quoted some of these stories, which he
conceives were invented in order to be a counterpoise to
the foolish romances of chivalry.   They long preceded any
such romances, and a heap of them—those which Mr. Hallam
quotes among the rest—may be seen in an eleventh century
MS. (Laud, No. F. 34), still preserved in the Bodleian
Library.   Nor was the papacy above sharing in these frauds.
I do not say that the alleged miracles at Becket's tomb were
deliberate impostures.   The circumstances under which
the unparalleled crime of Becket's murder was committed
were sufficient to strike every imagination in the twelfth
century, even that of the murderers themselves, when the
paroxysm of passion was over.   I can well believe that for
a long time "the martyrdom chapel" was full of apparitions
to the devout believer; the tomb of the saint a scene of
divine manifestations.   I can understand why the Black
Prince chose the proximity of the shrine, to which Becket's
body fifty years after the murder was translated, as the
place of his own sepulchre; and why Henry IV., who had
himself put to death another archbishop by form of legal
process, chose the same spot for himself and his wife.   But the

bargain under which the translation was permitted by the pope is most significant. The murder of Becket occurred in midwinter, a most inconvenient time for pilgrimage, and the monks sought for the pope's permission to put the day of translation in midsummer. The bargain was long and anxious. The pope claimed half the gross profits of the shrine, and on the monks insisting that they could not carry on the business on such terms, allowed himself to accept half the net profits. The pope was Honorius III., who had succeeded to the policy and pretensions of Innocent III., and the narrative of the transaction is in the archives of Christ Church, now the Canterbury chapter.

The more zealous was the reformer of Church discipline and doctrine, the more ferocious was his zeal. We owe the Inquisition to Dominic, one of the founders of the missionary movement at the end of the twelfth century; and the savagery of the Inquisition's orthodoxy at the commencement of its career was as implacable as that of its later organization and activity. The mission of the new order was, like that of its predecessors, to save society; but if any members, or all the members, declined the means which the mission laid down by the agents of the reform, the doctors of the new way were quite ready to destroy society, for the fundamental condition under which it would do good was that of unhesitating obedience, of a total surrender of the judgment to dictation, and of unquestioning faith in the authorised revelation. The Church in the twelfth century needed reform grievously, but the discipline of the orthodox reformer fell on those whom the Church had offended. So the whole Church became hopelessly corrupt in the fourteenth century, so corrupt that there seemed no prospect of an internal reformation such as that effected by Dominic and Francis, and only one remedy remained,—the submission of the hierarchy to the decrees of general councils. But the Council was as bloodthirsty, as perfidious, as the Inquisition. And when the Reformation became an accomplished fact, and a new race of obedient reformers sprang up in Loyola and his followers, there still was to be no truce, no faith, no mercy for the heretic; there was to be nothing but submission or death. If the Church of the middle ages strove to mitigate, to resist, to control, to subdue the evils of the age in which it found its work, it would do so only on condition that the progress of mankind went on the lines which it had sketched out, and to the limits which it had defined. Any onward movement was dangerous, suspicious, and, finally, intolerable.

It cannot be by accident that those parts of Europe which have been from time to time distinguished for manufacturing and commercial activity have also been, with one exception, and that capable of easy explanation, generally hostile to the pretensions of the Church, and that they have, when possible, revolted from it. It was so in Toulouse, before the crusade of Simon de Montfort wasted the fairest part of France. It was so in Flanders and Holland, in the Baltic towns, in Scandinavia, and in the eastern parts of England. It was so in the most industrious and opulent parts of France in the sixteenth century. It was not indeed so in Italy; but the papacy laid all Europe under tribute, and whatever may have been the lot of its own subjects, the presence of the papal court was an enormous factor in the wealth of Italy. It was not in human nature that it should willingly quarrel with the process by which it became opulent, though in the end it paid dearly for its advantages. Being necessarily disunited, for it hated the temporal power heartily and consistently, it became the prey of the strongest adventurer, of the tyrants which it bred within itself, till the close of the fifteenth century, when Charles VIII. gave the earliest occasion for that interference of foreign adventurers in Italy which continued to our own days. Nor again can it be by accident that those countries which have thrown off the yoke of the Roman see were and have been most distinguished for intellectual activity. The true literature of modern Europe is almost exclusively the work of those countries in which the Reformation has been finally settled—of England, of Holland, of Northern Germany.

Some years ago I remember to have heard of a Roman Catholic prelate in Germany who stated that Lingard's History of England was the fairest which he had ever read

But on being told that Lingard was a priest of his own creed, he exclaimed, " What an atrocious knave ! " The bishop took that clerical view of history which has been generally prevalent among all clergymen of all established, or dominant, or pretentious churches, who have written on ecclesiastical topics, even in the treatment of secular history. To suppress or colour inconvenient truths, to palliate ecclesiastical crimes when they cannot be ignored, to distort the motives, or traduce the characters, or ridicule the arguments, of reformers outside the Church, is the common vice of clerical historians. Such persons cannot be dispassionate. Any person who will be at the pains to read how Lingard, the fairest and most cautious instance of an ecclesiastical historian, deals with the attitude which Langton took towards Innocent and Honorius, of how he treats the resistance of Grostête to the papal provisions, can see how strongly he was biassed. Under such circumstances it is not reasonable to expect that he would be even commonly just to Wiklif and the Lollards, to Luther and the reformers ; or to wonder that he speaks of the first as an irresolute, impudent, and absurd fanatic, his followers as communists and rebels ; and of the Saxon reformer as a man whose motives are to be found in disappointed ambition, in vain-glorious love of display, and whose conduct in affairs is coarse, insolent, and offensive. He has little or nothing to say about the unparalleled misdeeds of the papal court from the accession of John XXIII. till that of Adrian VI.

England was planted full of monasteries and of capitular bodies. The monks, especially those of the Benedictine order, the most learned and respectable of the older bodies, generally chose some locality of great natural beauty, being often settled in some poorly peopled district. Here they built their magnificent churches and set up their conventual buildings. Some of these establishments were founded in times almost prehistoric, by kings, the boundaries of whose dominions can be no longer traced, and whose names alone have survived in their charters of donation. The towns were full of those ecclesiastical corporations, whose history and whose downfall is recorded in the vast work of Dugdale.

These monasteries were in the zenith of their reputation during the first half of the thirteenth century, when they had, it would appear, been stimulated to a beneficent activity by the rivalry of the two new orders of preaching friars, those of Dominic and Francis.   They had to be sure the fatal gift of wealth, but they seem to have used their wealth well.   They were founders of schools, authors of chronicles, teachers of agriculture, fairly indulgent landlords, and advocates of generous dealing towards the peasantry.   They drove to be sure an active trade in miracles and relics, and they were not very particular in scrutinizing reports of visions and dreams which portended honour to the saint on whose merits they depended and by whose good offices they were enriched.   It is, however, very difficult to put oneself in the place of those whose devotion to saints and reverence for relics seems to us so credulous and even degrading, but it would be intolerable to believe that the respect which they professed and imposed on others was a mere hypocritical grimace put on to serve the most sordid and dishonest ends.

It is not easy to understand how these monasteries declined in character and usefulness, till they came to the condition which is described so indignantly by Gascoigne,—a condition which renders probable the charges which Henry the Eighth's commissioners made against them.   But many causes appear to have contributed to the result.   Their wealth doubtlessly made them unpopular, especially when they had committed the fatal error in 1297 of praying Boniface VIII. to issue a bull by which the whole body of the clergy were forbidden to make any grant from their revenues to laymen without the express permission of the pope.   The extreme rashness and pride with which Boniface contrived at once to embroil himself with Edward and Philip is surprising enough, but that the English clergy should have sought his assistance against a monarch whose character and authority they had good cause to be acquainted with is still more strange.   The issue of the contest is well known.   The king was completely victorious, and really gained at a stroke all that his great-grandfather strove to obtain by the celebrated Constitutions

of Clarendon. The clergy, secular and regular, were forced
to submit, and never afterwards attempted to make head
against the king's will. It seems reasonable to infer that the
change from such high pretensions to such complete submission should have stimulated lay persons to try their own
strength against corporations which were wealthy, were unwilling to contribute to public purposes, and yet might be
cowed into acquiescence. A singular illustration of this
temper occurs in the ledger book of the Priory of Christ
Church, just thirty years after the struggle between Edward
and his clergy, the particulars of which I have extracted from
the original.

On May 27th, 1327, a letter came from the king to William
of Chilham, bailiff of Canterbury, and the citizens of the town,
requesting them to provide a contribution in men in order to
repel an invasion of Robert Bruce, who had taken advantage
of the disturbed state of England to renew his ravages on the
border. The bailiff and citizens agreed to equip and send
twelve men-at-arms to Newcastle-on-Tyne, and invited the
prior and monks of Christ Church to give their aid in the
undertaking. The prior declined on the ground that the
possessions of the monastery were, and always had been, in
free alms, and were, therefore, not liable to any such contribution ; and that, indeed, they could not make it without
the consent of the king himself. On the receipt of this
message the bailiff and citizens met in the field adjoining the
house of the preaching friars, and came to the following
resolutions :—(1) That they would pull down all the tenements in Burgate to the mill ; (2) that no one under penalties,
to be imposed by the city, should inhabit the prior's houses ;
(3) that all rents of 200 marks and upwards should be levied
for the benefit of the city ; (4) that no one should buy, sell,
or exchange drink or victuals with the monastery under
similar penalties ; (5) that all carts and horses from the
manors of the convent containing victuals or stock for the
monastery should be seized and sold with their contents ;
(6) that if the prior or any of the monks go out of their
church they should be spoiled of their clothes and goods and

be attached ; (7) that a deep ditch should be dug outside the great gate of the monastery, so that no one should go in or out ; (8) that no stranger should enter the church, unless he take oath first that he will offer no gift to the shrine of St. Thomas or elsewhere ; (9) each of the citizens swore that he would have from the shrine of St. Thomas a gold ring of the best, for each finger of each of his hands, from those which were hung up at the aforesaid shrine of St. Thomas. It was a common custom, when gifts of money and jewels were made to the shrine, to acknowledge them, and inform the donor that the ring had been hung on the shrine.

No further statement is made in the ledger-book of the consequences which followed from this transaction. The statement made to the prior is probably an exaggerated account of some violent language or threats used at the town's meeting ; for we can hardly imagine that these resolutions were formally committed to writing and forwarded to the monastery. But however much they may be softened down, they contain enough which must be real to show that, at a date long before the epoch at which monastic corruption was said to have commenced, there was a very active feeling of animosity against monastic privileges, even when the prior was so cautious as this ecclesiastic was. For the letters which precede this and are copied into the ledger express the prior's alarm at what was going on in England, his disinclination to take any side in the quarrel between the king and queen, and his request that all his communications on the subject should be burnt as soon as read. At this comparatively early date, in short, the lay tax-payers are beginning to be discontented with the wealth and the immunities of the clergy, and to cast about how they might relieve themselves from these recurrent claims, by insisting that their wealthy neighbours should share the burden.

The regular orders and (as long as their secular brethren identified themselves with the aims of the monks) the bishops and parochial clergy were supposed to sympathize with the policy of the pope. Now beyond doubt, the popes had exercised an enormous power, and, as many have recognized, for important objects,—objects which at the time seemed a public good,—over the affairs of Europe, especially in the German Empire. The struggle with the house of Swabia lasted from the days of Hildebrand till after the middle of the thirteenth century. But, to carry out their policy, the popes had taxed Europe severely; had spent largely, beyond question, in corrupting those persons who might resist the authority of the emperors; had constantly violated private rights; and had encouraged resistance to central and constituted authority. The long agony and weakness of Germany, continued for eight centuries at least, perhaps even from the days of Charles the Great's eldest son, were the work of the papal court. The pope did his best to make the German Empire and the German people powerless in Europe, and, to be just, the pope's policy was eminently successful; for it stereotyped the miserable German aristocracy, and created the German kinglets—the curse of the Teutonic race—from the earliest ages of later Europe. A divided and disunited Germany was the true temporal power of the pope, and the dissensions of Germany are his temporal power to this day. To effect this end, the pope wanted money. He gathered it from all his spiritual subjects by any pretext which he could devise, by capitation fees, by dues, by taxes on ecclesiastical successions, by exacting enormous bribes for confirmations in dignities, by the sale of canonizations, by the sale of relics, by the sale of pardons, licences, indulgences. He invented prohibitions in order to make a market of them. He invented affinities in order to sell dispensations; and he gave dispensations for the marriage of near blood relations, as, for instance, those of an uncle and niece. He borrowed and paid interest and principal by annuities, levied on anything which came handy. "The Roman Church," said Alphonso of Arragon to Eugenius IV., "is a veritable harlot, for she offers herself to every one who approaches her with money."

It was remarkable that the European sovereigns did not see that if the Roman court were successful in Germany it would follow out the same policy with every European state which it could influence. But the European kings and states-

men were like children in a nursery, where, though one of
the number may be convulsed with grief, the rest go on
unconcernedly with their games or their occupations. All
were indifferent. Still it is possible, if the popes had remained
at Rome during the fourteenth century, that the Reformation
might have been anticipated by two centuries. They migrated to Avignon, lost their political influence by being
simply the echoes of French policy, became more hungry
and rapacious than ever, and more disliked. Then came the
great schism, the epoch of the Councils, the decline of the
papal authority, and finally the Reformation.

The residence at Avignon, occurring as it did at the epoch
during which the English king carried on the first war with
France, made the pope still more unpopular in England.
He was believed to be the ally of the English enemy, the
adviser, counsellor, friend, mainstay of the usurper who kept
the Plantagenets out of their just inheritance. The attacks
of Wiklif and others his followers on the Roman Court,
on Roman doctrines, and the pope's adherents, the monks
and friars in England, were popular, and were encouraged
in high places. It seems to me highly probable that there
would have been a reformation in England on the lines of
Wiklif's teaching had it not been for the tremendous insurrection of Tyler and his associates. Thenceforward the
Church became the ally, the servant, the spy of the government, and earned the continuance of the wealth and influence
it possessed by the conviction which all the dynasties entertained, Plantagenets, Tudors, and Stuarts, that it was on
the watch against the common enemy of disaffection. As
it gave all its energies to this struggle, it ceased to be national,
and became the advocate of a party. As it became more and
more the advocate of a party, it was loyal only to that which
gave it security. As it concentrated its purposes on the
prosecution of its own wealth and place, it ceased to be
moral, and identified religion with acquiescence in secular
authority. As might be expected, the corruption of the
religious houses was greater than that of the secular clergy.
As again might be expected, the hierarchy of the secular

clergy were more time-serving, more negligent, more disloyal
to their true duty than the parochial clergy were. The
fifteenth century was the worst age of the Anglican Church.
It was the worst age of the papacy, at least since the time
when Hildebrand began to reform the Church with a view
to enslaving the state, and after denouncing simony, to
make simony the machinery of ecclesiastical government.

At the beginning of the fifteenth century, or at least after
the Council of Pisa, there were three simultaneous popes,
each claiming to be lawfully elected, each claiming the
allegiance of Christendom, and each cursing his rival and
his rival's supporters. As the schism was scandalous, another
Council, that of Constance, was summoned, and the unity of
Christendom was nominally restored. But it was impossible
to restore respect for the papal authority, or to revive that
empire over governments which had been the dream of
Gregory VII. and the achievement of Innocent III. There
still remained the vast and indeterminate influence over
men's minds, sanctioned by ancient tradition, supported by
every artifice which ingenuity could suggest and interest
insist on. I do not foolishly allege that the system of the
Roman Church was the outcome of a conscious and deliberate
conspiracy against every impulse that makes human nature
hopeful and courageous, because it insists that the individual
is responsible, for I am well aware that in the darkest age
of ecclesiastical morality, the fifteenth century, there were
men who were sincerely attached to Roman Christianity,
and would have been an honour to any religion. But the
degradation of the hierarchy in England and abroad was
conspicuous, the appeals to popular superstitions were gross
and scandalous, and, in this country at least, men who
recorded the facts and made an estimate of their necessary
consequences were being trained to accept the reform which
was inevitable in the following century, and might well have
been anticipated had not the English Government been
demoralized by prolonged and furious feuds.

I have stated frequently that the fifteenth century was
an epoch of peculiar prosperity, that the means of life were

cheap, that wages were high, that the price of land went rapidly up, that English commerce increased, that enterprise, according to the lights and opportunities of the age, was general, that the yeomanry and small gentry were firmly planted, and that remarkable opulence was attained by many. The Cannyngs and the Chicheles are examples of the wealth which was won by traders, the Fastolfes and the Cromwells of the opportunities given to knights and nobles. The solid and splendid buildings of this century denote its wealth and illustrate its profusion. The eulogy which Fortescue utters on the English constitution is testimony to the character and spirit of the people. The mass of the nation was thrifty and thriving. The Lollardy which is said to have infected all those who prospered and grew rich was very likely sour and contemptuous, but it was hardy and vigorous, like its descendant in the seventeenth century. It was sufficient to leaven the religious life of the English, though it was not, as yet, powerful enough to change it. The persecution which its adherents suffered (and the story of these persecutions could be gathered by laborious compilation from municipal archives, such as those of Norwich and Canterbury, where the charge for burning heretics is a recurrent expense on the city revenues) would point out how widely spread were the tenets of the sectaries. Now a hunted creed, if it be not extirpated, and is held by the most progressive of the industrial classes, makes its votaries reserved, concentrated on their callings, vigilant in their action, and, in the end, wealthy. These men had nothing to spare for monk and priest, least of all for the former. But there was no organization by which to give effect to the discontent which was felt, for insurrection was tried by Cade and failed, and in this remarkable uprising, political and social grievances are the staple of the complaint put forward by the Captain of the Commons.

On the one side is the picture of secure and progressive opulence, on the other of mismanagement, waste, debt, a corrupt aristocracy, and a still more corrupt Church. The whole machinery of government was hurrying the constitution into ruin. The Act of 1430, corrected by that of 1432, had made the county franchise, at that time by far the most important part of the representation, essentially aristocratical; and as from time to time, especially in 1450, the Court strove to neutralize the effect even of this restricted franchise, by granting representatives to what were from the beginning mere nomination boroughs, or, it would seem, to get a temporary influence, as much against the genuine boroughs as against the counties, the people were more and more deprived of any true place in Parliament. But it is clear that Parliament possessed considerable powers. It had begun to legislate. The Paston Letters prove that a seat in the Lower House was not only the object of ambition but of intrigue; and it is certain that the impulse which would lead persons in that day to seek for a place in the Commons was much more composite than a desire to earn the wages of knight or burgess, citizen or baron of one of the Cinque Ports.

On the accession of Henry IV., Arundel, who had been banished by Richard, was restored to the primacy. He held his place till 1414, when he was succeeded by Henry Chichele, a man of very humble origin, who occupied the see for twenty-nine years, longer, it is said, than any other primate before. Chichele was succeeded by Stafford, who was archbishop a little over nine years. Kemp followed, but was archbishop a little less than two years. He was followed by Bourchier in 1454, who remained archbishop till after the accession of Henry VII., dying in 1488. He was followed by Henry's partizan, Morton. Again, at the accession of Henry IV. Scrope was Archbishop of York, and was executed near his own residence in 1405. Two years after he was succeeded by Bowet, who had been Henry's agent or proctor, who was followed in 1426 by Kemp. Kemp remained archbishop till 1452, when he was succeeded by Booth. The see was after an interval filled by Nevil, the younger brother of the Earl of Warwick. Among other prelates of note are Wykeham, Beaufort, and Waynflete, bishops of Winchester successively from 1367 to 1405, from 1405 to 1447, and from 1447 to 1486; De Moleyns, Bishop of Chichester, Ayscough of Salisbury,

24

and the celebrated successor of De Moleyns, Reginald Pecok. The character of most of these prelates is known to us, generally from the comments of Gascoigne, an eminent clergyman, many times Chancellor of Oxford, a person whose fortunes and rank gave him access to much information, and whose piety and zeal led him to comment with severity on the scandals of his age.

Arundel was one of those prelates of noble birth who begin to appear in the highest dignities of the English Church after the Great Plague. He had taken part in the revolutionary movements of Richard's time, and had been a partizan of the appellants, was banished in 1397, and restored after Richard's deposition. He is noted for having procured the Statute *De heretico comburendo,* under which the sheriff in the county, and the chief magistrate in towns was compelled to carry out the ecclesiastical sentence of death pronounced by the bishop. With detestable hypocrisy churchmen pretended that they could not take life ; and, therefore, in a statute accepted by the king at the instance of the clergy, but not agreed to by Parliament, they put on others the duties which they declined. He also procured another statute, under which, on the pretence of silencing heretical preachers, the inferior clergy were obliged to take out a license for preaching, and to pay a fee for the privilege. This, we are told, was made the means by which the king was kept in ignorance of popular discontent consequent on mis-government. To the mind of the pious Gascoigne, the inhibition of the preachers by this prelate far more than counterbalanced the activity which he showed in denouncing heresy, purging the university from Wiklif's followers, and putting the obnoxious opinions to the test of fire and faggot.

Chichele, though of humble origin, was a dignified and popular prelate. He was noted for the courtesy with which he received those who came to him, for his munificence and liberality. But he was not above the charge of nepotism, as perhaps no archbishop ever has been. He owed his nomination to the pious zeal of the great Lancastrian conqueror. But if we can trust the account given of his favourite, Richard

Andrew, the primate was either unable or unwilling to check the scandals which became dominant at the time. He is said, which is probably untrue, to have counselled the invasion of France, in order to countervail the growing determination of the reformers to attack the wealth of the Church, and, with greater truth, to have acquiesced in the suppression of the alien priories, that is, those religious houses the surplus revenues of which belonged to foreign monasteries. The property of these priories was confiscated on the ground that they were the means of sustaining the king's enemies; and from their possessions the archbishop founded three colleges in Oxford and elsewhere, the king the great monastery of Sion and the splendid establishments of King's College, Cambridge, and of Eton. But it does not seem that Chichele took much part in the politics of the time, or even acted as the chief ecclesiastical minister of England. The first place in English affairs appears to have been taken by Beaufort, the king's great uncle, or by Gloucester, as the partizans of each had the ascendency.

Stafford, the successor of Chichele, was a scion of the house of Buckingham, descended through females from the youngest son of Edward the Third, and brother of the Stafford whom Cade defeated and killed at the battle of Sevenoaks in the summer of 1450. According to Gascoigne, he was of base birth and scandalous life, and lived with a nun, by whom he had sons and daughters. He had been a lawyer, and became ultimately Chancellor, and he is described as being insolent as well as profligate.

Kemp, who succeeded him, had a long episcopate, having been consecrated in 1419. He was for twenty-six years Archbishop of York, but was almost always absent from his duties and constantly in attendance at the Court, though he appears to have held no public office. Kemp was probably a person of considerable private fortune, who preferred the ease and comfort of his country seat in Kent to the fatigues and duties of the northern province. During his short episcopate at Canterbury he was Chancellor, and his death, while holding office, in 1454, rendered a visit to Henry necessary, and with it the discovery of the king's insanity and the appointment of York to the protectorate.

It is probable that the next archbishop, who held the see for thirty-four years, and whose tenure therefore exceeded that of Chichele, owed his elevation to the influence of York. Bourchier was brother to the Earl of Essex, who seems to have cautiously favoured the reforming party, of which York was the head. He sat in judgment on Pecok, and degraded him. But of all the bishops of the age, none equalled Bourchier in pliancy. One of those who was sworn to maintain the title of Henry VI., he deserted after to Edward IV., and crowned Henry's rival, deserted again to Henry in 1470, acknowledged Edward IV. again, recognized the title of his son, crowned Richard III., wheedled Elizabeth Woodville out of her children when she took sanctuary at Westminster, and concluded his contemptible career by crowning the conqueror at Bosworth. In every age of English history, except during the war of succession in the fifteenth century, pretenders and rivals have had their partizans on the episcopal bench who were willing to share the fortunes of those with whom they were associated. But the feuds of the fifteenth century furnished only two political victims in the whole of its course from the ranks of the prelates, Scrope and Pecok. The others were too time-serving and too contemptible to be distrusted or punished. Even Nevil was forgiven after he had shared the treasons of his family.

The political and social importance of the see of York was far less than that of Canterbury. After the execution of Scrope, a bold and startling act which seems to have been intended to strike terror into the malcontents of the North, the see appears to have been vacant for more than two years, when it was filled by one Bowet, who seems to have been attached to the king's court, as his successor, Kemp, was. His successor, Booth, who had been Margaret's Chancellor and was probably appointed for purely political reasons, was a person of no education, who had been at no university, and was rapacious, corrupt, and foolish. He is stated to have been the author of infinite scandals in his diocese, to have been notorious for his nepotism, and disreputable for the discouragement he gave to men of learning and character. Nevil, his successor, was raised to the episcopate by the influence of his family when he was twenty-three years old only, though, in consequence of his youth, he was disabled from consecration for a time, while he held the temporalities of the see.

The see of Winchester, though inferior in titular rank to those of London and Durham under the precedency established by Henry VIII., was next to Canterbury in influence, and superior to it in wealth. The bishop had noble castles at Farnham, Waltham, and elsewhere, and a London palace in Southwark. Three bishops of this opulent see have founded some of the richest of the Oxford colleges, St. Mary of Winton, known as New College, Magdalen, and Corpus. The first was the gift of Wykeham, a prelate who first conceived the idea of establishing a special training school for his beneficiaries before they came to the university, and thereby also of disassociating them from the teaching of the monks. As Merton was the founder of the collegiate system, so Wykeham developed the idea of uniting school and college, and making the former a regular feeder of the latter. He was exactly imitated by Henry VI., who similarly founded Eton and King's College. Wolsey intended to do the same by Ipswich and Cardinal College. But the system was not fully developed, a few only of such double institutions having been founded at and after the Reformation.

Beaufort is the most conspicuous English ecclesiastic in the first part of the fifteenth century. He was sent to Queen's College, Oxford, in his youth, for, oddly enough, this college was for a short time, and for some unexplained cause, the special place of education for young men of high birth. He was made a bishop when young, since he was for nearly fifty years a prelate, having been raised to the see of Lincoln in 1398, and made Bishop of Winchester in 1405. His nephew, afterwards Henry V., was sent to the same college, and was lodged over the great gate, in the provost's apartments, under his uncle's care. It is clear that he would not have been made bishop at an early age of the most extensive English diocese, had not Richard believed that his kinsman would be useful and loyal. His birth on the mother's side was not dangerous. Old John of Gaunt was still alive, and might well be pleased with the early elevation of his and Catherine Swinford's son. The Beauforts were not yet legitimated, though they were subsequently, and without reservation. It is needless to say, that a family which claims rights not yet awarded, is always more pretentious than one whose position is indisputable ; and that when the rights are admitted, it always remembers that they were disputed, and is proportionately sensitive and exacting. This is, I imagine, the key to the quarrels between the Cardinal of Winchester and the Duke of Gloucester. It does not, indeed, explain the unpopularity of Beaufort in his lifetime, for I set no store by the gossip of Holinshed, even though it has been immortalized by the genius of Shakespeare.

If the correspondence of Beaufort is ever discovered and published, I venture on predicting that, though the bishop was not averse to the continuance of the French wars, he was conscious that the pitiful personal ambitions of Gloucester were fatal to success abroad and the proper conduct of business at home. His mistake was that he trusted his own kindred, the House of Somerset, the most incompetent advisers and lieutenants which the unfortunate family of John of Gaunt employed. He lent money to his nephew's government (to have lent it to Henry would have been absurd), as he lent to his elder nephew, and, when he died, bequeathed money for the same purpose.

Beaufort occupied a very considerable place at the Council of Constance. The Church was in a very perilous position. The schism and the rapacity of three popes at once scandalized all Christendom, as it irritated all who were fleeced by these harpies. It was impossible to be indifferent. All the nations of the West were roused, and the German Emperor became an important personage for a time, as the nominal head of the European laity. Even John the Twenty-second or Twenty-third was constrained to agree to a general council, though he had every reason to dread it. He was believed to have poisoned his predecessor, he was known to be guilty of enormous and nameless vices, and was suspected of sorcery. He was deposed, and sentenced to perpetual imprisonment. The fathers of Constance proceeded, after deposing a licentious pope, to condemn Wiklif, and burn Huss and Jerome of Prague. Two years afterwards, after sitting in constant debate, Martin V was elected, as is said, owing to the intrigues of Beaufort, when a French doctor, who would have made a better pope, might have been chosen. Beaufort survived the marriage of Henry and Margaret for two years, the death of Gloucester for one year.

The third Bishop of Winchester with whom I am here concerned was Waynflete. He had been a *protégé* of Henry, taken from being Master of Winchester school to be the first Provost of Eton, and made Bishop of Winchester at Beaufort's death. Waynflete is the type of the pious founder in the fifteenth century. He determined on erecting a college at Oxford, and he succeeded by every kind of expedient, for he pursued with singular perseverance his project for thirty years, during which he employed every artifice towards enriching his college. He dedicated it, with great appropriateness, to the memory of the repentant sinner, Mary Magdalen. In secular matters he steadily crept after the successful party in the state, and was an apt pupil of his metropolitan Bourchier. I know no memories which are more hateful than those of the foremost prelates in the fifteenth century. Waynflete has probably been the most fortunate with posterity, for his college had, in the sixteenth century, a just reputation; in the seventeenth, a transient popularity, and since has been known to be opulent.

Three other bishops of the fifteenth century obtained a sombre notoriety—De Moleyns and Ayscough, who were murdered in 1450; Pecok, who was deposed in 1457. The fate of these three persons is so instructive and so suggestive of the social state of England during the last ten years of the House of Lancaster's existence, that I shall dwell for a short time on them.

De Moleyns was one of those official clergymen who, during

the whole of the middle ages, and for some time afterwards, rose through secular employment to ecclesiastical rank. A generation or two ago an editor of Greek plays was supposed to qualify himself for the episcopate by his labours in this field; in our own age, a schoolmaster is reputed to be the best raw material for a bishop; in the fifteenth century, the selection was made from those who had been conspicuous in the public service. In the case of De Moleyns, Bishop of Chichester, the elevation of the ecclesiastic is better justified than in most cases, if, indeed, he was the author of the " Libel of English Policy."

The " Libel of English Policy" is a poem in which the condition of English commerce is described, its security advocated, and its expansion suggested. The writer is evidently of opinion that the continuity of English trade depended on English supremacy in the narrow seas, and in the retention of the sea board on either side the Channel. As he was writing, the English were the real or reputed masters of the whole coast from Calais to Bayonne; they were friendly with Portugal, which was rapidly growing into an adventurous and successful mercantile kingdom; and they traded as far as the Straits of Gibraltar. Twelve years before the work was composed, the Bristol merchants had, by the use of the mariner's compass, reached Iceland from the west, and thus were able to compete with the eastern ports of England, especially Scarborough, in the cod fishery. But the writer's special interest, after the restoration and development of English trade, is the settlement of Ireland. Its produce, he says, is abundant, its gold mines excellent, its harbours the best in the world. But, he adds, that the wild natives are continually encroaching on the English settlement, and threatening its very existence, while, on the authority of the Earl of Ormond, the cost of a single year of the French war would entirely and completely settle the country, to the great commercial advantage of England. If, however, he concludes, either Ireland or Wales were to rise in rebellion against England, they would readily get the assistance of Spain or Scotland.

De Moleyns was Keeper of the Privy Seal. He had taken part in the negotiations which led to the unhappy marriage of Margaret and Henry, and was associated with the policy of Suffolk, whose unpopularity he shared. In the beginning of the year 1450, he went to Portsmouth to pay the soldiers and seamen there. He was set on by a mob, seized, subjected to a sort of rough trial, and, notwithstanding his protestations of innocence, was slain. In the summer of the same year, Ayscough, Bishop of Salisbury, was murdered by his own dependents and others, after he had fled from London upon the panic which followed the uprising of Cade. He was confessor to the king, had entirely neglected his diocese, except as a source of revenue, and was engaged in improving his large means by being the fraudulent trustee of an imbecile, who was loaded with ecclesiastical dignities and preferments, the revenues of which were appropriated by this scandalous and rapacious bishop. But, besides these men, there were the profligate De La Bere, Bishop of St. David's ; Lyhert, Bishop of Norwich, the queen's confessor and a courtier ; Lumley, Bishop of Carlisle, the Treasurer,—all, according to Gascoigne's authority, negligent, scandalous, and greedy. Only a little time intervened between the murder of De Moleyns and the impeachment of Suffolk ; but, in the interval, the minister succeeded in procuring the translation of the famous Pecok from the poor Welsh see of St. Asaph, where he had sat for nearly six years, to the more important and lucrative bishopric of Chichester.

Pecok was a Welshman by birth, and a fellow of Oriel College, Oxford, where he had a considerable reputation for learning and orthodoxy. He quitted Oxford for the Court at a rather early age, and soon achieved still greater notoriety by his writings. He was the most voluminous writer of the fifteenth century, for the titles of about forty of his books are preserved. After a time he fell under the displeasure of the king and court, was arrested on a charge of heresy, tried by Archbishop Bourchier, deprived, compelled to publish a recantation of his opinions, and was sent for the residue of his life to close confinement in Thorney Abbey. For a long time Pecok was

considered an arch-heretic, and was condemned as roundly
by Edward as he was by Henry, for his followers were rigidly
excluded from the foundation of King's College, Cambridge,
in the last revision of the statutes of that college ; and
Edward, according to Mr. Churchill Babington, denounced his
Oxford disciples.   He is rehabilitated by Fox, who, in his
search after witnesses, makes him a precursor of the Reformation, a pious prelate, who was hounded down by popish
bigotry.

Pecok was a defender of existing order, opinion, and practice,
on the ground that it was wholesome and convenient. The
peculiarity of his work lies in the method adopted in the treatment of the subject.   He abandons authority for reasonable-
ness.   Human opinion in the highest places, individually and
collectively, in pope, council, bishop, and priest, is liable to
err.   But the same contingency belongs to those who criticise
or repudiate these opinions.   The real question is, how do
what may be directed by authority, the existing practices of
an ecclesiastical organization, accord with the public good
and the general interests of mankind ?   Toleration is the
immediate condition of tenets which assert that the probable
and reasonable is the highest aim of the human mind and its
invariable limits, for no man can be responsible for inability
to accept what is, after all, not demonstrable.   But, on the
other hand, no one can be permitted to assail an existing
order of things contemptuously, because he is persuaded of
the absolute truth of his own opinion.   Every existing fact
can be excused or palliated on these grounds.   Pecok strove
to defend, and for a long time with great acceptance, the
wealth of the clergy and hierarchy, their absorption in secular
business, the monastic orders, the worship of images, and all
the practices of the Church.   His heresy, for which he was
ostensibly condemned, consists in the fact that he combated
the Lollards with the weapons of expediency instead of those
of authority, and affirmed that reason was a sufficient guide
in practical matters, while faith might be left to deal with
topics which were unproved and unprovable.   For a long
time the charges against him were chiefly that he excused

the bishops from their duties, and that he had no high opinion of the fathers of the Church as ultimate authorities. But the bishops were not displeased with their apologist, and it is probable that the charge of heresy would never have been made but for another event, which has not, as far as I know, been discovered and commented on.

Pecok, who, whatever his intellectual qualities were, and however much his rationalism was in advance of his age, was a person of inordinate vanity, sent in the year 1456—in what part of the year is not stated—a letter to Cannyngs, the Lord Mayor. This man was brother to the more celebrated Cannyngs, who built St. Mary Redcliff church at Bristol, and was brother-in-law to that Young who, being Member for Bristol, is said to have moved in the House of Commons that Richard of York should be declared heir-apparent. On May 22nd, 1455, occurred the affair of St. Albans. In November of the same year, York was made Protector for the second time, but with the significant addition that he should hold the office until discharged of it by Parliament. In February 1456, the king himself took the office away from him, at the instance of Margaret and some of the lords, probably the kinsmen of those who were slain at St. Albans. There was no parliament between February 1456 and November 1459, when the Houses met at Coventry, and York, with all his partizans, was attainted. After the dismissal of the parliament of 1456, the king, queen, and princes went away to Chester or Coventry, and there remained in seclusion. There is no public instrument existing of a date between July 26th, 1456, and January 28th, 1457. During the early part of the year 1457, the king was at Coventry, a Lancastrian stronghold. In August 1457, the king was at Westminster, where he remained till 1459, when he went again to Coventry. If this account of the king's movements, which is taken from Rymer and Gascoigne, be correct, Cannyngs must have kept the letter back till he found it possible and convenient to present it.

Cannyngs, on reading the letter, detected in it "very suspicious passages, tending to change of faith and to insurrection in the realm of England," and sent it on to the king. " When the king and the lords read it, they discovered the same tendencies, and great scandal arose about the great lords of the realm, who, as the bishop said, were on the side of him and his English works. Thereupon all the temporal lords, who were with Henry, demanded that he should be expelled from the king's council and the council of the lords, for no lord could state his opinion or give his advice in council till Pecok was driven out of the council-chamber." I cannot believe that this zeal was manifested by a body of Henry's lords on behalf of orthodoxy, or that Pecok could have been of such imbecile vanity as to have knowingly written a polemical letter to the London mayor which should precipitate a prosecution of him and his writings, or that the public would have taken so hostile an attitude against him as we are told that they did. He suggested, I am convinced, some political measures which might have been dangerous, and were certainly compromising, and all those who were about the king were anxious to be rid at once of so imprudent a counsellor. What, for instance, if he had proposed that sharp measures should be taken at once with Richard of York and the Neviles, now absent from the king's councils, for the skirmish of St. Albans was indecisive ? What, on the other hand, if he had advised that there should be genuine co-operation with the Yorkist or reforming party, in order to disarm public discontent and settle the administration, and this was conceived to be premature ? What if he had pointed out that York was ready on a favourable opportunity to claim the throne, and had given voice to what many believed, that even if this claim might be postponed, not one person in twenty who thought on the matter held that Edward was the legitimate offspring of Henry ? Hints on these dangerous topics in so critical a time, when men were so cautious that they abstained from committing themselves, or destroyed every scrap of writing, since hardly any correspondence of the time is preserved, were exactly what a conceited able man would make, and shrewd politicians would make much of. The council, therefore, resolved to remove Pecok on a charge of heresy, to make him abjure his theological opinions, and to take good care that his political tendencies should be forgotten in the discredit which would be cast by Catholic and Lollard alike on a man who had in those days been indiscreet enough, not only to set up reason as superior to the Church and the fathers and even the creeds, but to give it a seeming pre-eminence over the Bible itself.

The bishops of the fifteenth century till its close were, on the whole, bad men. But the parochial clergy were little better, and the monks were worst of all. The inhibition of preaching had made the former little other than mass priests, whom the people deserted for the stirring but secret exhortations of the Bible-men, or wandering Lollards, or, as they called themselves, as a password, the Known-men. The clergy fell into gross and evil practices, neglected the duties which once were reputed to belong to their profession, and adopted any trick to avoid residence on their benefices. Pluralities were common, ecclesiastical offices of considerable importance were given to children, to idiots, to laymen. Gascoigne speaks of one person in particular who was Arch-deacon of Oxford, though never ordained, and the holder of many prebendaries and livings, who lived at Oxford dissolutely, while the income of his many preferments went into the hands of the Bishop of Salisbury, a pretended trustee. The monks were worst of all, insatiate in getting money, in appropriating benefices, in ousting the parochial clergy, in squandering their ill-gotten gains in gluttony and drinking. The pious writer of the age suggests the confiscation of their ill-used wealth by the heirs of those who founded monasteries with very different objects, for the maintenance of piety, of learning, of education, and of other good works. The diatribes of Gascoigne have a strong flavour of the sixteenth century and Henry's wholesale devastation.

Perhaps the English Church might have been reformed and its abuses remedied by a strong hand within it or without it. Such a reform was not to be expected from the hierarchy, and would not be accepted from the Bible-

men. It might have come from a vigorous ruler, or from
a gradual growth of wholesome public opinion among men
of influence in the royal councils.   But the nobles, even
before the great feud broke out, were as greedy, as violent,
as unscrupulous as the clergy.   The lay-counsellors of the
Court were as averse to reform, even when suggested by the
more respectable among the clergy, as the prelates were.
For behind all this system was the papal court, poor because
committed to boundless expense, avaricious, and utterly
regardless of the means by which it could gather supplies.
In 1440, Engenius IV. sent one Peter de Monte to
England to sell indulgences, and Gascoigne denounces the
scandal with a warmth as sincere and almost as outspoken
as that of Luther.   He credits the papal court with infinite
crimes, though he allows that the Pope is either ignorant
of what is done or is coerced into acquiescing in the mischief,
or teased into allowing the practices which he condemns
in his heart and conscience.   Every one knows how, from
the testimony of writers whose orthodoxy has never been
questioned, the papacy went from bad to worse in the
fifteenth century, that the enormous vices of John XXIII.
were dwarfed by the still more scandalous iniquities of
Alexander VI., and that even the revival of letters which
purified the rest of Christendom was only made the stimulant
to even grosser depravity in papal Italy.   The facts may be
and have been denied, they cannot be gainsaid.

The first means by which this hideous mass of accumulating
and festering sewage began to be removed from English life
was the revival of letters to which I have referred.   The first
agents of the Reformation were the obscure, humble, austere,
devout, and persecuted Lollards and Bible-men, who grasped
at least one fundamental truth, that a religion which is
divorced from morality is the worst curse which human
societies can be called on to bear.   The next agents were the
Humanists, or reformers who, like More, Erasmus, and Colet,
were content to reform the Church from within, to purge
away the grossness which had been contracted by the cunning
and superstition of long ages, and to attempt the splendid

Utopia of a purified Church, founded on the old lines, with
a spiritual Cæsar at its head, who would be a Christian
Aurelius, a virtuous, wise, and paternal monarch who might
counsel and guide the soul of a regenerated Christendom.
The dream of these reformers came out of the ivory gate,
and England had to get her reformation from other hands.
It was to be begun by an overbearing, sensual, suspicious,
wasteful tyrant, who had only one spark of wisdom in his
nature, some judgment as to the temper of the people whom
he ruled over and ruined, to be continued by a camarilla
of the vilest adventurers who ever gathered in a Court, the
guardians of Edward VI., the best of the crew being successively removed by the worst, to be purified by a reaction
under Mary Tudor, and a persecution, which, thanks to the
new engine of liberty, the press, became known and duly
interpreted, and to be settled after a fashion by the constructive genius of Elizabeth, who could not, with all her
wisdom, see far enough to dispense with what was the most
powerful instrument of government, a despotic hierarchy,
or to trust herself to the energies of a free church on a reformed model. Her scheme has remained to our own day,
with as much strength as she could give its constitution,
and as much weakness as must inevitably belong to a
creature of political expediency and compromise.

I have dwelt on the position and character of the unreformed
Church of England because it is, as I have said, impossible to
form a true estimate of social life in this country unless some
account is given of those who represented its more manifest
life, and, as far as they could, directed its forces. And I do so
the more because, owing to the singularly outspoken comments of Gascoigne, whose great work I was the first to make
full extracts from, it is possible to learn precisely what the
condition of the Church was during this dark period of our
annals. Christianity and morality was not left without
witnesses even in that age. There were men among the
clergy who were worthy of their calling, whose zeal was far
above the smug opportunism of Pecok. But the life of
religion, I am persuaded, lay with the persecuted sectaries,

whose sufferings are unrecorded, whose history is perhaps irrecoverable.   Above them, what people call history was being enacted.   A depraved Church and a depraved aristocracy, splendid, wealthy, and surrounded by majestic memories which hid, as ivy does, the rottenness within, were hurrying to their ruin.   There was to come a war, the bitterness and treachery of which has probably not been equalled since the famous strife of the parties in that great struggle which destroyed the life of ancient Greece.   It occurred when Louis XI. and Castracani, Borgia, and Machiavelli were to become the types of political sagacity, the models of wise and far-sighted statesmanship.   It ended in the suspension of the constitution, in the abject submission of the aristocracy, in the enslavement of the hierarchy.   The king and the people stood face to face with each other, the people of whom no one took account during the great war of succession.

It was during the fifteenth century that the English yeomanry and smaller gentry took deep root in the land.   A nation is never ruined but by its government, and then only when a government does not fear the nation.   The English people was the only force which the Tudors feared, and the people saved the constitution and restored it.   The aristocracy was the only power which the French kings feared, and at last king and aristocracy were hurled into a common destruction.   But during the fifteenth century the under-current of English life went steadily on and prospered.   Most fortunately for mankind, the vices of churchmen and nobles are not and cannot be the vices of those who work and save.   In the evil days of Henry VI., in the turmoil and crimes which came to an ignominious end at Bosworth and England rested under the quiet rule of an adventurer whose political genius was no higher than that of a pettifogging lawyer, the English people were prosperous and grew opulent, to be almost ruined, I grant, by his successor, who ruled over his nobles like a king of Dahomey, but was over-reached and baffled by every European monarch in succession, who wasted his substance wildly, and died, after creating a crew who were worse than himself, in the act of cheating his people by a trick which they would have bitterly resented had they comprehended it. One can understand and even sometimes respect a despot, but the combination of a blood-thirsty tyrant and a thimble-rigger can only be admired by a lover of paradoxes.

Similarly, there was another epoch in English history, when to all appearance all that is noticeable is a mere scene of coarse, insolent frivolity, a society where all the men are sharpers and all the women courtesans, where honest public service was laughed out of existence, and the most capable statesmen were guilty of offences which deserved the gallows instead of peerages, pensions, and garters. Perhaps the ablest person in the reign of Charles II. was Shaftesbury. He did certain good services, by reason of which he has found an apologist. They chiefly concerned the upper and middle classes, for I fancy that the liberties of a ploughman or an artizan were not materially secured or enlarged by the Habeas Corpus Act. But Shaftesbury, after the Restoration, lent himself to the shameful fiction by which his old associates, the regicides, were left to a judicial murder, endorsed the king's worst and meanest acts, intrigued against his employer while making his fortune out of his employment, suborned Titus Oates, and after taking part in a reactionary plot, fled to leave other and better men to their fate. Shall we say that the English nation was represented by the Benets, the Osbornes, the Maitlands, the Spencers, the Finches, the Churchills, the Villierses, the Howards, by the sharpers, the bullies, the harlots of Charles's court?

The thrift and prosperity of the period which lies between the Restoration and the Revolution, the unseen and unrecorded life and work of the English people, created the spirit which developed the Revolution, and the wealth which defended it when it had been developed. The conspiracies against it were the work of the men who had been bred in the stew of Charles's Court. The hopes of the exiled Stuarts were centred on those who had betrayed every one who trusted them, and were constant to one thing only, their own gains and advancement. The strength of the New Constitution was the outcome of the time for which superficial history narrates the doings of courts and unravels the intrigues of diplomatists, but has not troubled itself with discussing the condition of the people.

CHAPTER XIV.

WAGES OF LABOUR AFTER THE RISE IN PRICES.

A N examination of the rise which was effected in the price of all articles of consumption during the last sixty years of the sixteenth century enables us to see clearly what was now become the condition of those who lived by wages. If we look at the money value of most articles, we shall see that, with very few exceptions, it keeps steadily increasing during each successive decade. This is not, it is true, precisely the fact with regard to wheat and other kinds of grain, for the money value of this produce is affected in each decade by the occasion of years of special scarcity and plenty. Hence, in the case of wheat or similar kinds of grain, it becomes necessary, if we would exactly interpret the change which had come over money values, to take a longer period, during which cheap and dear years neutralize each other. But the course of the seasons during the period which intervenes before prices have reached their true level and go on steadily rising, on the whole, for half a century, is striking and exceptional.

The issues of base money put into circulation by Henry were in the years 1545 and 1546. Those of Edward's guardians were in 1549 and 1551. In 1560 the currency was restored. It is important to remember these dates in estimating prices, and the immediate effect of the issue on them. There must have been, I conclude, some general impression at first that these moneys would be redeemed, and, under these circumstances, it appears that they did not produce the immediate effect which such a proceeding invariably does sooner or later. Now the harvest of 1545 must have been a very bad one, for the price of wheat was higher than it had been in any year since 1316, the great famine of Edward the Second's reign, though it was soon to be surpassed. But for the next three years wheat is decidedly cheap; in 1547 very cheap, the price being lower than it had been since 1510. Then follow three dear years and two comparatively cheap ones, Mary Tudor having come to the throne in the last year. Then follow three dear years, the third being dearer than in all previous experience, wheat being nearly five times the average price for the 280 years, 1261-1540, and standing, during the spring, at a price which must have indicated the worst anticipations of famine. In the next two years it is cheap again, a cheap year being now about double the old price. The years 1563 and 1573 are also dear. After the latter year, the ordinary price becomes about three times the old rate. The next dear year is 1586, when the price again goes beyond previous experience. But the harvest of 1588, the Armada year, was very abundant. Five years successively, 1594-98, are very dear, the last but one, 1597, being a veritable famine, the price being ten times what it was in the early period, and not being paralleled till 1648 and 1649. By this time, however, the average price had reached from five to seven times that at which it had previously stood for more than two centuries and a half. The price of wheat in 1649 was reached again in 1674, in 1661-2, in 1709, and 1710, and not again till 1767, 1774, and 1795.

Now up to the year 1540, the average wages of an artizan in the country were 3s. a week; of a labourer in husbandry, working by the day, 2s. a week. Such wages, in some cases rather more, are allowed by 11 Hen. VII., cap. 22 (1495), to which I shall presently refer. The labourer in harvest time, when working by the day, received the same wages as the artizan; and, in harvest time, the wages of the women labourers were only a little less than those of men. It should be remembered that this Act of Henry VII. is one which was intended to carry out the Statute of Labourers, and that therefore the minimum rate would be prescribed and, as far as possible, enforced. The price of wheat in 1495 was 4s. 0¾d.; of malt, 2s. 4½d.; of oats, 1s. 7½d.; and of oatmeal, 5s. 4d. a quarter. An artizan, therefore, earned nearly a bushel of wheat by a day's labour, and an ordinary labourer three-quarters of a bushel. A week's work would enable an artizan to purchase more than a quarter of malt, and a little more than seven days' work would supply the farm labourer with a quarter of malt. In so cheap a year as this, the peasant could provision his family for a twelvemonth with three quarters of wheat, three of malt, and two of oatmeal, by fifteen weeks of ordinary work; an artizan could achieve the same result in ten weeks. Such wages were regularly paid, and even more, particularly in London.

In 1533, a large proportion of Henry's artizans got 4s. a week, even during the winter months, the labourers earning, as before, 2s. In 1533, the price of wheat was, relatively speaking, high, 7s. 8d. a quarter, while malt was 5s. 5¼d., oatmeal 8s., and oats 2s. 9½d. the quarter. In this case, then, the farm labourer would have had to give nearly double the labour in wheat and oats, and more than double in the case of malt, though a good deal less than double in that of oatmeal, to make such a provision as his ancestor did in 1495; while the artizan at 3s., would have had to give between fourteen and fifteen weeks' work for a similar store. The first-named year is an exceedingly cheap one; the latter, though less advantageous to the labourer, is one in which he might still be able, as we see, to maintain his family, and lay by a considerable margin from the charges of his household, from a fourth to a half of his earnings.

In June 1564, the Rutlandshire magistrates met in order to carry out the provisions of the Act to which I have several times referred, and which had just been passed. The schedule of wages to which I am about to refer is printed by the royal authority among the proclamations of the Queen, and is preserved in the great collection of Elizabeth's instruments which was begun by Burleigh and continued by Cecil. It is without doubt a typical list, intended by the fact of the publication to be a guide to the other Quarter Sessions throughout the country. The list is drawn up "on consideration of the great prices of linen, woollen, leather, corn, and other victuals." The ordinary artizan is to have 9*d.* a day in summer, 8*d.* in winter; the heads of the craft, who are to be competent draughtsmen of plans, to have 1*s.* The labourers are to have 7*d.* in summer, except in harvest time, when they have 8*d.* to 10*d.*, and in winter 6*d.* The summer is from Easter to Michaelmas, the winter from Michaelmas to Easter. In 1563-4, wheat was 19*s.* 9¾*d.* a quarter; oats, 7*s.*, malt, 10*s.* 8*d.* The price of oatmeal has not been found, but it could not have been less than 25*s.* the quarter. The Rutlandshire schedule is a little lower than the prices actually paid in Cambridge and Oxford, as far as regards artizans' labour, for the artizan is paid, as a rule, not less than 1*s.* or 10*d.* a day. The wages of ordinary labour are those of the magistrates' schedule. Now the price of food is more than three times the old average, though malt, as we might expect, when wheat was at a scarcity price, is less than the corresponding price, being actually cheaper than barley. Now if we suppose the ordinary labourer to get 3*s.* 6*d.* a week through the year, by adding his harvest allowance to his winter wages, it would have taken him more than forty weeks to earn the provisions which in 1495 he could have got with fifteen, while the artizan would be obliged to have given thirty-two weeks' work for the same result.

In 1593, the magistrates of the East Riding of York met on April 26th, and fixed the wages of artizans and labourers in husbandry. The mower is to have 10*d.*, the reaper 8*d.* a day, or by the acre 10*d.* for meadow and 8*d.* for corn, it being clear that a man was supposed to mow an acre of corn or grass in a day. The winter wages of labourers are to be 4*d.*, in summer 5*d.* Ordinary artizans are to have 8*d.* and 7*d.*

The price of wheat in 1593 is 18*s*. 4½*d*. ; of oatmeal, 29*s*. 4*d*. ; of malt, 12*s*. 3½*d*. The work of a whole year would not supply the labourer with the quantity which in 1495 the labourer earned with fifteen weeks' labour. The artizan could procure it with forty weeks' labour.

In the same year, the mayor and others in the city o Chester fixed the wages of artizans and labourers who dwelt within their jurisdiction. The roll is unfortunately mutilated, and the day payments of artizan and labourer, without meat and drink, are torn off. But it is clear that the workmen here are even worse paid than in the East Riding,—that the wages of artizans were not more than 6*d*., those of labourers than 4*d*., and that there was actually no rise here from the older prices.

The year 1597 was one of fearful famine. The price of wheat was 56*s*. 10½*d*. ; of oats, 13*s*. 9½*d*. (I do not find that of oatmeal, but it appears to have been 64*s*.) ; malt, 28*s*. 9½*d*. It is said by the Mayor of Chester in his assessment to be a time of dearth and scarcity. The schedule is again unluckily mutilated ; but the extra allowance for the dearness of this year, the price being generally almost three times that of the year 1593, is only 10*s*. more for wages by the year without food than in the earlier year. The wages of artizans are from £5 10*s*. the year to £4 10*s*. ; those of husbandmen, £3 10*s*. It is not easy to see how they could have lived through the famine.

In 1610, the Rutland magistrates met at Oakham on April 28th, and made their assessment. The day wages of a mower are 10*d*. ; of a reaper, 8*d*., if a man, if a woman 6*d*., of ordinary labour from Easter to Michaelmas, 7*d*. ; from Michaelmas to Easter, 6*d*. Artizans are to have from 10*d*. to 9*d*. in the summer, 8*d*. in the winter. Master artizans, with skill as draughtsmen, are to receive 1*s*. a day in summer, 10*d*. in winter ; and it appears from the register of hirings that these rates were maintained till at least 1634. The price of wheat in this year was 40*s*. 4*d*., of malt 15*s*. 4⅓*d*. ; and it therefore appears that a Rutland artizan with 9*d*. a day wages, sup-posing oatmeal were worth, as its natural price should be, about 43*s*. 4*d*. a quarter, would have to work forty-three weeks in order to earn that which an artizan in 1495 obtained with ten weeks' labour; while the wages of the peasant, who got this supply by fifteen weeks' labour 115 years before, would be insufficient, even if he worked for fifty-two weeks in the year, and every day except Sunday, by 24s. 9½d., to win that quantity of provisions. Even the extra payments in harvest would not make up the deficiency.

In 1651, the Essex magistrates met at Chelmsford on April 8th, and fixed the wages for the county. Wages had now risen. The artizan had from 1s. 5d. a day in summer and 1s. 2d. in winter to 1s. 6d. and 1s. 4d., the latter prices being paid as usual to foremen or heads of gangs. Ordinary labourers had from 1s. 2d. to 1s., except in harvest time, when mowing was paid at 1s. 6d., reaping at 1s. 10d. the day. Women in the harvest field had 1s. 2d.; in the hay-field, 10d. Piece-work is paid at 1s. 8d. an acre for mowing, 2s. for making and cocking. The reaping of wheat, rye, beans, and maslyn is 3s. 4d.; of barley and oats, 2s. 6d., this including binding and shocking. Mowing and binding barley and oats is 2s. 2d. Threshing and winnowing are, for the quarter of wheat and rye, 1s. 10d.; barley, oats, and other kinds of grain, 10d. Sawing planks are paid at 2s. 6d. the hundred of six-score feet. The advent of the Commonwealth had induced some beneficial change on the workman's labour, at last in appearance. In 1651, the price of wheat was 51s. 4d.; of malt, 22s. 7d.; oats were dearer than malt, being 23s. 10d.; and oatmeal was from 64s. to 48s. the quarter. The artizan on an average could earn from 7s. 9d. to 8s. 6d. a week; ordinary workmen an average of 6s. 9d., except in hay and harvest time, when they could get from 9s. to 11s. a week; and the women reapers, 7s. Piece-work in the harvest field is calculated at a little less than an acre of grass a day, and a little more than half an acre of grain, if the reaper bound and stacked the sheaves. The sawing a hundred of planks, always estimated from early times as a day's work, is paid at the rate of 15s. a week between the two workmen, the upper and under sawyers being estimated at the rate of 8s. to 7s.

The cost of the stock of wheat, malt, and oatmeal is now in the aggregate £16 13s. 9d. If the artizan worked fifty-two weeks in the year, he could earn £20 3s.; and therefore it would still take him about forty-three weeks to earn his stock of provisions. The peasant, however, apart from his harvest earnings, could, with the same unbroken and continuous diligence, earn £17 11s.; and perhaps the sum could be made up to £18 by his extra wages in the hay and corn field. He is therefore distinctly better off than he was forty years before, at least in Essex.

The rate paid for mowing grass by the acre is a little in excess of that paid at Oxford in the latter part of the sixteenth century, where the price is 1s. 3¾d. for mowing, 1s. 7¼d. for making and cocking. But during this period, the average price of wheat was 14s. 2¼d.; of malt, 10s. 5d.; of oatmeal, 20s. 10¾d. To such rates of wages the corresponding price of wheat should be 18s.; of malt, 13s. 2¾d.; of oatmeal, 26s. 6½d., in order to equalize the real wages of mowing in the sixteenth and seventeenth centuries and a similar proportionate increase for the labour of tedding and cocking. The price of threshing is relatively high, being about four times the rate which prevailed in the period before the rise in prices began. The same difference characterises the prices given for reaping, binding, and stacking an acre of wheat; but the rate paid for cutting barley and oats is less. Already much of the two latter kinds of grain was mown. On the whole, then, though the wages of labour in 1651 are infinitely below what they were in the old times, and contrast unfavourably even with the rates paid immediately after the passing of Elizabeth's Quarter Sessions Act, they represent better rates than those which were prescribed under the same machinery forty years before, and as we see actually paid, as is proved by the register of hirings.

At the Easter Sessions of 1661, the Essex magistrates again revised the wages of labourers. The summer wages are still 1s. 2d., the winter 1s. a day. The woman gets 10d.; mowing is 1s. 6d., whether it be grass or corn; reaping by men, 1s. 10d.; by women, 1s. 2d. Mowing grass is raised to

1s. 10d. ; reaping wheat, rye, and maslyn is 4s. ; oats, 2s. 6d. ; beans, 3s. 6d. ; mowing barley and oats by the acre is 1s. 6d., the price of threshing and winnowing being unchanged. But in 1661 the price of wheat is 70s. 6d. a quarter ; of malt, 34s. 6d. The purchasing power of wages is, therefore, considerably reduced.

In Suffolk, 1682, the magistrates at Bury St. Edmund's fixed the day wages of haymakers—men at 10d., women at 6d. ; of male reapers in harvest at 1s. 8d., of women at 1s. ; and the regular wages at 1s. in summer and 10d. in winter. The wages of artizans are not given, but from other sources we may learn that they were from 1s. 6d. to 1s. 4d. In 1682, the price of wheat was 43s. 8d. ; of malt, 26s. 8d. ; and the natural price of oatmeal, about 48s. Either the wages were reduced as corn became cheaper, or the price of labour was ordinarily lower in Suffolk than it was in Essex. We shall see reason to arrive at the former conclusion.

On April 9th, 1684, the magistrates of Warwick met at the county town and assessed the wages for the year under the Act of Elizabeth. The assessment is said to have special regard and consideration to the prices at this time of victuals and apparel. The price of wheat was 42s. 0½d. a quarter ; of malt, 24s. 5½d. ; and the analogous price of oatmeal, 46s. 6d.

The artizans' wages are here 1s. a day, with the exception of the free mason, who has 1s. 4d., the only man of the class who gets this rate. The plasterer is to have only 8d. ; common labourers, except in harvest time, are to have 8d. ; the mower of grass and corn, 1s. ; the reaper, 1s. ; while the haymaker, if a man, has only 8d., the women 4d., and the woman reaper 8d. These are summer wages ; the winter pay is a penny a day less. The hours of labour are defined between March and September to be from five in the morning till between seven and eight at night, i.e., fourteen-and-a-half hours, from which two-and-a-half hours are to be allowed for meals. Of these half an hour is given for breakfast, an hour for dinner, an hour for "drinkings," and between the middle of May and the middle of August, half an hour for sleep.

From the middle of September till the middle of March he is to work from daybreak till night, and is to forfeit a penny an hour, that is at the rate of 50 per cent. above his earnings, for absence. Persons who give more wages than the prescribed assessment are to be imprisoned ten days and be fined £5; persons taking more than the assessment are to be imprisoned twenty-one days; and any retainer, promise, gift, or payment of wages in contravention is to be void and of no effect. The document is signed by eight magistrates, among whom we find the names of Mordaunt, Clopton, and Fielding, the last at this time knowing, it seems, how to spell his name.

The wages fixed by these Warwickshire magistrates are decidedly less than those allowed in Essex thirty-three years before. It is fair to them to state that the Lady-day prices of wheat and malt were lower than those which prevailed for the real hiring time (that from some date after Lady-day to a similar period in the following year), for wheat was 34s. 4d., barley 22s. 7d. a quarter on Lady-day 1684, when the justices met. It should also be remembered that these daily payments were for regular, not for occasional service, and that the master was as much bound to pay his man as the man was to stay in the service of his master during the term of his engagement. It is to this practice that we must ascribe, in part at least, the higher wages of harvest time and, occasionally, of piece work.

If we take the allowances of wheat, malt, and oatmeal employed for our calculations before, and fix that of oatmeal hypothetically at a low amount, say 46s. 6d. a quarter, we shall find that the cost of the stock of provisions in this year amounted to £14 11s. 6d., that the yearly wages of the artizan are £15 13s., and those of the farm labourer, exclusive of his earnings in the hay and corn fields, are £10 8s. 8d., i.e., insufficient in their aggregate, whatever addition may be made for harvest work, to purchase the stock which his ancestor was able to procure on such easy terms. I have always, throughout these investigations into the labourers' wages, taken his earnings only, without allowing for what his wife or his children might earn for him, and, in the case of an artizan, perhaps his apprentices. But in a contrast established between money values and payments at different epochs, it is above all things important to take the simplest elements of calculation and comparison. I am not discussing what might have been the aggregate earnings of a family, but what were the resources on which an individual labourer could rely for procuring the means of life for a family, when those means of life were confined to what, according to the fashions of the age, were the simplest materials of customary existence.

The magistrates of Lancashire met at Manchester on May 22nd, 1725, when certain "discreet and grave men of the county, having held conference respecting the plenty of the time and other necessary circumstances" (words costing nothing in a preamble, and, it is to be hoped, deceiving no one), determined on certain rates of wages for the county, and issued them, under the authority of George and Thomas Cheetham.

The best husbandry labourer is to receive, from March to September, 1s. a day; ordinary ones, 10d.; and during the other six months the payment is to be 10d. and 9d. Haymakers are to have—men, 10d. a day, women, 7d.; mowers, 1s. 3d.; shearers, *i.e.*, reapers—1s. men, and 10d. women; taskwork in husbandry being 10d. a day. All artizans are to receive a maximum of 1s. a day, and a pair of sawyers, 2s. It may be observed that the maintenance of labourers is generally put at 3s. a week. Piece-work is paid by a double kind of acre, one said to be seven yards to the rood, the other eight yards. For oats, the payments are 5s. for the former, 6s. for the latter; in barley, peas, and beans, the quantities paid are 6s. and 7s.; for wheat and rye (a proof by the way that wheat was cultivated in Lancashire in the eighteenth century), 7s. and 8s. Threshing and winnowing oats are paid at 1s. a quarter; barley, beans, and peas at 1s. 6d.; wheat and rye at 2s. It is interesting to note that colliers were paid 1s. a ton for getting coal in a low delf, 1s. 3d. for the same labour in a high one. The master workman in the various handicrafts is to have 1s. 2d. a day, except the tailor, who is to be content with 1s. The plenty of the time is not very conspicuous in

1725, as the price of corn is higher than it had been since 1713, being 46s. 1d. for wheat, 24s. for malt. Oatmeal should be 54s.

If one can arrive at a judgment from the language of the Lancashire magistrates' proclamation, these authorities appear to be alarmed at symptoms of combination and disaffection among the workmen. They order that these wages should not be exceeded in the county, though they think that they are a little too liberal for the northern part thereof, but they direct, that they should be proclaimed in every market town of the county by the authority of the sheriff, and that on market days, when business is at its height, proclamation should be solemnly made, and a legible copy should be set up and fixed in some open public place in each of the market towns, and that the rates decided on should be continued till an amended list be proclaimed. The justices then proceed to publish the penalties which are denounced by divers Acts of Parliament on offenders under the several statutes which are made to regulate the wages of labour.

They cite a statute of Edward VI., 2 and 3, cap. 15, under which a combination of workmen "concerning their work or wages" is to be followed by a penalty on conviction of ten pounds, or twenty days' imprisonment on bread and water for the first offence, a fine of twenty pounds or the pillory for the second, and a fine of forty pounds, the pillory, the loss of one of his ears, and judicial infamy for the third. This statute was confirmed by 22-23 Charles II., and was in force till the general repeal of all such prohibitions on the combinations of workmen which took effect under 6 George IV., cap. 129. The rest of the warnings are those derived from the statute of Elizabeth, and recited by the Warwickshire magistrates in 1684.

The best servants in husbandry, who must have been of a very exceptional character, are to receive 1s. a day for six months, and 10d. for the other six months, *i.e.*, taking every working day into the pay-days, £14 7s. a year. The ordinary peasant is to receive £12 7s. 10d. These persons, however, might increase their wages by harvest work, and probably did, so as to raise the total to £15 and £13. Artizans are to be paid at the rate of £15 13s. a year, if they are at work during the whole year. Now taking the test which has been supplied so many times, and putting oatmeal (for which I have not at present a price, but shall probably be not far wrong in my estimate) at 54s. a quarter, the aggregate sum is £16 2s. 3d., and as I repeat for the last time, what a husbandman earned with fifteen weeks' work, and an artizan with ten weeks' work in 1495, a whole year's labour would not supply artizan or labourer with in the year 1725, throughout Lancashire.

I have protested before against that complacent optimism which concludes, because the health of the upper classes has been greatly improved, because that of the working classes has been bettered, and appliances, unknown before, have become familiar and cheap, that therefore the country in which these improvements have been effected must be considered to have made, for all its people, regular and continuous progress. I contend that from 1563 to 1824, a conspiracy, concocted by the law and carried out by parties interested in its success, was entered into, to cheat the English workman of his wages, to tie him to the soil, to deprive him of hope, and to degrade him into irremediable poverty. In a subsequent chapter I shall dwell on the palliatives which were adopted in order to mitigate the worst and most intolerable burdens of his life—palliatives which were rendered necessary by no fault of his, but by the deliberate malignity of Governments and Parliaments. For more than two centuries and a half, the English law, and those who administered the law, were engaged in grinding the English workman down to the lowest pittance, in stamping out every expression or act which indicated any organized discontent, and in multiplying penalties upon him when he thought of his natural rights. I am not deceived by the hypocrisy which the preamble of an Act of Parliament habitually contains, and the assertions which are as habitually contradicted by the details of the measure. The Act of Elizabeth declares that "the wages of labourers are too small, and not answerable to these times ;" and speaks of the "grief and burden of the poor labourer and hired man," and thereupon enacts a law which effectually makes the wages small and multiplies the labourers' grief and burden, by allowing those who are interested in keeping him poor to fix the wages on which he shall subsist, and to exact a testimonial from his past employers and the overseers or church-wardens when he quitted a service, which he had to show before he entered another.

By construction of law, the offence of conspiracy; which was originally a combination for the purpose of bringing false evidence against others, or for the purpose of subsequently committing a crime; was extended to those associations of workmen, whose purpose it was to raise the rate of wages by such a combination, for the whole basis of the practice on the subject appears to be inferential from the statute of Edward VI., under which penalties are inflicted on those who combine not to do work, except at a certain price and for a certain time, and for implied violations of the 18th, 19th, and 20th clauses of the Act of Elizabeth, which must be forced in order to bear such a construction. But at the conclusion of the eighteenth century an Act of Parliament was carried, which declares all contracts, except between master and man, for obtaining advances of wages, altering the usual time of working, decreasing the quantity of work, and the like, illegal. Workmen who enter into such illegal combinations are punishable by imprisonment, and a similar punishment is inflicted on those who enter into combinations to procure an advance of wages, or seek to prevent other workmen from hiring themselves, or procuring them to quit their employment. Meetings and combinations for effecting such purposes are punishable in like manner, and offenders who inform against their associates are to be indemnified. This Act, it may be remembered, was passed when wheat was at famine prices, ranging from 100s. to 150s. a quarter, and the magistrates were beginning to confess the atrocious cruelty of the Quarter Sessions assessment of wages by adopting that system of Poor Law allowances which I shall comment on hereafter.

The imaginary offence which employers and lawyers invented for the purpose of keeping wages low is on a par with the crime of witchcraft. That no end, however excellent in itself, should be, indeed can be, aided by violence, is a commonplace in the law of all civilization. It is equally true that the pretence to a supernatural power of working mischief on others by a mysterious process which its victim cannot foresee, resist, or escape, is an offence against even a more rudimentary civilization. But the ordinary forces of law and police ought to be, and under a proper administration always are, sufficient against ruffians and cheats, though the phenomena of ruffianism and knavery ought to direct the attention of government to their causes, and to guide legislatures to preventive remedies.

A trade union conducted on legal and peaceful principles, by which I mean moral forces only, and with an entire abstention from violence, both in its inception and its administration, does not economically differ from any other joint stock partnership. When a number of persons combine their capitals, their energies, and their experiences in constituting a commercial undertaking, when they carry it on with integrity, and gain all the advantages they can by interpreting demand and regulating supply, so as to secure the greatest possible profit to themselves, the business is welcomed as legitimate, and the managers and agents of it are applauded. If the undertaking is greatly successful, the promoters of it are styled merchant princes, pioneers of industry, creators of public wealth, benefactors of their country, and guarantors of its progress. They are presumed to be peculiarly fit for offices and titles of honour, to merit places in Parliament, occasionally to be even qualified to transmit hereditary fortune, rank, and authority. Examine into the process by which individual or joint stock wealth is created, and you will always find that it has been developed from the practice of buying or producing judiciously, and by selling at as high a price as the market will consent to give. There is, indeed, no other process by which wealth can be accumulated or capital increased. The phrase may be varied as one wills, but it always means the same thing, that profits can be obtained only by selling at a better price than one has bought or made, whatever one may have obtained and is bringing into the market.

Now this is precisely what a trade union, or labour partnership as I prefer to call it, does for that which workmen possess,—their labour. They have something to sell in their strength and their skill. Like the capitalist, they wish to sell their property to the best advantage, that is, at a charge which will leave them something above, as much as possible above, the cost at which they are put in keeping themselves in an effective condition for their labour, and which exactly corresponds to the cost of production in the case of the manufacturer, and to the cost of acquisition in the case of the merchant or trader. They also know perfectly well that if they are constrained to sell their labour to the first comer or at a moment's notice, they sell at a disadvantage, and they are as much in their right in withholding their goods from the market till they can get their price, or, in other words, in refusing to work till they get satisfactory wages, as a shop-keeper is who will not sell his goods except at his price, or a manufacturer who will not bring his produce to market unless he gets his profit. In one particular, indeed, they are worse off than merchant and manufacturer. The goods in which they deal are very costly to keep, and therefore they have to be very circumspect in refusing to sell, because to withhold from the market is in their case a serious loss. In order to make this loss as light as possible, though at the best it is exceedingly heavy, they require to adopt the joint stock principle of mutual insurance against the loss of keeping their goods from the market, and on the widest possible scale. They seek to enlist the largest possible number of workmen in their association, to include all in the same trade if they can, to include all in a corporation of trades in the end, so that they may be able to strengthen, as far as possible, the exceptional weakness of their position. Now to do this successfully they should develop the most important of the social virtues. They should have consideration for the rights of others, in their own fellowship necessarily; in that of others, that they may not destroy the common agency by the harmony of which they can procure the greatest advantage: patience, and forbearance: shrewd foresight as to the condition, present and future, of the craft by which they live; and intelligence in proving that the machinery which they employ is for the common benefit of all, workmen, producers, and consumers alike. If they take their measures rightly, they can demonstrate all this. I confess that I look forward to the international union of labour partnerships as the best prospect the world has of coercing those hateful instincts of governments, all alike irresponsible and indifferent, by which nations are perpetually armed against each other, to the infinite detriment, loss, and demoralization of all.

Mr. Mill, misled by two positions which he takes to be fundamental, but both of which are equally baseless; the first that the amount payable in wages is a fixed and inelastic quantity; the second, that an increase of wages must necessarily be effected at the cost of the employer or consumer, or both, has entirely ignored trade unions in his estimate of the popular remedies for low wages, and speaks doubtfully or slightingly about the machinery of trade unions in bettering labour generally, though he does, as might be expected, condemn in becoming terms the spirit which dictated the Statute of Labourers. But in point of fact, if trade unions do or can raise wages, they may do so to the ultimate benefit of producers and consumers. It is very possible, late experience proves it to be a fact, that aggregate profits may be abnormally high and individual profits small, owing to the competition of capitalists in the same employment, and a tacit or avowed understanding that competition shall be directed not to selling cheaply, but to getting custom. Now if the operation of a trade union takes the form of reducing the number of competing capitalists or traders, the workmen may be better off, the survivors of the reduction better off, and the consumers better off, too. There is an unproductive consumption of a marked character in the presence of a number of persons engaged in the same calling who cannot all live well by the calling, but who do contrive in the scramble to load the charge of the goods produced by their presence and their profits. Men are beginning to find out that persons who were once conceived to be a beneficial class, the intermediaries of trade and production, are engaged in destroying profits to an infinitely greater extent than high wages do; that they have become customary in many callings, do mischief instead of service, are parasites, and not, in any sense, producers. There is, of course, a fixed quantity of merchantable wealth produced in any given time. It may be distributed among an excessive number of persons, many of whom are useless, many of whom, though in their degree serviceable, could be spared, and by the excision of both, profits and wages might be greatly enhanced for those who are essential to the operation, and the public be, after all, considerably benefited.

I do not defend the tactics which trade unions have sometimes adopted. They have, indeed, the poor excuse that they are imitative of practices which are sanctioned by custom or success in others. A strike, seldom, I believe, successful, though the contingency of it may be, is, to an economist, no way different from a speculative purchase by which the projector hopes to control the market by shortening supply. The violence which has characterized the action of workmen against those who abstain from their policy, compete against them for employment in a crisis, and, as they believe, selfishly profit by a process which they are too mean to assist, but from which they suck no small advantage, is indefensible and suicidal. But it has its parallel in the attitude taken by joint stock companies of trade to interlopers, and in the devices by which traders have over and over again striven to ruin rivals who will not abide by trade customs, or even seek to be independent competitors against powerful agencies. I see no difference, beyond the fact that law allows them, between the rattening of a Sheffield saw grinder and the expedients by which, in the Committee rooms of the House of Commons, railway directors seek to extinguish competitive schemes. Men who have not had the refinements of education, and who are not practised in the arts of polite malignity, may be coarse and rude in the expedients which they adopt, but when the process is essentially the same, when the motive is practically identical, and the result is precisely equal, the manner is of no importance to the analyst of motives and conduct.

There is but little alteration in the material condition of the artizan and labourer in husbandry up to the end of the second quarter of the eighteenth century. The wages of the former were generally 1s. 6d. to 2s. a day, those of the latter 1s. to 1s. 6d., though they are sometimes more, for the employer seems to have not infrequently disregarded the assessments of quarter sessions. In 1767 and onwards Arthur Young began and continued his tours through rural England, and constantly gives an account of the wages paid in different parts of the country. Thus, in Hertfordshire he reckons that the amount of a labourer's annual earnings is £18, of which his board, washing, and lodging amount to £12. This amounts to a little less than 7s. a week. In Northamptonshire it is £17 a year, and Young notes that day labour in that part of the country used to be only 4s. a week in winter, or even 3s., and that this was the rule ten years before. At Kettering, he tells us that labour has risen by one-third during the twenty years preceding his visit. In Derbyshire, he tells us that the price of labour (the annual earnings are set at £17) has increased 50 per cent. during the last twenty years; in Yorkshire, a fourth within the same period. In the fourth volume of his "Eastern Tour" he sets down the average wages of husbandmen at 7s. 10d. a week, this quantity being made up by the extra allowances of the hay and corn harvest; and he notes that in many places the wages had risen 50 per cent. within the last twenty years, and taking all places together, 25. This gives £20 3s. 4d. a year on an average. The house rent of the labourer is at an average of £2, his fuel at £1 6s. Bread, which he supposes to be wheaten, is 1¼d. the lb.; butter, 6½d.; cheese, 3¾d.; meat of all kinds, mutton, beef, pork, and veal, 3½d. Young comments on the equality of the price of bread throughout England as a singular and instructive fact. He also holds that such a rate of wages ought to nearly exclude parish assistance, adding that "sound and spirited husbandry, while products bear a fair price, will very well pay a high price of labour, and that thorough good farmers who are alive to their business do not complain of the rates of labour, provided men can be got." Wages, too, had again become higher in the neighbourhood of London.

Such a result is to be expected. Unless the rate of wages be artificially lowered, the cheaper products are, the higher wages are, provided, of course, that the cheapness is due to progressive industry. Now this is precisely what occurred about the middle of the eighteenth century. Agriculture made a prodigious start, and though population was evidently increasing with great rapidity, prices fell. Inclosures were general, and still prices fell; a bounty was granted on the exportation of grain, and prices were still declining. Now if prices fall with an increasing population, with a greater breadth of land enclosed and under cultivation, and even under the stimulus of a payment made by the State to such persons as would export grain, the natural inference would be that rents would fall. But, on the contrary, rents rose as prices fell. The value of land, according to Arthur Young, and on this point he was not likely to be deceived, was on an average thirty-three-and-a-half years' purchase; and the owner had, at least ordinarily, to do repairs to the homestead and buildings, to run the risk of vacant farms and bankrupt tenants. Now it is impossible that so high a price should be paid for land, unless the purchaser contemplated a prospective advantage in his acquisition, was convinced, in short, that what he expected to get 3 per cent. from as an investment to-day he could get a constantly increasing percentage from shortly after he had acquired it. The country was constantly producing more vendible commodities at less cost, and the advantage was shared by the labourer, the farmer, the landowner, and the consumer. And though much that Arthur Young says is crude, and not a little even foolish, as when he ascribes the progress of agriculture to the Corn Laws and the Bounty, much that he says about the necessary, the inevitable progress of opulence is true. The workman, it is true, got less of the profit than others did—less than the farmer, the landlord, and the general consumer, because his previous margin had been so low, but he did share in the advantage—the advantage of lower prices and higher wages. In 1768, when Young began his tour, prices to be sure were high, and the cheapness of the preceding forty years was beginning to give way to a series of harvests which were almost famine years; but it well might have been that these exalted prices were considered exceptional and likely to be reversed, and that at the most they would have afforded an additional impetus to the rise in the value of land.

In addition to the information which Young gives us so copiously about the price of agricultural labour, his tours supply us with the wages paid at various manufactories in different parts of England. The highest are those earned by colliers, which at Newcastle were 15s. a week, and at Wakefield 11s. The next are those in the iron and cutlery works, which are 10s. at Rotherham, and 13s. 6d. at Sheffield. The next highest paid are the workmen in porcelain at Liverpool, Burslem, and Worcester, who get respectively 8s. 11d., 9s. 6d., and 9s. The average payment for spinning and weaving is 8s. 7d., the lowest wages out of seven localities being paid at Manchester, for fustians, 7s. 1d.; the highest at Wakefield, for cloth, 10s. The average wages of women in textile manufactures is 4s. 2½d.; of boys, 2s. 11¾d.; of girls, 2s. 7d. The earnings, therefore, of the manufacturing population were already, as far as the men are concerned, greater than those of the hind; and, besides, the former calling gave a more regular and highly paid wage to women and children. The effect of the attraction to manufacturing districts may have been, indeed must have been, injurious to the health and vigour of the people who were drawn into these employments, but the fact of the attraction is plain. Again, the drugget weavers of Braintree earn about 9s.; the woolcombers, 12s.; the Wilton carpet weavers from 10s. to 12s.; the Gloucester pinmakers from 10s. to 15s.; the woollen manufacturers of Henningham 7s.;

the combers from 12*s.* to 14*s.*; the steel polishers of Woodstock, from 15*s.* to 42*s.*; the blanket weavers of Witney, from
10*s.* to 12*s.* The manufacturers of Woodstock, now extinct,
were the best paid of any.

The best paid workmen in textile fabrics were the woolcombers, who earned on an average, wherever they were,
about 13*s.* a week ; the lowest the say and calimanco weavers
of Lavenham at 5*s.* 9*d.* The best paid agricultural labourers
were those in Kent and Middlesex, with a weekly payment
of 11*s.* 4*d.* The worst are those of Gloucestershire and Wilt-
shire, at 5*s.* 2½*d.* The wages of the manufacturing labourer,
says Young, are, on an average, 8*d.* a week beyond those of
agricultural labourers, some of whom, in the West of England, get no more than 5*s.* and 6*s.* all the year round. Young,
who is an ardent advocate of high rents and high prices,
informs us that the rioting which had latterly disturbed
England had been invariably got up by those labourers who
earned the best wages. He evidently does not see that discontent and disaffection are frequently the outcome of
tolerable well-doing, rarely of penury and despair.

The old days of cheapness and abundance were now over,
and dear times succeeded. In 1744 and 1745, when the
upward movement of wages commenced, wheat was between
21*s.* and 22*s.* the quarter; after 1780, it was rarely below 50*s.*;
and towards the end of the century it rose to double that
price. It is possible that the deficiency in the English
harvests, prices being also elevated by the rapid growth of
population, and this being due to the growing demand for
hands in the factories, and especially for the labour of the
young, could not have been supplemented by foreign importation in the generally disturbed state of Europe at the outbreak of the continental war. But even if the supply had
been possible, the corn laws were a sufficient discouragement
to foreign trade in food. If the foreign producer had known
that the English people would buy corn in emergencies, he
could not tell when the emergency would arise, and at what
time he should make preparation for it. Trade rests upon
the anticipation of a market, and the legislation which makes

a market uncertain, adopts the most effectual means for destroying the market altogether. The scarcity which now became chronic for a quarter of a century in England, developed besides that detestable interest in the mind of the farmer and landowner, and keeps it still alive in that of the former, that the best profit which they can hope lies in the calamities, the miseries, the misfortunes, the losses, the impoverishment of their fellow-countrymen. Thanks to the efforts of those who established free trade in food, the farmer and the landlord are now deprived of the pleasure which they once felt when unpropitious seasons raised the price of food in so rapid and increasing a proportion, that a scanty harvest was bringing enormously increased gain to the agriculturist and the receiver of rents, and their satisfaction is limited to the prospect of interruption between the trade of this country and those regions from which food supplies are derived.

On May 6th, 1795, a meeting of the Berkshire magistrates was held at Speenhamland, after a public advertisement had been made of the intended meeting, when it was unanimously affirmed that the state of the poor required larger assistance than had been given them generally. The meeting also decided that it was not expedient for the magistrates to grant that assistance by regulating wages according to the Statute of Elizabeth, but that the magistrates should earnestly recommend the farmers and others to increase the pay of their labourers according to the price of provisions. They thereupon put out a scale, in which they calculated what should be the wages of workmen, according to the rise or fall in the price of bread, the scale being based on the same principle as the assize of bread. Thus when the gallon loaf should cost 1s., they reckoned that the labourer should receive, either by his own earnings or by an allowance from the poor rates, 3s. weekly for himself and 1s. 6d. for each of his family, and that with the rise of every penny in the loaf, he should receive an additional 3d. for himself and 1d. for each of his family. An unsuccessful attempt was made twice over in the House of Commons to enforce what was called the Speenhamland Act of

Parliament by law, and Bills to this effect were introduced in 1795 and 1800 by Mr. Whitbread.

There had been some rise in the rate of wages at the conclusion of the century. The poor could not have subsisted had not such a rise been effected; but it bore no proportion to the rise in the necessaries of life. In 1801, Arthur Young calculated that a Suffolk labourer could (at some date which he does not give, but it must have been nearly sixty years before) have bought with 5*s*. what, in 1801, would have cost him 26*s*. 5*d*., and that, therefore, as his wages and parish allowance would at the best have given him only 15*s*., he was virtually put on little more than half the scale of his earnings in the earlier period. The workmen of the time put out statements as to their condition, in which they admitted a slight increase, but showed how inadequate it was when contrasted with their present outgoings. Thus, the journeyman tailors stated that their wages from 1777 to 1795 had been 21*s*. 9*d*. a week, with which they could purchase thirty-six loaves at the average prices, that they had risen to 25*s*. in 1795, and to 27*s*. in 1801, but that they were only able to purchase eighteen-and-a-half loaves with the larger nominal sum. Compositors had secured an advance from 24*s*. to 27*s*. in 1795, and to 30*s*. in 1801, but were really worse off than they had been. A similar rise had been effected, and with the same consequences, in the labour of carpenters, bricklayers, and masons. The rise was from 3*s*. a week to 1*s*. 6*d*. and 1*s*. But it was proved that the cost of maintaining a household at the beginning of the last quarter of the eighteenth century was, by a comparison of prices, more than trebled at the close of the period. It should be noted also that while prices were so high in England they were remarkably depressed abroad, but that owing to the outrageous fiscal system in England, the famine in England was contemporaneous with a foreign glut. Now a free intercourse with other countries would have obviated much mischief and misery on both sides of the Channel. The report as to the state of the home trade is what might be expected. The trade of Birmingham was in a very distressed condition. A large number of workmen were out of employment, and those who got work had the utmost difficulty in subsisting, owing to the exorbitant price of food. The ribbon trade of Coventry was in a most deplorable state, the woollen trade of Yorkshire, if possible, still worse. The seasons had been unpropitious, and the law designedly intensified the scarcity.

Between 1800 and 1812 the nominal wages of agricultural labourers and artizans were considerably increased, either by actual payments or by parish allowances. Still the rise was not proportionate to the increased cost of living, for dearth had become an institution in the country. But the wages of persons employed in factories were not increased, or very partially, and many people were out of work altogether. In 1785, the poor rate was £2,004,238. In 1802, it was £4,267,965 ; in 1813, it amounted to £8,640,842. At the conclusion of the eighteenth century the rate of agricultural wages was 1s. 4d. a day. In the year 1810 it was 1s. 8d., and it is noteworthy that the carpenter's wages, generally about 50 per cent. above those of the agriculturist, did not go above the level of the latter at the time. For as Mr. Tooke ("History of Prices," ii. 71) said in 1837, "According to all experience, whether within modern observation or recorded in history, it may be laid down as an established maxim that labour is the last of the objects of exchange to rise in consequence of dearth or depreciation, and that commonly the price of labour is the last to fall in consequence of increased abundance of commodities or of increased value of money." The condition of labour was considerably bettered after the peace, was greatly benefited by the comparatively low prices which prevailed in the period intervening between the commencement of fiscal reforms and the repeal of the corn laws, and has, speaking generally, made further progress since that time.

The repeal of the ancient laws against the association of workmen for the purpose of raising their wages, led to the creation of trade unions. In course of time these associations took active steps, and especially in 1853 were successful in several directions. The lightermen on the river, the labourers in the docks, a number of artizans on the south of the river Thames, where there are great and important manufactures, the men employed in the building trades, masons, bricklayers, and carpenters, demanded and obtained an increase of 10 per cent. in their wages, and a considerable shortening in the hours of their labour. This movement has progressed, and at the present time the hours of labour are probably less in England than they are in any country, certainly considerably less than they are in the United States. Nor was this movement confined to artizans. The agricultural labourers, partly owing to their own action, partly to the greater mobilization of labour, brought about by the construction of the railways, which attracted numerous hands from the rural districts, partly to the easier means of communication, and the intercourse with other markets for labour which the railways opened up, made their demand also for a better remuneration, and generally achieved it. It is true that the wages of the farm hand are still low, and, as a consequence, country districts have suffered a great depletion of population, and it may be feared have lost their best hands, and, it is possible, the best stock. Emigration also became exceedingly active. Thousands went to the United States and the Colonies, although population, especially in the towns, continually increased, partly because, under better sanitary conditions, the number of births became greater and life was greatly prolonged, partly because there has been a steady inflow to the towns from rural districts, and even from foreign countries.

Working men have been far more effective in the combinations they have adopted than in the instrument which they have used for enforcing their demands. Strikes have so seldom been successful that a doubt has been expressed as to whether the rise in wages, fortunately an accomplished fact, has not been due entirely to demand, and in no case to the combination. But it cannot, I think, be doubted that however little the battle between capital and labour has resulted in the victory of the latter, the contingency of a battle must have frequently averted its occurrence. The tendency towards the struggle, too, is always when trade is bad and a reduction threatened, *i.e.*, at a time when the minimum of loss is put on the employer and a maximum on the workmen. But the fullest proof of the real efficacy of trade unions as a means for improving the condition of the labourer and increasing his material benefit lies in the stimulus which they have given to the construction of boards, which should conciliate both parties and arbitrate between them. Many of us can well remember the time when the master repudiated the interference of arbitrators with great warmth, and men looked on the proposal with cold incredulity. But this to a great degree is changed, and though the mechanism of conciliation works still with not a little friction, all persons testify to the infinitely improved tone with which trade disputes are avowed, carried on, and settled. It was not to be expected that persons unused to argument, and inexperienced in the analysis of facts, much more of motives, should not at first be violent when they were angry. The tendency, however, has greatly changed, and, in the opinion of most fair judges, with great rapidity.

Working men in England have now their future very much in their own hands. They see, I suspect, much more clearly than their critics do, what are the limits of their power over capital and prices,—on the former because the profits of capital depend on the sufficiency of the latter ; on the latter because they know that they may check or even destroy the market of what is voluntarily purchased, and may raise against themselves and their own order what must necessarily be used or consumed. But the joint action of working men is only in its infancy yet. As association becomes wider and more coalescent, many steps which have not yet been taken will become easy and natural ; as, for instance, the maintenance of a standard of honour and efficiency in work, and the protection of the public against the roguery of producers, of which at present workmen are the silent witnesses, but should not be the willing accomplices. I know nothing which would exalt the reputation and justify the action of trade combinations more than the establishment of a rule, that members of such unions would denounce and expose dishonest and scambling work, and protect those of their order who may suffer ill-usage or wrong-doing for having reported and checked such nefarious practices. As yet the rules of trade unions are principally confined to the process of bettering the whole class. Hereafter they will, or should, extend towards purifying the class, and making it a potent instrument for the moral and material advancement of all. Other professions exclude, either formally or informally, misbehaving, disreputable, or incompetent persons from their ranks. It cannot be doubted that in time to come artizans and labourers will elaborate those necessary police regulations, by which they will increase the usefulness, elevate the reputation, and cultivate the moral tone of those who ply the craft whose interests they seek to serve, and whose character they ought scrupulously to maintain.

CHAPTER XV.

THE ENGLISH POOR LAW.

THERE has always been poverty in human societies when men are settled on the soil, though not, perhaps, more poverty than exists among peoples who are still wanderers, or hunters, or herdsmen. I make no doubt that the ordinary hardships of human life in England were greater, and I am sure they were more general six centuries ago than they are now. Life was briefer, old age came earlier, disease was more deadly, the risks of existence were more numerous. The race was smaller, weaker, more stunted. But the extremes of wealth and poverty were, by the fact of these common conditions, less widely separated. Above all things, what is now characteristic of human life, that one-half of the world does not know how the other half lives, a very moderate statement of the fact, was not true of the early ages of English progress. Society was small, and not packed densely. Not only did each man know all about his neighbours' affairs, but the whole machinery of government pre-supposed that he did. The ancient jury was not a body of men brought together to interpret the relevance of a set of facts which they hear for the first time when they get into the jury-box, but a dozen men who were supposed to know all the facts of the case beforehand, who were held responsible for not knowing them, and still more responsible for not giving a satisfactory verdict on the facts which they knew.

As the English householder in the middle ages was supposed to know the acts and the character of every man in the neighbourhood, he was equally well-informed as to each person's circumstances. No doubt people hoarded, the more because taxation was on the visible means of the tax-payer; but it is certain that the periodical visits of the assessor must have brought out the fact of narrow circumstances, poverty, and want very plainly, perhaps over plainly, as destitution was, under certain circumstances, held to be a virtue, or, at least, the preparation for virtue. I cannot say that people did not perish from want in very bad times. I am tolerably sure that they did, and in considerable numbers, during the great famines of 1315 and 1316, when all but the very opulent must have been stinted. But fortunately for the English people, as I have frequently stated, their habit, even under the adverse circumstances of their existence and the uncleanly ways of their life, was always to subsist on abundant provisions of naturally high quality. They ate wheaten bread, drank barley beer, and had plenty of cheap though perhaps coarse meat. Mutton and beef at a farthing a pound, take what multiple you please, and twelve is a liberal one, were within the reach of far more people than they now are. The grinding, hopeless poverty under which existence may be just continued, but when nothing is won beyond bare existence, did not, I am convinced, characterise or even belong to mediæval life. That men died from want I can believe, but I do not think that they lived and died by inches, so to speak. There were many means by which occasional distress was relieved. I am not sure that I have been able to collect all the means.

In the first place, the relief of destitution was the fundamental religious duty of mediæval Christianity, I might have said of Christianity itself. In ancient polities it might be the duty of the state to relieve distress; it was always its prudence, if it cared for security. To get abundant supplies of food for the poorer citizens in one way or the other was the constant anxiety of democratic Athens and of imperial Rome. But from the very first Christianity transferred this duty from the state to the individual, and to the voluntary corporation. The early Church undoubtedly preached patience, but it much more emphatically inculcated the duty of almsgiving. The contribution of the tithe was enforced in order that a third part at least of the proceeds should go to the relief of the deserving poor. In the fifteenth century nothing moves the righteous wrath of Gascoigne more than the teaching of Pecok to the effect that ecclesiastical revenues enjoyed by churchmen can be disposed of according to the discretion of the recipient as freely as the proceeds of private property. After heresy, simony, and sorcery, the heaviest charge which could be levelled against a churchman was that of avarice, and a covetous priest who hoarded his revenues was lucky if the charge of avarice was not coupled with those graver vices to which I have referred. We may be certain, too, that the duty which was so generally imposed on them by public opinion—the force of which is not yet extinct—was inculcated by them on others. In times of plenty, too, food was often given with wages. A wealthy monastery or college would find a place at the servants' table for the artizans whom they employed without much grudging, and still more would the poor at the gate not be sent away empty-handed. Where mendicancy was no disgrace, almsgiving was like to be considered the most necessary and the most ordinary of the virtues.

It has been often said and often denied that the monasteries supplied the want which the poor law, two generations after the dissolution of these bodies, enforced. That the monasteries were renowned for their almsgiving is certain. The duty of aiding the needy was universal. Themselves the creatures of charity, they could not deny to others that on which they subsisted. But some orders were under special duties. The Hospitallers were bound to relieve casual destitution. Hence, when Waynflete procured the surrender of the house of the Oxford Hospitallers, he bound his college to the duties which the surrendered house had performed, duties which, it is almost superfluous to say, were speedily evaded. So again the preaching and begging friars were the nurses of the sick, especially of those who laboured under infectious diseases. There were houses where doles of bread and beer were given to all wayfarers, houses where the sick were tended, clothed, and fed, particularly the lepers. There were nunneries, where the nuns were nurses and midwives ; and even now the ruins of these houses contain living record of the ancient practices of their inmates in the rare medicinal herbs which are still found within their precincts. In the universal destruction of these establishments, the hardest instruments of Henry's purposes interceded for the retention of some amongst the most meritorious, useful, and unblemished of them. It is possible that these institutions created the mendicancy which they relieved, but it cannot be doubted that they assisted much which needed their help.

The guilds which existed in the towns were also found in the country villages. They are traceable to the period before the Conquest, and Hickes long ago printed some of the rules under which they were constructed and governed, though these are in the towns of Cambridge and Exeter. Blomefield finds some in the Norfolk villages. Vestiges of their halls remained long in small villages, these halls being devoted to the business and occasional feasts of the society. They were convenient instruments for charity before the establishment of a poor law, and they employed no inconsiderable part of their revenues, collected from subscriptions and from lands and tenements, in relieving the indigent and treating poor strangers hospitably. Blomefield, speaking of their feasts, says : " But as the poor of the parish always were partakers with them, I much question whether their revenues were not better spent then than they have been since they were rapa-

27

ciously seized from the parishes to which they of right belonged." (Norfolk, iii., 185). The guilds frequently survived
the Reformation, though, of course, they had lost their property,
and are probably represented in later times by the parish
feast. Their property, as I have already said, was finally
confiscated by 1 Edward VI., cap. 14, after having been comprised in the last of Henry's acts of rapine (37 Henry VIII.,
cap. 4).

Before the dissolution of the monasteries, but when this
issue was fairly in view, in 1536, an attempt was made to
secure some legal provision for destitution. The Act of this
year provides that the authorities in the cities and boroughs
should collect alms on Sundays and holy days, that the
ministers should on all occasions, public and private, stir up
the people to contribute to a common fund, that the custom
of giving doles by private persons should be forbidden under
penalty, and that the churchwardens should distribute the
alms when collected. The Act, however, is strictly limited
to free gifts, and the obligations of monasteries, almshouses,
hospitals, and brotherhoods are expressly maintained.

The Supplication of Beggars puts the contributions given to
the begging friars by the people at £45,333 6s. 8d. annually,
supplied by 520,000 households. There was a considerable
party in England which was willing enough to see the monasteries destroyed, root and branch, and one of the most
obvious means by which this result could be attained would
be to allege that all which could be needed for the relief of
destitution would be derived from the voluntary offerings of
those who contributed so handsomely to the maintenance of
indolent and dissolute friars. The public was reconciled to
the Dissolution by the promise made that the monastic estates
should not be converted to the king's private use, but be
devoted towards the maintenance of a military force, and
that therefore no more demands should be made on the
nation for subsidies and aids. Similarly when the guild lands
and chantry lands were confiscated at the beginning of
Edward's reign, a promise was made that the estates of these
foundations should be devoted to good and proper uses, for

erecting grammar schools, for the further augmentation of the universities, and the better provision for the poor and needy. They were swept into the hands of Seymour and Somerset, of the Dudleys and Cecils, and the rest of the crew who surrounded the throne of Edward. It cannot therefore, I think, be doubted that this violent change of ownership, apart from any considerations of previous practice in these several institutions, must have aggravated whatever evils already existed. It was idle to expect that they who saw ancient institutions, on which the duty of almsgiving was imposed, not only swept away, but devoted to entirely different purposes, in which these obligations were utterly neglected, would contribute of their free will to the relief of destitution, even if their resources were as considerable as before. But as I have already stated, there came upon this violent change another and far more formidable calamity, the issue of base money and the total derangement of currency and prices. Foolish people talk of the influx of the new silver. It had not reached England, and did not reach England till a generation after, and then superficially. What England wanted was silver, and the Government put it out of her power to get it.

The guardians of Edward attempted, in a savage statute passed in the first year of his reign, to restrain pauperism and vagabondage by reducing the landless and destitute poor to slavery, by branding them, and making them work in chains. The Act, however, only endured for two years. In the last year of Edward's reign two collectors were to be appointed in every parish, who were to wait on every person of substance and inquire what sums he will give weekly to the relief of the poor. The promises are to be entered in a book, and the collectors were authorized to employ the poor in such work as they could perform, paying them from the fund. Those who refused to aid were to be first exhorted by the ministers and churchwardens, and if they continued obstinate were to be denounced to the bishop, who is to remonstrate with such uncharitable folk. In Mary's reign, when the Act is renewed with a penalty on such collectors as decline the office, the reference to the bishop is accompanied with the hint that refusal to give might be construed as suggestive of heresy. This Act put the canvass for weekly subscriptions at Christmas in place of Whitsuntide. In the beginning of Elizabeth's reign (5, cap. 3) the unwilling giver, after being exhorted by the bishop, is to be bound to appear before the justices, in quarter sessions, where, if he be still obdurate to exhortation, the justices are empowered to tax him in a weekly sum, and commit him to prison till he pays. This Act precedes that enforcing apprenticeship and empowering the magistrates to fix wages, on which latter I have often and fully commented, and should probably be taken with it. The law has now proceeded from exhortation to compulsion.

It seems highly probable that destitution and vagabondage were still further developed by the decline of that manorial jurisdiction which had been so effective in the thirteenth and fourteenth centuries, and the transference of the machinery of police from the parish to the justice's office or to the quarter sessions. The old system, concentrating as it did the functions of local discipline in the steward and inhabitants of a parish, exercised a control and enforced a responsibility which was indifferently compensated by the authority of an individual or a bench of magistrates. And this impression is confirmed by the almost insensible change from a jury who are witnesses to a fact to a jury who are merely judges of a fact,—a change so gradual that we get the first hint of it in the celebrated case of Throgmorton, who was acquitted in Mary's reign ; though the legal irresponsibility of a jury which acquits in face of a judge's ruling, or what he conceives to be the law, was only affirmed by Chief Justice Vaughan as late as the reign of Charles II. in the Quakers' case.

There was only a step from the process under which a reluctant subscriber to the poor law was assessed by the justices and imprisoned on refusal, to the assessment of all property under the celebrated Act of 43 Elizabeth, cap. 3. The law had provided for the regular appointment of assessors for the levy of rates, for supplying work to the able-bodied, for giving relief to the infirm and old, and for binding apprentices. It now consolidates the experience of the whole reign, defines the kind of property on which the rate is to be levied, prescribes the manner in which the assessors shall be appointed, and inflicts penalties on parties who infringe its provisions. It is singular that the Act was only temporary. It was, by the last clause, only to continue to the end of the next session of parliament. It was, however, renewed, and finally made perpetual by 16 Car. I., cap. 4.

The economical history of labour in England is henceforward intimately associated with this remarkable Act. It was the result of a series of causes, each of which has been already commented on, the most dominant unquestionably being the rapid and serious rise in the money value of food and other necessaries, and the halting manner in which the rate of wages followed the rise. In the fourteenth and fifteenth centuries the labourer secured increased wages in the midst of decreasing prices. In the sixteenth, the reverse which he suffered was far more considerable than the advantage which his forefathers had gained. I do not, indeed, find that they who regulated his wages by Act of Parliament were aware how seriously his condition had been deteriorated, or that even those who busied themselves with the phenomena of social life, as Latimer did in the worst times of the bad currency, and Stafford and Harrison did in the days of Elizabeth, took any thought whatever of the labourer's condition under these deplorably altered circumstances. Even Eden, whose careful investigations into the condition of the poor, and whose comments on the various statutes which regulate their wages, their condition, and their movements, are fairly exhaustive, does not seem to have realized, though the facts were to a considerable extent before him, how great a change had come over the life of the labourer and the artizan. I cannot but think that a growing disaffection, which Elizabeth and her counsellors were not slow to discern, the remedy for which seemed to be the continuance of expedients adopted in the three previous reigns, was the cause which induced them and parliament to acquiesce in the Act of 1601. The Act was to be tentative, indeed, but in its general principles it lasted till 1835.

It is plain that had the Act of Elizabeth been carried out in all its details, the whole revenue of land would have ulimately been swallowed up in the relief of the poor. To some extent the framers of the Act saw that this was already locally possible, for the third clause of the Act contemplates the possibility of the resources of a parish being inadequate to the charge of maintaining the local poor, and directs that the deficiency, if any arises, shall be supplemented from the rest of the hundred. Now it was plain that if the magistrates in quarter sessions were to fix the rate at which labour should be paid, as they regularly did in the sixteenth and seventeenth centuries, they would have every motive to put the rate at the lowest sum which would sustain life, knowing well that if the labourer became destitute, all occupiers would have to assist in his maintenance, while the benefit of cheap labour would remain to those only who employed him, as, indeed, actually happened. In country places this would not at first be a very important matter, as there would have been few persons rated to the poor who, being occupiers, were not immediate employers of labour. But in the towns, the incidence of the poor rate was a very serious addition to the burdens of such occupiers as did not employ labour, and at the latter end of the eighteenth century it became a very heavy charge generally.

The effect of poor law relief on the wages of labour was to keep them hopelessly low, to hinder a rise even under the most urgent circumstances. This will be seen most clearly in the history of wages during the seventeenth century, when prices of corn were very high, and the labourer's standard of subsistence undoubtedly fell. For even if he were still able to maintain himself on wheaten bread, his power of purchasing other kinds of food was greatly curtailed. We must not be led into believing that because meat was comparatively cheap— it rapidly rose to three times the old rate, while wages did not increase more than fifty per cent. over the rate in Eliza-

beth's reign after the first exaltation of prices was established--
it was therefore within the range of his expenditure. On
the contrary, the comparative cheapness of meat, beside that
of corn, is proof that the power of consuming it was narrowed
by the deteriorated condition of the mass of the people. The
fact is, the relief of mere destitution was the removal of every
prudential restraint. If the labourer got scanty wages, he
was at least guaranteed against famine in sickness, in infancy
and in old age, and he was, therefore, discouraged from
exercising any foresight whatever. I am persuaded that the
singular indifference with which, on the whole, the condition
of the working classes was viewed in relation to profits and
rent was due to the impression, that as the propertied classes
had bound themselves by law to ensure the labourer against
the contingencies of life, the facts of the case needed no
further anxiety on the part of any person whatever, except
in so far as the maintenance of the destitute seriously trenched
on the value of land.

It has been said, and with great apparent justice, that the
legal relief of destitution, though perhaps incapable of an
economical defence, is justified on the highest political and
social grounds. If the relief of misery is left to private
charity, the assistance given is capricious and imperfect.
Besides, the destitute and unrelieved are always dangerous;
and though the forces at the command of modern society
are powerful enough to check any outbreak, they cannot be,
except at an enormous expense, so efficient as to protect
property against desperate distress. Again, serious as the
strife has been between labour and capital, when the former is
at least guaranteed against the worst contingencies; it would
be infinitely sharper were the guarantee repudiated. Nor
must one forget how harsh and bitter life becomes when it
is familiarized with the signs of unrelieved distress. I cannot,
indeed, doubt that in the magnitude of modern societies the
relief of the poor is a necessity which cannot be, however
much labour makes progress and betters itself, repudiated
or neglected. Society may not be responsible for nine-tenths
of the misery and poverty within it, but it will never restrain

poverty and misery unless it takes them in hand, and to do so is to relieve them.

But the English poor law, after all, was the outcome of great crimes committed by government, and is aggravated even now by customs permitted by government. It could not be free from the vices of its origin, and it is still in many particulars made mischievous and harsh by those provisions and those contingencies which arise from the customs to which it is partly due. I have referred to the crimes of the Tudor government. The customs to which I take exception have an earlier origin, and are even more enduring, for they have given occasion to two of the greatest problems of our own day,—the housing of our poor in cities and the settlement of agricultural labour in the country.

How far beggary, wretchedness, and crime, with their most fruitful concomitants, drunkenness and hopelessness, recipro-cally act on each other we cannot and never shall be able to tell. We know that they are the miserable circle in which thousands of our people, especially in London, revolve. We know that they have destroyed all interest, except in the means of the present day, in thousands. There is a large population which would, if it could, make war on society, which measures its own misery by the opulence of others, and is profoundly convinced that every power which society has and uses is employed against it. These people live in squalid dens, where there can be no health and no hope, but dogged discontent at their own lot and futile discontent at the wealth which they see possessed by others.

But it cannot, I think, be doubted that when prudence and thrift are deliberately discouraged, and recklessness is incul-cated by law or practice, the misery which must, it seems, accompany human life in society may become general and chronic. The legislature strove to tie the peasant to the soil, not, indeed, as a mere serf, for the Act of 1592 prescribed that every labourer's cottage in future should have four acres of land attached to it,—a law which roused the wrath of Arthur Young in 1770, and was no doubt habitually broken. But it also gave him, as a compensation for the policy which permitted entails and the accumulation of land in few hands, the right to be a pensioner on the soil, from all real and permanent share in which he was practically excluded. He had been robbed by the landowner, and he was to be hereafter quartered on the occupier. He had been impoverished by misgovernment, and was to be degraded by a charity which was to compensate him for the losses which he had sustained and for the hard measure which was being dealt out to him, but which would ultimately degrade him and make him helpless and hopeless. I can conceive nothing more cruel, I had almost said more insolent, than to condemn a labourer to the lowest possible wages on which life may be sustained, by an Act of Parliament, interpreted and enforced by an ubiquitous body of magistrates, whose interest it was to screw the pittance down to the lowest conceivable margin, and to inform the stinted recipient that when he had starved on that during the days of his strength, others must work to maintain him in sickness or old age. Now this was what the Statute of Apprenticeship, supplemented by the Poor Law, did in the days of Elizabeth. And if you go into the streets and alleys of our large towns, and, indeed, of many English villages, you may meet the fruit of the wickedness of Henry and the policy of Elizabeth's counsellors in the degradation and helplessness of your countrymen.

Still their evils have been aggravated by other agencies. The cost of living in large towns has been reduced by the excellent and regular services of supply. In the middle ages most articles of food and analogous necessaries were fully fifteen per cent. dearer in London than elsewhere. It is probable that at present they are as much cheaper. But to these economies there is one notable exception. The cost of house rent is enormous. Some of this cost is doubtlessly due to the density with which the people are packed, and the advantage contained in proximity to one's calling. But the cost is greatly increased by the power which the law confers on corporations and private proprietors to withhold land from the market at a minimum of cost. It will be clear that if the law encourages an artificial scarcity, it creates an unnatural dearness. By permitting corporations to hold land in towns, and by allowing private owners to settle land in towns, it gives such persons a power of exacting the highest terms possible for the use of their property, by keeping it out of the market till they can enforce their price. To use an American phrase, taken from the slang of speculators, the Russells and the Bentincks, the Cecils, the Portmans, the Grosvenors, and the rest, with the corporations, have had for a long period a ring or corner in the land market, and can force buyers to give famine prices. Now what is an injury to the moderately wealthy is oppression on the poor. It is well known that vile and loathsome buildings, probably the property of some opulent landowner, yield from the misery of their inmates a far larger rent than the plots on which the most luxurious and convenient mansions are built. Dives is clothed in purple and fine linen, and fares sumptuously every day from the crumbs which he sweeps out of the wallet of Lazarus; and if Lazarus has to be fed occasionally, and at last taken care of permanently, the fund which helps him comes, not from the pockets of those who grow wealthy from his want, but from those of others who are made liable in their degree to the same extortion. The law which levies rates on occupancy instead of on property makes the evil worse, for it puts the minimum inconvenience on the person who holds the strongest position. But they say, rates are paid by property in the end. If so, there can be no hardship in making the possessor of property pay them in the beginning. The facts and their effects may be dwelt on at greater length below.

In the ten years ending with 1590, the average price of wheat was 20s. 6d.; in the next decade, 31s. 11¼d.; the average being heightened by two years of famine, 1596 and 1597; in the next, 29s. 5½d.; in the next, 34s. 9½d.; in the next, 37s. 5¼d.; in the next, 43s. 0¾d.; in the next, 46s. 1¼d.; in the next, from 1651 to 1660, 44s. 6d.; the price being lowered in the last decade by the three abundant years 1653-5 inclusive. Now my readers will notice that the price of food is, on the whole, steadily rising, and he will readily discern that the two years of famine, 1596-97, when wheat was 46s. 3d. and 56s. 10½d., precipitated the passing of the Poor Law. At the commencement of the period, the artizan's wages were 1s. a day; the ordinary labourer's, 8d. At the conclusion of it, the former were 1s. 6d., the latter, 1s.; and at these prices they remained under the Act of 5 Elizabeth and the quarter sessions' assessment for a century and a quarter, since this is the rate at which they ordinarily stood in Arthur Young's time. In the time preceding the issue of base money, when the average price of wheat was below 6s. a quarter, they were 6d. and 4d. In the earlier period, then, an artizan could buy $\frac{1}{12}$ of a quarter of wheat, the ordinary labourer $\frac{1}{18}$ of a quarter by a day's work. But in the eight decades since 1581 they could get only $\frac{2}{41}$ and $\frac{2}{61}$ parts, $\frac{1}{32}$ and $\frac{1}{48}$ parts, $\frac{2}{69}$ and $\frac{2}{88}$ parts, $\frac{4}{139}$ and $\frac{2}{208}$ parts, $\frac{2}{75}$ and $\frac{2}{112}$ parts, $\frac{1}{4}$ and $\frac{1}{64}$ parts, $\frac{1}{10}$ and $\frac{1}{80}$ parts; while, in the last decade, when 50 per cent. was added to wages, owing, perhaps, to the charges of war and the circulation of money, they rose to $\frac{2}{63}$ and $\frac{2}{88}$ parts, omitting minute fractions throughout. Such figures show plainly how lessened the wages of the workman had become since the prosperous age to which I have so often referred.

Estimated by his power of purchasing wheat, the artizan and labourer in the last twenty years of the sixteenth and the first fifty years of the seventeenth century got progressively less, so that in the ten years from 1641 to 1650, their wages were little more than the fourth of that which had been earned by their grandfathers and great grandfathers. In the *Percy Ballads*, one of the speakers, called Ignorance, sings :—

> " I'll tell thee what, good fellow!
>   Before the friars went hence,
> A bushel of the best wheat
>   Was sold for fourteen pence ;
> And forty eggs a penny,
>   That were both good and new."

The price of the wheat in the song is a good deal above the average, though it does happen to be the price which prevailed just about the time of the Dissolution. The peasants naturally connected the change with the great event which had occurred before their eyes, and from which, chronologically, the decline in their condition commenced. It may have had its effect in the general cataclysm. It is certain that the majority of persons, most of all those who are quite unused to analyse the causes which lead to a result, ascribe to one or two events, occurring concurrently with an effect which makes them anxious or distresses them, the whole effect of which they complain. The event may have no relation to the phenomenon on which they rely, it may have a slight relation to it, it may have a partial relation to it, but be only one in a considerable congeries of causes, of which the principal remain undetected. Now the principal factor in the progressive decline of the labourer's condition was, as I have more than once stated, the issue of base money by Henry and Edward.

When the prices of the necessaries of life rise, the wages of labour do not rise with them. Even under the best conditions of labour this will not be found to be the case, or, what is the same thing to the economist, given a fixed order of things, under which the labourer is restrained from seeking employment in the best market, has his wages defined for him by a hostile authority, is made—as in the case of the agriculturist—the residuum of all labour, and is compensated by supplementary allowances raised by the taxation of occupiers, as under the Poor Law, the exaltation in the price of food is never compensated by a corresponding increase in the rate of wages, or, indeed, of the supplementary allowances. By contrast with the facts which prevailed before 1640, the labourer's service sank to the worst scale of remuneration during the first half of the seventeenth century, for the price of food increased, while wages remained stationary. By contrast with what prevailed during the first three-quarters of the eighteenth century, the wages of the labourer were again depressed during the last quarter of the eighteenth and the first quarter of the nineteenth centuries, when the old rates continued, and wheat kept rising ; for the average price between 1801 and 1810 was 96s. 4d., or more than double that which existed in the worst decade in the first half of the seventeenth century. At this time it is true that something slightly analogous to Henry's base money occurred—the issue of inconvertible paper; but the poverty of the poor was practically unalleviated, their wages only nominally improved, the assessment of their earnings unchanged, and no thought whatever was taken of their condition by the Legislature, unless it be that the attempt to repress by atrocious penal laws the violence which their unparalleled sufferings drove them occasionally to commit may be called thought.

As, therefore, wages do not rise with prices, no crime against labour is more injurious than any expedients adopted on the part of government which tend to raise prices. Unluckily for them, many working people have been misled by interested sophistry into believing that high prices for employers mean good wages for workmen. I do not deny that if an artificial stimulus is given to some particular industry, the demand for the produce of which is limited but continual, and the craftsmen in which are also limited, such a calling may get enhanced wages for a short time. But others soon crowd into the calling, and very speedily the thing is made dearer, and the producer remains no better off, having lost in the interval the knowledge which competition gives as to the best conditions under which industry can be exercised. But it is idle to argue that such an artificial stimulus can be given to every kind of industry. Were it universal, the country would be debarred from all intercourse with foreign commerce, and the legislature would raise a blockade round the ports far more effective than anything which the most successful belligerent could enforce. If it be partial, it will either affect all consumers or some. If all, it induces a universal scarcity without benefiting any one, for internal competition is sure to do its work on profits and wages; if some, it simply narrows the area of consumption, and with even more rapid results on profits and wages. These elementary principles, which one is almost ashamed to allege, could be illustrated by a thousand facts.

The case is rather more difficult when, in a country where

labour is free and mobile, a marked addition is made to the currency, in the only form in which the addition can be made, a debased coinage, or a large increase of circulating credit. Here we find temporarily all the appearances of great industrial activity,—wages rise, profits are large, at least when the labourer is free to choose his locality and his employer, though wages never rise to the level of profits. But the benefit is only for a time, and generally for a very short time. The labourer is the first to lose his advantage. Then profits shrink, and ultimately the collapse ensues, with its disappointments, its bitterness, and its degradation. The English labourer, indeed, has had little experience of such advantages as come from inflation, though something analogous to it occurred in 1873, when the capitalists made much money, and circulated a great many calumnies about the hands. But in the sixteenth century, whatever advantage ensued, was entirely on the side of the employers, on those who could interpret a base currency, could make the labourer pay for their commission on the exchange, and could succeed in permanently degrading him.

The first half of the seventeenth century is a magnificent political drama, in which the stage of public life in England is crowded with those historical characters on whom the better off and more educated of the English people dwell with a peculiar and lasting interest. We seem to see before us the Scottish king who had dropped into the English throne, who looked and spoke like a fool, but was not such a fool as he looked and spoke, with his strange brogue, his strange manners, his named and unnamed vices; and his son, who seemed grave and wise, but was hotbrained and foolish, proud and false, the type of those unlucky liars who are always found out. Then there is the first leader of the constitutional opposition, Phelips, and the wily but dangerous counsellor of the court, Cecil. There is Carr, with his wife, one of the harlots of the House of Howard, who had so bad an eminence in the century; and the grim Coke, loyal to the law and himself; and Bacon, whose splendid reputation has obscured the baseness of his life; the shrewd Cranfield, who almost made

James absolute; and Buckingham, who ruined the Treasurer, and bringing his schemes to nought, assisted in pulling down that which Cranfield had laboriously striven to build up; and behind, below, but infinitely above these, are those men of genius whose writings are the choicest treasures of the human race and the special pride of the English tongue, for the same generation witnessed the maturity of Shakespeare and the precocious intellectual wealth of Milton. As time passes on, the whole energy of the nation is concentrated on the struggle between absolutism and free institutions, free, alas! only for the few, but these, as yet, the best types of our race. The rare learning of Selden, the grave, inflexible patriotism of Eliot, the dexterous tact of Pym, the resolute gentleness of Hampden, the stern prescience of St. John, the wise moderation of Bedford, and, ultimately, the military genius and clear foresight of Cromwell, were to be arrayed against the perfidy of Charles, the passionate bigotry of Laud, the fierce energies of Strafford, against the herd of Finches and Noys, against bullies from the Thirty Years' War and pettifoggers on the Bench. The age was so dramatic, the men were so typical, that Hyde was able in his first exile to sketch their portraits as no one has sketched individuals since, because men were so individual; for the imaginative drama had died out, since living men were more characteristic than the subtlest pictures of the poet. There has been and there will be no period in English history which commands and deserves such attention as the first fifty years of the seventeenth century, for memory sees gods ascending out of the earth.

By the middle of the century there were probably four millions of people in England and Wales, for hardships and poverty do not always check the growth of population. The half at least of these lived by weekly wages. There are no annals of these people, of their work and their sufferings, except in the record of their wages and the cost of their living. We see the characters on the stage, and a little more, but nothing of those who enabled these great actors to play their parts, or of the work which was being done behind the scenes. History, which crowds its canvas with these great names, tells us nothing of the people. But they who take note of the pittance which the peasant or artizan earned, and of the cost at which he spent his wages on his needful food, can interpret the hardships of his lot, the poverty of his life, the barrenness of his labour, the growing hopelessness of his condition. The eager spirits who crowded into the House of Commons, the mounted yeomen who rode with Hampden, the men who fought and won at Marston Moor and Naseby, thought no more of the peasant and the workman, had no more care for bettering him, than the Irish patriots of 1782 cared for the kernes and cottiers on whose labours they lived. For in the midst of this battle of giants, when the king was made subject first, and his foe, the parliament, followed him in submission to the great army which Cromwell wielded as dexterously as a swordsman does his weapon, the English people who lived by wages were sinking lower and lower, and fast taking their place in the contrast with the opulence which trade and commerce began, and manufacturing activity multiplied, as the beggarly hewers and drawers of prosperous and progressive England. In 1651, the magistrates of Essex in quarter sessions at Chelmsford fixed the wages of artizans and labourers at 1*s.* 6*d.* and 1*s.* a day respectively; and this was the price which they generally secured. The price of wheat in this year was nearly 50*s.* a quarter.

I have little doubt that during the civil wars and the Protectorate there was some little stirring among the labourers. Their wages were raised, as I have said, fifty per cent. above what they stood at in the times which preceded these civil convulsions. It is probable, too, that trade and manufactures made progress; it is certain that agriculture did. It was natural that labour should seek after a better market, and should acquire some mobility. The government of the Protector was not likely to stop this movement, and it is plain that labour began to stir. But the Restoration came, the landed interest became dominant; the principle that the crown and the parliament should be employed in the interest of the landlord and the trader was stereotyped, and the law of parochial settlement was forthwith enacted. This law consummated the degradation of the labourer. It made him, as it has left him, a serf without land, the most portentous phenomenon in agriculture. It applied equally to the artizan, but he was able to extricate himself at an earlier period from the toils of this hateful law.

The Act 13, 14 Car. II., cap. 12 (1662), begins with a hypocritical preamble, that it was enacted for the good of the poor, for the correction of rogues and vagabonds, and for the proper employment of such as were legally chargeable to the parish of their settlement, and so empowers the churchwardens and overseers of any parish into which a person comes and occupies a tenement of less than ten pounds annual value, within forty days of such a person's coming, to apply to a justice of the peace for the removal of such a person to his place of legal settlement, under the hands of two justices. The person in question may, however, give security that he will not become chargeable, and may in any case appeal from the justice's decision to quarter sessions, *i.e.*, from Herod to Pilate. The Act, however, permits, with tender care for the farmer's interest, that strangers may, under proper precautions, be employed in harvest work.

The great Revolution, which established the authority of Parliament, put an end to arbitrary power, and relieved the consciences of those who could not accord themselves to the worship of the English Church, brought no liberty to the peasant and artizan. It stereotyped their servitude by constraining (3 William and Mary, cap. 11) that notice of newcomers should be published after service in Church. Labourers had ceased to be factors in political action, and are simply ignored for a century or more. But an Act of William III., 8 and 9 cap. 30 (1697), recognises the effect of the law of settlement passed thirty-five years before. It allows that persons are imprisoned in their place of settlement, where they cannot get work, though work may be wanted elsewhere, where the increase of manufactures would employ more hands, and that the provision of the Act of 1662, requiring the new-comer to give security that he would not be chargeable to the parish of his new residence, confines them to live in their own

28

parishes. It therefore permits churchwardens or overseers, who acknowledge their contingent liability, to give licenses to those who might wish to migrate, the effect of the license being that, if the incomer became chargeable, he could be forthwith removed with his children, even though they had been born in the new settlement. It is superfluous to say that such licenses would be looked on with suspicion, as expedients to relieve a parish of its quota of poor. Hence it became customary for those who employed foreign labour to give certificates of indemnity to the parish (often to a considerable amount, £100 or more) that they would bear the risk of the new comer's chargeability, the recognisance being stored in the parish chest. The effect of the law of parochial settlement was not only to annex the labourer to the parish of his residence, and to make him a serf. Those persons who possessed the whole of a parish took care, whenever they could, to pull down cottages on their estate, and rely on labour from a distance. By this system they hired labour at quarter sessions rates, *i.e.*, at factitiously low wages, while the parish of the man's residence had to supplement his wages and to bear all those contingencies which were enhanced by the labourer being constrained to travel a considerable distance to his work in all weathers. The law of settlement, therefore, not only fixed the tenant to the soil, but enabled the opulent landowner to rob his neighbour, and to prematurely wear out the labourer's health and strength. All this, too, was done when the patriots and placemen chattered about liberty and arbitrary administration, and fine ladies and gentlemen talked about the rights of man, and Rousseau, and the French Revolution, and Burke and Sheridan were denouncing the despotism of Hastings. Why at his own doors at Beaconsfield Burke must have daily seen serfs who had less liberty than those Rohillas, whose wrongs he described so pathetically and dramatically.

Most writers of the eighteenth century take the law of parochial settlement as a matter of course. There were persons who, such as Alcock and Burn, took a different view from the complacent landowners and farmers, but above all

Adam Smith. The former dwell upon the effects which the law of parochial settlement and chargeability had on the condition of the poor; but the great philosopher of social science detects the inherent injustice of the system. "To remove a man," says Smith, "who has committed no mis-demeanour from the parish where he chooses to reside, is an evident violation of natural liberty and justice, and an oppression, to which the people of England, though jealous of their liberty, but like the people of most other countries, never rightly considering in what it consists, have for more than a century together suffered themselves to be exposed without a remedy." The people of England have a very just view of what constitutes their own liberties when they are in a position to vindicate them, and can bring sufficient force to bear upon the machinery by which those liberties have been outraged and may be restored, but which has had no very great consideration for unrepresented and powerless interests. It is generally vain to expect political justice on behalf of those who can by their own action bring no pressure to bear on Parliament. And this is as much matter of modern as it has been of past experience.

It is one of the commonplaces of an ignorant optimism to allege that the remedy is supplied by taking away the cause of the disease; but the maxim that the effect ceases when the cause ceases, is true in inorganic nature only, and not always true there. The present condition of English society, its violent contrasts of opulence and penury, of profligacy protected by law and misery neglected by law, is the outcome of causes which have had a longer pedigree than the recorded generations of any family. The people of this country have become what they are by reason of events and acts which it is the duty of the genuine economist to discover, as contrasted with the economist who constructs a system out of a few axioms and a multitude of postulates. The reproach of political economy is that it is a hard and dry system, which has no sympathies, and only proposes to suffering humanity a bundle of unwelcome truths which it affirms to be natural laws. In many cases these are neither truths nor laws, but paradoxes, which have not even the merit of experimental inductions, but at the best are doubtful tendencies elevated to the rank of principles. I cannot take up any ordinary work on political economy without finding in every page a dogma which is controverted by facts, and, with the great exception of Adam Smith, I know no writer in England who has been at the pains to verify what he confidently affirms by the evidence of what has actually taken place. Mr. Mill is an ardent advocate of human liberty, and deserves all honour for his labours on behalf of it, but I do not remember that throughout his work on political economy he has been at the pains to point out how powerful a factor the law of parochial settlement has been in bringing about the unthrift and recklessness of the working classes, or how it has stereotyped improvidence and justified incontinence.

No trifling percentage of the funds collected for the maintenance of the poor was expended in litigation on the cases which sprang out of the Act of Charles II. It was an evil inheritance to the English people, perhaps the worst Act of the worst Parliament which ever sat, but it was a Potosi, an Eldorado to the lawyers. Many a barrister owed his place in Parliament and on the Bench to his skill in arguing settlement cases, to the ingenuity with which he was able to tighten the bonds on the peasant. The wealthy landowners clung to it with desperate tenacity, for it increased their rents at the expense of the occupiers and the poor. What mattered it to them that the English peasant's life was aged soon after his prime, if they could get cheap labour and increasing rents? The whole force of law was for nearly two centuries directed towards the solution of this problem, How much oppression can the English people endure, how much privation, misery, starvation, without absolutely destroying the labour on which growing rents depended? We, in our generation, though a portion of this evil has been prevented for the future, inherit the outcome of these two centuries, and with it problems of the gravest kind daily pressing for solution, and to which it is idle to offer the nostrums of over-population, emigration, competition, and the other formularies of an ideal society.

Towards the conclusion of the eighteenth century, the Berkshire magistrates, struck with the appalling discrepancy between wages and the price of food,—for the labour of the peasant could only procure him for several years one-eighth of the amount of wheat which the same person could have earned before 1540,—met and proposed, not that the mischievous law of Elizabeth which established quarter sessions wages should be repealed, or that the infamous law of parochial settlement should be done away, but that able-bodied labourers should have their wages supplemented by allowances from the overseer, proportionate to the number of their children or the general charges of their family. By this means they would be able to prevent a general increase of wages, to fix the wages of the single and the childless at a low amount, and compel all occupiers to contribute towards the cost of agricultural operations. This expedient, sanctioned by the courts, and, indeed, implied by 9 Geo. I., cap. 7, and 22 Geo. III., cap. 83, was known as the allowance system, and has been criticised adversely, not for its manifest harshness and injustice in giving that as charity which was due for work, but because it removed a check on population, at that time not much more than one-third of the number which now subsists in infinitely greater comfort in England than the lesser number did at the beginning of the century.

The English Poor Law would have ultimately devoured the rent of all open parishes, that is, those in which there were many owners, and consequently the possibility of housing the poor, and have enormously exalted the rent of all close parishes, *i.e.*, those in which there was one owner only, who cleared off every cottage on his domain, had it not been for the almost simultaneous discovery of steam power and the substitution of machine for hand-loom weaving. The capitalist inventors of these processes found that they wanted labour (though at first it appeared that the discoveries would dispense with labour), and were therefore indifferent to the contingencies of an unlicensed settlement. But it may be doubted whether their discoveries were an immediate boon to labour. The parochial system of relief must have been condemned long before it was imperfectly abandoned, when the system of close and open parishes had been thoroughly developed and the outrageous injustice of the practice had been exhibited in its fulness. The wages of the mill-hand were settled by the justices, like those of the artizan and peasant. Children and women were worked for long hours in the mill, and the Arkwrights and Peels and a multitude more built up colossal fortunes on the misery of labour. Any attempt on the part of workmen to combine for the purpose of selling their labour at better rates was met with stern repression, any overt act with sharp punishment. The English workmen earned all the wealth and bore nearly all the cost during that long war on which the fortunes of manufacturers and landowners, the glory of statesmen and generals, were founded. High profits were extracted from the labour of little children, and the race was starved and stunted while millowners, landowners, and stock-jobbers collected their millions from the toils of those whose wages they regulated and whose strength they exhausted. The student of economical forces can tell whence that wealth came by which England stood almost single-handed against Europe, and subsidized the wretched governments whom Napoleon humiliated,—governments which were saved by their subjects, but who repaid these subjects with the Holy Alliance, a name, after that of the League of the Public Good, which was the most hypocritical lie ever forged in the devil's chancery. The story of the workman's sufferings is told by Mr. Porter in his " Progress of the Nation."

At last, and not at its deepest midnight, a change began. The laws directed against the right of workmen to combine together in order to sell their wages in the best market, which had lasted for nearly five centuries, were repealed in 1824. So was the Quarter Sessions assessment of wages. The workman was not indeed free to find his market, for the law of parochial settlement remained, as the shadow of it remains to this day. But a trade union ceased to be a crime. It was no longer forbidden by law. It was not, indeed, under the protection of law; and I conceive that much of the savagery which for a long time characterized the conduct of trade unions was due to the outlawry under which those wholesome institutions were placed.

For nearly five centuries the legislature had declared that labour partnerships, that is, associations of working men formed for the purpose of selling their labour collectively to the best advantage, were under the ban of the law. The motive for this repression was never concealed. It was designed in order to increase and secure rents and profits at the cost of wages. For two centuries it failed, for nearly three it succeeded. The experience of the English workman had been of its success. It was therefore in human nature that he should believe in the efficacy of that which the legislature had so long striven to repress. It is commonly noted that those men who have been persecuted are more apt to be intolerant, when the persecution has passed away, than those who have never been oppressed. It is much more reasonable, then, that those who have been denied a right should conceive that the right is of inestimable value and should overrate its efficacy. Stolen waters are sweet, says the Hebrew apothegm, and bread eaten in secret is pleasant. But such joys are as nothing to the early delight of obtaining a liberty which has hitherto been forbidden. One has a right also to ask a reason for any restraint put on us. A workman might have laid out his money better at his master's tally shop than at the village store. But he objected to being forced to buy there, and rightly. The public-house may be a convenient place even for a total abstainer to receive his wages in, but a master should not be allowed, and latterly has not been allowed, t elect such a place, and constrain his workmen to take their money there, for all the Liberty and Property Defence League may say.

Eleven years after the repeal of the Acts against combination the new Poor Law was enacted. The change was needed, but it should have followed, not preceded, the repeal of the Corn Laws. The Corn Laws were defended on the ground that if they raised the price of food the Poor Law assured the peasant his subsistence from the land. The Act of 1835 took away this right, except under hard conditions, but it left the artificial scarcity. The result was that for once in English history a genuine communistic movement took root in the minds of the English workmen, for Chartism had only a political mask, the principal object of the organization being the repeal of the new Poor Law. When the Corn Laws were repealed, the movement collapsed. If it be ever revived, the motive force will be the laws and customs which direct the devolution and permit the settlement of land; laws and customs which are barbarisms, and would be infinitely grotesque, if they were not infinitely mischievous and infinitely dangerous. Already there is an ominous sympathy with the theory for making that a national estate which Englishmen have been studiously excluded from sharing by ordinary purchase as private owners. A political interest, like a political party, may seem to be strong when it is, after all, on the edge of a precipice. If it topples over, strength and weakness are all one.

Three processes have been adopted by the working classes, each of which has had a vast, and should have an increasing influence in bettering the condition of labour and making the problem of dealing with individual distress, however caused, easier and readier. They should be viewed by statesmen with unqualified favour, and be treated by working men as the instruments by which they can regain and consolidate the best interests of labour. They are trade unionism, or, as I prefer to call it, labour partnership; co-operation, or the combination in the same individuals of the function of labour and capital; and benefit associations, or the machinery of a mutual insurance society. So important do I conceive these aids to the material, intellectual, and moral elevation of the working classes to be, that I would, even at the risk of being thought reactionary, limit the privileges of citizenship, the franchise, parliamentary and local, to those, and those only, who entered into these three guilds—the guild of labour, the guild of production and trade, and the guild of mutual help. Nor do I think it extravagant to believe that were those associations rendered general, and finally universal, the social problems which distress all and alarm many would ultimately arrive at a happy solution. The first and third are only revivals of ancestral practice, the second is not very unlike the habit which prevailed in ages which I hope I have made in some degree familiar. I must, however, advert to them in another chapter, for this is already unduly long. Only let me assure my readers, that though it is a foolish dream to think that everything was better in the past, it is arrogant presumption to conclude that all progress is a modern acquisition, and that we can complacently despise the wisdom of our ancestors. Would that we could unite the opulence of the fifteenth century to the civilization of the nineteenth, and diffuse or distribute both.

CHAPTER XVI.

ENGLISH HUSBANDRY FROM THE RISE IN PRICES.

Identity of Agricultural Operations for Four Centuries—The Three Course System—The Communal Field a Loss—Enclosures in Early Times—The Price of Wool and Sheep Feeding—Causes Stimulating the Practice—Latimer's Account of Farmers—The Tenant's Charges and Profits Equalized, except in Labour on Land—The Margin for Increased Rent—The College Act of 1576—Fines on Renewal—The Monks and Fines—Their Adoption by Corporations and Private Owners—The Successive Tenancies of Lease on Fine, of Repairing Lease, and of Tenancies at Will—The Pamphlet of W. S.— The Cultivation of Hops—The Source of Better Agriculture, Holland—The War of Dutch Independence—Its Effects—The Truce of 1609—Agriculture in Herefordshire, 1610, and Vaughan—Gabriel Plattes, his Comments on the Tenant Farmer—The True Place of Rent—Blith and Hartlib—The Growth of Opulence after the Restoration—The County Assessments of 1636 and 1693—Houghton's Tables—Gregory King's Estimates of Population, Income, and Savings—Productive and Unproductive Classes—The Information this Gives as to English Society—The Origin of Savings—The Restoration of the Currency and the Bank of England.

THERE is no reason to believe that English husbandry was improved or even altered for nearly four centuries, *i.e.*, from the thirteenth to the beginning of the seventeenth century. There is even some reason to conclude, if we can trust the complaints of the first English writer on agriculture, Fitzherbert, whose two works were published at the latter end of the first quarter of the sixteenth century, that in certain directions husbandry had retrograded, that the crops of his day had become less plentiful than they were in a previous age, and that the use of such fertilizers as the skill of the age recognized was declining. This author expressly states that the uncertainty of the tenant's position, the risk that he may not recover his outlay, and the power which the landlord of a tenancy on a short lease had of raising the rent against a sitting tenant, were discouragements to the practice of marling and liming lands, and that the alarms and risks of the sitting tenant were paralleled by the slovenliness and want of energy which were now exhibited by the freeholder. Fitzherbert is the first to raise the complaint, reiterated by writers on agriculture in one form or another for two centuries and a half, that the danger to English husbandry lies in the insecurity of the tenant, in the rapacity of the landlord, and in the impossibility of developing self-reliance and courage under the terms of a precarious tenure.

The process of English agriculture during all this period was a three course system—of wheat in the first year, of a crop of oats or barley or beans, peas or vetches in the second, and a bare fallow in the third. This is the course regularly prescribed by the authorities at Christ Church, Canterbury, to their bailiffs on their numerous and valuable estates in Kent. The writer on husbandry in the thirteenth century, to whom I have already referred, contemplates the possibility of land being of such exceptional fertility as to bear an annual crop of corn. But I have found no such estate, though I have examined the records of the best and most careful cultivation on some of the most fertile land in England. The course, indeed, was inevitable. During all the period on which I am commenting the English farmer had nothing but arable crops, meadow hay, the pasture of closes, and the run of common grass to depend on. He had no winter roots and no artificial grasses with which to vary his rotation. The system of open fields made it impossible to pen sheep upon land, even if the grass on the balks or the weeds and straw left on the stubbles had been sufficient forage. Sheep were kept under cover from November to May because there was no forage for them out of doors. For the same reason cattle were housed. Animal manure was of the highest value, and was saved with care. The farmer was advised, when he was about to let his sheep out of fold, to drive them gently for a while round the fold, in order that they might add to his stock of manure within the fold during this exercise.

It is perhaps remarkable that systematic steps were not taken at an early period in the direction of that form of enclosure under which the lands in common arable or lammas fields might be assigned, to the advantage of any one, in severalty, according to the extent of each person's holding. At an early period it was recognised that land held in severalty was worth 25 per cent. more than land of equal quality held in the lammas field; and that when such distributions and assignments were made, the land was found to be far more serviceable. But the habits of agriculturists are very conservative, and the smaller proprietors had, or believed they had, a considerable advantage in the run of feed in which they shared when the crops were gathered. There were beyond question numerous enclosures in the fifteenth century. Much of this had been wood, always considered, even when pasture and pannage were permitted within it, as much more the lord's property than the ordinary common of pasture was, the fee simple of which, subject to communal rights, was also in the lord. But it appears that a considerable enclosure of ordinary common of pasture went on, under one plea or another, in the fifteenth and sixteenth centuries, particularly in the latter, for complaints are rife about the practice. It is said that Ket's Norfolk rebellion was due to discontent about enclosures in that county, and that similar disaffection was manifested elsewhere. It is probable that other and stronger motives were at work; but the statement that the peasantry were stirred to sedition by these practices is sufficient evidence of the fact that the practice was general.

For the first thirty years of the fifteenth century, wool was at a very high price, being 8s. $1\frac{1}{4}d$. for the tod of 28 lbs. During the next 110 years, the average price of the same quantity is 5s. $4\frac{1}{2}d$. In the forty years from 1541 to 1580, the price is 17s. 4d., *i.e.*, it had risen more than threefold in price. Wool growing, therefore, was the most profitable employment of agricultural capital. In the existing state of the English currency, and till its reformation by Elizabeth, it was also the most advantageous means by which the producer could obtain the benefit of good merchantable

money. I cannot, indeed, assert that the extraordinary
price of the tod of wool during Edward's reign, when it was
over 20*s.*, can be interpreted in good coin, but it is plain that
the stimulus of so exalted a price, four times the old average,
must have had its effect on agriculture. Even the moderate
rise of about eighteen per cent. in Henry's reign had powerfully assisted the development of sheep-farming in England,
and had drawn the attention of the king and the legislature
to the reputed evils of the practice; but the stimulus of later
prices was still stronger. Besides, a violent change in the
ownership of large tracts of land had followed the dissolution
of the monasteries, the confiscation of the guild lands, and
to some extent the spoliation of the secular clergy. The
new owners got the land, under conditions, burdened with
the leases which the monks had, foreseeing the coming storm,
made with their tenants. But unlike the old owners, the
adventurers of the Reformation were not in the older sense
of the word capitalist landlords, and to such persons sheep-
farming was the easiest and most profitable mode of increasing their revenues. The dissolution was virtually a new
conquest, and the successors of the monks had no motive
in dealing with their new tenants beyond that of interpreting
their own interests in the harshest manner.

Complaints made about the spoliation of the tenants' improvements and good husbandry by a penal rise in rents,
with the alternative of eviction and loss, are, as we have seen,
made by Fitzherbert before the king and the pope quarrelled,
and while the dissolution of the monasteries was only a talk
in the air, as it had been for more than a century. The complaint of Latimer in his Thirty-first Sermon is well-known.
"His father," he says, "had a farm of £3 or £4 a year," that
is, according to the regular rent of land at the time, of from
120 to 160 acres arable, with considerable communal rights
of pasture. "On this he employed six labourers. He had
walk for a hundred sheep, and his wife milked thirty cows,
which also, of course, must have mainly subsisted in
summer on the common pasture. He served on summons
as a mounted yeoman, and repaired to the king's banner

at Blackheath, receiving pay when he had joined his troop. He gave his daughters portions, £5 or 10 marks a piece, kept hospitality, and gave alms to the poor, from the profits of his tenancy. The present farmer gives £16 a year for the same holding, and has no surplus for the king's taxes, for his own savings, for his children's advancement, or for the poor." On such a tenancy and with such a rent the bishop's father might, in the cheap days of the previous generation, have lived plentifully and saved considerably.

An examination into the prices of the time will show that the tenant farmer, no improvement having been effected in the art of agriculture, and no economy in production being therefore possible, could only afford a very moderate increase of rent to his landlord if he were to remain in the same condition as he was in before. His corn, his wool, his cattle and sheep, his dairy products got far higher prices. But his outgoings, with one exception, were exalted in just the same proportion as his increased takings were. In point of fact, if we exclude from the average of his corn prices such years as 1551, 1555-6, 1563, 1573, 1576-7, which were years of positive scarcity, when the high prices only partially compensated for deficient harvests, the cost of his necessary expenditure, being greater, relatively, than the increased price which he obtained for his products, would leave him a very narrow margin for a possible increase of rent, an increase which might not be discovered by a fair landlord, and would certainly be disputed by a tenant. If any person is at the pains to draw up a balance sheet of a farmer's probable receipts and expenditure, calculated on the known prices of all which he needed, and on the equally well known market value of what he had to sell, he will find that, were the farmer to keep his old position, the increase of rent would be very small; and if such an inquirer were to turn, as I have been able to turn, to the actual rents paid and received by landlords for the occupation of land which had been rented before and after the change, he would find that a fair landlord got very little increase of rent during the sixteenth century.

In one item of cost his outlay would certainly be lessened.

He paid less for wages. But when we examine the outgoings
of such a tenancy as that occupied by Latimer's father, we
shall find that the gains here were inconsiderable. On a large
estate, such as used to be cultivated by the bailiff of a
capitalist landowner, the cost of labour is a considerable
sum. The landowner, besides the bailiff, whose time was
generally occupied by superintendence, and who did, I have
good reason to think, little more labour than that of sowing,
which was demanded of him, had to hire two or three carters,
two or three ploughmen, a shepherd or two, to make an
establishment for the dairy and cheese room, besides en-
gaging cowherds and other hinds. The labour of mowing
and harvesting, of thrashing and winnowing is generally
hired. But Latimer's father would have guided the plough,
sowed the seed, done most of the sheep-shearing, have taken
his part at least in the corn harvest, while his wife milked
the cows and superintended the dairy with her daughters.
The sons of such a husbandman could have done generally
the rest of the farm work. The six hands which he employed,
a complete staff for the extent which I have assigned to his
arable farm, being, with the farmer and his wife, one man to
every twenty acres, or precisely the labour which Arthur
Young, two centuries afterwards, thought was the full quota
of generous and effective husbandry, must have been employed for the greatest part of their time on work connected
with the common pasture, the carts, and the sheep-fold.
Now if, as is highly probable, these men in later times,
always provided there was room for their employment, were
boarded as well as paid wages, the expense of the former
part of the bargain would rise with the rise in prices, and the
saving on the latter part would be trivial. I concluded from
divers calculations that one estate which brought in rent to the
amount of £12 under the old system could not have been
raised to more than £16 to £18, even under the Act of 1576;
and on examining an account of the rent actually paid in the
existing accounts of its owners, I found that, in 1590, the rent
was £16 17s. 6d.

The Act of 1576 was passed in order to remedy the inelasticity of rents in the case of certain corporations. It provided that the colleges of Oxford and Cambridge, and those of Eton and Winchester, should receive a third of their rents in wheat and malt, or their equivalent values in money, at the best price on the market days of the four towns, Oxford, Cambridge, Windsor, and Winchester, which were nearest to Lady-day and Michaelmas. The converse of the rule prescribed in this celebrated law, from which all the information as to corn prices in the seventeenth and eighteenth centuries has hitherto been derived, had long been the practice in the Eastern Counties, where the land-owners had received part of their rents in kind under the covenants of their leases, the tenant stipulating to pay in wheat at 6s. 8d. the quarter, in malt at 4s., or in sheep at 2s., when the market price was greatly in excess of these rates. The merit of Elizabeth's Act is given to Burleigh. He copied it, I make no doubt, from a practice which had been familiar to him when he had been a student at Cambridge, and probably at the instance of those who found how difficult it was to increase rents. The rule which was prescribed in the case of a few corporations became the custom with others. But a commoner method, and one which in course of time became very characteristic of tenancies, especially those held from corporations, though far from infrequent in the case of individuals, was that of the fine on the renewal of a lease.

The circumstances of the case, as I have already indicated, made it difficult to procure increases of rack-rent, except very slowly. The population, especially that which was engaged in agriculture, was unwilling or unable to move, for law was powerfully assisting custom in stereotyping the distinction between town and country, artizan and farm-hand. Tenants from a distance were not to be expected, and tenants on the spot were, I suspect, very slowly willing to accept a rise in rents, except under strong compulsion. Either Latimer was exaggerating the case when he speaks of a farmer within his knowledge and in a single generation sub-mitting to a fourfold rise in rent, or the case must have been too exceptional to become the basis of an inference, as most persons have made it. That a rise in rents was directly effected I have no doubt. That in the course of the seventeenth century they were increased six or eight fold is exceedingly probable, if not certain. But that it required strong and continuous pressure to effect this result is more certain, and I am disposed to believe that the cases in which rents were earliest enhanced were those of the monastic lessees, when their terms came to an end.

The monks are credited with having foreseen the catastrophe which was impending, and with having invented or adopted the Fine. The customary tenants, who were the lineal successors of the serf, had always been liable to fines on alienation, which must at first have been excessively rare, and on succession, which must have been regular, and soon became fixed. In course of time and during the land hunger of the fifteenth century, persons of free, knightly, perhaps of noble origin, became purchasers of copyholds, and thereupon liable to such incidents of villeinage as still remained, while they aided in extinguishing others, which were derogatory and obsolete. But fines were assuredly paid both on surrender and admission. The practice was copied in the grant of leases. One can quite understand how a fine on admission to a lease of lands for a term of years, for a life, or for lives, which became exceedingly common, universal in the case of corporations, and general in that of private owners, should be employed by the monasteries with a view to getting a considerable lump sum at the commencement of a lease, which should be drawn up for a lengthy term, in place of the mere handsel which such a fine originally was. Now it is plain that a tenant, who was informed that, at a certain period during the continuance of his lease, when it had a long time still to run, he might surrender and renew it on the same terms if he were willing to pay a sum down, would discover in such a bargain an advantageous arrangement for himself; and the landowner might in such a manner believe that he could virtually get a better and a less invidious rent than he could by running out the term and making a fresh bargain.

29

I do not find the renewable lease on customary rents, and on the payment of a fine in anticipation of rents, prior to the sixteenth century, though I have examined many hundred rent rolls, and in particular those of the corporations, which invariably adopted the practice as soon as ever the event of greater crops at less cost made a rise in natural or economical rent, at first possible and next necessary. These leases, known afterwards as beneficial leases, were universal in the case of some owners, and frequent among others, and were exceedingly common, I am persuaded, during the whole of the seventeenth century. They were succeeded, in the case of ordinary landowners, by the long lease of the eighteenth, in which the obligation of doing repairs is often put by bargain on the tenant, and in the nineteenth by the tenancy at will, or from year to year, the common form of English occupancy at present, with the old liability on the part of the landlord to effect the permanent improvements, the tenant being tied down to good husbandry only. These are the outcome of the inflated prices which prevailed during the period 1780-1820. These prices were due to the stimulus given to population by the discoveries of Watt, Arkwright, and others, and the growing demand for labour, the continuance of unpropitious seasons, the incidence of a great European war, and the existence of a restrictive corn law.

A remarkable pamphlet, long supposed to have been written by Shakespeare, and now known to be the work of William Stafford, was published in 1581. It is a dialogue between five persons, a husbandman, a manufacturer, a merchant, a knight, and a doctor, *i.e.*, a person who was more or less competent to interpret the facts. All complain—the husbandman, that arable land is enclosed and turned into pasture, that rents are raised and labour is unemployed; the manufacturer, that labour is dearer and labourers worse off; the merchant, that the towns are decaying, and customers are scarce at these enhanced prices; the knight, that in the universal exaltation of prices rent has by no means followed, and that they who live by their land are stinted, and find no remedy except in keeping land in their own hands and

storing it with stock. The doctor, who deals with the situation, states that he does not think matters would be mended
if a successful attempt were made to revert to the old prices
by proclamation or by law. It is allowed that commodities
are plentiful; the question is why prices are high, why complaints are general and employment scanty. The facts were
plain enough,—prices had been rapidly rising since 1576.

We are in a better position to interpret the facts of the
situation than an observer, however acute he might have
been, was at the time when Stafford's pamphlet was written.
There can be no doubt that the persons who profited most
by the rise in prices were the yeomen freeholders, cultivating
their own holdings, and the tenant farmers; that the land-
holders had a struggle, and a very severe one, in pressing
their rents up to the rate which should compensate them for
the enhanced prices which they paid in their capacity as
consumers; that the mercantile and manufacturing classes were
hardly able to find compensation in the comparative opulence
of the occupiers, as contrasted with the stint which those
who lived on rents and fixed incomes had to endure; and
that the working classes, as is always the case when prices
are advancing, were worst off of all. The rise in prices was
first effected by the dishonest and fraudulent act of the
Government. This lasted so long, that prices accommodated
themselves to the facts, and when the reform came, they had
become habitual. Occasions arise during which the plenty
of the seasons seems likely to depress the price of corn to
nearly its old level, as in the nine years 1564-72, when wheat
was 12s. 1d. a quarter on the average, *i.e.*, about double the
old price. Soon, however, the price went up steadily, as
that of all other commodities had gone up and was increasing.

There was only one direction in which English agriculture
at this time took a new step. This was in the cultivation
of the hop. The use of hops was borrowed from the Low
Countries, and was introduced into Eastern England at the
conclusion of the fifteenth century. The practice of growing
hops attracted the attention of the legislature in 1552, when

it was permitted under some restraints. The earliest literature on hop-planting in England is a work by one Reynold Scot published in 1576. The statements made in this treatise prove that the whole details of hop-growing, picking, drying, and packing were borrowed from some place in which the process had long been familiar.

The first movement in the direction of general agricultural improvement came, like that of hop-growing, from the Low Countries, now divided into two parts,—the obedient Netherlands, which Alva and Parma had entirely ruined, and the great Republic of Holland, which had now, after exertions the most heroic, the most sustained, the most useful in the whole history of mankind, achieved its independence. The struggle of the united Netherlands against the power of Spain is in the history of modern civilisation what the struggle of Greece against Persia was in that of antiquity. I do not, indeed, affirm that if Holland had been vanquished the results would have been so considerable to the human race as those which would have ensued if a different event had been recorded from the fields of Marathon and Platea and from the bays of Salamis and Mycale, and if the spirit of continental Greece had succumbed to the same force which extinguished the genius of Ionia. We know fairly well what would have been the consequence had Persia been victorious from the desolation and beggary which now reign in those seats of ancient culture which the Turk has occupied. We have fortunately been unable to discern what would have followed if the Jesuit and the Spaniard had subdued Amsterdam as they subdued Antwerp, if Holland had been delivered over to the Inquisition, for the success of the Dutch struggle lightened the yoke of the obedient provinces, as well as broke the strength of their oppressor. To the philosopher and the statesman, the square of the Binnenhof should be the holy place of modern Europe, because there the greatest problem of modern history was solved, and the greatest of deliverances planned and carried out. Unhappily for Holland, the genius of three generations of the House of Orange was believed to be hereditary, and the historical republic was handed over, in 1815, to a new royal family, which might indeed claim descent from William the Silent, but is much more closely akin to Paul of Russia. The genius of the House of Orange perished with our William the Third.

The Hollanders conferred infinite benefits on modern civilisation beyond those which were derived from the spectacle of their obstinate struggle for freedom. There is nothing which they did not teach. They were the first people who practised toleration for all religions, though they were not always faithful to their principles. They were scholars, jurists, diplomatists, and statesmen. They developed navigation and commercial enterprise; founded factories and ruled colonies. They discovered the principles on which trade with the East could be safely and continuously conducted. They were the inventors of modern banking and of modern finance. The experience and the success of Holland aroused the wonder, the emulation, the envy of other states. At one time it seemed as though the empires of the West and the East, of the Indies of Alexander and the Indies of Columbus would pass under their sway. Unhappily for them, the Dutch democracy, always swayed by the House of Orange, took the side of the Stuarts during the great civil war, and quarrelled with Puritan England. It is not remarkable that Charles II., who owed his safety, his very life, to the Dutch friends of his family, should have done his best after his restoration to ruin his benefactors, to stereotype hostility between the two great commercial powers of Western Europe, and to plan the partition of the republic.

We owe the improvements in English agriculture to Holland. From this country we borrowed, at the beginning of the seventeenth century, the cultivation of winter roots, and at that of the eighteenth century the artificial grasses. The Dutch had practised agriculture with the patient and minute industry of market gardeners. They had tried sucessfully to cultivate everything to the uttermost which could be used for human food, or could give innocent gratification to a refined taste. They taught agriculture and they taught gardening. They were the first people to surround their homesteads with flower-beds, with groves, with trim parterres, with the finest turf, to improve fruit trees, to seek out and perfect edible roots and herbs, at once for man and cattle. We owe to the Dutch that scurvy and leprosy have been banished from England, that continuous crops have taken the place of barren fallows, that the true rotation of crops has been discovered and perfected, that the population of these islands has been increased, and that the cattle and sheep in England are ten times what they were in numbers and three times what they were in size and quality. Even now the ancient agricultural skill of the Hollander is not extinct. The gardeners of Haarlem still purvey roots and bulbs of flowers for the civilised world, and there is much which the English agriculturist of the present day could learn with advantage from the industry, patience, and skill of the Dutch farmer, and perhaps will learn, when England is relieved from the curse of her present land system, and her tenant farmers till the land under the same guarantees as the Dutchman does.

The introduction of improvements in agriculture from Holland begins with the truce which James negotiated, very much to his credit, between Spain and Holland in 1609. The Spanish Government, though wholly unable to carry on the war, was very reluctant to acknowledge the independence of the revolted provinces, and the Dutch, who were perfectly willing to accept the reality of independence and peace, under any form or no form, agreed to the truce, with the certain conviction that when it was over they would be stronger than ever. Just at the time this truce was made, and before the changes came, one Vaughan, a Herefordshire gentleman, in a project which he published in 1610 for establishing waterworks in the "Golden Vale" of the Wye, gives a picture of the social condition of the district where he lives. He tells us, that stretching for a mile and a half on either side of his house are five hundred poor cottagers, who are entirely engaged in spinning flax, hemp, and hurds; that when the harvest is over, he has counted three hundred persons gleaning in one field. He observes that in the mountains certain provisions are very cheap, that one may buy twenty eggs for a penny, and a bullock in good condition for 26s. 8d. But he says that not two sermons had been preached in the Golden Vale for the last two centuries, that there were twenty-four parishes in the hundred, not one of which could maintain a preaching minister, and that the people in the Vale surfeit on salmon as the Northamptonshire men do on fat venison. He proposes that to relieve the poor and unemployed population, water power should be employed for manufactures, and that some thirty looms moved by the abundant stream should be set up for spinning and weaving woollen, flaxen, and hempen fabrics, and even silk, promising that in this way a market would be found for a far larger amount of agricultural produce than could be profitably raised or grown at present. It is worth noticing that this Herefordshire squire suggested the adoption of a process which did not become a factor in English industry for more than a century and a half after the publication of his proposals.

Among the advocates of a better agricultural system than had prevailed was Gabriel Plattes, whose work on English husbandry was published in 1638. Plattes was probably a Dutchman by descent. He was as unlucky a person as nearly every one has been who has tried from his own observation and experience to benefit English agriculture, for though his reputation was of the highest kind in his generation, he fell dead in London streets shirtless and starved. During his experience, rents had risen, agriculture had improved, and though, as I showed in my last chapter, the condition of the labourer had become progressively worse, I do not dispute the fact that the landlord's rent and the trader's profit, as Clarendon tells us, were greatly increased. The proof of the former, and the effect on such agricultural industry as was not secured on a freehold tenure, is to be found in the following passages from Plattes' treatise. He tells us (chap. iv.), " I see no reason why tenants at will, for life or a term of years, should be industrious, whereas the benefit of their labours is to fall into other men's purses, unless there be a contract between landlord and tenant, whereby a just share may redound to both parties *answerable to their merit,* which, if this were done, then would the husbandman be much stirred up to try experiments." Again in the seventh chapter he tells us, "There would be many improvements if there were a law that every tenant, if he were put out, should recover double his charges of the succeeding tenant, which also may be done by contract between landlord and tenant, if they could agree. And then men would labour cheerfully, as for their posterity, if they were sure that another should not reap where they have sown."

In Plattes' criticism on the tendencies of the English land system we have the strongest, though not the earliest, indications of that obstinate determination to keep the tenant farmer a slave to his landlord's greed, or caprice, or ambition, or vice, till the true agricultural interest, which is entirely distinct from that of the landowner, has been involved in temporary ruin. If, under foreign competition or from domestic folly, (provided only English industry can get its food in exchange for its labour or the products of its labour,) all agricultural rent vanishes, industry, which alone makes man, is none the worse, perhaps all the better. Rent is the result of the fact that man, by his labour, can earn what is worth in the market more than his labour can earn for him. In that sense, and in that sense only, labour is paid by labour. Capital is worthless without labour, *i.e.,* the labour of using capital wisely and discreetly, and labour is immovable without capital, *i.e.,* the fund belonging to one kind of labour, which gives the handicraftsman the power of getting food as his work goes on. But no human being need trouble himself about a landlord's rents, other, to be sure, than the landlord himself. The happiest state which the human race could conceive is such a mobility of labour and such an extension of the cultivable land and the productive industry which man gives to cultivable land, as to produce that plenty, in which rent finds no place. To mourn over the decline of rent is to regret that one has extinguished friction and loss in the machinery of human industry and social life. To rail at rent is silly, to declare that one would confiscate it is dis-

honest,—to seek out such a machinery of industry as would
reduce it to a minimum is the best service one can render to
mankind, is the best answer to the insolence of unmerited
wealth, and to the bitter discontent of starved and ill-paid
labour. To fight against nature is always folly, and rent is
as much nature as dirt and disease and misery are ; but to
remedy the evils of ignorance and vice, which always grow
the greatest rents, is the true medicine for social misery. The
most impudent hypocrite of all is the great proprietor, who
being a principal cause of the misery which he affects to
deprecate, would be disgusted and furious if he were to be
shown in his true colours, and so trusts to ignorance and sophistry when he laments the condition of the poor, but
secretly and steadily adds to their burdens. "The bane of
husbandry," says Plattes again, " is the uncertainty of their
tenures, as may be seen in Ireland at this time." One might
think that this author of the seventeenth century had been
writing in the nineteenth, just as when one reads Swift, one
might imagine that the words of those who have denounced
the tyranny and injustice of the Irish land system—now, we
may hope, evil things of the past—were ringing in our ears.
But the misery which the English people have borne, and the
dangers which they now run, while they still endure the
hateful and disastrous traditions of our social system, have
never failed to attract attention, and although as yet vain,
remonstrance and warning.

The fact that English agriculture was making rapid progress
in the seventeenth century, though unfortunately the progress
was accompanied by a marked depression in the labourers'
position, is proved by other comments of Plattes. " An acre
enclosed," he says, " is better than four acres in common."
" A load of pigeons' dung exchanged for a load of coals, and
carried sixteen miles, though it would have done harm where
it came from, would confer a double value on the land where
it was put." " I have seen a hundred loads of earth sold at
Hampstead at 1*s.* a load, and carried three or four miles to
higher ground, and with great advantage." "I have known
meadow land so improved by irrigation that though it was

worth only 10*s.* a year, it has grown £10 worth of hay in a
dry season, and I have seen land near London, on which
irrigation at the cost of a shilling has raised the value by a
pound." Plattes says that all land must have once been sea,
and that all valleys have at some time been channelled by
water. "In Devonshire," he tells us, "they carry sea sand
many miles on horseback to inland fields in order to break
the clays."

This intelligent and unfortunate author tells us that the
best wheat in England was grown in the vale of Belvoir, and
states that he has seen a sowing machine at work, which he
describes, the saving of which is 15*s.* an acre and with the
result of a better crop ; comments on the uncertainty which
attends a crop of hops, the price of which varies according
to the year from 20*s.* to £10 the hundred-weight; warns the
farmer of the loss which comes from allowing any drainage
from his manure; states that he has observed that rot in sheep
is most prevalent when beehives are light, *i.e.*, in cold and
wet springs, for he adds, that when May and June are wet,
sheep are more liable to rot than when the same weather
holds in July, August, or September; warns the shepherd
against " frim and frothy grass," and bids him " keep his flock
on high land in May and June," assuring him that if he does
this " the tenant never need lay the key under the door, and
bid good night to his landlord." But keen as Plattes' interest
is in the fortunes of the tenant, he urges that "no common
should ever be enclosed without leaving a cow's grass to every
cottage."

In 1649, Walter Blith wrote on English husbandry. The
particulars of his work are those commonplaces of agriculture which are found in all treatises of the time. But there is
one passage in the preface which he writes, the interest of
which is high, because it is continuous testimony to the mischief which every one detected in farmers' ordinary rents :
" If a tenant be at ever so great pains or cost for the improvement of his land, he doth thereby but occasion a great rack
upon himself, or else invests his landlord with his cost and
labour gratis, or at best lies at his landlord's mercy for requital,

which occasions a neglect of good husbandry, to his own, the land, the landlord, and the kingdom's suffering. Now this I humbly conceive may be removed if there were a law enacted whereby every landlord should be obliged, either to give him reasonable allowance for his clear improvement, or else suffer him or his to enjoy it so much longer as till he hath had a proportionable requital." One seems to be reading the platform of the Farmers' Alliance in the preface to a work on seventeenth-century husbandry, and the demand for an Act of Parliament which should not only affirm the principles of justice, but guarantee its details. This absence of security is the principal "prejudice," as Blith calls it, to the farmer's industry ; the second is the drowning of land by miller's privileges, a fruitful cause at the present day of periodical floods, and by far the most important fact to grapple with in the treatment of river basin drainage ; the third is the existence of common fields and the absence of enclosures ; and the fourth is the right of common without stint on the open pastures. Blith informs us that land lets from 1s. to 10s., from 10s. to 20s. an acre, while some of the very highest quality, I presume he means naturally warped meadow, from 20s. to £4. But these figures are probably exaggerated. We shall see that even in the eighteenth century the rent of land was not such as to reach these amounts.

But the most considerable and voluminous writer on husbandry in the seventeenth century was Simon Hartlib, a Dutchman by birth, though naturalised in England, who enjoyed and esteemed the friendship of Milton. Hartlib made it his business to explain and inculcate the various processes by which the Dutch had become the most successful agriculturists in Europe, and were instructing the rest of the world. His information extends over the whole range of agriculture, and his "Legacy," as he called his principal work, contains suggestions which he did not see put in practice during his own time, though they were adopted with such signal success in the next century.

To the farmer and the merchant, the seventeenth century was a period of great prosperity. The twelve years' truce between Spain and Holland expired in 1621, and the two countries went again into strife. But Spain was also engaged in the deplorable Thirty Years' War, the last and the most ferocious, the most atrocious and most destructive of the religious wars. The quarrel between Charles and his Parliament enforced neutrality on England, even had Charles wished to assist his brother-in-law. But during this period, when England alone of the western nations was at peace, there was naturally a period of high prices, of considerable commercial activity, and not a little agricultural progress. On this prosperity Clarendon comments. But he gives no true cause of it, and he does not know, or care to know, that it was accompanied by great suffering, terrible poverty, and continuous degradation of the working classes.

From the Restoration to the Revolution occurred another period of even greater prosperity, as far as the traders and agriculturists were concerned, corn prices being, on the whole, moderate in the thirty years from 1661 to 1690. But during this time foreign trade made extraordinary strides. The English colonies were rapidly becoming numerous and thriving in the New World, and the foundations of many opulent houses were being laid on successful commerce with the East, where the English had become the successful rivals of the Dutch, and had inherited the possessions of the Portuguese in India, and, with them, a footing on its western coasts. In fact, ignominious and dishonest as the government of England was, stained as the court was with libertinism and profligacy, low as was the literary condition of England, for it had become a poor copy of the immodesties which characterised French literature half a century before, the country was at peace, and the mass of Englishmen were active, energetic, and uncorrupted, of austere morals, and acute, persevering enterprize. Macaulay speaks of the reaction which followed on Puritanism. The reaction was only superficial, and characteristic of that class only to whom accident and the absurd parody of representation, called the House of Commons, gave prominence and power. The English people at heart was the Puritan England of Cromwell and Pym, as a few years proved. Had the Revolution been followed by a Reform Bill, the history of the nineteenth century would have been anticipated in the eighteenth.

In the year 1636, the various counties in England were assessed for the levy of ship-money. An examination of the estimate of taxation by the acreage of each county shows how wealth had been displaced in England after little more than a century and a quarter had elapsed, and curiously Charles's levy of ship-money is almost exactly six times as much as Henry's aid. Of course Middlesex, including London, is put at the highest assessment. In 1503, its assessment per acre is twice that of the nearest county to it in wealth, Oxfordshire. In 1636, it is nearly twelve times as much as that of its nearest neighbours, Hertford and Bedfordshire. Oxford occupies the 17th place in the counties; Norfolk, before the third, is now the 25th. On the other hand, Bucks, from being the 19th is now the 4th. Lincoln, which was the 10th county in opulence in the earlier list, is 31st in the later. Lancashire and Cumberland are still the poorest of the English counties, standing almost exactly on the same level absolutely and relatively as they occupied in the several centuries for which information of this kind has been discovered. The industries which made certain counties and districts opulent at the end of the fifteenth century had left them at the beginning of the seventeenth, and had not yet been localised in their later abodes.

The ship-money of 1636 was calculated to yield nearly £207,000, and had not been contested yet in the law courts. Taking the existing acreage of England and Wales, the tax amounted to £1 on every 174,447 acres. In 1693, an assessment of 4s. in the £ was imposed by Parliament to meet the charges of the war with France; and this was also distributed through the counties. The total was £1,977,714, and when assessed on the whole acreage of England and Wales amounts to £1 on each 18,923 acres. The proportion which London and Middlesex bear to the rest of the country is not materially altered, is, indeed, slightly less, for in 1636 it was assessed at about one-fifth of the whole amount, and, in 1693, its contribution is about a sixth. The most considerable change is that in the county of Surrey. In 1636 it was 18th in the list of contributors; in 1693 it comes after London and Middlesex. The purely agricultural counties have made considerable progress. Oxfordshire, which was 17th in 1636, is now 8th; Kent, which was 14th, is now 9th; Essex, which was 15th, is 7th; Norfolk, which was 25th, is 18th. On the other hand, Lancashire, though still one of the poorest counties, which stood nearly fifty per cent. below Westmoreland, has now become, acre for acre, three times as wealthy as that county; while York, which was more than twice as opulent as Westmoreland, by the same test, is now four times better off. This change must be ascribed to the growth of woollen manufactures in the latter, and the general growth of nearly all textile industries in the former county.

At the latter end of the century, one Houghton, an apothecary living near the Royal Exchange, conceived the plan of issuing a weekly paper, which should contain on one side some short essay on natural history, or agriculture, or manufactures; and on the other a price list of the different kinds of grain, collected from the principal towns of the kingdom. He continued the work, though with one short interruption, from 1691 to 1702, and seems to have been the inventor of systematic advertising. We may learn from his short essays that the growth of agriculture was leading to even more extensive enclosures than had hitherto been practised, and that the science of forestry was attracting considerable attention. Potatoes were being largely cultivated in Lancashire, whence they were spreading over the kingdom. He tells us that barley bread had been used by the people in dear times, but only through the scarcity of wheat, which had always been, in every part of England, the customary food of the people. Houghton was a Fellow of the Royal Society, and was probably the person for whose election that association apologised to Charles, who assured them that so far from being dissatisfied at the election of a tradesman, he should be only glad to see more of such a stamp as the person whom they had latterly taken into their number.

During the seventeenth century the population of England had doubled. It could not have been more than 2½ millions at the conclusion of Elizabeth's reign ; it was nearly 5½ at the accession of Anne. This was due to the growth of agriculture during the century, and probably to the increasing activity of the English in textile industries. These were spreading in the west and the north, as the convenience of climate, and ultimately of climate and steam power, dictated. The various and independent calculations on which the estimates are made as to the amount of the population, and the closeness of the result in the several processes by which the numbers are arrived at, are stated by Macaulay, and are well known to the readers of his history. But the statistical account given by one of these persons, Gregory King, contains some other estimates, which have seldom, if ever, been commented on, but which suggest some considerations in connection with the subject which is before us.

King based his calculations of the population on the number of houses in the country, which were well known through the registers of the Hearth Tax, and the probable number of inmates in each house. These estimates were not made from what were likely to be the numbers born in each family, as most of King's critics alleged, but from the persons who constituted the establishments in the several houses. Thus he set down forty persons in the household of every temporal, twenty in that of every spiritual peer, and so on. The custom of the time was that most persons of substance kept a considerable number of domestics ; and there is abundant evidence that service in a household was one of the means by which part of the agricultural population was extensively employed. In King's estimate, the average income of a nobleman is set down at £3,200 a year ; of a bishop at £1,300 ; of a baronet at £880 ; of a knight at £650 ; of an esquire at £450 ; of a country gentleman at £280. The annual income of merchants and traders is estimated at from £400 to £200 ; of lawyers at £154 ; of the dignified clergy at £72 ; and of the inferior at £50. He states that there are 160,000 freeholders in the kingdom, with incomes ranging from £90 to £55 ; and 150,000 farmers, to whom he gives an average income of £42 10s. Those who are engaged in liberal arts and sciences earn each £60 a year. Shopkeepers and trades-men, whom he estimates at 50,000, get £45 a year. There are artizans and craftsmen, 60,000 in number, with wages amount-ing to £38 a year ; the residue being naval and military officers, whose average pay is from £80 to £60. Together these per-sons and their families constitute nearly half the population, and inhabit over 500,000 houses.

The agricultural labourers and country folk, those engaged in husbandry and divers local industries, inhabit 849,000 houses, earning at the best 1s. a day by their labour, and sometimes not more than half the amount. King sets the income of the more opulent classes of the community at 34½ millions, that of the country population engaged in unskilled labour or in analogous employments at nearly nine millions. In number they are a little in excess of those who are engaged in more profitable callings. To the labouring class King adds vagrants, thieves, and beggars by profession. Including the latter, he finds the average yearly income of those who are engaged in these ill-paid pursuits to be about £5, or less than 2s. a week ; and he reckons that their necessary sub-sistence must require at least an average of 7s. a year more. The thieves and beggars, he concludes, earn about as much as the poorest class of cottagers and those who are habitually receiving parish relief; but he naïvely concludes that their expense is greater, and that they cost the community as great a sum as they earn.

The issue of the whole is that the first schedule of persons, whose incomes have been given in detail, appear as the productive classes, who add to the wealth and in-crease the resources of the country, the second schedule as the unproductive classes who diminish it. He reckons that the gains which the former collect and add to the national capital are as much as £3,000,000, while the loss from the latter is about £600,000. This, with the loss which he assigns to the presence of predatory people and beggars, almost exactly corresponds to the amount which the poor rate reached at the end of the seventeenth century. Excluding a few of the more opulent classes, my readers will be struck with the smallness of the incomes which are earned at the end of the seventeenth century by the mercantile and professional classes, even when they are described as holding great offices and places, as being eminent merchants and eminent clergymen. The whole income from land, if we can set the nobles, clergy, country gentlemen, and freeholders together, is reckoned at $16\frac{1}{2}$ millions, or nearly half the income of the propertied and prosperous classes.

All working men, other than 60,000 artizans and handicraftsmen, in which we must, I presume, recognize capitalist workmen or employers of journeymen, are set down, from the point of view which contemplates the growth of national wealth, as unproductive people. Even the farmer is credited with only a fifth of the income and a sixteenth of the saving power in the gross total of this national progress. The farmer is supposed, and probably with reason, to have the scantiest margin apart from necessary expense out of which to accumulate. King thinks that the bishop has the largest available surplus, for he gives him a family of twenty and a saving power of £20 a year from each member of his household, while the temporal magnate is allowed £10, the merchant £13, the tradesman £1, the naval officer £2, and the artizan 10s. But the farmer's clear gain, with a household of five persons, is only 5s. a year per head. The calculations are, I am wholly persuaded, accurate, for Gregory King has rarely, even in modern times, been surpassed in the special and very exceptional power of understanding what is meant by statistical figures. King discovered the law which regulates the price of the necessaries of life on the occasion of a scarcity, and formulated a geometrical proportion which experience has proved, with some minor qualifications, to be a rule of safe action. Without knowing it, he demonstrated that the function of the corndealer was an indirect benefit to society, and that the pursuit of private gain, under ordinary conditions, may be of the greatest utility to the consumer by equalising prices.

We shall now be able, by the light of these figures, to

interpret the position of farmer and labourer at this time. As I have stated, the times were then of great prosperity and rapid opulence to the landowner, the trader, and the placeman. The exiles of the royalist party had learned in France the secret of official plunder and the mechanism of official bribery. They usurped the government, and wisely allowed the renegades of the old republican party to share their spoils, knowing that no knave can be trusted so thoroughly as the man who has been a traitor to his old associates. The landowner had found out how to compensate himself for high prices by enforcing high rents, had emancipated his own estates as soon as possible from their traditional obligations, and, much more important, had secured a strict law against imports of agricultural products, even from Ireland. He had contrived to make the condition of the poorer sister so uneasy, that even a Tory like Lord Anglesey winced when Buckingham told the Lords that Irish produce was a nuisance. The legislature had been degraded utterly during the Long Parliament of Charles, and though they took care after the Restoration that they should live, they lived in the uncleanest fashion. The traders had revived monopolies under parliamentary authority, and the chiefs of the mercantile classes manipulated the Commons when they could, as Osborne did, or bribed wholesale, as Child did, or when their opportunities were not so open, forged, as Duncombe did, and all founded noble families, and, as Gregory King thought, added to the national wealth.

They who created it, the farmers and the labourers, were the unproductive classes, who worked hard, benefited all, robbed nobody, and, as King informs us, saved little or nothing, for the aggregate gain from the savings of the farmers is about a third of the aggregate loss incurred by the waste of the labourer's existence. In point of fact, the principal savings of the wealth which was so rapidly accumulated by the few at the latter end of the seventeenth century were derived from the direct plunder of the public by placemen and the indirect plunder of the public by the great monopolist companies. who bribed the financiers with advances of money on loan to government, and besides the dividends which they received from this stock, appropriated a guinea of monopolist gain for every shilling which they lent on interest. It is not wonderful that the public at large, at least those who were able to interpret the machinery of government, aided by place-hunters out of office, should have striven, not always wisely, to arrest the process by which their scanty incomes were mulcted in order to build up the colossal fortunes which the trade in politics and the politics of trade were accumulating.

The evil reign of Charles had left one mischief with which the government of William had to cope. Charles had not committed the crime of Henry in issuing base money, but he had issued money in such a form as to invite its practical debasement. The folly of the age forbade its export, and thereupon assisted the exportation of it. Clippers of coins were hanged by scores, and it seems that not unfrequently a prosecution for clipping was set on foot in order to get rid of inconvenient persons. But these wholesale executions did no good, they did not improve the coinage, check crime, or prevent the exportation of bullion produced by melting the best pieces. At last the re-coinage was ordered, and Montague, by a bold stroke of administrative genius, set the currency on a sound basis. To the same accomplished financier was due the foundation of the Bank of England, and with it the establishment of credit and the economy of the currency. But the last institution, all-important as it was to the trade of London, and convenient as it was to the government, had little or no meaning beyond the metropolis. Better times were to come for both farmer and labourer by the operation of causes which were quite independent of governments and the utilisation of commercial credit,—a new departure in agriculture and the bounty of the seasons. But the change could not take effect till peace was restored. The Treaty of Utrecht closed the first great war waged on behalf of the balance of power, and closed it on this issue for nearly a century. The other wars of the eighteenth century were waged in the reputed interests of commerce, till the upheaval of 1792.

CHAPTER XVII.

AGRICULTURE AND AGRICULTURAL WAGES IN THE EIGHTEENTH CENTURY.

The Slow though Real Progress of Agricultural Improvements — The Passion for Agricultural Pursuits at the beginning of the Century, and its Continuance for some Time in the Next—Failures due to too much Land with too little Capital, and Slovenly Book-keeping—Motives for this Fashion of Agricultural Pursuits—The Gains of Commerce in the Eighteenth Century—The Pride of the English Nobility—The Immediate Benefit of Improved Agriculture—Arthur Young's Testimony—Increased Stocks of Animals—Manures, Marling — The Increase of Production estimated—Rental of England—Farmer's Profits—Leases Necessary and Universal—The Estimated Value of Stock in 1770, and of Wages in Agriculture—Rise in Rents—The Earnings of Labour—Young's Estimate of Earnings—Comparison of Wages in the Eighteenth and the Fifteenth Centuries—The Particulars of Agricultural Progress in 1770—Abundance and Scarcity, their Effects on the Landed Interest—Corn Laws—The Seven Barren Years of the Seventeenth Century—Enclosures in the Eighteenth and Nineteenth Centuries—The Period of Scarcity in the Eighteenth Century—The Corn Law of 1773 and 1791—The Rise in Rent at the Close of the Century—Eden's Information in 1795—Weekly Earnings and Annual Deficits—Porter on the Cost of Poor Relief in Wheat—Summary of the Action of Government on Labourers, and their Consequent Condition—Its Effects on their Minds now—The English Workman no Socialist—The Function of Employers and Labourers—The Attitude of Farmers—The Result.

I HAVE stated already that while the agricultural progress of the seventeenth century was chiefly in the direction of utilising the fallow for roots, that of the eighteenth was especially characterised by the extension of artificial pasture, and the increased use of clover, saintfoin, and rye grass. By this I mean that the development of each was the principal feature of agriculture in three successive centuries. The winter roots were known in gardens in the sixteenth century, at least towards its close, for Tusser speaks of them as garden plants. Saintfoin was known to be useful to the agriculturist as early as 1637, for in this year a small work was published in which its cultivation is strongly recommended. Clover seed is to be found in prices current some time before the end of the seventeenth century, and that not in the London market only. But these seeds are regularly bought from the beginning of the eighteenth century by any farmer who had any idea of improved agriculture. On the other hand, the extension of the cultivation and the improvement of the article were of very slow development. The roots were small, and the crop at first was scanty. In course of time the farmer procured good seed, and increased his produce by judicious treatment; and similarly he studied the best means by which to supply himself with clover and saintfoin hay, and to utilise the aftermath. No record, however, of the progress is left us. It is the characteristic of agriculture that its improvements are so gradual as to be almost imperceptible, and it is only by contrasting rents and produce at different times, and perhaps prices, that we are able to arrive at any exact conceptions as to the progress which was effected. Writing in 1772, Arthur Young says that "saintfoin, cabbages, potatoes, carrots, are not common crops in England. I do not imagine above half, or at most two-thirds of the nation cultivate clover. It is a surprising number of years that are necessary firmly to introduce the culture of a new plant." If gentlemen of the present age, says Young, "had not assumed a spirit in agriculture vastly superior to former times, I much question whether that excellent vegetable would make its way fairly through the island in a thousand years."

The Englishman of the eighteenth century was greatly addicted to agriculture as a business or a pleasure, or both. It was the "reigning taste" of the age. There was scarcely a nobleman or country gentlemen who did not betake himself to the cultivation of land, not merely in the sense of keeping a home farm in his hands, which he managed by his steward, but as an overseer of his land, and as an experimenter in husbandry. Writers of the time note that country gentlemen talked about land and its properties, the benefit of certain courses, the advantage of turnip fallows, and the economies of agricultural machinery, about breeds of cattle, sheep, and pigs, with the same interest which their fathers and grandfathers used to exhibit on the subjects of the stable and the kennel only. The fashion had been set in Norfolk by Lord Townshend, after his quarrel with Walpole and his retirement, when he devoted himself to agricultural pursuits, especially to turnip growing. "There have been," says Young, "more experiments, more discoveries, and more general good sense displayed within these ten years in agricultural pursuits than in a hundred preceding ones." And the same writer adds, that "if this noble spirit continues, we shall soon see husbandry in perfection, and built upon as just and philosophic principles as the art of medicine."

The pursuit was universal. Citizens who were engaged in London business five days in the week were farmers for the other two; men who had been brought up to other pursuits deserted them for a trade which appeared easy and independent. It was a bye industry with those who had other callings. Physicians, lawyers, clergymen, soldiers, sailors, and merchants were farmers as well. "The farming tribe," says Young, "is now made up of all ranks, from a duke to an apprentice." This habit continued till the beginning of the second quarter of the present century, especially in places remote from towns, out of the way of main roads, and before the first railways were constructed. Parson Trulliber, though perhaps an exaggeration, was not an imaginary character. Fielding must have seen such clergymen by hundreds. I am old enough to remember the type, very little changed, in my own youth; as I can also remember the doctor and country lawyer to have been as keen after the cultivation of their fields as they were after patients and clients, and a number of country gentlemen, with pedigrees of undoubted antiquity, as proud as the haughtiest noble and as coarse-mannered as the most illiterate rustic.

Of course, experimental farming such as this often was frequently ended in failure. The principal cause of ruin a hundred years ago was precisely the same as it has been and is to-day,—too much land in occupation, and too little capital to cultivate it with. Young considers an average of £6 an acre the minimum necessary for successful agriculture; and it is certain that stock, live and dead, and labour, some few items excepted, cost the husbandman less than half the sum which they do now, the produce, as a whole, being sold for much less than half the price it reaches in our days. If he were criticising English agriculture at present, he would certainly set down £12 an acre as the average minimum. Every one knows that much less than half this was, unluckily, the capital of the agriculturist when the course of bad seasons came five years or so ago. English agriculture has, as I have good reason to know, been in the course of the six centuries of its recorded history subject to severe strains. But there was no period in which the ordinary farmer was less able to stand the shock as he was when the present crisis came. Five years ago (1878) I was told by a land agent who managed a large amount of property in two of the most fertile among the arable counties in England, that the average capital of the farmer on land let at about 30s. an acre was considerably under £6 an acre.

Another frequent cause of discomfiture in the agriculture of this highly progressive period was the neglect of keeping proper accounts. Exact and careful book-keeping, Young urges, is the only way in which one can not only demonstrate the success of an experiment, but the prudence of imitating the experiments of others. In the case of a gentleman who farms with the aid of a bailiff, accurate book-keeping is the only satisfactory check which the landowner can employ in order to test his servant's integrity. The ordinary farmer, he tells us, guesses, and often with remarkable accuracy, at the items and the totals, though he is unable to reduce his profits to figures. But such a rule of thumb process is always unsafe, and is fatal to the inexperienced. I can imagine the delight with which Young would have studied the particulars and the accurate balancings of a bailiff's roll in the thirteenth and fourteenth centuries, and how his preconceptions as to the rudeness of the age four or five hundred years before his time would have been modified by an examination of the facts. Though the farmer of the eighteenth century was far better provided with agricultural appliances and far more competent for the work of agriculture than his ancestor of the thirteenth, —the rent he paid would be a sufficient proof if other proof were wanting,—he was, I suspect, more illiterate.

The fashion so prevalent of making agriculture a pursuit among the wealthy landowners was stimulated in many cases by the desire they felt of maintaining themselves against the new aristocracy of trade. There were some mercantile callings which were not beneath the reputation of cadets whose lineage was ancient. It is known that in the West of England this was particularly the case with the cloth trade, and that half the country gentlemen in the counties where this calling was general had son or cousin in the business. A brewer's occupation was also considered compatible with social rank. The advantage of direct dealings with the consumers of wool and barley was considerable and conciliatory. "Wheat," says Young, "from the sowing to the selling, goes through the hands of a set of pilferers, whose principal business it is to steal it, as every farmer in the three kingdoms knows." But it is perfectly clear that much of the rapid improvement made in agriculture from about 1720 to 1760 was due to the eagerness with which landowners strove to improve their estates. Such a fashion could not have been mere caprice.

The truth is, the gains of commerce in the first half of the eighteenth century were very large. Owing to the fact that most of this gain came into the hands of joint-stock companies, who possessed monopolies paid for by large advances to government, enormous fortunes were made by a comparatively small number of persons. The very low rate of interest which prevailed throughout the same period is a proof that profits must have been large, and saving, among the moneyed classes at least, general. Even in those trades, however, which were not protected by the monopoly of a joint-stock company under charter, the same result was attained by large capitals;

and my reader will remember how Walpole's famous excise scheme, under which bonded warehouses would have been established, the revenue improved, and the consumer benefited, was defeated by the combination of capitalist merchants. But comparatively few as the merchant princes were in the beginning of the eighteenth century, they were a new body, and becoming more numerous than the nobles and great landed gentry. That they were new is proved by Gregory King's estimate of their income, which he sets at half that of a baronet, little more than an eighth that of a nobleman, and little more than a third of that of a bishop at the end of the seventeenth century. In 1750, it is probable that the city of London had a larger commercial income than the rents of the whole House of Lords and the episcopal bench. Their savings supplied the elder Pitt with his enormous loans, the £75,000,000 which he borrowed during his administration, while the whole rental of England twelve years after the Peace of Paris was not more than £16,000,000, and the interest on the whole debt was almost one-third of the rental.

There is no period in English history in which the pride of the English noble was more absorbing and more obtrusive than during the time on which I am immediately commenting. It betrayed itself in a thousand affectations and a thousand insolences. Noble youth found a satisfaction in street outrages and indecencies, noble age in vapouring about the privileges of the peers, and in attempts to constitute themselves a limited order. Sometimes they dreamt of passing an Act and procuring a grant for the separate education of their own order in a special academy. Three-fourths of them would have restored the Stuarts, from sheer hatred to the moneyed men. They joined the patriots in denouncing the place-men, and swallowed public money with avidity ; for it is generally seen that as religion is imitated and mocked by hypocrisy, so public duty is parodied by patriotism. To countervail the growing interest of the city and its eagerness in buying land and honours, they supported Chamberlain's Land Bank, rushed into and denounced the South Sea Bubble, succeeded in exacting a property qualification in land for all members of the House of Commons, except the eldest sons of peers, and supported what they hated against Walpole, in the hopes of weakening it. But all their efforts were in vain. When Walpole met his rival Pulteney on the floor of the House of Lords, he described both as the two most insignificant fellows in the kingdom. Pulteney got a large pension for himself and his heirs, which the British public still pays,—to whom, Heaven and the Paymaster-General alone know. He had been a patriot.

The effort to improve their estates, to increase their profits, and to raise their rents, was the only wholesome outcome from this struggle. I am persuaded (on the rule that it is wise to assign action to the rational and intelligible motive of self-interest in matters innocent and in their effects laudable, instead of postulating mere whim) that the English landowners set the fashion of making the best of agriculture, because they desired to make one wealth-producing agency become a rival in personal interest and in popular sympathy with another. The inference is obvious, that a person who makes wealth is more useful than one who gets wealth. It is not clear that the man who gets wealth does not destroy at least as much as he gets, and sometimes more,—a thief does so plainly, as society concludes. A speculator often does, as those who have to purchase the materials of industry discover. A hundred men live in opulence on time bargains. Somebody pays for their enjoyments. There is a superstition among old-fashioned economists that all parties are the better for the middle man. Experience is gradually proving that the abstract theory is incorrect. Hence under competition producers are getting rid of the middle man, and the modern economist, who studies facts instead of spinning theories and dilating on tendencies, is beginning to prove that he is generally a nuisance. Now that a man who wins more food from the earth is more useful than one who wins more food from somebody else's labour without offering anything solidly desirable in return for his function, needs no proof. If you can entirely get rid of the middle man, all the better; if you cannot, it is

an economy, which even he can hardly dispute, to narrow
his functions and to curtail his profits.

It is curious to see how alive Arthur Young is to this
sentiment. He is no economist at all in the most shadowy
sense of the word, for he has no real conception of the
harmony of interests, the exposition of which is the true
function of the economist. His entire sympathy is with
agricultural production. Everything must lend itself to
this result. The labour must be cheap, whatever it cost
in penury to the workman. The produce must be increased
by every effort of ingenuity and skill. The energies of the
farmer must be stimulated, and his ignorance and sloth
cured by a rack-rent lease. The continuity of these beneficent processes must be secured by prodigal bounties on
the exportation of agricultural produce and judicious restraints on its importation. The great landowners have
been the pioneers of agricultural progress. Young is not
at all a lackey. He speaks plainly about the shortcomings
of those landowners who do not come up to his ideal.
But he is so grateful to those who do that he describes
their houses, measures the largeness of their reception
rooms, and comments on their pictures as learnedly as
Goldsmith's critic does in the story of his charming vicar.

The principal result which agricultural improvement exhibited on such estates as were cultivated with assiduity
and skill was the increased stock of animals. The general
adoption of root crops in place of bare fallows, and the
extended cultivation of clover and other such plants by the
use of the plough, supplied the farmer with a great increase
of winter feed, besides materially improving its quality and
sustaining powers. In consequence, on abundance of fodder,
abundance of stock followed. But abundance of stock implied
the great increase of barn-yard manure, the principal fertilizer
of the time, indeed of all times, on the spot. So great is the
increase that the farmer is in difficulty as to the means by
which he can adequately compost or dilute it before he
distributes it over his fields, and it is expedient to convey
the whole of the straw or stubble produced on the farm to

the yards.   The grazing of meadows in winter time he considers injurious to cattle and destructive to the pasture.   But the littering of cattle with straw will increase the litter in its conversion into manure five-fold in quantity, and the littering of pigs will increase it ten-fold.   Better, he concludes, purchase straw, fern, or stubble than sell a single truss.   The manure was mixed with earth, better still with chalk, best of all with marl.   A dressing of twenty loads an acre of barn-yard manure thus composted will give a four years' fertility to the land which is so treated.   The greatly increased produce of the eighteenth century was entirely due to the increased use of natural manures.   The lessened price of agricultural implements had the effect of diminishing generally the cost of production.

Marling had now been revived, and was, relatively speaking, far less costly than when it was practised in early English agriculture, as compared with the value of land ; for in earlier times, as I stated in Chap. III., the expense attending it was from half the value to nearly the whole value of the fee simple.   In Young's time it cost from 50s. to £4 the acre.   This is about twelve times the average price at which the improvement was made five centuries before.   In Young's day the operation cost, at the value which he assigns to arable land, from one-fourth to one-eighth of the fee simple.   The benefit of the operation, we are informed, lasts for twenty years ; but, he adds, it yields no advantage for the first year, and but little in the second.   In the third it is distinctly useful; but most of all from the fourth to the fifteenth, when its effect is nearly worn out.   Soils were also treated with clay, with chalk, and with lime.   But the principal agent in successful husbandry is stable and shed manure ; and my author estimates that land properly dressed with this fertilizer, and continually dressed, will yield, if the land be capable of such treatment, from 40 to 48 bushels of the different kinds of corn.   The average produce of the fourteenth century in prosperous years, and when low prices prevailed, was under 11 bushels of all kinds of grain.   Manure was carted from towns, but the price was high and the carriage costly.   The dressing of land with soot, ashes, bones, malt-dust, woollen rags, and even oil-cake was known; but the price was so high, and the evidence of the advantage so scanty, that the use of these articles had not yet transcended the stage of experiment.

The productiveness of agriculture in the eighteenth century was, it is plain, when land was properly cultivated, four times that of the thirteenth, both as regards corn and stock. The weight of the fatted ox was raised at least three-fold; for the maximum weight in the earlier period, and even up to the beginning of the eighteenth century, was 400 lbs., while in Arthur Young's time he constantly reached 1,200 lbs. A similar but not so extensive an increase had taken place in sheep, while the weight of the fleece had become fully four times above the average of the earlier period. Now if the produce of England in the middle of the fourteenth century was sufficient to feed two millions and a half, that of the middle of the eighteenth was sufficient for ten millions. But it is almost certain that when Young wrote, the population was only seven and a half millions, or possibly eight. England was, therefore, a considerable corn-exporting country, and would have been, even without the bounty, which was, of course, a virtual addition to rent. The bounty being, as was believed, a settled maxim in English policy, accounts in part for the fact that land, the value of which was constantly rising, sold in the beginning of the latter half of the century at $33\frac{1}{2}$ years' purchase.

Young tells us that in his northern tour he traversed and inspected more than 70,000 acres of land under cultivation, and that he registered the rent of the whole. He concludes, and with very good reason, that the parts which he visited are a fair sample of the whole of England. He sets the acreage of the whole country at thirty-two millions, a skilful calculation arrived at seventy years before by Halley the astronomer, by means of a most ingenious process, and only in error by about half-a-million acres. The rent of the land which he visited is, good and poor included, 10s. an acre; and he therefore concludes that the total agricultural rental of the country is £16,000,000. He continually urges that this rental, especially for good land, is too low, and that good husbandry and an enlightened self-interest suggest and even demand a considerable exaltation of rents. There is, he says, a proverb current among farmers that a man cannot pay too much for good land and too little for bad; and he illustrates his proverb by showing what is the rate of production and the cost of land rented at 5*s.* an acre and that which is rented at 20*s.* He makes out the profit of the former to be 8*s.* 8*d.* an acre, under the best known husbandry, and that of the latter 29*s.* It may be observed that, according to Young's calculations, the profit of the farmer, all charges deducted, is considerably in excess of the rent he pays. But it is considerably less than that procured under the ancient system of capitalist agriculture, or that which succeeded, the land and stock lease, and even than that of the short lease which followed.

Young considers it impossible that agriculture should thrive except under the security of a lease. Leases in his day were well-nigh universal, often with the obligation of repairs being imposed on the tenant. There was no motive as yet for keeping the tenant in a state of political dependence. No tenant on term of years had a vote, not even a copyholder had one. The only county voter was the freeholder; and even the freehold for life would not guarantee subservience. I suspect that the Chandos clause in the first Reform Bill is to a great extent answerable for precarious tenancies, though the constantly rising rent of land in the fifty years preceding that famous clause is more responsible for the result. When the country gentlemen became passionately protectionist, it was an aid to their policy that the tenant farmers should be not only enlisted in the same interest with themselves, but should be plainly informed that their livelihood depended on the interpretation which the country party chose to give of that interest.

In the estimate which Young makes of the capital value of agricultural wealth in England, land is put at 33½ years purchase of the rent and valued at 536 millions, farmers'

stock at nearly 110 millions, while house property is estimated at 100 millions. He reckons the wheat and rye crop
at over 9 millions of quarters annually, that of barley at
11½ millions, that of oats at 10¼ millions. It will be seen
that this estimate, which he bases on the amount of those
kinds of grain which he found to be actually produced in
the district over which he travelled, corresponds closely
with the inference which I have arrived at as to the possible
population which could be maintained on English produce
at two periods which are separated from each other by an
interval of five centuries. The tithe payable from the produce he estimates at 5½ millions; and he is clearly alive to
the injury which a tithe in kind inflicts on progressive agriculture. The whole earnings of agricultural labour are set
at 14½ millions, shared among 836,235 persons; or, in other
words, the cost of agriculture, as far as labour is concerned,
is supplied at nearly £17 9s. per head of persons. The
estimate includes harvest labour, but not that of the tenant
himself, which Young says was general, and, for farmer's
profits, necessary.

The average rent of land is, he tells us, actually 9s. 11d.
an acre, but for the sake of convenience he puts it at 10s.
In the middle ages, and down to the rise in prices, it was
let at not more than 6d. an acre. The payment, therefore,
made for the occupation of land has risen twenty times.
The average rise in the price of wheat is about six-and-
a-half times, and the average rise in the price of labour
is almost exactly three-and-a-half times, for the price of
wheat is set at about 40s. a quarter, while that of the
labourer is 7s. 1d. per week, the corresponding prices in the
earlier period being 6s. and 2s.; and it should be remembered that while the labourer in Young's time had his
earnings of hay and harvest time included in the aggregate
average, the labourer of the earlier period had his harvest
earnings over and above. The agriculturist of the eighteenth
century called the forty-one weeks which remained before
and after the harvest period winter, when the regular wages
were about two-thirds of the better paid eleven weeks. As,

however, I have often said, the agricultural labourer in the first half of the eighteenth century was better off than he had been at any period since the fifteenth and the first half of the sixteenth.

The rise in rent is the result of diffused agricultural skill. The cost of production had so far diminished, that the farmer could afford to pay out of the enhanced general profits twenty times as much for the use of land as his ancestors did some two centuries before. If the peasant's wages had risen with the general progress of that skill, in which he shared to the full with the farmer, the rise in rent would have been checked. The labour bill on a 500 acre farm in Young's days, on his estimate, was £335 8s. 4d.; the rent, £250; the profit, about £400. But assuming the profit to remain the same, and the labourer to have received a rise of wages at all proportionate to the rise in the price of wheat, rent would have again sunk to zero. The farmer's profit is estimated at from 14 to 18 or even 20 per cent. on his capital, a return on the smallest of the figures, which is sufficient to account for the popularity of agriculture and for the generally prosperous condition of the farming class.

Two facts exceedingly puzzle this careful statistician. He finds that the local price of labour does not correspond with the local dearness and cheapness of provisions, and that relatively high and low wages are not connected with relatively low and high poor rates. It never seems to have struck him that the Law of Parochial Settlement, and the consequent temptation put before the owner of a whole parish to check the local growth of population, would, directly there arose a demand for labour in particular localities, tend to decrease the liabilities of one district and increase those of another, but that the demand for labour and the consequent rise in local wages might very well go on with pauperism and overcrowding. Similarly he does not in the least discern the effect of the quarter sessions assessment in stereotyping apathy and helplessness. What he complains of is the occasional prodigality of the justices in their valuations of labour and the rate at which they fix the price of the peasant's contribution to the general growth of opulence.

In estimating the earnings of labour, Young gives many and elaborate tables based upon a preposterous postulate, the unreality of which he admits. The labourer is supposed to be in constant work, and to earn the average of the three seasons, hay-time, harvest-time, and winter, the latter being forty-one out of the fifty-two weeks. His wife is to work in hay and harvest-time, and to get six weeks' work in winter. His eldest son is to be a first-hand, his second an ordinary hind, his third a farmer's boy, each at the average wages which such a calling supplied. One of his daughters is to be a dairy-maid, and the other a common maid. This family of seven are all capable of work, all at work, and are all collecting their wages into a common fund. He finds the average of such a family's wages to be close to £51 8s. a year. Now it is plain that not one family in a thousand corresponded at that time or afterwards to Young's hypothesis, and that, therefore, the calculations based on the statement are, as regards the remuneration of labour, entirely fictitious. What they do represent, and as I believe accurately, is the average cost at which a farmer in the Eastern Counties could procure the services of seven persons in the distribution of occupations in husbandry. Each of these services was necessary, and was, indeed, traditional in English husbandry on the large scale from the very earliest times, and they would be and could be proved to be equally necessary in the economy of modern English agriculture. How far the figures which Young has collected fell short of the facts in the case of an agricultural labourer's aggregate earnings will be shown in the evidence supplied by Sir Frederic Eden, on which I shall hereafter comment.

Now if any of my readers will take the pains to calculate what a family of seven, engaged as Young contemplates, would have received in the aggregate under the Act of 11 Hen. VII., cap. 22, in the year 1495, he will find that it amounts to £24 10s., or nearly one-half of that which the same persons employed in identical industry received in the tenth year of George III. In 1495, the four-pound loaf of bread cost ½d.; in 1770, 5d.; and to take and contrast Young's other prices with those of the earlier year, butter, 1d. and 7d.; cheese, ¼d. and 4d.; meat, ¼d. and 4d. Of these prices the first is very low, for the year 1495 is a very cheap year. The others are the average price for the whole period of 283 years. Now if we apply the same rule to bread, we should raise the price of the four-pound loaf to ¾d.

If, therefore, it were the case, as it certainly was not, that the same amount of labour was required to secure the produce which was obtained in the eighteenth century as was needed in the fifteenth, it is clear that had wages in the later period been made to possess the same purchasing power which they had in the earlier, the family of seven would have received, in nominal or money wages, seven and a half times more than they received in 1495, in order that they might obtain the same amount of the necessaries of life, *i.e.*, £183 15s. instead of £51 8s. It will be plain that such a rate of wages would have reduced rent first, and profits afterwards, and have left no opportunity for the growth of the former, except in so far as labour might be economised by the increased productiveness of land at less cost, by substituting mechanical for manual labour, by cheapening the carriage of goods, by increasing the fertility of the soil, and by improving seed and stock. All these were, except perhaps the second, effected. But I do not think that any one who examines the facts will doubt that much of the increase of rent which was effected in the first half of the eighteenth century, and nearly all which was obtained in the seventeenth, was obtained at the expense of the agricultural labourer, whose real wages were, as I have shown here and elsewhere, reduced by all the difference between their earlier and their later purchasing power.

The advance which agriculture had made by the year 1770 was great and remarkable. Tools and implements were far cheaper and far better. The breeds of cattle and sheep were greatly improved, threefold in many cases within living memory, and the comparative cheapness of agricultural produce, a cheapness which is general and fairly uniform,

is proof that, apart from the continuous abundance of the
seasons and the success of agricultural operations, for a time
at least production had gone ahead of population. Of the
character of the seasons, Young asserts that a proper distribution of cultivation over the area of the farm, and especially
the adoption of that husbandry which recognises the place
of root and hay or grass crops in connection with crops of
corn, will practically make the farmer independent of the
weather, since he will get his compensation, in the vast
majority of cases, for what he loses in one kind of produce
by what he gains in another. Now I am ready to admit
that much of this improvement was due to the public spirit
and enterprise of some who had turned their attention to the
good of their own estates, and (as the farmer must work in
the open, and has neither the inclination nor the power to
make a secret of a profitable process) who had benefited
their neighbours by the proof of their success. It is possible,
if wages had advanced on the same lines as rents and profits
did, that the margin of advantage would have been so
narrowed that there would have been little impulse given
towards either experiment or improvement. An industry
may be discouraged by the excessive cost of labour, especially when the product is of optional use. But the production
of food is not so much affected by these considerations, at
any rate in the same degree, as long as rent exists and profits
are large.

When there were seasons of great abundance and, consequently, of low prices, there was general complaint on the
part of the landed interest, who considered, because nature
was propitious and prices were low, that the country had
become poor. We are told that in the few cheap years
in the first half of the seventeenth century the tenants could
not pay their rents, and that land was reduced in value from
twenty to sixteen or seventeen years' purchase. The abundance
of the seasons between 1666 and 1671 led to the prohibitive
Act of 22 Chas. II., cap. 13, under which a duty of 16*s.* 4*d.* was
imposed on wheat as long as it was below 53*s.* 4*d.* a quarter,
and one of 8*s.* when it was below 80*s.* The Act. which was

intended to keep up prices, failed of its effects, for the prices again became low. In order further to secure high prices and full rents, a bounty of 5*s*. a quarter, when the price did not exceed 48*s*., was granted immediately after the Revolution. To the operation of these two enactments the scientific agriculturists, who affected to discuss the economic bearings of husbandry on the growth of opulence, ascribed the development of agriculture in the eighteenth century and the plenty of its produce. It is probable that the belief in the efficacy of these legislative remedies led to the very numerous enclosures which begin under the authority of Parliament in the reign of Anne, under which, in the eighteenth century, nearly 3,000,000 acres were enclosed, and in the nineteenth, up to 1854, nearly 6,000,000 more. The amount so enclosed is more than one-third of the whole cultivable surface of England and Wales.

The seven barren years at the conclusion of the seventeenth century were long noted for the distress of the people and for the exalted profits of the farmer, as they probably gave occasion to the celebrated law of Gregory King, that when there ensues a scarcity in an absolute necessary of life, and the quantity falls off in an arithmetical ratio, the price is exalted in a geometrical one. But when prices fell, as they did in the period between 1715 and 1765, there was a general outcry of agricultural distress, which, when it comes to be analysed, is always resolved into the shrinkage of the landlord's rent. Noblemen and country gentlemen demanded the aid of the legislature in order to enable the farmers to pay their rents. In eleven years nearly £2,000,000 were paid in bounties. But much new land was brought under tillage, and the price of labour, as I have said, rose twenty per cent. Mr. Malthus accounted for the rise characteristically, by alleging that there was no proportionate increase of the population, for that the English people, having now achieved a notable increase in the real wages which they received, decidedly elevated the standard of their comforts and conveniences. It is doubtful whether moral or prudential reasons had much to do with the matter. Wages are always, both in nominal amount and in real power, greater when food and the other conveniences of life are cheap; and the demand for labour was receiving an additional stimulus from improvements in agriculture and the increasing area of land which was taken into cultivation. But whatever may have been the cause, a reverse was near at hand.

Up to 1765, England had been an exporting country in divers agricultural products. Subsequently it became an importing country. It was supposed to have suffered this change from the fact that the population increased rapidly. The view is untenable on two grounds. In the first place, an increase of population cannot take place at a bound; in the next, it has always been found that a time of distress, when food is dear, checks population. Undoubtedly after the Peace of Paris an extraordinary development of English trade occurred. The colonial empire of England was doubled, and the monopoly of the trade, according to the accredited policy of the age, was conferred on English shippers and merchants. Undoubtedly, too, the manufacture of textile fabrics took a great start, the production of them being cheapened and the market for them widened by the successful application of machinery to the process. But the displacement of industries must have produced much local suffering, and the check to population which this loss of revenue induced must have more than counterbalanced the miserable stimulus given to it by the increased demand for the labour of the young. In the long run, labour has gained by the inventions of Arkwright, of Watt, and of Cartwright, but the process which preceded the gain was accompanied by profound suffering, part of which, to the benefit of all parties, was remedied by the prohibitive regulations of a later time.

The seasons from 1765 were as generally unpropitious as those up to that period were abundant; and in 1773, the opponents of the existing corn law secured the alteration of the Act of 1671. By this law importation was permitted at 6*d.* a quarter, when wheat was at or above 48*s.*, and the bounty was to cease when it was at or above 44*s.* But whenever the seasons happened to be abundant, the old cry was raised that landlords were distressed and farmers ruined. As a consequence, in 1791, a new corn law was enacted, under which a very heavy duty was imposed while wheat was below 50s., though it was slight when the price rose above this amount. But the general scarcity of these later years produced its effect on rent. Arthur Young, writing more than forty years after the date of his celebrated tours comments on the singular and rapid rise in rent which took place after 1782, and the development of competition for occupancy. The landlords were alarmed at their own good fortune, and for a time hesitated to take advantage of it; but tenants rushed into the occupation of husbandry, which was thenceforward highly profitable when scarcity ruled, as was the case generally till 1820, and was correspondingly depressed when occasional abundance intervened.

After the deficient harvest of 1795, wheat rose to 104s. a quarter, and remained at that amount, or near it, for a whole year. It was during this time that Sir Frederick Eden collected his evidence as to the wages of labour and the cost of maintenance. The facts are in remarkable contrast to the hypothetical earnings which are drawn up with such fulness by Arthur Young. It must be admitted that the government of the day adopted very active measures against the dearth. They seized all neutral ships laden with corn and bound for France, and compelled them to discharge their cargoes at English ports, and at a handsome profit to their owners. They offered a bounty of from 16s. to £1 on imported corn. But the scarcity was universal, extending even to the United States, though the barren lands of the eastern and central states could never have been relied on for any great amount. The two Houses of Parliament signed an engagement to reduce their domestic consumption by at least one-third, and the distillation of corn spirits was prohibited. Many of the poor perished by want, and nearly all persons were stinted. But it was a time of great prosperity to the landed interest,— to the landlords whose rents were rapidly rising, and to the farmers who were realising enormous gains during the currency of their leases. The deficiency was variously calculated at from one-fifth to one-third short of an average crop.

During the first two months of the year 1796, Eden collected the amount of wages actually earned by families engaged in agricultural labour in different parts of England, many of them being records of 1795 wages. Five are taken from Clopshill, in Beds; four from a village near Carlisle; four from Buckden, in Hunts; six from Hinksworth, in Herts; four from Kegworth, in Leicester; four from Lincolnshire parishes; four from Diss, in Norfolk; five from Northampton; six from near Oxford; six from Suffolk; four from Stogursey, in Somerset; and one from Yorkshire,— fifty-three in all. The collective earnings of these families average 11s. 9d. a week in Beds, ranging from 9s. to 14s. 6d.; and these wages fall short of their expenditure, poor enough, by an average of £3 15s. 9d., though a part of this deficiency is made up by harvest earnings.

At Carlisle the average earnings are 10s. for the whole family, and the average deficiency in the whole is £3 2s. 4d. In Hunts the average wages are 9s. 3d., and the average deficiency £2 15s. 4d. The six families in Herts earn an average of 12s. 6½d., but their necessary expenditure exceeds their receipts by an average of £22 3s. 6½d. The average earnings of two families in Leicester are 13s. 9d., and the average deficiency is £18 0s. 3¾d. In one family in Lindsey the earnings are 11s. 6d., the expenditure in excess of wages being £21 18s. 4d.; another family is only 7s. 4d. short, but the wages of man, wife, and child are only 11s. 3d., and the family live on bread alone. In the case of three Norfolk families, the total earnings are 11s. 3d., and the average deficiency £13 11s. 4d. In Northants, four families earn an average of 10s. 7½d., but are on an average £3 15s. short on the year. The six Oxfordshire families earn an average of 12s. 10d., the total being heightened by one household in which three boys earn nearly as much as their father does. Here the average deficiency is £3 5s. 9d. In Suffolk, four families, in each of which the children contribute largely to the earnings, the average wages are 15s. 1d., and the average deficiency £12 13s. 6d., which in these cases is slightly lessened by harvest wages.   In Somerset, four families earn an average of 8s. 9¾d., and their annual expenses exceed their annual income by an average of £11 3s. 10d.   The Yorkshire labourer is worst off.   His own earnings are under 6s. a week, his wife's a little over 1s., and his child's an infinitesimal sum.   His expenses exceed his income by £12 13s. a year, though his fare is the humblest conceivable.   I have taken those rates of wages only which were paid in 1795 and 1796.   Between 1792 and 1795 such provisions as these labourers could procure had risen by about 125 per cent. The poor rate rose to £4,000,000, and yet the people were starving.   Mr. Porter has acutely observed, that in years of dearth, in which the largest sums have been expended on the poor, the amount estimated in wheat is the lightest borne by the community.   He has inferred, indeed, that this is right, that the poor in seasons of dearth should suffer with those by whom they are supported, and feel the inconvenience which the niggardliness of nature has put upon the whole community.   The inference is just, if it be also true that the position which they occupy is one which they have chosen for themselves, and for which they are therefore responsible.

The examination of the facts shows that this was not the case.   We have been able to trace the process by which the condition of English labour had been continuously deteriorated by the acts of government.   It was first impoverished by the issue of base money.   Next it was robbed of its guild capital by the land thieves of Edward's regency.   It was next brought in contact with a new and more needy set of employers—the sheep-masters who succeeded the monks.   It was then, with a pretence, and perhaps with the intention, of kindness, subjected to the quarter sessions assessment, mercilessly used in the first half of the seventeenth century, the agricultural labourer being still further impoverished by being made the residuum of all labour.   The agricultural labourer was then further mulcted by enclosures, and the extinction of those immemorial rights of pasture and fuel which he had enjoyed so long.   The poor law professed to find him work, but was so administered that the reduction of his wages to a bare subsistence became an easy process and an economical expedient. When the monarchy was restored, his employers, who fixed his wages by their own authority, relieved their own estates from their ancient dues at the expense of his poor luxuries by the excise, tied him to the soil by the Law of Settlement, and starved him by a prohibitive corn law. The freedom of the few was bought by the servitude of the many. Fletcher of Saltoun, an ardent republican for a narrow class, suggested hopeless slavery as the proper doom of the labourers, argued that the people existed only to work, and that philosophical politicians should have the power to limit their existence by labour. Throughout the eighteenth century the most enlightened men gave the poor their pity, occasionally their patronage, sometimes would assist them at the cost of other workers ; but beyond a bare existence, never imagined that they had rights or remembered that they had suffered wrongs. The weight of taxation fell on them in every direction, and with searching severity. It was necessary to find funds at all risks and from every source, and it is obvious that the most fruitful source of taxation is that of necessary consumption and cheap luxuries. It was, of course, impossible to tax the absolute necessaries of the individual workman, else he would starve and perish. But the process left him nothing but a bare subsistence. The interpretation of his wages is always incomplete unless one takes into account the virtual reduction which taxation made of them ; and to know this would require an exact and searching analysis of the customs and excise, and of their incidence. Even this would be insufficient, because to adequately interpret the situation we should have to estimate the privation of enforced abstinence, as well as the contribution of universal taxation, and measure the labourer's losses not only by what he consumed but by what he was forced to abstain from consuming. And withal the existing condition of things bred and strengthened that mean and malignant passion for profiting by the miseries of others which became the policy of the landed interest, and to some extent even now remains a dominant hope in the minds of landlords and farmers. To crown the whole, the penalties of felony and conspiracy were denounced against all labourers who associated together to better their lot by endeavouring to sell their labour in concert, while the desperation which poverty and misery induce, and the crime they suggest, were met by a code more sanguinary and brutal than any which a civilized nation had ever heretofore devised or a high-spirited one submitted to.

Such was the education which the English workman received from those evil days, when the government employed and developed the means for oppressing and degrading him. It is no marvel that he identifies the policy of the landowner, the farmer, and the capitalist employer with the machinery by which his lot has been shaped, and his fortunes, in the distribution of national wealth, have been controlled. He may have no knowledge, or a very vague knowledge, as to the process by which so strange, so woeful an alteration has been made in his condition. But there exists, and always has existed, a tradition, obscure and uncertain, but deeply seated, that there was a time when his lot was happier, his means more ample, his prospects more cheerful than they have been in more modern experience. From one point of view, the analyst of "the good old times" may be able to show that life was shorter, disease more rife, the market of food more unsteady, the conveniences and comforts of life fewer and more precarious than they now are. From another point of view, and that by far the most accurate and exact, the relative position of the workman was one of far more hope and far more plenty in the days of the Plantagenets than it has been in those of the House of Hanover; that wages were, relative to their purchasing power, far higher, and the margin of enjoyable income over necessary expenditure was in consequence far wider.

The remarkable fact in the history and sentiments of the English workman is that he is neither socialist nor anarchist. He believes, and rightly believes, that in the distribution of the reward of labour his share is less than it might be, than it ought to be, and that some means should be discovered by which the unequal balance should be rectified. He does not indeed detect the process by which this advantage can be secured to him, and relies, though doubtfully, upon certain expedients by which he thinks he can extort better terms. He has good reason for believing that he can gain his ends, in some degree at least, by association with his fellows; for he cannot have forgotten how angrily any action of his in this direction has for centuries been resented and punished, and how even now it is assailed by sophistical and interested criticism. But he has never dreamed of making war on capital or capitalist. In his most combative temper he has simply desired to come to terms with capital, and to gain a benefit by the harmonious working of a binding treaty between himself and his employer. He is wise in his contention, though not always wise in his strategy.

Food and the materials of industry constitute the capital of a community, of which money is the symbol. Labour is engaged, whether of head or hand, in replacing the former as it is consumed, and of imparting utility to the latter. The produce of the former is that upon which all subsist, those by whom it is procured and those who, by one plea or another, are able to make good their claim to a portion in the common stock. All who are engaged in industry strive to complete their work in the briefest and easiest manner. The employer of labour works as truly as the peasant and artizan, with head and hand, though in a different manner. His principal function, as far as the common interest is concerned, is to interpret the means by which labour may be continuously employed. When the product is secured and exchanged, always ultimately for food and other necessaries and conveniences, this question is always arising, What is the share, all expenses being deducted, which the employers shall have on the one hand, and labourers on the other, of the residue? The quarrel between capital and labour, as it is called, but as it would be more accurately styled, between employer and employés, is, What is the amount of the share each should have in profits and wages? For centuries the law and the government interposed on the side of the employer in order to lessen the labourer's share. For a very long period, two centuries, the efforts of law and government were unsuccessful. At last they gained their object, and gradually reduced the labourers' share to a bare subsistence, so bare that in order to get their necessary work from him they supplemented his wages by a tax on the general public, as they do in a less degree to this day. The worst time, however, in the whole history of English labour was beginning when Eden collected the facts which he gives us as to the labourer's earnings. This condition of things was continued for twenty-five years.

The farmers competed against each other for occupancies, and constantly offered higher rents, which the enforced cheapness of their labourers' wages enabled them to pay, and the necessities of the public artificially created by the corn laws enabled them to increase. They made common cause with the landlord, and worked against the interests of the labourer and the general public, the body of consumers. They saw that if they pledged themselves to higher rents, they must needs procure the means by lowering the cost of what they produced and by heightening its price. They achieved the former by driving wages down to a bare subsistence, and the latter by maintaining an artificial dearth.

Now it is plain that contracts founded on such unnatural conditions were certain, sooner or later, to bring mischief on those who agreed to them. It was certain that at an early period the nation would resent the existence of laws which were designed to stint them. It was certain that manufacturers and traders, now secure of a foreign market, if trade were open to them, would demand that they should be able to sell their goods for that which the people would always readily consume, and would, therefore, be the best and safest object of exchange. It was probable that workmen would not be for ever content to accept nothing but a bare subsistence, and that they would seek to extricate themselves from so ungrateful a position. But the vitality of the old system was singular. It took the active agitation of a quarter of a century before free trade in food was granted. The labourer, unused to the action which springs from the consciousness of a common purpose, even when the liberty of union was given him, was too ignorant and too apathetic to use that force of combination which his ancestors five centuries before had employed with such effect. He fled from his calling. Other and better paid industries hired him from the farmyard and the harvest field, sometimes, indeed, to his ultimate injury. The most enterprising sought in the United States and the colonies a future which was denied them here.

But though there was a shrinkage on both sides in the quality and quantity of labour, in the price of certain farm products, and in the profits of agriculture, rents went on steadily increasing. It was an open secret that even when these enhanced rents were being paid, the farming class had so narrow a margin of profits that even slight reverses would become serious. It was known that agricultural capital had greatly diminished, and that the cultivation of the soil was gradually becoming slovenly and imperfect. At last the crisis came, and the foolish payment of excessive rent, and the equally foolish receipt of excessive rent, have led to disasters in English agriculture to which there is no parallel in the annals of that industry. The case is made worse by the fact that there appears to be no prospect of an early and vigorous recovery, even though much rent is sacrificed

CHAPTER XVIII.

WAGES IN THE NINETEENTH CENTURY.

The Rate of Wages and the Price of Food—Pressure on the Operatives in Factories and the Weavers—Machine Breaking—The Manufacturing Districts worst off —Causes raising Wages—These not Operative till Late—Difficulties in the formation of Labour Partnerships and their Management. The Competition of Capitalists, and its Effects on Labour—Recent Events—Effects of a Relaxation of Foreign Tariffs—The Depreciated Currency of the War—Abrogation of the Quarter Sessions Assessment—The Allowance System—Illustrations of its Working—The Abolition of Compulsory Apprenticeship—The Defence of Apprenticeship—The Objection to it—The Cost of the War—Hostility of Capitalists to the Workmen's Advance—Their Sinister Predictions—Animosity felt by the Workman towards the Combination Laws—Hume's Committee— The Unions—The Agricultural Labourer—History of his Wages and the Poor Law—The Factory Acts not Extended to the Children of Peasants— Agricultural Gangs—Mr. Girdlestone—Joseph Arch—The Difficulties of an Agricultural Labourers' Union—The Work of the Primitive Methodists—The Attitude of the Farmers Erroneous—The Moral Education of Labour Partnerships—The Present Position of Agriculture.

DURING the first twenty years of the nineteenth century, the price of wheat was on an average 98s. 6d. a quarter, i.e., 16·4 times the rate which prevailed on an average for the 280 years in which there was practically no variation in money values, beyond those which arose from exceptional scarcity. In the year 1800, when the working man was within the range of this extraordinary exaltation in the price of his food, the average wages of artizans were 18s. a week in London. They gradually rose by about 75 per cent. during the years of dearth, being generally highest in the years which were characteristically dear. When greater plenty prevailed, they fell. In the country they were about one-third less than they were in London. It does not appear that artizans had their wages supplemented by the allowance system, for when, in 1824, Lord John Russell moved for a committee to inquire into the consequences of a practice which had now become general, and drew his motion in such general terms as to include all kinds of labour, Mr. Peel objected that the reference to the committee would include superfluous subjects, and, in consequence, the inquiry was limited to agricultural wages.

These wages, which I shall refer to more particularly, in so far as evidence is forthcoming, further on in this chapter, were largely supplemented by parish allowances. The maximum sum expended in the relief of the poor under the old law was in 1818, when it was nearly eight millions, or 13s. 9d. per head of the population. The factory hand was even worse off than the labourer, and, as machinery was gradually being introduced into the manufacture of textile fabrics, the hand-loom weaver was worst off of all. Great as was the demand for labour under the new system, it was, unfortunately, not countervailed by an increase of real wages, hardly of nominal wages, for the demand was for both sexes and nearly all ages. But the severest penury fell on those who had been, in the older days of manufacture, the specially skilled artizans in textile fabrics, for the effect of machinery is to reduce labour as much as possible to the functions of attention and guidance. The weavers, therefore, who either could not or would not accommodate themselves to the new order of things, suffered the direst reverses. It was no wonder that they looked on machinery with the profoundest hostility, that riots and machine breaking were frequent, and that the bitterest animosities were engendered. Thus in 1811-12, stocking and lace frames had been applied to the staple manufactures of Nottingham, and the discontented labourers, foreseeing or fancying that their livelihood would be imperilled, broke into houses and destroyed frames. The legislature thereupon passed an Act inflicting, as usual, the punishment of death on the frame-breakers. The Act only lasted two years; but on the occasion of its second reading, Lord Byron warmly attacked it, and recommended that if the Act were carried, it should be so amended as to provide that the jury should always consist of twelve butchers, and that a judge of the temper of Jefferies should be always engaged to preside in the court. Such a judge would not have been hard to find at that time.

It is easy to prove that the great movement of modern days, the employment of mechanical in the place of human forces, operates ultimately in cheapening produce and in bettering the wages of labour. But until that is brought about, the producers on the old lines may be subjected to severe privations. Nay, unless precautions are taken against the abuse of labour on the part of employers, it is very possible that the mass of those who work under the new system may sink into a lower position than that which they previously occupied when they were engaged with the old. The efficiency of labour may, by the use of mechanical expedients, be greatly enhanced, but unless the demand for labour is simultaneously enlarged, the profits of the employer may be increased enormously, while the wages of the workmen may even be lessened. Such a result may be further assisted by the temporary monopoly of patents. That the patents of Arkwright and Peel secured enormous fortunes for these inventors or purchasers of inventions we all know, that they ultimately cheapened production is equally clear; that they gave England well-nigh a monopoly in the supply of textile fabrics is as manifest; but it does not strictly follow that the English workman was better paid. The handloom weaver was undoubtedly impoverished, but I do not find that the machine weaver bettered his position. His wages remained low, his means were even straitened, and the misery of the manufacturing districts was even greater than that of the agricultural.

There are three processes by which the wages of artizans may be increased concurrently with the adoption and development of mechanical appliances. Any of these has its effect on the fortunes of labour, and as they have worked together, though at a comparatively recent period, they have had a marked influence on their wages, in results which can be clearly traced. They are restraints imposed by law on the employment of labour; restraints imposed by the joint action of labourers ; and the competition of capitalists as producers. Further, since the existence of such restraints and such a competition sharpen those inventive faculties which are ever on the look out for the means by which the process of production is cheapened, and when, in addition to these causes, there is the further stimulant of a market restricted by the policy of other countries, and therefore only open under the conditions of such a further cheapening as will enable the product to get over the barrier of foreign protection, the most powerful stimulants are applied to mechanical intelligence and productive invention.

Now for the early part of the nineteenth century, for nearly the first half of it, these conditions did not exist concurrently with the development of mechanical appliances. There was no control put on the employment of the young in any calling, and the manufacturer who had cheapened his production by the introduction of machinery could add to his profits by the employment of children in that kind of work which, under an earlier system, was carried on by adults. He could further, the poverty of workmen assisting the silence of law, make a saving by paying his wages, in part at least, by tallies on a shop which belonged to himself, and could add the profits of retail trade to the profits of cheap labour. The Factory Acts, which prohibited the employment of some persons altogether, and regulated the hours during which some other persons could be employed, increased the wages of labour absolutely and relatively, and, as has been shown, without diminishing, as also did the prohibition of the truck or tally system, the legitimate profits of the employer. The restraints which could be imposed by the joint action of labourers, though legally possible at an earlier date, were very slow in their operation. The illegal combination, branded as a conspiracy and sometimes treated as a felony, was certain to resort to violent action when its aims were thwarted, and in the earlier days of its imperfect legality constantly outraged the liberty which it purposed to secure. The trade unions of the earlier period had very much to unlearn, in that they were to substitute confidence for distrust, prudence and judgment for haste and

32

rash action, conciliation for force, foresight for passion, and a
careful interpretation of their powers in place of headlong
vengeance for the wrongs which they conceived that they were
still suffering. They who try to combine individual forces and
purposes, and to substitute joint-stock action, with its methodi-
cal subservience to a central authority, for independent action,
find that they may make serious errors before they discover the
proper use of the new powers which they are wielding. The
founders of the Bank of England collected subscriptions from
their shareholders, and applied them with all the judgment
they possessed in a novel way to trade and finance. During
the first twenty years of its existence, the managers of the
Bank committed errors which, had it not been for the great
commercial and political value of the institution, would have
been fatal to its existence. The errors and failures of joint-
stock enterprise have been incessant and disastrous. The
railway passenger in England would be providing ample
dividends to the shareholders in those companies if he paid a
half-penny a mile on the most convenient conveyance, had
not these undertakings been permanently burdened, and their
nominal capital increased threefold by the blunders of those
who projected them, by the rapine of those who gave them
a legal status, and by the follies and recklessness of those who
have managed them.

But no undertaking requires more care, more prudence,
more tact, more patience, more watchfulness, than the application of the joint-stock principle to labour. In the first place,
persons whose means are exceedingly slender have to make a
sacrifice for an object highly advantageous if it can be
secured, but the success of which is always problematical and
generally doubtful. In the next, they have to surrender their
judgment to the determination of those who have to interpret
the most difficult of problems,—the question whether the
market for labour will bear the cessation of labour. My
readers are aware that the leaders and managers of labour
partnerships have very rarely formed a correct estimate of
the powers at their disposal, and the powers which they
strive to resist and overcome, for the immediate object of a

strike has only occasionally been obtained. In the next, they who combine for these ends have the mortification of knowing and seeing that their sacrifices and labours in the machinery of their organization are made by a small portion of the order to which they belong, while the benefit of their action, if it be successful, is shared by those who decline to participate in the movement, and even take advantage of the occasion to baffle those who assert, and with perfect sincerity, that they are labouring for the common good of all their fellows. I do not wonder that passion and violence have in past times accompanied the action of trade unions, when the promoters and members of them have felt that they were thwarted, not by the resistance of employers, but by the selfishness, as they hold it, of those who profit by their policy and take advantage of them in the crisis of their struggles.

The third cause which has affected favourably the position of labour and wages is the competition of capitalists, aggravated, though not perhaps adversely affected, by the restrictions put on foreign markets. This competition is rendered intense by the occurrence from time to time of exceptional demand and of real or imaginary scarcities. Thus the waste of wealth and the demand for foreign products consequent upon the civil war in America added largely to the permanent industries of this country, and induced the investment of great masses of capital in undertakings from which the capital could not be extricated or the capitalist disengage himself. Within ten years of this event, a war, brief in its duration but exceedingly destructive and dislocating, occurred in Europe. By a financial blunder of the gravest kind, the vanquished nation was called upon to pay a vast ransom to the victor. This, a new capital, was at once thrown on the market, and beyond doubt Germany paid, in enhanced prices and inflated but unsafe activity, far more than she exacted. Now the waste of wealth, which had to be restored by foreign imports in the one country, and the vast exaltation of prices, which for a time levelled the dam of protection in the other, called other masses of English capital into active and permanent investments for such industries as were stimulated at the time. Hence, with

increasing production, we hear of declining profits and unremunerative trade. But, on the whole, wages have not
declined. The phenomenon, often adverted to in these pages,
that a time of low prices is a time of good wages, has been
exhibited during the last ten years. I make no doubt that
there are compensations. It is admitted that the efficiency
of labour in attention, rapidity, and exactness keeps pace
with the growing perfection of the machinery which it
manipulates ; that the special skill of the mill-hand is getting
more marked and complete ; and that, perhaps, were it not
for the increasing number of those who share in the employers'
profit, the cheapening of the process would more than compensate for the cheapness of the product.

Undoubtedly, if a relaxation of foreign tariffs were to take
place, this concurrent efficiency of machinery and labour in
England, which, as far as I can observe, is far greater than
in any country which I have visited, would be followed by a
large increase of profits, and, relatively speaking, a far larger
increase of wages. At present I believe that the workmen
of this country, speaking of them in the mass, are better paid
than those of any other settled and fully peopled community,
if one takes into account not merely the money wages which
they earn, but the power which these wages have over commodities. But the rise is entirely of the last thirty years,
and, unfortunately, it has not been shared by all in equal
proportion, while the case of some has been rendered worse.

The distress of the English workman during the earlier
years of the nineteenth century was heightened by the issue
of a depreciated paper currency. The history of that depreciation, the causes which brought it about, and the consequences
which followed from it, have been told so exactly and so
exhaustively by Mr. Tooke, that, in my opinion, that branch
of monetary science which is concerned with the functions of
paper currency has had no substantial addition to it since he
wrote, though one frequently meets with the heresies and the
fallacies which this acute writer detected or refuted by anticipation. The effects of the depreciated currency fell, as usual,
with more severity on labour, and on those generally who had

small incomes, than it did on those who could interpret the discount on the currency, and make a profit by their interpretation. In 1813, the premium on gold—*i.e.*, the depreciation of the paper—was nearly thirty per cent., and nominal wages were therefore in reality little more than two-thirds of their reputed value. The injury which was done to all was made a pretext for continuing the mischief beyond the time in which it could have been removed; but it has often been found to be the case in the economical history of England that a demonstrated wrong has been defended and its continuance supported on the plea that to do justice to the many would inflict a loss on the few.

In 1814, the quarter sessions assessment and the compulsory apprenticeship enacted by the Act of Elizabeth were abrogated. They had done their work thoroughly, and the regulation of the labourers' wages had been so completely successful that they were made mechanically to follow the price of food—a sure proof that wages are down to the level of subsistence. Thenceforward they were regulated by the farmers and the employers. There had been symptoms already that the justices were a little too considerate of the labourers' necessities. Besides, the Speenhamland Act, as it was called, of 1795, had authorized the allowance system, under which the employer of labour paid half the wages, and the ratepayers, employers or not, contributed the other half. The farmers, therefore, had only to meet together, when wheat was 100s. a quarter, and meat by the carcase was 7½d. a pound (having been less than half the price twenty years before), and agree that they would pay their workmen a shilling a day, with the rider that the rest of the public should pay him another shilling, which they took care to assess, collect, and distribute at their discretion. It is no wonder that, except in the fact that the breadth of arable land was greatly increased, and that locally certain improvements were made in the breed of sheep, very little real progress was made in agriculture during the sixty years between 1780 and 1840. The Board of Agriculture, over which Young presided with such efficiency and diligence, was dissolved, and agriculture has never since, unfortunately, been made the object of a department of State. For some unexplained reason, the political party which has had the principal management of public affairs since the first Reform Bill has always been averse to the revival of this department, and their rivals, who are perpetually talking about the necessity for it when out of office, have as strangely neglected to renew it when they have been in.

Vicious, demoralizing, and unjust as the allowance system was in principle, it occasionally gave an opportunity to individuals who had sufficient prudence and thrift to make use of it. In my native village in Hampshire, I well remember two instances of agricultural labourers who raised themselves through the machinery of the allowance system to the rank and fortunes of small yeomen. Both had large families, and both practised a bye industry. The village was peculiar in its social character, for there was not a tenant-farmer in it, all being freeholders or copyholders. The rector was opulent and generous, and there were a few persons of some private means in the parish. But, on the whole, the rates and the allowances came from the resources of occupying owners, and were, therefore, the contribution of the vestry from its own resources, the only non-employers being one or two humble tradesmen, the rector, and a country gentleman, whose house and grounds were not a hundred acres in extent. There was no poverty in the whole place. Most of the labourers baked their own bread, brewed their own beer, kept pigs and poultry, and had half-an-acre or an acre to till for themselves as part of their hire. But they had regulated wages, and, when their families were large, allowances. There were not infrequent sales of land in the village, as families came to an end, but rarely in large quantities. The rector built extensively, parsonage, schools, and finally church, from his own means, and, therefore, employment was pretty general. The village mason became a considerable yeoman. But the two labourers of whom I am speaking had their allowances, lived on their fixed wages with the profits of their bye labour, one being pig-killer to the village, and, therefore, always busy from

Michaelmas to Lady-day, at a shilling a pig, and the offal, on which his family subsisted, with the produce of their small curtilage for half the year. In the end, the allowance, saved scrupulously, and, I presume, made a profound secret, was invested in land by each. The one bought some forty acres of poor soil, on which he got a comfortable and independent living; the other some twenty, on which he did still better, for the land was some of the best in the village.

The abolition of compulsory apprenticeships in such callings as were specified in the Act of Elizabeth, or had been interpreted to come under its conditions, and the settlement of wages by the quarter sessions assessment or other magisterial authority, was not considered a boon by the artizans in 1814. In the first place, the repeal of Elizabeth's Act was demanded by the employers of labour, and it was, therefore, suspicious. In the next, the legislature from time to time had referred trade disputes between employers and employed to certain permanent authorities. Besides, the capitalists were exceedingly averse to any restraints on the employment of apprentices under the old system; and it was concluded, not without reason, that the repeal of the legal necessity would be followed by a rush into the calling. It should be remembered also that the change was effected at a time when the distress of the working classes was the deepest, that the avowed object of the repeal was to cheapen labour, and that every effort was made then and thereafter to sharpen the edge and expedite the use of the hateful laws which had been constantly enacted up to 1800 against combinations of workmen, and were still strictly enforced.

The defence of apprenticeship is two-fold. It secures, if the apprentice is adequately taught, a supply of good workmen, thoroughly instructed in the craft. It lessens the number of persons employed in the calling, by putting an impediment in the way of earning full wages. In the former of these ends the public is interested, though it may be doubted whether, in the absence of a trade regulation under which the workman should refuse to work for a dishonest manufacturer, and should be assisted by his union, and probably protected by the law, in case the denunciation is made a means of oppressing him, the skill of the workman is not sometimes enlisted in concealing the dishonesty of the employer. In the second aim of those who insist on or advise apprenticeship, the trade alone is concerned. The further precaution taken in some callings of limiting the proportion of apprentices to journeymen, though defensible on certain grounds, is much more open to challenge. It is a restraint on the choice of callings, and is, therefore, apparently at least, an injury to those who are kept outside a calling which they would desire to enter. Mr. Howell has stated the case in his work on capital and labour with great fairness. But it would appear from his own admissions that while up to 1814 the practice of unlimited apprenticeship was general, and the results disastrous, the abolition of the law and the consequent discontinuance of the practice has been followed by an epoch of better and continually increasing wages. Now, though wages were said to have been less in the twenty years between 1820 and 1840 than they were in the previous twenty years, it is admitted that the intrinsic value of these wages, as measured by their purchasing power, was greatly increased. But if we can rely on Mr. Leoni Levi's figures, taken from the record of prices paid at Greenwich from 1800 to 1820, and between 1821 and 1840, we shall find that, in the former period, the rate of wages as compared with the cost of food was at 55·25 to 232·5, the first figure being the daily wages in pence, and the second the aggregate cost in shillings of seven chief necessaries; while in the latter period, the wages stand at 62·75, and the same articles cost only 146·35. Wages, then, had actually risen, and the price of the necessaries of life had greatly fallen.

The chief economical objection to apprenticeship, which has not been anticipated by Mr. Howell, is that it tends to create an ever-increasing residuum of unprotected labour. That all human societies as they grow more populous will have a proportionately larger element of helplessness, misery, and crime within them, is apparently inevitable. It is most visible in countries where emigration goes on largely from the best and most vigorous stocks, and immigration into towns from poorer districts and foreign countries is active; for when immigration is from near localities, the least desirable addition to the growing population is likely to take place. Now during the existence of the famous Statute of Apprenticeship, the residuum was driven to agricultural labour, or to the new industries where apprenticeship did not prevail. That the whole body of working men suffered greatly is only too manifest; that those callings suffered most which consisted of the non-apprenticed classes is proved, if by nothing else, by the resistance which the workmen made to the abolition of the custom. The common defence for the limitation of apprentices is that if bad times come, it is better for few to suffer than that many should, and that the limitation of hands is analogous to and identical with a limit of output in production. But the answer is, that the restraint puts a permanent suffering on those who would otherwise enter a better paid calling, and reduces an increasing number to permanently low wages.

In point of fact, the sufferings of the working-classes during the dismal period on which I have dwelt might have been aggravated by the practices of employers, and were certainly intensified by the harsh partiality of the law; but they were due in the main to deeper causes. Thousands of homes were starved in order to find the means for the great war, the cost of which was really supported by the labour of those who toiled on and earned the wealth which was lavished freely, and at good interest for the lenders, by the government. The enormous taxation and the gigantic loans came from the store of accumulated capital, which the employers wrung from the poor wages of labour, or the landlords extracted from the growing gains of their tenants. To outward appearance, the strife was waged by armies and generals; in reality the resources on which the struggle was based, and without which it would have speedily collapsed, were the stint and starvation of labour, the overtaxed and underfed toils of childhood, the underpaid and uncertain employment of men. Wages were mulcted in order to provide the waste of war, and the profits of commerce and manufacture. It is no wonder that workingmen have no great trust in government by party, for the two great historical parties have fleeced and ground them down with impartial persistence.

Employers have constantly predicted that ruin would come on the great industries of the country if workmen were better paid and better treated.   They resisted, and have resisted up to the present day, every demand which workmen have made for the right of association, for the limitation of children's and women's labour, for the shortening of hours, for the abolition of truck, for the protection of their workmen's lives and limbs from preventible accidents, and are now appealing to the doctrine of liberty of contract, after having for centuries denied the liberty.   This misconception as to the consequences which would ensue from just and, as events have proved, wise concessions, has not been due to a cunning selfishness, but to the natural disinclination which all men have to make those efforts which have always compensated the loss which they thought that they foresaw, and have frequently turned it into a gain.   For it is a remarkable and an indisputable result of those interferences with what is apparently free action, that when their justice or necessity has been demonstrated, and the change or reform or restraint has been adopted, benefit instead of injury to the imperilled interest, strength instead of weakness, have been the consequence.   The concession of the right of combination was thought to be an infinite peril, and the workmen have gradually learnt their proper strength, and what is far more important, the strength and solidity of the calling in which they are engaged, and the profits which are required in order to secure its continuity and their employment.   They are getting to know what is the point at which cost will cripple production, and may be safely trusted not to destroy by excessive exactions that by which they live.   The Factory Acts were believed to be the death-blow to English manufacture, and they have made labour more efficient, more intelligent, more decent, and more continuous, without trenching on profits.   Only three years ago, the legislature determined on abolishing some of the fictions which lawyers had induced over the theory of common employment, and the same predictions of ruin were uttered. The law was passed, however, and a concession being made to the employers, under which, as is so often mischievously done, they were allowed to contract themselves out of the law, they eagerly clutched at the opportunity, as though the whole life of their industry depended on their being able to save a few shillings a year in remedying the losses of their own heedlessness, or a few pounds which might, properly spent, obviate the risk and ensure that justice should be done. The Parliament and the Law, which never do better work than when they arbitrate between timid interests, have over and over again by their action demonstrated the futility of these apprehensions and the folly of these fears. The only pity is, that Parliament has not had the courage to extend its action.

The old laws against combination and the doctrine of trade conspiracies were so dangerously wide, so capricious and uncertain, that at last the exasperation and anger of the workmen became excessive. The country was honeycombed with secret societies, and political disaffection was coupled with social discontent. The complaints of hungry workmen were met by the Peterloo massacre, and the demands for political reform, which the workmen had been instructed to consider remedial, by the Six Acts. In the early history of the English people, the bias of judges and law courts was directed towards the emancipation of the peasant and the maintenance of personal rights. The process by which the serf became the copyholder was greatly assisted by the interpreters of the common law. But from the days of the Stuarts, the judges were servile, timid, and the enemies of personal liberty. Over and over again Parliament has interposed to sweep away precedents which have coerced natural liberty, and interpretations which have violated justice. For generations it seemed that the worst enemies of public and private liberty were those courts whose duty it was to adjudicate equitably and to state the law with fairness. The English people owes much to the persevering acuteness of Bentham and the high-minded courage of Romilly that it was delivered at last from the Kenyons and the Eldons.

The credit of abolishing the combination laws is due to Joseph Hume. He procured a committee in 1824, took evidence, reported to the House, and obtained an instruction from it to the Chairman of Committees that a Bill should be drafted on the lines of eleven clauses dealing with the combination laws, and four which examined the effect of certain prohibitions put on artizans going abroad. The Committee declared itself unable to express any opinion on the propriety of removing the prohibition then put on the exportation of machinery. The Bill appears to have passed without debate or opposition, for I find no record of any such debate in Hansard. The Act inflicted penalties on such combinations as attempted to further their ends by violence.

It was inevitable that the working classes should immediately take advantage of the powers which the law had at last awarded to them. For nearly five centuries law after law had been passed under which the workman's wages had been regulated, for the reputed advantage of their employers. The English law has never affected to fix the price of food, though sometimes proclamations have pretended to do so, and local authority has occasionally been empowered to publish fair prices. But when a scarcity of labour occurred, due to natural causes, it attempted to control the claims of the workmen. For more than two centuries the law was a complete failure. For nearly three, as I have shown at length, it was a complete success. Now it was entirely natural for the workmen to believe that what they had gained at last was a boon, since their employers had so long and so successfully deprived them of its use. The employers and Parliament became alarmed, and revised the Act of 1824, though they did not venture on materially modifying it.

The ingenuity of the judges, always interested in the defence of property and very little friendly to that of liberty, discovered that the common law against combinations was still alive, and a series of prosecutions on false or frivolous grounds was undertaken, convictions recorded, and punishments inflicted. Mr. Howell has collected several instances of these trials, and comments on the general dissatisfaction felt among working men at the administration of the law. The ultimate emancipation of trade unions or labour partnerships from the difficulties and hindrances to which they were still exposed, and from the disabilities which precedents had put on them, is of very recent date.

The condition of the agricultural labourer has been different from that of the artizan. Scattered and incapable of combined action with his fellows, bowed down by centuries of oppression, hard usage, and hard words, with, as he believes, every social force against him, the landlord in league with the farmer, and the clergyman in league with both, the latter constantly preaching resignation, and the two former constantly enforcing it, he has lived through evil times. Under the allowance system, he seems to have been guaranteed against starvation, and under the law of parochial settlement he avenged himself on some of his oppressors, though not on the worst, those who, on one pretext or another, quartered him on another parish, employed him on quarter sessions or farmers' vestry assessment wages, and left others to supplement his wages by the allowance, and to support him when they had worn out his body, as they had worn out his spirit long before. There is nothing in the history of civilisation more odious than the meanness of some English landlords, except it be their insolence. They have been abetted by the foolish farmers, who ground down their labourers in order to enrich the landlords, and have finally sacrificed themselves to the rent-rolls of profligates and gamblers.

The sharpest trial they had to bear was the wholesome surgery of the new poor law. This famous measure, which was so necessary, so harsh, so inopportune, so unjust, was modelled on the practice which had been adopted in two Nottinghamshire parishes, Southwell and Bingham, in the former of which the workhouse test was organised by Sir George Nicholls, in the latter by Mr. Lowe, the father of an eminent statesman and very rigid economist of the *laissez-faire* school. The experiment of these two parishes was made the type of the new system. It is only just to say, that what might have been fairly equitable to all, though still severe in the last degree to the agricultural labourer, was mutilated by the owners of the close parishes, who succeeded in making others pay for the maintenance of their labourers, as all the landed interests had made the occupiers pay.

The average wages of the agricultural labourer, according to Arthur Young's calculations, had been 7s. 6d. a week from 1767 to 1789; 10s. from 1799 to 1803; and 12s. from 1804 to 1810. In 1811, they were 12s. 9d. They continued at this rate for three years; sunk about 17 per cent. from 1814 to 1818; about 20 per cent. more in 1819-20; about 12 per cent. more in 1821; and 5 per cent. more in 1822. Then they began to rise, and, according to Mr. Villiers' returns in 1861, were 9s. 4d. in 1824; 10s. 4d. in 1837; and 11s. 7d. in 1860. In 1866, Mr. Levi sets them at 13s. It may be doubted, however, whether these several increases of money wages were not, so far as the labourers were concerned, more than counterbalanced by the increase of house rent, the curtailment of allotments and similar indirect aids to labour, to say nothing of the excision of the allowances under the old poor law. In 1837, the cost of maintaining the poor was less than in any year since 1800, and was three millions below what it had been in 1832, though the average price of wheat in the former year was 58s. 8d.; in the latter, 52s. 6d.,—a difference in the ordinary consumption of a labourer's family, as estimated in bread, of about 4d. a week. The rise thus effected in 1837 probably represents the compensation for the loss of the allowances, for some expenses under the new poor law were considerably increased. I may add, that Young argued in 1813 that the wages of the agricultural labourer were below his necessary food, omitting all estimates as to house rent, fuel, clothing, and extras.

The beneficent restraints of the Factory Acts were not extended to the children of agricultural labourers engaged as helps to the paternal employment. Much of the activity which assisted the agitation for those excellent acts and insured their success, was the hostility felt by benevolent landowners to over-prosperous manufacturers. Even if the language employed by them did not warrant this inference, and the tactics they adopted did not confirm such a conclusion, the fact that agricultural children were not protected against premature labour would prove my contention. One does not see why they should not have been protected. The exposure of young children to weather, the custom of putting them under brutal carters and ploughmen, the common practice of sending them to drive birds from newly-sown fields in the most inclement seasons of the year, with scanty food and clothing, was, I imagine, as likely to be injurious to their health and growth as employment in mills. But the desire to secure an increasing rent, to be procured by the stint of the labourer, is, I imagine, as keen a passion in the bosom of the landlord as that of getting an increased profit from the unsuitable labour of women and children or from the misery of the factory hand has ever been in the constitution of the manufacturer.

I do not remember, in the very extended study which I have given to the history of agricultural labour and wages during the six centuries for which there is recorded and continuous evidence, that, in the worst experiences of the labourer, he was till very recently open to the risk of having his young children of either sex taken from him, and put under the care of a gangmaster, with a view to their labouring in the fields, being housed for the night in barns, without the pretence of decency, not to say comfort, and apart from the obvious degradation of their condition, exposed to the coarse brutalities of the manager of children's labour. But in the Eastern Counties it appears to have been till recently the practice, perhaps still is, for farmers to contract for the services of agricultural gangs, *i.e.*, of crowds of children set to work under an overseer who had hunted them up. The practice, I remember, was defended on the ordinary ground of cheap labour being a necessity for profitable agriculture, which, when it is interpreted, means that tenant farmers are too cowardly to resist rents which they cannot pay, except by the degradation of those whom they employ. That a peasantry, underpaid and underfed, should be constrained to submit their children to such an odious and demoralising slavery, is unhappily intelligible ; that the middle-man can be found to undertake the office of such an agency, is a fact to be regretted but expected ; that farmers should allow themselves to employ such an expedient, is scandalous; but that they who pretend to consider the condition of the poor, and to be active in the interests of humanity, should be complacent and silent, is a negligence which ought to bring its punishment, or is an acquiescence in ill-doing which I do not care to characterize.

Some twenty or more years ago, Mr. Girdlestone, a clergyman in a country parish in the west of England, and then or subsequently a canon of Bristol, called attention to the miserable condition of agricultural labour in that part of England with which he was familiar. The agricultural labourers of Devon are more than ordinarily numerous, for within the memory of man, a lucrative local industry, cloth weaving, has decayed, and the ordinary population has been swollen by the accession of unemployed weavers. Mr. Girdlestone had the ordinary fate of those who attack the doings of the landed interest. His better behaved opponents denied the accuracy of his statements, and published their own account of the facts. His rougher critics, the farmers, threatened him with violence and the horse-pond. It is not quite clear that his poor clients thought him their kindest friend in letting the world know what was their condition, for employers in country places have many opportunities of letting their workmen feel that discontent or complaint, even if expressed by an advocate, is dangerous. Quarter sessions' justice is very often, apparently, partial, but the tender mercies of farmers to their labourers are the reverse of gentle. Nor, indeed, is there much good done in calling attention to such facts as Mr. Girdlestone disclosed, unless the remedy is clear and can be applied immediately. Even the activity of the press, now far more searching than it was twenty years ago, and the tenderness of the public conscience, are apt to be transitory. Besides, though modern England is curious and sensitive, we may be certain that much unrecorded wrong is done. The public prints do not know everything, and might find it inconvenient to know everything.

Some years later, Joseph Arch, a Warwickshire peasant, undertook the heroic task of rousing the agricultural labourer from his apathy, of bearding the farmers and the landowners, and of striving to create an agricultural labourers' union. I believe that I was the first person in some position who recognised his labours, by taking the chair at one of his meetings, and I have been able to see how good his judgment has been, how consistent his conduct, and how prodigious are his difficulties. I believe he has done no little service to his own order, but I conclude he has done more for the general interests of labour, if only by showing how universal is the instinct that workmen can better their condition only by joint and united action. And it should be said, that other workmen, trained for a longer period in the experience of labour partnerships, have aided, and that not obscurely, the undertaking in which Arch is engaged.

The difficulties in creating and maintaining a labour partnership of agricultural hands are very great. In the darkest period of their history, artizans, even when their action was proscribed by the law, still clung together, had common purposes, took counsel, though secretly and in peril, and struck against oppressively low wages. But for three centuries at least, agricultural labourers have had no organization whatever on behalf of their class interests. I shall have written in vain if I have not pointed out how effectively the employers of rural labour contrived to enslave and subdue them. It is hard to see how any one could have hoped to move them. But even when they were moved, it was still more difficult to make the units cohere. I remember that an eminent clergyman of my acquaintance, now deceased, told me that when he first took a country living,—some of Arch's kindred were among his domestic servants, and he was entirely friendly to Arch's policy,—nothing struck him more painfully than the evident suspicion with which the labourers in his parish met kindness. He said that he very early despaired of their confidence, for he noticed that invariably any trust he showed in them was distrusted, was supposed to be tendered with the object of overreaching them. I do not comment on the experiences which must have induced this habit of mind on them, but simply say that this was the material with which Arch had to deal.

I am willing enough to admit that my clerical friend's position was more awkward than that of other persons. The landlord, generally non-resident, is, ordinarily speaking, as unknown to the English peasant as if he were a foreign potentate, and I suspect that the Arcadian pictures we now and then get of the peasant-labourer, his wages and his allowances from the great house, are, with rare exceptions, rustic ornaments in the immediate neighbourhood of the country seat, cottages with trim gardens, with honeysuckles trained on the walls, and neat borders of old-fashioned flowers in the little garden by the road, the creations of a benevolent despot, who from some good-nature and more ostentation keeps his poorer neighbours in apparent content. But the peasant who has to do with the tenant-farmer enjoys none of these amenities, and the parson who took the peasant's part would be thwarted in a hundred ways, and perhaps threatened with the horse-pond. I do not doubt that most country clergymen are kindly and conscientious, but they are poor hands at arbitrating between employers and labourers ; and when the former are farmers and the latter are hinds, I have generally found that the clergy put a personal interpretation on the apostle's advice, and seek to live peaceably with all men.

But though, being one of their order, the advocate of an agricultural union occupies a more independent and more confidential position than the intelligent parish clergyman, the temper of the peasants must be, even to an enthusiast, no easy instrument to play on. He has to combat with the persistent apathy of despair. He has to contend with the sluggishness of ignorance. He has to interpret the habitual mendacity of distrust. He has to rebuke the low cunning with which the oppressed shirk duty, for only those who are worthy can take a good part in the emancipation of the English serf. I well remember that a friend of mine, earnestly anxious to better his labourers on his model farm, gave them high wages, regular work, and showed them infinite consideration. At last he despaired and sold his property, because they thought him, in their poor puzzled way, a fool ; and he found that he had made them worse knaves than he found them.

Again, such a man, constrained to be a leader of men, is obliged to assert an authority and exercise a decision, which others, inevitably less informed, cannot understand and are loath to submit to. This difficulty is universal. The most awkward persons to deal with when debate is needed are two mobs, one of uneducated, and the other of fairly educated persons ; for the former are generally suspicious, the latter generally conceited. Neither will concede to the expert unless there is danger, or till patience wearies conceit. The greatest difficulty, we are told, even with the comparatively well trained artizan, is willing obedience to necessary discipline. It is said that the ill-success which has attended various schemes of co-operation has been due to the disinclination of operatives to obey the necessary orders of one who is of their own order, whom they have invested with authority. They will obey an overlooker whom their employer selects, even though his rule be harsh and severe; but it is not so easy to induce them to acquiesce in the directions of those whom they could depose at their pleasure. But the difficulty is greater the less instructed persons are, and the less familiar they are with the process by which the reality of liberty is achieved, —by the sacrifice of a portion of liberty itself. I have heard that in Mr. Arch's efforts he has been constantly baffled for a time by revolts from the necessary authority with which the manager of a labour organization must be invested.

Again, the scattered character of the agricultural population must needs be a great difficulty in the way of adequately organizing them. The heads of a trade union in towns can summon their men speedily ; and take action, if action seems desirable, promptly. But it is far more difficult to manipulate the scattered elements of an agricultural union, especially when the hostility to it is so marked, as has been generally shown, and the opportunities of giving effect to that hostility are so numerous. I do not believe that the mass of peasants could have been moved at all, had it not been for the organization of the Primitive Methodists, a religious system which, as far as I have seen its working, has done more good with scanty means, and perhaps, in some persons' eyes, with grotesque appliances for devotion, than any other religious agency. I have often found that the whole character of a country parish has been changed for the better by the efforts of those rustic missionaries, who possess many of the qualities, and have reproduced not a little of the discipline which the preaching friars of the thirteenth, and the Lollard Bible-men of the fourteenth and fifteenth century displayed or enforced. I believe it is true that all successful religious movements have aimed at heightening the morality and improving the material condition of those whom they have striven to influence.

The poverty of the agricultural labourer is a serious bar to the organization of the order. If trade unions have done, as I feel persuaded they have, much to raise the moral and better the material condition of artizans and operatives, they still cost money. I see from the excellent and, on the whole, complete apology for trade unions written by Mr. George Howell, that the charges put on the members by the machinery of the union of engineers amounts to an annual average of £1 17s. 2d. for the last six-and-twenty years ; and, if I remember, my friend Mr. Broadhurst told the foreign workmen at the Paris conference, that the funds necessary for the mechanism which he recommended would be a shilling a week from every member. But though the work of an agricultural union is greater than that of an urban association, there is no hope that peasants will be able to contribute at this rate. The economies of the agricultural labourers' union are rigid, the expenditure is cut down to the narrowest limits.

I am persuaded that the jealousy which the farmers feel

and the resentment which they express against Arch and his union are mistaken. The first condition under which a workman can be expected to be honest and intelligent, efficient and effective, is that he should have a sense of self-respect. Half a man's worth, says the Greek poet, is taken away on the day that he becomes a slave. The increase in the labourer's pay, if it be obtained, will be much more than compensated by the moral education which he has got by submitting to discipline and by understanding the principles of a labour partnership. When working men make a free contract, and they can never make such a contract as individuals, I am persuaded that they will make more intelligent and more beneficial bargains for the use of their labour than they ever will if they are hindered from corporate and collective action, remain under the impression that their wages are fixed without any discretion on their part, or are constantly called upon to defend or apologize for what they believe is their undoubted right,—a right which no consistent economist would dispute. The public is profoundly interested in the efficiency and the independence of the working man. By the former the industrial success of the country is guaranteed and secured. In the latter, there lies the only hope that we shall ever be able to realize in our day what the trade guilds of the middle ages aimed at, and in some directions unquestionably secured,— the character of the workman, as contained in his moral and professional reputation, and the excellence of the work which he turned out, to say nothing of the practical refutation of social fallacies. Among the members of the Agricultural Labourers' Union, sobriety, independence of public charity, and education, are conditions. The trade unions of London and other large towns do not perhaps exercise the moral discipline over their members which they might do if their fellows more generally enlisted in the system, and they will do, as they get stronger and better informed. But I am abundantly convinced that the English trade unionists include in their numbers the most intelligent, conscientious, and valuable of the working men.

I have referred to the difficulties which beset those who

strive by the machinery of trade partnership to better the condition of the agricultural labourer. At all times they would be many, but they are sensibly enhanced at the present time. It is patent to every one, that a vast amount of English land is going out of tillage. It is known that the value of land during the last five years has sunk to panic prices, for much of the price of land was due to the expectation, realized during three centuries, that agricultural land would continually rise in value. Now the mischief cannot have come from lowered prices, for they are incontestably higher than they were ten years ago. It cannot have come from the fact that effective agriculture is a lost art; for if one takes every particular in the schedule of the conditions under which agriculture is successful, the progress of the art in the United Kingdom is as remarkable and as continuous as it possible to conceive it. Agricultural machines are better, breeds of animals are better, seeds are vastly better, manures have been multiplied by chemical skill and tested by elaborate experiments, and in every direction progress of a solid and substantial kind has been made. But in spite of all this, there is serious agricultural depression and serious national loss. For once, at least, the complaints of the farmers are substantial, for they have in numbers abandoned their calling.

There is only one explanation possible for the decline of agricultural profit. It must be that the income is not proportioned to the outlay, that the cost of agriculture with a number of individuals who have hitherto followed the calling has been excessive. Now there may be four causes for this result, any one of which would be serious, but all together may be now, as in past times, fatal. They are, first, insufficient capital; second, excessive rent; third, insecure tenure; fourth, inefficient labour. No writer on agriculture has ever hesitated to ascribe disastrous consequences to the occurrence of any one of these incidents. What may we expect if all four are coincident? That there are many agriculturists who during the last few years have escaped these evils I can readily believe. But that many have failed through the pressure of the whole is manifest. And it should be remembered that excessive rent is a relative term ; that rent is excessive to one farmer which is easy to another ; and to discover what was the rent that not only the land but the cultivator could bear should have been, as it assuredly has not been, the business of the landowner and his too often most dangerous adviser, the agent or surveyor. Of this I am convinced, that the effect of unpropitious seasons has been trivial when compared with the other causes. Foreign competition has had no effect except in the muddled and selfish heads of protectionists, as may be proved by obvious and measurable facts. Whether the partial and halting security which the late Act gives to the tenant will have any solid effect is too problematical for any one to anticipate.

The inefficiency of agricultural labour, its alternate scarcity and abundance, is, I believe, to be admitted. Low wages, harsh usage, and the temptation of advantage in other localities, explain much of the evil. Perhaps changes in the mode of cultivation, the extension of pasture, and the use of machinery may have contributed in some slight degree. But the most hopeful prospect in this direction appears to me to lie in the extension of union principles among agricultural labourers. It is quite possible to pay too little for labour. Low wages, as economists have frequently demonstrated, do not always mean cheap labour. What Young says about land, that you cannot give too little for poor soil or too much for good soil, is true of your workmen. Some few years ago, an eminent agriculturist of my acquaintance told me that he preferred to have union men on his land, and bore testimony to their sobriety, steadiness, and integrity. Discontent with one's lot is not always a vice ; it may be the prelude to many virtues, the parent in the end of that which its timid or jealous critic would be the first to welcome. It seems that the foolish and frantic calumnies which have been told about labour partnerships have this foundation. They who utter these statements are uneasy at the supreme utility of labour, and are afraid that it will destroy public prosperity. Labour knows the conditions of its existence and continuity better. Meanwhile the retention of foolish and suicidal privi leges has created a dangerous interest, as yet wild and undefined, about the relation in which the people of England stand to the land of England.   The lack of wisdom and foresight is, I am convinced, more prevalent among those who have governed the nation than in the nation whom they have governed

CHAPTER XIX.

THE PRESENT SITUATION.

Summary of the Preceding Statements—Mr. Newmarch's Inferences—Labour Partnerships—Views of Senior, Thornton, and Mill—Trade Unionists and Political Economists—Certain Writers and their Views—Utility of Rigid Theories — The Statesman's and the Social Philosopher's Use of these Theories—Effect of Interference with the Natural Development of Society —This Universal in all Civilised History—The Services of Political Economy to Free Trade—The Distribution of Wealth, its Importance in the Theory— Restraints on Some Labour Necessary—The Remaining Facts of the Past which need Reform—The Land System and Local Taxation, Exceptional Advantages Given in Each to Certain Classes, and the Results—Rent of Land in Towns—Mr. George—Effects of Putting Local Taxation on Occupiers, on Public Opinion, on the Value of Land—Incidence of Local Taxation—The Common Statement—The Fact—Effects on Agriculture, Trade, Labour— The Practice in America—The Effect on Workmen of State Paid Dwellings —Comparison of Fifteenth Century Wages in Building Trades and Present Rates—Women's Wages at the Two Epochs—Allowances other than Wages now and then—Effects of Machinery on Agriculture—The Old Day of Eight Hours—The Character of the Work Done under it—Effects of Great Business in which Labour is Employed—Spontaneous Increases of Wages—Power and Weakness of Labour—The Course of History.

I HAVE now, I trust, stated with sufficient distinctness the facts which bear on the history of wages and labour for six centuries in England. The evidence is taken from unimpeachable sources, from the record of what was actually paid, and the power which the wages earned had over the necessaries and conveniences of life. For nearly half the period, I have myself supplied all the evidence from which the inferences have been derived, or could be as yet. For another century I have relied on the notes which I have already collected for the history of prices during the period extending from the middle of Elizabeth's reign to the accession of Anne. For the rest I have trusted to Arthur

Young and Eden to the end of the eighteenth; to Tooke, Porter, and others for the nineteenth. I have been able, I hope, to discover and explain the special causes which affected the labourer from the middle of the sixteenth century to the end of the first quarter in the nineteenth. I have shown that from the earliest recorded annals, through nearly three centuries, the condition of the English labourer was that of plenty and hope, that from perfectly intelligible causes it sunk within a century to so low a level as to make the workmen practically helpless, and that the lowest point was reached just about the outbreak of the great war between King and Parliament. From this time it gradually improved, till in the first half of the eighteenth century, though still far below the level of the fifteenth, it achieved comparative plenty. Then it began to sink again, and the workmen experienced the direst misery during the great continental war. Latterly, almost within our own memory and knowledge, it has experienced a slow and partial improvement, the causes of which are to be found in the liberation of industry from protective laws, in the adoption of certain principles which restrained employment in some directions, and most of all in the concession to labourers of the right so long denied, of forming labour partnerships.

Though the materials before him were exceedingly inadequate, and in many particulars quite untrustworthy, my late friend Mr. Newmarch, one of the very few persons who have been competent to interpret related statistics, discovered and announced in the last volume of the " History of Prices," that the best condition of the English workmen was during the fifteenth century, and subsequently, but in a less degree, in the first half of the eighteenth; the worst in the first half of the seventeenth and in the first quarter of the nineteenth. The periods, however, for which his information was defective were the fifteenth and seventeenth centuries, for one of which, till I published my third and fourth volumes, no evidence of value had been adduced; for the other, none has been printed. I am glad to have the opportunity of referring here to the great synthetical abilities of my late friend, the more so because one is so constantly vexed by the rashness of many who attempt the work of one who did it so well and thoughtfully, and even put their names to it.

My reader will observe that I set great store by the reparative energy of labour partnerships or trade unions in improving the material prospects of the working classes. These institutions were repressed with passionate violence and malignant watchfulness as long as it was possible to do so. When it was necessary to relax the severities of the older laws, they were still persecuted by legal chicanery whenever oppression could on any pretence be justified. As they were slowly emancipated, they have constantly been the object of alarmist calumnies and sinister predictions. I do not speak of the language used by newspapers and reviews which merely take the capitalist side of the question and give anonymous utterance to the passion of the hour. Far graver were the allegations of such persons as Senior and Thornton, economists whom I knew and respected for their clearness of sight and the excellence of their intentions. Even my friend Mr. Mill treated these forces of industrial life with a strange indifference. I confess to having at one time viewed them suspiciously ; but a long study of the history of labour has convinced me that they are not only the best friends of the workman, but the best agency for the employer and the public, and that to the extension of these associations political economists and statesmen must look for the solution of some among the most pressing and the most difficult problems of our own time. I shall hope to show this after I have dealt with the facts of the present situation.

The trade unionists speak with considerable bitterness of political economists, and with some reason. The ordinary teaching of political economy admits as its first definition that wealth is the product of labour ; but it seldom tries to point out how the producer should obtain the benefit of his own product. It treats of the manner in which wealth is produced, and postpones or neglects the consideration of the process by which it is distributed, being, it seems, attracted mainly by the agencies under which it is accumulated.

Writers have been habituated to estimate wealth as a general
does military force, and are more concerned with its concentration than they are with the details of its partition.   It
is not surprising that this should be the case.   Most writers
on political economy have been persons in opulent or at least
in easy circumstances.   They have witnessed, with profound or
interested satisfaction, the growth of wealth in the classes to
which they belong, or with which they have been familiar or
intimate.   In their eyes the poverty of industry has been a
puzzle, a nuisance, a problem, a social crime.   They have every
sympathy with the man who wins and saves, no matter how;
but they are not very considerate for the man who works.
Ricardo, an acute stockbroker, went so far as to say that there
should be no taxation of savings, so profound was his interest
in the process of accumulation by individuals.   It was strange
that he did not see that the only fund which can be taxed is
what the individual may save.   To tax what he must spend is
to destroy industry.

In point of fact, ordinary political economy does not go
further than to describe the process and some of the consequences of a state of war.   The war is industrial, in which
each man is striving to get the better of his neighbour, to
beat him in the struggle for existence.   Malthus and the elder
Mill laid down the Darwinian hypothesis before the modern
prophet of the physical life of the future and the past began
to speculate on natural forces.   Malthus, a most excellent
and benevolent person, was so convinced that the limitation
of what produces wealth should be effected in the interests of
wealth, that he proposed to do away with all relief to destitution.   The elder Mill endorsed the dismal and absurd
theorem of Ricardo that the production of food was obtained
only in diminishing quantities by increased labour, and his son
insisted on it with pious zeal.   John Mill was so impressed
with the risk of over-population that he hints, not obscurely,
at unqualified restraint, at even more than the coercion of
prudential foresight.   It is needless to add that these
writers magnify the function of the capitalist employer, are
under the impression that capital can be transferred from

object to object with almost the facility of a balance from one banker to another banker, and are alarmed at the risk that national wealth may be sacrificed by a change in the relation which exists at any given time between profits and wages. Nothing illustrates this alarm better than Mr. John Mill's famous paradox that the fund available for paying wages was a fixed quantity. The countenance which he gave to this doctrine has been made the basis of a perennial attack on trade unions. It insists on the inference that when the representatives of one industry strive to better themselves, they can do so only at the expense of other labourers. This doctrine, which Mill at last saw was an error, has been the greatest difficulty in the way of the trade unions. It is as baseless in industrial life as the quadrature of the circle is in mathematics. But this postulate would not, I think, have been gravely alleged had not Mr. Mill been affected by the supreme significance of the production of accumulated wealth, the ideal of the speculative economists.

It is exceedingly useful for men to know what will be the consequences of an industrial war, of a struggle for existence in society, of the results of that kind of competition, in which the strongest is entitled to use all his strength, and the weakest is to be judged, not by his utility, but by his success in the scramble. In these days we are told that the inferences of the economist are only tendencies. Had they been veritable, living realities, society would have long since collapsed, for they would have left only the alternative of two conditions —the relentless despotism of the few, or the anarchy of the many. I do not believe that, however great are the forces at the control of government, the logical consequences of rigid political economy would have been suffered to ensue. Force could extinguish discontent for a time, but the extinguisher would have had to be hired, and would in the end itself take fire.

The political economist of the strict school tells you what will happen (though he seldom tells you all that will happen) under certain conditions. Fortified with this information, and warned by it, the statesman in the true sense sees what must not happen, and takes his precautions, applies his remedies, and neutralises the disastrous consequences. The struggle for existence, interpreted strictly, is not progress but retrogression, and civilization is constantly engaged in moderating the struggle, even at the risk of sometimes burdening itself with indefinite liabilities. The information as to what will come to pass under the unrestrained action of certain social laws, is a boon which we cannot over-estimate, provided, of course, that the antecedent causes are fully stated and properly estimated. The student of social science thus discovers, or tries to discover, which of these causes are preventible, and the statesman, if he be worthy, deals with the problem. In the sense that the researches of the economist tell us the truth, his laws are beneficent, just as the physical laws, which connect disease with its causes, and show us thereby the means of prevention, are also beneficent. It is only when the economist becomes arrogant, and avows that he is a guide to all social action, instead of being the interpreter of certain definite results, that he is informed by the workman that his conclusions cannot be accepted as final in the practice of life, and by the statesman that they may consist with the constitution of another planet, but not with this.

The case is rendered infinitely more complicated, and abstract political economy becomes still more unpractical, when the social condition of any community has not grown naturally, but has been distorted by selfish laws and mischievous practices, the effects of which still survive, though the causes have passed away, and more difficult, when some of the most potent among these causes still survive. There has never yet been a civilised society in which nature was allowed to have her way, and where, in consequence, the economical condition of the people is one of spontaneous growth. One class has oppressed another; and even when the oppression has been remedied for the future, the present still bears, and for a long time will bear, the inherited tendencies of the past. Even in a country which, like that of the United States, has had an apparently spontaneous development, and has been freed from tyrannous customs, the immigrants bring with them the traditions, the weaknesses, the resentments of the country which they have quitted,—feelings and habits which have been engendered by past experience,—and have been cunningly introduced to political and social heresies, promulgated for the benefit of the few, in their new home.

Political economy has indeed taught one lesson of enormous value, though the truth has only been accepted in its fulness among ourselves. It is that any hindrance put by law or custom on the purchaser's market is a wrong to every one— to the community first, to the labourer next, to the capitalist employer last. It is due to the facts that the injury comes last to the capitalist, and that before the mischief is worked out such a person is able to gain abnormal profits by the losses of others ; and that they who get these profits are an organization, the consumers and the labourers, as a rule, are only a mob ; that protectionist laws, as they are called, exist for a day. When labour is thoroughly organised, and workmen find out the significance of the truth, which I have insisted on and illustrated in this work, that wages have always increased absolutely,—*i.e.*, in their money amount, and relatively, *i.e.*, in their purchasing power, when prices were low,—they will be still less disposed to listen to the insidious advice of those who counsel them to help the movement for raising prices, through restraints on trade, under the plea of fairness. But it will be found that all the best inferences of the political economist have had the advantage of being inductions from experience, and have been supported by practice after they have been demonstrated in theory.

Had economists worked out the most important part of their science, that which deals with the distribution of wealth, instead of merely busying themselves with hypothetical theories about rent, profits, and population, they would have inculcated every one of those legislative acts which have seemed to control the production and distribution of wealth, but in reality have assisted the former, and have made the latter more natural, and therefore more equitable. I think that my contention, which I see quoted by Mr. Goschen, could be exhaustively proved, that every act of the legislature which seems to interfere with the doctrine of *laissez-faire*, and has stood the test of experience, has been endorsed because it has added to the general efficiency of labour and, therefore, to the general well-being of society. A civilised people desires that they who produce its wealth should be intelligent, honest, thrifty, far-seeing, prudent, and, to the fullest extent possible, cultivated and well-mannered. It is impossible that these advantages should be secured, and the economies which they invariably effect secured with them, unless the workman is adequately remunerated for his labour, and is encouraged to hope. "The liberal reward of labour," says Adam Smith, "as it is the necessary effect, so it is the natural symptom of increasing national wealth. The scanty maintenance of the labouring poor, on the other hand, is the natural symptom that things are at a stand, and their starving condition that they are going fast backward." The first sentence is indisputably true; but the phenomena referred to in the second may be artificially induced, and were induced for a generation or two after Smith wrote. Employers will get labour cheap if they can; it is the business of the State to prevent them getting it so cheaply, that they imperil the future of the race by the process; and it is the business of particular crafts of workmen to sell their labour at as good a price as they can. They never have ruined, and they never will ruin, the capitalist employer by the process, for they may be trusted not to ruin themselves, since they are quite as acute as their employers in discerning what price the market will bear.

There still exist in all their mischievous force two factors in the evil legacy of the past, which exercise a mischievous influence on the fortunes of English industry. One of these is the permission still given to accumulate land under settlements, and to suggest its devolution by primogeniture. The other is the unfairness which puts local taxation on the occupier in place of putting it, in part at least, on the owner. The first of these is partly an inheritance of the Norman conquest, partly a result of the great War of Succession in the fifteenth century, partly the acquiescence of corrupt courts of justice in conveyancing practices, which were contrary to public policy and to the declared purposes of the common law. The second begins with the poor law of Elizabeth. At that time the occupier was generally the owner, and the rule was commended for its simplicity. But the slow operation of the former practice changed the conditions of the latter, and the occupier is rarely the owner, and can rarely become the owner. The convenient rule of Elizabeth's law became the interested practice of every other kind of assessment imposed by Parliament. The cost incurred in the maintenance of roads, the police of town and country, the health of towns, the education of the young, are imposed on the occupier; and the owner, except when he happens to be the occupier, is freed from all direct payments. As the revision of assessments is put into the hands of the quarter sessions, and the magistrates are not only generally landowners, but have a necessary property qualification, these authorities have invented a special system of valuing their own property, and on the plea that they assess their houses and grounds at what they would let for, have put nominal rates on themselves.

Now that the owner of land should be allowed to get the best price he can for that which he has to sell or let is, I conceive, as fundamental a right as that of the manufacturer to secure the fullest price which the market will allow him for his produce, and the labourer the best price for his labour. Nothing is, I think, more foolish than the theory that the State should regulate the prices of land, produce, or labour, should fix a maximum or minimum of either. Nothing, I think, could the theory become a practice, would be more disastrous to all. The English law attempted to carry out the theory with regard to labour, as I have shown, for centuries, and with the most mischievous results to land, produce, and labour. But, on the other hand, nothing is more natural and proper than that a person who owns land, produce, or labour should get the best price he can for it; should not, in short, be constrained to sell it to the first applicant, either at that person's price or at a fixed price determined by law.

But it is another thing for the legislature to give any vendor

34

exceptional powers under which he can enhance the price of
what he has to sell by constraining him to keep out of the
market a large portion of that which is strictly limited in
quantity. The custom was originally permitted, in order to
protect the successors of an existing generation of landowners
against the consequences of their own vices, and the result
has been to make them more vicious. This might be of no
consequence, except in so far as it is not in the public
interest that profligates in high position should be deliberately
engendered by law; but the protection accorded to them is
injurious to others, however good the personal character of the
protected individual may be. It stands to reason that if the
market of a necessary of life is deliberately straitened, its cost
will be enhanced. I have not the slightest doubt that the
miserable condition of the poorer classes in our large towns is
greatly due to the accumulation of land in few hands in such
towns, and to the possession of land by corporations. I cannot
doubt that if settlements of land were forbidden by law, and
corporations were constrained to grant leases in perpetuity to
purchasers, the market for convenient sites would be adequately
stocked, and the price of land in towns would fall. It is, of
course, impossible to find a parallel object to the existing area
of a country, its land. But if we could conceive that the supply
of the precious metals in any given country became a rigid
quantity, and the law permitted individuals to take portions
of this quantity out of currency, and hinder its natural distribution, it is certain that all prices but those of the precious
metals would constantly fall. Something analogous to the
case is to be found in the fact that the paper currency in the
United States is limited by the necessity of purchasing
government stock by the issuing banks. The debt in the
States is rapidly being decreased, and the price of the residue
is gradually advancing. It has been found necessary to permit
an issue based on silver certificates, that is, on deposits of silver
estimated at the factitious value of the silver coin. This
expedient will, however, soon be ineffectual, and it will become necessary, unless the paper currency is to bear a
premium, to find a further basis for the security of the issues.

or to discover some new means for supplementing the paper circulation.

No parallel, however, can be found to exactly illustrate the effect of an artificial stint of marketable land. It is a perpetual corner, to use an Americanism, created or permitted by the law to the injury of the multitude and for the advantage of the few. It gives the owner the power, not only of constraining the public to purchase in an artificially narrowed market, but of compelling him to part with capital which he has laid out on a terminable lease at the expiry of the term. Now this may be no injury to the middle man, for he will recoup himself from the necessities of the public, his customers. It may be no injury to the trader, though there are signs, not very obscure, in the growth of so-called co-operative shops, that the public are beginning to see that enormous rents for shops enter into the price of commodities purchased in them ; and it may be no injury whatever to persons whose transactions are very large, because the addition of a percentage to cover office expenses is infinitesimal under such circumstances. But where rent is the most important and the most increasing part of the cost of subsistence, as it is with the urban labourer, especially in large towns, the mischief is prodigious. The self-complacency with which some persons— owners of land to a great extent in London, for the temporary use of which the severest terms which the law allows and the market gives are extorted, to say nothing of taxes on renewal, equivalent to the appropriation of the tenant's good-will— advocate the housing of the London poor at the cost of the London occupiers, and, of course, to the enormous benefit of those who hold this induced monopoly, and will be vendors under forced sales, would be absolutely amazing in any other country besides England. But this kind of complacency is dangerous.

While in the United States in 1881, I found that the reading public was interested and amused by Mr. George's work on "Progress and Poverty." A clever man had caught up a few real facts and a few doubtful theories, and had constructed from them a sketch of social life, which was characterized by growing evil and waning hope. The sketch was not lacking in dramatic force, and in that probability which is frequently unreal, because it is based on, or appeals to, narrow or exceptional experiences. For this misery of the present and the future, Mr. George prescribes a single and, in his opinion, a complete remedy, just as the owner of a patent medicine is ready to assert and advertise that his nostrum will prevent or cure every disease to which either sex and every age is subject. The book was written with great clearness. The Americans, always pleased with clever paradoxes, and not devoid of that interest in speculative pessimism which well-to-do people like to indulge in, especially when it is illustrated from foreign practices, read the book, not seriously, I conclude, and have, I presume, forgotten it. In England it has run through numerous editions, and is said to be eagerly accepted as a new gospel of labour by multitudes of intelligent workmen, who recognize in the English land system the aggravation of their discomforts, the spoliation of their wages, and the present beggary of agriculture. The situation, it seems to me, is sufficiently ominous, and the attitude which landowners take, have taken, and appear likely to take in the future, discourages the defence of what is their proper right in the minds of competent and disinterested advocates. It is clear that class is set against class ; but who is to blame, in the past and in the present? for this distrust is not always made manifest. It is certain, however, that if discontent retaliates injustice by injustice, they are most in fault who gave the original provocation, and affect to be ignorant that they gave it, and continue to give it.

The other serious cause of dissatisfaction is the practice of putting all local taxation on the occupier. This is especially felt in towns, where local taxation is increasingly severe. The industries which aggregate in towns have, by their natural competition for building sites, aggravated by artificial scarcity induced on a limited area, continually enhanced the ground value of house property in densely peopled localities. I could show, if the nature of my work required the proof, that land for two miles round St. Paul's has increased during the last

hundred and fifty years a thousandfold in value. In so far as such
an exaltation in value is not the arbitrary creation of a partial
law, it is a natural result. If it could be shown to be the
entire creation of labour and capital, as the Thames Embank-
ment was, it is as much the property of the producers as a
bale of cloth or a cask of sugar. Now it is the opinion of
many, and these very respectable persons, that a very large
portion of this enhanced value should become the property of
the tax-payer, and that the revenue of it should be employed to
diminish his burdens. Others go further. As a matter of fact,
the owner contributes nothing to local taxation. Everything is
heaped on the occupier. The land would be worthless without
roads, and the occupier has to construct, widen, and repair
them. It could not be inhabited without proper drainage,
and the occupier is constrained to construct and pay for the
works which give an initial value to the ground rent, and, after
the outlay, enhance it. It could not be occupied without a
proper supply of water, and the cost of this supply is levied
on the occupier also. In return for the enormous expenditure
paid by the tenant for these permanent improvements, he has
his rent raised on his improvements, and his taxes increased
by them. The occupier in towns is worse used by far than
the Irish tenant was before the changes of the Land Act, for
if the landlord made him pay interest on his own outlay, the
cost of local taxation was shared between the parties.

It is commonly and confidently said that these taxes are
only paid through the occupier, and not by him ; that if they
were shifted to the landlord or the owner of the ground-rent,
the price would be enhanced by all the tax. To this it is a
sufficiently practical answer to say, that in such a case no wrong
can possibly be done by transferring local taxation to the ground
owner and building owner in towns, where the tenancy is precarious ; and where the tenancy is a term, by dividing the charge
between house landlord and ground landlord, according to the
respective capital values of their interest, with the object of
imposing the whole of the taxation on the ground landlord at
the termination of the lease. When this period arrives, the
ground landlord may, if he pleases, not now being supplied

by the law with a protected market, and under another condition to be stated hereafter, make his subsequent bargain
with the tenant.   Such an arrangement would test the truth
of the allegation, and would clearly not mulct the owner of
the unearned increment, since it would come back to him
in an increased rent.   I have never found that ground landlords welcome or even relish this proposal, which, on their
own showing, would only involve a re-arrangement.

The fact is, the statement is not true.   It is, of course, the
case, that when a tenant-farmer takes a farm he inquires about
and calculates the outgoings before he offers a rent.   A tithe
rent charge, he knows, is only part of the rent, and if the land
be tithe free or if the landlord pays this rent charge, he gives
all the more for the land.   If the two other charges were
remitted, it entirely depends on the way in which they are
remitted whether he will include them in his rent or not.   I
am referring to poor rates and highway rates.   If the legal
relief of the poor were extinguished, he would pay less rent,
for he would assuredly have to pay more for labour, plus what
those pay in poor rates who do not employ labour.   If the
highway rates were extinguished, and the state of things recurred which was general before the Act of 1773, under which
every occupier or owner was bound to find at least six days'
labour on the roads, he would probably pay less rent, because
the cost of carriage would be enhanced, and the charge of
taking goods to market would be increased.   The fact is, the
two principal rates levied on rural occupancy are in reality
beneficial outlay, since without labour and roads no land has
value.   They are antecedent conditions of agriculture in the
first place, and rent in the second, in satisfying which the
landowner and the farmer get subventions from other occupiers, who do not employ labour and yet contribute to the
double fund.

These taxes are transferred from the farmer to the landowner in the shape of a reduced rent, because they are
associated with what is essential to agricultural operations.
A tax levied on an individual remains with him, unless he has
some relation of exchange with another person, when he always

strives to transfer that tax to such a person. If an income tax is levied on a farmer, he cannot transfer it to his landlord, or to the purchaser of agricultural produce : not to the former, because there is no transaction to which it can be annexed ; not to the latter, because it is excluded by the competition of the market. A landlord who pays an income tax cannot make his tenant or any one else reimburse him. A tradesman who pays an income tax can possibly add it to the price of his goods, and would certainly attempt to do so, and it seems, from what tradesmen have said, may succeed in doing so. But in the case of beneficial outlay, such as that on poor rates and roads, the poor really pay the former in stinted wages, and the landowners do, and should do, most of the latter.

These operations do not apply, or do not in anything like the same degree apply, to dwellings in towns. That the tenant takes the outgoings into account is certain. But what determines his rent in the vast majority of cases is not the profit which he makes on the occupancy, but the proportion which rent bears to his income. It has been long since seen that the ground-rent of shops, and also the rates, in popular and business thoroughfares, are compensated for by enhanced prices to purchasers, or, at least, by a much more rapid turnover, the latter being frequently a matter of personal reputation. If the local taxation were transferred from the tenant to the ground-landlord, he might lower his prices, but there is no reason to believe he could be made to pay more rent. A man does not pay an increased rent because he makes more profits, but because the owner of his place of business can reduce his profits by offering, when opportunity occurs, this site to a rival tradesman. The local tax, therefore, tends to remain with him, but is transferred along with the greater portion of his rent to the customer, under the head of trade charges, in so far as his energy and ingenuity can affect the transfer.

With the mass of those who live in town tenements, these circumstances do not apply. A London labourer, I conclude, does not get better wages because he lives in London and pays a higher rent, but because, as a rule, the best labourers gravitate to the best market. I have pointed out before, that during the period in which the best wages were paid to the labourer, London wages were about 25 per cent. more than country wages of the same kind, and that when labour was depressed universally, the London labourer lost his advantage. During the first twenty years of the present century, London wages were higher than country wages, but then both were on the margin of existence. At present, the more important orders of artizans in London are in receipt of higher wages than those who ply the same craft in the country; but I have always been told that this was because they were worth all the difference. I have been constantly informed that it pays the employer to take London workmen into the country, at London wages, because their superiority is so marked.

The practical immunity of ground rents from all taxation except income tax raises, naturally, the cost of sites. Local taxation in London is in the aggregate about one-third the annual value of ground and building rent together, the proportion of the two varying from many times more in the ground rent, to equality, and to the reverse. I am persuaded from my experience as a director in an industrial dwellings company, whose buildings are erected in the borough which I represent (1883), that if the charge of local taxation were distributed equitably over the ground landlord and the building landlord, the effect on the cost of sites would be such as to render the housing of the industrious poor, in a two-roomed flat, with all conveniences of decency and cleanliness in each habitation, a matter of comparative ease and of moderate commercial success. The solution of the problem would be easier still, if the law permitted a cheap registration of title and an inexpensive mortgage on advances made by Government, with a wide margin for security. The unnatural cost of sites and the unnatural cost of legal instruments are the great hindrances to the economical housing of the poor in large towns. In the worst parts of London the ground rent is almost the whole of that for which rent is paid; and it is well known that when the Metropolitan Board of Works purchased the rookeries, they often paid for a filthy and dilapidated tenement the price of a mansion in a fashionable square.

In the eastern and middle states of the American Union, local taxes are levied on owners, and not on occupiers; upon property, and not on the use of property; no kind of property being exempt from contribution, as is, I think, absolutely just and necessary. Hence the owner of a magnificent house, with well-appointed and ample grounds, does not, as in England, escape with a nominal assessment, on the ground that the letting value of the property is problematical and, therefore, low. Again, the owner of void tenements is not excused from contributing on their assessed value. It is not the duty, American statesmen argue, of the public to remit an obligation on the ground that an owner does not dwell in his own house or discover a tenant for it. This system of taxation values stock-in-trade, furniture, even the balances of customers at bankers, and taxes all. There is no reason why an empty house or shop should escape, because the owner does not employ it for the purpose which led to its erection. Hence, while in England landowners, being relieved from a tax on void tenements, escape everything but loss of interest on their property, and, therefore, if rich, are able to withhold their property from the market, under terms of special advantage, the American owner gets the sharp reminder of local taxation that it is his business to inhabit or sell or let his tenements.

I have no doubt that strenuous efforts will be made to impose the expenditure necessary for the adequate housing of the industrial classes in London and other large towns on the local ratepayers or on the general public; and that, if possible, the purchase of sites for the erection of such habitations as are needed will be made a means for procuring exaggerated prices for those owners of town property who have been able hitherto to evade all contributions to local purposes from their property, and to employ the machinery which the law allows them or confers on them in order to enhance the price of that which is needed to satisfy what either social danger, or a sense of moral duty, or an awakened humanity declares to be urgent. What the other cities may do, I do not pretend to predict, nor how far they will realise that they will be called on to perform a duty at a great cost to themselves and at a great profit to the landowners. But London is helpless. Nothing can be conceived more ludicrously incompetent than the Board which manipulates its expenditure and at present transacts its municipal business. It is to be hoped that London may have an audible voice given it before the Legislature attempts to aggravate its burdens. But as yet London is administered, and not self-governed.

It is noteworthy that the demand for some action on the part of the Legislature for the better housing of the poor has not proceeded from labour itself. The working classes have made no claim on the State for the supply of one of the necessaries of life at an arbitrated rate. It is probable that they can foresee that this process is not friendly to the object which they have before themselves,—to sell their labour at the best possible price ; and to effect that object by selling it collectively, and on the joint-stock principle. On the other hand, they have not resented, except when the action proceeded from the masters, the competition of foreign workmen. Nor have they been, in the only capacity in which they deliberate, deluded by the sing-song of the fair trade syrens. To commend them for this is to patronise their good sense ; for it is certain, and they are, I conclude, as convinced as any one can be, that state gifts, like charitable donations for purely business transactions, are always more than compensated by the reduction of what is, without them, the natural market rate of wages. If they are wise, they should be resolute in determining that the conditions under which they will engage in the social warfare and the social harmony are that those with whom they are concerned shall have or shall retain no privilege, and that they will be beguiled with no gifts, the most insidious manner in which the workman may be led to sacrifice the advantages of his position.

Some of the working classes in London, and those who have been long educated in the machinery of labour partnerships, have at last regained the relative rate of wages which they earned in the fifteenth century, though, perhaps, in some particulars, the recovery is not complete. I can illustrate what I mean by giving the details which I promised above. From 1449 to 1450, divers workmen were engaged in building at Oxford. The head mason got 4s. a week for nine months in the year; the others, 3s. 4d. for ten. For two months the under masons got 2s. 10d. Now a multiple of twelve will fairly represent, except in house-rent, the general difference in the cost of living at the present period and that to which I have referred. In modern values, then, these sums represent 48s., 40s., and 34s. Mr. Howell informs us that the building trades in London in 1877 had reached 7s. 1½d. a day, or 42s. 9d. a week. I am not informed whether this rate is for the whole six days, and for how many days in the year it may be reckoned on. The workman of the fifteenth century only missed eighteen days of the year, of which a fortnight was at Christmas, three days at Easter, three at Whitsuntide, and six on other days scattered over the year. My reader may care to see the average prices for the two years 1449-50. Wheat was 5s. 10d. a quarter; malt, 3s. 10½d.; oatmeal, 5s.; beef, 4s. 1d. the cwt.; mutton, 4s. 6d.; pork, 5s.; geese, 4d.; fowls, 1½d.; pigeons, 4d. a dozen; candles, 1s. 1d. the dozen pounds; cheese, ½d. a pound; butter, ½d.; eggs, 5¾d. the hundred of 120; firewood, 1s. 10¼d. the load; shirting 6d. a yard; and cloth, 1s. 5¼d. If my reader cares to construct a table for himself from these facts, he will find, I think, that, leaving out house-rent, the most formidable item in modern, the most trivial in ancient times, my multiple of twelve is moderately low.

I have taken the best prices of artizan labour in the best English market for such labour in order to contrast them, improved as they are by the mechanism of a trade union, with the prices paid spontaneously in a county town in England 434 years ago. I will now contrast the lowest prices of the most poorly paid labour (not, indeed, that in London, where the extremes of poverty are to be expected and are witnessed, but) in places where, if kindness can discover and aid struggling and ill-paid industry, the search will be made and the assistance accorded, with the remuneration of the same kind of labour more than four centuries ago.

Women's labour in agriculture is rare in the fifteenth century. When it is found, it varies from 2s. a week paid in hay and harvest time to 1s. 6d.; for ordinary field work, such as hoeing corn, I have found it as low as 1s., the rate paid old women for weeding pitched pavements. In the calculations made as to the rate of women's wages in the agricultural districts supplied by Mr. Villiers in 1860, the average given is 4s. 2d. But if the price of this kind of labour had risen as highly as that of other commodities has, the wages of a woman labourer in husbandry would be from 24s. the best paid, and 18s. the ordinary rate, to 12s. the most poorly paid. I do not know whether any material increase has occurred in such wages since 1860, very little information being given as to the amount generally paid, and I think that such an outgoing would have been put prominently forward as a further cause of agricultural distress; but even if it be the case that it has increased some twenty-five per cent. and is now at 6s., the wages of ordinary agricultural labour earned by women are not more than a third of the amount which they were four centuries ago.

In almost all comments on the wages paid the agricultural labourer, they who invite our attention to the facts in the public prints, and are invariably the landowners, dwell with satisfaction on the indirect allowances made to the peasant, his low-rented house and garden, his bit of potato ground, his occasional payment in kind by a periodical bushel of unsaleable wheat, and the concession of collecting wood or getting an allowance of loppings and roots as fuel, and insist that these are substantial additions to his weekly earnings. Undoubtedly he would be worse off without them, and generally when they are given they are an addition to such wages as the labourer could not live upon alone. But it should be remembered that these are to be compared with the facts of far better days, of a time in which the peasant's hut and curtilage was occupied at a fixed rent of 2s. a year, which, treated by the multiplier given above, would be less than sixpence a week at present; that the curtilage of his cottage was far larger than the villager's garden is in our time ; that he had his share in the common of pasture; that he was able to keep poultry, probably a cow, certainly pigs ; that his employers constantly gave him portions of food, under the name of nonschenes, daily; and that in harvest-time his wages were not only increased, but he was frequently boarded as well. I do not imagine that the present privileges and allowances of labourers in husbandry are to be reckoned as spontaneous acts of generosity on the part of employers, in whom I have never seen any such tendency, but simply as the curtailed and by no means equivalent survivals of much larger and more solid advantages, which could not, perhaps, with safety be suddenly and entirely extinguished.

It is probable, too, that the wages of labour were far more continuous in agricultural operations than they are at present. The farmer, before the use of machinery in substitution for human forces was adopted, and for a considerable time after it was familiar, employed his hinds in many kinds of service for which mechanical means are now found. We learn from Young that many improvements had been made in the implements employed in agriculture, and his English tours are full of engravings of such machines as he found in use. But sowing, reaping, mowing, and threshing were all done by hand, ploughing, of course, and the building of ricks. It was Young's great desire to see improved ploughs adopted, and with them much more rapid and clean work, with less wear for man and cattle. Now, many of these necessary processes are effected by machinery, sowing universally, mowing generally, reaping and binding frequently. Ricks are often built by means of elevators, and the threshing of corn is invariably done by machines. But the six or eight weeks of the labourers' hay and corn harvest were what he relied on for supplementing the scanty earnings of the rest of the year, and were constantly the source from which he supplied himself with the extras, over and above the bare food, of fuel, house-rent, clothing, and casualties. He expected to have much work in the barn during winter at threshing, and now the use of

the flail is a lost art. It is more than likely that the shortening of his exceptional advantages, and the change which has
come over the previous regularity of his occupation, would be
very indifferently compensated by a rise of 25 per cent. in his
wages when he is employed.

I stated in a previous chapter that the day was one of
eight hours' work, and grounded my opinion on the fact that
winter wages were reckoned to be payable only in the
months of December and January, and from the fact that
extra hours, sometimes as many as forty-eight in the week,
are frequently paid for by the king's agents when hurried
work was needed. These hours, of course, were not continuous, being broken for nonschenes, dinner, and supper in
the summer, and for nonschenes and dinner in the shorter
days. During the winter solstice it seems that only the
dinner-time was allowed. Even when the Act of Elizabeth
and the regulations of the quarter sessions prescribed a day
of twelve hours all the year round, for this is in effect the
meaning of the clause, two hours and a half were allowed for
rest, and the day was brought down, on an average, to nine
hours and a half. But this was precisely one of those pre-
scriptions which labourers would be sure to resist and
employers would find it expedient not to insist on. That it
was evaded is, I think, clear from the fact that the quarter
sessions' ordinances constantly call attention to the law, and
remind artizans of the penalties they incurred,—a penny for
every hour of absence. Employers were very likely to
discover that the labourer's resistance to an excessively long
day was not entirely personal, and that the work might suffer
from the workman's weariness or exhaustion. Now the quality
of the work in the old times of which I have written is
unquestionable. It stands to this day a proof of how excellent
ancient masonry was. The building from the construction
of which I have inferred so much as to work and wages, is
still standing as it was left four centuries ago. I am persuaded
that such perfect masonry would have been incompatible with
a long hours' day. You may still see brickwork of the next
century, which I venture on asserting no modern work would

parallel; and within five minutes' walk of it Roman brick-work, probably sixteen centuries old, which is as solid and substantial as when it was first erected. The artizan who is demanding at this time an eight hours' day in the building trades is simply striving to recover what his ancestor worked by four or five centuries ago. It is only to be hoped that he will emulate the integrity and thoroughness of the work which his ancestor performed. According to Mr. Leone Levi, the average amount of hours in the building trades at the date of his work on the wages of the working classes (1867) was fifty-five hours.

The magnitude of commercial undertakings, due to the cheapening which ensues when business is concentrated in few hands, is a characteristic of modern times. In some particulars it is better for the working classes; in some it induces in-conveniences; in all it makes the organization of labour a necessity, and, as I hope to show hereafter, a solid advantage to the public. I have already stated that in the past, which I have been contrasting with the present, the relation of employer and employed was exceedingly direct; nor do I doubt that it was to this directness that the high remunera-tion of the artizan was due. A church or a mansion was to be built, a new wing or new offices to be added to a conventual house or college. Perhaps the owner supplied the plans. If not, the master mason knew how "to draw his plot," and the master carpenter his. The employer bought all the raw materials direct from the manufacturers, and put them ready for use on the spot. He could calculate within a very moderate margin what the whole would cost, and what would be the charge of labour. In the building to which I have referred, the cost of materials, on much of which labour is expended, was £54 10s. 3½d.; of labour, £73 0s. 0½d.; and the extras connected with the structure, but not immediately associated with the materials and labour, £14 9s. 0½d. Thus in the aggregate charge, the cost of materials is 38·3 per cent.; that of labour, 51·4 per cent.; and of extras, 10·3 per cent.

The multiple of twelve would put this structure at a cost of £1,703 12s. 6d., from which should be deducted the sale of certain cranes, worth, on the same estimate, £73 12s., and therefore leaving £1,630. Now I make no doubt that at the present day the tower would cost from £4,000 to £5,000, and I infer that the additional cost would be entirely due to the charge of contractor's profit, architect's commission, and middlemen's advantage. It is upon the saving of this enormous waste that the energies of the intelligent employer are directed, and the advocates of increased wages for workmen should be. When the economy is effected, it will be found, concurrently with another reduction of charge alluded to already, that workmen may get better wages and may be more cheaply housed. It is assuredly from the stint of wages that the profits of middle-men have been derived.

The employer in our day is unknown probably to nine-tenths of his workmen. Their relations are generally with his agents and overlookers only, and probably must remain so. But it will be evident that the more able and shrewd the employer is, the greater will be his profits, because such mental qualities are rare ; and the more difficult his workmen make his position, either by slackness or slovenliness of work, or by the necessity of supervision, the greater do they themselves make his profits to be. He has a large margin from which he can save in the competition with those who are engaged in the same calling, by the reduction of the middleman's charges. He has another large margin from which he can save, in the character of his workmen and the goodness of their work, for the better this is than the average, and the greater its efficiency is, the cheaper it is to him. If, however, this quality of excellence becomes general in workmen, they ultimately have it in their power to attach a portion of his profits, by a demand for higher wages, and by a conviction that he will not forego a cessation of his advantage by refusing to part with a portion of it. It will be found, I believe, that those heads of firms who best know their business are most amenable to the reasonable demands of their workmen, and the analysis given above shows that the reason of this is that they make greater profits than their rivals. For though it is true that, in the first place an increase of wages can only be derived from profits, and where rent is a principal result from profits, as it is notably in agriculture, from rent, the efficiency of labour may be so increased in the end that profits and rent may rapidly recover themselves. This is the way in which the judicious employment of machinery tends to raise wages. That it lessens the demand for labour immediately is possible, just as a successful demand for more wages lessens profits, but in the end it increases them, for it cheapens production, and thereupon sets up a fresh demand for labour, and lessens cost, and thereby leaves a larger margin of gross profits to be divided. The increase in the wages of agricultural labour between 1730 and 1760 was not merely due to the fact that agricultural produce was cheap, but to the fact that profits in agriculture were large, that a rapidly increasing area of cultivation was taken in hand, and that a rapidly increasing capital was put into the land.

Now it cannot be denied that capital may seek labour, and that labour may, without an effort, be able to gain the advantage of this demand. Such an event has occurred when there has been a sudden deficiency of labour, as after the great pestilence of 1348. It has occurred when the distribution of employment has become so exactly proportionate to the current demand for labour that demand has been always in excess of supply, as was the case in the fifteenth century, and is normally the case in countries where labour is scarce and the opportunities of wealth are great, as in the western, and especially the mineral districts of the American Union. Such an event has occurred when there has been a sudden and increasing demand for special products, as happened to the coal and iron trades in 1865 and 1873. It does to some extent when the supply of labour is in equilibrio, and the competition of capitalists is great,—a rarer phenomenon. But in the great majority of cases, the whole advantage of a new discovery, a new process, and a new machine rests with the capitalist employer. The great inventions of steam and the machinery employed in textile fabrics remained with those who invented and applied these capital forces and processes. The artizan, by whose labour the development of this wealth was alone possible, became more impoverished and stinted. If population was stimulated, it was made more miserable, and population will grow rapidly when the condition of the people is deteriorated. Now it is impossible to doubt that had labour partnerships been general and legal in the latter part of the eighteenth century, the Englishman of that epoch would have been as assuredly able to make better terms with his employer as we are told he did in the fourteenth, when the legislature vainly strove to put down the combinations of those ancient trade-unions.

It would be possible to go through the various kinds of labour which were carried on in those remote times, and are still special industries. But enough has, I trust, been said to sustain the main conclusions at which I have arrived. From what is supposed to be the natural, and, on the whole, justifiable, tendency of the parties to a contract, the employer strives to enlist the services of the common factor with himself of profit and wealth on the most favourable terms for his part of the bargain. The labourer or workman, on the other side, seeks as naturally to achieve his advantage, though he is seriously hindered by his individual impotence and by the urgency which disables him from lingering long over the terms of the bargain. But in the process of settling it, he has on very rare occasions been put in the position of using his power with prodigious force, so as almost to annihilate interests which seemed secure and progressive, as in the middle of the fourteenth century, and to effect a social revolution. From time to time, in a minor degree, he has been able to produce, by his discontent and the temporary cessation of his industry, great inconvenience. The power which he possessed, and the use which he made of it, suggested that the rare occasions on which he could act should be anticipated and restrained, and the legislature at last succeeded in binding him, though he struggled vigorously, and in the end proved that his liberty was less dangerous than his servitude.

Then began a new departure. The policy of the past had

done mischief to the interests which it professed to further, and the new poor law was enacted. The policy of repression had led to results which seemed to threaten the very existence of a large class of artizans and of the future of the nation, and the Factory Acts were passed. The soil of England became too narrow for its people, and employment, even under the circumstances of those restraints on employment which the Factory Acts induced, became precarious. There was danger in the air, and perhaps the Legislature became alive to the duty of considering other interests than one, and free trade in food was established.

Meanwhile the working classes were not idle, and not a few of them adopted, though still with great risks, the new freedom which was accorded them, and founded labour partnerships. These have grown; and whatever the capitalist and some of the public may think of them, they are believed by many workmen to be a far greater and more powerful instrument for good to those who have conceived, developed, and supported them than any guarantee of law or custom. The advocates of the system have demanded as yet but little from the Legislature beyond what is essential to their free action. It remains to be seen whether they have not been a benefit in the past, and are a principal hope in the future, not of that labour merely for whose ends they have been severally established, but of labour in general, of human progress; and lastly, whether they do not form the readiest means, perhaps the only means, by which the gravest social and political problems may be stated and solved. I shall try to make an estimate of this question in the next and concluding chapter.

CHAPTER XX.

REMEDIES.

Changes Necessary for the Improvement of the Social State Incomplete—The Remedies for the Present rendered more Difficult by the Errors of the Past—Labour in Other Countries during the Past—Protection against Foreign Competition, and its Effect on Wages—In the United States—Fair Trade—Extension of the Functions of Government an Error—The Meaning of Frankenstein's Demon—The Population of Large Towns, though in a Bad State, Better than it was—Foreign Immigration—Theory of Lodging being Provided by the State—Nationalization of Land, Origin of the Movement for—Effects of such a Policy—Emigration of the Young—The Agricultural Remedy—Mr. Vallis on a Peasant Occupier's Earnings—Trade Unions, the Factor in Improving the Condition of Artizans—Their Prevalence in the Fifteenth Century —Duty of the Workman as Regards his Labour—The Economy of Waste—The Effect of Machinery may be Mischievous if not Counteracted by Labour Combinations—Labour Combinations and Rent, especially Ground Rents—Domestic Servants' Wages—Overcrowded Callings often Relievable by Trade Unions—Extension of Trade Unions to Women's Work.

THE English Government, till very recent times, having been administered by opulent landowners and successful traders, did its best to depress the condition of those who live by labour. Parliament has, indeed, within the last sixty years, done much in abrogating severe and repressive laws, in giving freedom to labour, in making the United Kingdom a free market, and thereby educating its industry, in restraining the greed which employed immature labour, in disabling women from certain degrading employments, in constraining employers to deal fairly with their workmen, and in arbitrating between rapacious landlords and defenceless tenants. It has, indeed, by no means completed its duties to the public. It must sooner or later, the sooner the better, sweep away the distinction between real and personal estate, forbid the settlement of land, and release conveyances from the grip of the attorney by establishing a cheap and compulsory registration of title. It has been reckoned that the conveyance of real estate in the United Kingdom is mulcted in law charges, exclusive of taxes, to the extent of £12,000,000 annually. I do not answer for the accuracy of the figures, or know, indeed, what are the elements from which they are derived. But I know that such charges are a present loss, which are not only without any equivalent whatever, but constantly bring about an insecurity from which properly registered titles would be free. And, again, there must be a revision of local taxation, under which landowners shall be made to bear their just share in local burdens; and to which, as I readily admit, all property should, except in the case of poor rates and roads, contribute by relieving occupancy and taxing property. But though much remains to be done, more has been done in this country than in any other to remove the legal disabilities of labour, and give it freedom of action. The result of this wisdom is manifest. The unwise delay in other needful reforms will soon be plain.

It is, indeed, impossible to do away at once with the effects of the past. The growth of society has been distorted by partial and injurious laws, and the distortion will not be removed by the removal of the causes which induced it. You cannot, as the adventurer in the Greek comedy does, take the nation, and, by some magic bath, restore it from decrepitude, disease, vice, dirt, drunkenness, and ignorance, to manliness, health, virtue, self-respect, sobriety, knowledge, forethought, and wisdom at a stroke. It will need long years of patient and disappointing labour before the marks imprinted by centuries of misrule and wrong-doing are effaced. And furthermore, the renewal, if it is to come, cannot be imposed from without. It must be developed from within. Beyond the removal of positive mischief, which it has in past times created, the legislature can do little more that give every freedom it can for innocent energy, and check all the mischief, as far as is possible, which comes from the strong domineering over the weak. If it does too much, it enfeebles enterprize and discourages practical wisdom. If it neglects to adequately protect the weak, and thereby gives license to selfishness and fraud, it permits a trouble, for which it has assuredly to find a remedy. Nor can the aid of well-meaning persons outside the mischief which has to be remedied do much beyond perhaps, disclosing the disease and indicating a means of cure. If there be evil at work in the condition of those who live by wages, most of the cure must come from themselves. There is no means for it but self-help. The constitution is needed more than the medicine, and, without it, the medicine is naught. Philanthropy is superficial, intermittent, transient, partial, at best. There is infinite danger that it may become a scheme by which attention is diverted from causes which contribute to or create the mischief, and duties may be enforced vicariously. I can easily imagine a great proprietor of ground rents in the metropolis calling attention to the habitations of the poor, to the evils of overcrowding, and to the scandals which the inquiry reveals, while his own income is greatly increased by the causes which make house-rent dear in London, and decent lodging hardly attainable by thousands of labourers. It is quite possible for the indirect agents of these evils to denounce the mischief to which they are the contributors, and to claim from others the funds by which to remedy the injuries which they cause and from which they profit. When a London landowner invites the public to consider how the London poor are housed, he should simultaneously recommend that the laws and privileges which aggravate the evil should be repealed or abandoned.

Bad as the condition of labour has been in England, it has been worse in other countries. When, five centuries ago, the insurgents under Wat Tyler and his associates brought about the emancipation of the serf, the peasantry of Western Europe were thrust into gradually increasing misery. I have already commented on the beggary of the French peasant and the failure which attended his early efforts for freedom. The Peasants' War in Germany was the result of intolerable oppression. The conquest of Egypt had closed the last of the ancient routes to the East, and the traders of Italy and the Rhenish cities were impoverished. In the profits of this trade the nobles shared, and when these profits declined, they strove to reimburse themselves by extortion from the peasantry. The peasants claimed to be freed not only from these new exactions, but from their ancient dues, revolted, were put down, punished severely, and driven back into more hopeless bondage. The Thirty Years' War in the next century completed their misery. It is noteworthy that as the Black Prince and the Captal de Buche suspended hostilities and united their forces in order to chastise the Jacquerie in France, so, in 1525, the Duke of Guise, on behalf of the French king, who was then at war with Charles the Fifth, and was his prisoner, took an active part in punishing the boors in Germany. So both the historical parties in England have been equal adepts in oppressing labour.

At the French Revolution, the people turned on their ancient oppressors and rent them, avenging the wrongs of centuries by a savage butchery. The cruelties of the Terror were due to a reaction from the sense of accumulated wrongs, and to the dread which freed slaves feel that if they are not thorough in their work, the latter end will be worse than the beginning. When, in his old age at Brussels, the infamous Barrère was asked to explain the mad fury into which the French Revolution rapidly developed, and the ferocity which the Mountain exhibited, he merely answered, *"Nous étions des lâches."* The answer is an epitome of the Terror and of its doings.

Modern governments still wrong labour by pretending to protect it against foreign competition. What they really do, is to swell the profits of the capitalist, to cripple the energies of the workman by narrowing his market, and to shorten the means of the consumer by making that dear which he wishes to purchase. The establishment of protective duties is a confession that the industry cannot thrive at home, still less be successful abroad, unless the people at home pay an increased price for its use. There is nothing done by levying such a tax on consumption, unless it be imposed on those articles which are in general demand, and therefore are the necessaries or conveniences of the many; for the more voluntary the use of an article is, the less does it serve the ends which are proposed by the *régime* of protective duties. It is very likely true that an industry may be developed by protection, and a foreign market found. This is said to be the case with German iron, and that the manufacturers of this article undersell Belgian and English iron masters. But a moment's reflection will show that they can do so only at the expense of the German consumer, who not only pays an enhanced price for what he uses, but finds the profit which reimburses the manufacturers for what would otherwise be a loss in the foreign market.

In the United States, the process is being exhibited on the most gigantic scale. The freest people in the world, whose administrations and parliaments have been able to study and avoid the errors and crimes which older governments have committed against labour, have submitted to a tariff which clips the wages of the workman to the extent of fifty per cent., under the pretence of supplying him with variety of employment. It is a trifle that heavy duties are imposed on a few foreign luxuries, except in so far as they give a semblance of equity to those which are laid on common necessaries, on the clothing of the workman, and on his tools, and on the farmer's implements of husbandry. The motive of the impost is, of course, to increase the profits of capital; and this has hitherto been the result, and the impoverishment and dependence of labour,—a consequence as certain though not so manifest. The more remote but inevitable consequence, a bitter distrust and a growing enmity of the labourer towards the employer, has been occasionally seen in the furious outbreaks which have from time to time occurred in America, and are likely to recur whenever, as is frequent in protected trades, a great depression comes over the special industry.

From sheer folly, or from interested motives, a belief that better profits would ensue to employers, or in order to serve party ends by giving a false interpretation of economical phenomena, there are persons who are foolish or wicked enough to advocate the return to a protective policy in

England under the name of fair trade. The good sense of the better educated and more experienced English workman shows him that his acceptance of this doctrine would be nugatory in articles of voluntary use, and suicidal in those of necessary use, and he has, therefore, rejected the suggestion. There are, moreover, persons who have the effrontery to invite workmen to accept and acquiesce in a tax on their food, in order that landlords may keep up their rents at the expense of the general public. Such shameless mendicancy is in keeping with the traditions of aristocratic government, which has, in the history of English finance and legislation, put the burdens of state on the many, and freed the property of the few ; but when it is fully understood, it will not serve the men who advocate it, or the party which has the meanness to encourage it. Unless his nature is changed, there is nothing which the average Englishman more thoroughly distrusts than a politician who gives furtive and occasional support to a proposal which he publicly condemns.

When a Government goes beyond its proper functions, which are to maintain the public safety, to propound useful and equitable legislation, to arbitrate between interests when it is necessary, to extinguish privileges, to unite efficiency with economy in the administration of affairs, to punish fraud and violence, and to undertake those great offices for which private action, individually or collectively, is inadequate, and attempts to distribute employments among its people, to favour one class at the expense of another, to meddle with the innocent habits of its subjects, and to mould their lives after its own pattern, to coerce the open expression of opinion, and to silence criticism on its own proceedings, it makes itself, or those whose affairs it administers, responsible for all the failures of its action, and engenders the belief that if man is made unhappy, the Government has brought about the result. The English Government from the days of the Pale till the passage of the second Irish Land Act, has attempted to create or support an aristocracy of race in Ireland, and has thereupon developed a democracy of discontent, hatred, and violence. Half the German army is engaged in protecting the German soil from an invasion of revenge, and the whole believes it is. But the other half is engaged in restraining that wild outburst of socialism which a meddling and pedantic administration has induced the German people to believe to be the only opposition which the government really recognises and fears. The huge empire of Russia is undermined by a universal conspiracy. The Austrian administration lives by setting race against race, and achieves an apparent union by nourishing implacable aversions. When the traditional purposes of a government are detested, its best intentions are distrusted.

The strange story of Frankenstein was, I make no doubt, suggested to Mary Godwin out of the opinions which she received from her father. Frankenstein had contrived to put life into a gigantic being which he had constructed, and on which he intended to bestow superhuman strength, stature, and beauty. His creation had strength and stature, but was unutterably and shockingly hideous. The maker of the monster abandoned the horrible creature, which had to shift for itself, and to learn the arts of life in solitude, as all fled with loathing from the sight of it. It possessed infinite powers of endurance, infinite capacity for learning, great determination and cunning, irresistible strength. It yearned for society, for sympathy, and for kindliness; and meeting with none of these, being rejected by all and made a loathsome outcast, after it had been called into being, it became an infuriate fiend, which pursued with implacable hate and with the most cruel wrongs the man who, being the author of its existence, was thereupon its most detested enemy. This remarkable conception was intended, it is clear, to personify the misery, the loneliness, the endurance, the strength, the revenge of that anarchic spirit which misgovernment engenders, the suddenness with which its passions seize their opportunities, and the hopelessness of the pursuit after it, when it has spent its fury for a time. Most European governments have been engaged in the work of Frankenstein, and have created the monsters with whom they have to deal.

The great cities and towns of England contain a vast

population which lives, one hardly knows how, on mean and precarious wages, in dismal and unwholesome dens. Some of this poverty is merely miserable, some of it is vicious, some is criminal. The growing population of these English towns is partly of local origin ; for though apparently a century ago the deaths in London exceeded the births, the increase of sanitary appliances have made London so healthy that the relations are reversed ; every week the amount of the births equals the number of a large village. There is also a large immigration into London and other towns. The German population of London is fully equal to that of a first-class town in the German empire. The Irish population is probably larger than that in any Irish town, except Dublin and Belfast. London, it is probable, also receives a considerable part of that population which has deserted the agricultural districts. Now London is the greatest manufacturing town in the world. Naturally its inhabitants are engaged in an infinite variety of occupations. But these occupations are stinted by the fact that an octroi duty on coal is levied to an amount which seems insignificant, but is sufficient to kill such manufactures as depend on a prodigal consumption of this source of power. The tax was first imposed, I believe, to supply a fund for rebuilding St. Paul's Cathedral, was continued for the use of that absurd and obsolete Corporation of the City Proper, and now forms part of the fund for the purposes of a hardly less grotesque institution—the Metropolitan Board of Works.

Evil as the condition is of destitute and criminal London, with its misery and recklessness, it is not, I am persuaded, so miserable and so hopeless as nearly all urban labour was sixty years ago. It is not, I believe, so bad as it was at the beginning of the eighteenth century, when, as one sees from Luttrell's diary, the executions at Tyburn formed a notable percentage in the weekly bills of mortality. It is not so ignorant nor so unclean as it was twenty years ago, though, as usual, the pedantry of the Education Department, in driving all children through a rigid examination, produces a distaste afterwards for books and learning, which makes the standard of proficiency a barrier towards subsequent study and learn-ing, which is nearly as insurmountable as ignorance. In order to enable the Government officials to calculate the charge of national education in the easiest manner for themselves, they pay by results, and in consequence induce results which are very adverse to those for attaining which public money is expended.

It is a matter of great gravity whether we should welcome or even permit the perpetual immigration of a foreign element into the country. The American people, with an unlimited extent of territory, decline to allow themselves to be the recipients of European pauperism, and keep a sharp look-out on the character of the steerage passengers to the States. They suspend the rights of citizenship during a considerable period of probation. They have decided, for reasons which are very intelligible, though not very convenient to be published, not to allow their population to be polluted by the presence of a Chinese proletariat. Now it is quite certain that the English people at one time gained considerably by the influx of foreigners. Some of our best industries were developed before the Reformation by the inflowing Flemish artizans from the time of Henry II. onwards. Others owe, it seems, their development in England (though not without some remonstrance, as we find from an Act of 1454 directed against foreigners engaged in the silk manufacture) to the exiles whom religious bigotry and persecution drove away. Such were the workmen who fled from the Spanish Inquisi-tion in the Low Countries, and the Bourbon Dragonnades in France. We owe, indeed, some of our best stocks in England to these migrations. No Englishman can regret, for the sake of his country, that it was an asylum for a Romilly.

But it is quite another thing, when cheap transit being provided, the great towns in England swarm with pauper foreigners. Perhaps the readiness with which this kind of population is accepted, is a survival of the experience in which the addition of the foreign element was an indisputable good; perhaps it is a convenience to those capitalists who make large profits out of degraded and impoverished labour.

Working men, who understand the interests of their order, are alive to the risk which their organizations run from the competition of foreign immigrants, and with characteristic public spirit have suggested to foreign labour that it should seek to raise itself, not at the expense of other labourers, but in concert with other labourers. The advice which Mr. Broadhurst gave last autumn (1883) at the Paris conference of workmen was in the best interests of all workmen. In brief it is, Raise yourselves, not by depressing others, but by acting with them. You cannot escape, try whatever you can, from the influence of competition, any more than from the survival of the fittest. But the survival of the fittest may be the survival of the analogue to Frankenstein's demon, while the effort of all true civilisation is to improve those who are improvable, and to deal with the residuum. It is possible that the struggle for existence, unless controlled and elevated, may be the degradation of all. It nearly came to be so during the first thirty years of the present century.

Various remedies have been proposed for the immediate benefit and the permanent improvement of the working classes, especially the industrious poor in large cities. It may be expedient that I should state, in this conclusion to my inquiry, what appears to me to be the value of the several projects which have been propounded.

I am persuaded that an attempt to relieve distress, provide proper lodging, and find work for the inhabitants of large towns would in the end produce even worse evils than that condition which the expedients would seek to relieve. No one disparages kindliness and charity. For certain calamities, such as those which are relieved in hospitals, they are indispensable. For extraordinary casualties they are invaluable. But as a universal process they would be disastrous, especially if the charity is compulsory, or provided out of the funds which the Government raises by way of taxation. To adopt such an expedient would be to despair of the recuperative power of honest industry. If the London ratepayers, or even the London landlords, are to find the means by which homes are to be provided for workmen at prices which are unremunerative to those who supply the homes, and work on products for which there is no market, or an overstocked market, it needs no particular acuteness to discover that the emigration into such towns will be more rapid than ever, and the restraints on improvidence, not now over strong, will be entirely removed, and the old allowance system restored in its worst form. It seems plain, too, that in the end, what was seen to be not very remote under the old poor law, will ensue, and the relief of poverty will absorb nearly all the products of labour.

The nationalisation of land is a favourite project with those who believe that socialism is the true remedy for low wages. Now I cannot believe that this project, from the extreme form which it takes in Mr. George's proposal, that the property of all landowners, great and small, should be confiscated, to the milder proposal, that after due compensation secured to existing interests, the state should constitute itself the universal landlord, and appropriate for public ends all future accretions of value in land, would have been ever gravely contemplated had it not been for the policy of English landlords, who have clung to the obnoxious privileges of primogeniture and the right of settling land. The instinct of the public leads them to conclude that there is a very strong motive for the maintenance of these customs, and naturally that the motive is a selfish one. They are aware that the soil of this country is limited in extent, that what is scarce is dear, and that if what is scarce can be made artificially more scarce, it will be made more dear. That this impression is correct cannot, I think, be doubted. It is not indeed easy to discover the precise amount of additional or unnatural dearness which the application of Gregory King's Law, which formulates the effect of scarcity on the price of a necessary of life, would prove to be induced on building sites in the metropolis. But it is clearly understood that the cost is greatly enhanced, and discontent at an unfair advantage conferred by law on the owners of certain kinds of property, exaggerates the

impression formed as to the amount. I am at least persuaded that the socialism which desires in a more or less
drastic manner to curtail the present rights of landowners
will become more prevalent and more threatening as long
as the invidious privileges to which I have often referred
are maintained. These mischievous privileges explain the
popularity of Mr. George's theory and his remedy of universal confiscation,—a confiscation which will include not
only palaces and parks, mansions and farms, but every freehold cottage or homestead in which working men have
invested the savings of their lives. Discontent constantly
accepts ludicrous and even suicidal paradoxes.

The policy which would make the state the universal
landlord, after providing for the compensation of existing
interests, would be only less fatal and foolish than that
which confiscated them without compensation. It would
confer on the state the most gigantic functions, which would
require for their administration a machinery which, were it
entirely honest and thoroughly efficient, would cost more
than all which the project hoped to gain, would create an
enormous body of fundholders, the recipients of the rents
which the government received for the use of the national
estate, fundholders who would not be, by the very terms
of the bargain, tied by a single responsibility to the society
which paid them the dividends on the new stock, and would
cert inly lead to a bureaucracy which would be vexatious,
inquisitorial, and corrupt. If the state is to revise its
contracts with its tenants periodically, the tenant will be
divested of all motives to improve his holding; if the new
tenancy is to be a permanent one, the state of things which
the nationalisation of land was intended to obviate will
instantly recommence. But the progress of human liberty
is always connected with the restraint of government interference, except when government, by arbitrating between
conflicting interests, saves the weak from the tyranny of
the strong, and thus secures justice, and benefits the whole
community by its police. Again, the object of the wise
economist, that result to which all the practical teaching

of his science and all the experience of social history tend, is the distribution of wealth into as many hands as possible. A country is infinitely safer, infinitely stronger, infinitely more capable of genuine progress, in which the many are in comfort and content, than that is in which much wealth is accumulated, but the process of distribution is artificially hindered.

Another remedy is emigration, or migration. Spontaneous emigration is almost invariably a loss to the community from which it proceeds. It is supposed to relieve the country of a surplus population, and thereupon to be a remedy against the danger of over-crowding. But a process which takes away the best of the working classes, as must be the case with spontaneous emigration, since only the most vigorous and enterprizing are influenced by the movement, is the reverse of a gain to the country which loses them, and if their places are filled, as it seems they are, by immigrants of inferior type, and, as is generally the case with such types, of greater fecundity, the loss becomes a double one. The fact that the emigration is a benefit to the emigrant does not alter the result. Now emigration is a boon to the country from which it takes place only when it relieves society from that class of the industrious and honest workers which is certain to be over-crowded, and from which, therefore, depletion is a good to all,—to the people which runs the risk of being constrained to support the excess, and, far more important, to the labour which is likely to be in excess. The class which most exactly fulfils the conditions referred to, is the young of both sexes; and it is well known that this is the class of immigrants that our colonies eagerly welcome, and are willing in their new homes to surround with every safeguard.

I am persuaded, from reason and experience, that the emigration of the young is the best remedy for hereditary pauperism. Some years ago, when I was a guardian of the poor in my own city, my Board took pains to carry out this kind of emigration, through the agency of Miss Rye, and with absolute success. Nor do I doubt that in London and other large towns, especially as education is sharpening the faculties and developing the intelligence of the young, such a system of emigration would be welcome and highly beneficial, especially if care were taken that the parent should be carefully and exactly informed of the way in which the child was going on, and the child was made to understand the duty of relieving the parent, perhaps of finding him or her a home in the new country to which he or she may have gone. The children of the poor are not undutiful or ungenerous to their parents. I am convinced from my personal knowledge that the wages of domestic servants are freely given by young women to their parents, and that the miserable earnings of agricultural labourers are constantly eked out by the wages of daughters in service. In the case of pauper children, I hold that they who have put upon others the charge of their maintenance have morally forfeited the right of determining their career; and that in the case of criminals and persons of infamous character, they should be, in the interest of the children, deprived of parental rights at once and altogether. It is the interest of honest and industrious workmen that pauperism should be diminished as much as possible in the present and obviated in the future, and that crime should be isolated and watched. Everything which increases the cost of administering human societies, and still more everything which involves the waste of wealth, diminishes the resources available for the employment of industry.

The disastrous dissociation of agricultural skill and competent capital has led to a diminution of the rural population, and to the abandonment of tillage over a large and, it is to be feared, an increasing area of English land. The poverty of the towns has been swollen by agricultural immigration, and the necessary cultivation of the country has been injured by the lack of hands. Hence it has been proposed, and with great reason, to revive and extend the system of small holdings, so as to attract a rural population to the land before it is too late. My friend, Mr. Jesse Collings, in the House of Commons, has already procured some legislation in this direction, and the system has the warm support of Mr. Arch's practical experience. I believe that the only reason why farmers are hostile to such an arrangement is that they fear it will make the agricultural labourers too independent. It seems that it is disliked by landowners because they are wedded to the tradition of having large farm tenants and a system which is plausible in itself, and, until the recent agricultural break-down, has been apparently successful. But at the present crisis one would think that any and every expedient which would tend to replace labour on land and attract new capital to land would be advantageous, and should be eagerly adopted. Though the individual capital of peasant holders (I am thinking of much more than miserable acre allotments of the worst land in the parish, at double the rent of the best) is small, the proportionate capital is large. I am sure, at least, that if intelligent labourers had the prospect of getting a ten or fifteen acre farm, with a decent dwelling and corresponding farm offices, the amount of capital per acre with which they would stock their holdings would soon be relatively far higher than that of the large farmer, and that the produce per acre would be far larger, especially if they betook themselves to dairy farming and ensilage, as the small fifty acre farmers of the Eastern States in America are doing, and with such marked success, on the worst land in the world. Fortunately small farms are under the protection of the Agricultural Holdings Act.

I have before me a little work, written by a national schoolmaster some fifteen years ago, and to which I then put a preface. I stated in it that "the position of the agricultural labourer in husbandry was one which pressed for a solution, and that speedily, or that the country would have to face difficulties which cannot be evaded, difficulties which, unless foreseen and provided against, may be in the highest degree serious." The crisis has come, and it is worse than I anticipated.

Mr. Samuel Vallis, in the little book to which I have referred, gives a balance-sheet of his receipts and expenditure on five acres of land cultivated by spade husbandry. He shows a gross return of £109 10s., his live-stock being two cows and two pigs, his grain crops being an acre of wheat and half an acre of green peas. He puts down on the other side £3 an acre for rent,—an unconscious avowal as to the enormous rent procured for cottage farms,—£5 10s. for seeds, and £20 16s. for labour, the latter item being of course one which was necessary for the schoolmaster, but would not be incurred as a money payment by the labourer, and so shows a profit of £68 4s., which he states, almost superfluously, is more than double the wages of the ordinary farm labourer. He steadily pursued what he calls "the soiling system" with his cows, *i.e.*, they were constantly fed under cover, and he reckons that the advantage of this over the "exposed system" is fully 25 per cent. He adds that if young agricultural labourers remained single till twenty-five, and saved half their wages, they would soon find the necessary capital for such a little holding, or, indeed, for one three times the size.

I do not doubt that it is still possible to recall a rural population to the English soil, to renew and extend the productiveness of English land, and to find abundant high-class labour for the capitalist farmer when he reappears. It is true that the occupiers of peasant holdings might demand higher wages than they now earn. But what of that? They might illustrate anew the doctrine that low wages do not mean cheap labour, and that high wages may. It is certain that the possession of property is the best, nay the only means under which people are educated into respecting property, and that diligent labour on a small holding will lead to diligent labour on another's tenancy. I am told that the experiment of a beneficent despotism, under which the labourer has been gifted with enough land for cow and pigs to his cottage, with the condition that he worked honestly for an employer at hire, has been tried successfully, the landowner being the arbiter as to the wages paid. The system is the revival in our own day of the old tenancy in villeinage, though with less land and on an uncertain tenure. If this system succeeds, though the intrinsic faults which belong to it were found out and commented on in the earliest agriculture, I should anticipate that a more generous tenure would be still more successful, and that the most obvious solution of the agricultural difficulty would be to win back the labourer to the land by the temptation that there is annexed to his cottage such an amount of land as would give him an interest in the soil, and by leaving him free to contract for his time and skill with the larger tenants.

In course of time it may be possible to reunite capital and agricultural skill, and bring back the labourer to the soil. It is necessary to do both, and to face the solution of the problem. At present, the parties immediately interested will not see the facts, and the public at large, which is profoundly interested in the rehabilitation of agriculture, is kept in the dark. No more deplorably unsatisfactory and incomplete account of the situation can be conceived than that contained in the report of the Duke of Richmond's commission, which is crowded with irrelevances, and destitute of true information on the real facts of the situation. So ill-informed are those who are concerned for agriculture, or pretend to be, that there are persons addressing working men who imagine that they can by bold assertions induce industry to believe that it will benefit itself by replacing taxes in the form of a sliding scale on wheat, by so restricting the foreign market, and thus rendering the wages of the workman more uncertain than they otherwise would be, and by raising the price of food, and thus diminishing their purchasing power.

The future of the artizan, factory, and urban population has yet to be discussed. For this there is but one remedy,—the extension of labour organizations on the trade union principle, but with considerable improvements in detail. If it be found that those callings alone have prospered in which labour partnerships have been developed, and those have prospered most in which the fundamental principles of such labour partnerships have been most prudently kept in mind and acted on, it stands to reason that an extension of the system to other callings, now notoriously underpaid, is the most obvious remedy for low wages and uncertain prospects. Such associations are a revival of the best traits in the mediæval guilds.

I confess that in my earlier writings, before I had studied

the history of labour and its strange vicissitudes in England, I was of opinion, though with some misgivings, that the organization of a trade union was directed against the consumer through the employer, that it appropriated out of an elastic but common fund from which labour was paid (though I never agreed with Mr. Mill's wage-fund theory), an undue share, and that it aimed at establishing an aristocracy of labour, from the benefits of which the great mass of working people would be excluded. An inquiry into the history of labour has dispelled these opinions. I do not aver that the organizations of the middle ages are models for working men in modern times to imitate. They were partly concessions to artizans in towns, partly encouraged in so far as they were benefit societies; but they were much more a reaction against interested oppression. The modern labour partnership is freed from the enforced vices of the older organization, and has generally purged itself from the equally adventitious vices which were engendered by the interpretations which the courts put upon the atrocious combination and conspiracy laws.

Now the existence and development of the ancient system, described in detail in the previous pages, was accompanied by remarkable and general prosperity, for the vices of society in the fifteenth century were mainly those of the Church and the nobles. Every one throve, except the foolish people who, after wasting France, came back to England and wasted each other. The singular prosperity of the age has greatly puzzled those who have even in part recognised its character, but was easily seen, to such experienced eyes as those of Tooke, to have had no relation to the reputed value of the currency, or to the other explanations which had been given of so remarkable a phenomenon.

I can discover no other cause for this remarkable material progress beyond the universal associations of labour. I admit that the situation was in itself favourable to high wages. Land was greatly distributed. The seasons must have been singularly propitious. The country was permeated by a religious feeling which scorned the worldliness and immoralities of the established system, was severe, parsimonious, ardent, secret, and personal. Unfortunately, the mass of the people either could not or would not use what power they had to check the growing violence of the nobles, the scandals of the Church, and the vices of the administration. They sided, it seems, with the reforming party among the nobles, the Yorkist faction, and found, as people always find who entrust popular interests to a noble partizan, that they were made tools of and deluded.

It is probable, too, that the success of their private organizations, necessarily a secret, made them indifferent to such political action as they could take. The towns, and even the villages, had their guilds, and it is certain that these guilds were the agencies by which the common interests of labour were protected. In a prosperous people, legal persecution develops cautious resistance and judicious organization. In an unprosperous one, it encourages the growth of violent opinion and a passion for destructive remedies. I can quite believe that the working classes of the fifteenth century grew indifferent to politics, or found that they could not grapple with lawless domestic feuds. I am certain that the factions let them alone, just as I am certain that when the working classes became impoverished and powerless in the sixteenth century, the destruction of the guilds was seen by their oppressors to be the best way of breaking up their organization. In the same way the modern trade union has had to fight for two generations in order to get its funds protected against fraud or embezzlement.

The evidence of the present and the example of the past appear to prove that labour partnerships are the remedy for low wages. They undoubtedly put the employer in a difficulty. They claim a greater share for labour in the gross profit of industry. They constrain him (if he is to hold his own in the struggle) to find his remedy in the economy of waste, in the development of invention, or in the reduction of rent. The analysis of these agencies requires a fuller exposition of the circumstances.

The workman should seek to make his labour as efficient

and fruitful as possible. The honourable desire to protect every workman in the same craft, by seeking to establish a minimum of wages, may lead to the suggestion of a minimum standard of efficiency. It is entirely essential not only to the dignity but to the strength of labour that it should do what it has to do as well as it possibly can. I am sure that the workman of the fifteenth century was as proud of the integrity of his work as he was of the agencies by which he was independent. We can, even at the present day, measure and appreciate its excellence. And in order to maintain their own character, workmen are, in my opinion, justified in denouncing incompetence, sloth, or scamping work in their own order, and in exposing fraud and dishonesty among employers. If it were possible for the employer to dispense with overlookers, and trust his workmen, much saving would be effected, for in order to get a larger share in the joint profits of the capitalist and workmen, it is essential that the deduction from gross profits should be as little as possible. But it must, I fear, be admitted, that in the modern strife between labour and capital, the importance of securing that every care should be taken of the employer's interest by the workmen has been lost sight of, and, in consequence, that fund from which alone the condition of the workman can be bettered, the net profits of the whole industry, has been needlessly and injuriously diminished. It cannot be too strongly insisted on that employer and employed have a common interest,—the production of a maximum profit from their common industry ; and that the only question which ought to arise in the partnership between them, is that of the respective shares which each should receive in the equitable distribution of the profit. But I venture on asserting that the economy of this kind of waste is the most important of all.

There are various other forms of it. The extraordinary application of natural forces to purposes of human utility is the most striking fact in the history of modern industry. The economy of waste is the discovery of the process by which the force may be used with the least friction and loss, and the success which has attended individual effort in this direction is a commonplace in the history of industry, manufacture, and wealth. Such discoveries, secured as they are by patents, exist entirely for the benefit of the capitalist, and the profits derived from them can be appropriated in no degree by any one. In just the same way the special skill of the individual agriculturist, who cannot protect his processes by patent, remains with him as a profit-bearing agency, and cannot be appropriated by labourer or landowner till the economy is diffused among all persons engaged in the same calling. But other economies, some of which have been alluded to already, —viz., the extinction of middle profits and the moral development of industry,—immediately become the object on which labour may ground its claims to a share in the enhanced profit of the undertaking, though here again, until the economy is diffused over all the operations of a similar kind, the appropriation of the part is hindered. And perhaps the monopoly of the patentee (the natural justice of which I do not dispute, though the grant of the monopoly is constantly inequitable in fact) may help to break that immediate loss to labour which often follows for a while on the economy of productive processes, and so give time to prepare for the re-arrangement with labour, which the greater profits of the employer justify. In illustration of what I say, I may refer to the effect of sewing machines. It was calculated that this invention would materially lessen the toils, and, in the end, increase the gains of tailors and seamstresses. It has not done so, because the tailors' union is not strong enough to enable the members to claim better terms from employers, and the seamstresses have hardly any union at all. That they who have employed the labours of such artizans as I refer to have made prodigious profits, is pretty evident. I find no fault with the advantage which they have acquired, my only regret is that it has not been shared with those who have created the wealth, as it would have been under a proper organization.

The circumstances under which rent may be made to bear a larger share of public duties, in return for the enormous benefits which industry and the progress of society have conferred upon landowners, have been already in part referred to. The well-being of the mere landowner is a matter of no concern to anybody but himself. The well-being of the labourer, or of the capitalist who gives the concentration of intelligence and administrative power to the affairs of a complicated instrument of profit, or of the artizan, who conscientiously and faithfully carries out the details of work, is of interest to all. I cannot join in the chorus of exultation which comments on the virtues of a middle-man who, having saved ten or twenty millions, dies in the odours of the peerage and of sanctity. I do not care for the opulence which, beginning with questionable gifts or grants or plunder, has, through generations of fools or profligates, at last, and by the labour and even by the presence of others, contrived to take enormous tolls on enterprize, on industry, and on population, and is ever on the look-out to fleece all, if they will submit to be fleeced. To suggest that the owner of land should be deprived of his property is dishonest, and, were it carried out, would be disastrous. To value his present interest, and to appropriate the future increase of the area which he possesses, would be an enormous task, and would make government, society being a vague force of which government must be the agent, an ubiquitous function, the jobs of which would be demoralizing, the discontent with which would be dangerous, the cost of which would be enormous, and the risks of which would be formidable. Suppose in 1870 the English Government had adopted Mr. Mill's suggestion, had accepted the position of universal and immediate landlord, and had agreed to pay in perpetuity the agricultural rents which were then raised, it would have made an excellent bargain for the landowners, and an exceedingly bad one for the public. The doctrine that agricultural rent will always rise, which was at the bottom of Mr. Mill's theory of decreasing production from land, is one of the most dangerous, and I may add erroneous notions conceivable. A knowledge of the history of rent, in the third quarter, for example, of the seventeenth century, and the first quarter of the eighteenth, would have entirely dispelled a delusion which was founded on the accidental conditions under which rent was increased in the first half of the nineteenth century.

But the case is quite different with ground rents. Here the State has a right to interfere with that exceptional accretion of value which comes from other than the outlay on the land. It is easy to separate the ground value from the building value, and to tax the one on the principle which should be applied to all property, and the other on the principle which should be applied to property whose only or principal value is derived from the existence and action of others. That the reformers of local taxation should insist on the ground landlord contributing to the fund, which is necessary for the very existence of those who create his wealth, is plain ; that they should anticipate the necessity, by joint action, of lessening the exorbitant rents which their supineness induces them to pay for sites, is wise; for in many branches of business there is clear enough evidence that trade customers will be no longer willing to pay them ; and that what is called co-operative shop-keeping, a system already in its infancy, and still exposed to the risks of inexperience, will seriously limit the future of those traders who are too slovenly or too servile to resist extortion.

The organization of labour, with a view to its sale in the aggregate, is incomparably more important, when the condition of any class is such that the wages it earns are not progressive, or are retrogressive, than it is when the demand is generally less than the supply. Persons have often stated that there has been no trade union among domestic servants, and that the wages of such persons have greatly risen by the mere operation of demand and supply. There is no doubt of the increase ; and it bears indirect testimony to the fact that the profits of the higher branches of industry are greater than those of the lower, and that there is m re employment for domestic labour in consequence. But it is also certain that the demands made on such labour cause that it should be increasingly select. The domestic servants who satisfied the simple habits of a generation or two ago, were very inferior in tact, in manner, and in function to those which are needed in very moderate households at present. Besides, it is not quite clear that there is not an understanding among domestic servants which is just as effective as a trade union. The training of an efficient domestic servant is a long apprenticeship. Those who enter into this calling know what is expected of them, and what is the reputation which they must acquire and keep, and are very fully aware of the claims which they can make for wages. Good as the position is, and, relatively speaking, high as are the wages of peasant girls who enter into domestic service and are carefully trained in it, the calling is not in itself attractive, and young women often exchange it for a married life of much toil and little hope, for the poor earnings of dressmakers and seamstresses, and even for a ruinous freedom. The supply always tends to fall short of the demand, and those who enter the calling are fairly cognisant of the fact.

But there is no doubt whatever that many callings are, in technical language, overcrowded. I say technically, for they may not be under a better distribution of profits. I find no fault with employers for attempting to arouse the common scare of those who are threatened with the risk of having to pay higher wages, that the industry will be driven from the country, but I am not called on to believe them. The prediction is made so freely, and has so rarely been verified, that any person who hears it may be pardoned for doubting it. It is certainly not an imminent risk if the profits of the capitalist continue to be large, and there is plenty of evidence that in those callings where the labour of the employed is worst paid, the profits of employers are abnormally high, as in the case, for example, of ready-made clothes. There is plenty of evidence as to the enormous profits of most employers in the manufacture of textile fabrics in the days when factory-hands were very ill-paid. Never, I imagine, was wealth more rapidly accumulated in Lancashire and Yorkshire than it was between 1800 and 1840. It is rarely the case, however, that the liberal reward of labour is followed by a material enhancement of price. No one believes that if the London seamstresses, tailors, and match-box makers received double the wages which they do at present, there would be an appreciable difference in the price of the products sold, or any present risk that any of those industries would cease to be plied in this country.

There is some evidence that the principle of organization as applied to labour is extending even to the poorest paid work-people. It is gratifying to see, for instance, that the process is gradually spreading among women. The first step is the modest benefit society, which provides a fund against sickness, and gradually for accidental or enforced abstinence from employment. The habit of making provision against casualties arising from the weakness of the individual's own position in relation to the risks of sickness or other contingencies, is soon extended towards making provision against the risks which attend the employment. Thence it is an easy stage to the process by which some slight barrier is made against an arbitrary lessening of wages. This step is aided by the avowed sympathy of those who are convinced that labour should be helped, or, at least, not hindered, in selling its work at the best price which it can get; and is justified in resisting, by all the means it can command, the process which would compel it to a forced sale of the only article of value which it possesses. In course of time, employers become habituated to the process under which workpeople sell their labour, on the same principle which others adopt in selling their goods, for the dealer knows the ruinous effect of a compulsory and sudden sale. And perhaps, finally, the sternest economist will come to see, not only that workpeople may adopt the principle of the capitalist in withholding goods from the market till a remunerative price is obtained, but that the process as applied to labour is ultimately as beneficial as most persons see it is when applied to trade. The market price, they tell us, must in the long run conform to the cost of production, plus the profit of the capitalist. Is this to be true of one of the factors in production only, and to be false in the case of the other?

The moralist might dwell at length and with satisfaction on

the education which the principle of mutual aid gives to human
nature. The rational economist knows that the best way in
which the various forces which contribute to a common result
can carry out their end is by the harmony of these forces. But
the harmony is impossible if there be a well-founded distrust
as to the equity with which the distribution of profits is
effected. There will be a longing for violent remedies if law is
plainly enlisted on behalf of any one interest, and to the detriment of all others. For, I repeat, the excellence of the social
state does not lie in the fulness with which wealth is produced
and accumulated, but in the fact that it is so distributed as to
give the largest comfort and the widest hope to the general
mass of those whose continued efforts constitute the present
industry of the nation and the abiding prospect of its future
well-being.

To the historian, however, as distinguished from the mere
annalist, the narrative of the varying fortunes which have
attended on these centuries of work and wages is immeasurably instructive. Whatever claim other people may make to
a share in the common work of civilization, the English race
may justly affirm that the English people has instructed mankind in the machinery of government, and in the process by
which freedom may be secured in the fullest measure to all,
and the administration of public affairs may be effectively
carried on. The institutions of England have been copied,
with more or less success, by all civilized races. They may
be faulty, but they contain the best agencies which experience
has discovered and practical wisdom has adopted.

We do not owe them to the dynasties which have ruled in
England, for the English constitution has been wrested from
the several families who have been permitted from time to
time to be at the head of affairs, and have one and all con-
spired against the welfare of those who have endured them,
till, more frequently than any other people, the English have
deposed them, and driven them away. We do not owe them
to statesmen and lawyers, for they have constantly abetted
their employers in those purposes which have been so happily
ffled. We do not owe them to the English aristocracy,

which has been by turns turbulent, servile, and greedy, and is now probably the most unnecessary, as a body, that any civilized society exhibits and endures. We do not owe them to the Church, which has been, since the days of the first Edward, the willing servant of statecraft, and has rarely raised its voice against wrong-doing. Had the English people relied on the mere machinery of its government and the character of those who have manipulated this government, it would have never been an example and a model of civilized organization. To my mind, England was at its lowest degradation during the twenty years which intervened between the destruction of the monasteries and the restoration of the currency, when the worst possible government was carried on, but with strict adherence to parliamentary forms.

The fact is, even in the darkest time there still was something which despotism feared or discovered that it must fear. England has never been entirely without a public opinion, which has been constantly acute, and has not infrequently been dangerous. There have always, too, been public men who could give effect to that opinion, and make it strong by marshalling it. The traditional parties have in turn thriven or become powerful,—the one by appropriating at its convenience the work of those who have interpreted and formulated popular demands; the other by putting itself at the head of all interests which are hostile to the public good, and by relying on the organization which is sure to be developed on behalf of such interests, and on apathy, ignorance, or unintelligent discontent. But by dint of patience and by watching for opportunities, the English people has developed a system which, though far from perfect, has achieved much of that which had long been the Utopia of philosophers. But the reforms which have been effected are the work of the people, and they are to be traced in that history only which is rarely written, of the stubborn perseverance with which Englishmen have criticised their own condition, have discovered that from themselves only, whoever may be the agent of the remedy, the remedy can be found, and have, under infinite discouragements, effected so much. The student of social forces will find, that in order to understand the order of things in his own time, he must take account not only of the process by which the machinery of our social condition has been made and constantly marred, but much more of the opinion and action which have developed and moulded the character of the English people.

S. MARTIN'S COLLEGE OF EDUCATION · LANCASTER ·

INDEX.

A

Artizans, wages of, in eighteenth century, 406.
Arundel, Archbishop, episcopate of, 370.
Assessments, of wages in Quarter Sessions, early, 353.
Assize, of bread and malt, the, 61.
Attainders, parliamentary, generally remitted, 294.
Avignon, migration of popes to, 246.
Ayscough, Bishop, his murder, 377.

B

Bank of England, the, in its earlier days, 467.
Bailiff's roll, description of the, 48.
Bankruptcy, law of, another form of usury law, 142.
Barére, anecdote of, 551.
Beaufort, Bishop, his career, 373.
Becket, murder of, 27.
—— translation of, 359.
Beggars, supplication of, on alms, 418.
Benevolences, reputed character of, 317.
Bills, tradesmen's, of the fifteenth century, 165.
Bishops, cadets of noble familes in the fourteenth and fifteenth centuries, 93
—— English, principal in the fifteenth century, 369.
—— the, of the fifteenth century, their character, 381.
—— in 1450, unpopularity of, 311.
Black death, origin and history of, 219.
Blith, Walter, on English husbandry, 458.
Blomefield, on Norfolk guilds, 417.
Boar, the fatted, a dish at feasts, 83.
Boarding, contracts for, by Elizabeth, 354.
Boccacio, on the Plague, 224.
Boors' war, the, in 1525, 157.
Bounty, the, at the Revolution, 484.
Bourchier, Archbishop, episcopate of, 372.
Bread, equality of price of, in England in eighteenth century, 404.
Bribes, paid to assessors, 214.
Broadhurst, Henry, his experience of trade unions, 516.
—— in Paris, his advice, 557.
Bruges, embassy to, in 1371, 247.
Building, cost of, in fifteenth century, 543.
Burgundian Duchy, the formation of, its importance in European history, 300.
Butter, cheapness of, 93.
Bye industries, in villages, common, 47.
Byron, Lord, on the frame-breaker's Act, 495.

C

Callings, overcrowded, remedies for, 571.
Cambridge, riot at, 264.
Capitalist, agriculture, clearly impossible after 1381, 274.
Cannyngs, Lord Mayor, his letter from Pecok, 379.